'[The] . . . narrative is unified by his analyses of literary and political figures, party formations . . . new forms of mass entertainment. Together these studies link party, class and culture . . . They include the author's classic interpretation of blackface minstrelsy as Jacksonian ideology, and his equally persuasive placement of the western dime novel in postbellum, free-soil Republicanism.'
Michael Rogin, *American Historical Review*

'. . . a penetrating analysis of how popular and literary culture spread the gospel of white racial supremacy. This book is a gem of historical craftsmanship.'
Gary Nash, University of California, Los Angeles

'The socialist intellectual who participates in . . . radical activity has the potential of developing left-wing thought in increasingly rich and complex ways. Such is the case with Alexander Saxton, the proletarian novelist of the 1940s and 1950s turned Marxist historian in the 1960s and after. *The Rise and Fall of the White Republic* is testimony to the sophistication and power of the antiracist imagination as it has evolved over five decades of cultural and political struggle . . .'
Alan Wald, *Monthly Review*

The late Constance Coiner, author of *Better Red: the Writing and Resistance of Tillie Olsen and Meridel Le Sueur*, was one of Saxton's graduate students. She refers to him in her dedication as 'member of the Old Left, beloved teacher of the New'. Tillie Olsen, author of *Tell Me a Riddle*, *Silences* and *Yonnondio*, wrote of Saxton's work: 'honor to you for this book and for your others; for your vision, steadfastness, integrity . . . [for] the contribution which your life and work have made'.

The Rise and Fall
of the White Republic

THE HAYMARKET SERIES

Editors: Mike Davis and Michael Sprinker (1950–1999)

The Haymarket Series offers original studies in politics, history and culture, with a focus on North America. Representing views from across the American left on a wide range of subjects, the series will be of interest to socialists both in the USA and throughout the world. A century after the first May Day, the American left remains in the shadow of those martyrs whom this Haymarket Series honours and commemorates. These studies testify to the living legacy of political activism and commitment for which they gave their lives.

Bestselling Titles

ANYTHING BUT MEXICAN: Chicanos in Contemporary Los Angeles *by Rodolfo Acuña*

THE INVENTION OF THE WHITE RACE, VOLUME I: Racial Oppression and Social Control *by Theodore Allen*

THE INVENTION OF THE WHITE RACE, VOLUME II: The Origin of Racial Oppression in Anglo-America *by Theodore Allen*

CITY OF QUARTZ: Excavating the Future in Los Angeles *by Mike Davis*

PRISONERS OF THE AMERICAN DREAM: Politics and Economy in the History of the US Working Class *by Mike Davis*

THE CULTURAL FRONT: The Laboring of American Culture in the Twentieth Century *by Michael Denning*

MECHANIC ACCENTS: Dime Novels and Working-Class Culture in America *by Michael Denning*

RED DIRT: Growing Up Okie *by Roxanne Dunbar-Ortiz*

THE ASSASSINATION OF NEW YORK *by Robert Fitch*

NO CRYSTAL STAIR: African Americans in the City of Angels *by Lynell George*

THE HISTORY OF FORGETTING: Los Angeles and the Erasure of Memory *by Norman M. Klein*

AN INJURY TO ALL: The Decline of American Unionism *by Kim Moody*

LABOR IN A LEAN WORLD: Unions in the International Economy *by Kim Moody*

YOUTH, IDENTITY, POWER: The Chicano Movement *by Carlos Muñoz, Jr.*

WHITE GUYS: Studies in Postmodern Domination and Difference *by Fred Pfeil*

THE WAGES OF WHITENESS: Race and the Making of the American Working Class *by David Roediger*

TOWARDS THE ABOLITION OF WHITENESS: Essays on Race, Politics and Working-Class History *by David Roediger*

BEYOND THE PALE: White Women, Racism and History *by Vron Ware*

The Rise and Fall
of the White Republic

Class Politics and Mass Culture
in Nineteenth-Century America

---◆---

ALEXANDER SAXTON

With a new foreword by
DAVID ROEDIGER

V

VERSO

London • New York

First published by Verso 1990
© Alexander Saxton 1990
This edition first published by Verso 2003
© Alexander Saxton 2003
Foreword © David Roediger 2003

1 3 5 7 9 10 8 6 4 2

Verso
UK: 6 Meard Street, London W1F 0EG
USA: 180 Varick Street, New York, NY 10014–4606

Verso is the imprint of New Left Books

ISBN 1-85984-467-7

British Library Cataloguing in Publication Data
A catalogue record for this book is
available from the British Library

US Library of Congress Cataloging-in-Publication Data
A catalog record for this book is
available from the Library of Congress

Typeset by NorthStar
San Francisco, California, and M Rules, London
Printed in Finland by Werner Söderström Oy

Chapters 4, 7 and 9 first appeared in slightly different form in
American Quarterly under the titles 'Blackface Minstrelsy and
Jacksonian Ideology', 27 (March 1975): 3–28; 'George Wilkes:
The Transformation of a Radical Ideology', 33 (Fall 1981): 437–58;
and 'Problems of Class and Race in the Origins of the Mass
Circulation Press', 36 (Summer 1984): 211–34; copyright 1975,
1981 and 1984, respectively, by the American Studies Association.
Portions of the Introduction appeared as 'Historical Explanations of
Racial Inequality' in *Marxist Perspectives*, 2 (Summer 1979): 146–68.
A section of Chapter 8 was earlier published as 'The Racial Trajectory of
the American Hero', *Amerasia* 11 (1984) 2: 67–79, published by the
Asian American Studies Center, UCLA; copyright Regents of
the University of California.

Contents

To Trudy

Acknowledgements

For expert guidance and assistance I am grateful to the staffs of many libraries, manuscript departments and archives. Among these are the historical society libraries of Colorado, Kansas, Massachusetts, New Mexico, New York; the Museum of New Mexico at Santa Fe; the university libraries of Columbia, Duke, Harvard, the University of California at Berkeley and Los Angeles, and of the universities of Colorado and Virginia. Also I stand indebted to the public libraries of Boston, Denver and New York, to the Peabody Department of the Enoch Pratt Free Library of Baltimore, to the Division of Archives and Public Records of Colorado and to the Veterans' Records sector of the National Archives. Special thanks are due to the Theater Collection of Harvard Library and to the Lincoln Center Theater Collection of the New York Public Library. Above all - since I have taxed them more heavily than any of the others - I owe thanks to the Bancroft Library of the University of California at Berkeley, the Huntington Library in San Marino, and to Special Collections of the University of California at Los Angeles.

Time for the research and writing of this book was made possible in part by a grant from the National Endowment for the Humanities; by multiple research grants from the Academic Senate of the University of California at Los Angeles; and by the flexibility and generosity of my Department in arranging leaves at critical junctures. I have been working on this project for a long time. Even now it would not be finished except for the input of research assistants. I have been extraordinarily fortunate in the research assistants who have worked with me, most of them graduate students at UCLA: Sherry Katz, Lesley Kawaguchi, Ben Keppel, Dan Lund, Michael Prendergast, Keith Topper, Sandra Zickefoose, and Teresa Strottman of the Española library in New Mexico. Nor could this project have been finished without the aid of Jane Bitar and her word processing staff at UCLA. I will not forget the skill and patience of Nancy Rhan who has been straightening out my typescripts for twenty years.

Many of my colleagues have read portions of this work and improved it by their comments and suggestions. I am grateful to Lucie Cheng, Edna Bonacich, Jon McLeod, George Rawick and Michael Sprinker. In this same connection I want to thank the Los Angeles Social History Study Group for evenings of intense and critical discussion: Hal Barron, Roberto Calderon, Nancy Fitch, Jackie Greenberg, John Laslett, Gary Nash, Steve Ross, Cynthia Shelton, Frank Stricker, Dorothee Schneider and Devra Weber. I am especially indebted to Gary Nash, Dave Roediger, Bob Rydell and Ron Takaki for comments on the conceptualization and structure of the entire undertaking which were of great value to me. Copyediting, for the first time in my experience, was a pleasure rather than a burden. My thanks to Steven Hiatt, who made this necessary task a shared intellectual enterprise.

Foreword

Somebody needs to check what they put in the water in Great Barrington. That small Massachusetts city gave the United States its greatest activist-intellectual of the twentieth century, W.E.B. Du Bois. In 1935, nearing seventy years of age, the Harvard-educated Du Bois followed a series of novels, plays, poems, editorials, sociological studies and essays with *Black Reconstruction*, the most poetic and best work of history yet written in the US. It was, among much else, the beginning of the study of whiteness as an historical problem. Introducing 'the white worker' as a central figure in his drama, Du Bois never allowed readers to suppose that the adjective could be understood without the noun, or vice versa. His theorization of a 'public and psychological wage', supplementing the cruder monetary payoffs of white supremacy, has proven one indispensable starting point in understanding why some workers would think it important to be white. Du Bois's lifetime of experiences in social struggles lent a passion and precision to the questions that he posed. Not surprisingly, given his long time away from Great Barrington in the African-American South, Du Bois wrote a history of national power rooted in the tumultuous history of that section of the nation. In the short run, readers and reviewers struggled to catch up with a book far ahead of its time. Some managed to miss the fact that Du Bois had seized the traditional narrative of nineteenth-century US history by its throat. Others disparaged the study precisely because they knew what was at stake. Many admired the erudition and grace of the book and began to make corners of its arguments cornerstones of their own work. In the longer run, we still struggle to catch up with all of *Black Reconstruction* but its place as a classic is secure.

Fifty-five years later, another child of Great Barrington, Alexander

Saxton, published the book you hold. At seventy, the Harvard-educated Saxton had long produced important fiction and political journalism as well as history. Like that of Du Bois, his activist career already spanned half a century. Much of that career was spent in the Communist Party, which Du Bois would apply to join in the early 1960s. Reflecting his long time spent away from the Northeast, Saxton passionately helped to write a new section of the nation, the West, into the national story of race and class. The book ran far ahead of its time. Many critics managed to miss the point that Saxton had seized received narratives by the throat – utterly refusing to cast the relationship between racist brutality and white egalitarianism as simply ironic or paradoxical and showing it instead to be chillingly reflective of a popular logic. Others carped because they knew what was at stake. Some gloried in Saxton's insights – with Louis Kushnick, Alan Wald, Noel Ignatiev, Paul Buhle and Barry Goldberg providing especially inspired critical commentary. With this new edition, the kind of extended process that made *Black Reconstruction* a word-of-mouth classic matures.

I introduce this comparison between Professors Du Bois and Saxton knowing that the former is in many ways incomparable. Moreover, the two books, though broadly compatible, have quite different concerns: the Civil War and more especially what Du Bois calls 'abolition-democracy' are somewhat marginalized in *The Rise and Fall of the White Republic*, while the West and Indian policy are scarcely central in *Black Reconstruction*. Still less do I wish to make a serious case for Great Barrington's magical influence. However, the comparison does give us entry into the two major concerns of this brief foreword: where to place *The Rise and Fall of the White Republic* among critical studies of whiteness in the United States and how to account for its excellence and insight. Those two concerns so fully merge for me that I shall make no serious effort to keep them entirely separate.

I have long had a highly personal interest in how *The Rise and Fall of the White Republic* was received. It appeared just months before my own study of race and class in the nineteenth century, *The Wages of Whiteness* (1991), was published in the same Haymarket Series by Verso. That series would go on to publish Theodore Allen's superb two-volume *The Invention of the White Race*, Fred Pfeil's rollicking *White Guys* and Vron Ware's *Beyond the Pale*, making Verso the leading force in the expansion of what Richard Delgado and Jean Stefancic call 'critical white studies'. But in the early 1990s, only *Rise and Fall* and *Wages* were out there. Moreover, I had been the internal reviewer of Saxton's book and regarded it as so utterly superior – more comprehensive, politically astute and poetic – to *Wages* that my fondest hope was that the two books might be considered as companions, enabling mine to travel in the wake of his. Whatever graduate student miseducation I had received regarding the alleged undesirability of someone else intruding on 'my' topic evaporated at once in a combination of my admiration for Saxton's wonderful earlier book, *The Indispensable Enemy: Labor and the Anti-Chinese Movement in California*, and the happy feeling that *Rise and Fall* confirmed the sanity of *Wages* at a time when few historians wrote in this vein. Thus it turned out that the very first compliment that I received on *Wages* was one I couldn't accept. An old acquaintance had hailed me after a lecture by enthusing over my then-new book, but added that it was particularly impressive when compared to Saxton's tendentious tract. My crestfallen response doubtless sounded sullen: 'I like his lots better.'

I still decidedly like it far better, but it must be said that some of the virtues of *Rise and Fall* did not go unpunished. Though it remains the best historical work on whiteness published since 1990 (and, I think, since *Black Reconstruction*) and ranks with the work of Cheryl Harris and Toni Morrison in defining the leading edge of recent scholarship in critical white studies generally, Saxton's work has not always been thought of in that way. The son of a leading figure in the publishing industry, Saxton understands the happenstances and blips of literary reputations as well as anyone and is in any case quite without a need for aggrandizement. Nonetheless, for the sake of critical white studies and not for Saxton, it seems worth emphasizing that *Rise and Fall* was both the first and the best of a new wave of historical studies of whiteness. The brevity and punch of my *Wages* and of Ignatiev's important *How the Irish Became White* ensured that our arguments could be more readily reduced to succinct formulations and our books more manageably assigned in courses. Our activism around the 'abolition of whiteness' also made for a readership crossing disciplinary lines and moving beyond academia.

But there could be no doubt that Saxton's work posed the weightiest challenges to those wanting to practice history-as-usual. It paid a fair bit for doing so. While the racism of antebellum white workers discussed in my book, or that of Irish immigrants in Ignatiev's, could be gainsaid without necessarily changing the whole story of US history, Saxton implicated the ruling political coalitions of the nineteenth century as well as popular culture and the American Federation of Labor. Even as they sometimes nodded towards the boldness of parts of *Rise and Fall*, negative reviews used intemperate language rarely found among academics. Words like 'ridiculous' and 'implausible' echoed alongside wholesale rejections of Saxton's Marxism, and of his use of varied literary evidence. That such charges could equally easily have been made against *Wages*, but by and large were not, suggests the extent to which some reviewers, faced with the deep challenges Saxton presents, were in fact saying, 'This *can't* be right.'

Ironically, just as mixed early reviews helped to keep *Rise and Fall* from being recognized as the pioneering and preeminent study among the new histories of whiteness, a more recent critical foray seeks to isolate it from recent scholarship on whiteness altogether. In his broadside attack on what he calls 'whiteness studies', in *International Labor and Working Class History*, Eric Arnesen simultaneously absolves and dismisses Saxton's *Rise and Fall*: since 'whiteness studies' is poisoned by the psychoanalytic framework of *Wages*, and since Saxton criticizes psycho-historical explanations for racism's origins, *Rise and Fall* is not a book Arnesen feels a need to grapple with. Apart from being less than accurate – later in *Rise and Fall* Saxton holds that broadly psychological explanations for the *reproduction* of racism do have force – Arnesen's position is embarrassingly facile. Though he professes to identify with the assumptions of Saxton's study, he maintains his argument that studying whiteness offers little or nothing to historians by simply writing the book out of the picture altogether. Again Saxton's ideas, and their place in critical white studies, go unconfronted.

Attempting to account for the boldness and force of *Rise and Fall* doubtless matters more than placing the book historiographically. The literary scholar Alan Wald offers an apt framework at the outset of his essay on Saxton's work. 'The socialist intellectual who participates in several generations of radical activity', Wald writes, 'has the potential of developing left-wing thought in increasingly rich and complex ways'. As Saxton observes in a memoir attached to a recent republication of his 1948 novel *The Great Midland*, it was not the schools of Great Barrington which introduced Saxton to Du Bois and his ideas. They ignored Du Bois. Nor was he ever mentioned during Saxton's time at Harvard, even though Du Bois was that university's first African American PhD. 'What I learned about Du Bois, and most of what I learned about racial discrimination in US history', Saxton recalled, 'I learned in the Communist Party'. The Communist literature agent for Saxton's Chicago circle of party members in the early 1940s distributed *Black Reconstruction*.

At the time, Saxton was agitating for racially fair employment practices in the railroad industry, where he worked. At one point, officials of the Jim Crow railway union brotherhoods favored keeping Blacks from participating in fair employment hearings. They argued that African Americans would behave out of racial self-interest and could not be impartial. 'Apparently white men', Saxton bitterly noted, 'belong to no race'. This early emphasis not only on white racism but on the ability of white presumptions to go unexamined anticipated much of Saxton's work over the next half-century. *The Great Midland* imagined interracial unity among railroad unionists by considering examples of such unity in steel and other mass production industries. It had to imagine since, as Saxton recalls, in his intense railway activism he had 'never heard of any white shop steward on any railroad who defended black workers'. (His later and longer activism as a building tradesman gave Saxton experience in another bastion of craft and caste unionism, and produced some modest successes in breaching the color line.) Whiteness, and especially the whiteness of the weak, was an urgent *problem* for Saxton, as it was for Du Bois. He has refused, in both his fiction and his histories, an easy dismissal of that problem as one of 'false consciousness' in which elites simply misled white working people. 'Lower orders', he insists, 'shared willingly, if not equally, in the profits of racial exploitation'. Garnet, the craft union boss in *Bright Web in the Darkness* (1958), Saxton's most ambitious novel, is repellent in what one critic calls his 'foul-mouthed' racism, but he is also tragically consistent in his hardbitten defenses of the manhood, union brotherhood and privileges his whiteness has helped him to secure.

Wald's emphasis on generations of resistance has further resonance in Saxton's case. After leaving the CP in 1959, Saxton joined with other Communists and ex-Communists and with Trotskyists and former Trotskyists in a loose socialist network which helped to form a strong Bay Area chapter of the Fair Play for Cuba Committee. In graduate school at Berkeley and then in teaching at UCLA, Saxton embraced the anti-war and anti-imperialist movements of the 1960s and 1970s. *The Indispensable Enemy* led to especially close associations with Asian American students. This new set of solidarities and tasks, no less than his labor organizing and fiction writing, gave form and urgency to the questions Saxton posed in *Rise and Fall*.

Indeed in many ways *Rise and Fall* culminates a series of works in history and American Studies conceived in the context of mass opposition to the atrocities, the policies and the racism of the US in Southeast Asia. These studies include the late Michael Rogin's inspired *Fathers and Children*, Richard Drinnon's mammoth *Facing West*, Richard Slotkin's challenging *Regeneration Through Violence* and *The Fatal Environment*, and, perhaps most importantly, *Iron Cages*, by Saxton's former UCLA colleague Ron Takaki. All of these authors make imperial expansion, terror, capitalism and anti-Indian racism central to reinterpreting the nineteenth-century US, and many join Saxton in extending the discussion to include Asian exclusion. One weakness of recent work on whiteness has, as I argue at length in *Colored White: Transcending the Racial Past* (2002), been its failure to connect with this earlier literature and to see how thoroughly empire joined with slavery and proletarianization in forming the white race in the US. Thus it is doubly important that critical white studies claim Saxton's work. It is, as Paul Buhle's remarkable review essay on *Rise and Fall* in *The Nation* showed, about empire without ever ceasing to be about slavery, industrialization and class formation.

The Rise and Fall of the White Republic, for all its ambition and deliberate sprawl, does not do everything. As the late literary scholar Constance Coiner and the great novelist Tillie Olsen have recently observed, Saxton's fiction is peopled by memorable female characters. One of them, the African American shipyard worker and musician Joyce Allen in *Bright Web in the Darkness*, strikes Olsen as 'one of the rarest, most beautiful creations in literature'. Another, the Polish American Stephanie Koviak in *The Great Midland*, fully captured the imagination of Coiner, who found her 'conflicted, depression-prone, ambitious and independent'. This same attention to the dynamics of gender is only episodically found in *Rise and Fall* – for example in the remarkable passages on Harriet Beecher Stowe and on blackface minstrelsy and sexuality. Saxton's focus on party politics in the years before women's suffrage makes his omissions on this score understandable but does not quite keep readers from wishing for more. Similarly, *Rise and Fall*'s nuanced treatment of James Fenimore Cooper's fiction – so fully informed by an appreciation of the ways in which important writers hold social contradictions in tension – deepens a wish that Saxton had also discussed Herman Melville's complex writings. Like every other major work in critical white studies, *Rise and Fall* leaves us plenty to do. But it also does much to show us how, and in what spirit, to proceed.

David Roediger
University of Illinois
March 2003

Introduction: Historical Explanations of Racial Inequality

This study in nineteenth-century political and cultural history is directed to the problem of ideology and change. Its focus is on a single but extended relationship – that between white racial domination in the United States and ideas and attitudes about race. My purpose is not to produce another intellectual history of racial thought, but to trace the continuity and modification of a major ideological construction. Three assumptions govern the sequence. They are that a theory of white racial superiority originated from rationalizations and justifications of the slave trade, slavery and expropriation of land from non-white populations; that this theory continued to hold a central place in various syntheses of ideas legitimizing power because it continued to meet justificatory needs of dominant groups in the changing class coalitions that have ruled the nation; and that these legitimizing syntheses, including specific constructions within them, remained in flux through ongoing processes of modification and readjustment. This book explores these assumptions within the time span of the nineteenth century.

Explore may be less presumptuous than *demonstrate*. What I intend by it is an effort to integrate the starting assumptions into a set of plausible and economical explanations for known developments, which I take to be the closest one can come to demonstrating causality in history. Limitation to the nineteenth century seemed advisable on two grounds. First, the complexity of carrying this inquiry into the twentieth century is large enough to warrant a separate project; and second, although these assumptions apply in part to an era before 1800, they have been more widely accepted for eighteenth-century America and therefore have been more fully elaborated. It is the explanation of continuity that remains tenuous

1

because, since it has not been widely accepted (scholars generally having relied on economic competition or psychological factors to explain the continuity of white racism in the nineteenth and twentieth centuries), it has not been tried out over any long span of American history.

The motivations that led to this study certainly were less abstract than my statement of its topic. Experience as an industrial worker and labor unionist faced me with perceptions of the centrality of race and racism in American society. Later, when I became a historian, I fixed the effort to arrive at some historical understanding of race as my chief goal. The project of the book, then, will be to bring together a viable historical explanation of the origin, and especially the continuity, of racial inequality in the United States. Why I see this as a study in ideology I will attempt to make clear in the remainder of this introduction.

For a book that focuses on racism and racial domination, terminology presents a special problem. In principle, any people to whom historical experience has imparted a shared identity ought to be known by whatever name they choose to give themselves. Yet there is no escape from the underlying problem, which is that the scars of racial subordination continue to mark any set of terms we select. The terms I have used – aside from the obvious designations of nationality and origin – are African American, American Indian, Euro-American and Mexican American. The latter remains appropriate for the late nineteenth century even though it may no longer be so for the late twentieth. *Black* and *white* I have used generally as adjectives. In treating the central subject matter, white racism, it has often been necessary to speak of Europeans or Euro-Americans in juxtaposition to those 'others' who were the targets of racist ideology. The 'others' were in effect the remainder of the population of the world. I refer to them in this context as peoples of color, or simply as non-whites.

Explanatory Strategies

Contemporary literature on race falls mainly into the categories of histories of ideas about race,[1] narrative or descriptive accounts of how race prejudice works, social surveys of its impact, and polemics against it. Awareness of a need for historical explanation is relatively recent. Until about the third decade of the present century, most people in the so-called western world, including most social scientists and historians, took for granted the hereditary inferiority of non-white peoples. Differential treatment required no special explanation so long as it could be understood as a rational response to objective reality in the same way that differential treatment of women and children was supposedly so understood.

Nineteenth-century racial doctrine began to be challenged during the first decade of the twentieth century. That critique took more than a generation and is probably not yet fully completed. It was only when racist doctrine showed signs of crumbling under the impact of scientific criticism and political and economic changes throughout the United States – indeed, around the world – that the differential treatment of non-whites came up for scrutiny as a phenomenon requiring special attention. Even then, causal explanations of racism had low priority because it was still assumed that exposure of the falsity of racist doctrine would automatically explain the differential treatment of non-whites as the result of misunderstanding or ignorance. This was the outlook, initially at least, that informed the Carnegie Corporation's 'comprehensive study of the Negro in the United States', launched in 1937 under the direction of the Swedish social scientist Gunnar Myrdal.[2]

The Carnegie report lies fifty years behind us, yet the gravitational field of that massive enterprise has influenced virtually everything since written on the subject of race in the United States. For this reason it offers a logical starting point from which to begin a survey of historical explanations of racial inequality. Myrdal's explanation ran roughly as follows: Africans in North America were not at first treated differentially. Their status approximated that of European indentured servants. But as black servants 'gradually were pushed down into chattel slavery while the white servants were allowed to work off their bonds, the need was felt, in this Christian country, for some kind of justification above mere economic expendiency and the might of the strong.' A rationalization was constructed, mainly from the Old Testament. Africans had descended from Noah's son Ham, whose progeny had been cursed, and blackened, by God, and so forth. As these figments of religious mythology wilted under eighteenth-century Enlightenment scrutiny, there came a shift – disastrous for the Africans – from 'theological to biological thinking'. Given the new premise that human beings belonged to the 'biological universe', it was 'natural' for 'the unsophisticated white man' to arrive at the opinion that blacks were biologically inferior.[3]

In America, this opinion contravened what Myrdal called the 'American Creed' – a composite of values of liberty, equality and civility derived from the Enlightenment, from Christianity, and from English Common Law – which, in his view, served as a collective conscience or superego for the American nation. The title of his study, *American Dilemma*, referred to the dichotomy between this set of values and actual treatment of Africans, for here the 'Creed' operated in a 'double direction' – on the one hand forbidding inequitable treatment of any human being, while on the other requiring dehumanization of the black victims to justify the departure, in their case, from its proclaimed values. 'Race prejudice' was needed 'for defense on the part of the Americans against their own national Creed'.[4]

Thus racism proliferated, not only with the expansion of slave-based cotton culture before the Civil War; but afterwards as a rationale for the 'caste system' that became the 'social organization of Negro-white relations'. Racist beliefs were seemingly verified in everyday experience. African Americans did in fact fall below whites in social and economic status, in health, in life expectancy. Myrdal stressed the cumulative effects of deprivation and 'the early conditioning of the Negro child's mind by the caste situation'. Whites perceived these stigmata not as the wounds of imposed poverty, but as proofs of biological inferiority.[5] Were they 'deliberately deceiving' themselves? 'Our hypothesis', Myrdal explained, 'is that *the beliefs are opportunistic* and have the "function" to defend interests.' Whose interests? The next sentence specified the interests of the 'ordinary American'; while an earlier section had described 'Negroes and the poor whites' as 'placed in an intensified competition'. Myrdal then quoted a Swedish proverb: '"When the feed box is empty the horses will bite each other."' Yet the concept of competition did not lead him to a conclusion that non-whites and working class or immigrant whites were equally badly off. 'The Negroes are set apart, together with other colored peoples, principally the Chinese and Japanese. ... Considerable efforts are directed toward "Americanizing" all groups of alien origin. But in regard to the colored peoples, the American policy is the reverse. They are excluded from assimilation.'[6]

Myrdal's collaborator, Ashley Montagu, went beyond Myrdal in contending that economic stress unleashed accumulated resentments that might cause aggression against racial minorities as well as others. This argument was based in part on the psychoanalytic theory of infant deprivation which had already become a standard feature in studies of prejudice. As Montagu outlined it, separation from 'the nipple, the mother's body, uncontrolled freedom to excrete and to suck' thwarted 'expected satisfactions'. Frustration led 'to fear, to hatred and to aggressiveness', which 'must in one way or another find expression – "Race" hatred and prejudice merely represent familiar patterns of the manner in which aggressiveness may express itself.'[7]

Myrdal's and Montagu's arguments are ideological in that they place white racism as a necessary cause for the differential treatment of non-whites. Racism they explain as the rationalization of an exploiting group.[8] Neither Myrdal nor Montagu noted, apparently, that this argument might be criticized as circular: a system of ideas and attitudes that allegedly causes differential treatment of non-whites is said to originate as a result of such differential treatment. Both authors believed that racism, once it came into existence, would not only perpetuate itself but continue to reproduce similar patterns of behavior. Since this explanation involves a time span of several centuries, the authors attempted to bolster their construction by using additional factors (economic competition, frustration-aggression) to explain the continuing vigor of the original ideology. These additions, however, undermined the main argument because the added factors seemed to run counter to the starting assumption. An ideological argument, for example, must assume or demonstrate that racism exists because it serves the needs of an exploiting class or group; whereas the competition argument attributes racism to an exploited lower class. Or again, the ideological argument has racism serving socio-economic or political needs of an exploiting class, while frustration-aggression arguments stress a set of factors centering on the psychodynamics of individual personalities, presumably irrelevant to class situation. Moreover, frustration-aggression theory makes the victim extraneous to the generation of hostility. If racism is equated to other forms of internally generated, irrational prejudice it could focus as well on Catholics, Jews or Ulstermen as on African Americans. Frustration-aggression thus tends to undercut the interpretation of racism as a product of the rationalizing of slavery and imperialism to which Montagu as well as Myrdal had assigned priority.

Myrdal and Montagu both ended their examinations on notes of ameliorative optimism. Montagu concluded by assigning to education the keys to the future, a prognosis unfortunately negated by his ideological and psychological interpretations of racism.[9] When Myrdal's report was published at the end of the Second World War the world situation was one in which the United States found itself competing for the allegiance of the world's largely non-white peoples. Racism was becoming dysfunctional, internationally at least. Myrdal invoked the 'American Creed' for his finale. America at last must reject racial favoritism in the name of liberty, equal opportunity, and due process of law.[10] It would be difficult to pinpoint more precisely the central contradiction of Myrdal's study. While racism, especially as manifested in earlier centuries, is dealt with in the blunt language of dominance and exploitation, the American Creed – relied upon to right the wrongs of racism – is handled throughout in the non-ideological terminology of abstract idealism.[11]

These contradictions and gaps in the work of Myrdal and Montagu are themselves illuminating since they point to logical difficulties that have proved recurrent. Thus the dilemma of the circular argument; the problem of joining supplementary to long-range arguments; and the disjuncture between psychological and either economic or ideological explication continue to appear in the literature on racial subordination. Beyond that, and more importantly, the report managed to identify major strategies that would dominate the complex debates it helped set in motion. Those strategies – economic, psychological and ideological – provide a convenient frame of reference for discussion of more recent work. The last of these three strategies – the ideological – might be taken as a subset of the first; that is, ideological explanations are economic in derivation since their starting concept is that of a collective rationalization of class or group interest. In what follows, however, I will separate ideological from economic explanations because the introduction of collective consciousness as part of the apparatus of class domination adds such different dimensions to economic explanation as to comprise a distinct category.

Economic Strategy

The simplest form of economic explanation for the differential treatment of racial minorities is the argument from job competition. Two groups of workers compete for a limited supply of jobs; the less established undercut the more established, who respond with efforts to ostracize and exclude their competitors. Ostracism and exclusion are accompanied by expressions of distaste and hostility. If the more established have access to political power they may be able to give their exclusionary efforts the sanction of law. This argument has the effect either of obscuring racism as a factor, or of reducing it to the sort of rational 'economic' resentment that in America has often been directed against recent European immigrants, or against strikebreakers, or both. It tends to exonerate members of the excluding group from charges of bias or bigotry, since the existence of job competition is clearly not their fault and they can hardly be blamed for protecting their economic interests. For these reasons it is likely to be invoked by representatives of organized labor, as well as by their liberal or radical sympathizers. The argument of course may be applied to either ethnocultural or racial minorities, its major weakness being the inability to distinguish between the two. Thus, while satisfactorily explaining differential treatment of minorities as such in reference to a dominant majority, it cannot explain how a Chinese minority, for example, might be treated differently from an Irish minority.[12]

The simple model summarized above has generated complex variations. One of these is split labor market theory, which provides a conceptual framework for examining and comparing racial, ethnic and gender separations in the labor force in industrializing or postindustrial societies.[13] Labor markets in the United States have generally been split into more than two segments. Most European immigrants worked their way out of disadvantaged split labor market situations within two or three generations, a time span sufficient to equalize their cultural and economic 'resources' with those of the dominant group. The experience of nonwhite workers, by contrast – whether native-born or immigrant – has been distinctly different because racial hostility precluded any such equalization. Split labor market theory, no better equipped to offer an autonomous explanation for this racial differentiation than the original job competition model, must necessarily begin with some particular market, and usually begins by assuming a certain level of racism as one of the historically given conditions of that market.[14]

Another variation on the job competition argument has gained some celebrity through the work of free market economists like Thomas Sowell.[15] Job competition here becomes, not the source of discriminatory treatment, but the arena through which disadvantaged minorities win redress. African Americans are indeed heavily disadvantaged, in Sowell's presentation – less, however, because of white hostility than because their rural and slave past impoverished their cultural and economic resources. Yet in this respect they differ little if at all from European immigrants of rural background, some of whom, especially Irish and southern Italians, had suffered comparable deprivations.[16] All racial and ethnic minorities (generally lumped together under *ethnic*) have achieved some upward mobility in America and in so doing have encountered ethnocentric resistance from the dominant society. Such resistance seems to be conceptualized in this argument as a set of fixed obstacles like mountain ranges that all newcomers must somehow find their way across. Varying rates of success at surmounting these obstacles are partly dependent on the cultural and economic resources of the several minorities; primarily, however, they depend upon the workings of the free market in an expanding economy.[17]

Not only did that market in times past offer openings of some sort to all comers, but it served also to cancel out the competitive disadvantages of minorities. Thus nineteenth-century European immigrants of rural origin, only marginally employable because they lacked industrial skills and work disciplines, might nonetheless find jobs at substandard wages and overstandard hours while their children supplemented the family income by working in factories. Any who found themselves marginalized by irrational prejudice could follow the same route. High though the individual cost might be, upward mobility for the group as a whole was achieved. That, in Thomas Sowell's view at least, is how the labor market once worked. Alas, it no longer remains as free as it was then. Impediments such as wage and hour laws, social security, unnecessarily long years of education – together with standardized criteria for hiring and promotion imposed by social reformers or by corporate, union and government bureaucrats – have bogged the market down. For African Americans, most of whom entered urban areas and commenced industrial employment only in the mid-twentieth century, the door to upward mobility that once stood open for their European predecessors has been slammed shut. Presumably, the prospects for disadvantaged minorities would be as bright as ever should the market ever be liberated from its welfare fetters.[18]

The thrust of the sequence just summarized is to attribute differential treatment of African Americans to departures from free market principles (chattel slavery, followed by enslavement to the welfare state), and to minimize white racism as a causal factor by stressing the similar situations of African Americans and pre-industrial European immigrants. Yet that similarity of situation rests upon an assertion that African Americans entered urban labor markets only in the mid-twentieth century.[19] While for a majority this may in fact be true, it is also true that *some* African Americans reached urban industrial areas as early as the 1840s. Encountering ferocious white resistance, they were generally excluded from industrial labor because of that resistance in conjunction with the abundant availability of European immigrants. Had their reception been more favorable, it seems likely that more black Americans would have moved into industrial labor much sooner than they actually did. The circumstances foreclosing such a move (white resistance, employer preference for European immigrants, selective federal migration policies) were themselves involved in white racism – which, having been expelled from the visible equation, reasserts itself in the necessary historical context.

The free market version of economic explanation, then, although doubtless serving political sympathies opposite to those of the liberal, or even radical, job competition and split labor market versions, nonetheless shares with them an incapacity to effectively exclude white racism as a causal factor, or to explain it autonomously, without recourse to non-economic linkages. Subsuming *racial* within *ethnic*, such arguments direct their inquiry solely to the differentiation of minorities from the general population, neglecting the differentiation of racial minorities both from the general population and from ethnic minorities. If this simplification corresponded to reality, one would anticipate that non-white Americans after two or three generations would have found their way into the skilled trades, supervisory positions, union leadership, small business and local politics, as European immigrants generally have done. Since this was by no means the pattern, at least before the Second World War, economic explanations per se cannot account for the differential treatment of racial minorities. They can of course serve as auxiliaries to larger explanatory constructions. In that case they posit the pre-existence of racism as part of the environment within which immediate economic factors operate.

Psychological Strategy

Of the several strategies for explaining the differential treatment of racial minorities, the psychological is the most prolific and multifaceted. Psychological explanations, which usually stand at a distance from questions of class or socio-economic power, can fit harmoniously into either the consensus or progressive variety of American national consciousness; and this doubtless is a reason for their popularity. Two distinct types of psychological strategy have appeared. One seeks its answers in the presumed psychic and cultural deficiencies of racial minorities. The other seeks them in hypothetical tensions within the collective and individual psyches of the white majority.

The first type, well represented by the work of Nathan Glazer at Harvard, begins with the historical delineation of an American character reminiscent of Myrdal's 'American Creed'. Thus the 'American orientation' is said to be toward openness and liberality, and against bigotry and prejudice. For this reason, the Anglo-American melting pot never totally succeeded in reducing the long succession of newcomers in America. What resulted was neither ethnic homogeneity nor cultural pluralism, but something in between. Minorities shared a common experience through willing acceptance of certain basic ingredients in the culture: language, interest group politics, upward mobility. Americanized but not homogenized, each group emerged 'beyond the melting pot', transfigured from what it had been, yet retaining unique characteristics that comprised a continuing matrix for group identification. Ethnicity could then replace class as the dynamic of an intergroup politics combining the realism of self-interest with the more generous, value-oriented ties of cultural affinity. Even the old conflict between minorities and Anglo-American dominance would eventually fade away as WASPs became one more minority in the multi-ethnic society of the future.[20]

Thus far no distinction has been made between ethnic and racial minorities. It quickly becomes apparent, however, that racial minorities have fared less well in America than European immigrant minorities, and the familiar question confronts us: *why?* The argument turns at this point to a second historical proposition, specifically that American slavery inflicted psychocultural damage on African Americans that extended far beyond those generations actually exposed to slavery. The historical wounds are then said to reappear in the incapacity of adult black males to function as heads of families, thus leading to a self-perpetuating downward spiral of social pathology:

> The experience of slavery left as its most serious heritage a steady weakness in the Negro family. There was no marriage in the slave family ... no possibility of taking responsibility for one's children. ... What slavery began, prejudice and discrimination, affecting jobs, housing, self-respect, have continued to keep alive. ... This is the situation in the Negro community; it will be the situation for a long time to come.[21]

For a long time to come, also (if we extend Glazer's premise to its apparent corollary), African Americans will be treated differentially relative both to the population as a whole and to ethnic minorities because of the negative characteristics presumably implanted long ago by slavery and transmitted culturally from generation to generation. The ultimate blame of course is placed on slavery. But nothing can be done about that now; nor can much be done to alter differential treatment of black Americans if such treatment is believed to result from pathological deficiencies seen as self-perpetuating in African-American culture.

Obviously, it would not be difficult to construct parallel sequences for other racial minorities using similar models. The conclusions suggested by such beginnings seem not very different from the standard conclusions of old-fashioned racism. Ironically, they enter scholarly discourse as the purported findings of an interdisciplinary analysis that rejects racism and expresses keen sympathy for its victims. Leaving aside these conclusions, however, the entire construction remains flawed by the failure of historical evidence to sustain it.

America's supposed openness to newcomers throughout most of its history has been racially selective. By the time of Jefferson and Jackson the nation had already assumed the form of a racially exclusive democracy – democratic in the sense that it sought to provide equal opportunities for the pursuit of happiness by its white citizens through the enslavement of African Americans, extermination of Indians, and territorial expansion at the expense of Indians and Mexicans. If there was an 'American orientation' to newcomers it was not toward giving equal opportunity to all but toward inviting entry by white Europeans and excluding others. It is true that the United States absorbed a variety of cultural patterns among European immigrants at the same time that it was erecting a white supremacist social structure. Moderately tolerant of European ethnic diversity, the nation remained adamantly intolerant of racial diversity. It is this crucial difference that has been permitted to drop from sight.[22]

A shortage of historical evidence similarly undercuts the concept of a psychocultural deficit imposed by slavery. Since its original formulation in 1959 this proposition has been examined and re-examined. A phalanx of distinguished scholars, who agree perhaps on little else, has demonstrated beyond much possibility of doubt that African Americans, under slavery and afterward, created a distinct, partially autonomous culture including a viable and enduring family structure. That critique has reduced the credibility of the psychocultural deficit argument to a vanishing point.[23]

The second main tendency of psychological explanation has sought to avoid the neo-racist implications of the first by focusing on psychological aspects of the dominant culture. The trend goes back to Gordon Allport's *Prejudice* and especially to Theodor Adorno's classic study, *The Authori-*

tarian Personality. It goes far beyond these earlier works, however, in its reliance on Freudian theory to explain not merely why certain personality types might be receptive to prejudice; but why hatreds directed specifically against African Americans and American Indians have found mass acceptance among the white population of the United States. The pioneering work of this tendency was certainly Winthrop Jordan's *White Over Black*.[24]

Jordan, like Myrdal and Montagu, has made racism the keystone in his account of the differential treatment of African Americans. His task is to find the originating and continuing causes of white racism. Jordan shows that in Elizabethan England blackness and darkness were widely used as symbols of evil, whiteness and light as symbols of virtue and wisdom. Treason, betrayal, murder, were black deeds. The carnal instincts, particularly sensuality, were dark. So were things repulsive such as excrement; and Jordan here hints at the Freudian concept of anality. He then develops a complex argument in which these associations, operating metaphorically, serve to explain the enslavement of black Africans on one hand and the extermination of red American Indians on the other. His argument runs as follows: the English, when they colonized America, began to enslave Indians because they were dark-skinned, savage – and available; but they did not go far in this direction because, since Indians were not black, they did not meet the needs of the English psyche for the symbol of blackness.

Yet Indians did meet another symbolic need that required a different role for them: by being driven off the land, they demonstrated the English dedication to civilization and rational progress. Africans, by contrast, symbolized the carnal instincts – those internal enemies of civilization whose domain included sexuality, the womb, excrement – having always to be hugged close yet kept under rigid control. '... Indians and Africans rapidly came to serve as two fixed points from which English settlers could triangulate their own position in America; the separate meanings of *Indian* and *Negro* helped define the meaning of living in America'. Indian extermination and African enslavement are thus derived from subjective needs of the English psyche.[25]

Jordan's psychological and intellectual interpretations are sometimes brilliant and always interesting. The basic problem with his presentation is not a paucity of information or shortage of historical evidence, but rather a priori assumptions that govern his evaluation of causes. Fully aware of the military, economic and political factors favoring African over Indian enslavement, and which eventually favored African slavery over European indenture, Jordan dismisses such factors as insufficient. Only subjective factors are brought forward as the decisive ones. Masters refrained from enslaving their European indentured servants, Jordan writes, not because they lacked the power to do so, but because they 'did not believe themselves so empowered'. And of the original decision to enslave Indians and Africans rather than Europeans, he comments that 'to ask such questions is to inquire into the *content* of English attitudes'.[26]

Certainly this is not the place for a critique of Freudian theory, but it is worth noting that Jordan and other psychohistorians dealing with white racism rely on segments of that theory – anality, for example, or infant deprivation – as if they were bedrock. Some of us, on the other hand, may feel that formulations that invoke presumed instinctual drives are vulnerable to criticism and that a willingness to take them as universals of human behavior tends to subvert historical thinking. Yet the major difficulty presented by Freudian theory for historical explanation is at a simpler level. It is, to put it bluntly, that of credibility.

Doubtless one of the special conditions confronting all psychohistorians is that so much of their material is metaphorical – as illustrated in Jordan's treatment of white-black symbolism. Every external action then becomes a metaphor for internal processes that are alone the real causes of historical events. These internal processes, however, can only be known by decoding the external actions metaphorically. Since metaphor is indefinitely expansible in its range of meanings, the psychohistorian remains at liberty to tap in at any level that suits the needs of the argument.

Another difficulty inherent in the notion of symbolic acting out of inner tensions is the gap between the psyche allegedly experiencing the tensions and the human beings who presumably act them out in history. Jordan attempts to bridge this gap by assuming a collective psyche to which the techniques of psychoanalytic theory can be applied. Since that collective psyche does not yet exist, it has to be constructed by the historian. There is then no great difficulty in achieving symmetry between the collective psyche-as-constructed and the resultant historical actions; but the construction itself lacks much in the way of evidential validation. Like a work of fiction, it must depend upon its power to induce the willing suspension of disbelief on the part of the reader.

Most other psychohistorians have avoided this particular dilemma by using the form of the biographical study. Given a prolific public figure such as the young Luther, or Andrew Jackson, abundant evidence is likely to be available upon which to base an interpretation of the individual psyche.[27] But how to get from the tensions of that psyche to the actions of people in history? There appear to be two possible routes. One posits the subject of study as a representative figure whose inner dynamics typified those of his contemporaries. The other places him as a creator, a kind of culture hero, who publicly acted out symbolic resolutions that masses of fellow citizens could then internalize as their own. Not only are these routes conceptually contradictory, but it is difficult to demonstrate the actuality of either, let alone distinguish between them. Again, the reader is left to accept, or reject, the psychohistorian's creative intuition. It is true of course that epistomological questions may be raised with respect to any mode of historical explanation. But the difficulties seem exceptionally severe for psychohistory because of its assumption that *real* causes are psychic ones that can be approached only through metaphorical interpretation of external actions.

Ideological Strategy

In constructing explanations for the differential treatment of racial minorities, Myrdal and Montagu began with an ideological formulation, then shifted ground to economics and psychology. Direct economic explanation, however, turned out to be incapable of standing by itself; while the two main trends of the psychological approach have either retrogressed to neo-racist polemics or become locked into the metaphors of psychohistory. Ideological strategy remains; but ideological explanation has suffered from so bad a name in the not very distant past that scholars often felt obliged to repudiate its influence, as did Winthrop Jordan when he wrote that to describe racism as 'merely the rationalizing ideology of the oppressor' was to 'advance a grievous error'.[28] There are, of course, ideological reasons why ideological interpretation stood in disrepute. Most basic among them is simply the obverse of the reason suggested earlier as to why the psychological approach has been so widely accepted: ideological interpretation does *not* fit harmoniously into either the consensus or progressive varieties of American national consciousness because it stems from a class analysis of historical change. The Cold War intensified that lack of harmony to the point of driving ideological interpretation underground in American academic and intellectual circles.

As the Cold War itself went underground, ideology gradually found its way to the surface again. Its return to visibility was heralded by the widely influential work of the historian Bernard Bailyn and the anthropologist Clifford Geertz. Both gave central billing to ideology; yet these scholars in different ways stripped the ideological concept of most of its class linkages. The actual reuniting (in America, at least) of ideology with class analysis, resulted from – or coincided with – publication of the prison writings of the Italian Communist Antonio Gramsci, and their extraordinary impact in Europe and the United States. Post-Gramscian ideology, however, differs from the ideology of many earlier Marxists or even from that of the Frankfurt scholar Karl Mannheim. The concept has become at once broader and less optimistic.

It is less optimistic because it has abandoned the Enlightenment belief in self-evident social truths that need only the ripping away of obscurantist ideology to be revealed to universal perception.[29] At the same time, the older, limited notion of ideology as willful distortion of reality has yielded to a broader concept of 'principles, programs and goals' through which a particular class strives, in Gramsci's phrase, to achieve hegemony – to impose 'its values and attitudes', its sense of direction, on the society it dominates or hopes to dominate.[30] Since literature and art as well as socialization, education and political debate furnish the substance of ideological construction as so conceived, studies of that construction must cope with a vast terrain. As applied to the differential treatment of non-white peoples in American history, it is not surprising therefore that ideological explanations remain scattered and fragmentary. So far there has been no single study of the problem as a whole. Nonetheless it is not difficult to piece together a summary of what presently exists by way of definition and explanation.

1. Racism is the pivotal concept for the ideological argument. It is defined as a system of beliefs and attitudes that ascribe central importance to real or presumed racial differences. Physical differences between groups may be easily visible and are certainly real, but racism reaches beyond them to assert that moral, intellectual and psychological qualities are also racially characteristic; that they are transmitted, along with physical traits, by heredity; and that these together constitute a major chain of historical causation. Racism is thus fundamentally a theory of history. Like other theories or systems of beliefs and attitudes, such as liberalism or nationalism, it exists as a phenomenon in history, capable of explication in terms of historical causation.[31]

2. Racism entered history as a product of that complex sequence of events, which about the middle of the fifteenth century impelled peoples of Western Europe to an outward surge of exploration, conquest and exploitation. Since these events accelerated the accumulation of capital, they set the stage for the capitalist industrial revolution in Europe.

3. Thus the same sequence that led to expansion gave to western Europeans long-sustained advantages in social and economic organization and in industrial and military technology. By the end of the nineteenth century, European empires controlled most of the earth.

4. Since Europeans are generally white-skinned, while the peoples they encountered are generally dark, for three and a half centuries basic human relationships centered on the domination of whites over people of color.

5. Racism has stemmed from the appearance of social reality. It expanded into a rationalization and a means of justifying and perpetuating that reality. Rationalization began with speculative accounts of the divine origins of white Christian civilization. As European thought shifted from a religious to scientific orientation, racism assumed the form of a scientific doctrine.

6. Linked to the beginnings of the social sciences, racism became part of that massive synthesis of physical, biological and historical explanation that nineteenth-century science bequeathed to humanity. It then confronted every informed person, white or non-white, in the dual guise of existing social reality and established scientific knowledge. Each individual, although perhaps rejecting certain moral or political implications of racism, remained powerless to dispute its standing as social reality and scientific truth.

7. Racism retained its prominence until the early twentieth century, when the combined effects of scientific criticism and of historical changes that it was incapable of explaining began to undermine its foundations. Even then it continued a vigorous existence within the cultures and institutions of predominantly white societies. The institutional embodiment, as a kind of residual class base, has generated continuing endeavors to reestablish its earlier claims to scientific credibility.

There are obvious gaps in this sequence. One is the already familiar proclivity to circular argument. Thus it might appear in Point 5 that racism is simultaneously cause and result of the differential treatment of non-whites.[32] Ideological explanation understands social behavior as ultimately moved by consciousness of class or group interests. Morality then centers on definitions and interrelationships attributed to self (as the necessary locus of consciousness); to class (as trustee of rational – if not always perceived – self interest); and to group (as the assignee of dedications and purposes). Hegemony, in this reading, becomes simply the establishment or preservation by a ruling class of identifications between *class* and *group*. But why should it be supposed that seventeenth-and eighteenth-century Europeans experienced spontaneous convictions of self-interest and group dedication that required them to burn up their lives on plantations and slave ships in order to accumulate capital for entrepreneurs back home?

What is needed to resolve the dilemma of circularity is an ideological explanation for the initial act of differential treatment that does not invoke racism or any variant under some other name as a causal factor. Edmund Morgan in a study of the origins of slavery in Virginia offers an example of precisely such an explanatory process. Morgan reverses Jordan. Instead of insisting on the primacy of subjective factors in the English psyche, Morgan shows how Virginians established African slavery through a series of rational responses to real situations, each step illuminated for them by concepts of labor, class and wealth that they had brought from England. Racism is not a necessary cause in Morgan's account of the origin of slavery in Virginia. Rather it results from that origin and becomes a necessary cause for what follows.[33]

More formidable than the problem of circularity is that of continuity. How has racism reproduced patterns of racially differential behavior for more than three centuries through shifts of ruling class power and across a spectrum of labor systems from slavery to wage labor? As would be expected, the most successful ideological explanations of continuity have dealt with slavery. There is no great difficulty, for example, in understanding the planters' defense of slavery, or that, although racism need not have caused any particular act of racial exploitation, it must have become a central factor in justifying a class that achieved wealth and power through such systematic exploitation. 'Wherever racial subordination exists', as Eugene Genovese put it, 'racism exists. ...'"[34]

But how can such an understanding of planters explain why non-slaveholding whites acquiesced either in planter dominance or in its ideological justifications? And what of the North and West? Slavery was only one segment of time and space occupied by racism in American history. The 'world the slaves made' existed for at least half a century within an egalitarian white society described by the sociologist Pierre van den Berghe as '*herrenvolk* democracy'.[35] The same democracy eventually destroyed slavery, yet retained the doctrine of white supremacy as keystone in its new legitimizing synthesis. Upon that democracy rose an industrial capitalist order. As labor power assumed its characteristically capitalist form of commodity, economic theory might have predicted that racial characteristics would lose their relevance in the labor market. On the contrary, they dominated the labor market. From what socio-economic nutriments, in the era of modernization, did the ideological component, racism, draw its sustenance?

The question is crucial. It cannot yet be answered adequately, since no systematic explanation for the differential treatment of racial minorities has been developed for Jacksonian, or Gilded Age, or Populist America – let alone for America of the progressive or New Deal or Cold War periods. Nor has ideological analysis been applied to such historically baffling phenomena as the shift of federal policy with respect to race and racism after the Second World War, or the cult of ethnicity and beginnings of neo-racism in the 1960s and 1970s. In default of such projects, the ideological strategy will remain tentative, more broadly based on expectations than on achievement.

Nonetheless, it seems fair to say that of the several approaches surveyed the ideological appears the most promising. It promises, in the first place, a conceptual frame for more limited explanatory sequences such as that of the split labor market examined above, or theories of labor market segmentation in advanced capitalism, which begin by assuming racism as a factor of the environment under study. At longer range, it promises to meet a pressing need by providing a historical explanation for the differential treatment of racial minorities in the United States that could command general acceptance simply because it works. The purpose of this book is to offer a modest contribution in that direction.

The book is divided in three parts. Part One begins by posing class and racial hierarchy as the basis of Whig politics, taking American whiggism not in the once-standard mode of a reaction to Jacksonian initiatives, but as the established order against which those initiatives were directed. The focus then shifts to the Jacksonian side with examinations of the press and theater selected to exemplify the reworking of racist ingredients in mass culture to justify white egalitarianism. Part One ends with an interpretation of the Jacksonian Democratic party.

Part Two brings forward three transitional sequences: the first involving the popularization of regional vernacular heroes; the second and third stemming from urban artisan radicalism on one hand and New England National Republicanism on the other. All three pursued separate routes (by way of the Free Soil alliance) into the Republican coalition. Part Three begins with the Republican party and the new Republican West. In the context of western working-class experience, it explores the problem of class consciousness in a racially segmented labor force. The last chapter but one – continuing earlier discussions of vernacular characterization in drama and fiction – traces the class and racial components of western heroes from Leatherstocking to Owen Wister's Virginian. The book ends with an inquiry into the failure of late nineteenth–century challenges to industrial capitalism, and the degree to which white racist ideas and institutions tended to inhibit effective opposition to ruling-class legitimacy.

My effort throughout this work is to get at the actual processes of ideological revision. Whether animated by deliberate intent of leadership or through individual compulsions of 'ideological innovators', those processes reaffirmed the credibility of the racist component. They added necessary adjustments of conceptualization and tone to conform, first, to shifts in the class structure of the ruling coalitions; and, second, to changes in the scientific, religious and attitudinal mix of world-reality as perceived. I have worked from a conviction that consciousness mandates an effort to impart meaning and coherence, including some system of purposefulness or moral commitment, to experience. Not all experience is social but the consciousness of it is framed in social experience. The starting point, therefore, is the collective inheritance, differentiated by class or social group background – the received wisdom each individual copes with, repetitively for the most part, sometimes innovatively. What results is an ongoing 'social construction of reality'.[36] Conflicting ideological components, such as a defense of racial exploitation on one hand or an assertion of racial equality on the other, must depend in part for their effectiveness upon a degree of correspondence with that ongoing construction. It is within this rather narrow perimeter of correspondence, seemingly, that anticipations of creative input to historical change must find their place, if they are to have a place.

Notes

1. Although my focus is not on studies of ideas about race, such works are crucial to any investigation of racial ideology. I have relied especially on George M. Fredrickson, *The Black Image in the White Mind: The Debate on Afro-American Character and Destiny, 1817–1914*, New York 1971; Thomas F. Gossett, *Race: The History of an Idea in America*, New York 1963; Dwight W. Hoover, *The Red and the Black*, Chicago 1976; William Stanton, *The Leopard's Spots: Scientific Attitudes toward Race in America, 1815–1859*, Chicago 1960; Reginald Horsman, *Race and Manifest Destiny: The Origins of American Racial Anglo-Saxonism*, Cambridge, Mass. 1981; and Roy Harvey Pearce, *The Savages of America: A Study of the Indian and the Idea of Civilization*, rev. ed., Baltimore 1965.

2. Gunnar Myrdal assumed directorship of the Carnegie Corporation's project in 1937, and his final report was published in 1944. Page references are to 'The Twentieth Anniversary Edition'. Gunnar Myrdal, *An American Dilemma: The Negro Problem and Modern Democracy*, New York 1962. Myrdal's account of the project is appears on pp. *li–lxii*. Parallel citations are included in Arnold Rose, *The Negro in America: The Condensed Version of Gunnar Myrdal's An American Dilemma*, New York 1948.

3. Myrdal, pp. 85, 97; Rose, pp 31, 35.

4. Myrdal, pp. 8–14, 78–80, 89; Rose, pp. 1–5, 20–30, 33.

5. Myrdal, pp. 88, 98; Rose, pp. 33, 35.

6. Myrdal, pp. 102, 111, 69–70, 28, 53–54; Rose, pp. 37, 41, 27, 12, 21.

7. Ashley Montagu, *Man's Most Dangerous Myth: The Fallacy of Race*, Cleveland and New York 1965, pp. 151, 154–55.

8. Montagu, Appendix A, pp. 34, 36–371.

9. Montagu, pp. 351–59.

10. Myrdal, pp. 1015–1024.

11. See Rose's summation, p. 320, presumably concurred in by Myrdal; Rose, p. *xii*.

12. Two examples among many: Philip Taft, *Organized Labor in American History*, New York 1964, pp. 301–4, in contrast to pp. 306, 308; Philip Foner, *History of the Labor Movement in the United States*, Vol. 1: *From Colonial Times to the Founding of the American Federation of Labor*, New York 1947, pp. 272–76.

13. Job competition and the opposite side of the same coin, the argument that racial division in the labor market functions to benefit employers by weakening the ability of the labor force to act collectively in its own interest, appear in a wide variety of economic explanations. See, for example, Harold M. Baron, 'Racial Discrimination in Advanced Capitalism: A Theory of Nationalism and Division in the Labor Market', in Richard C. Edwards, Michael Reich, and David M. Gordon, eds, *Labor Market Segmentation*, Lexington, Mass. 1973, pp. 203, 207–8; Raymond S. Franklin and Solomon Resnik, *The Political Economy*

of Racism, New York 1973, p. 22; David M. Gordon, ed., *Problems in Political Economy: An Urban Perspective*, Lexington, Mass. 1977, pp. 147–49; Robert Cherry, 'Economic Theories of Racism', in Gordon, ed., *Problems ...* , p. 173; Victor Perlo, *Economics of Racism, USA: Roots of Black Inequality*, New York 1975, pp. 146, 149, 163–64.

14. The comments on split labor market theory are directed to several essays by my colleague and friend, Edna Bonacich: 'A Theory of Ethnic Antagonism: The Split Labor Market', *American Sociological Review* 37 (October 1972): 547–59; 'A Theory of Middleman Minorities', *ASR* 38 (October 1973): 583–94; 'Abolition, the Extension of Slavery, and the Position of Free Blacks: A Study of Split Labor Markets in the United States, 1830–1863', *The American Journal of Sociology* 81 (November 1975): 601–28; 'Advanced Capitalism and Black/White Race Relations in the United States: A Split Labor Market Interpretation', *ASR* 41 (February 1976): 34–51. William Julius Wilson, *The Declining Significance of Race: Blacks and Changing American Institutions*, Chicago 1978, pp. 144–54, arguing for the rising significance of class in the disadvantaged situation of non-white minorities, recognizes that racism has played a major role in determining the over-representation of non-whites in the new industrial 'underclass'.

15. Thomas Sowell, *Race and Economics*, New York 1975.

16. Ibid., pp. 54–55, 71–90, 131. Sowell, *The Economics and Politics of Race: An International Perspective*, New York 1983, extends his free market analysis to the world at large in a wide-ranging and interesting book. The historical explanation of racial inequality in the United States, however, remains basically unchanged.

17. Sowell, *Race and Economics*, pp. 61–80, 127–31, 143. For a striking contrast to Sowell's view, see James P. Comer, *Maggie's American Dream: The Life and Times of a Black Family*, New York 1988, especially pp. 212–15.

18. Sowell, *Race and Economics*, pp. 143–44, 149–50, 153–56, 192, 202–3, 208.

19. Ibid., pp. 4, 5–21, 116, 142–50, 153–56.

20. Nathan Glazer and Daniel Patrick Moynihan, *Beyond the Melting Pot: The Negroes, Puerto Ricans, Jews, Italians and Irish of New York City*, Cambridge, Mass. 1963; Glazer and Moynihan, eds, *Ethnicity: Theory and Practice*, Cambridge, Mass. 1975; Glazer, *Affirmative Discrimination: Ethnic Inequality and Public Policy*, New York 1975; see especially pp. 5, 6, 3–22.

21. Glazer and Moynihan, *Beyond the Melting Pot*, pp. 33, 52; Glazer, *Affirmative Discrimination*, pp. 72–73.

22. In contrast to Nathan Glazer's 'American orientation', see Pierre L. van den Berghe, *Race and Racism: A Comparative Perspective*, New York 1967, p. 77; Ronald Takaki, *Iron Cages: Race and Culture in Nineteenth Century America*, New York 1979, pp. 11–15. For a more recent examination by Takaki, 'Reflections on Racial Patterns in America', Takaki, ed., *From Different Shores: Pespectives on Race and Ethnicity in America*, New York 1987, pp. 26–37.

23. As Nathan Huggins points out in 'Herbert Gutman and Afro-American History', *Labor History* 29 (Summer 1985): 323–35, Glazer and Moynihan could have taken most of their descriptive material on African-American families from the Chicago School sociologists, E. Franklin Frazier *The Negro Family*, 1941, and Charles S. Johnson, *Shadow of the Plantation*, 1936, who attributed presumed family malfunctions to a presumed total destruction of the African culture. The psychocultural deficit theory stems mainly from Stanley M. Elkins, *Slavery: A Problem in American Institutional and Intellectual Life*, New York 1963, first published by University of Chicago Press in 1959. For refutations of this theory, see Andrew Billingsley, *Black Families in White America*, Englewood Cliffs, N.J. 1968; John Blassingame, *The Slave Community*, New York 1972; Eugene Genovese, *Roll, Jordan, Roll*, New York 1974; Herbert Gutman, *The Black Family in Slavery and Freedom, 1750–1925*, New York 1976.

24. Gordon W. Allport, *The Nature of Prejudice*, [1954], abridged ed., Garden City, N.Y. 1958. Winthrop D. Jordan, *White Over Black: American Attitudes Toward the Negro, 1550–1812*, Chapel Hill, N.C. 1968. Theodor Adorno et al., *The Authoritarian Personality*, New York 1950. Martin Jay, *Adorno*, Cambridge, Mass. 1984, pp. 38–41.

25. Jordan, *The White Man's Burden: Historical Origins of Racism in the United States*, New York 1974, pp. 22, 49, 46–54. *The White Man's Burden* is a 'quite drastic abridgement with minor modifications', p. *viii*, of the author's longer and vastly more detailed *White Over Black*. Since the argument is the same in each, I have cited the shorter version.

26. Jordan, p. 50 (italics in original); David Brion Davis, *Slavery and Human Progress*, New York 1984, p. 38.

27. Fawn Brodie, *Thaddeus Stevens: Scourge of the South*, New York 1959; Brodie, *Thomas Jefferson: An Intimate History*, New York 1974; Eric Erikson, *Young Man Luther: A Study in Psychoanalysis and History*, New York 1958; Michael P. Rogin, *Fathers and Children: Andrew Jackson and the Subjugation of the American Indian*, New York 1975.

28. Jordan, p. *ix*.

29. Bernard Bailyn, *The Ideological Origins of the American Revolution*, Cambridge, Mass. 1967; Clifford Geertz, 'Ideology as a Cultural System', in *The Interpretation of Cultures: Selected Essays*, New York 1973; Antonio Gramsci, *Selections from the Prison Notebooks*, New York 1971; and *Selections from the Political Writings, 1910–1920*, New York 1977; Carl Boggs, *Gramsci's Marxism*, London 1976. For an account of the changing meanings of the term *ideology*, see Martin Seliger, *Ideology and Politics*, London 1976. My own usage of the term will be clear enough, I think, from my comments on 'post-Gramscian ideology'. For a more formal definition, with which I generally agree, see Seliger, p. 119. Mannheim, *Ideology and Utopia* [1929], New York 1936, stands between early Marxian and post-Gramscian notions of ideology, since Mannheim allows at least the possibility of self-evident perceptions of social reality by occasional utopians or chiliasts.

30. George M. Fredrickson, review of David Brion Davis, *The Problem of Slavery in the Age of Revolution*, in *New York Review of Books* 16 October 1975, pp. 38–40.

31. The definition of racism corresponds to a fairly widely held view (for example, van den Berghe, p. 11) with a historian's twist at the end. Points two through seven are a composite drawn from many sources, most of which I cannot individually identify. The book review by George Fredrickson referred to in note 30 above, and an essay by the same author, cited in note 32 below, have been helpful; likewise Davis, *Slavery and Human Progress*, pp. 51–82. I should also refer to *Caste, Class and Race: A Study in Social Dynamics*, by Oliver Cox, Garden City, N.Y. 1948, as a work with which I have both deep agreements and strong disagreements. Barbara Fields, 'Ideology and Race in American History' in J. Morgan Kousser and James M. McPherson, eds, *Region, Race and Reconstruction: Essays in Honor of C. Vann Woodward*, New York 1982, pp. 143–47, generally parallels the argument I have set out. Fields's essay becomes, I think, unnecessarily confusing because of a failure to distinguish between *race* as an objectively visible fact and *racism* as an ideological construct.

32. Historically oriented scholars have generally rejected ethnocentric explications of racism because they invoke instinctual drives or 'universals' of human nature. Frederickson, 'Toward a Social Interpretation of the Development of American Racism', in Nathan Huggins, Martin Kilson and Daniel Fox, eds, *Key Issues in the Afro-American Experience*, New York 1971, 1:246. Frederickson distinguishes between an 'implicit' or 'societal' racism, which he says characterized the white society of North America until the early nineteenth century, and 'ideological' racism, said to have come into existence in the 1830s as a conscious defense of slavery against attack. Neither appears to be equal to, or directly caused by, ethnocentrism. Van den Berghe, pp. 12–13, accepts ethnocentrism as a nearly universal human trait, but separates it decisively from racism.

33. Edmund Morgan, *American Slavery – American Freedom: The Ordeal of Colonial Virginia*, New York 1975. For an admirably succinct application of a comparable argument to colonial slavery as a whole, see Robin Blackburn, *The Overthrow of Colonial Slavery, 1776–1848*, London 1988, pp. 3–31, especially pp. 9–11. These two works suffice to destroy the foundation of Winthrop Jordan's psychological explanation.

34. Genovese, *Roll, Jordan, Roll*, pp. 4, 7–49.

35. Van den Berghe, p. 77.

36. I have borrowed this phrase from the title of Peter L. Berger and Thomas Luckman, *The Social Construction of Reality: A Treatise in the Sociology of Knowledge*, New York 1966.

PART I

National Republican Thesis, Jacksonian Antithesis

1

National Republicans

Public discussion of questions of political power and social structure in the United States before the Civil War developed largely within the forum of party controversy. Soon after ratification of the Constitution the characteristically American pattern of two parties locked in ambivalent hostility crystalized briefly in the rivalry of Federalists and Republicans. Federalism, increasingly pro-British and regional to New England, disintegrated after the War of 1812, as some of its partisans receded into political impotence while others, especially outside New England, came to terms with the ascendant opposition. By contrast, the Republicans swept on to a decade of unchallenged dominance. Often misleadingly referred to as the Era of Good Feeling, this interval of one-party government actually nourished a ferocious intraparty factionalism that erupted into rebellion against the last Republican administration, that of John Quincy Adams. Andrew Jackson's victory over Adams in 1828 led to a renewal of overt party competition known to historians as the Second American Party System. Jacksonians became *Democratic*, while supporters of Adams at first annexed the adjective *National*, then took to themselves the ancient and revered name *Whig*.

Common usage has made these terms indispensable, whether conceptually accurate or not. *Democratic* did in fact designate a substantial portion of what the party of that name stood for and against. Such was not the case with the Whigs. Their naming had been opportunistic and contingent: opportunistic, in that positive reference to the English champions of parliamentary liberties and the heroes of American independence implied exclusive claim to traditions no more in the domain of one party than the other; contingent, in that the stressed issue (fear of executive encroachment on the legislative branch), however real it may have been, was merely contingent to Whig principle. As the opening battles of the second party system made clear, control over the federal executive conveyed massive advantages in securing and maintaining congressional majorities. Whiggish slogans directed against 'King Andrew' were tactical weapons of a minority party. Had Adams defeated Jackson in 1828 and pushed to fulfillment the national programs set forth in the messages of his first term, his Jacksonian opponents might with equal logic have styled themselves Whigs while berating 'King John' for executive usurpation.

There was of course more than contingency in the fact that the Whigs became the minority party. While it might be roughly accurate to say that Democrats and Whigs alike were the progeny of Republicanism, it would be mistaken to assume that the new parties simply divided the old constituency. The Jacksonian breakaway was a revolt from outside and down under directed against what, perhaps not Jackson himself, but certainly masses of his partisans, perceived as an oligarchic trend in the Republican succession. Instead of evoking patriotic echoes of 1812, the adjective *National* now conveyed suspicions of upper-class pretension that attached to the administrations of Monroe and especially of Adams, whose debacle made the party name a liability. Technically, then, the line of descent was Republican: National Republican: Whig. The term *Democratic* entered the arena in rebuttal to *National Republican*, while *Whig* made its entry as an effort to evade the class impact of the Democratic attack on the National Republican establishment. *National Republican* will be taken as the primary term, or thesis, in this polemical sequence.

The rise of John Quincy Adams to the presidency parallels the historical events that led to National Republicanism. Inducted by his father's revolutionary career into national leadership, Adams, during the quarter-century that bracketed the War of 1812, moved through the *cursus honorum* of public office. United States senator, envoy to Russia, chief of the American negotiating team at Ghent, minister to Great Britain, Adams became secretary of state under President Monroe in time to gather in the delayed fruits of the War of 1812. These were what patriots had long dreamed of: total control over the Mississippi Valley and a foothold on the Pacific. Adams's accession to the presidency in 1825 seemingly reaffirmed the hope for government through nonpartisan consensus. 'We are all Republicans, we are all Federalists', Thomas Jefferson had prophecied in 1801. To enthusiastic public servants like Adams, *National* Republicanism seemed to fulfill that prophecy. Son of the last Federalist president, he had come to Republicanism not without deep distrust, reinforced by the French Revolution, of its subversive potential. But *national* served as reassurance against *republican*.

In arriving at this happy combination, two opposite *anti*-national infections had been shuffled off: Republican commitment to world revolution on one hand, and Federalist faith that only Britain could save the upper-class world from revolution on the other. Weaned of such illusions, the Republic had not only outlasted the Napoleonic wars but used them to gain its own ends. Vis-à-vis Europe and the new republics of America, it could pursue its own proper and specific interests. Its commerce circled the globe. The western regions would become the site for architectural statesmanship of a new order. Its magistrates would speak to America and the world in the measured, authoritative, educated voices of a coalition of landholding and commercial affluence. Adams assembled a cabinet of notables headed by Henry Clay, his fellow commissioner at Ghent, chief of the congressional War Hawks of 1812, and, as secretary of state, heir apparent to the presidency. Among the others were James Barbour, Secretary of War – planter, lawyer, war governor of Virgina, former United States senator; William Wirt, attorney general – dean of the Maryland bar, biographer of Patrick Henry; and Richard Rush, a son of Pennsylvania's famous revolutionary doctor, former comptroller of the United States and minister to Britain – as secretary of the treasury. Not quite one of the administration but still linked to the nationalist coalition was John C. Calhoun of South Carolina, the vice president.

Together these men comprised a regional cross-section of upper-class leaders committed to the *National* Republican vista. Publicized through messages and official papers, their program carried forward as the ideological heritage of American Whigs. In its broader manifestations it will be referred to henceforth as the National Republican thesis. Certainly the most celebrated exposition of that thesis was John Quincy Adams's presidential message of 1825, which provides the focus of the present chapter. The first of the sections that follow reconstructs the ideas and attitudes about race available to John Quincy Adams in the milieu of his youth, and presumably accessible to other young men of his class and generation. The second shows Adams modifying and adjusting those ideas and attitudes to suit the strategic needs, as he perceived them, of the class coalition that was moving him forward as a leader. A third and final section examines the 1825 message. Since, however, racial relations entered that message only as silences in the studied rhetoric, it will be necessary to examine also a corollary statement on Indian policy by Secretary of War James Barbour. That will be the opening topic of Chapter 2, which turns then to the Whig party and its somewhat tarnished efforts to carry the National Republican program into mass politics.

The Racial Component

In the summer of 1785, John Quincy Adams, eighteen, returned from Europe to Americanize his largely European education with a degree from

Harvard. Landing at New York, he journeyed north through Connecticut, stopping to visit friends and political colleagues of his father, then minister to the Netherlands. Among them was the nationalist poet and Congregational pastor Timothy Dwight, whose work the young Adams took to be on a par with the best writing in Europe.[1] Grandson of Jonathan Edwards, later the ultra-Federalist president of Yale College, Dwight had ample credentials as an enunciator of Puritan values.[2] What he had to say about Indians offers a convenient introduction to the outlook into which New Englanders of John Quincy Adams's generation were being socialized. Dwight's epic, *The Conquest of Canaan*, was dedicated to George Washington and published in the year of the younger Adams's visit; it allegorized Anglo-Americans as children of Israel redeeming a promised land from Indian hordes so devilish that 'wives wade[d] in nuptial, sires in filial, gore'; and even their 'babes ... by vile affections lur'd, in guilt, and years ... alike matured.' Satan ruled unchallenged in America, until 'This sea of guilt unmeasur'd to prevent / Our chosen race eternal justice sent. ...'[3]

So harsh a verdict expressed the hatred of early times rekindled by the rage of revolutionary patriots against frontier Indians allied with the British. Nine years later, in *Greenfield Hill*, Dwight's sentiments had mellowed but not fundamentally changed. Looking out over the meadows of his own parish, Dwight reflected that here Pequot warriors once had battled New England's defenders of the faith. Slain more than a century and a half earlier, the Pequots could now be likened to such reputable pagans as Phoenicians and Etruscans whose overthrow had made way for Roman civilization and Christianity. The classic comparison imparted a tragic glory to the New World contestants, thus furnishing a substitute for that heroic antiquity deemed indispensable to the growth of a national literature. The mood became one of pensive melancholy:

> Indulge, my native land, indulge the tear...
> To me each twig from Adam's stock is near
> And sorrow falls upon an Indian tomb.[4]

John Adams, to whom *Greenfield Hill* was dedicated, could also shed a nostalgic tear. To his former friend, and former enemy, Thomas Jefferson, he wrote in 1812 that he had 'interest in the Indians and a commiseration from my childhood. ...There was a numerous family ... whose wigwam was within a mile of this house ... and I, in my boyish rambles ... never failed to be treated with whortleberries, strawberries or apples ... but the girls went out to service and the boys to sea, till not a soul is left. ...'[5] In this sad outcome, Adams conceded no shade of injustice. 'I see not how the Indians could have been treated with more equity or humanity than they have been in general in North America. ...What infinite pains have been taken and expenses incurred ... to convert these poor, ignorant savages to Christianity! and alas! with how little success!'[6]

The ambivalent wisdom conveyed by such messages was that Indians were human, presumed to be children of God, capable of religious perceptions and moral concepts; yet blind to Christianity, locked into stubborn pagan rejection of 'agriculture and civilization'.[7] All that could be done for them had conscientiously been done; if they sank down into oblivion, that was their choice.

Were there other signals with respect to Indians that might have made themselves audible to the young Adams? One other significant voice must certainly have been that of Thomas Jefferson. Jefferson seems to have furnished an alternative father figure for Adams who, during his Paris childhood, had known and revered Jefferson as a man of reason and science, embodying in contrast to Europe the balance and equanimity of America. The father must have known this too, since in the year of their deaths he wrote Jefferson referring to 'our John', and explained, 'I call him our John, because when you was at Cul de Sac at Paris, he appeared to be almost as much your son as mine.' If one thinks not primarily of region but of the shared experience of making a revolution, there was much truth in what John Adams said.[8]

As to Indians, the view from the Chesapeake buttressed that of Massachusetts Bay. Jefferson's *Notes on Virginia*, published in Paris and London in the year John Quincy Adams returned to enroll at Harvard,[9] must have been read by both Adamses before publication. Jefferson's Indians also were marked for extinction; liquor, smallpox and war being assigned as principal causes, together with the loss of their food supply resulting from the 'abridgement of territory to a people who lived principally on the spontaneous productions of nature.' Although by no means unaware of the extent of Indian agriculture, Jefferson repeatedly described their economic system as hunting and gathering, and asserted that they remained in a state of barbarism, or savagery. Barbarism could be in certain respects an admirable condition, since it nurtured virtues akin to those associated with classical antiquity such as loyalty, courage in combat, and fortitude to endure suffering and death.[10] Yet it contained fatal defects. Because of the men's addiction to hunting and war, women were subjugated and exploited. So must be the case, Jefferson reasoned, 'with every barbarous people. ... The stronger sex imposes on the weaker. ... It is civilization alone which replaces women in the enjoyment of their natural equality. ... Were we in equal barbarism, our females would be equal drudges.' Due to their laborious existence, Indian women deliberately reduced their birth rate; and this, added to the nutritional deficiencies of a hunting and gathering economy, held natural increase among Indians lower than among Africans or Europeans in America.[11]

Jefferson's argument made Indian decline a result of their stage of culture. He contended for example that when individual Indian women moved into civilized households by marrying white traders, they reproduced at the same rate as white women. Separated from the barbaric environment, 'we shall probably find', he wrote, 'that [Indians] are formed in mind as well as in body, on the same module with the "Homo Sapiens Europaeus".'[12] Might they not, then, collectively opt out of barbarism? Curiously, Jefferson offered no clear answer to this question. He apparently believed that somehow, through culture or biology, Indians were locked into their primitive stage. In isolation, barbarism might go on forever; when confronted by civilization it could only retreat into a vanishing wilderness until it perished. This was the expectation that shaped Jefferson's later proposal for an Indian wilderness preserve within the Louisiana Purchase; and it is the view he must have conveyed in 1785 by conversation as well as through the chain of reasoning implicit in the *Notes*.[13]

In their thinking about Indians, Jefferson and John Adams both drew upon Enlightenment concepts of international relations, especially as set forth in Emmerich de Vattel's famous treatise, *The Law of Nations*.[14] John Quincy Adams, reading law at Newburyport, likewise thumbed Vattel, noting in his journal that the author's 'sentiments and principles' were derived from 'that law of nature, which every person of common sense and honesty must wish to prevail: Do as you would be done by.'[15] In Vattel, Adams must have read the following:

> The earth, as we have already observed, belongs to mankind in general, and was designed to furnish them with subsistence: if each nation had from the beginning resolved to appropriate to itself a vast country, that the people might live only by hunting, fishing, and wild fruits, our globe would not be sufficient to maintain a tenth part of its present inhabitants. We do not therefore deviate from the views of nature in confining the Indians within narrower limits. However, we cannot help praising the moderation of the English puritans who first settled in New England; who, notwithstanding their being furnished with a charter from their sovereign, purchased of the Indians the land of which they intended to take possession.[16]

No doubt Adams agreed with this judgement. Visiting his father, the vice president, in 1795, he attended a presidential reception for a delegation of Chickasaw chiefs. In what appears to be his earliest written reference to American Indians, Adams compared their speech to the neighing of horses which 'more than once reminded me of the Houynms. ...'[17]

The direct evidence of Adams's youthful thoughts about African slaves is almost equally sparse. But here too it is not difficult to reconstruct what must have come to him in the process of socialization. Africans, unlike

Indians, he had often seen in Boston and Braintree. The Adams family owned no slaves; but the Quincy side, from which came his mother Abigail, had, and perhaps still did at the time she was born.[18] Anglo-Americans in Massachusetts seem for the most part to have experienced little difficulty in living with African slavery, at least until their own controversy with England.[19] Slavery was never actually abolished in Massachusetts. It came to an end in 1783 when the state supreme court construed the bill of rights of the state Constitution of 1780 as incompatible with bondage. John Adams had written that bill of rights. Yet neither he nor his fellow citizens who voted for ratification could have anticipated with certainty that the 1780 Constitution would outlaw slavery, since its relevant language was virtually the same as that already familiar from the Declaration and currently being written into the new state Constitution of Virginia, where no one expected emancipation to result. Yet this may underestimate John Adams. While he had undoubtedly sought to avoid political confrontation over the issue, it seems likely that he, as well as his southern colleagues, Jefferson and leading Virginians of that generation among them, perceived the Declaration and bill of rights as pointing towards eventual emancipation. John Adams may not have expected the result so quickly in Massachusetts; certainly he never opposed it.[20]

In this, as in other matters, Abigail Adams was more radical than her husband. 'I wish most sincerely there was not a slave in the province', she wrote in 1774. 'It allways appeared a most iniquitous Scheme to me to fight ourselfs, for what we are daily robbing and plundering from those who have as good a right to freedom as we have.' And she added, doubtless referring to previous words between them, 'You know my mind upon this Subject.'[21] Her son John, while the father was at Philadelphia during the Revolution, saw his mother struggling to manage the family homestead despite inflation and a labor shortage. Sometimes she hired black workers because they were cheaper or the only ones she could get.[22] Wage labor, white or black, was liable to be swept off by calls for militia enlistment. She lamented in the summer of 1777 that the 'High Bounty ... has tempted my Negroe Head ... just in the middle of our Hay.'[23] Eleven years later, when John Adams had become vice president and Abigail presided not over subsistence farming but official households at the national capital, she informed her sister back in Braintree of the vicissitudes of the servant problem. Both in New York and Philadelphia the racially mixed market still included slaves. The vice president's wife could find no cook in the whole city of New York 'but what will get drunk'; and 'as to Negroes I am most sincerely sick of them.' Later, distinguishing between free blacks and slaves, she wrote that the 'servants here who are good for anything are Negroes who are slaves. The white ones are all vagabonds.'

She entreated her sister to send down a respectable black woman from Boston who understood pastry.[24] There appears little racial differentiation in these observations except to the extent that blacks (especially black slaves) were thought less likely to be 'vagabonds' than whites, especially white 'Foreigners'. What Abigail Adams was displaying could hardly yet be called, but eventually would become, the classic racial stance of American Whigs. We may assume that the son took it from her virtually intact.

With the father, by contrast – perhaps because of more recent yeoman origins – the style was quite different. John Adams believed that white men were demeaned by acting in the way black men were expected to act. From Philadelphia in 1777 he wrote to his wife Abigail forbidding the dispatch of a particular white servant on the ground of his 'playing Cards with Negroes and behaving like a rival with them for Wenches.' His correspondence regarding black soldiers in regiments of the line shows his major concern to have been that they might bring discredit upon Massachusetts since, like 'Lads and old men', they were 'Such as are unsuited for the Service. ...'[25]

A decade earlier, under the pseudonym Humphrey Ploughjogger, John Adams had published a series of vernacular epistles against the Stamp Act. These letters solicited yeoman and artisan support through excoriations of aristocracy and assertions of a white egalitarian ethic. 'I'de rather the Spittlefield weavers should pull down all the houses of old England', Ploughjogger declared, 'and knock the brains out of all the wicked great men there, than this country should lose their liberty. ... We won't be their negroes. Providence never designed us for negroes, I know, for if it had it wou'd have given us black hides, and thick lips, and flat noses, and short wooly hair, which it han't done, and therefore never intended us for slaves. This I know is as good a sillogism as any at colledge, I say we are as handsome as old England folks and should be as free.'[26]

Such were the signals with respect to Africans and African slavery reaching John Quincy Adams from his parents, and from the community he grew up in. By the time of his adolescence, the signals had converged upon a consensus, slightly flawed, yet nonetheless a consensus, that slavery ought not to have legal sanction in a republican order. But what of the status of Africans as social beings and members (or non-members) of the human family? All Africans, in the young Adams's experience, slave or free, occupied lower-class positions. His mother treated them no differently from white wage workers or servants, whom clearly she considered to be part of the human family. His father, on the other hand, like the general run of the community outside, spoke of blacks in terms of physical contempt that included, but went beyond, class difference.

As in the case of Indians, the view from the Chesapeake reinforced, initially, the thrust of socialization begun in Massachusetts. Jefferson's *Notes on the State of Virginia* favored legal termination of slavery, but with the proviso that blacks receive instruction at 'public expense' in 'tillage, arts or sciences', and then be colonized. Why was separation necessary? Because the 'deep rooted prejudices' of whites, together with 'ten thousand recollections, by the blacks of the injuries they have sustained', would inflame hatreds that could end only 'in the extermination of the one or the other race.' Inevitability of racial conflict stemmed, in Jefferson's argument, from physical difference 'fixed in nature' and 'as real as if its seat and cause were better known to us.' The outward manifestation of inner difference was color, crucially important in itself because from whiteness sprang the supreme beauty of white women. Blacks themselves testified to this fact by preferring white women over black 'as uniformly' as 'the Oranootan' sought 'black women over those of his own species.'[27]

Jefferson's color comparison proceeded from the outside in, from appearances to essentials. Skin and hair texture led to sweat glands that disseminated a 'disagreeable odor', then to the sexual apparatus by which blacks became 'more ardent after their female' than whites, yet remained deficient in the 'tender delicate mixture of sentiment'. Arriving at the mental faculties, Jefferson concluded that blacks were equal to whites in memory, but inferior in reason. Scarcely would one be found, he thought, able to comprehend 'the investigations of Euclid'; and as to imagination, any expression 'above the level of plain narrative' or 'even an elementary trait of painting or sculpture' was beyond their reach.[28]

To this indictment Jefferson attached a cautionary note: 'To justify a general conclusion requires many observations … ' especially 'where our conclusion would degrade a whole race of men from the rank in the scale of beings which their Creator may perhaps have given them.' Science must pursue the matter further. Meanwhile, he would propose hypothetically, 'as a suspicion only, that the blacks, whether originally a distinct race, or made distinct by time and circumstances, are inferior to whites in the endowments of body and mind.' Since, however, he had left scant elbow room for any alternative hypothesis, the trend of his thought was conveyed by the presumably scientific analogy of the 'Oranootan'. In any case, the practical arrangements of society must be based upon preponderant probability. Rome could relatively easily free its slaves since a freed slave mixed into the general population 'without staining the blood of his master'. In America, emancipation must be followed immediately by removal 'beyond the reach of mixture'.[29]

That at least was what Jefferson had written. At Paris, John Quincy Adams must have known Jefferson's household slaves, among them the coach driver, James – only a few years older than Adams – Sally Hemings's brother. It is unlikely he ever met Sally Hemings, since he left Paris two years before she came there; but his parents knew her well.[30] John Adams in 1802 accepted the authenticity of Thomas Callendar's exposure of the Sally Hemings relationship and commented that such was the 'natural and almost unavoidable consequence of that foul contagion in the human character, Negro slavery.'[31] The elder Adams's ready acceptance was doubtless facilitated by the fact that Jefferson had by then become a political enemy, yet also suggests corroboration of what he and Abigail previously suspected or knew. When the parents returned to Braintree in 1788, their oldest son must have asked about Jefferson, of whom he had once written in his diary, 'spent the evening with Mr. Jefferson, whom I love to be with.'[32] Such a perspicacious youth at twenty-one might have picked up clues from his parents' responses, or silences; but that is conjecture. However he heard of the Hemings connection, the connection itself could only have struck him as a betrayal of the moral obligation contained in Jefferson's own teaching.

In autumn 1788, during a full dress oration before the Phi Beta Kappa Society, the young man alluded to *Notes on the State of Virginia* as a landmark in the development of American letters. His parents went to New York for the inauguration of the new national government; and the crisis of his adolescence, pinpointed in the diary, began shortly afterwards.[33] Suffering something like a nervous breakdown, he interrupted his study of law and passed the winter of 1788/89 recuperating at his aunt's house in Haverhill. When well enough, he walked, rode, hunted ducks in the marshes; and fell in love for the first time, half in earnest. The young set at Haverhill whiled away winter afternoons with the games and sham battles of sexual awakening. A favored recreation of upper-class youth was the exchanging – and the occasional publication of – verses addressed to, or aimed at, young ladies of their circle.[34] Among several contributions of John Quincy Adams to this genre is a poem published in the Boston *Herald* in the winter of 1789. After a conventional declaration of enslavement to 'DINAH's charms', the poem continues,

> The partial gods, presiding at her birth,
> Gave DINAH beauty, and yet gave her worth;
> Kind nature ting'd with blackest hue her skin,
> As emblem of her innocence within.
> A jetty fleece adorns her lovely head,
> Her sparkling eyes are bordered round with red. ...
> Thy choice alone can make my anxious breast
> Supremely wretched or supremely blest.[35]

'Scipio Africanus', the signature, appears also as an entry in Adams's diary under the same date. The verse itself paraphrases a poem written by Adams in his notebook and presumably intended as a serious statement of love, or of longing for love. The structures are parallel, the opening and closing couplets the same except that 'DINAH' has become 'Clara'. The fourth lines also are identical but carry different meanings since for Clara 'the emblem of innocence within' is a skin of 'purest white'.[36]

To present Clara and DINAH as interchangeable must, for Adams's set, have seemed the ultimate *reductio ad absurdum* of romantic love. This might serve an immediate purpose in shielding the vulnerable egos of young men playing courtship games. It could do so because the young males (and the young women they were addressing) had been collectively socialized into a culture that perceived Africans as something like Oranootans – creatures sharing the biological powers of the human animal but so deficient in mental and moral faculties that they could neither grasp such self-evident truths as those of Euclid nor spiritualize sexual ardor with 'tender delicate' mixtures of 'sentiment'. Two aspects dominated this perception: that the deficiencies remained 'fixed in nature', and that physical sexuality was the culmination, the essence, of Africanness. Courtship games at Haverhill might come and go, but the social construction of Africanness was an enduring artifact that could be put to many uses.

Practical Applications of Racial Ideology

John Quincy Adams was born at the periphery of, but not *in*, the commercial wealth of Massachusetts. The family was of upper yeoman background. His father, the first Adams to become president, was also the first to attend Harvard College. College education, bringing within reach an upwardly mobile marriage to Abigail Quincy, established John Adams as a young lawyer at the start of the great controversy with England; thence he moved into national leadership through effective and courageous organizational activity. One of the 'young men of the Revolution', his career exemplified the co-optation of lower-class talent as well as the central role of Harvard College in that process. Modest increments of fortune accompanied successful revolution. By the late 1780s, the Adams family was investing in government securities, and ten years later had acquired a mansion in Braintree and real estate in Boston. The younger Adams, as a Harvard undergraduate, expressed concern over the threat posed by Shays' Rebellion to the stability of the currency and the pledged faith of government: that was the topic of his commencement day oration in 1787.[37] After college, family influence placed him in a local but distinguished law firm and later aided him to a first rung of the diplomatic ladder. By the time the young man completed his tour of overseas missions and at the age of forty assumed the office of secretary of state, he could estimate his fortune (separate from family properties) at about $100,000, a sum promising independent income for the remainder of his life. His own son, Charles Francis, completed this three-generation sequence by marrying into the highest echelons of Boston commercial wealth.[38]

That outcome, however, was by no means visible in earlier years. As a youth, resentfully aware of his ambivalent class status, John Quincy Adams had felt himself disadvantaged relative to wealthier young people of his set by the lack of what he considered a substantial family inheritance. He feared this deficit might damage his legal career and limit his marriage prospects. Reading law in the office of Theophilus Parsons, Newburyport's leading attorney, Adams constantly worried about wasting time, admonishing himself that his hope of becoming 'anything but an object of charity and contempt' depended solely on his own exertions.[39] This was the year of debate over ratification of the federal Constitution. With Newburyport strongly Federalist and the redoubtable Parsons heading the town's Federalist delegation to the Massachusetts ratifying convention, Adams identified with the minority. 'Nor do I wonder that he should approve of it', he wrote of Parsons in his diary, 'as it is calculated to increase the influence, power and wealth of those who have any already. If the Constitution be adopted, it will be a grand point in favor of the aristocratic party. ... For my own part, I am willing to take my chances under any government anywhere; but it is hard to give up a system which I have always been taught to cherish and to confess that a free government is inconsistent with human nature.'[40] Harboring such sentiments, it apparently came as a shock to learn that his father supported ratification. The son quickly readjusted his own orientations: 'I did not expect it and I was glad to find that I was mistaken, since it appears probable that the plan will be adopted.'[41]

Three years later when Adams first ventured into public politics, no trace remained of adolescent antifederalism. His 'Letters of Publicola', published in the summer of 1791, were a critique of Paine's *Rights of Man* and a rebuke to the incumbent secretary of state, Thomas Jefferson, for endorsing the American edition of Paine's work. Equating democracy with mob rule and indicting Paine as an instigator of class violence, the young Adams not only adhered to the Federalist line as it crystallized in the first Washington administration but contributed to defining that line.[42] And how was his indictment to deal with a father figure such as Jefferson? Adams moved through cycles of withdrawal and reconciliation with respect to Jefferson. Perhaps it was the influence of Jefferson that authorized his anti-Federalist phase at Newburyport: in order to come back to his own father he had to deny Jefferson. Perhaps also he felt himself obliged to repudiate Jefferson's relationship to Sally Hemings in order to come to terms with his own sexuality. The internal and external crises seem to have intertwined. Yet the 'Publicola Letters' – vitriolic against Paine – were merely quizzical and ironic in their reference to Jefferson. At most they chided him for letting party passion so cloud judgement that he had permitted scum like Paine to enter the precincts of political discourse. This was like bringing a mob into the consultative chambers, not quite the same as being one of the mob.[43]

Thus the denial of Jefferson remained indecisive. When, after ousting John Quincy Adams's father from the presidency in 1800, Jefferson invoked the shared Americanness of Republicans and Federalists, he was in a sense acknowledging the young man's earlier accusation. Doubtless Adams was fortunate that his father, forced into retirement, blamed the disasters of his administration in part on sabotage within the Federalist ranks, since that left the son elbow room for his own manoeuvers. Jefferson's victory had fetched him home from his first diplomatic post in Europe. Setting up his new family in a Boston town house, John Quincy Adams resumed his law practice and performed, briefly, a stellar role in Federalist politics. In 1802 he was summoned to Plymouth for an oration commemorating the landing of the Pilgrims.[44] It would be difficult to find a more perfect example of ideological construction. Using the occasion for an assertion of the class alliance to which he believed New England's ruling elite must commit itself, he called for unity among the children of all the great founders – of Raleigh, Calvert, Penn, Oglethorpe as well as of Bradford and Winthrop. To what purpose he made clear in his peroration: '"Westward the star of empire takes its way."' Let us unite in ardent supplication to the Founder of Nations and the Builder of Worlds, that what was then prophecy may continue unfolding into history … that the last may prove the noblest empire of time.'[45] Yet since empire building in America required possessing lands occupied by Indians, could such possession be justified? In the opening portion of his speech, Adams constructed an account of New England colonization to answer this question.

The Puritan colonies, he said, had surpassed all others in America because the energy of their founders rested not on hopes of material gain but on religion and devotion to conscience. So exalted had been the religious commitment of Puritan settlers that they erred at first on the side of visionary impracticality. They fell prey to an error common among the philanthropically minded from the days of Plato to Rousseau and the French Revolution – the delusion that commonality of goods provided the essential basis for a godly commonwealth. Here Adams could take his stand on the solidest rock of New England Federalism. 'Wiser and more useful philosophy' must recognize the limitations of mankind, prone to weaknesses 'no wisdom can remedy', vices 'no legislation can correct'. Happily, from their own experiment, the Puritan fathers had learned that 'community of goods without community of toil' was 'oppressive and unjust', and contrary to 'the laws of nature', since it made the 'virtuous and active members of society slaves and drudges of the worst.' With this understanding, the founders had altered their polity to one of private property and individual enterprise.[46]

Having rescued New England's forefathers from Jacobinism, Adams moved to exonerate them of any injustice to Indians. Here Vattel's argument, clericalized of its humanist thrust, came providentially to hand. 'Shall the fields and valleys which a beneficent God has formed to teem with the life of innumerable multitudes be condemned to everlasting barrenness?' The question, stated so as to admit only a negative answer, required a conclusion that the Puritans had acted in accord with natural law. Going even beyond natural law, Adams insisted, they had confirmed their right by purchase and tempered possession with mercy. At the final judgement they would stand forth 'in the whiteness of innocence.' And if any doubt lingered as to whether divine intelligence would underwrite a human interpretation of natural law, the witness of good deeds well intended must speak to the point. 'Let us indulge in the belief', he proposed, 'that they will not only be free from the accusation of injustice to those unfortunate sons of nature, but that the testimony of their acts of kindness and benevolence towards them will plead the cause of their virtues, as they are now authenticated by the record of history upon earth.'[47]

In exculpating the Puritan fathers, Adams had carried Vattel's argument into an arena of theological controversy in which the rationalist Vattel would probably have taken little interest. Adams, however, was keenly concerned in the question of justification by works and so doubtless were many of his Federalist listeners in 1800. It seems likely that they misconstrued the political tendency of his doctrinal niceties; yet there is no reason to suppose that Adams did not think they understood him fully. The Federalist-controlled state legislature sent him to the United States Senate; where, in precise adherence to the program of his Plymouth address, he felt obliged to support Thomas Jefferson's Louisiana Purchase. The Federalists then drummed him out of the party.[48]

Throughout the sequence here summarized, class identification worked as a salient factor. The two Adamses, retained for their organizational services, identified with and gradually entered New England's merchant oligarchy. Adams the son acted out his crisis of adolescence by flirting with opponents of that class, but when confronted with the reality of his father's allegiance, yielded and placed himself in the line of paternal succession. What finally enabled him to establish his own political autonomy (and, psychologically, to resolve the adolescent crisis) was a split in the merchant oligarchy over interpretations of class interest. Would that interest best be served *narrowly* by a struggle for continued regional dominance, or *broadly* by participation with other regional elites in a westward expanding nation? The difference between Adams and the old guard of New England Federalism was that while the Federalists envisioned a regional enclave of city-states dominated by an overseas commerce functioning under British suzerainty, Adams projected a continental nation within which agriculture and domestic manufacturing would provide the underpinnings of an independent world commerce. He never differed from Federalism on the preeminence of commerce nor on the necessity of class hierarchy for civilized social order. But a nation – a continental nation – unlike a city-state, could not be governed unilaterally by any regional oligarchy. It was at this juncture that the younger Adams broke decisively with the New England Federalists and staked his career on his own understanding of the upper-class interest.

The break with Federalism opened another cycle of reconciliation with Jefferson. Under Republican auspices, Adams resumed his interrupted diplomatic career. He accepted the ministry at St. Petersburg, then went on to Ghent as one of the United States commissioners to negotiate an end to the War of 1812. At Ghent, Adams outdid the emigré Republican Albert Gallatin and the western Republican Henry Clay in his intransigence on the western question. The British brought forward as their opening gambit an autonomous Indian nation to surround the Great Lakes on the south, thus interposing a buffer between the American Northwest and Canada. While the English commissioners spoke of ensuring Canada against surprise attack and shielding their Indian allies from 'perpetual encroachment', the Americans took them to mean that the Indian enclave, as an extension of Canada, would convey unilateral control over the lakes and revise the treaty of 1783 by bringing Canada down to the Mississippi.[49]

Among themselves they agreed they could not transmit such a proposal. At the same time they suspected that Britain, now victorious in Europe and reportedly preparing vast military campaigns in America, intended to force a rupture of negotiations.[50] To break off on the issue of an Indian state in the Northwest would be disadvantageous to their side, the Americans thought, since it would tend to exacerbate northeastern – and especially New England – dissatisfaction with continuing the war. Consequently, they manoeuvered for a more general issue to stand on if negotiations failed. Only Adams among them insisted on ideological justification.[51] Outraged at the 'insolent charge ... against the Government of the United States, of perpetual encroachment upon the Indians under pretense of purchases', he drafted a response invoking 'the moral and religious duty of a nation to settle, cultivate, and improve their territory ... the only solid and unanswerable defense against the charge of the British note.'[52]

Cornering the British commissioner, Henry Goulburn, Adams assured him that wherever Indians would 'form settlements and cultivate lands' – as in the case of 'the Cherokees, for example' – their rights 'always were respected by the United States.' No one had the right to monopolize land solely for hunting; nonetheless, the United Staes compensated Indians whose hunting grounds were taken over for settlement. American policy in this respect had vastly improved on 'the former practice of all European nations, including the British. The original settlers of New England had set the first example of this liberality. ... To condemn vast regions of territory to perpetual barrenness and solitude that a few hundred savages might find wild beasts to hunt upon it, was a species of game law that a nation descended from Britons would never endure. ...' No government, he warned Goulburn, would be able to enforce closure upon the people of the United States. Already in 1810 they had passed seven millions and 'at this hour ... undoubtedly passed eight'. Britain would find it easier to exterminate 'the whole American people' than to oppose 'against them her barrier of savages'.[53]

Goulburn wrote to his superiors, probably in reference to Adams, 'I had ... no idea of the fixed determination which prevails in the breast of every American to extirpate the Indians and appropriate their territory; but I am now sure that there is nothing which the people of America would so reluctantly abandon as what they are pleased to call their natural right to do so.'[54] Adams considered his conversation with Goulburn so important that he not only recorded it in his diary but sent a résumé by personal letter to the secretary of state, James Monroe. Important for what? Historians generally attribute Britain's change of front and the successful outcome of the Ghent negotiations to events in Europe rather than to the eloquence of the American commissioners. We know from Adams's own account that the cosmopolitan and erudite Gallatin expected Adams's defense of United States Indian policies to be ridiculed, while the politically astute westerner Henry Clay described it as 'canting'. Both expressions convey a sense of embarrassment at what they feared would be taken for hypocrisy.

But that was in Europe. Monroe was in America; and as heir apparent to the presidency would soon be in position to name the next in line. Leaving Clay to take his chances in the House of Representatives, Monroe sent Adams from Ghent to the Court of St. James and in 1817 appointed him secretary of state. Samuel Flagg Bemis's account has it that Monroe selected Adams over Clay because the Republican succession, pure Virginian since the fall of the first Adams, needed the candidacy of a northern man more than that of a westerner, particularly a Virginia-born westerner like Clay. Doubtless this account is correct; yet it misses the point that Adams's strength as a New Englander lay in his western orientation. He had constructed and brought into action at Ghent a justification in moral, rational and religious terms for the adherence of eastern establishments to western expansion. That, in postwar politics, was the ideological cement of 'National' Republicanism.[55]

During eight years as secretary of state under President Monroe, Adams's most famous accomplishments were promulgation of the Monroe Doctrine and completion of the Transcontinental Treaty with Spain. Conflicts involving American Indians proliferated, triggered by Adams's relentless pressure on Spain, by Andrew Jackson's invasion of Florida; and by the struggles of Cherokees, Creeks and Seminoles against infiltration, principally by Georgians, of what they regarded as their homelands. These issues intertwined. The federal government, responding to surges of nationalist sentiment after the War of 1812, hastened to follow out the corollaries of that war by establishing sovereignty over the Gulf Coast of Florida. In the South, aspirant entrepreneurs enflamed by the first great cotton boom, swarmed to carry the slave plantation system into the fertile Indian lands immediately to the west and south. And on a continental scale, with settlers moving into the now wide-open Mississippi Valley and the borderlands of the Great Lakes, men like John Quincy Adams could begin to think seriously about rivers and harbors on the Pacific.

As the Spanish Empire disintegrated, the Floridas drifted toward the American shore.[56] Spanish authority existed in only a few fortified posts. Elsewhere were rallying points of Latin American rebels and privateers; nests of pirates and slave hunters; and sanctuaries for Indians hard-pressed by American expansion as well as for slaves who escaped the plantations. Andrew Jackson, commander on the southern frontier, offered in a letter to President Monroe to clean up the situation without 'implicating' the administration. When Monroe did not specifically repudiate this suggestion Jackson in 1818 crossed the border, captured the major Spanish forts, court-martialled and executed two British subjects, and killed or sent into slavery without benefit of court-martial an unknown number of Indians and Africans. This created a crisis with Spain, which was helpless to retaliate, and with England, which was not. It also triggered a crisis in the presidential circle. Monroe was surrounded by presidential aspirants. Two, John C. Calhoun, secretary of war, and William Crawford, secretary of the treasury – supported by Henry Clay, now Speaker of the House – saw a chance to chop down a formidable rival and pushed for court-martialing Jackson for disobedience. Adams spoke in Jackson's defense and Adams's view prevailed. Although the president ordered withdrawal from Florida, he did not reprimand Jackson, leaving open the ground that in the general's own understanding he had not exceeded instructions. That completed the *pro-forma* of non-implication.[57]

Adams, however, went beyond *pro-forma* in his public exoneration of

Jackson. His key statement was a letter of instructions to the American minister at Madrid.[58] Released immediately to the press, its rhetorical style was obviously intended more for public than ministerial instruction. What had confronted General Jackson in Florida, Adams explained, was that certain British subjects, in connivance with Spanish officials, had gathered a 'banditti' of 'lawless Indians and negroes', whom they incited to 'wage an exterminating war … with all the horrors of savage warfare …' against 'defenseless citizens … peaceful inhabitants' of the United States. Jackson's conduct, far from meriting presidential 'censure', was 'founded in the purest patriotism', vindicated in 'every page of the law of nations'. Here Adams turned again to his old counselor at international law. 'When at war (says Vattel) with a ferocious nation which observes no rules … a general … may take the lives of some of his prisoners. …'[59] Convinced that he now had England by proxy before the bar of justice, Adams moved from the particular to the general. '… all the Indian wars with which we have been afflicted have been distinctly traceable to the instigation of English traders or agents. Always disavowed, yet always felt; more than once detected but never punished; two of them … have fallen, *flagrante delicto*, into the hands of an American general' who had 'fixed them on high, as an example … of that which awaits unauthorized pretenders of European agency' meddling in the relationships 'between the United States and the Indians within their control.'[60]

The Erving letter left Spain no escape from the boundary settlement demanded by the United States unless Britain chose to go to war over the Florida executions. Adams had understood, correctly, that Britain, gearing for commercial penetration of Central and South America, would not prop up the Spanish Empire. What made his intervention a *tour de force* was that he paralleled the as-yet-unspoken commercial aspirations of Great Britain by setting out the inner core of the Monroe Doctrine – two years before its enunciation in the Latin American context – as a gospel of continental nationalism. From Monticello, Jefferson urged President Monroe to send out copies in French and English to all United States diplomatic and consular officials. '[It is] … among the ablest compositions I have ever seen', Jefferson wrote. 'It is of great importance to us … to maintain in Europe a correct opinion of our political morality.'[61]

For Adams, dedicated to continental nationalism, ideological problems of race had centered largely on American Indians. Comparable problems involving African Americans remained marginal. With respect to African slavery only two issues – and these, by contrast to the invasion of Florida or the boundary that carried the United States to the Pacific, of minor import – required his public commitment as secretary of state. One was the claim of reparations for slaves seized (or liberated) by the British; the other the matter of search at sea in suppression of the African slave trade.

At Ghent, American claims of reparations for slaves carried off by the British had been set aside to expedite the major settlement, and were eventually referred to the Czar of Russia for arbitration. The American position was simply that slaves, as private property not contraband of war, must be returned or the owners compensated. Adams instructed the American minister to St. Petersburg to stress to the Czar that emancipation could not be recognized as 'legitimate warfare. ... No such right is acknowledged as a law of war by writers who admit *any* limitation [in war].' '[P]utting to death all prisoners ... might as well be pretended as a right of war; or the right to use poisoned arrows. ...' Whether or not the Czar concurred in Adams's formulation that emancipating slaves and slaughtering prisoners were equivalent atrocities, he favored American claims by awarding a lump sum to be parcelled out among the aggrieved slave owners.[62]

The difficulties raised by British efforts to end the African slave trade were more complex. Both nations had outlawed slave trading; but Adams took the stand that the Constitution would not permit American citizens, if apprehended as slave traders, to be judged by foreign or international tribunals; and that American sentiment against impressment would never tolerate search and seizure by British warships. A roundabout effort to break this *impasse* through defining the slave trade as piracy and pledging both nations to its suppression (with a proviso that crews of captured vessels were to be tried only by courts of their own nation) seemed more promising. Approved by President Monroe and his cabinet, agreed to by the British, the treaty was finally killed in the United States Senate, largely by southerners who accused the administration of abandoning American rights at sea. Although doubtless disappointed, and perhaps also forewarned of what might be expected from the South, Adams's confidence in the persuasive logic of continental nationalism remained apparently undented. From the viewpoint of the South and West, his record thus far could appear impeccable. He did not mar it by taking a position on the Missouri debate. Privately he wondered if it might not be wiser to meet the slavery issue head-on; but as a practical matter he favored compromise. He was, after all, next in line for the presidency. To his wife he wrote in October 1822:

> It is my situation that makes me a candidate. ... The acquisition of Florida ... the extension of the territories of the Union to the Pacific Ocean ... the formal admission of our right to border upon the South Sea [Pacific], both by Spain and Great Britain, has been obtained, I may confidently say by me.[63]

Through the portion of his career that led to the presidency, Adams employed racial constructions essentially to justify the continuing alliance between northern commerce and southern slave-owners in a westward-expanding nationalism. Such an alliance required two thrusts of its racial legitimation. The first was to reassure southerners and westerners that northern commercial leaders held ideas on racial matters similar to their own. The second was to undermine the moral stance of regional separatism among northern commercial spokesmen and religious leaders.

Northern regional separatism was linked historically to the declining years of the Federalist party. Its civic ideal was that of an oligarchical city state, or confederation of cities, nourished by overseas commerce under the aegis of Britain, and insulating itself as fully as possible from the turmoils of the hinterland to which it was attached. Westward expansion figured negatively in this view, not only because it led to collisions with Britain, but because it entailed taxes and recruitment of youth for wars in the West that seemed irrelevant to the interests of the seaboard cities. Worse, as expansion brought in new western states, the political supremacy of the cities would be lost and their economic foundations shattered by hostile legislation and by the drain of capital and manpower to the West. This argument in political economy stood buttressed by moral and religious scruples against alliance with slavery and complicity in the destruction of Indians. Since the Atlantic cities had long since purged themselves of Indians and were for the most part located in states that had terminated slavery, exploitation of such scruples remained readily available to northern separatists. Adams's racial constructions were aimed at outflanking these moral obstacles by putting forward 'a correct opinion', to use Jefferson's phrase, as to the 'political morality' of Republican policies.

To this end, affirmations of racial inferiority were necessary but not sufficient. Natural law required that bearers of advanced civilization replace or dominate primitive and savage peoples. It also required – supplemented perhaps by Christian doctrine which in Adams's view extended or perfected natural law – that such peoples be dealt with justly. Slavery was patently unjust; yet under historically unjust circumstances it was not impossible for a moral nation to act justly. 'What was vital to the success of the Republicans was not abolition but rather their being able to divorce slavery from their social vision.'[64] Britain having imposed slavery, what was required of the United States was to avoid abusing its power over the victims and to terminate slavery as soon as reasonably possible. Northern states had already done so. For the South, the teachings of men like Jefferson marked the path to be followed. Whether or not colonization should be joined to emancipation would be decided at some appropriate time, on grounds of practical expediency since that question was auxiliary to the main moral issue. So long as these avenues remained open, no indictment could be brought against the nation for injustice to African slaves. With respect to Indians, the argument from Vattel validated the justice of what had so far been done. Adams apparently entertained no doubt of that validation prior to his accession to the presidency.

The 1825 Message

Adams in 1825 could believe that his own triumphant rise to the highest office demonstrated general acceptance of the racial legitimations reconstructed in the preceding section. Taking them as *faits accomplis*, he directed his first annual message to what must have seemed to him the key problem in a federal republic – that of the extent and proper purpose of centralized power. The result was an ode to commerce in the manner of Schiller's 'Ode to Joy' or the choral section of Beethoven's Ninth Symphony. Every device of rhetorical embellishment contributed to declare the beneficent role of commerce. Mathematics and written language stemmed from that source. Such intellectual achievements as weights and measures, celestial navigation, astronomy, science itself, all were the progeny of commercial exchange. Revising the order of Jefferson's priorities, which made commerce auxiliary to agriculture, Adams set commerce as the keystone of his social order. To enhance it thus became the chief axiom of government policy, other considerations following in corollary positions.[65]

Known as one of the architects of westward expansion, Adams seems to have had little direct interest in the West. His only western tour came in 1845, when he was seventy-eight, long after the collapse of his ambitions as a national leader. He was in fact always oriented toward Europe. The West – like agriculture and manufacturing, for which it provided the essential land base – would serve the national interest as an auxiliary to commerce. Without such a base, the United States would be unable to enter the ranks of leading commercial nations and would remain merely an appendage to Britain's commercial system. From the Louisiana Purchase and his efforts at Ghent to gain control of the Mississippi, through the defense of Jackson's sortie into Spanish Florida and insistence in the Transcontinental Treaty with Spain on a Pacific beachhead, determination to break out of commercial dependency on Britain governed his western diplomacy.

Even the sacred obligation of extending to mankind the benefits of republican institutions, Adams argued, could best be fulfilled through commerce. Liberty's most basic units were not yeoman freeholds but commercial exchanges. Equal access to the ports of the world advanced the rights of man more than wars of revolution. As secretary of state under Monroe, Adams had opposed recognizing the new Latin American republics, until, with British backing, they had consolidated their independence from Spain.[66] American diplomacy must then aim at preventing their reentrapment in closed trading partnerships, whether directly with Britain or under clandestine British auspices, with the former colonial metropolis. Thus the Monroe Doctrine, promulgated by Adams, and accurately describable even in 1817 as an Open Door policy. Adams explained in his 1825 message that by insisting on two principles of commercial relationship – 'the one of entire and unqualified reciprocity, the other the mutual obligation of the parties to place each other permanently upon the footing of the most favored nation' – the United States could educate the new republics to the opportunities and duties of national independence. He recommended congressional approval of a delegation to the upcoming Congress of Panama to push this educational process 'as far as may be compatible' with neutrality.[67]

From foreign affairs, the president turned to finances. Aside from servicing and retiring the federal debt, expenditures had gone to the diplomatic apparatus and military arms, to internal improvements authorized by Congress, and to the expenses of Indian treaties. Each item justified itself as accessory to commerce. Adams's admiration for naval prowess raised his language to an early crescendo. Although unprepared (through no fault of its own), the Navy nonetheless had won 'unfading glory' in the war with Britain. Since then its squadrons had protected American ships from the Mediterranean to the West Indies, while along the 'unsettled Pacific Coast' the presence of 'the flag and the firmness of our commanding officers' made possible 'a flourishing commerce and fishery extending to the islands of the Pacific and to China.'[68] No such commerce 'could exist … without the continual support of a military marine – the only arm by which the power of this Confederacy can be estimated or felt by foreign nations, and the only standing military force which can never be dangerous to our liberties at home.'[69] Adams asked Congress for a 'naval school of instruction, corresponding with the Military Academy at West Point.'[70] In the Navy, he seems to have perceived a model of National Republicanism. The contrast between the matter-of-fact prose alotted to military matters and the epic style of his naval allusions underlines this ideological affinity, as well as making clear the primacy of overseas commerce in his vision of the future.

Public lands, tariffs and the national debt then fell into place as corollaries to the primacy of commerce. Adams regarded the federal debt, undertaken to pay for territorial acquisitions and meet the cost of the War of 1812, as a mortgage secured by the public domain.[71] As soon as the debt could be paid off, federal revenue would 'reflow in unfailing streams of improvement from the Atlantic to the Pacific Ocean.'[72] Actually, in 1825, tariff receipts were running about nine times the return from land sales. Absence of any reference to the tariff as a special problem in Adams's message suggests that he concurred in the existing trend of legislation aimed doubly at revenue and protection. He anticipated that protection, by speeding the growth of manufactures, would shift commerce away from imports to domestic interchange and exports. Such a long-range trend, doubtless beneficial to the nation as a whole, would yield the negative result of reducing tariff revenues. Eventually this would oblige the federal government to shift to other sources of income. Public lands, meanwhile, had scarcely begun to realize their potential revenue; but as roads and canals brought them into the market, they could be expected not only to cover current costs of government, but to generate funding for the program of internal improvements Adams was about to unveil. Obviously the 1825 vista allowed no room for anything like a homestead program.[73]

Not until 1828, one month after his defeat for reelection, when the tariff of 1828 had blown up into a political hurricane, did Adams permit himself a detailed discussion of protection. 'The great interests of an agricultural, commercial and manufacturing nation', he then began, 'are so linked in union that no permanent cause of prosperity to one of them can operate without extending its influence to the others.' Safeguarding domestic industries against the competition of foreign nations (notably Great Britain) would redound to the benefit of agriculture and commerce as well. Adams gave explicit endorsement to the principle of protection, while conceding that the Tariff of 1828, which he himself had signed into law, might want readjustment if 'practical experience'[74] proved it unduly burdensome on any particular section or interest. Again commerce provided the keystone. Just as he had dissented from Jefferson's notion of commerce as auxiliary to agriculture, he also rejected the view of some of his later whiggish colleagues that it ought to be subordinated to manufacturing. Consequently, protection, essential though it was to the growth of manufactures, could never be treated as an end in itself. By placing 'agricultural, commercial and manufacturing interests' in alphabetical order, Adams in one sense avoided the divisive question of priority. At the same time, his words evoked an image of commerce at the center while agriculture and manufacturing guarded the right and left sides of the throne as constituent but slightly subordinated elements in the trinity. Clearly this image, although not yet explicitly set forth in 1825, governed his thinking on tariffs and their relation to commerce.[75]

Adams came to his grand finale through an examination of governmental responsibility. The 'great object' of all government was to improve the 'condition of those who are parties to the social compact.' He then unleashed a full-scale assault on doctrines of federal limitation. Enumerating once again the enumerated as well as implied powers, Adams argued that if such powers could be used for 'the improvement of agriculture, commerce and manufactures, the cultivation and encouragement of the mechanic and elegant arts, the advancement of literature and the progress of science', to refrain from so using them would be 'treachery to the most sacred of trusts. ... The spirit of improvement is abroad upon the earth. ...' Underlying all temporal mandates conveyed by laws and constitutions was the ultimate duty: ' ... tenure of power by man is, in the moral purposes of the Creator, upon condition that it shall be exercised to the ends of beneficence to improve the condition of himself and his fellow man.'[76]

Improvements were to be graded on a scale beginning with material assets such as roads and canals and moving up through social and political amelioration to the highest level of all, which was the advancement of knowledge. Spectacularly successful at the lower levels, the new republic as yet had failed to contribute its 'share of mind, labor and expense to the improvement of those parts of knowledge which lie beyond the reach of individual acquisition, and particularly to geographical and astronomical research.' Americans could take scant pride in the fact that Europe with its 'comparatively small territorial surface' now had 'upward of 130 of these lighthouses of the skies', while 'throughout the entire American hemisphere' there was not one.[77] From this invocaton of republican moral responsibility, Adams wound down to a restrained coda. He would simply await recognition by Congress of the obligations inherent in the powers it possessed.[78]

Rhetoric was a serious matter for National Republicans (and Whigs), especially so to John Quincy Adams, who as professor at Harvard College had helped to create and systematize the art. Whig political culture placed rhetoric in a context largely derived from Scottish moral philosophy and faculty psychology.[79] As, within every well-ordered individual, moral sense and the faculty of intelligence would be expected to control passions and animal faculties, so the educated elite of any well-ordered society must govern the inferior levels. Rhetoric provided an intermediate language by which rational and moral ideas – self-evident to the intellect or logically deducible – could be transposed into emotional, metaphorical, even sensual images, palpable to each individual's animal faculties and therefore comprehensible at the inferior levels of the social order. True rhetorical discourse, using the lower to convey the higher, inspired and persuaded yet never abused its art to make the worse appear the better cause.

At the climax of his message, Adams had evoked one of the central metaphors of the Age of Reason: the universe viewed as handiwork of the divine clockmaker. Illuminated in the night sky, separated from earthbound contingency, the stars and planets marked off through eternity the absolute rationality of creation. It followed, for Adams, that astronomy, the highest branch of natural religion, must become the special pursuit of that highest of political structures, the republic. From their observatories reading the dials of a law-governed universe, republican scientists would transcribe for mankind ever more perfect perceptions of the divine purpose. Yet oddly, a crucial phrase – 'lighthouses of the skies' – negated the metaphoric meaning. Lighthouses, logically, are opposite to observatories: instead of receiving light from outer sources, they project their own feeble candlepower into the darkness.

It would be hard to believe, with his rigorous standards of rhetoric, that Adams was merely exploiting the impressive sound of his words without regard to their meanings. What seems more likely is that he tolerated an inappropriateness to his primary meaning because the words expressed his meaning once removed. Their actual effect is to call into question the lucid optimism of the metaphor. On one hand they reach behind the Enlightenment to the Calvinist notion of a deity totally beyond the scope of man towards which the human mind can only send out impotent and incoherent pulsations. On the other, they reach forward to the era of romantic despair: Ahab on the quarterdeck.

There is a connection between these images. What they have in common is an unrelenting burden of individual responsibility. The difference – a vast difference – lies in the direction of the responsibility. For seventeenth-century Calvinists, the cosmos, ruled by an omnipotent hand, remained intact; it was the integrity of their own souls that had to be doubted. A nineteenth-century man like John Quincy Adams, by contrast, for all the anxiety that permeates his diary, apparently had little doubt as to the good intentions of his soul. Contemptuous of old-style theological hair-splitting, he assured himself that a life of Arminian good works dedicated to his fellow men would be adequate for salvation in the judgement of any benevolent and all-seeing deity – if there was such a one. The earlier anxiety, turned inward, had required an endless probing of the soul for hints of grace. That of the nineteenth century, outward bound, hammered against history and the universe itself for a righteousness to match one's own. Throughout his life Adams attended service on 'sabbath morn' and often used part of that day for composing devotional poems. Usually these were renderings of the psalms, but he also wrote: 'All-seeing God, the doubt suppress; / The doubt thou only canst relieve. ...'[80]

Despite the achievements of science and astronomy, only God could reveal the order upon which the universe surely must be founded. Meanwhile, 'in the moral purposes of the Creator' (as Adams warned Congress in 1825), man also was obligated to bear his share of that task by illuminating the darkness adjacent to him, creating order in whatever section of chaos came within his reach. Here, at the highest level, rested the duty (and justification) of government. For most Whigs, I think, this would be the binding tenet of their beliefs about government. Adams had hoped to demonstrate through his administration how much might be accomplished by a vigorous and well-intentioned exercise of federal power toward the improvement of man. Instead, he found himself engrossed in the deteriorating conditions of Indians.

Notes

1.   Robert A. East, *John Quincy Adams, the Critical Years: 1785–1794*, New York 1962, pp. 15–27; Richard Drinnon, *Facing West: The Metaphysics of Indian Hating and Empire Building*, New York 1980, pp. 65–69. For New England attitudes toward Indians in the colonial and early national periods, see Richard Slotkin, *Regeneration Through Violence: The Mythology of the American Frontier, 1600–1860*, Middletown, Conn. 1973, especially Chapters 1–8.

2.   Drinnon, *Facing West*, p. 65.

3.   Timothy Dwight, *The Conquest of Canaan, a Poem in Eleven Books*, in William J. McTaggart and William K. Bottorf, eds, *The Major Poems of Timothy Dwight, 1752–1817*, Gainesville, Fla. 1969, pp. 82–83.

4.   Dwight, *Greenfield Hill*, in McTaggart and Bottorf, eds, *Major Poems*, pp. 462–63. My use of both these selections I owe to Drinnon's *Facing West*.

5.   John Adams to Thomas Jefferson, Quincy, 29 June 1812, in *Microfilms of the Adams Papers*, Boston 1955, Part 2.

6.   John Adams to William Tudor, Quincy, 23 September 1818, *Microfilms of the Adams Papers*, Part II.

7.   John Adams to James Lloyd, Quincy, 21 March 1815, ibid.

8.   John Adams to Thomas Jefferson, Quincy, 22 January 1825, in Drinnon, *Facing West*, p. 103. Robert H. Wiebe, *The Opening of American Society: From the Adoption of the Constitution to the Eve of Disunion*, New York 1985, p. 4.

9.   Thomas P. Abernethy, 'Introduction', Thomas Jefferson, *Notes on the State of Virginia*, New York 1964, p. *xi*.

10.   Jefferson, *Notes*, pp. 57–58, 59, 60, 90, 91, 93.

11.   Ibid., pp. 57–58, 86.

12.   Ibid., p. 59.

13.   Annie Heloise Abel, 'The History of Events Resulting in Indian Consolidation West of the Mississippi,' *Annual Report of the American Historical Association, 1906*, Washington, D.C. 1908 (New York 1972), 1:233–450, and pp. 241–49.

14.   Emmerich de Vattel, *The Law of Nations, or, Principles of the Law of Nature Applied to the Conduct and Affairs of Nations and Sovereigns*, London 1797. This work had been in circulation since at least 1773.

15.   John Quincy Adams, 15 September 1787, *Life in a New England Town: 1787–1788: Diary of John Quincy Adams While a Student in the Office of Theophilus Parsons at Newburyport*, ed. Charles F. Adams, Boston 1903, p. 33 .

16.   Vattel, *Law of Nations*, pp. 100–101.

17.   John Quincy Adams, 11 July 1794, *Memoirs of John Quincy Adams Comprising Portions of his Diary from 1795–1848*, ed. Charles Francis Adams, Philadelphia 1874, 1:34–35 .

18.   George H. Moore, *Notes of the History of Slavery in Massachusetts*, New York 1866, p. 51. Charles Francis Adams, *Three Episodes of Massachusetts History*, Boston 1903, 2:923. 'Will of Deacon John Adams [7 January 1760] with Comments by his Son [29 April 1774]', Robert J. Taylor, ed., *Papers of John Adams*, Cambridge, Mass. 1977, 1:33–35. Charles W. Akers, *Abigail Adams: An American Woman*, Boston 1980.

19.   Moore, *Notes*, pp. 100–108; Jeremy Belknap, 'Queries Respecting the Slavery and Emancipaton of Negroes in Massachusetts, Proposed by the Honorable Judge Tucker of Virginia and Answered by the Rev. Dr. Belknap,' *Massachusetts Historical Society Collections*, Ser. 1, Boston 1795, 3:199, quoted in Leon Litwack, *North of Slavery: The Negro in the Free States, 1790–1860*, Chicago 1965, pp. 8–9; John Quincy Adams to George Mifflin Dallas, Washington, D.C., 9 October 1822, *Writings of John Quincy Adams*, ed. Worthington Chaun-

cey Ford, [1916] New York 1968, 7:319–20.

20. John Adams, *Works of John Adams*, ed. Charles Francis Adams, Boston 1856, 10:315, quoted in Moore, *Notes*, p. 110. *Papers of John Adams*, 3:*xvi–xviii*, 18–20, 388–90, 411; 4:455, 469; John Adams to Jonathon Sergeant, Philadelphia, 17 August 1776; Moore, *Notes*, pp. 191–92, 200–209; William W. Freehling, 'The Founding Fathers and Salvery', *American Historical Review*, 77 (February 1972): 81–93.

21. Abigail to John Adams, 'Boston Garrison', 22 September 1774; L. H. Butterfield, ed., *The Adams Papers*, Series II. *Adams Family Correspondence (AFC)*, Cambridge 1963, 1:161–62. Abigail to John Adams, Braintree, 31 March 1776, *AFC*, 1:369–70.

22. Abigail to John Adams, Braintree, 27 May 1776, *AFC*, 2:323–24.

23. Abigail to John Adams, Boston, 22 August 1777, *AFC*, 2:323–24.

24. Abigail Adams to Mary Cranch, 9 August 1789, 28 April 1790, 12 March 1791, 28 April 1790, 18 April 1791, 23 June 1797, 21 November 1800, in Steward Mitchell, ed., *New Letters of Abigail Adams, 1788–1801*, Boston 1947, pp. 20, 48, 70, 72, 99, 156–57.

25. John to Abigail Adams, Philadelphia, 11 August 1777, *AFC*, 2:304; John Adams to William Heath, Philadelphia, 5 October 1775, and William Heath to John Adams, Camp at Cambridge, 23 October 1775; *Papers of John Adams*, 3:183, 230.

26. 'Humphrey Ploughjogger', *Boston Gazette*, 19 January 1967, 14 October 1765, *Papers of John Adams*, 1:146–48, 181–82.

27. Thomas Jefferson, *Notes on the State of Virginia*, New York 1964, pp. 132–33.

28. Ibid., pp. 133–35.

29. Ibid., pp. 138–39.

30. Fawn Brodie, *Thomas Jefferson: An Intimate History*, New York 1974, pp. 186–89, 216–28, 248.

31. Brodie, *Jefferson*, pp. 353–54; John Adams, quoted in Page Smith, *John Adams*, Garden City, N.Y. 1962, 2:1094.

32. As quoted in Samuel Flagg Bemis, *John Quincy Adams and the Foundations of American Foreign Policy*, New York 1949, p. 14.

33. East, *Adams, Critical Years*, pp. 103–4; John Quincy Adams, *Life in a New England Town*, pp. 165–70.

34. East, *Adams, Critical Years*, pp. 105–12.

35. Ibid., pp. 113–15.

36. John Quincy Adams, 'A Vision', pp. 9–17 in notebook titled 'Fugitive Pieces', Microfilms of the Adams Papers, reel 223. John Quincy Adams, *Poems of Religion and Society*, Auburn, N.Y. 1853, pp. 109–116.

37. *Papers of John Adams*, 1:33; Stanley Elkins and Eric McKitrick, 'The Founding Fathers: Young Men of the Revolution', *Political Science Quarterly*, 76 (June 1961):181–216; 'Will of Deacon John Adams', *Papers of John Adams*, I:33–35; East, *Adams: Critical Years*, pp. 70–74. Bemis, *Foundations*, pp. 4–7, 20–22; Marie B. Hecht, *John Quincy Adams: A Personal History of an Independent Man*, New York 1972, pp. 3–5; George A. Lipsky, *John Quincy Adams: His Theory and Ideas*, New York 1950, pp. 9–17; Charles Francis Adams [and John Quincy Adams], *The Life of John Adams.*, rev. ed., Philadelphia 1871.

38. Bemis, *Foundations*, pp. 35–42, 25; East, *Adams, Critical Years*, pp. 86–95; John Quincy Adams, *Life in a New England Town*, pp. 1–11; Martin Duberman, *Charles Francis Adams, 1807–1886*, Stanford, Calif. 1960, pp. 28–35.

39. East, *Adams, Critical Years*, pp. 110–15; John Quincy Adams, *Life in a New England Town*, pp. 83–84, 134, 169–70.

40. John Quincy Adams, *Life in a New England Town*, pp. 46, 55, 95–96, 105–6, .

41. Ibid., pp. 106, 128, and entries dated 12, 17, and 29 October; 20 and 23 November; 1, 11, and 23 December 1787; and 9 January; 7 and 11 February; and 4 and 5 March 1788, pp. 46–106.

42. Bemis, *Foundations*, pp. 25–28; East, *Adams, Critical Years*, pp. 131–35; John Quincy Adams, 'Letters of Publicola', *Writings*, 1:68, 71.

43. John Quincy Adams, 'Letters of Publicola', pp. 67–69. Bemis, *Foundations*, pp. 112–20. John Quincy Adams later joined anonymously in Federalist ridicule of the Jefferson–Hemings liaison. Linda Kerber, *Federalists in Dissent: Imagery and Ideology in Jeffersonian America*, Ithaca, N.Y. 1970, pp. 50–51, 71n; Winthrop D. Jordan, *White over Black: American Attitudes Toward the Negro, 1550–1812*, Chapel Hill, N.C. 1968, pp. 465–69; Dumas Malone,

Jefferson the President: First Term, 1801–1805, Boston 1970, pp. 211–16, 494–98; Brodie, *Intimate History*, 348–54, 540–41; Richard Dillon, *Meriwether Lewis, A Biography*, New York 1965, pp. 269–77.

44. Bemis, *Foundations*, pp. 111–13.

45. John Quincy Adams, 'Oration at Plymouth', 22 December 1802, in David J. Brewer, ed., *The World's Best Orations*, Chicago 1899, 1:65–79.

46. Ibid., p. 74.

47. Ibid., pp. 75, 76.

48. Bemis, *Foundations*, pp. 112–20; Joyce Appleby, *Capitalism and a New Social Order: The Republican Vision of the 1790s*, New York 1984, p. 94.

49. Bemis, *Foundations*, pp. 199–213; Lynn Parsons, '"A Perpetual Harrow Upon my Feelings": John Quincy Adams and the American Indian', *New England Quarterly* (September 1973): 344; John Quincy Adams to Secretary of State James Monroe, Ghent, 11 August 1814, *Writings*, 5:175–82; John Quincy Adams, 25 September 1814, *Memoirs*, 3:41.

50. John Quincy Adams, *Writings*, 5:93–94, footnote 1; John Quincy Adams to Louisa Catherine Adams, Ghent, 16 and 19 August, 9 September 1814, *Writings*, 5:82–83, 89, 120; John Quincy Adams to Secretary of State James Monroe, Ghent, 17 August, 5 September 1814, *Writings*, 5:87, 110.

51. John Quincy Adams, *Diary, 1794–1845*, ed. Allan Nevins, New York 1951, pp. 130–35, 142–43.

52. 25 September 1814, *Memoirs*, 3:41; John Quincy Adams, 'Answer to the British Commissioners', 24 August 1814, *Writings*, 5:93–101.

53. 25 September 1814, *Memoirs*, 3:41–42.

54. Henry Goulburn to Earl Bathurst, 25 November 1814, in Arthur Wellesley, Duke of Wellington, *Supplementary Dispatches, Correspondence and Memoranda*, London 1858–92, 9:452, 454, quoted in Parsons, '"A Perpetual Harrow"', p. 340; John Quincy Adams to Secretary of State James Monroe, Ghent, 5 September 1814, *Writings*, 5:110–20; Harry L. Coles, *The War of 1812*, Chicago 1965, pp. 251–55.

55. Bemis, *Foundations*, pp. 242–55.

56. John Quincy Adams to George William Erving, Washington, D.C., 28 November 1818, *Writings*, 6:488; hereafter referred to as *Erving Letter*.

57. Bemis, *Foundations*, pp. 313–16; Robert V. Remini, *The Election of Andrew Jackson*, Philadelphia 1963, p. 161.

58. Parsons, '"A Perpetual Harrow"', p. 349; Bemis, *Foundations*, pp. 308–9.

59. *Erving Letter*, pp. 476, 481–82, 485, 486–88, 496, 498.

60. Ibid., p. 499.

61. Thomas Jefferson to President James Monroe, quoted in John Quincy Adams, *Writings*, 6:502.

62. John Quincy Adams to Henry Middleton, Washington, 6 November 1820, *Writings*, 7:82–93. Bemis, *Foundations*, pp. 293ff.

63. John Quincy Adams, 29 June 1822, Microfilms of the Adams Papers, Part 1, 332–35; Coles, pp. 251–55; Bemis, *Foundations*, pp. 414–18, 423–35; John Quincy Adams to Louisa Catherine Adams, Washington, 7 October 1822, *Writings*, 7:316–17; George Dangerfield, *The Awakening of American Nationalism, 1815–1828*, New York 1965, pp. 125–26.

64. Appleby, *Capitalism*, p. 102, argues that by focusing on grain production by yeoman farmers in the Mid-Atlantic states, Republicanism freed itself of moral responsibility for slavery. My point is that Republican leaders like Jefferson (and John Quincy Adams) sought to justify a regional alliance with slavery for the purposes of continental nationalism.

65. Kerber, *Federalists in Dissent*, pp. 23–66, shows that New England and other Federalists linked their polemics against the Jefferson administration, Virginia and the South to a critique of slavery that laid out the main lines of later Abolitionist arguments. John Quincy Adams, long before his break with the Federalists, was separating himself from such positions: Kerber, pp. 32–33, notes 27, 28.

66. Lipsky, *Adams, Theory and Ideas*, p. 118. Bemis, *Foundations*, pp. 345–46, 365–66.

67. John Quincy Adams, 'First Annual Message', 6 December 1825, in James D. Richardson, ed., *A Compilation of the Messages and Papers of the Presidents*, New York 1897–, 2:868.

68. 'First Annual Message', 2:869, 873, 875–876.

69. Ibid., 2:876.

70. Ibid.

71. See 'Third Annual Message', 4 December 1827, 2:954. 'First Annual Message', 2:871.

72. 'First Annual Message', 2:871.

73. 'First Annual Message', 2:924. See also 'Third Annual Message', 2:957.

74. 'Fourth Annual Message', 2:979–981. See also 'Second Annual Message', 2:924.

75. 'Fourth Annual Message', 2:979; William W. Freehling, *Prelude to Civil War: The Nullification Controversy in South Carolina, 1816–1836*, New York 1965, pp. 93–297; Dall W. Forsythe, *Taxation and Political Change in the Young Nation, 1781–1833*, New York 1977, pp. 76–104; John D. Macoll, 'Representative John Quincy Adams and the Compromise Tariff of 1832', *Capitol Studies*, vol. 2 (Fall 1972): 40–58.

76. 'First Annual Message', 2:877, 881, 882.

77. 'First Annual Message', 2:877–80.

78. 'First Annual Message', 2:883.

79. John Quincy Adams, *Lectures on Rhetoric and Oratory*, New York 1962, and 'Introduction', J. Jeffery Auer and Jerald L. Banninga, 1: unnumbered pages *v–xxxi*. Daniel Howe, *The Political Culture of the American Whigs*, Chicago 1979, pp. 24–31.

80. John Quincy Adams, *Poems of Religion and Society*, pp. 60–61.

2

Whigs

The Indian problems confronting John Quincy Adams as president arose from the fact that the United States, in order to negotiate its own survival, had bargained with both Indians and individual states. To Georgia, in return for waiver of that state's western territorial claims, the federal government had in 1802 promised to extinguish Indian titles inside the state as soon as that could be carried out peacefully. The titles were mainly Creek and Cherokee; but to secure an alliance with or the neutrality of these powerful tribes – urgently needed during the Revolution and War of 1812 – the government had pledged to recognize their sovereign status. Soon after his inauguration, Adams signed into law a treaty negotiated during Monroe's administration by which the Creek nation purportedly surrendered all its lands within the state of Georgia. The treaty turned out to have been fraudulently promoted despite the protests of major Creek leaders. Although Adams, following the same reasoning by which he had justified Jackson's invasion of Florida, must have approved the result, he could not condone the means, and announced his intention to cancel the treaty. Georgia, however, insisted on enforcement; and congressional leaders doubted that Congress would support the administration against Georgia. Adams sought to escape this dilemma by pressuring the Creeks to yield the same lands through a new treaty more legitimately ratified. This involved intimidating, or bribing, Creek chiefs into concurrence. As the laundering process was pushed toward completion, Georgia, impatient of delay, sent survey teams into the disputed territory. Adams countered with civil proceedings in federal court, which Georgia's governor and attorney general ignored.[1]

The Indian titles could justly be extinguished (following Vattel's arguments) only by virtue of the right and duty to bring arable land under cultivation. Justice required an empirical finding that particular Indians were not in fact practicing stable agriculture. Adams doubtless recalled his own assurance to Henry Goulburn, the British commissioner at Ghent, that if and when Indians would 'form settlements and cultivate lands' – he had even cited the Cherokee as an example – their rights 'always would be respected by the United States.'[2] He must also have remembered a discussion of the upcoming Georgia crisis near the end of Monroe's administration when Calhoun, then secretary of war, observed 'that the great difficulty arises from the progress of the Cherokees in civilization.' Adams entered this remark in his diary, noting that the Cherokees in Georgia numbered 'about fifteen thousand ... increasing in equal proportion with the whites; all cultivators, with a representative government, judicial courts, Lancaster schools, and permanent property. ...'[3] What would become of such Indians after their titles were extinguished? Georgia demanded removal. Adams's secretary of war, James Barbour, angered by the populistic demagogy of Georgia's Governor Troup, suggested instead that the United States abrogate its Indian treaties and incorporate Indians directly into the general population, subject, like whites, to the laws of the states or territories wherein they resided. Adams apparently reminded Barbour that without federal protection Indians in states like Georgia would be left defenseless since the states would not concede them any rights whatever.[4]

The diary shows Adams, for a time at least, uncertain of his own moral commitment. He could find no escape from the fact that constitutional obligations of the federal government stood in opposition to the sovereign powers of Georgia.[5] For a National Republican there could be no question which ought to prevail. And so devoted a reader of scripture as John Quincy Adams could hardly have failed to ask himself if his role were not more like that of Pontius Pilate than John the Baptist. When Georgia brought its militia against the Creeks, he withheld military intervention, and washed his hands of the matter by placing it in the lap of Congress, which he knew would do nothing. Thus was played out in dress rehearsal a nullification drama seven years ahead of time, but with an opposite outcome.[6]

James Barbour's Proclamation Line

Secretary of War Barbour had meanwhile turned to more systematic study of Indian removal. Early in 1826, midway in the Creek controversy, the House Committee on Indian Affairs sent the administration a draft bill for removing eastern Indians beyond the Mississippi, accompanied by a request for comments. Barbour wrote the reply. This document was discussed by members and friends of the administration, among them

Barbour's Virginia neighbor, James Madison, who praised it. Adams himself gave his approval at least to the extent of permitting transmission to Congress. Clearly Barbour's response comprised something of a position paper for the administration. And since, after formation of the Whig party, Whig views on American Indians would generally be expressed as negative criticisms of Jacksonian measures, the 1826 letter stands among the few positive expositions of the National Republican – subsequently Whig – Indian program. In this light it deserves to be read side by side with Adams's 1825 message to Congress.[7]

Barbour began with a review of previous policies. Obviously directed against Georgia, this opening part of his letter remains one of the harshest indictments ever written of Anglo-American treatment of Indians. 'One master passion, common to all mankind, that of acquiring land', had driven 'the white man on the Indian'. It is now, therefore, that a most solemn question addresses itself to the American People. ... Shall we go on quietly in a course, which, judging from the past, threatens their extinction, while their past sufferings and future prospects, so pathetically appeal to our compassion?'

Barbour carefully exempted 'the humane efforts of the Federal Government' from the main thrust of his accusation. 'Unabated desire to bereave them of their lands' had subverted the nation's 'original plan', substituting hypocrisy and deceit for its 'spirit of benevolence'.

> Missionaries are sent among them to enlighten their minds. ... Schools have been established. ... They have been persuaded to abandon the chase ... implements of husbandry, and domestic animals have been presented to them, and all ... accompanied with expressions of a disinterested solicitude for their happiness. Yielding to these temptations, some of them have reclaimed the forest, planted their orchards and erected houses, not only for their abode, but for the administration of justice, and for religious worship. And when they have done, you send *your* agent to tell them they must surrender their country to the white man, and recommit them to some new desert. ... They see that our profusions are insincere. ... What new pledges [they ask] can you give us that we shall not again be exiled when it is your wish to possess these lands? It is easier to state than to answer this question.

Barbour's answer was removal on a grand scale. He proposed that Indians of the eastern states be transported to 'the country West of the Mississippi, and beyond the States and Territories, and so much on the East of the Mississippi as lies West of Lakes Huron and Michigan.' This would have 'set apart for their exclusive abode' a region from Texas to Canada including the lake country of Minnesota, the Great Plains, the Rocky Mountains, as well as a slice of the Pacific Coast between California's northern tip and the mouth of the Columbia. Barbour's concept, dwarfing the modest proposition put forward by the British at Ghent, would have reinstituted something like the Proclamation Line of 1763, a thousand miles to the west. Other features of his plan were equally drastic. Removal by 'individuals in contradistinction to tribes' would dissolve existing treaties and eliminate tiresome negotiations with tribal chiefs. Chiefs and leading men, Barbour suggested, having grown rich through possession of farms or plantations within the old tribal homelands, would be least likely to favor moving west. Better to let such persons stay behind in 'unaltered' condition. They would of course have to abandon tribal status, taking their chances under local and state laws that might or might not protect them; in any case that was hardly a drawback since the intent of the proposal was to encourage migration.

As for those who did migrate, would they do so voluntarily? Barbour said yes: nothing ought to be done without consent. Yet having already allowed for abolishing treaties and bypassing tribal chiefs whether they liked it or not, his notion of consent was clearly dwindling. He disposed of the problem of consent entirely when he explained that his purpose was simply to bring these ideas before Congress and that Congress, in his opinion, possessed the power to move Indians collectively or individually whenever it saw fit. Nor was consent to figure much more in the Indian territories in the West. Because Indians clung so tenaciously to their tribal identities, they would be incapable of peaceful coexistence until their tribal identities had merged into a homogenous Indian identification. That might be a long time coming. Meanwhile, Congress must establish a territorial regime with governor, secretary and judges appointed by the president, but allowing for gradual stages of self-government. From the beginning to the end of this argument, Barbour stressed the goal of destroying tribal entities. His system of removal by individuals could be expected to accomplish that result for eastern Indians. The western tribes could be brought more gradually to the same point by empowering the president to provide for 'the extinction of tribes and their amalgamation into one mass.' This would clear the way for a final step – the transition, likewise by presidential decree, from communal ownership of land to distribution in severalty:

> Nothing, it is believed, has had a more injurious influence on our efforts to improve the condition of the Indian than holding land in common. Whether such a system may succeed, on a very limited scale, when under a beneficial patriarchal authority, is yet to be ascertained. Past experience has left the strongest evidence against its practicability. … The attempt of the kind in the first settlement of Virginia, and I believe, in the early settlements elsewhere, conducted the colonists to the very brink of ruin, from which they were rescued only by abandoning it. The distribution of the soil, and the individuality imparted to the avails of its cultivation, history informs us, instantly gave a new

and favorable aspect to their condition. ... If, therefore, the position be a just one, that every attempt at a community of property has eventuated unsuccessfully, even with civilized man, it is not matter of wonder that it should have been equally so with the savage.[8]

Historians, if they mention Barbour's letter to the Committee on Indian Affairs at all, have generally focused on its accusatory preface and ignored the legislative proposals.[9] Doubtless this is because the proposals were never enacted; even more because, viewed in the light of triumphant Jacksonianism, they appear irrelevant, almost frivolous. How could a project for closing the West to American settlement be broached seriously in the midst of the age of manifest destiny? Barbour seems to be speaking from an earlier century. Yet in reconsidering his letter, it is worth noting that although he recapitulated Adams's argument in the Plymouth oration of 1802 on the saving grace of private property, he also anticipated the central thrust of the Dawes Act, seventy years in the future.[10]

Barbour's contemporaries did not see him as irrelevant. In their estimate he figured as a bombastic politician, eager for power and applause; sparsely self-educated, infatuated with the sound of seemingly erudite phrases; a shrewd, successful planter and slaveholder; practitioner and propagandist of scientific methods in farming; a man of intelligence, and – at least for those who shared his political directions – integrity.[11] Adams, whom no one then or now could characterize as irrelevant, took Barbour seriously. It is true that he wrote in his diary, 'I fear there is no practical plan by which they can be organized into one civilized, or half-civilized government';[12] and certainly Adams was aware that the Indians, on the one hand, would struggle to preserve tribal identities, while on the other hand the projected closure of western regions to white settlement would rouse ferocious resistance in Congress and out. But that did not mean he thought Barbour's proposals impractical.

Viewed as a position paper pointing out advantageous directions rather than a blueprint, the strategic possibilities of Barbour's project become impressive. By no means did it preclude piecemeal approaches to western closure selected to divide or disarm opponents. On the contrary, it put forward incentives for wooing support in areas otherwise likely to be hostile. To states containing substantial Indian populations – among them Georgia, North Carolina, Pennsylvania, New York, as well as all the lands west of the Alleghanies – the project offered either removal of the Indians or their subjugation to local law, or both. But that was exactly what Georgia clamored for. Should such states in return permit the establishment of federally controlled Indian regimes in portions of the national domain as yet unorganized, the plan would have achieved its main purpose by delaying indefinitely the advent of new white settler territories and states.

The key to Barbour's plan was the idea of using Indian communities to perpetuate central control of the national domain by retarding white settlement. The Indian regimes, he wrote, would be 'exclusively under the control of the United States, and, consequently free from the rival claims of any of the States.' The nation as a whole could then guarantee 'that it [*it* here referred to the western region into which the Indians would have been transplanted] shall be theirs forever.'[13]

What was 'theirs', although closed to white settlement, need not remain forever closed to white enterprise. Barbour probably thought mainly of backcountry commerce governed by federal licensing; but some of his National Republican and Whig colleagues would soon be thinking of extractive enterprises and overland routes to commercial entrepôts on the Pacific Coast. Beyond that, the 'eventual' shift from hunting grounds held in common to farms owned in severalty was certain to release excess lands. The time and manner of release, however, would be decided by the federal government, and the lands themselves would initially come into the national domain. It would thus be possible to regulate western development by orderly stages, no new region being opened till older regions had attained population densities and land valuations comparable to those of eastern states. The flight of capital and labor power from the East would then be minimized; rising land values would accrue to the central government – to sustain internal improvements – rather than to squatters and speculators.

That Barbour thought more or less systematically in such terms is indicated by views he expressed on the decline of agriculture in Virginia. Through his own achievement he had demonstrated how profitably Virginia capital could be invested in agricultural technology and the diversified training of slave labor. Addressing the Albemarle County Agricultural Society while he was secretary of war (Barbour followed James Madison as president of the society in 1825), he dwelt with obvious satisfaction on his own successful farming techniques, but warned that the state's best resources no longer flowed into its most important occupation, which was, or ought to be, agriculture. Pursuing the same theme in a speech to Virginia's first agricultural convention in 1836, Barbour recalled once rich farm regions now returning to brush and forest. A chief cause of this decay was the emigration of our people, 'drawn by cheap new lands in the south and west.' The migrants took with them 'capital for which they have sold their property'; worse, they carried away capital they had gained by mining their farms for quick profit, 'leaving the skeleton they have made to their successors.' Those left behind – a few very wealthy, 'too comfortable to move', and a much larger number 'so poor they cannot' – comprised only the 'head and tail of society', while the 'vital part' vanished over the western horizon.[14]

A market-oriented slave plantation owner like James Barbour shared with other landed and commercial proprietors scattered through different regions and diverse occupations this ambivalent attitude toward the West. Such congruencies were the essence of political coalition. National Republicans (and Whigs) craved continental nationalism as the basis for commercial empire, but feared internal disruptions that might be triggered by too rapid opening of new lands. Indian policy promised a means of centralized regulation. Barbour, in offering his plan to Congress, had proposed a bargain: to withdraw federal protection of Indian lands inside the states in return for permanent federalization of the public domain.

The Whig Party

The administration launched with great expectations of continental nationalism quickly lost steerageway. For what follows it is important to stress the sequence of these events. First came promulgation of the National Republican thesis — explicitly in Adams's 1825 message and Barbour's 1826 critique of Indian policy; implicitly in a cautious reticence with respect to slavery, which even after the Missouri debates could enable northern and southern nationalists (Adams and Rush; Barbour, Calhoun and Clay) to collaborate. Next came the Jacksonian counterattack. The regional notables in Adams's cabinet and hundreds of comparable figures scrambled amid the wreckage of their class coalition to put together a new vehicle as much like the old one as possible. The result was the Whig party, created to embody and carry forward the National Republican thesis. In this case, at least, the ideological construct proved more durable than its material implementation. Although Whigs – and subsequently Republicans – would rally around that thesis for the next seventy-five years, the Whig party may be said to have been impossible before it began.

The reason for this failure was that its constituency was breaking apart. US economic growth since the War of 1812 had diversified the original class coalition underlying the National Republican thesis. Slave-based agriculture in the South and manufacturing in the mid-Atlantic and northern states tended toward separate constituencies and regional differentiation of class interests. North of the Potomac the process intensified upper-class adhesion to the National Republican thesis; southward it tended to split the upper class into Whig and regionalist (states' rights) factions. These structural changes first erupted into national politics with the Missouri debates of 1820–21. Factionalization of the South was already well-advanced prior to John Quincy Adams's inauguration.[15] Seeking a transregional alliance, southern states' rights factions moved rapidly into the Jacksonian coalition.[16] With respect to Indians – and in sharp contrast to the proposals Barbour had set before Congress – the Jacksonians proposed not merely an end of federal protection for Indians inside the states but the unlimited opening up of western lands as well – in return for the use of federal power to sustain slavery.

Southern nationalists like Calhoun, Clay and Barbour at once found themselves on the defensive, in danger of being stigmatized as enemies of their own class interest. Calhoun, a tower of National Republicanism in the South, embraced regionalism under heavy fire in his own state. Clay, although retaining a tenuous grip on Kentucky, lost standing as a favorite son of the South and for that reason would be passed over by the Whig party in favor of such politically noncommittal candidates as Harrison and Taylor.[17] Barbour's declining political fortunes predicted what lay ahead for southern Whigs. Already undermined in Virginia by the devious course he had pursued as United States senator during the Missouri debates, Barbour had expected that national office would reestablish his career. Instead, the administration's resistance to Georgia in the Creek controversy and his own Indian policy letter further weakened him. He persuaded Adams in the final year of the administration to send him as minister to London, hoping to stave off the day of reckoning in his own state. But Jackson fetched him home to Virginia. There Barbour tried, like Adams at Quincy, to carve out a local bailiwick. Running for the House of Delegates, he squeezed through in a close contest only to be challenged and unseated. In his farewell speech to the Virginia legislature (in which his public career had begun thirty-three years earlier) he assured his adversaries that class loyalty ran deeper than party affiliation or national sentiment. James Barbour, he promised, would be at the front ranks of his class should slavery ever be threatened in the South.[18]

Ideologically, the Whig party's fatal weakness lay in a contradiction between principles and tactics. This contradiction stemmed not so much from the relationship of the party to its own class base as from the nature of its opposition. The Jacksonian coalition will be examined in some detail in a later chapter. Here it will suffice to point out that the return to party competition in the late 1820s occurred in a recently developed but irreversible context of potential mass participation.[19] The Jacksonian leaders (slaveowners included), who were challenging an established regime, effectively exploited this potential. Whig leaders, obliged to defend their regime within the new political context, found themselves more seriously hampered than their opponents by the fact that their constituency was elitist, not egalitarian.

Most Whigs believed, as Adams's Massachusetts colleague, Daniel Webster, put it, that power properly followed wealth. Like their fathers – some of whom had signed the Declaration of Independence – they saw no conflict between republicanism and a class location of political power.

What was required, simply, was an understanding that the Declaration, in speaking of unalienable rights, said nothing of any right to participate in government. On the contrary, the best efforts of devoted governors alone could suffice to preserve the rights of life, liberty and pursuit of happiness for the run of mankind. The Constitution guaranteed to states a republican form of government because that form seemed most likely to place in office men whose interest would coincide with the rights of their constituents. A republic would yield that result, however, only so long as it was administered by responsible men; and responsibility, in the Whig view, adhered to that share in the social order conveyed by owner-ship of property. Without the continuity of upper-class culture, without the refinements of education and moral sensibility that flowed from it, a nation – especially a new nation like the United States – would find itself intellectually impoverished, defenseless against ignorant leaders or vicious pretenders. This was so because the lower social orders, while certainly indispensable and perhaps no less virtuous in a moral sense than their social superiors, could act only destructively outside their proper spheres. Given political power, they were likely to use it to violate the property rights of the upper class upon which stable government depended. Any system that permitted separation of property from political representation set itself on a disastrous road. That was the delinquency John Quincy Adams had charged against Tom Paine and Thomas Jefferson in his 'Publicola' letters: 'the hideous form of despotism' would then 'assume the party-colored garments of democracy.'[20]

This same theme was worked over relentlessly in Whig polemics. Half a century after 'Publicola', for example, the Baltimore lawyer John Pendleton Kennedy, who was occasionally a congressional colleague of Adams, satirized Jacksonian country oratory in the following terms:

> Do we not know [said the speaker] that in every community the majority are poor? that there are two men without property for every man with it? Of course then, it follows logically, that, as two heads are better than one, the sole right, as well as the sole power of legislation is in the poor; and that they may make laws for the government of the rich. ... Besides, who would be the most impartial in such a matter, the man legislating for his *own* property, or the man legislating for his neighbor's? This requires no reply.[21]

Kennedy, like his fellow Baltimorean William Wirt, Adams's attorney general, was more than a lawyer: he was a novelist, essayist, civic leader, textile manufacturer and railroad promoter. Privately he wrote to his uncle, a Whig lawyer in the Virginia town that probably furnished the setting for the satire just quoted, 'The war is and shall be forever between the ignorant, the idle, the dissolute, and their antagonists in the social frame.'[22]

This explicit insistence on class hierarchy, typified in Kennedy, contrasted sharply with an ambiguity in political manoeuver that often appeared, to their opponents at least, like outright hypocrisy. Electoral tactics brought Whigs up against the disjuncture between their goal of upper-class dominance and their actual inability to preclude lower-class political participation. In this respect the long flow of eighteenth- and early nineteenth-century history ran against them. By the time of Adams's inauguration in 1825, property qualifications for voting and eligibility to office had been eliminated in many states and were being stripped of substance in others. White manhood suffrage had become the norm beyond any possibility of rollback. Whig leaders were consequently in the position of urging the mass of voters to choose candidates who believed voters ought to be controlled, for their own good, by men of the upper class. If they said what they believed in campaign broadsides, they were likely to alienate the majority; if they said what they did not believe, or less than they believed, they taxed the faith and sophistication of upper-class constituents (their source of campaign funds) to the breaking point.[23]

The dilemma became acute in presidential elections; and since a keystone of the National Republican thesis was maintenance of a coalition of regional elites in support of national development, the party's credibility required presidential victories. The Whigs had only two victors, however, both of whom were military men who endeavored to place themselves above politics as if washing their hands of the interests that motivated their own partisans. Both candidacies involved misrepresentation of central tenets of Whig doctrine, and in neither case did presidential victory convey power to enact a Whig program, in part because so much of their electoral effort had gone to evade rather than teach the necessity of that program. The Harrison–Tyler campaign of 1840, bringing two sons of Virginia first families – the one a substantial landholder in the Northwest, the other a Tidewater planter – into the arena as log-cabin egalitarians, appeared ludicrous to contemporaries and has furnished entertainment for historians and social scientists ever since. Eight years later, Zachary Taylor, after declaring not only that he had never run for office, but that he had never previously voted, won the presidency as the hero of a war the Whigs had opposed from the outset.[24]

By 1848, of course, the issue of slavery in the territories was displacing other issues. Leaving aside for the moment the special problem of slavery, Whig views on expansion were scarcely more acceptable in the framework of white manhood suffrage in the 1840s than were Whig scruples as to the inseparability of wealth from honorable government. Most Whigs, having experienced political awakening during the War of 1812, accepted continental nationalism in substantially the terms set forth by John Quincy Adams; but their proprietary anxieties inhibited them from turning this commitment to the advantage of the party. They feared rapid western settlement would drain capital and labor from the East; leave currency and credit to the imagination of wildcat bankers; and – in lieu of using the public domain to capitalize internal improvements – give it away to speculators and drifters. While by no means unrealistic, these fears trapped Whig thought within the old Federalist counting-house mentality of family commercial enterprise. The result was to foreclose any possibility of expanding the class base of their coalition by *populizing* capitalist accumulation in the West. This was precisely what some Whigs – among them William Seward and Richard Hildreth – were grasping for; but given the reluctance of their colleagues to tolerate deviation from inherited doctrine, such ideas had to wait another generation and another party.[25]

Conscientious Whigs were embarrassed by their party's evasiveness and sought to apologize for it. Thus the Baltimore Whig John Pendleton Kennedy, a delegate to the Harrison–Tyler nominating convention, regretted (afterwards) that he had not held out for the ideologically more forthright Henry Clay. His occasion for retrospection was a 'defence' of the party's dismal track record during the two congresses that followed the election of 1840. Kennedy, who carried a leading part in the action, put the blame on vetoes of Whig measures by Vice-President Tyler, who had succeeded to the presidency after Harrison's death. Tyler had of course been nominated by the same convention that chose Harrison. Knowing little about Tyler, Kennedy explained, the convention delegates had taken his alleged intimacy with Henry Clay and his eagerness for nomination as pledges of adherence to Whig principle. 'I acknowledge for my part', he wrote, 'a grievous delinquency.'[26] What Kennedy did not say was that Whig leaders, himself among them, had known (or thought they knew) what they were buying in John Tyler. They were buying a political foe of Andrew Jackson as well as a highly conscious member of Virginia's planter class. In that respect, Tyler was the sort of man to whom Whigs, in theory, wished to entrust power. But he turned against their program for reasons Kennedy could only attribute to personal villainy.[27]

As a slaveowner, Tyler had ample reasons for blocking Whig legislation aimed at enhancing the economic powers of the federal government. Tyler's opposition to such legislation reflected the changes in social and economic structure that were rendering whiggery obsolete in the South. Were party leaders unaware of those changes? Obviously they were aware of them. Yet most of them were unable to perceive causal links between structural change and ideological conceptualization. By no means were Whig leaders uniquely obtuse, but they labored under unique disadvantages because they were encountering problems for which no historical precedents yet existed. Although upper-class coalitions prior to theirs had struggled against rival coalitions or factions, none had ever had to defend itself in electoral competition with a mass political party. The reason was, simply, that before the United States there had been no mass culture, and before the Jacksonian assault on National Republicanism, no mass party. To this extent, America was indeed a new world.[28] The National Republican thesis as set forth by Adams and his colleagues in 1825 and 1826 had not been designed as an electioneering instrument. When a party subsequently gathered around that thesis, its leaders were obliged to improvise by trial-and-error tactics for defending upper-class privilege in the brave new world of mass politics.

In the long run it is hardly surprising that the Whig party disintegrated in the South after separation of its class constituency; nor that it failed, North and South, to persuade a majority of the electorate. What is surprising, given its minority base and demonstrated inability to control the federal apparatus, is that it sustained itself over two generations and across several great surges of population movement. This continuity must have resulted from the reproduction of whiggish ideological types through economic and geographical expansion.[29] Survival under adverse circumstances seems to have nourished, and indeed fed upon, a self-image with deep historical roots. Adams, as he never forgot, had made his way into the commercial ruling class of Massachusetts from outside. He was not totally in it. The old guard Federalists, against whom he waged the battles of his youth, he judged to be an aristocratic segment of the upper class corrupted by excess wealth to the brink of treason. National Republicanism, on the other hand, had represented a middle ground of civic virtue. When as president he chose his cabinet, he selected men from precisely that middle ground. Rush, his man from Philadelphia, was not a merchant prince or Pennsylvania land baron, but son of an austere republican doctor. Wirt had come to Baltimore not as one of the Chesapeake gentry, but the son of a Swiss immigrant. The southerners Barbour and Clay, substantial slaveowners both, had begun their journeys from the Piedmont, not the Tidewater. Upper-class leaders these men certainly were, but leaders unaccustomed to taking wealth for granted and for whom shared obligations of class remained part of everyday consciousness.

Here, again, Barbour's career epitomizes the anxieties of an upwardly mobile middle estate. Descended from an old but impoverished Piedmont family, Barbour had by the time he was fifty-five accumulated more than 21,000 acres and 130 slaves. By 'conservative estimate' worth a quarter of a million dollars, he had advanced himself from virtually nothing to substantial wealth.[30] Lacking a college education himself, he sent his son to Harvard, where he besieged him with angry rebukes for extravagance and warnings against being duped by his 'more cunning school fellows'.[31] To go to Harvard was to go among aristocrats so 'cunning' and rich that hard-earned money was only a joke to them. Adams, although mainly blaming Jackson and the South for his defeat, also believed that New England Federalists had conspired against him. This widely held persuasion of conspiracy from above lived at least as long as whiggish politics. John Pendleton Kennedy, who came into the party with the second generation, insisted that Federalists had initiated and continued to dominate the Jacksonian movement. Since, in Kennedy's view, the rank and file of that movement were ignorant and gullible, his concept was that of a rabble led by renegade aristocrats – 'a meeting of both ends'.[32] However disingenuous, Kennedy's argument implied a corollary that corresponded to his own political reality. If Jacksonians united the top and bottom of the social order, men like Kennedy – natural targets of urban Jacksonianism – must stand at the center.

Kennedy was the son of a once prosperous emigrant from northern Ireland, bankrupted during the years of embargo and non-intercourse. The boy had grown up poor at the fringes of the upper class. He attended a short-lived, unprestigious Baltimore college and served as a private in the Maryland militia during the battles of Blandensburg and North Point. Due perhaps to military enthusiasms left over from the war, he entered local politics as a would-be Jacksonian. Kennedy found his permanent political affiliation through marriage to the daughter of a man much like his own father – James Gray, a Protestant emigre from northern Ireland who had flourished in commerce only to be ruined by the War of 1812; but who had gone on to become proprietor of a successful cotton mill on the Patapsco River outside Baltimore. Gray championed stable currency, sound credit controlled by a national bank, internal improvements to facilitate manufacturing ventures like his own, and a protective tariff. Not long after his daughter's marriage he gave the young husband a gift of a hundred dollars in token of his admiration for a pamphlet Kennedy had published attacking Jacksonian tariff policy and criticizing the doctrines of free trade. Gray made his son-in-law legal counsel and partner in the Patapsco cotton mills, which by 1851 were valued at between $200,000 and $300,000.[33]

Kennedy's adoptive politics brought occasional successes and frequent disappointments. As a spokesman of young Baltimore at the state legislature he lost out to the Chesapeake gentry over the issue of internal improvements; Baltimore voters subsequently defeated him for Congress in favor of the son of a revolutionary general and old-line Baltimore Federalist, John Eager Howard. Howard's son, the incumbent congressman, was the official Jacksonian candidate.[34] Kennedy later wrote that Andrew Jackson had called into flux 'the mass of men ... who, in every country are the flatterers of military renown ... stirred by patriotic impulse, but ever most apt to fall into an excessive admiration of heroical achievement, permitting the sentiment to preclude all doubt, silence all distrust. ... ' Jackson, like Napoleon, exploited the incapacities of the lower class; like Napoleon declared himself 'the only real Representative of the People'.[35] Leadership, even demagogic leadership, required intelligence and moral stamina that the lower class seldom could generate. Under the current dispensation, however, lower-class votes offered a standing temptation to disaffected members of the upper class to gratify ambition by pandering to those beneath them. The main danger came from leadership spun off by the upper class – from the 'meeting of both ends'.[36]

Kennedy and his Baltimore circle embodied locally, as had the Adams cabinet nationally, a stance generally characteristic of Whigs – that of an embattled middle establishment. The masses below were being manipulated by renegades from above. For Adams the manipulators were old guard Federalists. For southern Whigs like Barbour, they were Tidewater aristocrats; for Kennedy in Baltimore, the Chesapeake gentry. For Henry Clay in the West they were the old border captains and military men such as Humphrey Marshall, by whom Clay was wounded in a nearly fatal duel; and of course Andrew Jackson himself.[37] And for multitudes of Whigs scattered across western New England, upstate New York and Pennsylvania, the manipulators were those proprietors and land barons who, having ensconced themselves during an earlier era, continued to dominate state and local governments and courts of law through the network of the Masonic Order. In New York state this network was called the Regency, a political epithet epitomizing the entire concept.

With due respect for the work of those historians who have stressed the role of paranoia in American politics and who have scoffed at conspiracy theories, I doubt that any adequate explanation of Anti-Masonry can be provided solely by psychology, especially abnormal psychology. The Anti-Masonic movement remains one of the more dimly lighted chambers in nineteenth-century American social and political history: no fully satisfactory interpretation yet exists. It is clear, however, that intelligent and seemingly sane individuals (Adams, Richard Rush, William Wirt, William Seward, Thurlow Weed, Horace Greeley, Thaddeus Stevens, among many) took the *politics* of Anti-Masonry seriously. When a persuasive historical interpretation does come into existence, it is likely to fit within the framework of structural change and ideological construction upon which I am relying.[38]

As structural change differentiated the interests of slave-based commercial agriculture from the general interest of the merchant-landlord oligarchy, the new Whig party disintegrated in the South, undermining the efforts of its proponents to construct a fortress of National Republicanism. Like many other National Republicans who became

Whigs, John Quincy Adams, while vigorously class conscious, had sought to avoid the issue of racial exploitation. Nonetheless he recognized immediately that the downfall of his own administration came about through Georgia's dispossession of the Creeks. Attributing that dispossession to the slave interest, he afterwards concluded that if the American republic were to survive, its slaveholding class must be destroyed. Adams thus anticipated the movement of main-line whiggery from National Republicanism to Republicanism by about twenty years – and I will suggest in the next chapter that he not only anticipated that movement but guided it as an ideological innovator. The point to be stressed here, however, is that outside the South the party's gradual alienation from slavery reproduced the characteristic stance of the middle establishment. Those renegade manipulators customarily denounced by Whigs could readily be identified with the master manipulations of the slave interest. Political and economic goals converged on the single goal of excluding the planter class from federal power. Such innovations of Whig ideology can best be examined through the interrelations of the party system within the mass culture. But before turning to that wider focus, it may be helpful to pick out certain aspects of racial ideology that remained peculiarly whiggish.

Whig Racism

Whigs generally opted for moderate or 'soft' solutions to racial problems. Thus James Barbour in his 1825 address to the Albemarle County Agricultural Society argued that kindly treatment coincided with both the welfare of slaves and the self-interest of masters. 'The relation of master and slave ... deprived of its otherwise harsh and unfriendly characters' would then blossom into harmonious cooperation and rising productivity.[39] Since Barbour recommended incentives, technical training, and special rewards for profitable work, the logic of his position pointed toward wage labor, although he held back from that conclusion. Many southern Whigs undoubtedly hoped for an end to slavery along the lines suggested by Jefferson. During the Virginia legislative debates of 1831, the minority voted to seek a plan of gradual emancipation. This, in the South, marked the last flurry of public debate on the issue. Henceforth southern Whigs, like Henry Clay in Kentucky, kept silent. Yet Clay, having given up all presidential aspirations near the end of his life, felt obligated to reaffirm his adherence to gradual emancipation as one of the earliest commitments of his political career.[40] Through the North and Northwest, Whigs consistently favored this solution, usually tying it, as did Clay and Lincoln, to colonization. In New York, Pennsylvania, and the Old Northwest, Whigs were more likely than Democrats to support suffrage and public education for African Americans.[41]

Their Indian policies also were characteristically 'soft'. From Whigs came the main opposition to Jacksonian Indian removal and the sharpest criticisms of the Second Seminole War. Chief Justice John Marshall, once a Federalist foe of Jefferson, had by the 1830s become a whiggish opponent of Jackson; his final decision in the Cherokee cases, concurred in by National Republican or Whig colleagues on the court, was widely applauded by Whig leaders. And as Barbour's earlier letter to the House Committee on Indian Affairs had made clear, some Whigs at least could contemplate without mental anguish the possibility of Indian participation in the governing of federal territories that might eventually become states.[42]

The racial policies of Whigs differed categorically from those of their main adversaries, the Jacksonian Democrats. This, however, was not because they were less racist in ideas or attitudes. Measured by the terms of the definition put forward in the Introduction, John Quincy Adams, for example, was hardly less racist than Andrew Jackson himself. The same may be said of other leaders previously referred to as exponents of Whig ideology. Clay – to whom Indians 'as a race' were not worth preserving – rated Africans also as 'a servile and degraded race'.[43] Barbour expected the inherent 'obstinacy' of Indians, together with 'their prejudices, their repugnance to labor, their wandering propensities', to hinder, perhaps prevent, 'their complete civilization'.[44] And so subhuman were Africans in his opinion that enslavement had uplifted them, whereas manumission would leave them 'ignorant, insolent and demoralized', unable to subsist except 'from prostitution, from theft and from begging'.[45]

As early as 1832, John Pendleton Kennedy, in his nostalgic novel of Virginia, *Swallow Barn*, had perfected a childish, animalistic, comically contemptible cartoon of the plantation darky that would shamble through American fiction and popular culture for generations to come:

> At a most respectful distance behind trotted the most venerable of outriders – an old free negro, formerly a retainer in some of the feudal establishments of the low countries. His name was Scipio. His face, which was principally composed of a pair of protruberant lips, whose luxuriance seemed intended as an indemnity for a pair of crushed nostrils, was well set off with a head of silver wool that bespoke a volume of gravity.

At Swallow Barn, the master's thirteen-year-old son, red-headed and freckle-faced, had as 'compeer', especially for fishing expeditions, 'a little ape-faced negro' nicknamed Beelzebub. And again: 'There is a numerous herd of little negroes about the estate ... darting about the bushes like untamed monkeys.' When the master, for 'diversion', ordered a footrace, they 'ran with prodigious vehemence. ... These young negroes have wonderfully flat noses, and the most oddly disproportioned mouths, which were now opened to their full dimensions, so as to display their white teeth in striking contrast with their complexions. They are a strange pack of antic and careless animals. ...'[46] The tone is condescending; but the deliberate dehumanization unmistakable.

If scarcely less racist in ideas and attitudes than the Jacksonians, why were Whigs more prone to favor 'soft' racial policies? In part, perhaps, because Whig leaders, more likely to have grown up in affluent circumstances, were also more likely to have been educated into the high culture of the days of their youth, which was Enlightenment rationalism. Rationalism favored a unitary origin of the human species and an optimistic view of its prospects. Shying away from theological explanations like the curse of Ham, rational thought explained the inferiority of non-white races (if they were inferior) as due to environmental bad luck that might in time be reversed.[47] Meanwhile the advantaged situation of whites furnished no ground for moral complacency because it too had resulted from environmental luck. Racist ideology, stemming from the world expansion of Western Europe, from the African slave trade and dispossession of non-white peoples in the Americas and the Pacific islands, had to jell within this rather restrictive mold. A person educated to Enlightenment rationalism might maintain the inferiority of non-white races, or even look forward, like Jefferson, to their natural extinction; but would tend to regard deliberate extermination as a crime against humanity. Although ready enough to use racism in justifying racial exploitation, such a person scarcely could pursue to a logical extreme that passion described by Melville as the metaphysics of Indian hating.[48]

Especially for the first round of Whig leaders, Enlightenment thought loomed large and the influence of Jefferson and the Virginia school remained pervasive. That influence is obvious in Adams; clearly visible also in such men as James Barbour, Richard Rush, William Wirt, and John Pendleton Kennedy. Nor was it merely coincidence that the two most celebrated national spokesmen of the Whig party were westerners, though Virginia-born – Henry Clay and William Henry Harrison. Both profited from slavery; both throve through the destruction of Indians; both, in the republican enthusiasms of their youth, took stands against slavery; both championed republican revolution in Latin America; and both made peace with slavery at home.[49]

At most, however, Enlightenment influence provides only a partial explanation for the difference between hard and soft racial policies. The Enlightenment shone on incipient Jacksonians as well as Whigs. And while it may have illumined upper-class minds more generously than others, it was by no means unavailable to the minds of the urban working class.[50] Moreover – and most important – its illumination faded rapidly in the nineteenth century. Younger leaders in both parties would be increasingly distanced from it. But although by itself the rationalist explanation proves inadequate, it points, by virtue of its emphasis on class and education, to a more general, and satisfactory, argument.

Since the goal of the Whig coalition as an alliance of commercial and landed upper classes was to perpetuate upper-class political power, its ideological construct necessarily accepted and revered class hierarchy. The various classes comprising that hierarchy would differ in their obligations and privileges, their life styles and moral codes, even in language and dress. Within this spectrum of differences racial difference could be viewed, not as overriding all others, but simply one among many. What was crucial for Whigs was the willing acceptance by each class of its assigned position and role. Racial inferiority then presented no special problem, provided the inferior race occupied an appropriately subordinate position in the social structure.

In America, because of its accelerating economic growth, class hierarchy had always been more fragile than in Europe. The Revolution and War of 1812 had broken down some of the outer fortifications; the Jacksonian insurgency, invoking an egalitarian ethic for white republicans, attacked the citadel head on. In defense, Whigs proclaimed their counter-ethic of class deference. Upper-class leaders of an earlier period might have taken that for granted, but by the 1830s it had to be searched out and re-imagined. Here again, Kennedy furnishes a set of vivid examples. In *Swallow Barn* he included a scene in which the young squire fights an aggressively egalitarian upstart at the country store. The young squire, who had luckily studied scientific pugilism in his college days, chastises the Jacksonian bully without suffering a bruise or even working up a sweat. While at one level this scene expressed every boy's dream of glory, as a message of class superordination in 1832 it could hardly have been totally reassuring. How many young landlords learned pugilism at college? Or suppose the hero had encountered one of the new breed of frontier ruffians, half-horse, half-alligator, that were spreading over the landscape?[51]

In his next novel – which, like the Leatherstocking stories of James Fenimore Cooper, had two heroes – Kennedy sought to construct a firmer foundation of class deference. The two heroes of *Horse Shoe Robinson*, published in 1835, were a young, upper-class squire and a yeoman-artisan, farmer-blacksmith whose nickname, Horse Shoe, established his calling. Together they pursued a dangerous mission against Tories and Redcoats in revolutionary North Carolina. Although the odds seemed stacked against them, their chances of success rated high because Horse Shoe's prowess made him equal to legions of Tories and regiments of Redcoats. He was in effect the half-horse, half-alligator of the 1830s pushed back into a less problematic time period. The young squire, major in the Continental Army though he was, could never have mastered Sergeant Robinson in a fist fight. Fortunately there was no need to make the attempt. Kennedy had fixed the relation between his two heroes in the opening scene:

> As they stopped to eat beside a stream in the Blue Ridge, the young squire called out, 'Get down, man: rummage your haversac, and let us see what you have there.' Robinson was soon upon his feet, and taking the horses a little distance off, he fastened their bridles to the impending branches of a tree; then opening his saddle bags, he produced a wallet with which he approached the fountain where Butler had thrown himself at full length upon the grass. Here, as he successively disclosed his stores, he announced his bill of fare. ...[52]

The scene is worth remembering because it expresses so precisely the Whig idyll of prelapsarian innocence. Whigs always hoped to reconstruct native American artisans and yeomen farmers in the image of Horse Shoe Robinson. Sometimes they succeeded. But a sector of the labor force that remained inaccessible to them was the one occupied by recent immigrants. Whigs were never able to cut off naturalization and limit suffrage. Because these alien citizens amassed political power and seemed determined to use it in defiance of the politics of deference, they became for Whigs the most threatening element of society. Kennedy recorded in his journal an encounter on a train trip to Albany with 'two tall, bony, begrimed and rough looking fellows' who had taken a seat he thought properly belonged to a woman traveler. When the men declined to move, Kennedy said sarcastically that he was sure 'some of her own countrymen' would 'give her a seat. She couldn't expect *you* to do that.' '"How do you know I am not an American myself?"' one of the men demanded, rising with his fist doubled. 'Everybody in the car knows that', Kennedy replied. 'An American is never uncivil to a woman.' Realizing that 'there was a considerable native force ... to see me through the affair', the two then 'muttered their malice in low tones ... and at last discreetly but sullenly became silent.'[53]

After the 1844 presidential election, Kennedy, apparently attributing Henry Clay's defeat to the foreign vote, warned in a letter to the New York *Tribune* that the voice of the 'true people of America' was in danger of being suppressed 'by fraud and violence' at the polls and 'outweighed by voices *unAmerican*'. What was needed were more rigorous 'Laws of Naturalization ... greater care in the introduction to citizenship' to guarantee 'that no man shall vote in our elections who has not a heart to feel with American people, and a mind so acclimated as to understand, at least, the difference between American and Foreign interests. ...'[54]

In contrast to their resentment toward immigrant working people,

Whigs tended to accept non-white populations with humorous tolerance. Generally, of course, such populations, like black slaves in the South, or Indians, were politically powerless. But even where they had been allowed the suffrage, as in New England and to a limited extent New York, their small numbers and the overpowering hostility of white society forced them into clientship or dependency upon the upper class. In sum, Whigs, although they entertained racist ideas and attitudes to approximately the same degree as their Democratic adversaries, tended toward soft racial policies for three class-related reasons. First, non-whites in those days posed no conceivable threat to the privileges and social standing of the upper classes. Second, the existence of a racially divided labor force where it did exist, and the possibility of such a division where it did not, circumscribed the economic aggressiveness of lower-class whites. Third, non-white populations might under certain circumstances – such as, for example, those hinted at by James Barbour in his 1826 letter to the House Committee on Indian Affairs – be pressed into service as tools or proxies of the commercial and landholding establishment. The same class-related reasons that directed Whigs to soft policies inclined their adversaries to ruthless ones.

In pre-Jacksonian days such differences of tactical approach, as they pertained to upper-class interests, could be discussed frankly in counting houses and dining rooms and in the press of the seaboard cities. More hotly contested in legislative chambers, they might trigger a few affairs of honor and would eventually be disposed of, by compromise or division, among spokesmen of the merchant–landlord oligarchy.[55] After the Jacksonian upsurge, political decision making entered the realm of public spectacle. The political process infused not only the new parties but also the mass media of communication and entertainment which the Jacksonian upsurge itself was calling into existence. Harvard rhetoricians like John Quincy Adams would now be obliged to offer their declamations on the same stage with the half-horse, half-alligators of the southwestern frontier, or remain silent.

Notes

    1. Annie Heloise Abel, 'The History of Events Resulting in Indian Consolidation West of the Mississippi', *Annual Report of the American Historical Association*, Washington, D.C. 1908, 1:233–450; see especially pp. 339–40, 344–57; John Quincy Adams, First Annual Message, 6 December 1825; Letter of Transmission, 31 January 1826; Special Message, 5 February 1827; Letter of Transmission, 22 January 1828, in James D. Richardson, ed., *A Compilation of the Messages and Papers of the Presidents*, New York 1897, 2:827, 890–92, 936–39, 960–61.
    2. See the discussion of the Ghent negotiations in Chapter 1, p. 38.
    3. John Quincy Adams, *Memoirs of John Quincy Adams Comprising Portions of his Diary from 1795–1848*, ed. Charles Francis Adams, Philadelphia 1874–1877, 6:271–272.

4. Abel, p. 370; John Quincy Adams, *Memoirs*, 7:89–90, 22 December 1825.

5. Adams, *Memoirs*, 7:221, 231–32, 4, 25 February 1827; Abel, pp. 244–45, 322–23, 355.

6. Abel, pp. 354–55.

7. Barbour's report and draft of a proposed bill are in Barbour to James Cocke, Chairman of the House Committee on Indian Affairs, 21 February 1826, House of Representatives Documents, 19th Cong., 1st Sess., Document 102, pp. 3–12; Charles D. Lowery, 'James Barbour, a Politician and Planter of Ante–Bellum Virginia', Ph.D. diss., University of Virginia, 1966, pp. 289–90; John Quincy Adams, *Diary*, 21 November, 22, 23 December 1825; 4, 5, 6, 7 February 1826, Microfilms of the Adams Papers, Boston 1955, Reel 40; James Madison to T.L. McKenney, 27 March 1826, James Madison Papers, Library of Congress, Microfilm, Reel 21.

8. Barbour report, pp. 5–10.

9. Abel, pp. 365–67; Samuel Flagg Bemis, *John Quincy Adams and the Union*, New York 1956, pp. 84–85. See also Charles D. Lowery, *James Barbour: A Jeffersonian Republican*, University Station, Ala. 1984, pp. 164–66.

10. *Statutes at Large of the United States of America from December 1885–March 1887 and Recent Treaties, Postal Conventions and Executive Proclamations*, Washington, D.C. 1887, pp. 338–91.

11. William Faux, *Memorable Days in America, Being a Journal of a Tour to the United States...*, London 1823, pp. 367–74; Stephen Collins, M.D., *Miscellanies* Philadelphia 1845, pp. 209–30; W. S. Long, 'James Barbour', *The John P. Branch Historical Papers of Randolph–Macon College*, June 1914: pp. 34–64; Adams, *Memoirs*, 4:226, quoted in Lowery, Barbour diss., p. 160. Lowery, 'James Barbour: A Progressive Farmer of Antebellum Virginia', in John B. Boles, ed., *America, the Middle Period: Essays in Honor of Bernard Mayo*, Charlottesville, Va., 1973, pp. 168–87.

12. Adams, *Memoirs*, 7:113, quoted in Lowery, Barbour diss., p. 290.

13. Barbour report.

14. James Barbour, *Address of James Barbour, Esq., President of the Agricultural Society of Albemarle at their Meeting of 8th November, 1825*, Charlottesville, Va. 1825, pp. 7–13; 'Address to the Agricultural Convention of Virginia, Delivered by the President, James Barbour, Esq., in the Hall of the House of Delegates, 1836', *Farmers' Register*, vol. 3, March 1836: pp. 685–89. On the land policy context of Barbour's views, Daniel Feller, *The Public Lands in Jacksonian Politics*, Madison, Wis. 1984, pp. 80–81, 190.

15. George Dangerfield, *The Awakening of American Nationalism, 1815–1828*, New York 1965, pp. 212–15, 221–25; William W. Freehling, *Prelude to Civil War: The Nullification Controversy in South Carolina, 1816–1832*, New York 1965, pp. 102–42.

16. The axis of that coalition – at least until William H. Seward won the New York gubernatorial election in 1838 – was an entente between state's rights parties in the South and the Regency in New York, led by Martin Van Buren. Lee Benson, in *The Concept of Jacksonian Democracy: New York as a Test Case*, New York 1966, pp. 40–41, makes clear why the Regency's interest in states' rights coincided with a similar interest on the part of the southern planter class: 'In 1825, as a United States senator, Van Buren had fought the plan of the Adams administration to have the federal government play a broad, positive role in respect to internal improvements, and had proposed a constitutional amendment to prevent federally sponsored public works. ... the defense of state's rights formed the doctrinal core of his faction's *Address* in 1830. ... Emphasizing that New York had paid for its own canals and in particular the Erie Canal, the *Address* argued that it would be an "unequal and unjust" policy for the federal government to use "our money to build internal improvements for other states." ... If we recognize that the Maysville Road controversy firmly fixed "the just right of states" as the central dogma of Jackson's party, we can more easily understand New York politics after 1830.' Michael F. Holt, 'The Democratic Party, 1828–1860', in Arthur M. Schlesinger, Jr., *History of United States Political Parties*, New York 1973, 1:500–505.

17. Charles M. Wiltse, *John C. Calhoun*, Indianapolis, Ind. 1944, 1:285–98, 349–98; Clement Eaton, *Henry Clay and the Art of American Politics*, Boston 1957, pp. 73–83, 97–98, 103–5; Glyndon G. Van Deusen, *The Life of Henry Clay*, Boston 1937, pp. 248–54, 309–36; Lowery, Barbour diss., pp. 219–21; Harry Ammon, 'The Richmond Junto, 1800–1824', *Virginia Magazine of History and Biography*, 61:413–15; 'Missouri Compromise Letters to

James Barbour, Senator of Virginia in the Congress of the United States', *William and Mary Quarterly* (1902): 10:5–24; Dangerfield, pp. 97–140.

18. Long, pp. 54, 60; *Richmond Enquirer*, 3 January, 17 February, 7 March 1831.

19. Holt, 'Democratic Party', in Schlesinger, ed., 1:503. David Hackett Fischer, *The Revolution of American Conservatism: The Federalist Party in the Era of Jeffersonian Democracy*, New York 1965, pp. *xii–xiii* and note 3.

20. Richard N. Current, *Daniel Webster and the Rise of National Conservatism*, Boston 1955, pp. 37–38. John Quincy Adams, 'Letters of Publicola', in *Writings*, ed. Worthington C. Ford, New York 1913–17, 1:68, 71. The best general treatment of the Whigs and the best introduction to Whig culture and politics is Daniel Walker Howe, *The Political Culture of the American Whigs*, Chicago 1979. See especially the portrayals of John Quincy Adams, pp. 43–68, and Joshua Giddings, pp. 167–80; Glyndon G. van Deusen, 'The Whig Party', Schlesinger, Jr., ed., 1:333–63.

21. John Pendleton Kennedy, *Quodlibet: Containing Some Annals thereof ... Edited by Solomon Secondthoughts ...*, Philadelphia 1840, p. 129.

22. Kennedy to Philip Clayton Pendleton, 17 October 1844, in Charles H. Bohner, *John Pendleton Kennedy: Gentleman from Baltimore*, Baltimore 1961, pp. 70–71.

23. Chilton Williamson, *American Suffrage: From Property to Democracy, 1760–1860*, Princeton, N.J. 1960, especially pp. 76–78. Benson, *Concept of Jacksonian Democracy*, pp. 7–10. Arthur M. Schlesinger, Jr., *The Age of Jackson*, Boston 1945, pp. 283–88. Schlesinger, perhaps more perceptive of hypocrisy among Whigs than among Democrats, is illuminating on Whig resistance to doctrinal innovation.

24. Freeman Cleaves, *Old Tippecanoe: William Henry Harrison and His Time*, New York 1939, pp. 1–45; Robert Gray Gunderson, *The Log Cabin Campaign*, Lexington, Ky. 1957; Brainerd Dyer, *Zachary Taylor*, Baton Rouge, La. 1946, pp. 265–301.

25. See Chapter 11.

26. Kennedy, *Defence of the Whigs by a Member of the Twenty–Seventh Congress*, New York 1844, p. 66.

27. Kennedy, 'Whig Manifesto', *Niles National Register*, 18 September 1841, 61:35–36.

28. Ronald P. Formisano, *The Transformation of Political Culture: Massachusetts Parties, 1790–1840*, New York 1983, pp. 3–54, especially 3–5.

29. Feller, *Public Lands*, pp. 16 and 79: 'The state [Ohio] passed a milestone in 1825, when it began building a mammoth canal system. ... As its economy matured, Ohio looked to manufacturing and commercial agriculture, not to migration and land sales, as the keys to future prosperity, and the American system of protective tariffs and internal improvements assumed first importance for its citizens.'

30. Lowery, Barbour diss., pp. 338–41.

31. James Barbour to James Barbour, Jr., 25 July 1816, James Barbour Papers, University of Virginia, Manuscript Department, 91486, Box 1.

32. Kennedy, *Defence*, pp. 25–35, 45–46.

33. Kennedy, Journal, January 29, 1851, vol. 7e: 151–152, John Pendleton Kennedy Collection, Peabody Institute, Baltimore.

34. Bohner, pp. 123–24.

35. Kennedy, *Defence*, pp. 34–35, 39–40.

36. Ibid., p. 46.

37. Bernard Mayo, *Henry Clay, Spokesman of the New West*, Cambridge, Mass. 1937, 1:301–3.

38. The classic text on Anti-Masonry is Charles McCarthy, 'The Antimasonic Party', American Historical Association, *Report*, 1902, 2:365–574. A more recent overview is Michael Holt, 'The Antimasonic and Know–Nothing Parties', Schlesinger, Jr., ed., 1:575–620. Other helpful accounts are Howe, pp. 54–60; Whitney Cross, *The Burned Over District: The Social and Intellectual History of Enthusiastic Religion in Western New York, 1800–1850*, New York 1965; and Formisano, *Transformation*, pp. 197–221. See also Formisano and Kathleen Smith Kutolowski, 'Antimasonry and Masonry: The Genesis of Protest, 1826–1827', *American Quarterly* 29 (1977):139–65. As Formisano, *Transformation*, pp. 198, 217, points out, the dominant trend of Anti-Masonic historiography has treated Anti-Masonry itself as a hysterical fanaticism and the transformation of Anti-Masonry into effective politics as a deliberate manipulation by skilled operators like Thurlow Weed and William H. Seward.

This trend is represented by Dixon Ryan Fox, *The Decline of Aristocracy in the Politics of New York, 1801–1840*, [1919] New York 1965, pp. 337–43; and in Schlesinger's *Age of Jackson*, pp. 248, 288. It appears more recently in Seymour Martin Lipset and Earl Raab, *The Politics of Unreason: Right Wing Extremism in America, 1790–1970*, New York 1970, pp. 39–49, and in Sean Wilentz, *Chants Democratic: New York City and the Rise of the American Working Class, 1788–1850*, New York 1984, pp. 190, 209.

39. James Barbour, *Address, Agricultural Society of Albemarle*, p.10.

40. Henry Clay to Richard Pindell, 17 February 1849, 'Letter on Gradual Emancipation in Kentucky', Epes Sargent, *The Life and Public Services of Henry Clay ... Edited and Completed at Mr. Clay's Death by Horace Greeley*, New York 1856, pp. 619–27. See Feller, *Public Lands*, pp. 148–50, 165–66, for Clay's inclusion of a colonization clause in his 1833 bill for distributing the proceeds of public land sales to the states.

41. Howe, especially pp. 150–180; Leon Litwack, *North of Slavery: The Negro in the Free States, 1790–1860*, Chicago 1965.

42. Barbour report; see notes 7 and 8 above.

43. John Quincy Adams, 22 December 1825, *Memoirs*, 7:90. 'Letter on Gradual Emancipation', Sargent, p. 626.

44. Barbour report, notes 7 and 8 above.

45. Barbour, *Address, Agricultural Society of Albemarle*, p. 11.

46. John Pendleton Kennedy, *Swallow Barn; or, A Sojourn in the Old Dominion*, New York 1854, pp. 21, 40–41, 107, 308–10. *Swallow Barn* was first published in 1832: J.V. Ridgely, *John Pendleton Kennedy*, New York 1968, pp. 13–15.

47. Thomas Jefferson, *Notes on Virginia*. For a variation of environmentalism, see Ronald Takaki's discussion of Benjamin Rush's views on the origins of the blackness of Africans in *Iron Cages: Race and Culture in Nineteenth-Century America*, New York 1979, pp. 28–35. David Brion Davis, *Slavery and Human Progress*, New York 1984, pp. 42–43, 86–87.

48. Herman Melville, *The Confidence Man*. For a brilliant discussion of the complex interrelationships among anti-slavery, the Enlightenment and Protestant evangelicism, see Davis, pp. 129–53.

49. Sargent, *Henry Clay*, especially pp. 13–14, 19–21, 39–78; Dorothy Burne Goebel, *William Henry Harrison: A Political Biography*, Indianapolis, Ind. 1926, pp. 1–19, 36–74, 75–78, 222–24, 256–94; J. P. Dunn, Jr., *Indiana: A Redemption from Slavery*, new and enlarged ed., Boston 1905, pp. 294–324.

50. Eric Foner, *Politics and Ideology in the Age of the Civil War*, New York 1980, pp. 57–76, especially 65–67.

51. Kennedy, *Swallow Barn* 1854, pp. 359–68.

52. Kennedy, *Horse Shoe Robinson: A Tale of the Tory Ascendancy*, Philadelphia 1835, 1:22.

53. Kennedy, notes for an essay on 'National American Chivalry', Kennedy Papers, vol. 58, quoted in Charles H. Bohner, *John Pendleton Kennedy: Gentleman from Baltimore*, Baltimore 1961, p. 167.

54. Kennedy, letter in New York *Tribune*, 29 November 1844, in Bohner, p. 165.

55. Fischer, especially pp. 29–49. Federalist experience after 1800 partially foreshadowed that of the Whigs during the 1830s. In both cases 'conservatives' suffered from a division in the governing oligarchy. In 1800, however, there was no decisive shift away from deferential politics. Federalist failure was due not to the advent of mass democracy but to an inability to cope with the continental nationalism of their previous partners in the oligarchical coalition. Fischer describes his 'Young Federalists' in terms similar to those I have applied in following chapters to Whig 'ideological innovators'. Differences between the Federalist and Whig situations could be pinpointed by noting that 'Young Federalists' proved to be quite effective party organizers but lacked any unifying national vision, pp. 97–109, 150–81. Whig 'ideological innovators' had such a vision in the National Republican thesis, but remained unable to adjust their class consciousness to the necessities of the new mass politics.

3

Mass Media, Mass Mediators

Late in the fall of 1827 a real half-horse, half-alligator came over the mountains from Tennessee and stopped, according to his own account, on a cold, wet night at a tavern in Raleigh. As he elbowed toward the fire, one of the locals shouted a hurrah for Adams in his face. The Tennessee traveler, unlike Horse Shoe Robinson, had little tolerance for the politics of deference. 'Fresh from the backwoods', he responded, '[I] ... can wade the Mississippi, leap the Ohio ... whip my weight in wildcats – and if any gentleman pleases, for a ten dollar bill, he may throw in a panther – hug a bear too close for comfort, and eat any man opposed to Jackson.'[1] This was David Crockett, a newly elected congressman, on his way to do battle with Adams's men in Congress. Whether he actually spoke the lines he claimed to have spoken there is no telling; but certainly he had already reckoned the impact of the printed word on his public image, since he explained to the writer of this episode that he had never before used the 'above expression'; he had simply felt 'devilish' and it popped into his head; nor would he have thought of it again except that he saw it 'so much in print'.[2]

There really was a David Crockett. His eventful if brief career has been overshadowed by a more lasting incarnation as one of that group of comic, regional dialect speakers for whom Henry Nash Smith's characterization of 'vernacular' provides a perfect fit.[3] The construction of vernacular heroes – as I will attempt to demonstrate in several later chapters – remained crucial to the ideological process in America throughout the nineteenth century. David Crockett (or the Southwestern type he represented) came second in a line of vernacular heroes, the first-born being the Down East Yankee, prototype of Yankee Doodle and Uncle Sam. The Yankee and Crockett both were linked to theater and to the press, especially the new mass circulation press of the 1830s. I turn first to Crockett (although the Yankee preceded him) because Crockett's life in history and his vernacular re-creations offer illuminating counterpoints to John Quincy Adams's second and post-presidential career.

David Crockett: The Making of a Vernacular Hero

Crockett's life in history is quickly summarized. He was born in East Tennessee in 1786 to Scotch-Irish parents who migrated from North Carolina after the Revolution. The father had probably fought at King's Mountain; two of his grandparents were killed by the Creeks. Three times during Crockett's childhood his family moved west and shortly after his own early marriage he moved west again. At twenty-six he was fixed in the pattern that shaped the lives of his parents and thousands like them: without capital for improvement they opened new land, hacked fields out of the forest, succumbed to debt incurred in purchasing the land; and as the region filled around them and land values rose, sold out and moved west, hoping for better luck on the next round.[4]

Crockett served not very glamorously in the War of 1812. After the death of his first wife he married a war widow whose farm 'considerably improved his status in life'. Together they moved with their children to Indian lands from which the Chickasaws had recently been expelled. Here for the first time Crockett's fortunes took an upward turn. He acquired a grist mill, powder mill and distillery on Shoal Creek; his labor force included slaves. Justice of the peace, commander of the local militia, he was elected to the state legislature, where he defended the new settlers of Indian cessions – many of whom were technically squatters since they had moved in before surveyors' lines were run. A flood destroyed the mills and distillery on Shoal Creek, and with no reserves to meet this disaster, Crockett and his wife sold what remained of their property to pay off debts and moved again in the fall of 1822 to the Obion River, then a 'complete wilderness'. His fame as a settlers' champion had preceded him, and no sooner was this new region organized into Gibson County, Tennessee than Crockett returned to the legislature.[5]

Again he defended squatters and recent, or prospective, settlers. Although he condemned banks as 'a species of swindling on a large scale',[6] he supported the state-owned Bank of Tennessee in the interest of cheaper credit. Generally he favored land sales at the lowest prices and credit in lieu of cash. Often he stood in opposition to James K. Polk.[7] If land could only be bought with 'ready money', Crockett said, 'poor people would get very little of the land'; as for himself, he had not come here 'to legislate for ready money men'.[8] Elected to Congress in 1827, he spoke as a Jackson man and worked closely with Polk, chief of the Tennessee delegation, on behalf of a bill to turn over to Tennessee all federal public lands in the state. Shortly after Jackson's victory in 1828, Crockett apparently became aware that the land bill offered little protection for squatters against speculators. He sponsored an amendment that would convey free title to already established settlers (squatters) on federal lands. If he had supposed his fellow Tennessee congressmen would support this amendment, he was disappointed. They unanimously opposed it, as did the new administration. This rift enabled opponents to table both the bill and the amendment. Blaming defeat on the other Tennessee congressmen, Crockett charged that they were controlled by the state legislature, which in turn was dominated by land speculators. Polk blamed Crockett.[9]

The Jackson regulars put up a candidate against him in 1829. Assuming the stance of a loyal party man who believed the party mistaken on one particular issue, Crockett was comfortably reelected. Yet whether he liked it or not, he was now beginning a *de facto* alliance with the National Republicans. When the regulars, led by Polk, fielded another campaign to unseat him in 1831, Crockett, desperate for money, accepted a loan from the Second Bank of the United States on the understanding that he would support Whig efforts to recharter the Bank.[10] Failing reelection, Crockett attributed defeat mainly to his having opposed the administration on Indian removal, for which he had been 'hunted down', he said, 'like a wild varmint'. He had earlier conceded that he knew of no one within five hundred miles of his home who would have voted against Indian removal. The Indian question, however, was central to the crystalizing Whig thesis; and doubtless this was part of the price Crockett paid for votes on his land bill amendment, and for financial subsidy. Repayment of his loan from the Bank was postponed, and later cancelled, by order of Nicholas Biddle.[11]

Returning to Congress in 1833, Crockett found himself a national celebrity. He toured the Northeast as the honored guest of Whig merchants and millowners, and spoke enthusiastically of New England factories and the Lowell system. Andrew Jackson he denounced as a traitor to the principles of Jacksonian democracy, and allowed himself to be put forward as presidential timber, perhaps for 1840. At a mammoth Independence Day rally in Philadelphia he shared the platform with Daniel Webster, and in 1835 went back to Tennessee to campaign for reelection. Crockett's political future rested on the squatters' preemption amendment he had been pushing ever since he entered Congress and which in the spring and summer of 1835 he tried to steer through committees and procedural votes. A bipartisan fraction supported him. But since the proposition flew in the face of traditional Whig principle (as expressed, for example, in John Quincy Adams's excoriations of frontier land-grabbing) and remained, for other reasons, distasteful to regular Democrats, he failed. Thus he confronted his Tennessee constituents in 1835 as a proclaimed foe of Andrew Jackson, an associate of Whigs, perhaps even a hypocritical exploiter of his constituents' most urgent need, toward which he had promised much and produced nothing. He lost that election.[12]

The construction of Crockett as vernacular hero had begun in 1830 when James Hackett, a New York actor who specialized in comic renderings of Yankees, announced a five hundred dollar contest for a comedy appropriate to his theatrical needs. Seeking to widen his repertory, Hackett urged the New York writer James K. Paulding to enter the competition, even suggesting a title and hero, '*viz*: the *Lion of the West* and Nimrod Wildfire'. Word of this arrangement got around, and news stories identified the central character of Paulding's still unwritten play as the Tennessee congressman, David Crockett. Crockett was not offended. When Hackett brought his play to Washington, Crockett rose in the audience to exchange bows with Wildfire on stage.[13]

Hackett was probably mildly Democratic, Paulding strenuously so. Crockett had entered Congress as a Jackson man and stayed with Polk and the Tennessee regulars at least until the end of his first term. When he finally acknowledged disagreements with Jackson, he did so by way of a circular letter published in his Tennessee congressional district. That information may have been a long time getting to Paulding and Hackett; and since party formation was still very much in flux, may not have impressed them strongly when it did. Clearly, the political purpose of the play was to lionize political friends, among whom they took Crockett to be. Especially from eastern urban audiences, Wildfire evoked laughter and admiration, not ridicule, since his role was that of an effective advocate of democracy against upper-class snobbery and American self-reliance against British domination.[14]

In August 1831 – three months before the first performance of *Lion of the West* – Crockett lost his election in Tennessee; yet the contest had been close, and he began planning his comeback at once. Early the following year the first of the David Crockett narratives appeared anonymously in Cincinnati. The narration, set forth in impeccable English, recounted the author's visit to Crockett's frontier cabin; enclosed within the narrative were reminiscences and anecdotes presumably by Crockett himself. These, making up a large part of the text, comprised a brilliant fabrication of Southwest vernacular, undoubtedly based on Crockett's own speech, but borrowing heavily also from Paulding's Nimrod Wildfire. The author (although this was not known at the time) appears to have been a Pennsylvania Whig, Mathew St. Clair Clarke, who had served as clerk of the House of Representatives until severed from that situation by Jackson's victory in 1828. Crockett had entered Congress in 1827; he and

Clarke were reported to have traveled together in the West, and Clarke may have been his guest in Tennessee. Clarke's ghostwriting dramatically advanced the process begun in *Lion of the West* of establishing Crockett as a national celebrity.[15]

Meanwhile, through a political colleague and friend, Thomas Chilton, a former Whig congressman from Kentucky, Crockett opened negotiations with the prestigious Philadelphia publishing firm of Carey and Hart for a full-dress autobiography 'written by himself'.[16] Chilton played the role of ghostwriter. A Kentucky lawyer-politician, partisan of Henry Clay, Chilton probably knew the West better than Clarke. The autobiography, which came off the press early in 1834, made money for Carey and Hart, for Crockett, and perhaps for Chilton as well. More important, it laid the basis for Crockett's triumphs of 1834: the tour of the Northeast, the hints of presidential candidacy in 1840, the Fourth of July ceremonies with Daniel Webster. For Crockett, all this pointed toward great expectations, provided he won reelection to Congress in 1835. Failure of the land bill foreclosed that possibility. Losing, he went to Texas and his death at the Alamo.[17]

Following the autobiography, Carey and Hart issued three more David Crockett volumes. The first two, in 1835, both credited to Crockett, were the *Tour of the North and Down East* and *The Life of Martin Van Buren*. The third, in 1836, recounted Crockett's pilgrimage to the Alamo and the last battle.[18] This too was alleged to have been written by Crockett, on the totally spurious ground that it reproduced pages of a diary found on the author's body. Crockett may have had some input into the first two, virtually none in the third.[19] The *Tour* – mainly a paste-up of newspaper clippings and summaries of speeches – was compiled for publication by William Clark, a Whig congressman from Pennsylvania.[20] A Georgia Whig, Judge Augustin Smith Clayton, who was well acquainted with Crockett, wrote the life of Van Buren; it was a neo-Jacksonian critique that portrayed Van Buren as swaggering 'like a crow in a gutter ... laced up in corsets such as women in a town wear.'[21] As to the *Texas Exploits*, authorship has been clearly established for Richard Penn Smith, a Philadelphia attorney, journalist, playwright, gentleman of education, affluence and generally whiggish persuasion.[22]

In the role of vernacular hero, then, Crockett emerges as the collective product of several political collaborations. The first, for Jacksonian purposes, was that of Paulding the writer and Hackett the actor, in creating a comic but admirable frontiersman modeled on Crockett. The enterprise was then captured by Whigs. Five widely circulated books, each ghostwritten by a Whig author, boosted Crockett into national orbit. The firm of Carey and Hart played a crucial role, since it produced and published four of the five.

Carey and Hart was at that time the name of the Carey family publishing house. Mathew Carey, the founder, was an Irish Catholic who had been a young rebel editor in Dublin and who had migrated to Philadelphia to escape British prison. As a friend and protege of Lafayette, Carey quickly moved into the republican intellectual elite. The house of Carey, upon which the family's fortune rested, became under his direction and that of his son, Henry C. Carey, the outstanding book publisher in America during the 1820s and 1830s. Dropping his father's Catholicism but preserving his intellectual zest and business acumen, Henry C. Carey divided his energies among publishing, profitable investments in Pennsylvania iron and coal, and the study of political economy, in which he established an international reputation. A crusader for the manufacturing interest and protective tariff, his politics, predictably, were National Republican, Whig, Republican.[23]

It is worth noting that although the Careys underwrote and produced four Crockett books, they brought out the last two under dummy imprints.[24] This may have been due to fears of libel, especially in the case of the Van Buren diatribe. More likely it was because the Careys and their associates wished to avoid linking the vernacular hero too closely to a firm well-known for its Whig connections. Exclusive Whig sponsorship tended to push the Crockett persona towards a deferential yeoman role comparable to that of John Pendleton Kennedy's Horse Shoe Robinson. That might serve the nostalgic needs of historical romance (Kennedy was also a Carey and Hart author) but scarcely those of the new mass politics. In retrospect it is easy to see the relationship between David Crockett in history and the artifact created by Whig publicists as pointing to an alliance between the eastern commercial manufacturing establishment and squatters and marginal farmers in the West – thus adumbrating the marriage of eastern capital with the homestead movement and Free Soil that eventually would bring together a base for the Republican party. Something of that sort entered the presidential campaign of 1840, since the work done in orbiting Crockett as vernacular hero and in vilifying Martin Van Buren served to define the role that would be imposed on William Henry Harrison. Yet even in 1840, as the disintegration of their party after its presidential victory demonstrated, Whigs remained incapable of consummating such an alliance because of the ideological time lag that characterized decisive segments in their constituency.

It has sometimes been suggested that the real Crockett was duped by the Whigs.[25] I think this is a misreading of the record. On both sides the interchange was one of convenience rather than principle. Crockett paid the price the Whigs demanded and they gave what he desperately needed – cheap credit by way of Nicholas Biddle and a scattering of individual votes for his land bill; not much, perhaps, but more than was to be had in Tennessee. A spokesman for squatters and marginal farmers in a slave plantation state, Crockett was in a bind from which the Whigs could not rescue him whether they wished to or not. His transactions had to be with the Democracy, which was already mortgaged to the land speculation and land engrossment essential to the plantation system. Like Tennessee's Andrew Johnson later and in comparable circumstances, Crockett remained a Jacksonian Democrat in the South despite alliance with anti-Jacksonians in the North.

Thus he went where his northern allies directed on the Indian removal act; but expressed different thoughts even in the ghostwritten autobiography they made for him. His decision to volunteer in the War of 1812 he explained as a result of unprovoked aggressions by the Indians. And of an attack on an Indian village in which he enthusiastically participated:

> ... the Indians soon saw they were our property. The women and others ran out to surrender and some were taken prisoner. ... I saw some warriors run into a house until I counted forty-six ... then [we] set the house on fire, and burned it up with the forty-six warriors in it.

Crockett added that they afterwards found some potatoes in a root cellar under the burned house and having been several days without rations, ate them although 'they looked like they had been stewed with fat meat'.[26] The Cherokee trail of tears, for which Whigs from Webster in Massachusetts to Clay in Kentucky condemned Andrew Jackson, could hardly have discommoded Crockett.

Less controversial in the 1830s than Indian removal, yet key to all political commitments, was the attitude toward Africans and African slavery. In Paulding's *Lion of the West*, the vernacular hero in a scene given considerable prominence, exhibited his comic yet admirable white egalitarian identity by baiting and mocking a free black serving man.[27] This probably represents accurately enough Crockett's actual style. The five Crockett books that followed, however, are largely free of anti-black invective, perhaps because they were ghostwritten by Whigs. In only one of them, and briefly, does racist language break through, when the hero, in order to emphasize his own independence of Jackson, equates African-ness with submission and subservience: ' ... I am no man's partizan; I don't mean to wear no man's collar; for I would as lief belong to a nigger, and be a racoon dog, as the partizan of any man.'[28]

Crockett, in history, whatever his language about Africans may have been, owned and bought and sold slaves to the extent that his meager fortunes permitted.[29] Like many southern yeomen, he made political war against land engrossment and planter domination, but his notion of upward mobility was to become a slaveowner and planter. Had he won the election of 1835 and solidified his constituency, he might have negotiated the crossing. Or had he emerged from the Alamo not as a dead hero but a live one, he would doubtless have acquired land in Texas and stepped into the planter class. He would then have moved again into political leadership – as a Jacksonian Democrat.

The achievement of national popularity by regional and vernacular heroes like David Crockett early in the Jacksonian era was by no means fortuitous. Both were products of mass politics. Despite the virtuosity displayed by Whig publicists in lofting such figures as the Yankee Major Downing or Colonel Crockett (or General Harrison, for that matter), the natural affinity of vernaculars remained Jacksonian. Competition in manipulating vernacular characterization was one aspect, perhaps a crucial one, in the transformation of previously upper-class institutions – not only political parties but the press and theater, schools and denominational churches, even the anti-slavery movement – into mass media of ideological expression and controversy. Whigs and Democrats vied for preeminence, but the Democrats won most of the rounds. Efforts of Whig publicists to outdo the Democracy in these mass mediations probably hastened the collapse of their party; yet resulted at longer range in assembling the materials from which the legitimizing synthesis of a new party would ultimately be constructed.

The Second Career of John Quincy Adams

It was to this task that John Quincy Adams, proving an apt pupil in the school of mass politics, devoted his second and more remarkable career. After his defeat for reelection in 1828, his diary shows him struggling to put behind him his reactions of self-pity and loss of self-esteem.[30] The monotonous recordings of rancor and humiliation build to an extraordinary transformation. Within two years the former president was back in Washington as congressman from his own miniscule district of Quincy. In old age he played out a new role – Galahad of the anti-slavery cause.[31]

No serious issue concerning slavery had surfaced during his presidency. It was Indian problems that had caused controversy. Why then should he turn to antislavery rather than defense of Indians for his political reincarnation? Certainly he had ample opportunity for the latter course. His former attorney general, William Wirt, carried the Cherokee case to the Supreme Court; Adams could have done so. He presented petitions in their favor in the House of Representatives, and assuaged his guilt for not doing more by noting in his diary that he could not bear the pressures such a commitment would bring upon him. Partly, perhaps, he withheld commitment because he saw the Indian case as hopeless in the sense that most white Americans must concur with Georgia no matter how indignant they might be at the methods Georgia used.[32] But that was not enough, since by 1829 he would hardly have avoided a conflict merely on the supposition that it might be lost. This particular conflict he considered not worthwhile in its own right – because, I think, he regarded both Indians and Africans as marginal in the vast unfolding of God's will. He was not morally obligated to the welfare or survival of either group.

Significant others, whether good or evil, were white: and it was against white adversaries that God's battles had to be fought. For Adams, good, in its historical manifestations, coincided with the political morality of that commercial upper class with which he consciously identified. In his first career, laboring for an alliance of regional upper classes, he had projected the master plan of continental nationalism; but the slaveholding South betrayed him. Although the immediate issue was Georgian access to Indian lands, the heart of the matter was slavery on which had been nourished a class interest that challenged the interest of his own class.[33] To focus on Indians would strengthen the slaveholding South because, although few Americans were slaveholders, almost all willingly acquiesced in the displacement of Indians. Only through slavery could he attack the slaveholding class.

He had earlier had intimations of this necessity. During the Missouri debates of 1820 (in which, for the sake of his diplomatic tasks, he took no part), he had written in his diary: 'Slavery is the great and foul stain upon the North American Union and it is a contemplation worthy of the most exalted soul whether its total abolition is or is not practicable. ... A life devoted to it would be nobly spent or sacrificed.' And near the end of that year: 'A dissolution of the Union for the cause of slavery would be followed by a servile war in the slave-holding States, combined with a war between the two severed portions of the Union. It seems to me that its result must be the extirpation of slavery from this whole continent ... as God shall judge me, I dare not say that it is not to be desired.'[34] After his defeat in 1828 he constructed step by step an indictment of the plantation system as a class enemy.

'General Jackson' was saddling an 'overseer ascendancy' upon the national government. Jackson's vetoes destroyed the 'system of internal improvement ... the only path to increasing comforts and well-being, to honor, to glory, and finally to the general improvement of the condition of mankind.' Purchasing support by surrender of 'Indians to the States within the bounds of which they are located', the Jackson administration threw the weight of federal influence 'into the slave-holding scale. ... The system of internal improvement, and the promotions of domestic industry ... will be abandoned ... the doom of the National Bank at the expiration of its charter is already sealed.' Slavery – 'the support, the perpetuation and the propagation of slavery' – he told northern tariff advocates in 1842, dominated federal policy. Its thrust was to destroy 'every measure which could contribute to promote the manufacturing interest or the domestic industry of free labor.'[35]

Leaving the problem of Indian titles behind him, he focused on the distribution of public lands. 'The slave-holders of the South have bought the cooperation of the Western country by the bribe of the Western lands. ...' Land sales in the Southwest directly augmented slavery. In the North, they brought results almost equally disastrous: 'The thirst of a tiger for blood is the fittest emblem of the rapacity with which [congressmen from the new states] fly at the public lands. The constituents upon whom they depend are all settlers, or tame and careless spectators of the pillage.' Constituents and congressmen together comprised the output of a social chaos that converted Americans into a rootless, brutalized rabble, ready for political demogoguery and military adventure. Their voracious egalitarianism made them willing allies of slavery.[36]

So single-minded was Adams's war against the slave plantation system that it is tempting to think of him as having undergone something like a religious conversion. Yet it would be a mistake to suppose, on the basis of such evidence as, for example, his magnificent argument in the *Amistad* case, that he had been converted to any belief in racial equality. At least with respect to race, Adams seems to have readjusted and systematized the thoughts of his youth rather than abandoned them. In 1845, in an essay published in the *American Review: A Whig Journal of Politics, Literature, Art and Science*, he took up again the theme of savagery and civilization that had informed his Plymouth oration four decades earlier, as well as his polemics at Ghent. He now expanded his original dichotomy into a four-stage history of man, a sequence he could have taken from Scottish moral philosophy or from Condorcet.[37] These stages were hunting, pastoralism, agriculture and urban commerce. Each was necessarily prerequisite to the one that followed; but all four could exist simultaneously; and the third and fourth must do so, the materials of commerce being, for Adams, mainly agricultural. Throughout his life he never made any clear distinction between commerce and manufacturing.[38]

Human society moved upward through history from the first to the final stage. Because this progress followed natural law it was necessary or preordained. Adams did not pursue the question whether all peoples advanced through all four stages (Jefferson also had chosen not to pursue this question at a corresponding juncture in his own work).[39] Consequently, it remained possible to suppose that they did, or could; possible likewise to suppose that some might not. The latter alternative was strengthened by Adams's stress on the correspondence of mental and moral characteristics to the exigencies of the several stages. Thus it might prove difficult for a hunter, socialized into the alternating frenzies and passivities of the chase, to accept the monotony of herding sheep; or for the herdsman to advance from his lyric pastoral mode to the disciplines of the counting house.

Adams allotted separate but not quite equal accommodations to the secular and sacred. One could read man's progress from savagery to civilization either in science and history or in holy scripture. Each bore the stamp of divine authorship, offering parallel accounts of the same reality. Yet two crucial leaps, essential to the improvement of moral behavior, must have been impossible for human reason (after the fall of Adam) solely on the basis of science and history. These were knowledge of the omnipotent one-ness of God and of the immortality of the soul. The first, in Adams's belief, could have been arrived at only by revelations of the Old Testament prophets, the second only through the Christian gospel.[40]

Staunchly Arminian, Adams believed that salvation was available at will to any soul.[41] He probably would not have maintained that knowledge of Christianity was indispensable to salvation; and since he committed himself not once but twice (Adam and Eve, then Noah and his wife) to the descent of all mankind from a single parental couple, presumably heaven stood open to African and Indian as well as European souls. To what purpose, then, was sacred knowledge, or any other sort of knowledge, for that matter? It is at this point that the symmetry of the edifice begins to disintegrate. The purpose of knowledge was to furnish instruments for carrying out that overriding duty God had assigned to man, the improvement of the human condition, physically and morally, on earth. Thus progress was enjoined by religion. Yet knowledge, including religious and moral knowledge, was itself the outcome of progress from the ignorance and bestiality of the savage to the rational understanding and Christian conduct of the agricultural and urban-commercial stages.[42]

Since Adams linked the highest morality to individual land ownership, monogamous marriage and monotheism – all three having made their historical entries only in the agricultural stage – it is hard to imagine, if heaven were entered by any sort of strait gate, how savages on one hand and Christian merchants on the other could enjoy equal access.[43] As far as I know, Adams never specified a strait gate; so it remains possible that he modeled his heavenly city on a well-ordered mercantile oligarchy in which salvation ensued from knowing one's proper place in the class hierarchy and gracefully accepting the functions and rewards suitable to it. All this points toward what seems an unavoidable conclusion: that Adams linked non-white races to lower stages of development (Indians to savagery, Africans to somewhere between pastoralism and primitive agriculture – which is probably where he would have placed the slave plantation system) and saw them as fixed at those levels in history and in the cosmic hierarchy. How such variations had come about within the progeny of a single couple he did not explore.

Enlightenment thought has often been said to provide no place for evil other than equating it to ignorance. Jefferson could serve as an example. The same weakness – if it is a weakness – follows through to the sunny side of American romanticism. The dark side, by contrast, assigns to evil a structural role, individually and collectively, in man's fate. On a continuum from Jefferson to Hawthorne, Adams would fall somewhere between: intellectually closer to Jefferson, emotionally closer to Hawthorne. Evil, for Adams, in any guise that could enter public discourse, was political. Throughout his first career it came largely from Great Britain. This was a thoroughly Jeffersonian evil in that it could be defined rationally and attributed to objective historical causes. Thus British conduct toward the United States during the Revolution and War of 1812 resulted from unjust institutions that stemmed from ignorance, superstition and inertia. The main evil of Adams's second career emanated from the slaveholding South. Here too the phenomenon could be described objectively and understood as a consequence of historical causation. Yet the evil of slavery, in Adams's expression, seemed to exceed rational links to any historical antecedents. It spread like a plague, sickening the moral fiber of individuals, honeycombing the soul.[44]

Touched on the issues of slavery, as they had first been by the Missouri debate, slaveowners 'betrayed the secret of their souls. ... They look down upon the simplicity of a Yankee's manners, because he has no habits of overbearing like theirs and cannot treat negroes like dogs. ... False estimates of virtue and vice', polluting private 'sources of moral principle', led relentlessly to public corruption.[45] The people would learn to applaud their elected leaders in shameful acts. Annexation of Texas fulfilled for Adams the long transition of 'the North American Confederation into a conquering and warlike nation. Aggrandizement will be its passion', he predicted; ' ... the skeleton forms of war and slavery will stalk unbridled over the land'. 'The deepest of my afflictions is the degeneracy of my country from the principles which gave her existence ... under the transcendant power of slavery'. 'The Constitution is a menstrous rag, the Union is sinking into a military monarchy. ...'[46]

Such a phrase as 'menstrous rag' could never have entered Adams's public rhetoric. Obviously not confined to the unconscious, since he had written it out in his notebook, it remained part of his ceaseless dialogue within himself. His choice of words makes clear, I think, the connotation of an essay on Shakespeare he had published in 1835, at the height of the debate over the Second Seminole War. Adams maintained that *Othello* failed as tragedy because its dramatic evocation of audience sympathy for the young heroine worked at cross-purposes to its moral intent. That intent, according to Adams, was to show 'how black and white blood cannot be intermingled in marriage without a gross outrage upon the law of Nature'. The outrage, however, was due less to Othello, who in seducing a white woman of 'splendid and lofty station' merely followed out his own 'blackamoor' nature, than to Desdemona whose sexuality had shattered civilized restraint. 'The blood must circulate briskly in the veins of a young woman, so fascinated, and so coming to the tale of a rude, unbleached African soldier. ... Upon the stage, her fondling with Othello is disgusting.' At the end, 'when Othello smothers her in bed', audiences instead of experiencing 'the terror and pity' proper to tragedy would more likely 'subside immediately into the sentiment that she has her deserts.'[47]

I am of course bringing forward here an argument previously rejected, to the effect that white European Americans constructed metaphors linking African blackness to shameful acts and to the dark passions of sexuality.[48] While I consider this argument unpersuasive as an attempted explanation for the initiation of African slavery, it seems to work plausibly when placed in a dependent relationship to prior ideological constructions. Thus Adams in his first career employed the metaphor selectively, in its simplest form, to underpin official orthodoxies such as that slaves could justly be treated as private property, or that runaway slaves in Florida merited execution without trial. During his second career he invoked the same metaphor to convey the moral degradation of the planter class. Here the usage became more complex, since it rested on an assumption that African amorality permeated the white South through sexual permissiveness, through the mixing of 'black and white blood' institutionalized by slavery in every upper-class white household.

Although Adams wrote despairingly of the nation's future in private dialogue with his diary, his public deportment was in a different key. Two years before his death he made his first trip west, or at least to what had been west in the days of his youth. The journey turned into a triumphal progress across New York, south through Ohio to Cincinnati, even into Kentucky.[49] Its occasion – laying the cornerstone for an observatory to be erected by the Astronomical Society of Cincinnati – demonstrated that he had been too pessimistic in supposing the West must be overrun by the influence of the Slave Power. Despite that influence, whiggish ideas happily had taken root, bringing portions of the West, such as Ohio, up to the condition of the eastern seaboard at the time of the great National Republican administrations. Adams could readily enough find an explanation for this phenomenon in his theory of stages: having progressed rapidly from the first to the third and fourth stages (from hunting to stable agriculture and urban commerce), Ohio now entered the realm of a more advanced 'political morality'.[50]

'We – you – *you*', he told his audience – each building individually from the Christian obligation 'to improve the condition of himself and his fellow men'[51] – had deployed the arts and sciences to convert 'the wilderness into a garden. ... You see you are no longer in the wilderness of savage men. ...' Towns, churches, farms 'attest that the hunter is no longer there: that the forest is falling under the axe of civilized man, and rising again under the hammer and trowel of the carpenter, the farmer and the mason. ...' But were not such practical achievements principally valuable as foundations for a more perfect comprehension of the divine order? And then the old question again, 'whether, among these monuments of civilized industry, perserverance, ingenuity, there is one light house of the skies – one tower erected ... to enable the keen-eyed observer ... to watch from night to night through the circling years ... and report to you and all the civilized races of man, the discoveries yet to be revealed? ...' As yet there was not one. The structure about to be commenced, he hoped, would wipe away this 'reproach from the fair fame of our beloved country'.[52] Adams did not live to make the final turn of the argument by admonishing his western listeners that no lighthouse of the skies could really be built in America until the racially tainted slaveholding class south of them had been destroyed. Yet he could hardly have doubted, given the stage of civilization arrived at, that this understanding would soon become self-evident; nor that he himself had done his share toward improving 'the condition ... of his fellow men' by revealing the true nature of the Slave Power.

Notes

1. New York *Sun*, 18 November 1833.
2. Ibid. The *Sun* was quoting from *The Life and Adventures of Colonel David Crockett of West Tennessee*, published anonymously in Cincinnati early in 1833, or from a second edition of substantially the same text published by Harper & Brothers, New York, later in 1833, under the title *Sketches and Eccentricities of Colonel David Crockett of West Tennessee*. I have used this version for citation and will refer to it hereafter as *Eccentricities*.
3. Henry Nash Smith, *Mark Twain: The Development of a Writer*, New York 1974, p. 4. For the historian the most valuable work on Crockett is that of James A. Shackford and Stanley J. Folmsby, eds, *A Narrative of the Life of David Crockett of the State of Tennessee*, Knoxville, Tenn. 1973, especially the excellent Introduction, referred to hereafter as Shackford and Folmsby, 'Introduction'. The text is the Crockett autobiography, first published by Carey and Hart, Philadelphia 1834, which I will refer to as Crockett, *Narrative*. James A. Shackford, *David Crockett: The Man and the Legend*, ed. John B. Shackford, Chapel Hill, N.C. 1956; Stanley J. Folmsby and Anna Grace Catron, 'The Early Career of David Crockett', East Tennessee Historical Society, *Publications* 28 (1956): 58–85; 'David Crockett, Congressman', East Tennessee Historical Society, *Publications* 29 (1957): 40–78; 'David Crockett in Texas', East Tennessee Historical Society, *Publications* 30 (1958): 48–74. Shackford has little patience with folkloristic treatments of Crockett. While I have admired the work of Walter Blair and Constance Rourke in other contexts, I agree with Shackford's criticism of their writings on Crockett: Blair, 'Six Davy Crocketts', *Southwest Review* 25 (July 1940): 443–62; 'Col. Crockett Goes Visiting', *National Republic* 17 (October 1929): 24–25, 39; 'Col. Crockett in New York', *National Republic* 17 (November 1929): 28–29, 39;

Constance Rourke, *Davy Crockett*, New York 1934. See Shackford, *Crockett*, pp. *viii–ix*, 204–5, 274–75.

4. Folmsby and Catron, 'Early Career', p. 61; Crockett, *Narrative*, pp. 17–69. For a description of this process in the background of his own family, see Bray Hammond, *Banks and Politics in America from the Revolution to the Civil War*, Princeton, N.J. 1957, pp. 281–82.

5. Crockett, *Narrative*, pp. 72–73 and following; also pp. 125–37, 143, 147, 166n, 168–69; on slave ownership, p. 145: 'I had some likely negroes, and a good stock of almost everything about me. ...' Shackford, *Crockett*, pp. 33–35; Folmsby and Catron, 'Early Career', pp. 71–73.

6. Folmsby and Catron, p. 80, quoting Charles Sellers, 'Banking and Politics in Jackson's Tennessee, 1817–1827', *Mississippi Valley Historical Review* 41 (June 1954): 61–74.

7. Folmsby and Catron, 'Early Career', pp. 76–84.

8. Ibid., p. 77.

9. Folmsby and Catron, 'David Crockett: Congressman', pp. 45–48, 49–51; Polk to David McMillen, 16 January 1829, quoted in Shackford and Folmsby, 'Introduction', p. *xiv*.

10. Folmsby and Catron, 'David Crockett: Congressman', pp. 51–52, 54–55, 61–62, 65, 67; Crockett, *Narrative*, p. 205; *Eccentricities*, pp. 166–71, 186, 200–203; Shackford, *Crockett*, pp. 128–30, 134–36, 171.

11. Crockett, *Narrative*, pp. 205, 207; Shackford, *Crockett*, p. 135.

12. Ibid., pp. 155–60, 167–70, 175, 176, 189–95, 205; Folmsby and Catron, 'David Crockett: Congressman', pp. 70–72, 76–77.

13. On vernacular heroes, see below, pp. 116–20. On Seba Smith and Major Jack Downing, Milton and Patricia Rickels, *Seba Smith*, Boston 1977. On interchanges between Jack Downing and David Crockett, Crockett, *Narrative*, p. 16; Crockett, *An Account of Col. Crockett's Tour to the North and Down East in the Year of Our Lord Eighteen Hundred and Thirty–Four*, Philadelphia 1835, p. 32; Shackford and Folmsby, 'Introduction', pp. *ix–xx*. Shackford, *Crockett*, pp. 196–202, 253–56; Folmsby and Catron, 'David Crockett: Congressman', p. 75; Francis Hodge, *Yankee Theatre: The Image of America on the Stage, 1825–1850*, Austin, Tex. 1965, p. 118; Walter J. Meserve, *Heralds of Promise: The Drama of the American People in the Age of Jackson, 1829–1849*, Westport, Conn. 1986, pp. 109–11; James K. Paulding, *The Lion of the West*: Retitled *The Kentuckian, or a Trip to New York*, ed. James N. Tidwell, Stanford, Calif. 1954.

14. This is inferred from the fact that Hackett included on his prize committee William Cullen Bryant, William Leggett and Fitz-Greene Halleck: Nelson Frederick Adkins, *Fitz-Greene Halleck: An Early Knickerbocker Wit and Poet*, New Haven, Conn. 1930, p. 222; Joseph L. Blau, ed., *Social Theories of Jacksonian Democracy: Representative Writings of the Period, 1825–1850*, Indianapolis, Ind. 1954, pp. 371, 373–74; James Grant Wilson, *The Life and Letters of Fitz-Greene Halleck*, New York 1869, pp. 353, 411–12, 415; Amos L. Herold, *James Kirke Paudling, Versatile American*, New York 1926, pp. 73–74, 114–15, 128.

15. Shackford, *Crockett*, pp. 132–34, 253, 255–57; Folmsby and Catron, 'David Crockett: Congressman', pp. 66–68. At the beginning of his *Life of Martin Van Buren*, Philadelphia 1835, p. 23, Crockett or his ghostwriter modestly declared that if he, President Jackson and Black Hawk went on tour together they would draw larger crowds than any other three men in the United States.

16. Shackford and Folmsby, 'Introduction', pp. *xv–xvi*; Shackford, *Crockett*, p. 148, 154–55, 264–73.

17. Crockett, *Narrative*, p. 4. Shackford, *Crockett*, pp. 193–94, 204–6.

18. David Crockett, *Col. Crockett's Exploits and Adventures in Texas*, Philadelphia 1836.

19. Shackford, *Crockett*, pp. 277–81.

20. Ibid., pp. 184–87.

21. Ibid., pp. 186–89; Crockett, *Life of Van Buren*, pp. 80–81.

22. Shackford, *Crockett*, pp. 274–76; especially p. 274, quote from J. S. Derby, *Fifty Years Among Authors, Books and Publishers*, New York 1884, pp. 552–53; Neda McFadden Westlake, 'Introduction'; Richard Penn Smith, *Caius Marius: A Tragedy...*, Philadelphia 1968; David Grimsted, *Melodrama Unveiled; American Theater and Culture, 1825–1850*, Chicago 1968, pp. 148–49, 167–69, 216–18; Arthur Hornblow, *A History of the Theatre in America from Its Beginning to the Present Time*, Philadelphia 1919, 2:61; Bruce W. Mc-

Cullough, *The Life and Writing of Richard Penn Smith*, Menasha, Wis. 1917. Smith, *The Sentinels and Other Plays*, Ralph H. Ware and H. W. Schoenberger, eds, Princeton, N.J. 1941, pp. *v–x*. On Crockett ghostwriters, see Michael A. Lofaro, ed., *Davy Crockett: The Man, the Legend, the Legacy, 1786–1986*, Knoxville, Tenn. 1986, pp. *xx–xxi*.

23. Kenneth Wyer Rowe, *Mathew Carey: A Study in American Economic Development*, Baltimore 1933, pp. 1–18; Arnold W. Green, *Henry Charles Carey: Nineteenth Century Sociologist*, Philadelphia 1951, pp. 1–49.

24. *The Life of Van Buren* bore the imprint Robert Wright, *Exploits ... in Texas* that of T.K. and P.G. Collins; Shackford, *Crockett*, p. 319.

25. For example, Folmsby and Catron, 'David Crockett: Congressman', p. 70; Shackford, *Crockett*, p. 156.

26. Crockett, *Narrative*, p. 72. On Crockett's vote against Indian removal, Crockett, *Tour*, p. 70; Shackford, *Crockett*, p. 116; Folmsby and Catron, 'David Crockett: Congressman', p. 63, 65. The quotation is from Crockett, *Narrative*, pp. 88, 90.

27. See below, pp. 120–21.

28. Crockett, *Tour*, p. 80. See also pp. 44–45, 74.

29. Crockett, *Narrative*, p. 145; Shackford, *Crockett*, pp. 136, 144.

30. John Quincy Adams, 31 December 1828–1 January 1829, *Memoirs*, 8:88–89.

31. Samuel Flagg Bemis, *John Quincy Adams and the Union*, New York 1956, pp. 161–75. Daniel Howe, *The Political Culture of the American Whigs*, Chicago 1979, pp. 43–68.

32. For much of what follows, I have relied on Lynn Parsons, '"Perpetual Harrow Upon my Feelings": John Quincy Adams and the American Indian', *New England Quarterly*, 46 (September 1973): 339–79, especially pp. 361–63.

33. Parsons, '"A Perpetual Harrow"', p. 368.

34. John Quincy Adams, 24 February and 19 November 1820, *Memoirs*, 4:531, as quoted in Samuel Flagg Bemis, *John Quincy Adams and the Foundations of American Foreign Policy*, New York 1949, p. 418.

35. John Quincy Adams, 6 and 22 June 1830, 13 January 1831, 26 March 1842, *Memoirs*, 8:230–32, 273; 9:117.

36. John Quincy Adams, 6 August 1835, 14 June 1838, *Memoirs*, 9:247, 10:19. Referring to the Webster–Hayne debate in 1830, Adams had described 'the mutual surrender of the lands to the West and of the American System to the South ... of which this debate has marked the project' as a 'nefarious conspiracy' to apply nullification not only to the tariff, but to the nation's obligations to Indians and to federal ownership of the public lands: John Quincy Adams to Alexander Everett, 15 April 1830, in Daniel Feller, *The Public Lands in Jacksonian Politics*, Madison, Wis. 1984, pp. 116–17. On Adams and public land policy, Feller, *passim*.

37. Howe, *Political Culture*, p. 49; Michael Keith Baker, *Condorcet: From Natural Philosophy to Social Mathematics*, Chicago 1975, pp. 360–71; *John Quincy Adams before the Supreme Court of the United States in the Case of the United States, Appellants, vs Cinque, and Others, Africans, Captured on the Schooner AMISTAD ... Delivered on the 24th of February and 1st of March, 1841. ...* Reported in the 10th, 11th and 12th volumes of Wharton's *Reports*, New York 1841 (Microfilm, Louisville 1962). William S. Owens, *Slave Mutiny: The Revolt on the Schooner AMISTAD*, New York 1953.

38. John Quincy Adams, 'Society and Civilization', *American Review: A Whig Journal of Politics, Literature, Art and Science* 2 (July 1845): 80–89.

39. Ibid., p. 81.

40. John Quincy Adams, *The Letters Addressed by John Quincy Adams to His Son on the Study of the Bible*. Appendix to Abigail Adams, *Letters of Mrs. Adams, the Wife of John Adams, with an Introductory Memoir by her Grandson*, Charles Francis Adams, 4th ed. rev., Boston 1848, pp. 427–72, especially Letter 2, pp. 432–35.

41. John Quincy Adams, 19 March 1820, *Memoirs*, 11:340–41; *Letters to his Son*, pp. 430–31, 434, 438–39; Howe, *Political Culture*, p. 58.

42. 'Society and Civilization', pp. 88–89; 1825 Message, Richardson, ed., 2:82–83.

43. 'Society and Civilization', pp. 83–84, 86–88.

44. As his views on slavery hardened, Adams revised his perception of Jefferson: compare 27 December 1819 and 12 January 1831, *Memoirs*, 4:492 and 8:272.

45. John Quincy Adams, 3 March 1820, *Memoirs*, 5:10–11.

46. John Quincy Adams, 29 May and 16 June 1844, 19 February 1845, *Memoirs*, 7:37, 57, 171.

47. 'Q' [John Quincy Adams], 'Misconceptions of Shakespeare upon the Stage', *New England Magazine* 9 (December 1835):438–39. See also John Quincy Adams, 'The Character of Desdemona', in Rufus Wilmot Griswold, *Prose Writers of America, with a Survey of the Intellectual History, Condition and Prospects of the Country* ..., Philadelphia 1870, pp. 100–106.

48. See Introduction, pp. 10–11.

49. John Quincy Adams, 1–14 November 1843, *Memoirs*, 11:417–31.

50. Feller, *Public Lands*, pp. 16, 79, for a discussion of the transition from frontier to 'Old West'. On the development of Cincinnati since the frontier stage, Steven J. Ross, *Workers on the Edge: Work, Leisure and Politics in Industrializing Cincinnati, 1788–1890*, New York 1985, especially 'The New City: The Capitalists' View of Growth and Progress', pp. 67–93.

51. John Quincy Adams, *An Oration Delivered before the Cincinnati Astronomical Society on the Occasion of Laying the Corner Stone of an Astronomical Observatory on the 10th of November 1843*, Cincinnati 1843, p. 62; 1825 Message, Richardson, ed., 2:882.

52. Adams, *Oration*, pp. 63–65.

4

The Jacksonian Press

While John Quincy Adams from his solitary niche in Congress was devising stratagems to checkmate the queen of slavery in the South, a host of less notable citizens followed up promising leads opened by the Jacksonian assault on the politics of deference. The most visible of these leads clustered around organizing a mass political party. Yet electoral activities were only part of a wider upsurge that challenged and frequently overturned elite dominance in the cultural media. Cultural insurgency furnished the context of egalitarian politics. Parallel sequences might easily be demonstrated in many realms of culture. I have selected the press and theater (treated in Chapter 5) for primary emphasis because they responded to political stimuli more directly than other cultural institutions; and because they displayed an apparently spontaneous outflow – in contrast to the studied labors of John Quincy Adams – of class-determined racial images. In this respect they served as workshops, studios, cutting rooms for the construction and testing of racist components.

Daily newspapers in the United States when John Quincy Adams yielded the White House to Andrew Jackson belonged to and served the upper-class coalition that had dominated politics throughout the era of national independence and constitution making. In 1830 there were sixty-five dailies in the United States with an average circulation of 1,200. Selling for six cents a copy and described as 'blanket sheets' (35 inches by 24, they unfolded to a four-foot width), such papers obviously were intended to be spread out on the library table at home, or across the counting-house desk.[1] Circulation was by subscription, and subscriptions cost ten dollars a year, the equivalent of a week's wages for a skilled journeyman.[2]

Within the next twenty years the spread of the penny press expanded both the numbers and class base of newspaper readership. In 1840 there were 138 dailies; in 1850, 254. Average daily circulation rose from 1,200 in 1830 to just under 3,000 in 1850. New York alone had fourteen dailies in 1850 with a combined circulation running well over 150,000. This amounted to 1 newspaper a day for every 4.5 inhabitants, in contrast to 1 for every 16 twenty years earlier. Democratization of newspaper reading sprang from the same sources as did the upsurge of the Jacksonian coalition, paralleling it and initially reinforcing it. Just as political revolt against the National Republican thesis opened the era of mass politics, so the cultural transformation of the 1830s and 1840s swept the nation into the age of mass media. Although the Jacksonian coalition was both urban and rural, its most radical egalitarian tendencies flowed from the artisan culture of the cities and entered the Democracy through the Workingmen's movement. The first wave of penny dailies duplicated this sequence. Their appearance coincided with the formation of the Democratic party. Their territory comprised the cities of the Atlantic seaboard. Pioneered by artisan printers, these dailies remained predominantly urban artisan in both their readership and their ideological responses. Innovators of the new mass press included influential veterans of the Workingmen's parties, whose grudging adherence to the Democratic coalition mirrored the suspicious separatism that had characterized the relationship of the Workingmen to the Jacksonians.[3]

The first successful penny daily, the New York *Sun*, was founded in September 1833 by a 23-year-old journeyman printer, Benjamin Day, who might have been the model for Mark Twain's Connecticut Yankee. A New England artisan of Protestant Anglo-American old stock, proud of his common school education, combining vast enthusiasm for money and machinery with an egalitarian contempt for the higher learning of colleges and universities, Day typified the pioneers of the penny dailies; and for this reason his career is worth following in some detail.[4] The son of a West Springfield, Massachusetts hatter, Day apprenticed on the Springfield *Republican* when it was still a weekly edited by Samuel Bowles, Senior. Drawn like other young artisans to the metropolis, Day hired out on the New York *Evening Post* and soon opened his own job shop.[5] The Workingmen's movement was just beginning. Many of its activists were young printers, their lives centered on shops like Day's, who poured their energies into short-lived radical journals. When Robert Dale Owen and Frances Wright came east from Indiana in 1829, these young artisans grouped around the *Free Enquirer*, first issued from the New York shop of George Henry Evans, a journeyman printer of English parentage who had served his apprenticeship in small-town printing offices of the Burned Over District.[6]

The initial outburst of Workingmen's activity during the summer and fall of 1829 thrust Evans, Owen and their associates into political leadership.[7] Wright, concentrating on her course of lectures, remained some-what in the background but supported the collective endeavor by urging *Free Enquirer* readers to form associations for the 'protection of Industry and for the Promotion of National Education'.[8] In 1829 and 1830 members of the New York association functioned as a radical caucus inside the Workingmen's party. When it became obvious that the *Free Enquirer*, with its commitment to anticlericalism and shocking the bourgeoisie, was by no means the most effective vehicle for mass mobilization, Evans, at the end of October 1829, began the *Workingmen's Advocate*. Generally regarded as the nation's second labor paper (the *Mechanics' Free Press* of Philadelphia preceded it in 1828), the *Workingmen's Advocate* served for the next fifteen years under a variety of formats as a major voice of artisan radicalism.[9]

Soon after the first issue of the *Advocate* appeared in November 1829, the New York Workingmen's ticket demonstrated impressive strength in city elections. The party at once came under redoubled attack from the established press. Leaders of the Workingmen, recognizing the need for a mass circulation daily, launched the *Daily Sentinel* early in 1830. Subscriptions at $8.00 a year were to be somewhat cheaper than those of the blanket press. Prepublication announcements listed Day as one of six directors. Among the other five were two activists in the Workingmen's party, P.C. Montgomery Andrews, a printer, and William Stanley, also probably a printer. Wright's *Free Enquirer* and the *Workingmen's Advocate* boosted the new paper enthusiastically and Wright herself lent $1,000. Day apparently dropped out of the directorship before publication began. By that time, however, the Workingmen's party was breaking up and it was obvious that the *Sentinel* was already a dying cause.[10]

The notion of a mass circulation daily based on New York City's working class must have been intensely discussed by directors of the *Sentinel*. Within three years of its demise, Day launched the *Sun*, and soon afterwards William Stanley, with two partners, founded the New York *Transcript*. Whereas the *Sentinel*, retaining the general style of upper-class dailies, and with only a modest reduction in price, had relied on the shift from conservative to radical politics to win readers, Day and the Stanley group experimented with massive changes in format, price and distribution, as well as content. In contrast to the blanket sheets, the new papers measured 8 1/2 by 11 inches.[11] Selling for a penny a copy, they relied on street vendors rather than prepaid subscriptions.[12] To radical politics they gave scant visibility. What remained of 120 column inches after 4 columns had been sold to advertisers was divided among financial items, shipping, local news – and crime. Both the *Sun* and *Transcript* covered the city police court. Since these reports brought forward primarily the city's brawlers, burglars, pimps and prostitutes, they furnished local news par excellence:

crime, violence, humor, sex in a single package.[13] Outstripping their six-penny rivals, the new papers increased their advertising and brought in handsome profits. Success bred competition. Scores of penny dailies entered the field between 1834 and the depression of 1837. Some lasted only a few weeks; most of the rest collapsed during the depression; one, James Gordon Bennett's New York *Herald* (1835), lived to become a giant.[14]

Of more lasting consequence than proliferation was the spread to other cities. By 1837 three of Day's journeyman printers – Arunah Shepherdson Abell, Azariah Simmons and William Swain – had successfully applied Day's methods to establish the Philadelphia *Public Ledger* and the Baltimore *Sun*. The *Daily Times* in Boston broke into the mass circulation orbit in 1836.[15] Of the penny dailies so far referred to – three in New York, one each in Philadelphia, Baltimore and Boston – all but one (the exception was the New York *Transcript*) survived the depression to continue as circulation leaders into the booming 1850s. These were the majors in what I have described as the first wave of the mass circulation press. They institutionalized working-class readership in the great cities of the Central Atlantic seaboard. Opening out possibilities, they created methods and models, applied existing technology and promoted new.[16]

Benjamin Day had started the New York *Sun* with a hand-cranked flatbed press capable of 200 copies an hour. 'Capital! Bless you, I hadn't any capital', he recalled. 'I had no capital except my job office. ...'[17] Day's recollection accorded with the Jacksonian producer ethic. His job office and a journeyman's mastery of the craft were acceptable forms of capital since they accrued from his own labor. Reinforced by the success of the *Sun*, they gave him access to other capital that enabled him to invest in steam-powered presses. This additional capital probably took the form of credit from paper wholesalers and manufacturers of printing equipment. Whatever the details of financing, Day's investments added to the fixed charges of the enterprise. The larger the circulation, the greater the fixed costs. Aside from printers and reporters, the *Sun* carried engineers, firemen, mechanics, bookkeepers and salesmen on its payroll. Entire outfits of type wore out every few months.[18]

Such costs were fixed because mass circulation was the source of financial success. But circulation could not guarantee success. What produced revenue was advertising, which varied directly with circulation, but varied also with the cycle of boom and depression that characterized capitalist growth in the nineteenth century. Advertising revenues dropped off in 1837. In 1838 Day sold the *Sun* to his brother-in-law, Moses Beach, for $40,000.[19] Beach, like Day, was a Connecticut Yankee. Born to an old-stock New Haven family, he had apprenticed in a cabinet shop, shifted to paper manufacturing and invented a rag cutter used in paper mills.

Moving to New York, he joined Day as head of the mechanical department, later as partner. Whether or not the *Sun* could have survived without the modest infusion of capital Beach brought, we know that most dailies founded before the depression failed before 1840. Day, after selling the *Sun*, dropped out of the penny daily field; Beach rose to wealth and national prominence.[20]

Of the seven men identified as founders of pioneer penny dailies, available biographical data indicates that six began as artisans – five printers and one cabinetmaker; that all six artisans followed their trades to New York, four of them coming originally from old stock New England or upstate New York backgrounds. Two of the seven (Stanley and Day) had been directly involved in the New York Workingmen's party; while four others (Swain, Simmons, Abell, Beach) flourished in the penny daily field as a result of their association with Day. The seventh was in some respects a maverick. Neither an artisan nor a New Englander, James Gordon Bennett, founder of the *Herald*, was born in Scotland of middle-class Catholic parentage. Migrating to America in 1819, he worked as a reporter on the Charleston *Courier* and later was Washington correspondent for the grandest of New York's blanket sheets, the *Courier and Enquirer*. But like the others, Bennett was a wage earner, and in 1836 he was unemployed and nearly broke. Speaking in the same egalitarian vein as Day, he claimed he had started the *Herald* with only $500.[21]

Men such as these – on the basis of their journeyman's and editorial skills – might have had access to working credit, scarcely to large capital. One reason for the affinity of their newspapers to Workingmen's and Jacksonian politics was the anger many of these editors felt at seeing upper-class blanket press dailies subsidized by bank loans – especially by the Second Bank of the United States – while they themselves were starving for capital.[22] Given the favorable coincidence of technology, flush times and politics in the early 1830s, these artisan editors created the mass circulation press; men of their economic and social status would not have that opportunity again. This did not mean that artisan editors ceased to play a role in American political and intellectual history; but that their sphere would be limited to small circulation newspapers in western towns (Mark Twain and Dan DeQuille in Virginia City, for example) or to the radical and labor press (Henry George, George Swinton and a host of others).

Majors in the second wave of mass circulation dailies were more likely to be Whig than Democratic.[23] Horace Greeley, founder of the New York *Tribune* in 1841, came of old New England stock like many founders of the first wave, and like them began his career as a journeyman printer; yet with respect to capitalization and credit his sponsorship by the New York state Whig apparatus gave him entry to a different world.[24] Henry

Raymond, who launched the New York *Times* in 1851, had few if any links to the artisan tradition. Born in Lima, New York, graduate of the University of Vermont, his class background was that of editors of the old six-penny press. When he set up his own paper he enjoyed the backing of a group of investors who subscribed $100,000 not after, but before, the first issue of the *Times* came off the press.[25]

The transition from Day's hand-cranked flatbed press to the $100,000 capitalization of the *Times* suggests that within that span of less than twenty years two lines of development already several centuries old converged briefly and then separated. Since the first application of modern technology to reproducing written words there has been a continuing trend to reduce the unit cost to consumers; and a trend toward a higher price of entry into the field. By comparison with the monk who transcribed manuscripts by hand, the Gutenberg press marked the beginning of mass communications. It expanded readership at the cost of a fixed investment in technology as prerequisite to entry. At one end of this sequence lay a minimal price of entry and a prohibitive unit cost; at the other, a unit cost curve approaching zero and an investment curve rising almost vertically: mass illiteracy at one end, oligopolistic or monopolized control of communication at the other. Differing value ascriptions would define the optimal relationship between these two curves in different terms. Egalitarianism certainly would seek to combine low unit cost with a minimal cost of entry. For the United States such an optimum occurred some time in the first half of the nineteenth century – say during the twenty years from 1833 to 1853. To Jacksonians this may have seemed a happy coincidence. Viewed retrospectively, it appears not as a coincidence but as one of several necessary conditions for the era of mass politics and the party system. It made possible, while it lasted, something like a free market in ideological commodities that corresponded to the Jacksonian ideal type for the economy as a whole.

Penny dailies of the first wave – in contrast to the heavily political focus of their immediate predecessor, the New York *Sentinel* – gave politics low visibility. They emphasized crime and sex.[26] It has sometimes been proposed that journalistic sensationalism served to divert mass readership from political and social issues.[27] What is often overlooked in this connection is that crime and sex were not politically neutral. New York's Robinson-Jewett murder trial, covered in pitiless detail by the penny dailies, offers a revealing example.[28] On the acquittal of Robinson – an upper-class young man accused of murdering a prostitute – the New York *Sun* commented that 'an opinion is prevalent and openly expressed that any man may commit murder, who has $1500 to give to Messers Hoffman, Price and Maxwell.' The Ogden Hoffman referred to was a successful New York lawyer and leading Whig.[29] Concurring in the *Sun*'s opinion, the editor of the Philadelphia *Public Ledger* added: 'We believe it too, and we think that no calm observer of the whole trial would believe otherwise'.[30] By turning traditional morality against its upper-class sponsors, the penny dailies contributed to the construction of a counterculture that challenged upper-class culture on many fronts.

Characteristic of penny-press editors of the first wave was their identification with wage-earner interests. Reporting on labor trials, they often expressed indignation against courts that convicted workingmen for trade union activities and against judges who meted out severe sentences.[31] Following the New York conviction of twenty-five journeymen tailors for combination to obtain higher rates, the Philadelphia *Ledger* quoted with approval an assertion that 'the whole aristocracy of this city [New York] have been arrayed against the journeymen tailors, for the purpose of frightening the mechanics and workingmen of this country. During this trial we have every reason to believe that justice has been kept as far out of sight as possible ... [by men who] set themselves up as the lawful organs of keeping one class as the mere slaves of the other.' The editor of the *Ledger* had no need to remind his readers that the judge who sentenced the twenty-five journeymen tailors was the same who presided over the acquittal of Robinson.[32] 'There can be no doubt', the New York *Sun* declared, 'that owners of factories obtain more real benefit from ten hours work of hale, hearty and willing hands, than twelve hours from sickly and puny persons. Confinement wears out the constitution.'[33] The Philadelphia *Ledger* hoped that striking mechanics at the Brooklyn Navy Yard would 'be able to stand out long enough to bring their oppressors to terms'.[34] 'Since the *Sun* began to shine upon the citizens of New York', Benjamin Day wrote, recalling the early years of his paper, 'there has been a great and decided change in the condition of the laboring classes and the mechanics. ... They understand their own interest, and feel that they have numbers and strength to pursue it with success. ...'[35]

A common misapprehension with respect to mass circulation dailies of the Jacksonian era is that they were politically nonpartisan. Certainly the editors themselves contributed to this illusion since they ostentatiously denied party affiliation. What they meant was that they were not subsidized by parties or candidates, hence not in the condition of subserviency they charged against their sixpenny adversaries.[36] When penny-daily editors described their counterparts of the sixpenny press as 'partisan controlled editors', and 'loathesome and pestilent fungi',[37] they acted in the context of a belief that parties, prior to the overthrow of John Quincy Adams, had been dominated by elites. Day and many of his printer colleagues had once hoped for an independent party of artisans and producers; failing this, they conceded that Democrats more often than Whigs spoke for what the Workingmen had put forward; but they never lost their suspicion that Democratic leaders might revert to the politics of deference and consequently never felt secure in their party commitments. In this respect (as in many others) they differed sharply from the Whig editors in the second wave of penny dailies, who were likely to be less inhibited about partisanship.[38]

Of the origins of the New York *Tribune* in 1841, Horace Greeley recalled that he had been 'incited to this enterprise by several Whig friends who deemed a cheap daily, addressed ... to the laboring class' urgently needed; especially so, Greeley added, because New York's existing mass circulation dailies, the *Sun* and the *Herald*, 'were in decided, though unavowed, and therefore more effective, affiliation with the Democratic party'.[39] Greeley's assessment was undoubtedly accurate. While avoiding endorsements of candidates or electoral tickets, penny-daily editors in the first wave usually managed to come down on the Democratic side of issues controverted between the major parties.[40]

Their most spectacular display of solidarity was on the issue that united them most closely with the Jacksonian party: territorial expansion.[41] They pushed for Indian removal, supported the government in the Second Seminole War, and rejoiced at Texan independence.[42] They applauded Polk's expansionist politics and supported the war to which those politics led, celebrating battle by battle the advances of the American army into Mexico. More than any other newspapers, the *Suns* of New York and Baltimore, the *Herald* and the *Public Ledger* stretched technology to its limits in providing detailed and rapid coverage of the war. Special steamers, pony-express couriers, news trains and telegraph – previously used mainly for promotional stunts – now became standard fare.[43]

Underpinning these positions was a line of thought developed in the *Workingmen's Advocate* by the printer and former Workingmen's party leader, George Henry Evans, that western land offered the solution for social and economic problems of eastern cities.[44] First-wave editors liked to combine Evans's economic argument with the mysticism of manifest destiny.[45] Thus the Philadelphia *Public Ledger* at the end of 1848 – after the Treaty of Guadalupe Hidalgo with Mexico and after the great upsurge of European revolutions – declared that the 'mission' of the United States was to extend 'political Christianity' across the continent 'under federal democracy'. The nation, in order to carry out this mission, must learn the lessons of history. These lessons, according to the editors of the *Ledger*, related to land distribution. Peace and prosperity always had accompanied wide land tenure, whereas nations that permitted monopolization of land perished by internal dissension or foreign conquest. 'History gives solemn warnings against landed monopoly. Let us profit by them'. The *Ledger*'s historical essay bore the title, 'Land! Land!'[46]

Territorial expansion in alliance with the slaveholding South necessari-

ly rested upon assertions of racial superiority. First-wave penny dailies –
and the Democratically oriented mass circulation papers that followed
them – methodically propagated such assertions. Indians, as in Jackson's
Indian Removal message of 1830, were always bloody savages blocking
the path of civilization.[47] More closely than any other segment of
American culture in the 1830s and 1840s, urban artisan culture remained
linked to the radical republicanism of the Age of Reason.[48] Since the
Enlightenment had stressed the one-ness of humanity and sought historical explanations, through geography and environment, for racial differentiation, one would expect to find some ambivalence regarding assertions
of white racial superiority in mass circulation dailies of the first wave.
With regard to American Indians, however, there seems to be no trace of
such ambivalence. Perhaps because Vattel and his rationalist colleagues
had done their work so well; or for the reasons John Quincy Adams had
perceived when he dedicated his second career to anti-slavery rather than
defense of Indians, editors of these papers appear to have adopted and
elaborated racist justifications for westward expansion without demur.

No such acquiescence, however, applied to justifications of African
slavery. Here the republican tradition, exemplified for artisan editors by
Frances Wright, Robert Dale Owen and George Henry Evans, bucked
strongly against the onset of racist apologetics for slavery.[49] What resulted
was a division of loyalties within the first wave of penny dailies, despite
their prevailing Jacksonian orientation. Early issues of the New York *Sun*,
coinciding with the beginnings of Abolitionist organization, contained
scatterings of anti-slavery material. Benjamin Day later explained that he
and George Wisner, the journeyman printer who became his police court
reporter and, briefly, partner, had disagreed:

> We split on politics. You see, I was rather Democratic in my notions; Wisner,
> whenever he got a chance, was always sticking his damned little Abolitionist
> articles. We quarreled. ... I kept the paper, paying him $5,000 in cash for his
> share.[50]

The *Sun* regularly denounced anti-slavery petitions and characterized
John Quincy Adams as an 'uneasy and splenetic agitator'.[51] It charged
Joshua Giddings with rendering 'aid and comfort to Britain' when he
introduced a resolution in Congress commending the black slaves who
had seized control of the American brig *Creole* and taken it to a British
port. Warning that Giddings advocated slave insurrection, the *Sun* likened
him to 'Robespierre, Brissot and Marat', who 'set themselves up as champions of the freedom of speech and of the negroes, and led the way to
deeds of blood, the history of which will appal the world throughout all
time to come.'[52]

The *Herald* pursued approximately the same lines as the *Sun* with respect to slavery. Bennett, who had learned the newspaper business in South Carolina, remained loyal to the slaveholding South until after the outbreak of the Civil War. Bennett liked to use racist invective to affect a belligerently egalitarian style.[53] Thus, he would refer to the *Sun* – the competitor upon which his own paper largely had been modeled – as that 'decrepit, dying penny paper, owned and controlled by a set of woolly-headed and thick-lipped Negroes'; or, 'our highly respected, dirty, sneaking, drivelling contemporary nigger paper'.[54]

Despite these tokens of hostility, the *Sun* and *Herald* represented the dominant trend among first-wave dailies. Arunah Abell, the journeyman printer from Providence, Rhode Island who had shared in setting up the Philadelphia *Public Ledger* and gone on to found the Baltimore *Sun*, apparently adapted without rancor to southern transplantation. After purchasing an estate outside Baltimore for nearly half a million dollars, Abell became so overtly secessionist in sympathy that his paper narrowly missed being shut down by federal order in 1861.[55]

His Philadelphia partners, Swain and Simmons, on the other hand, moved the *Public Ledger* from an opportunistic and wavering anti-slavery position before the Mexican War to a clear commitment afterwards.[56] The Boston *Daily Times*, traveling a parallel route, was eventually bought out by a second-wave rival of whiggish persuasion.[57] Yet divergent stands on slavery did not necessarily differentiate these editors in terms of their racial concepts. The *Ledger*'s opening gambit on Texas in the spring of 1836 had been unmistakably against slavery: the editors wanted the federal government to buy Texas from Mexico and terminate slavery. Conceding that the Constitution precluded federal action against slavery in any state where it presently existed, they denied the 'sophistical extension of this objection to territory yet to be acquired'; and then,

> We believe the best course would be to exclude colored population entirely, bond or free. This would save Texas from the curse of slavery; and from that greater curse, a free negro population, and save the neighboring states from the curse of its being a receptacle of runaway negroes.[58]

Anticipating the Wilmot Proviso by ten years, the *Ledger* helped to fashion a political climate that made the proviso viable in Pennsylvania.

The mass circulation press, then, came into existence as a nearly identical twin to the urban artisan wing of the Democracy. Pioneer editors of the first-wave dailies had been deeply influenced by the Workingmen's movement. Reluctantly entering the Jacksonian coalition, they soon made their papers indispensable. Their rapidly expanding readership created the urban constituency, first of the Jacksonian party itself, afterwards of the party system in its entirety. Artisan editors and publishers brought forward a republicanism rooted in the anticlerical humanism of the Enlightenment. Through continuing national dominance of the Democratic party, this artisan radicalism entered into the crystalization of American national consciousness. Democratic dominance prior to the Civil War rested on alliance with slavery and aggressive advocacy of territorial expansion. Reportage and editorials in the mass circulation dailies provided a setting in which the complex problems of linking artisan republicanism to slavery and expansion could be grappled with imaginatively and intellectually. The same dailies celebrated the marriage of democracy to white racism, of homesteads to Indian extermination.

Mass circulation dailies, although originating in conjunction with the rise of the Democratic party, were not inherently limited to that party's purposes. By bringing forward artisan editors, the low costs of entering the mass circulation field during the 1830s bridged a dichotomy, characteristic of the old blanket press, between the interests and class identity of owner-publishers on one hand and working printers on the other. Technological innovation, spurred by mass circulation, then escalated costs of entry. The result was to reestablish the earlier internal dichotomy; and at the same time to open a new and more formidable gap between owner-publishers and their mass readership. Egalitarian rhetoric, which for the artisan editors had served as a weapon against the oligarchy, would become for their successors a means of obscuring newly developing class separations. Thus the Jacksonian transformation of journalism introduced a totally new relationship, certain to alter the conditions of ideological construction.

Notes

1. On the 'wider upsurge', Robert H. Wiebe, *The Opening of American Society: From the Adoption of the Constitution to the Eve of Disunion*, New York 1985, pp. 143–67; Frederic Hudson, *Journalism in the United States from 1690 to 1872*, New York 1873, pp. 408–15; Edwin and Michael Emery, *The Press and America: An Interpretive History of the Mass Media*, 4th ed. Englewood Cliffs, N.J. 1978, p. 120; Alfred McClung Lee, *The Daily Newspaper in America: The Evolution of a Social Instrument*, New York 1947, pp. 715–17, 728; Louis H. Fox, 'New York City Newspapers, 1820–1850: A Bibliography', *Papers of the Bibliographical Society of America*, 21: Parts 1 and 2, Chicago 1927, pp. 4–5; Clarence S. Brigham, *Journals and Journeymen: A Contribution to the History of Early American Newspapers*, Philadelphia 1950, pp. 19–22.

2. Hudson, pp. 408–15; Gerald W. Johnson et al., *The Sun Papers of Baltimore*, New York 1937, p. 35; Calder M. Picker, 'Six New York Newspapers and Their Response to Technology in the Nineteenth Century', Ph.D. diss., University of Minnesota, 1959, p. 28; U.S. Department of Labor, Bulletin of the U.S. Bureau of Labor Statistics no. 475, *Productivity of Labor in Newspaper Printing*, Washington, D.C. 1929.

3. There is a vast literature on the Jacksonian press, most of it piecemeal and pedestrian. Two important, recent exceptions are Michael Schudson, *Discovering the News: A Social History of American Newspapers*, New York 1978, pp. 3–60, and Dan Schiller, *Objectivity and the News: The Public and the Rise of Commercial Journalism*, Philadelphia 1981. Both works enlarge our understanding of the period, especially Schiller's, which has a more

extensive class analysis of the penny dailies and their readership. Neither requires me to revise my own interpretation, which was set forth in 'Problems of Class and Race in the Origins of the Mass Circulation Press', *American Quarterly* 36 (Summer 1984): 211–35. See also A.M. Lee, *The Daily Newspaper in America*, pp. 717, 730–31.

4. For comparisons, see pp. 98–99.

5. For biographical information on Day: William G. Bleyer, *Main Currents in the History of American Journalism*, Boston 1927, p. 158; Frank Luther Mott, *American Journalism*, New York 1941, pp. 222–28; Frank M. O'Brien, *The Story of the Sun: New York, 1833–1928*, New York 1928, pp. 23–24.

6. William R. Waterman, *Francis Wright*, New York 1924, pp. 176–200; Edward Pessen, *Most Uncommon Jacksonians: The Radical Leaders of the Early Labor Movement*, Albany, N.Y. 1967, pp. 69–75; Walter Hugins, *Jacksonian Democracy and the Working Class: A Study of the New York Workingmen's Movement, 1829–1837*, Stanford, Calif. 1960, pp. 3–20, 83–88; Helen S. Zahler, *Eastern Workingmen and National Land Policy 1829–1862*, New York 1941, pp. 18–25, 32–40; Whitney Cross, *The Burned Over District*, New York 1965, *passim*.

7. Pessen, pp. 58–79; Waterman, pp. 198–205.

8. Waterman, pp. 197–98.

9. Hugins, pp. 10–24; Waterman, p. 197; New York *Courier and Enquirer*, 14 June 1830, in Waterman, p. 220; New York *Workingmen's Advocate*, 31 October 1829; Louis Arky, 'The Mechanics' Union of Trade Associations and the Formation of the Philadelphia Workingmen's Movement', *Pennsylvania Magazine of History and Biography* 76 (April 1952): 142–76; Fox, 'New York City Newspapers', p. 117; Waterman, pp. 200–201.

10. These events are summarized in Hugins, *Jacksonian Democracy and the Working Class*, pp. 10–23, and Pessen, *Uncommon Jacksonians*, pp. 9–32, 58–75. They may be followed in detail in the *Workingmen's Advocate* and the *Free Enquirer*, autumn 1829 through summer 1830; *Free Enquirer*, 26 December 1829; 20 February, 13 March, 8 May 1839. *Workingmen's Advocate*, 31 October, 12, 19, 26 December 1829; 16, 23 January, 13, 20 February, 20 March, 29 May 1830. Robert Dale Owen to Frances Wright, 19 April 1832, cited in Waterman, p. 208; Hudson, p. 420; Mott, p. 237; A.M. Lee, p. 190; Fox, pp. 89, 117.

11. Fox, pp. 98, 106–7; Bleyer, pp. 158, 163. They increased in size as the amount of advertising increased.

12. Hudson, pp. 417–18; Fox, pp. 106–7; A.M. Lee, pp. 262–63; Bleyer, p. 161; Frank Presbrey, *The History and Development of Advertising*, Garden City, N.Y. 1929, p. 190.

13. Hudson, pp. 417–18; Mott, pp. 222–23; Bleyer, pp. 164, 166–67.

14. Presbrey, pp. 190–95; Hudson, p. 424; Mott, p. 228; Hudson, pp. 428–60; Oliver Carlson, *The Man Who Made the News: James Gordon Bennett*, New York 1942.

15. Gerald Johnson et al., pp. 3–20, 28–33; Mott, pp. 239–40; Harold E. West, 'The History of the *Sun*', Baltimore *Sun*, 14 May 1922; Hudson, pp. 505–7; Presbrey, p. 201; Thomas J. Scharf and Thompson Wescott, 'The Press of Philadelphia', in their *History of Philadelphia*, Philadelphia 1884, 3:1958–2062; 'In Memory of William M. Swain', Philadelphia *Public Ledger and Daily Transcript*, 17 February 1868; Bleyer, pp. 174–75; Mott, pp. 238–39.

16. On the circulation growth of first-wave penny dailies: Fox, pp. 98–106; O'Brien, p. 24; Bleyer, pp. 160, 166–167; Hudson, pp. 424, 431, 439; Mott, pp. 232, 237, 238–41; Presbrey, 201; Johnson et al., p. 46; Sidney Kobre, *Development of American Journalism*, Dubuque, Iowa 1969, p. 227. On the circulation growth of second-wave dailies after the Depression of 1837: A.M. Lee, pp. 76–77; and Tables 13 and 17, pp. 725, 730–31. On newsprint technology: Joel Munsell, *Chronology of the Origin and Progress of Paper and Paper Making*, New York 1876; reprinted 1980, pp. 61–72, 78, 81–95; James Melvyn Lee, *History of American Journalism*, Boston 1923, pp. 93, 99–105. On the development of printing presses: Presbrey, pp. 194–195; Hudson, p. 418; James Lee, pp. 114–117; A.M. Lee, pp. 117, 166; O'Brien, p. 71; Carlson, p. 217; Kenneth E. Olson, *Typography and Mechanics of the Newspaper*, New York 1930, pp. 406–9; Robert Hoe, *A Short History of the Printing Press*, New York 1892, pp. 31–37; Augustus Maverick, *Henry J. Raymond and the New York Press for Thirty Years*, Hartford, Conn. 1870, p. 95.

17. Pickett, p. 89.

18. O'Brien, pp. 79–81, 107; Pickett, p. 122. *Sun*'s profits and costs: Bleyer, p. 163; Mott, p. 226. Size of daily operations, New York *Herald*, 1840: Carlson, p. 228.

19. A.M. Lee, p. 166; 'Moses Yale Beach', *Dictionary of American Biography*, New York 1964, 1:82–84; Bleyer, p. 163.

20. *DAB*, 1:82–84; O'Brien, pp. 127, 138–40, 166; A.M. Lee, p. 168; Fox, pp. 106–7; Johnson et al., pp. 23–24; Mott, p. 239.

21. A.M. Lee, p. 166; Hudson, pp. 425–28; Carlson, pp. 5–57, 80–94, 132.

22. New York *Sun*, 8 February 1834, 10, 15 July 1837; Philadelphia *Public Ledger*, 16, 23, 26 August 1837; Johnson et al., p. 43; A.M. Lee, pp. 180–81; Carlson, pp. 109–17, 132–34; Hudson, pp. 434–36, 507.

23. In addition to the New York *Tribune*, 1841, the New York *Times*, 1851, and the Boston *Herald*, 1846: Bleyer, p. 175; Mott, p. 239.

24. Fox, p. 108; Horace Greeley, *Recollections of a Busy Life*, New York 1868, pp. 37–75, 107–13, 124–26, 133–40; Glyndon Van Deusen, *Horace Greeley: Nineteenth–Century Crusader*, [1953] New York 1964, especially pp. 5–15, 50–57.

25. Maverick, pp. 15–95.

26. Bleyer, p. 166; Fox, p. 4.

27. For examples, Bleyer, pp. 163–64, 180; Mott, pp. 225–26.

28. Bleyer, pp. 181–84; Carlson, pp. 158–63. The Robinson–Jewett murder trial can be followed in the New York *Herald*, New York *Sun*, New York *Transcript*, Philadelphia *Public Ledger*, 15 April–15 July 1836.

29. Quoted in Philadelphia *Public Ledger*, 11 June 1836. On Ogden Hoffman, Saxton, 'George Wilkes: The Transformation of a Radical Ideology', *American Quarterly* 33 (Fall 1981): 440–41.

30. Philadelphia *Public Ledger*, 11 June 1836; also 29 June 1836.

31. For reports of labor trials, New York *Transcript* as quoted in Philadelphia *Public Ledger*, 28, 30 May, 1, 2 June 1836. Philadelphia *Public Ledger*, 31 May, 11, 14, 25, July 1836; 12 October 1837; 23 July, 26 October 1840.

32. New York *Union* quoted in Philadelphia *Public Ledger*, 2 June 1836. *Ledger* 2, 4 June 1836: Judge Ogden Edwards presided at both trials. For the *Ledger's* criticism of the conviction and sentencing of the tailors, 23 June 1836.

33. New York *Sun*, 12 December 1845; Carlson, pp. 128, 136–37.

34. Philadelphia *Public Ledger*, 1 November 1836. See also New York *Sun*, 20, 21 February, 14 March 1834; Philadelphia *Public Ledger*, 26 March, 4 May 1836; 2, 13 February 1844.

35. Bleyer, pp. 162–63, quoting O'Brien, p. 129. On the self–identification of penny daily editors, see Carlson, p. 99; Hudson, pp. 363–64; Fox, p. 59; Philadephia *Public Ledger*, 25 March, 16 July 1836; also 26 March, 9 July 1836; Baltimore *Sun*, 30 October 1844.

36. A.M. Lee, pp. 181–82, notes the illusion and refutes it. Bleyer, pp. 185–60, 167, 171, 180; Carlson, p. 169; Johnson et al., pp. 29, 44–47; Nevins, pp. 109–10, accept claims of nonpartisanship more or less at face value. For statements by penny-press editors of their own nonpartisanship and allegations of party control over the sixpenny papers: New York *Sun*, 26 September 1840. The New York *Sun's* handling of charges of voter fraud by New York Democrats against the Whigs, 24 October–5 November, especially 26 October 1840. Also 24 April, 21 May 1836; 24 August 1837; 13 November 1840. Baltimore *Sun*, 16 June, 19 August, 2 November 1840. Also see Carlson, p. 169, and Hudson, pp. 432–34.

37. New York *Sun*, 24 April and 21 May 1841.

38. Maverick, pp. 27–28, 89. On the tendency of nonpartisan penny daily editors to favor the Democrats, Mott, p. 237; Pickett, p. 176.

39. Greeley, p. 137.

40. Bank war: New York *Sun*, 8 February 1834, 10 July 1837, 23 September 1840, 16, 20 October 1841; Philadelphia *Public Ledger*, 16, 23, 26 August 1837, 22 October 1840; Carlson, pp. 109–17, 132–34; Hudson, pp. 434–36, 507. Imprisonment for debt, payment for jury duty, militia service, contracting of prison labor: New York *Sun*, 12, 17 December 1833, 24 January 1834, 21 September 1841, 6 November 1845. Sympathetic to immigrants and Catholics: New York *Sun*, 12, 17 July 1837, 15 October 1840, 11 February 1847; Baltimore *Sun*, 9, 11, 13 July 1844. Favoring cheap or free land: New York *Sun*, 24 June 1842, 31 January 1846; Philadelphia *Public Ledger*, 10 November 1846. Opposed to, or ambivalent on, protective tariff: New York *Sun*, 23 March, 24 June 1842; Philadelphia *Public Ledger*, 12, 14 October 1837, 24 October 1840; Baltimore *Sun*, 21 August 1840. Favorable to Tyler

after his break with Whigs: New York *Sun*, 24 September 1841, 4 April 1842. Favoring James Fenimore Cooper in his dispute with Whig editors over the battle of Lake Erie: New York *Sun*, 25 May 1842; Philadelphia *Public Ledger*, 25 September 1840. Critical of leading Whigs: New York *Sun*, 6 January, 22 February, 25 March 1842.

41. Carlson, p. 193; Emery, p. 142; Hudson, pp. 443, 476, 480; Johnson et al., pp. 73–83; O'Brien, pp. 113, 142, 166; Pickett, pp. 117–19, 202–3.

42. New York *Sun*, 4 March 1834; 3, 4, 10, 14, 17 July 1837, 28 March 1842. Philadelphia *Public Ledger* (stories on Texas and Seminole war), 26 March, 3, 14, 18, 20, 24 May 1836, 17 August 1837, 12 November 1844; Carlson, p. 213.

43. Hudson, pp. 476, 480, 508–9; Johnson et al., pp. 73–83; Pickett, pp. 117–20; New York *Sun*, 8 May 1847. Circulation increased. But so of course did operating costs; and so likewise the trend toward monopolistic control. The first meeting of what became the Associated Press was held in the offices of the New York *Sun* in 1848: O'Brien, p. 142; Hudson, pp. 365–67; Mott, p. 166; Pickett, pp. 13–14.

44. Helen Zahler, *Eastern Workingmen and National Land Policy*, New York 1941.

45. New York *Sun*, 14 July 1837; 1, 11 November, 12, 17 December, 1845; 31 January 1846.

46. Philadelphia *Public Ledger*, 10 November 1848.

47. Philadelphia *Public Ledger*, 26 March 1836; 20 October 20 1837; 2, 3 February 1844; New York *Sun*, 24 March 1834, 10 July 1837.

48. Eric Foner, *Tom Paine and Revolutionary America*, New York 1976, especially pp. 19–66.

49. Celia Morris Eckhardt, *Fanny Wright: Rebel in America*, Cambridge, Mass. 1984, pp. 108–67; Eric Foner, *Paine*, pp. 73, 89, 127; Eric Foner, *Politics and Ideology in the Age of the Civil War*, New York 1980, pp. 61–62.

50. Interview with Day quoted in New York *Sun*, 2 September 1933, quoted in Mott, pp. 222–23.

51. New York *Sun*, 22 and 23 February 1842. See also 21 September 1841 and 1 November 1845.

52. New York *Sun*, 25 March 1842.

53. Carlson, pp. 173–175.

54. Ibid., pp. 173–174, 183.

55. Johnson et al., pp. 31–33.

56. See, for example, on the rescue by free blacks in Boston of an escaped slave, Philadelphia *Public Ledger*, 6 September 1836; and an editorial on rejection in the United States Senate of the treaty to annex Texas, 13 June 1844.

57. Bleyer, p. 175.

58. Philadelphia *Public Ledger*, 26 March 1836.

5

Theater

Theater in America, like politics and the press, remained an upper-class enclave through the first decades of the nineteenth century. Then, revolutionized by the Jacksonian upsurge and paced by the extraordinary popularity of blackface minstrelsy, theater expanded into an industry of mass entertainment. Circuses and traveling stock companies planted outposts throughout the Mississippi Valley; and blackface minstrelsy – proliferating into a distinct, highly politicized genre that will be examined in Chapter 7 – opened channels to audiences never before touched by drama. New methods and models replaced old ones. As class exclusiveness yielded to popular participation, the structures of eighteenth-century drama disolved into the polymorphous genre of melodrama.[1]

Transformation of the American theater paralleled the ongoing transformations from deference to egalitarianism in politics and from subscription to mass circulation for the press. Yet these sequences were by no means identical. Theater lagged behind the others, both because American urban elites, long after throwing off English political control, continued to revere England as the fountain of culture; and because the problems of building a national theater proved more intractable than those of organizing political parties or publishing newspapers. Consequently, efforts to nationalize the American theater merged with pressures to open it up to new, mass audiences, and both assumed aspects of an assault against high culture. Contestants in this arena reconstructed the received wisdom about class and race current in the merchant–landlord republic of 1800 into new patterns projecting the essential relationships of a racially bounded democracy. Racial imagery as a result assumed a metaphoric function seemingly unique, at least in that time period, to American culture.

The Contrast

Potential conflicts between upper-class dominance and national autonomy had been vividly set forth in a play appropriately titled *The Contrast*, which opened in New York in the year of ratification of the Constitution.² The first work by an American playwright dealing with American themes to be produced professionally in the United States, *The Contrast* was a comedy of manners imitative of Sheridan's *School for Scandal*. Its author, Royall Tyler, son of a wealthy Boston merchant and valedictorian of his graduating class at Harvard, had served as an officer in the Revolution and aide-de-camp to General Lincoln during the suppression of Shays' Rebellion. He read law under John Adams, opened a successful law firm and purchased 'one of the finest houses in Braintree'. The subscription list for publication of his playscript in 1790 was headed by George Washington. Tyler himself went on to become chief justice of the Vermont Supreme Court.³

The title of his play referred actually to several overlapping contrasts. Most immediately visible of these was the standard eighteenth-century dichotomy between rural purity and city sophistication. But Tyler was not criticizing urban culture. He was attacking the importation of English aristocratic modes which in America undermined republican virtue and threatened the achievements of the Revolution. Colonel Manly, late of the Continental Army, makes his first visit to New York on business involving congressional land grants – not, however, to further his own interests but those of soldiers who served under his command. Shocked by the extravagance and immorality of the social set to which his sister Charlotte introduces him, the Colonel collides with the leader of that set, Dimple, wealthy heir to a Hudson River manor. Dimple has just returned from the grand tour of Europe, where he learned to ape the manners and morals of aristocrats. In exposing Dimple's duplicity and attempted seduction, the Colonel wins the hand of Maria, a romantic young lady who prefers serious reading (Richardson and Sterne) to idle chatter about style.

All ends well, as comedy requires; yet there are several ominous notes in *The Contrast*. The most prominent emerges through the funniest portion of the play – its portrayal of servants. Like his eighteenth-century models, Tyler uses servants ostensibly to underline qualities of their masters. Dimple's anglicized valet mimics upper-class seduction through his frank avowals of contempt for the chastity of housemaids. Manly's man Jonathon – by contrast – is a sturdy yeoman from the New England hills. Jonathon marks an early (perhaps the earliest) appearance of the Yankee hero – firstborn of those regional vernaculars who would dominate American popular culture and literature throughout the nineteenth century. But the Yankee is no hero for Tyler; that incarnation would have to await the age of Jackson. When Dimple's valet asks if he is not the servant of the recently arrived Colonel, the Yankee replies indignantly, 'Servant! Sir, do you take me for a neger, – I am Colonel Manly's waiter.' Pressed as to whether or not he shines the Colonel's boots, the Yankee concedes: 'Yes; I do grease them a bit sometimes; but I am a true blue son of liberty for all that. Father said I should come as Colonel Manly's waiter to see the world, and all that; but no man shall master me. My father has as good a farm as the Colonel.'[4]

In the unlikely circumstance that anyone in 1787 might have missed this point, Tyler has the Yankee recapitulate before going on. 'I swear we don't make any great distinction in our state between quality and other folks.' The valet now challenges him directly:

'This is indeed a levelling principle, – I hope, Mr. Jonathon, you have not taken part with the insurgents?'
'Why, since General Shays has sneaked off and given us the bag to hold, I don't care to give my opinion; but you'll promise not to tell – put your ear this way – you won't tell? – I vow I did think the sturgeons were right.'
'I thought, Mr. Jonathon, you Massachusetts men always argued with a gun in your hand. Why didn't you join them?'
'Why the Colonel is one of those folks called the Shin – Shin – dang it all ... you know who I mean ... Now the Colonel told father and brother ... [Here the Yankee is temporarily sidetracked trying to recall the names and ages of various sisters and cousins, and of the numerous brothers who fought in the Revolution.] Colonel says that it was a burning shame for the true blue Bunker Hill sons of liberty, who had fought Governor Hutchinson, Lord North and the Devil, to have any hand in kicking up a cursed dust against a government which we had, every mother's son of us, a hand in making.'
'Bravo!' [says the valet].[5]

The Yankee has here avowed his allegiance to the politics of deference. Educated men like Colonel Manly, who know how to pronounce such difficult words as 'insurgents' and 'Cincinnati', are the properly responsible persons to govern the republic. But the valet's ironic 'bravo' – calling attention to the taint of hypocrisy that infuses all the Yankee's speech – suggests that his allegiance may not be altogether reliable.

What this sequence appears to convey is that in a society of open economic opportunity ('My father has as good a farm as the Colonel'), lower-class loyalty cannot be taken for granted. The duty and privilege of governing rest on the moral and intellectual superiority of the ruling class. The Revolution may be over; but republican virtue must continue to be practiced, as indeed it is by men like Colonel Manly. Tyler's prologue confirms this reading:

> Exult, each patriot heart! – this night is shown
> A piece, which we may fairly call our own;
> Where the proud titles of 'My Lord! Your Grace!'
> To humble *Mr.* and plain *Sir* give place.

The couplets then make a conventionally nationalist assertion that American cities equal those of Europe in culture, affluence and refinement; and immediately call in question that boast:

> Our free-born ancestors such arts despis'd;
> Genuine sincerity alone they priz'd; ...
> Or, if ambition roused a bolder flame,
> Stern virtue throve, while indolence was shame.[6]

The warning conveyed by the Yankee and reiterated in the author's prologue is obviously central to the structure of the play. There are, however, two other problematic episodes in this comedy, both involving race, and both apparently peripheral. One is the Yankee's use of the term 'neger' – the only time it occurs in the script – to set his own class status above that of menials. The other is a curiously involuted intrusion of the notion of the noble savage. Our first encounter with the heroine, Maria, finds her alone in her boudoir singing to herself a melancholy ballad:

> The sun set in the night, and the stars shun the day;
> But glory remains when their lights fade away!
> Begin, ye tormentors! your threats are in vain,
> For the son of Alnomook shall never complain.
> ...
> Remember the wood where in ambush we lay,
> And the scalps which we bore from your nation away;
> Now the flame rises fast, you exult in my pain;
> But the son of Alnomook can never complain.[7]

This certainly is burlesque. Knowing Tyler's background, we can assume he held ideas about Indians similar to those that John Quincy Adams would later announce in his Newburyport address. Moreover, since the connotations of the song lead Maria immediately to a soliloquy on the status of women in her society and the reasons why women find warlike virtues attractive in men, it is clear that Tyler was aware of the sexual innuendo inherent in Maria's fixation on torturing a naked and noble warrior. In these two episodes, peripheral though they may have been, Tyler adumbrated scenarios that would become part of the racist stock in trade of blackface minstrelsy and melodrama; apparently they were good for laughs even in 1787. Apart from that, it is worth speculating what

Tyler intended by them.

The first fits logically into his negative portrayal of the Yankee. We know, from an earlier glimpse of John Adams in action,[8] how accurate it is. Tyler then is saying: yes, the Yankee may now acknowledge the deference due to educated and responsible upper-class leaders; but he is not forgetting his father's farm; nor does he hesitate to discount the class distance between himself and Colonel Manly by focusing on the racial disparity that separates both from the 'neger'.

The second is more difficult to decode. The best clue, I think, lies in the fact that Tyler obviously expected his audience to ridicule the heroine's romantic aberrations and sexual fantasies – just as it could laugh at Colonel Manly's obtuse squareness – while at the same time admiring the values both characters represent. That would be sheer treachery in melodrama; but with Tyler we are still in the universe of social satire. Could social satire then transcend class? Certainly not for Tyler. In using a comedy of manners to explore class hegemony, he seems to have been trying to locate a point of view that would correspond to the ideal intelligence of his class; an observation post through which the revolutionary republican bourgeoisie might survey the social fabric – including its own possibilities and follies – with an ironic but enlightened rationality. *The Contrast* would soon be out of style.

Problems of an Infant Industry

By the time Tyler wrote *The Contrast*, seaboard cities (even Boston) had built theaters and these were becoming professionalized in the last years of the century.[9] The professionals, however, were English. Many, as in the parallel migration that brought editors like Tom Paine, William Duane, Mathew Carey, and Robert Dale Owen, transferred their allegiance to America. In journalism such expatriates were influential but never dominant; in theater they saturated the field. Regardless of intentions, their background and training institutionalized cultural subordination.

The prestige of English repertory reinforced this dependency. England's theatrical heritage could no more be repudiated for patriotic purposes than could the common language or literature. On the contrary, patriotism required the new nation to prove itself by its excellence at reproducing the traditional repertory. And where could competent performers of Shakespeare, Ben Johnson, and Sheridan be found except in London? Before the War of 1812 almost no actors or theatrical managers in the United States were native born.[10]

Moreover, for the development of national theater new writing is at least as important as the nativity of actors and managers. Here too the problem of professionalization presented a formidable obstacle. 'An American audience', wrote Major Mordecai Noah, an aspirant playwright who earned his living at law and journalism, ' ... would be highly pleased with an American play, if the performance afforded as much gratification as a good English one.' In England, theater had become a potentially profitable profession: '... hence a dramatic author ... employs all his faculties ... a knowledge of stage effect – of sound, cadences, fitness of time and place, interest of plot ... which are required to constitute a good dramatic poet, who cannot in this country, and while occupied in other pursuits, spring up overnight like asparagus. ...'

Noah dealt lightly with a subject he obviously took seriously. In setting forth the plight of native drama, he used terms similar to those applied by protectionists like Henry Clay and John Pendleton Kennedy to domestic manufactures. Noah, subsequently a Jacksonian, invoked the laws of liberal economics to right the balance. 'We will succeed in time, as well as the English, because we have the same language and equal intellect. ...' Yet it was clear that the fires of nationalism pressed hard on liberal orthodoxy: 'National plays should be encouraged. They have done everything for the British nation, and can do much for us; they keep alive the recollection of important events by representing them in a manner at once natural and alluring. ...'[11]

The occasion for Noah's commentary was the preface to a 'bagatelle' he had thrown together precisely to keep alive recollections of American military prowess in the War of 1812. His comedy, *She Would Be a Soldier; or, The Plains of Chippewa*, performed in New York in 1819, was one of a postwar outpouring of patriotic celebrations that provided a brief stimulus to American playwrights, since the field was one in which English authors could hardly compete.[12] In a more fundamental way, also, the war marked a turning point in efforts to construct a national theater. American victories in the West opened the Mississippi Valley. Traveling stock companies invaded the plains of Chippewa. When Edwin Forrest at fifteen scored modest acclaim in a juvenile role, he asked advice of an older actor, who told him to go where he could learn theater from the bottom up. Previously that could only have meant London; by 1821 it meant Cincinnati, St. Louis, New Orleans.[13]

Theater in the West enlarged the national audience, a development not unobserved across the Atlantic. The English began to dump their surplus stars – or, more accurately, the surplus time of their stars – on the Americans. These visitors differed from the naturalized professionals of the earlier period. Coming with established reputations, they were eager to make money in America and return home. By imposing a traveling star system on the proliferating American stock companies, they skimmed the cream from the market.[14] Now, however, young Americans like Forrest had their feet in the stage doors. Many, again like Forrest who delivered the New York Democracy's Fourth of July oration in 1838, identified with Jacksonian politics. It was these changes that carried national theater into the streets and into politics.

The campaign to nationalize the theater employed exhortation, product differentiation (the analogy to domestic manufactures seems inescapable) and consumer boycott. Thus Walt Whitman, denouncing English 'usurpers of our stage', exhorted readers of the Democratic *Daily Eagle* that 'the drama of this country *can* be the mouthpiece of freedom. ... '[15] Product differentiation generally began with acting styles. Edwin Forrest, especially in his Shakespearean roles, strove for a bombastic, 'muscular' sentimentality, in contrast to the cooler analytical style preferred in Britain.[16] Forrest was moving tragedy toward melodrama; but there was not sufficient flexibility in the traditional tragedies to carry the process very far. Hence the effort to Americanize tragedy had to be conducted by other means, chiefly consumer boycotts. Significantly, it was only in reference to Shakespearean tragedy that the issue of national theater provoked violence. Edmund Keane, the English tragedian, had been prevented from performing in Boston in the 1820s and mass efforts to protect Forrest's *Hamlet* from English competition led in 1849 to a battle with police and militia in which twenty persons lost their lives and many were wounded.[17] More was involved in the Astor Place riots, of course, than acting styles; but the fact that Jacksonian egalitarianism and Irish anglophobia could share the stage with national theater illustrates the sympathetic harmonies that pervaded all three.[18]

Forrest tried to harness these energies for the Americanizing of tragedy, which remained the most prestigious form of dramatic art. Beginning in 1821, he sponsored a series of contests for American-authored tragedies. Some two hundred were submitted, of which nine won prizes ranging from $500 to $1,000. Since awards usually included half the third night's proceeds, the return to a winning author might amount to more than an average year's income. The contests advertised Forrest's patriotism as well as his stardom; and given the understanding that entries were to focus directly or indirectly on American themes, the effect was to subsidize production of native American tragedies in which American actors could enjoy product differentiation in a highly competitive field. Forrest included several prize-winners in his repertory. Despite Forrest's support, however, they quickly vanished from the stage, apparently incapable on their own of inducing any willing or widespread suspension of disbelief among American audiences.[19] Certainly this failure was not for lack of national themes, since the tragedies portrayed struggles against enslavement by foreign tyrants, egalitarianism triumphant, and the sad but inevitable doom of noble savages.[20] Nor was it, probably, because of their manifest artistic shortcomings. Rather, the structure of traditional tragedy seems to have been inhospitable to what the authors were trying to say.

Presuming a world in which class hierarchy and moral law stood preordained by the stability of the universe, tragedy had traditionally viewed conflict as the outcome of flaws or derelictions recurrent in the human condition: jealousy, pride, divided loyalties, the will of the child against obligation to the parent, duty versus ambition. Such conflicts unbalanced the universal order, and tragic resolution restored the balance.

These dynamics worked themselves out within a realm of moral choice coextensive with the educated upper class. Members of lower classes entered only as bearers of messages or grotesque porters at castle gates; they were not moral agents in their own right. Consequently, tragedy had no way of encompassing conflicts of class, race and nationality that arose through history and social change. These were the conflicts that preoccupied most Americans in the Jacksonian era; yet tragic structure reduced them to irrelevance because no single moral code now defined the tragic resolutions, nor could any universal order conceivably be restored. Forrest's prize-winners kept trying to reinstate the traditional conflicts, thus preserving a formal show of tragedy, while camouflaging the real issues that had been raised but could not be done justice.

From this deadlock an escape was eventually found by way of melodrama; and melodrama after the Civil War would reproduce certain aspects of the tragic mood. The road to melodrama, however, was not through traditional tragedy; it was through the proliferation of comedy and farce.

The Comic Vernaculars

Despite the high prestige of tragedy, comedy doubtless held greater appeal for mass audiences. It also presented a less forbidding threshold of education requisite to writing and revising works in the genre. Such factors, however, could not have come into operation had there not been an influx into comedy, beginning with Royall Tyler's Yankee in 1787, of regionally distinct vernacular characters. The enormous popularity of Tyler's Yankee actually hindered presentations of the play because actors eligible for leading roles feared to share the stage with a character who stole their scenes.[21] Audiences responded almost automatically to the Yankee's language, which made him an authentic personification of American identity. There was of course a problem in that the first stage Yankee began his career as a servant. While this may have reflected the author's class outlook, he had little choice in the matter since vernacular speech could only be lower class. The dividing line between those who spoke English purely and those who did not was neither national nor regional in the early nineteenth century; the difference was education, and education corresponded to class. Upper-class English travelers in the United States found the speech of those they met as social equals indistinguishable from their own.[22] Since for theater, speech furnishes the chief arbiter of characterization, it was easy to portray lower-class characters as distinctively American, difficult or impossible to do so with upper-class characters.

In making his Yankee a servant, Tyler had followed a dramatic convention by which servants underlined or parodied relationships that were treated satirically or sentimentally in the upper structure of the play. Derelictions of language in that context served to emphasize the reality or inevitability of class hierarchy. But with Tyler's Yankee there is already a hint that deviant language may be used to challenge the cultural hegemony of those who speak pure English. It was this aspect of regional dialect on stage that would bring it into alliance with the Jacksonian assault on the politics of deference. Vernacular characters simultaneously championed the national identity against foreign detractors and egalitarianism against the pretensions of the upper class. Although Tyler could never have intended that result, he was on target when he had his Yankee servant – rather than Colonel Manly who was also a Yankee – burst into the song 'Yankee Doodle'.[23] Vernacular characters thus marked a long step in the direction of nationalizing theater.

If for theater-goers the entry of American speech enhanced aesthetic enjoyment, for young American actors and actresses it was a matter of bread and butter. The linguistic demands of vernacular characterization put it beyond reach of foreign competitors. Here was a miracle of product differentiation that provided the cutting edge of changes that followed. In tragedy there was little room for product differentiation but in comedy and farce there turned out to be a good deal. Many stock comedies and farces centered on blank-check roles intended to be filled in by actors using their own specialities. Farce usually provided the afterpiece that followed a feature performance of tragedy or comedy, although the afterpiece might also be a skit tailored to the occasion, or musical numbers, dancing, or acrobatics. Into these niches moved the vernacular characters.[24]

The Yankee, after his strong beginning in 1787, hung back rather diffidently until after the 1820s, then depended on a visiting English star, Charles Mathews, to bring him forward. Mathews, acclaimed in England for humorous but kindly renderings of Scots, Yorkshiremen, and other regional types of the British Isles, toured the United States in 1822–23.

His style was admired by several American aspirant comedians, including James Hackett, a 22-year-old Utica merchant. Born of a well-to-do Long Island family, Hackett had married an actress and dreamed of a career in theater. During his American tour, Mathews developed Yankee characterizations, intended for the English public, comparable to his British dialect types. Inspired by Mathews' example, Hackett abandoned merchandizing to throw his enormous energy and considerable talent into pursuit of the Yankee. He succeeded spectacularly.[25] As Hackett's portrayals moved from afterpiece to central billing, the construction of new repertory avoided scene-stealing difficulties by placing the Yankee in star roles. Hackett's audience appeal approached that of Forrest, while his younger competitors like 'Yankee' (George) Hill and Dan Marble probably surpassed both.[26] Francis Hodge writes in his *Yankee Theatre: The Image of America on the Stage* that for twenty years comedy in America was Yankee comedy.[27]

Where the Yankee led, other vernaculars dared to follow. In 1830 a sort of variety show titled *The Times; or, Life in New York*, starring Hackett as 'Industrious Doolittle … a native of the Eastern States', listed among its *dramatis personnae* 'Mr. Pompey, a dandy Negro waiter, leader of the Broadway fashions.'[28] The urban free black had previously found a tenuous foothold in conventional servant roles;[29] he now became the second oldest of the nation's vernaculars. That same year in the autumn, taking a leaf from Forrest, Hackett announced his own prize contest for a three-act comedy.[30] The winner was James K. Paulding's *Lion of the West; or, A Trip to New York*, featuring the half-horse, half-alligator of the western frontier, David Crockett. Four years later another *Life in New York*, obviously an imitation of Hackett's earlier show of the same title, and billing one of Hackett's Yankee competitors as 'Major Jack Downing', contained a spot for T.D. Rice to dance Jim Crow.[31] If *Life in New York* could accommodate Yankees, free blacks, and plantation slaves, why not urban workingmen? Francis Chanfrau in 1848 brought a New York audience to its feet with a portrayal of Mose the Volunteer Fireman that he carried 'triumphantly through every theatrical town in the Union.'[32] Although entering the theater under the wing of the earlier established Yankee, each of these vernaculars marked out an independent track. Each, like the Yankee, moved from afterpiece to full-length performance and collectively they developed the variety show into a major component of post–Civil War melodrama. Two of them, the Broadway dandy and the plantation black, teamed up to create a new genre, blackface minstrelsy, that did for show business approximately what the penny press had done for journalism, ushering it into the era of mass communications.[33]

For vernacular characters, lower-class status was the basic factor upon which all other attributes depended. In the first place it determined their language. Second, it set limits of occupational mobility that for some changed slowly and for others not at all. The Yankee and the Broadway dandy both began as servants modeled after the European comic tradition. By the time Hackett took hold of him in the mid-1820s, the Yankee had become an independent operator on a small scale – shopkeeper, peddler, commercial traveler. The Broadway dandy remained a servant, Jim Crow a slave until after the Civil War. The western frontiersman and Mose the urban workingman, on the other hand, had never been tainted by menial service. The frontiersman's occupation scarcely needed to be specified; he was hunter, trapper, boatman, Indian fighter, occasional agriculturalist, in the 1850s a gold miner.[34] Mose stayed an urban workingman, generally a butcher's boy or mason's helper.

Although Yankees and frontiersmen, unlike other vernaculars, exhibited some occupational mobility, they shared with the others a fixity of lower-class status. Always evidenced in their language, their class status was dramatized in their sexual behavior: they were endogamous. Love affairs, if they had any, must be with partners in their own class, humorously portrayed, like servant-quarter coupling under the old regime. Romantic love was not for vernaculars. That remained the bailiwick of performers specializing in pure English, even though they might be second-stringers relative to the vernacular stars. Doubtless there was increasing pressure to break through these barriers. The long-range trend among all vernacular characters except those in blackface was to merge into a homogenized western hero speaking a composite of lower-class clichés and slowly – very slowly – transcending the rigid boundaries of occupation and marriage. But mainly the western hero developed as a post–Civil War phenomenon, linked to the dime novels and melodramas of a later era.[35] For the pre-war period, lower-class status remained the decisive element of vernacularness. Yet that element never determined the values ascribed to any vernacular characterization. Ascription of values depended rather upon the class identification and ideological intent of individual authors.[36]

This point leads to a comparable set of observations regarding the politics and racial attitudes of vernaculars. Because vernaculars asserted national identity in lower-class voices, they were naturally implicated in the Jacksonian upsurge. Mose the Volunteer Fireman illustrates this proclivity since his class background links him to artisan ideology and to such radical movements as the workingmen's parties of the 1820s.[37] The same generalization applies, although less obviously, to the other vernaculars as well. Their 'natural' political tendency, like their class status, came as a corollary to their vernacularness. But specific party affiliations remained to be manipulated by authors as, in a more general sense, the ascription of values could be manipulated. Seba Smith showed this in his construction of the Down East Yankee, Major Jack Downing, one of the most subtly delineated of all vernaculars.[38] Smith's Major Downing naturally adheres to the Jacksonian side; Smith, a Whig, used that adherence as a means of putting down the Democrats. The same is true of John Pendleton Kennedy's vernacular characterizations in the political satire *Quodlibet*.[39]

James K. Paulding, a New York Democrat,[40] likewise recognizing vernacularness as necessarily Jacksonian, assumed David Crockett to be a political ally – which publicly he still appeared to be when Paulding in 1830 gave birth to his half-horse, half-alligator, Nimrod Wildfire. Since Wildfire carried a Jacksonian label, the positive value assigned him in Paulding's *Lion of the West, or A Trip to New York* worked to promote the Democracy and downgrade its foes.[41] Paulding's Democratically identified Nimrod Wildfire and the narrator of the four Davy Crockett accounts (ghostwritten by Whigs) are recognizably the same vernacular frontiersman.[42] All display natural Jacksonian proclivities. This was what made Crockett a gold mine for the Whigs. The Crockett experience doubtless helped them learn how to use mass media to their advantage in the new politics of mass participation. In this sense Crockett provided a dress rehearsal for Harrison.

Vernacular characters, including those in blackface, displayed the ideas and attitudes of *herrenvolk* democracy. Their natural proclivity was to the hard side of racism.[43] Like lower-class origin and natural Jacksonianism, this became one of the constants of vernacularness. Values attached to this proclivity, like those attached to other vernacular constants, varied with the ideological intent of particular authors. Intent might be ambivalent. Royall Tyler probably found the term 'neger' spoken by his Yankee in *The Contrast* amusing and expected audiences to laugh at it. Yet he must also have intended to disavow the Yankee's self-serving use of white egalitarianism and warn of potential dangers to class hierarchy. George Aiken, dramatizer of *Uncle Tom's Cabin*, displayed similar ambivalence in handling the dialogue between his Yankee, Gumption Cute, and Topsy. Aiken pumped the scene for laughs by having the Yankee address Topsy as 'Charcoal', 'Stove Polish', and ask whether she were a 'juvenile specimen' from a currently well-known blackface minstrel company.[44] The context nonetheless identifies the Yankee as a scoundrel and hypocrite.

Such encounters between white and blackface vernaculars had become standard fare in American theater long before *Uncle Tom's Cabin*.[45] In *Lion of the West*, Nimrod Wildfire shouts at a black hotel waiter, 'Hullo! skulk, you black snake.' The astonishment expressed by an English female traveler ('Mrs. Wollope') that a 'free citizen of America' can be averse to freemen of 'a different skin' stands discredited by her prior identification with Frances Trollope. Wildfire says, 'The Niggers! why no, madam but they're such lazy varmints. I had one once myself, he caught the fever and ague – the fever he kept, but the ague wouldn't stay with him, for he was too lazy to shake.'[46]

It is worth recalling that Paulding's play was written after David Crockett entered Congress but before his alienation from the Jacksonian side could have been widely understood outside Tennessee.[47] Its curtain line leaves little doubt as to the author's value ascription or political prognosis. As the romantic hero and heroine are united – thanks to Wildfire's fearless assistance they have surmounted all obstacles – he promises to share with them and his new eastern friends 'free gratis for nothing' his lands on the Big Muddy and Little Muddy rivers. Then, turning to the audience: 'Look here, ladies and gentlemen, strangers, I know I'm a pretty hard sample of a white man, but I don't want to skeer nobody; and as you see I'm in want of a little more education, I hope I may be indulged occasionally in a "trip to New York".'[48]

Were New Yorkers like Paulding then more tolerant of vernacular racism than Yankee dramatists? The Boston playwright and physician, Joseph Jones, author of *The Green Mountain Boys*, attached the moral endorsement of positive portrayal throughout to his Yankee, Jedediah Homebred. Homebred's encounter with a black servant runs as follows:

> '... Say, you, when did you wash your face last? Can't tell,
> can you?'
> 'Who's you sarsen dere, you know?'
> 'Are you a nigger? I never seen a real one, but I guess you be.
> Aren't ye – you?'
> 'Who's you call "nigger"?'
> 'Well, I only ask'd you. Why he's mad as a hen a'ready.
> Did your mother have any more like you?'

Jones' Yankee, after having the good fortune to kiss a pretty housemaid of his own vernacular (and racial) status, bursts into song – not 'Yankee Doodle', but 'Hail Columbia!'.[49]

If Jones ascribed positive value to Jedediah Homebred's racism, so must George ('Yankee') Hill, also Boston born, and reputedly the most perfect of all Yankee impersonators. *The Green Mountain Boys*, a gift from Jones to Hill, became one of Hill's trademark pieces. Close friends, the two men met in 1832 on the occasion of Hill's breakthrough from afterpiece skits to featured performance.[50] The vehicle for that transition was Samuel Woodworth's *The Forest Rose; or, American Farmers* (1825). Woodworth had grown up poor in Scituate near Boston; poet, playwright, and editor, overworked and underpaid, often unemployed – the last job of his life was in the Boston Navy Yard – he is best remembered today for 'The Old

Oaken Bucket'.[51] Separated by almost a generation from vernacular stars such as Hackett and Hill, Woodworth holds a place halfway between upper-class theater and mass entertainment; a natural Jacksonian like Seba Smith's Jack Downing, nonetheless he had one foot still in the politics of deference. His curtain line for *The Forest Rose* would have satisfied Royall Tyler – or George Washington: '... remember that while we are lords of the luxuriant soil which feeds us, there is no lot on earth more enviable than that of AMERICAN FARMERS.' This patriotic finale is entrusted not to the vernacular Yankee, but to the village 'squire', reminiscent of Colonel Manly in *The Contrast*.[52]

Woodworth's Yankee appears transitional. While he has moved up from servant to shopkeeper ('I guess you'd think so, if you saw my name on the shop, down by the bridge'), his class status remains inferior to that of the squire and his family. But more important, his moral status changes within the play. The plot interweaves three simultaneous courtships. Of these, two are romantic loves, linking Harriet, the Squire's daughter, and Lydia Roseville, the squire's ward, to two worthy young suitors. The third is the Yankee's comic wooing of Deacon Forrest's vivacious daughter. At the outset, as a newcomer (from Taunton, Massachusetts) to the village, the Yankee appears self-centered, humorless, constantly protesting his adverse circumstances in a phrase repeated often enough to become a *leitmotif*: 'I wouldn't serve a negro so.'[53] Midway, the Yankee faces a crisis of conscience: a sum of money has been placed in his hand by a dissolute English aristocrat, Bellamy, who then demands his assistance in a scheme to decoy and seduce Harriet. The Yankee ponders his dilemma:

> I don't calculate I feel exactly right about keeping this purse; and yet I believe I should feel still worse to give it back. Twenty-three dollars is a speculation that an't to be sneezed at, for it an't to be catch'd every day. But will it be right to keep the money when I don't intend to do the job?[54]

As he partially persuades himself that the Englishman deserves to lose his money for attempting so evil a deed, it becomes clear that the Yankee will not serve as accomplice, but intends to thwart the plot. In the remainder of the play he brings about the exposure and discomfiture of the Englishman. At the end, hand in hand with the deacon's daughter, the Yankee has become part of the village community in contrast to his alienation at the beginning. His moral standing has progressed from ambivalently negative (like that of Tyler's Yankee) to strongly positive (like that of Paulding's Nimrod Wildfire).

Described by Richard Moody in a recent introduction as a 'nineteenth century Oklahoma', and 'the first hit show of American theatre', *Forest Rose* remained a favorite for more than forty years in theaters scattered from London and New York to New Orleans and San Francisco.[55] Subtitled 'A Pastoral Opera', Woodworth's creation is, in certain respects, a gem of early Victorian sentimentality. It is sprightly, funny, loving. Especially its young women sparkle with that sensuous independence that Henry James so loved, from a distance, in well-bred American girls. It is also incredibly cruel. The redemption of the Yankee rests on two comic scenes borrowed from Chaucer. In the first, to rebuke the Yankee for his offensive self-centeredness, the deacon's vivacious daughter lures him into a blindfold kiss, then substitutes – not her unveiled posterior as in the Chaucerian original – but the lips of Rose, a black servant woman ('Deacon Forrest's negro wench. – They call her the black Rose.').[56]

In the final scene a similar trick is arranged to punish the dissolute Englishman. Led to believe that the veiled lady who comes to meet him in the forest is the squire's daughter, the Englishman finds himself suddenly surrounded by the entire company. He protests he has done no wrong since the lady came to him of her own accord; and she, nodding her head in confirmation, thanks him 'cause you kissee me so sweet, in the grove, just now.' One wonders whether Woodworth's sentimental vision could have perceived his blackface vernacular as a young woman in the alien surrounding of that American village. If so, he was quick to repudiate it. Amid general hilarity, the black Rose stands unveiled. The Englishman is now merely the butt of humor. Peering through his eyeglass, he exclaims, 'A damn black affair, sure enough'; while the sprightly young couples joke about 'love in the *dark*', and the smell of onions on Rose's breath. The play ends in a round robin led off by the country squire in which each character sings an *envoi* to the audience. When the black Rose takes her turn, she has dropped vernacular speech and assumes the identity of a white performer in league with the others:

> Ye city beaux, accept a hint,
> If forest roses please you best,
> Be sure there is no sable in't
> Or you may rue the jest ... [57]

In the three decades since *The Contrast* the Yankee's views on class and race have moved to center stage. Class differentials dissolve into a sentimental oneness of the white *herrenvolk* for which race becomes the only denominator. By transforming the convention of theatrical make-up into a collusion between white audiences and white performers, Woodworth anticipated the triggering mechanism of blackface minstrelsy whose practitioners would prove the most independent and enduring among the vernaculars hatched out of comedy. They also proved the most indestructible of 'natural' Jacksonians. More than any other segment of pre–Civil War popular culture, blackface minstrelsy was directly linked to politics, specifically to Jacksonian politics.

Notes

1. David Grimsted, *Melodrama Unveiled: American Theater and Culture, 1800–1850*, Chicago 1968; Francis Hodge, *Yankee Theatre: The Image of America on the Stage, 1825–1850*, Austin, Tex. 1964. See also Richard Moody, *America Takes the Stage: Romanticism in American Drama and Theatre, 1750–1900*, Bloomington, Ind. 1955; Arthur H. Quinn, *A History of American Drama from the Beginning to the Civil War*, 2d ed., New York 1946; Hyman H. Taubman, *The Making of the American Theatre*, New York 1967; Isaac J. Greenwood, *The Circus: Its Origins and Growth Prior to 1835. With a Sketch of Negro Minstrelsy*, [1898] New York 1909.

2. Richard Moody, ed., *Dramas from the American Theatre, 1762–1909*, Cleveland 1966, p. 27.

3. Moody, *Dramas*, pp. 27–32.

4. Royall Tyler, *The Contrast*, in Moody, *Dramas*, p. 42.

5. Ibid., p. 43.

6. Ibid., p. 33.

7. Ibid., p. 36.

8. See Chapter 1, p. 30.

9. Taubman, pp. 53–55, 77.

10. Hodge, p. 23; Walter J. Meserve, *Heralds of Promise: The Drama of the American People in the Age of Jackson, 1829–1849*, Westport, Conn. 1986, pp. 9–10, 31–33, 34.

11. Mordecai M. Noah, 'Preface' to *She Would Be a Soldier; or, The Plains of Chippewa*, in Moody, *Dramas*, pp. 123–24; Isaac Goldberg, *Major Noah: American Jewish Pioneer*, Philadelphia 1936.

12. For example, James K. Paulding, *The Bucktails; or Americans in England*, 1835: see Moody, *America Takes the Stage*, p. 126; Richard Penn Smith, *The Eighth of January: The Battle of New Orleans*: see Smith, *The Sentinels and Other Plays*, Ralph H. Ware and W. W. Schoenberger, eds, Princeton, N.J. 1941, p. v; Smith, *The Triumph at Plattsburg*: see Arthur Hobson Quinn, ed., *Representative American Plays*, New York 1923, pp. 165–180. Noah himself contributed *The Siege of Tripoli*, 1820, *The Hero of Lake George*, 1821, and *The Seige of Yorktown*, 1824; see Moody, *Dramas*, p. 122.

13. Sol Smith, *The Theatrical Journey Work and Anecdotal Recollections of Sol Smith*, Philadelphia 1854, pp. 15–18; Arthur Hornblow, *A History of the Theatre in America from Its Beginning to the Present Time*, Philadelphia 1919, 2:32–33.

14. Grimsted, p. 29; Taubman, p. 77.

15. Edwin Forrest, *Oration Delivered at the Democratic-Republican Celebration of the Sixty-Second Anniversary of the Independence of the United States*, New York 1838, quoted in Grimsted, p. 71. See also Grimsted, p. 151, on the politics of M.M. Noah and James Nelson Barker; and Hodge, pp. 191–92, on the Jacksonian orientation of George Hill. Prosper M. Wetmore, 'Prologue' to *Metamora* in Moody, *Dramas*, p. 205; Walt Whitman, Brooklyn *Daily Eagle*, quoted in Taubman, pp. 82–83.

16. Hornblow, 2:36, quoting William Winter, *The Ballet of Time*, New York 1918; Montrose J. Moses, *The Fabulous Forest: The Record of an American Actor*, Boston 1929.

17. Grimsted, pp. 65–67; Hornblow, pp. 38–39; Taubman, pp. 89–90; Richard Moody, *The Astor Place Riot*, Bloomington, Ind. 1958.

18. New York *Tribune*, 9 and 15 May 1849, quoted in Grimsted, p. 73; Taubman, p. 89; Grimsted, pp. 72–73. Supporters of Macready's right to perform included several leading Democrats. Grimsted, p. 71n: 'The list of forty–seven signers included Washington Irving, Herman Melville, Benjamin Silliman, and the playwrights Mordecai M. Noah and Cornelius Mathews.'

19. Richard Moody, *Edwin Forrest, First Star of the American Stage*, New York 1960. John Augustus Stone, *Metamora*, and Robert Montgomery Bird, *The Gladiator*, are in Moody, *Dramas*, pp. 205–27. See Moody's introduction to each. Bird, *Orallosa*; Richard Penn Smith, *Caius Marius: A Tragedy*, ed. and intro., Neda McFadden Westlake, Philadelphia 1968; and see Westlake's introduction. Grimsted, pp. 148–49, 167–69, 216–18; Hornblow, 2:61. Bruce W. McCullough, *The Life and Writing of Richard Penn Smith*, Menasha, Wis. 1917; Smith, *The Sentinels and Other Plays*, Ralph H. Ware and H. W.

Schoenberger, eds, Princeton, N.J. 1941, pp. *v–x*. Mary Mayer Bird, *The Life of Robert Montgomery Bird, Written by His Wife Mary Mayer Bird*, C. Seymour Thompson, ed., Philadelphia 1945.

20. Smith, *Caius Marius*, pp. 54–55; Bird, *The Gladiator*, in Moody, *Dramas*, p. 264; Stone, *Metamora*, ibid., p. 209; Bird, *The Gladiator*, ibid., p. 247.

21. Moody, *Dramas*, p. 30. Milton and Patricia Rickels, in *Seba Smith*, Boston 1977, note that the concept of the vernacular character was developed by Henry Nash Smith in *Mark Twain: The Development of a Writer*, Cambridge, Mass. 1962. See also Smith, *Virgin Land: The American West as Symbol and Myth*, Cambridge, Mass. 1970, pp. 94, 238–41. Rickels and Rickels, p. 26, describe Smith's 'vernacular perspective' as designating 'a language, set of values, and ethical and esthetic assumptions.' I would add, in reference to nineteenth-century American vernaculars, that these attributes are largely class–derived.

22. Hodge, pp. 6, 77, 255.

23. Tyler, *The Contrast*, in Moody, *Dramas*, p. 48.

24. Hodge, pp. 21–22, 103.

25. Hodge, pp. 60–77, 81–86.

26. See Hodge on Hackett, pp. 81–151; on George Hill, pp. 155–218; on Dan Marble, pp. 221–40.

27. Hodge, pp. 255–61. Gumption Cute in George Aiken, *Uncle Tom's Cabin* in Moody, *Dramas*, pp. 360–96; Salem Scudder and Jacob M'Closky in Dion Boucicault, *The Octoroon; or, Life in Louisiana*, in Quinn, ed., *Representative Plays*, pp. 431–58.

28. Hodge, p. 107.

29. Moody, *America Takes the Stage*, pp. 63–67.

30. Hodge, p. 118.

31. Ibid., pp. 146–47.

32. Moody, *Dramas*, pp. 476–78; Hornblow, 2:132–33, quoting Joseph N. Ireland, *Records of the New York Stage*, New York 1867; Meserve, pp. 120–27.

33. See Chapter 7.

34. Charles Mathews, the English actor, recognized the servant origins of the Yankee by having his Yankee in *Jonathon in England*, London 1824, treated as a servant in England due to a confusion of identity: Hodge, pp. 69–76. In *The Forest Rose*, New York 1825, the Yankee is clearly established as a shopkeeper: Moody, *Dramas*, p. 160. James K. Paulding, *The Lion of the West*, ed. James N. Tidwell, Stanford, Calif. 1954, p. 21. 'Sweet Betsy from Pike' and 'Oh! Susannah', frequently sung in minstrel shows, take the western vernacular hero into mining.

35. Compare Nimrod Wildfire, below, p. 160, with Frank H. Murdock's *Davy Crockett*, 1872: Isaac Goldberg and Hubert Heffner, eds, *Davy Crockett and Other Plays*, Princeton, N.J. 1940, pp. 115–48.

36. Yankee characterizations by Royall Tyler, James Hackett, George Hill and George Aiken are recognizable as Yankees; but the first and last convey negative values, the middle pair, positive: Royall Tyler, *The Contrast*, in Moody, *Dramas*, pp. 35–39; James H. Hackett, *The Times, or Life in New York*, Hodge, pp. 105–7; *Old Times in Virginia; or, The Yankee Pedlar*, adopted by George Hill as one of his trademark pieces, Hodge, pp. 179–81; George Aiken, *Uncle Tom's Cabin*, in Moody, *Dramas*, pp. 360–96.

37. Eric Foner, *Tom Paine and Revolutionary America*, New York 1976; Alexander Saxton, 'George Wilkes: The Transformation of a Radical Ideology', *American Quarterly* 33 (Fall 1981): 26–47.

38. Seba Smith, *The Life and Writings of Major Jack Downing of Downingville, Away Down East in the State of Maine. Written by Himself*, Boston 1833. P. T. Barnum perfectly exemplifies the 'natural' Jacksonian proclivity of the vernacular Yankee: see P.T. Barnum, *Struggles and Triumphs*, first published in 1855, Carl Bode, ed., New York 1981, pp. 73–75, 315–16.

39. Rickels and Rickels, *Seba Smith*, pp. 36–38; John Pendleton Kennedy, *Quodlibet*.

40. Amos L. Herold, *James K. Paulding: Versatile American*, New York 1926, pp. 65, 73–74, 114–15, 128.

41. See James A. Shackford and Stanley Folmsby, 'Introduction', in David Crockett, *A Narrative of the Life of David Crockett of the State of Tennessee*, James A. Shackford and Stanley Folmsby, eds, [Philadelphia 1834] Knoxville, Tenn. 1973; Stanley J. Folmsby and

Anna Grace Catron, 'The Early Career of David Crockett', and 'David Crockett: Congressman', East Tennessee Historical Society, *Publications* 28 (1956): 58–85, and 29 (1957): 40–78. Paulding won the Hackett prize contest in November 1830, and the play was first produced in April 1831. Hackett staged a special performance in Washington at Crockett's request, and he and Crockett exchanged bows to applause from the audience. See James N. Tidwell, 'Introduction', Paulding, *The Lion of the West*, pp. 7–9. Tidwell, p. 9, notes that Paulding wrote Crockett denying that Wildfire was modeled on him. This may have been ex post facto; in any case the public generally identified Wildfire with Crockett. As late as fall 1833, Democratically oriented papers like the New York *Sun* carried an installment of the first Crockett narrative portraying Crockett as an ardent Jackson man: New York *Sun*, 18 November 1833.

42. See above, pp. 80–84.

43. See Chapter 7.

44. Aiken, *Uncle Tom's Cabin*, in Moody, *Dramas*, pp. 386–87. William L. Van de Burg, *Slavery and Race in American Popular Culture*, Madison, Wis. 1984, pp. 17–24, 39–49, provides a useful survey of early dramas containing African or African–American characterizations.

45. Among many others, and in addition to those already referred to: William Dunlap, *A Trip to Niagara*, New York 1828, and Anna Cora Mowatt, *Fashion*, New York 1845: Moody, *Dramas*, pp. 178–97, 317–47.

46. Paulding, *Lion of the West*, pp. 36–37.

47. Meserve, pp. 109–111, shows that there were two revisions of *Lion of the West* by other authors prior to March 1833. The parody of Trollope was added in the last revision, but the characterization of Wildfire remained substantially the same throughout.

48. Paulding, *Lion of the West*, p. 62.

49. Quoted in Hodge, p. 171. On Joseph Jones, see Meserve, pp. 94–104.

50. Hodge, pp. 165–71.

51. Moody, *Dramas*, pp. 143–46; Kendall B. Taft, 'Samuel Woodworth', Ph.D. diss., University of Chicago, 1936.

52. Woodworth, *Forest Rose*, in Moody, *Dramas*, p. 173. The term 'squire' is used only by the Yankee and the Deacon's daughter: Moody, *Dramas*, p. 161, 169; Taft, 'Samuel Woodworth'.

53. Ibid., pp. 159–61.

54. Ibid., p. 169.

55. Moody, *Dramas*, p. 147.

56. Woodworth, *The Forest Rose*, in Moody, *Dramas*, pp. 159–60.

57. Ibid., pp. 172–73, 174.

6

The Democracy

Views of the mass circulation press and theater in the preceding chapters were intended to establish the contours of the urban culture within which the Jacksonian Democracy's northern wing took shape and within which Democratic ideology, outside the South, was mainly elaborated. In both press and theater, egalitarian republicanism stemming from artisan and working-class populations played a dominant role. White racism defined the boundaries of republicanism and justified the problematic empathy developing between urban egalitarians and planter oligarchs in the South. The legitimizing synthesis of the Democratic party reproduced (or paralleled) this construction.

As suggested in the earlier discussion of John Quincy Adams's administration, the starting dynamic of the Jacksonian upsurge was disarticulation of the class base of National Republicanism in the South set in motion by planter anxiety over the defense of slavery. One faction, clinging to National Republicanism, eventually joined the Whigs. The other supported Jackson while moving sideways toward southern regionalism. There could be no doubt of Jackson's nationalist commitment; what his southern partisans advocated was in effect a *regional* nationalism aimed at defending slavery not by interposing state against federal power (except in last resort), but by controlling federal power from the strongholds of their states to bring the federal apparatus to the defense of slavery. These were the originating architects of the Jacksonian coalition. That they foresaw an alliance with urban egalitarians in the North seems unlikely, yet certainly they were bidding for political allies outside the South, and offering attractive prices.[1] Probably their prospectus in 1828 went no further than putting together a package that would unseat Adams. What resulted – given the nation's open economic expansion, the prevalence of white male suffrage, and revolts against the politics of deference already shaking many cultural and political institutions – was the creation of a mass party, national in scope.[2] Moreover, since the opposition was not destroyed but merely stunned and scattered, the new party called into existence an opposite bower that would soon become its formal partner in the so-called Second Party System.

While there is no need to trace here the evolution of the notion that parties and party competition might serve useful purposes, it is important to note that this idea had become increasingly familiar during the first quarter of the nineteenth century.[3] Political leaders could engage in acrimonious debate confident that their hearers understood them to be soliciting votes rather than bloodshed; and that the other side would do likewise. John Quincy Adams, defeated but unguillotined, could reappear as congressman from Quincy. This degree of sophistication was essential to the working of the party system as a means of mobilizing the new mass electorate and holding together more or less stable coalitions upon which governmental policies could be based.[4] Of the sections comprising this chapter, the first discusses party systems; the others examine structural and ideological aspects of the antebellum Democracy that seem particularly relevant to development of the racial component of the party's legitimizing synthesis.

Party Systems

By the early 1830s, then, a party system roughly similar to the one known to us today had come into existence and would soon be recognized, even celebrated, as the glory of American democracy. The system was in effect a binary constellation each member of which was a voter coalition held together by shared economic interests, cultural, religious and ethnic sympathies or antipathies, and regional loyalties. Party affiliation frequently reached across generational lines not because American sons especially venerated their fathers but because – despite the much heralded mobility of American society – sons were likely to remain in the same class, religious tradition and ethnic or cultural milieu as their parents. For the most part geographical mobility did not negate these class and cultural continuities.

Why binary rather than multiple? Why not a spectrum of parties as in European parliamentary systems? This question has been debated in the extensive literature on party systems, with answers generally converging on the unique role of the American presidency. Thus Richard P. McCormick wrote in the introduction to his *Second American Party System*: 'Basically, I share ... the understanding that American parties are above all electoral machines, engaged in nominating and electing candidates. ...

Party formation', McCormick added, 'was most directly conditioned not by divisions in Congress or by explicit doctrinal issues but rather by the contest for the presidency.' Theodore Lowi, referring to deadlocks between president and Congress that sometimes punctuate the constitutional separation of powers in the United States, has suggested that any shift to a multiparty system, by continuously depriving the president of congressional majorities, would tend towards a presidential subordination to the legislature comparable to that of chief executives in parliamentary regimes. David Feller, examining the politics of public lands, offered a similar point with respect to the shift, in the early 1830s, from sectional pluralism to a two-party system. One can turn these formulations around: American presidents, as leaders of national coalitions, have used executive power to preserve their constituent majorities both in Congress and in the nation at large. Executive power quickly emerged as decisive among the countervailing powers that resulted from the federal compromise. Its key was presidential office. Unlike parliamentary ministers chosen through bargaining among elected delegates already ensconced in their legislative chambers, American presidents had to be elected in national referenda. Whereas a parliamentary system would tend to encourage independent parties, each with its tightly prepared legislative program, the American system placed a premium on broad coalitions aimed at assembling nationwide majorities prior to elections.[5]

Party systems in the United States are generally periodized on the basis of dominant partners. For the nineteenth century this yields three periods distinguished by dominance of (1) the Jeffersonian (National) Republicans (1801–1829); (2) the Jacksonian Democratic party (1829–1861) and (3) the Republican party (1861–1933). The first period – and I am stretching my argument by describing it as a system, since the Federalists virtually went out of business after 1817 – lasted through seven presidential terms without interruption of dominant party control. The second spanned eight presidential terms, six to the dominant Jacksonians, two to the subordinate Whigs. The third period, by the end of the century, had run through ten terms, eight Republican, two Democratic.[6]

Each of the three systems was characterizd by the continuity in power of the dominant party. Control over the federal apparatus brought cumulative accretions of power because, among other factors, federal patronage enhanced the electoral chances of that party's congressional and senatorial candidates. Thus Jeffersonian Republicans from 1800 to 1822 'won three quarters of all contests for presidential electors and congressmen, and four fifths of all senatorial contests.' During the second party system, the Democracy accounted for about two-thirds of all congressmen and three-fifths of all senators. To initiate and execute new governmental policies requires simultaneous control over the presidency and both houses of Congress. Democrats exercised such control for nine years, Whigs for only two. Moreover, any legislation pushed through by the subordinate party in its brief tenures of power might face Supreme Court review. Twenty justices occupied seats on the Supreme Court during this period, and of these twelve owed their appointments to Democratic presidents. The court had become firmly Democratic by 1836. These specifics point to a general conclusion that dominant parties, although seldom able to achieve one-party rule since they usually faced effective opposition, succeeded in monopolizing the initiation of federal policies for long periods.[7]

It follows from what has been said that a small independent party of the European type, lacking access to the advantages flowing from federal administration, would be hard pressed to maintain itself in America unless it could show promise of winning such access in a coming election. To maximize its chances of doing so, it would be impelled to merge into coalition with other political forces. Thus, while the turbulent politics of growth continually generated new parties, the party system kept pressing them into its duality of dominant and subordinate partners.[8]

Political leadership in the United States has rested on the art of orchestrating diverse, sometimes contradictory interests within broadly framed programs. The emphasis has been less on specific items of legislation than upon dominant themes, areas of ideological harmony that could unite potential adherents. Participants in a coalition could then be expected to postpone or compromise some of their demands for the sake of the program as a whole. If, however, no area of ideological harmony could be maintained, the coalition would begin to disintegrate and the party would lose its ability to win national elections – as had been the case with the Federalists after 1800 and the National Republicans after about 1825. Obviously, no party controlling the federal apparatus would fall apart easily or yield power without a struggle. Time spans of these sequences for the nineteenth century have ranged from twenty-eight to more than forty years. Between periods of party dominance have come chaotic intervals in which a newly forming majority fought to consolidate its own constituency. The intervals thus appear as indices to alterations of the political superstructure corresponding to basic structural changes in the society. 1801 registered a swing from counting-house commercialism dependent upon the British Empire to an independent commercialism based on continental nationalism. 1829 marked the separation of class interests within the National Republican oligarchy; 1861 the overthrow of the planter class.[9]

A phenomenon so striking in its elegant simplicity as the American party system has understandably elicited a scholarly literature that in itself offers a field of ideological investigation. I will not pursue that investigation here except to dissociate myself from two recurring, and I believe misleading, interpretations. The first – which appears in many forms – traces the finished product to some prior blueprint. The American party system thus might be said to have evolved in its particular way because it was functionally necessary to democratic government of a mass society. To this could be added a comparison of social structures to organisms, suggesting that the right sort of social structures came equipped with something like genetic codes to predetermine the development of their essential parts. More recently the elusive blueprint has been located in the presumed necessities of modern industrial civilization and – like gravity working at a distance through space – is understood to operate backward through time. My own inclination is to reject teleological explanations as undemonstrable and to rely on the more humdrum concept that historical outcomes accrue from multitudes of individual and collective actions aimed, successfully and unsuccessfully, at diverse, often contradictory goals.[10]

The second interpretation from which I would dissociate myself is more specifically American. It is the tendency to avoid reference to class power as a factor in historical change. The tendency enters the study of parties and party systems by proposing that because major parties in America have been coalitions of cultural, religious, ethnic and regional groupings, they have therefore transcended or escaped class influence. The origins of particular parties are then deduced from historical contingencies of geography, religion and ethnicity, while their durability is ascribed to the function they have performed in furnishing convenient mechanisms for mass decision making. But while major parties in the United States certainly have not resembled European parliamentary parties, they nonetheless have been responsive – and I think primarily responsive – to economic or class interests. I agree with Joel Silbey in his *Political Ideology and Voting Behavior in the Age of Jackson* that recent research on the Jacksonian period has brought forward the 'importance of clashing religious and ethnic perspectives in shaping group values and attitudes toward politics', but when Silbey concludes that 'class divisions were usually not central to the political conflicts of the time', he has, I think, overstated his case. The notion that in America culture has banished class from the political arena seems to me an exercise in self-mystification.[11]

Class Components of the Democratic Party

Class components of the Democratic party included urban workers and small middle-class, yeoman farmers, aspirant entrepreneurs and southern planters. The first three of these terms would be imprecise under any circumstances. They become more so by application to a time in which yeoman farmers seldom existed in pure form, while the industrial working class and industrial capitalist class were still in the early stages of formation. I use these terms because no better ones are available.

Urban workers in the 1830s were mostly artisans. Artisans might be masters of their own shops who employed others, or they might be wage earners. Some moved back and forth from one status to the other. Moreover, the circumstances of artisanry were changing as manufacturing increased in volume and scale. A few artisans would move up into the new class of industrial capitalists. Others would convert their skills to the specializations of machine designers, millwrights, industrial mechanics, foremen and superintendents; and some remained journeymen in lines like the printing, building and metal trades that survived as craft skills. Some also moved down to join the growing ranks of industrial workers. And there had of course always been the unskilled in the cities – porters, stevedores, seamen, day laborers.[12]

After the War of 1812, most of the diverse groups collectively referred to as urban workers and the small middle class, if they participated in politics, must have been Jeffersonian, then National Republicans. Did they become Democrats? Not all, by any means. In cities of the central and eastern seaboard, a significant number joined workingmen's parties, from which they opposed both Adams men and Jacksonians. Essentially these parties spoke for independent artisans facing the onset of industrialization.[13] Short-lived, since the logic of the party system tended to isolate them or force them into the major parties, the workingmen's parties nonetheless furnished a conduit of radical thought from the revolutionary era to the romantic egalitarianism of the nineteenth century. Their heroes were Thomas Jefferson and Ethan Allen, Tom Paine and Frances Wright, Irish rebels and English Chartists. Clearly the main transit of workingmen was into the so-called Locofoco wing of the Jacksonian Democracy, from which emanated the most radicalizing impulses of American politics, including proposals for land distribution that eventually found their way into the Homestead and Free Soil movements.[14]

Other wage earners followed different routes. Free blacks in New England and New York, most of whom certainly worked for wages, solidly backed the Whigs. So also, though not so solidly, did native-born Protestant workers in cities where recent immigrants, especially if they were Irish or German Catholics, became prominent in Democratic politics. Despite these exceptions, however, it seems reasonable to conclude from secondary literature, based on vast amounts of primary evidence, that American workingmen during the Jacksonian era, skilled and unskilled, East and West, were more likely to be Democrats than Whigs.[15] So marked was this preference that by the 1840s it had become traditional:

Whigs like John Pendleton Kennedy described their opponents as 'Locofocos', meaning that they belonged to the party of the urban working class and immigrant radicalism. Ralph Waldo Emerson, certainly more tolerant than Kennedy, wrote in his journal in 1838, 'I passed the shop and saw my spruce neighbor, the dictator of our rural Jacobins, teaching his little circle of villagers their political lessons. And here, thought I, is one who loves what I hate; here is one wholly reversing my code. ...'[16]

With respect to yeomen farmers, as to urban workers, the difficulty of generalization is compounded by ambiguities of definition. Farmers often hired out for wages and in some areas moved between agrarian and industrial pursuits. In eastern Massachusetts farmers were likely also to be shoemakers or fishermen; in New Hampshire, granite quarriers; in Pennsylvania, coal miners or iron workers. John Brown, a yeoman farmer in the last years of his life, had run a tannery, herded sheep and gone into business as a wool merchant. On the Tennessee frontier, David Crockett was basically a farmer, although much of his food came from hunting; he also cut shakes for the New Orleans market and tried his hand at a saw mill, a grist mill and a powder factory. William Henry Harrison, the nation's symbol of self-sufficient western yeomanry, speculated in land, invested in a distillery and became part-owner in a Cincinnati iron foundry.[17] The problem is not so much one of terminology as of history. Farmers in nineteenth-century America comprised a vast matrix of class formation; the yeoman identity constantly played host to speculative, entrepreneurial and wage worker identities.

As to their politics, what can be said is that nationally they divided about equally between Whigs and Democrats in the early years of Democratic dominance and had become more favorable to the Democrats by the 1850s. Given the volatility of their class tendencies and the limited choice offered by the party system, it is hardly surprising that yeoman farmer status proved insufficient by itself to dictate a national commitment to one party or the other. Certainly there were marked regional preferences. Areas of upper New York and the Old Northwest into which New England population migrated were likely to be whiggish. South of the Yankee corridor, areas in transition from a frontier economy (characterized by dependence on current migration for agricultural markets and cash flow) to an 'Old West' economy (characterized by commercial agriculture, developing urban markets and beginnings of manufacturing) also were likely to show whiggish proclivities. On the other hand, the careers of agrarian radicals like Thomas Hart Benton and Andrew Johnson demonstrate how solidly the Democracy had established itself in the lower Mississippi Valley.[18]

Does the introduction of regional and cultural factors obviate class inquiry? I think not, since such influences necessarily interlock with class. Many years ago Charles Francis Adams, describing the transformation of Quincy, Massachusetts, from a National Republican village to a Jacksonian town, traced the mesh woven by class, region and culture. When the second Adams became president, his home town was still governed by a local elite with the willing consent of the long-established yeoman families – 'slow, conservative, and generally disposed to show much deference to the opinions of the gentry.' In 1825 the Bunker Hill Monument Association bought control of Quincy's little-used stone quarry. By 1826 a railroad had been built. The quarry ten years later employed 500 men, old stock, rural Yankees from New Hampshire who came down every spring by wagon for a summer's work. 'Noisy, muscular, hard-living Americans, with small reverence', Charles Francis Adams described them. 'A foreign voting element', they voted Democratic.[19] But the railroad also quickened the pace of the shoemaker's trade by opening access to wholesale markets.

Shoemakers congregated in Quincy. They worked at home, talking politics in their backyard shops, Adams reported, and they too tended towards the Democracy. Meanwhile, children of the old yeoman families were leaving the countryside for Boston or the West. Filling their places as 'farm hands' came Irish immigrant laborers. In 1824 the village had unanimously endorsed its native son for president. At the next election there were three Jackson votes. In 1836, running for Congress, Adams carried Quincy more than 2 to 1 over a Democratic opponent. In 1838 he failed to carry the town for the first time, although he won the congressional district.[20]

Once a rural hinterland of Boston, Quincy became more Democratic as it became more urban. The South, on the other hand, which showed vast agricultural expansion but little urbanization during this period, became more Democratic as it became more agrarian. The contrast underlines the impossibility of broad generalizations about rural politics and the necessity in any causal explanation for a tight focus on the web of class, region and culture. The South, crucially important in the Jacksonian party system, will be discussed separately in this connection. Here, for the purpose of enumerating major class components of the Democracy, a sampling of presidential electoral returns suffices to demonstrate that large rural areas, especially in the South and West, consistently gave support to the Democratic party.[21]

A third element of the Democratic coaliton was a group even more troublesome to define than the first two. Perhaps it is better identified as a state of mind than a class. According to the great tradition every white American boy born in a log cabin was supposed to cherish ambitions of becoming president. This tradition was Jacksonian; it had not existed before the advent of the first mass party. Jackson himself had not been born in a log cabin, although his frontier experiences served as proxy; Harrison had actually grown up in one of the grandest mansions of Tidewater Virginia. Lincoln would thus become the first genuine log cabin president. But the prototype was David Crockett. Crockett had been born in a log cabin and certainly dreamed of becoming president. Before that, however, we know that Crockett had dreamed of achieving less exalted goals. He had wanted to be a land speculator, a planter, a proprietor of milling and manufacturing enterprises.[22] Other young men in similar circumstances hoped to be lawyers, surveyors, saloon keepers, railroad promoters, bonanza miners. Those who pursued such aspirations – frequently butting their heads against established structures of enterprise and wealth – might best be described as aspirant entrepreneurs, people on the make. Crockett was one of them; his western enterprises failed largely because he lacked access to capital; both in Tennessee and in Washington he was desperate for loans. Militant egalitarianism might break open closed doors. Crockett entered politics under the Jacksonian banner, and after his disastrous marriage with the Whigs he redeemed himself by fighting to erect an egalitarian slaveholder republic in Texas. Had he survived he probably would have surfaced as a Texas Democrat.

America produced legions of Crocketts. 'To the dissatisfied, whether through distress or ambition', Bray Hammond wrote in his study of banks and Jacksonian politics,

> ... Andrew Jackson offered a distinct and attractive change. ... He became champion of the common man, even though the latter might be no longer either frontiersman or farmer but speculator, capitalist or entrepreneur of a new, democratic sort, who in every village and township was beginning to profit by the Industrial Revolution, the growth of population, and the expanding supply of bank credit. This new common man was manufacturer, banker, builder, carrier and promoter. He belonged to the 'active and enterprising', in the luminous contrast put by Churchill C. Cambreleng, as against the 'wealthier classes'.[23]

Hammond has left a revealing gallery of Jacksonian entrepreneurial portraits.[24] John Pendleton Kennedy, who received a hundred dollar gift from his father-in-law for a pamphlet attacking Cambreleng, recorded his own confrontation with the president of the Union Bank of Baltimore, which Kennedy served as legal counsel. The bank president had determined to support the Jackson administration against the Second Bank of the United States, hoping thereby to rid himself of irksome controls over note issue and anticipating the transfer of federal deposits to his own bank. Kennedy's response was to plunge into organizing the Whig party in Baltimore.[25]

The fourth component of the Jacksonian coalition – southern planters – presents no difficulty of definition. Not all slaveowners, of course, were planters. Kenneth Stampp has made the convenient distinction that owners of thirty or more field hands, because they would be obliged to employ overseers (and could afford them), enjoyed an affluent life-style that separated them from yeoman farmers and from the small gentry who owned slaves. By his reckoning there would have been approximately 25,000 planters in 1860. Allowing five members to a family, planter families would have numbered 125,000, about 1.5 percent of the white population of the South.[26] During the 1840s and 1850s planters tended to shift from the Whigs to the Democracy. This shift contributed to the creation of a virtually solid South prior to the Civil War.

The Solid South

The cotton boom following the Napoleonic Wars had pumped new wealth into slave plantation investments. Simultaneously, a northern effort to block admission of Missouri as a slave state alerted southerners to the accelerating growth of population in the North and West, by which the South already had lost control of the House of Representatives in any regional division and might soon lose parity in the Senate. Southern 'regional nationalists', attempting to rekindle the republican fervor of the Virginia and Kentucky Resolutions in defense of states' rights, initiated the Jacksonian movement.[27] Meanwhile, upper-class dominance in the South as elsewhere came under attack from below. The slave population, declining relatively in the Upper South, had concentrated in the Tidewater and Black Belt of the Deep South, which now extended, as a result of the cotton boom, into the new states of the Mississippi Valley.[28] Yeoman families who owned few slaves or none settled the back country – the hills and piney woods – of the new states. In older states a similar social stratum, increasing in relative numbers, became more politically active. Together they furnished the mass base of the southern Jacksonian party. Pressing for white manhood suffrage in regions where it had not yet penetrated, demanding equal apportionment in representation and taxes, they challenged planter domination at local and state levels.

The democratizing surge in the South was marked by battles at legislative sessions and constitutional conventions – in Virginia in 1829–1830; Mississippi in 1831; North Carolina in 1835; Louisiana in 1845; North Carolina again in the late 1840s and Virginia and Louisiana again in the early 1850s.[29] A new crop of Democratic leaders built careers out of these struggles. The conflict in North Carolina, according to the suffrage historian Chilton Williamson, 'benefitted the Democrats more than the

Whigs, giving them control of the state and winning for them the support of the non-slaveholding poorer whites.'[30] A comparable movement in Virginia brought Henry Wise, 'defender of poor whites … a believer in suffrage democracy … and equitable representation of the various sections of the state … above all a defender of the southern way of life and the peculiar institution',[31] to the governorship in time to sign the death warrant of John Brown.

White egalitarianism, invincible at the polls, presented a formidable problem to the planter class. Members of this class who had earlier moved from Federalism or National Republicanism to the Whig party found it increasingly difficult to win even local elections as Whigs. A three-way division was taking shape within the South. The back country and piney woods became Democratic; the Black Belt and Delta, suitable to large plantations, were likely to remain Whig; counties that were mixed became battlegrounds. The balance of this division varied from state to state. Yet everywhere Whigs suffered from the fact that where they had their strongest bases, black slaves outnumbered whites. Consequently, Whigs were impelled to fight to retain total population, or at least the federal three-fifths ratio, as the basis of representation.[32] This outraged their Jacksonian opponents and compounded for southern Whigs the difficulty Whigs everywhere encountered when forced to carry their principles into the arena of mass democracy. They were defeated in the mixed counties, while those elected from Black Belt counties found themselves outvoted in the state legislatures.

As a ruling class, the planters might have accepted minority political status – relying on courthouse rings and inside manipulation to protect them locally – if adherence to the Whig party had brought increased strength at the national level. The opposite was the case. The National Republican thesis now appeared detrimental to their class interest. A moment of truth came after Harrison's victory in 1840, to which eight slaveholding states had contributed their electoral votes.[33] Whigs, at last in control of Congress, showed themselves relentlessly committed to the thesis in all its aspects: internal improvements, a protective tariff, encouragement of manufacturing, tight federal controls over western lands. Tyler, the Tidewater planter who succeeded to the presidency after Harrison's death, expressed in his vetoes southern ruling-class opposition to these measures. He was denounced by his own party as a traitor and scoundrel. Soon afterwards the elusively abstract issues of protection, improvements, graduation, and distribution of land sales revenue were translated into concrete metaphors that no backcountry white egalitarian could fail to understand: annexation of Texas and war against Mexico. The Whig party nationally took positions on Texas and Mexico that southern Whigs found indefensible.[34]

What resulted for their party can be shown by a simple comparison between counties with high and low slave populations. Table 1 shows the results of five presidential elections, 1840–1856, for the states of Alabama, Georgia, Mississippi, Louisiana and Tennessee; and for two sets of 50 counties (or parishes), each set composed respectively of the highest and lowest 10 from each state in percentage of slaves to the total population. At the state level, returns show a Democratic preponderance of 16 to 9 in 25 possible outcomes, together with a Democratic trend throughout the period from the 1840 division of 4 to 1 in favor of the Whigs to the 1856 Democratic sweep of all five states. Similar general tendencies show up for the two sets of counties, together totalling 100. Of 500 possible outcomes, 275 were Democratic, 212 Whig. In 1840 the 100 counties divided 55 to 38 for the Whigs; sixteen years later they showed a 72 to 28 preference for the Democracy.

A comparison between the two sets shows that the fifty counties with the highest percentage of slaves recorded 168 Whig victories (67 percent) and 80 Democratic (32 percent) through the five elections. The fifty counties with the lowest slave percentage favored Democrats over Whigs 195 (78 percent) to 44 (18 percent). In 1840 the counties with a high slave population gave 43 victories to Whigs (87 percent), and only 6 to Democrats (12 percent); the same counties in 1856 divided 26 (52 percent) to 24 (48 percent) in favor of the Democrats. The fifty counties with the lowest percentage of slaves went Democratic 32 (73 percent) to 12 (27 percent) in 1840; in 1856, 46 (92 percent) to 4 (8 percent). Within a general Democratic preponderance, then, and throughout a secular trend favoring the Democrats, the fifty counties with low slave percentages began strongly Democratic (in a year when the five states stood four to one for the Whigs) and moved to become almost unanimously Democratic. The 50 counties with high slave percentages, which began almost totally Whig, showed narrow Democratic preferences in the last two elections in the period. As early as 1852, to judge by this index, the Whig party was virtually defunct in the South.

The Barbour family of Virginia again offers an instructive example. At the time of the Missouri debates, Philip Barbour, a younger brother of James, was a member of the US House of Representatives, where he defended states' rights, while his older brother in the Senate juggled nationalist principles against tactical expediency.[35] Perhaps as a result of his states' rights position, Philip Barbour acquired something of a reputation, in the Southwest at least, as a man of the people. David Crockett was reported in the first of the Crockett narratives to have expressed admiration for Thomas Hart Benton of Missouri – and for Philip Barbour, whom he would have 'preferred for president to Jackson or Clay.'[36] The younger Barbour presumably spoke for the family at the Virginia Con-

SOUTHERN ELECTIONS, 1840–1856

Outcomes of Presidential Elections

	1840	1844	1848	1852	1856	
Alabama	D	D	D	D	D	OW/5D
Georgia	W	D	W	D	D	2W/3D
Louisiana	W	D	W	D	D	2W/3D
Mississippi	W	D	D	D	D	1W/4D
Tennessee	W	W	W	W	W	5W/0D
Totals	4W	1W	3W	1W	1W	10W
	1D	4D	2D	4D	4D	15D

Presidential Elections in Counties with the Highest Percentage of Slaves

	1840	1844	1848	1852	1856	
Alabama	10W	6W	10W	3W	5W	34W
	0D	4D	0D	7D	5D	16D
Georgia	9W	9W	10W	1W	3W	32W
	1D	1D	0D	8D	7D	17D
Louisiana	7W	7W	8W	6W	4W	32W
	2D	3D	2D	4D	6D	17D
Mississippi	10W	8W	9W	4W	6W	37W
	0D	2D	1D	6D	4D	13D
Tennessee	7W	7W	7W	6W	6W	33W
	3D	3D	3D	4D	4D	17D
Totals	43W	37W	44W	20W	24W	168W
	6D	13D	6D	29D	26D	80D

Presidential Elections in Counties with the Lowest Percentage of Slaves

	1840	1844	1848	1852	1856	
Alabama	0W	0W	1W	0W	0W	1W
	9D	9D	8D	10D	10D	46D
Georgia	1W	1W	2W	0W	0W	4W
	9D	9D	8D	10D	10D	46D
Louisiana	3W	2W	3W	1W	1W	10W
	2D	6D	6D	9D	9D	32D
Mississippi	2W	0W	1W	0W	0W	3W
	8D	10D	9D	10D	10D	47D
Tennessee	6W	5W	6W	6W	3W	26W
	4D	5D	4D	4D	7D	24D
Totals	12W	8W	13W	7W	4W	44W
	34D	39D	35D	43D	46D	195D

SOURCE: Compiled from U.S. Bureau of the Census, *Seventh Census of the United States, 1850,* and *Eighth Census of the United States, 1860,* Washington, D.C. 1853, 1863; *Whig Almanac and United States Register*, New York 1844–57.

stitutional Convention of 1829–1830 when he opposed white manhood suffrage and advocated a 'compound ratio' of white population and property (by which he meant slaves) as the basis of apportionment for legislative representation. He began his long argument by warning that the words, 'all men are by nature equally free', if taken literally, would emancipate slaves 'not far short of a moiety of our entire number', and would 'as a natural consequence' result in such 'scenes of horror and desolation' as those 'produced in St. Domingo by a declaration of much the same tenor, issued by the famous national assembly of France.' For those of his colleagues who might still cherish the old revolutionary slogans, Barbour then explained that freedom considered as a natural right could not logically require equal 'civil and political rights', since these were not natural rights at all, but came into existence solely as products of some particular institution of government.

There was little need to debate the question of manhood suffrage at this convention, since the possibility of moving Virginia from its existing freehold qualification was scarcely considered by the delegates. The big issue was the basis of representation, and here Barbour stood solidly on the principle of responsibility: 'It is the natural desire of all to lay the foundation of this Constitution in such a manner that it shall stand and endure. If that be our purpose we must rest it on these two great columns: persons and property. Withdraw either and you have a weak and tottering edifice. ...'[37] While Philip's older brother James was serving the Adams administration as secretary of war, Philip – despite his explicit commitment to traditionally conservative views on suffrage and representation – helped to build the Jacksonian party in Virginia. The older brother, after surfacing briefly to preside over the Harrison–Tyler nominating convention at Baltimore in 1839, went down to political oblivion. The younger brother became a judge in Virginia and was appointed by President Jackson to the United States Supreme Court.[38]

The careers of many southern political leaders traced similar trajectories. John C. Calhoun, a nationalist in 1812, embraced the central proposals of the National Republican thesis before separation of the ruling class in the South forced him into the state's rights orbit. He then suffered the misfortune of being pushed too fast by the impetuosity of his constituents, and so collided with President Jackson over nullification at the very moment when their respective class positions called for alliance. By 1837, however, when Georgia's war against the Creeks and Cherokees had made nullification successful and respectable – and after Jackson had yielded the presidency to Martin Van Buren – Calhoun brought his South Carolina fire eaters into a working relationship with the Democratic succession. John Tyler, who had been elected to the vice-presidency on the Whig ticket in 1840, was manoeuvering for the Democratic presidential

nomination four years later. Albert Gallatin Brown, governor of Mississippi and United States senator, exemplified what was probably a more
typical two-generation sequence. His father, recently risen to planter
status in the new Southwest, had become a Whig; and Brown's opening
gambit in local politics was a blast at Jackson's removal of deposits from
the Second Bank of the United States as a 'gigantic step toward
DESPOTISM'. But Brown quickly 'threw in his lot with the Democrats,
who were predominant in the more recently developed poorer sections
of southern and eastern Mississippi.'[39]

In the last years of the 1850s an Alabama Whig wrote to the
Washington *National Intelligencer*: 'I cannot overlook the fact that the
South, as the weaker section, cannot afford to divide its strength. It ought
to present an unbroken front. . . An undivided South as the base of a great
Constitutional party, embracing the conservative men of all sections is
what I desire to see. ... What have we got to gain by opposing
Mr. Buchanan's administration, or by weakening the Democratic party?'[40]
What he meant was that southern planters defending the institution of
slavery desperately needed the allegiance of a white South united across
class lines. Judah P. Benjamin, Louisiana's most flamboyant Whig, had
earlier expressed this political need in symbolic action by changing his
party designation in the United States Senate. Son of immigrant Jewish
parents from St. Croix, Benjamin had grown up in South Carolina, briefly
attended Yale, then moved to New Orleans where he became an attorney
and sugar planter and married into the Whig creole aristocracy. In a
speech to the Senate Benjamin set forth the reasons for his Democratic
conversion:

> Property – for a billion dollars cannot purchase at a low average price the
> slaves which now belong to the people of the South.
> Existence – aye, existence itself, because the history of Haiti is written in
> characters so black, so prominent, that we cannot be ignorant of the fate
> which awaits us if measures similar to those that have produced that result
> there are also to be inaugurated in the Southern States.[41]

Capture of the Jacksonian movement in the South by planter leadership was a difficult manoeuver executed with impressive skill and sparkling
class solidarity. It carried enormous consequences for the Democratic
party outside the South. As the southern states became consistently
Democratic, the ability of the party to win presidential elections increased, thus blessing northern and western leaders with accretions of
political power that they could not have achieved on their own. Patronage
and federal appointments ranging from the humble level of customs in-
spectors, navy yard laborers, and postmasters, up through marshalls,
clerks of court, consuls, Indian agents, and supply contractors, and on to

such exalted posts as judges, ministers, cabinet members – even the presidency (reserved, after Zachary Taylor, for northerners willing to follow the mandates of the South) – all now came regularly within the gift of Democratic politicians.

To continue this flow of life-giving manna, northern Democrats realized that they had to support the southern planters in policies they deemed essential to preserve slavery; and to avoid potentially divisive discussions of slavery within the party ranks. Both conditions doubtless at first seemed easy to meet. For the time being no one of much consequence was demanding a debate on slavery. The planters seemed to be making peace with white egalitarians on their own home ground. The southern critique of tariffs, internal improvements and high land prices dovetailed – outside the South – with Jacksonian allegations that monopoly and special privilege permeated the old commercial landlord establishment. Such criticisms brought urban and rural voters to the new mass party. Moreover, Democrats North and South could rejoice together in the most visibly dramatic usage of federal power – national expansion. The disparate coalition that composed the Democracy rode the high tide of manifest destiny.[42]

The Jacksonian Legitimizing Construct

The ideological process in its largest sense creates and recreates consciousness. It pervades human experience and, like consciousness itself, appears as a necessary condition of human existence. But the term *ideology* has customarily been used more narrowly to refer to justifications of particular regimes of class domination. To distinguish this political focus from the broad meaning of ideology (which must be kept within mental reach, especially when the focus is political) I have used the term *legitimizing construct*. A complex modernizing society could be expected to have more than one legitimizing construct within a matrix of shared ideology; and as I suggested earlier in this chapter, any class coalition must generate its own legitimation in order to maintain cohesion sufficient for the exercise of governmental power. The National Republican thesis was such a legitimation. Jacksonians attacked it by offering a competing legitimation. Since their legitimation began as a counterstatement to the National Republican thesis, a convenient starting point from which to trace its construction is egalitarianism.

Jacksonian Democrats asserted the political, civil and moral equality of white male citizens. This did not mean that they advocated equality by act of government, rather that they advocated the equal opportunity of all white male citizens to engage in the pursuit of happiness and to get ahead – not necessarily ahead of their fellow citizens, but ahead of where they had been last year and the year before. In America, presumably, people got ahead by diligence and skill at producing goods and services for which there was a market demand. Disciples of Adam Smith, devotees of the labor theory of value, and Jacksonians all proclaimed free competition among individual producers. This view was incompatible with slavery; yet so long as the immediate political needs of slaveholders, yeoman farmers, urban workingmen and aspirant entrepreneurs ran parallel, the contradiction could be held off by rhetorical skills and selective concessions to other partners in the coalition. Southern Democrats like Virginia's Henry Wise or James Hammond, one of South Carolina's most affluent planters, spoke for manhood suffrage. Hammond and John C. Calhoun expressed solicitude for the welfare of northern workingmen. Walt Whitman, on behalf of Brooklyn Jacksonians, reciprocated. 'We like John C. Calhoun. ... We believe that a higher-souled American patriot never trod on American soil.'[43] Philip Barbour, in his address to the Virginia Constitutional Convention of 1829, stated a belief widely held by Democrats of all regions when he denied that wealth and property, individually owned, in any way restricted opportunity for other members of the society. 'The wheel of fortune never stands still, but is in a perpetual state of revolution. He who was on the summit yesterday may be at the bottom today. ...' In Virginia, Barbour explained, primogeniture and entail had once artificially sustained an aristocracy; but such props were long gone. 'There exists not the slightest danger of a concentration of wealth, in any one portion of our country, or among any particular class of our citizens.'[44]

Jacksonians agreed with Barbour that inequality of wealth was not in itself to be feared. All that was necessary to ensure free competition and open opportunity was that no privileged group gain access to an inside track or be allowed permanent advantage created by government. For that constituted special privilege; and special privilege, the essence of old world aristocracy, had no place in new world democracy. It followed that legal monopolies and corporate charters subverted the republic because they created special privileges. Acts of incorporation by state legislatures, then, must be viewed with suspicion; even worse were enactments by the national Congress; most obnoxious of all the Second Bank of the United States. Thousands of voters supported President Jackson in his campaign to destroy the Bank Monster, not for the most part because they opposed paper currency and credit, but because they believed that the bank had become a vested interest of whiggish aristocracy in eastern cities.[45] Similar arguments shaped Democratic tariff policy. Although party leaders, Andrew Jackson among them, had initially favored protective tariffs in the interest of national self-sufficiency, they later concurred in denouncing them as class legislation designed to benefit a particular interest – manufacturing – at the expense of other interests throughout the nation, especially agriculture. Internal improvements were vulnerable to the same attack. Each could be discredited individually as favorable to an interest or region; collectively they benefitted manufacturing over agriculture, mid-Atlantic and northeastern cities over the hinterland; and virtually every project floated some government-created corporation. If, as Thomas Hart Benton declared, land belonged 'to the people', it would be the duty of true Democrats to resist any effort to reserve the public lands whether for special interest or federal revenue. Thus from its egalitarian rebuttal of the National Republican thesis stemmed the Democracy's rejection of the economic measures projected by that thesis.[46]

Egalitarianism, posed as high principle, requires either a policy of leveling – that is, expropriating wealth to bring all to a common level; or else a denial that differences in wealth carry any invidious significance. Whigs like John Pendleton Kennedy customarily accused their opponents of leveling.[47] In fact, the Jacksonians chose the other alternative. While making no direct effort to eliminate the economic base of class difference, they consistently rejected the concept of class hierarchy as applicable to the American nation. This was in line with their understanding of egalitarianism as equal opportunity; and of course indispensable to a coalition aimed at combining divergent class interests into a single nationwide majority.[48]

Jacksonian legitimation grouped these components under a single head. They were *producers* – 'planters, farmers, mechanics (with a slight infusion from the commercial and professional classes)' – the 'productive and burthen-bearing classes' of the nation.[49] That Senator Thomas Hart Benton, the Missouri agrarian, used *class* in its plural form signals the polemical thrust of his thought. He was refuting class with *classes*. In a society composed of many classes, equally 'productive and burthen-bearing', class was reduced to mere category or division of labor. Producers might be poor and humble, or they might win fame and fortune through their own efforts applied to opportunity, as Benton himself and Andrew Jackson had done. Such achievements, creating the abundance by which the nation lived and prospered, merited the acclaim of fellow-citizens. No matter how great or how modest their success, producers would never lose touch with the soil and the workbench, with the shared life of productive labor from which they came. Far from being a class, they comprised the nation itself, the 'bone and sinew of our country', as President Jackson addressed them.[50]

Even within the producers' nation, however, there resided an enemy that had to be defeated again and again. Not long after the overthrow of the Adams administration, Benton had identified this foe as a 'Federal' party that 'discouraged the settlement of the West by refusing ... to vote for equitable prices for the public lands. ...'[51] *Federal* by this time had become a term of abuse directed by each side against the other. In Whig rhetoric it usually denoted upper-class renegades who betrayed their class origins by serving the Democracy as demagogic leaders. In Democratic rhetoric the term did not so much refer to a native upper class as to an alien element rendered subservient to foreign influence through its own corrupt hankering after aristocratic pretensions. The real nation, the producers, Jackson warned in his farewell address, must stand ever vigilant against the selfish minority that enriched itself, not by producing, but by manipulating money and credit: bankers, monopolists, masters of 'great moneyed corporations'.[52] So successful was the Democratic party in propagating this populist idyll that farmers and workingmen for generations to come would look back on Jacksonian America as a classless society in which the fraternity of citizen producers had directly controlled governmental power.[53]

Just as its economic policies and social theory flowed from the egalitarian premise, so did the Democracy's enthusiasm for territorial acquisition. In a predominantly agricultural society it would appear obvious that equal opportunity for an increasing population must depend on opening new regions to settlement. Each component of the Jacksonian coalition anticipated gains from expansion. For southern planters, these included new cotton lands, perhaps sugar in Cuba and Tamaulipas as well; and the entry of additional slave states to enhance the political power of the South.[54] For yeoman farmers the gains were more and cheaper land for themselves and their children. For aspirant entrepreneurs new territory always seemed the realm of the big chance. Even to workingmen and the middle class of the eastern cities, territorial expansion appeared promising. It is unlikely that many urban artisans expected to stake out homesteads, yet it was not illogical to suppose that open land in the West would reduce competition for jobs in the east and might speed the growth of western industrial centers to which working people could (and did in fact) remove.[55] Major L. Wilson, discussing the concepts of time characteristic of the two parties, has contrasted the Whig ideal of controlled growth through time in a limited space with the Democratic aspiration for spontaneous expansion without geographical limit, carried out in the immediate present.[56] The latter concept is the more charismatic. Here the Jacksonians stood on high ground *vis-à-vis* their Whig opponents whose well-known ambivalence toward expansion seemed to confirm accusations of anti-national tendencies.

Although territorial aggrandizement raised particular class aspirations, the practice of mass politics evoked larger visions of the producers' republic. Democrats successfully appropriated the emblems of nationalism. This crucial achievement resulted largely from the efforts of new professionals, distinct from the older and already abundant professional politicians in that their goal was not merely to win office (although they sometimes did) but to fashion marketable commodities from the raw materials of information and ideas. Outstanding among such intellectual artisans was the historian George Bancroft, himself a party leader in Massachusetts and chief theoretician of the Democracy. In his popular *History*, Bancroft celebrated the yeoman farmers' defiance of British tyranny at Lexington as the fulfillment of a beneficent preparation 'of providence and of time'. 'The light that led them on' had originated from 'Republican Greece and Rome', from Christianity 'as taught by Paul of Tarsus and Augustine, through Calvin and the divines of New England.'

> ... All the centuries bowed themselves from the recesses of the past to cheer in their sacrifice the lowly men who proved themselves worthy of their forerunners, and whose children rise up and call them blessed.[57]

Born too late to stand with the farmers at Lexington, Bancroft was nonetheless able to carry on what he considered their mission by serving simultaneously as secretary of war and of the navy under President Polk. In these offices he detailed arrangements for the seizure of California and the invasion of Mexico.[58]

If the War of 1812 had provided an earlier stimulus to nationalism, it was war against Mexico – and the vast territories thereby laid open to conquest – that brought the sentiment to full maturity. 'We love to indulge in thoughts of the future extent and power of this republic', Walt Whitman, then editor of a Jacksonian party paper in Brooklyn, the *Daily Eagle*, wrote in 1846. ' ... It is for the interest of mankind that its power and territory be extended – the farther the better.'[59] Not long before the Mexican war, Whitman's political colleague, John L. O'Sullivan, editor of the *Democratic Review*, had invented the famous phrase 'Manifest Destiny', which in O'Sullivan's argument conveyed the right 'to possess the whole continent' given by Providence for 'the great experiment of liberty and federated self government entrusted to us.'[60] In the year following the treaty of Guadalupe Hidalgo, Thomas Hart Benton, addressing a national railroad convention at St. Louis, proposed to erect a statue of Columbus at the rail crossing of the Great Divide, with an extended arm pointing to Asia.[61]

This spread-eagle style was well-suited to the rough-and-tumble of mass meetings and conventions. Yet the ideas of Manifest Destiny could also be expressed in the language of transcendental philosophy. Walt Whitman, product of the urban artisan culture of New York, was also a disciple of Ralph Waldo Emerson and was eager to fill the role of American poet that Emerson predicted. In 'Passage to India' – which, although published after the Civil War, originated in the same associations that inspired Benton's vision of Columbus at South Pass – Whitman transformed the Pacific Railroad into a symbol of universal brotherhood:

> Passage to India!
> Lo, soul, seest thou not God's purpose from the first?
> The earth to be spann'd, connected by network,
> The races, neighbors, to marry and be given in marriage,
> The oceans to be cross'd, the distant brought near ...
> (Ah Genoese thy dream! thy dream
> Centuries after thou art laid in thy grave,
> The shore thou foundest verifies thy dream.)[62]

For Whitman, the American nation became the new redeemer. Manifest Destiny, outward bound, passed through conquest and domination to eventual reunion with the universal oversoul. Nationalism was thus operative at several levels. It could justify territorial conquest as readily as inspire the search for national theater or for a distinctively American voice in art and poetry.

A fact sometimes noted, although seldom linked to the power of the Jacksonian party, is that outside New England America's high culture before the Civil War belonged to the Democracy. So of course did American low culture. The middle adhered generally to the Whigs. *Uncle Tom's Cabin* was Whig; *Moby Dick* – and blackface minstrelsy – were Democratic. In the South John Pendleton Kennedy was a Whig, William Gilmore Simms a Democrat. In New York, Greeley was a Whig; so was Lewis Gaylord Clark, editor of New York's arbiter of literary taste, the *Knickerbocker Magazine*. But Washington Irving, James K. Paulding, Cornelius Mathews, Evart Duyckinck, Bryant, Cooper, Melville, and Whitman were Democrats. Even in New England there was George Bancroft, the nation's most famous historian – Harvard graduate, first American to study historical method at a German university, minister to Great Britain by appointment of the grateful President Polk; and Hawthorne, who held a patronage job in the Boston customs house and wrote a campaign biography of his college friend Franklin Pierce in return for the consular post at Liverpool. Poe, vacillating between Baltimore and New York, supped at whosoever table would feed him, but his most enduring political orientation remained, through Duycknick, to the Democracy.[63]

An editor and critic of rising prominence in the early 1840s, Evart Duyckinck drew together a network of Democratic men of letters, based in New York City but with outposts at Charleston, Massachusetts Bay, and the Berkshires. The members of this set called themselves Young

America and exchanged publication and laudatory reviews in magazines they influenced or controlled, borrowed ideas from one another as well as money, and waged war on cultural subservience to England. They hoped to create a national literature that would sink its own uniquely American pipelines to truth. Until about 1847 their chief journal was O'Sullivan's *Democratic Review*, for which Duyckinck sometimes shared editorial responsibility. Whitman – still ten years from his own annunciation as solitary singer in the West – contributed occasional pieces to the *Review* and applauded Young America in the Brooklyn *Eagle*.[64]

Emerson, a Whig, observed that although the Whigs put up the more dependable candidates, Democrats offered the more generous and exciting program. Emerson referred explicitly to the egalitarian premise and opening of opportunities 'for the young and the poor to the sources of wealth and power.'[65] The ideological construct that compelled Emerson's grudging admiration as well as the allegiance of so many of his talented contemporaries made use of white racism to legitimize slavery, territorial expansion at the expense of Mexico and the removal or the extermination of Indians. In the South, Democratic doctrine sustained the planter class in several interrelated ways. It reassured planters themselves that slavery, being neither their fault nor within their power to change, would, so long as it remained in their hands, function as a benignly Christian social system. It neutralized the potential opposition of non-slaveholders by offering equal partnership in the *herrenvolk* democracy, while simultaneously threatening them with the fate of the whites of Santo Domingo should they fail to sustain the hegemony of the planters. Finally, it encircled the slaves by making the ongoingness of their daily lives depend upon perceiving the master's imposed view of their circumstances as divinely ordained in nature. Slavery could hardly have existed in the American South without these three transactions.[66]

Racism in the South, as throughout the nation, showed both hard and soft sides. At first these corresponded directly to class and party separation: planters soft, yeomen hard; Whigs soft, Democrats hard. Planters favored controlled nurture; like James Barbour they were apt to practice diversified training, incentives and rewards.[67] Yeomen (together with white workingmen in the South) were more likely to speak for segregation, denial of training, exclusion from labor markets, deportation; ultimately for extermination, if that could be brought about by natural means.[68] Pierre van den Berghe, the sociologist from whom I borrow the term *herrenvolk democracy*,[69] has described these two tendencies as paternalist and competitionist. In his comparative study of racism, he associated the first with plantation societies, classically exemplified by the West Indian sugar islands in which European masters, always a small minority, lived in close proximity with African slaves, yet separated from them by a vast social distance. The second he linked to settler societies such as South Africa, where dominant and subordinate races, relatively equal in numbers and at no great social distance, live in physically segregated communities.[70] In the American South, these tendencies coexisted, one prevalent in the Black Belt, the other in the hills and hinterland.

Out of these paired characteristics arose one other crucial set. The soft side, appropriately to paternalism, envisioned the object of racism as a child. John Pendleton Kennedy's slave children at Swallow Barn precisely convey the image: little bright-eyed animals, comic, sometimes lovable, always troublesome; yet less than human because incapable of maturing beyond the mental and moral limits of childishness.[71] For the hard side, by contrast, childishness was mere camouflage hypocritically connived at by slaveowners themselves. The real African was grimly adult: a sexual colossus, a Dominican ravisher, worse than savage because clothed in the false garb of civilization.[72] The two images counseled opposite modes of treatment – good-natured manipulation, on the one hand, suppression and terror, on the other.

In the South the images of slaves and the modes of treating them tended to merge, because the plantation, as a labor system, required both. The planter could laugh at – or even with – and manipulate his slaves so long as the overseer (likely to be of yeoman origin) wielded the whip. More important, they merged because the paternalist and competitionist societies coexisted. Planters' sons rode out with yeoman farmers in the security patrols. When political parties divided on class lines, planters found themselves in an untenable position since they could not exclude yeomen from political activity. Planters, once they turned Democrats, adopted the hard side as part of their egalitarian rhetoric; but egalitarianism could be relevant only to the external relations of their class. In domestic affairs – in justifying class dominance to themselves, and at home with their families and slaves – the soft side remained indispensable. As the South moved from two-party competition to one-party solidarity, the hard and soft sides of racism became optional styles of speech, each appropriate to certain situations or audiences.

Convergence of the two sides rested ultimately on the oneness of racist doctrine. This is not to say that racism was unified in an intellectual sense. It always included multiple, contradictory ingredients drawn from religion, history, science and pseudoscience, medical practice and malpractice, as well as from the beginnings of anthropology and sociology. To recapitulate the origins and inner tensions of this melange would be redundant since the task has been fully dealt with in one of the more satisfactory areas of the history of slavery and the South.[73] The point is that despite its intellectual diversity, racist doctrine remained unified as an ideological construct brought into existence through a particular sequence of historical circumstances.[74] The hard and soft sides were mutually reinforcing. Together they presented themselves, ready for uses old and new, to successive generations of slaveowners and non-slaveowners, planters and yeomen, Whigs, Jacksonians – and Southern Democrats.

Moreover, in the arena of mass politics, racist doctrine acquired that pragmatic, anti-intellectual unity characteristic of the legal brief. Logically incompatible arguments offer alternate routes by which divided juries (or voters) may arrive at common verdicts. Whether believers in the curse of Ham ought to reconcile their differences with environmentalists, or orthodox Christians share the Lord's Supper with separate creationists, were issues of relatively small concern, for example, to Virginia legislators confronting the aftermath of Nat Turner's rebellion. More immediate verdicts took precedence. In 1831 and 1832, non-slaveholding Virginians, mainly from western counties, argued publicly for the last time in the South for a plan of gradual emancipation. They lost.[75] After the Virginia constitutional debates the South moved from its traditionally Jeffersonian apology for slavery as a burden imposed by history to an aggressive assertion that slavery not only worked to the advantage of the South, but was the best possible system man could devise.[76] ' ... [T]he greatest strength of the South arises from the harmony of her political and social institutions', James Hammond of South Carolina explained to the United States Senate in his 'mudsill' speech in 1858:

> In all social systems there must be a class to do the menial duties ... or you would not have that other class which leads progress, civilization and refinement. It constitutes the very mud-sill of society and political government ... Fortunately for the South, she found a race adapted to that purpose. ... We do not think that whites should be slaves either by law or necessity. Our slaves are black, of another and inferior race. ... Yours are white, of your own race. ... They are your equals in natural endowment of intellect, and they feel galled by their degradation. ... If they knew the tremendous secret, that the ballot box is stronger than 'an army with banners', and could combine, where would you be?[77]

Hammond's statement was in part directed to allies and potential allies in the North and West. Its effectiveness depended on their understanding of the racist component of his argument. Southern Democrats like Hammond knew that white racism was not a local product that had to be exported. As part of the common heritage of the Anglo-American society, it served to explain and justify the populist nationalism brought forward in egalitarian and expansionist rhetoric. Tactical applications of racism, however, differed in the North and West from those of the South. Southern planters who might still need the paternalistic metaphor at home had shuffled off earlier linkages to the Whig party nationally and sought instead to cement their alliance with the Jacksonian coalition. Consequently the initial thrust was on the hard side of racism. At the cutting edge were northern and western party leaders whose political careers depended upon the southern connection. What they perceived as a main danger to their expectations came not from traditional Whig projects like internal improvements and protective tariffs, but from anti-slavery agitation emanating in part (but by no means entirely) from whiggish sources.

Their response was to identify all anti-slavery agitation with special interest, especially that of manufacturing capital; and to use racist invective to discredit the sincerity, patriotism, even sanity, of anti-slavery advocates. This was the hard side at its hardest. It reinforced the already widespread conviction that Whig softness on racial questions cloaked an intent to use Africans and Indians to undermine the status of white producers. In the countryside, especially in the West, this led to denunciations of sentimentally romantic pampering of Indians;[78] in cities it intensified fears that Africans, freed from slavery, might undercut the wages and living conditions of white workingmen.[79]

James K. Paulding provided what may be regarded as an official statement of the northern Democratic position on slavery and anti-slavery. A friend and collaborator of Washington Irving, Paulding figured prominently in New York literary circles from the War of 1812 to the war against Mexico. His brother-in-law – Washington Irving's older brother William – was a New York congressman, and his own older brother served as Tammany mayor of the city. Paulding himself, after accepting appointment in 1815 as secretary of the Board of Navy Commissioners, occupied civilian posts in the Navy Department continuously until his retirement from public service in 1841.[80] He published *Slavery* to aid Martin Van Buren's 1836 presidential campaign, his reward being the secretaryship of the Navy, which he held till the end of Van Buren's administration.[81] Paulding recapitulated the southern defense of slavery, adapting it to what he considered the sensibilities of northern readers. He separated himself from the extreme 'positive' defense by conceding that if slavery were to be established *de novo* he would not favor it; but as it presently existed in the United States he found it by no means 'of such surpassing enormity as to demand the sacrifice of the harmony and consequent union of the states.'[82] On the contrary, so valuable was the Union in itself and to human progress 'that no beneficial consequences to any class of mankind or to the whole universe' could 'counterbalance' the evil that must result from its 'dissolution.'[83]

'The government of the United States, its institutions and its privileges', Paulding wrote, 'belong of right wholly and exclusively to white men; for they were purchased, not by the blood of the negroes, but by that of our fathers.'[84] Africans, like Indians, had showed themselves incapable either of participating in, or standing against, the white republic. Failure of the 'late insurrection in Lower Virginia', and its inevitable outcome in a 'most terrible retribution' demonstrated this truth.[85] Even were they given their freedom they could never provide for themselves. 'The mind of the African, not only in his native country, but through every change, and in all circumstances, seems in a great degree divested of this divine attribute of improvement.'[86] To educate and impart aspiration to those too dull to pursue it was like giving the curse of Tantalus.[87] Yet, if simply left as they were they would remain happy and well cared for, 'never beset by the gnawing cares of the free white man, whose whole life is one continued effort to provide for himself and his children.'[88] How could any right-minded person advocate uprooting these limited and dependent creatures by freeing them? The answer was that none could. Opponents of slavery then must be either enemies of the nation or mentally ill. For Paulding the bottom line of anti-slavery was miscegenation. 'The project for intermarrying with blacks is a project for debasing the whites by a mixture of that blood, which, wherever it flows, carries with it the seeds of deterioration ... a scheme for lowering the standard of our nature by approximating the highest grade of human being to the lowest. ... They are traitors to the white skin, influenced by madbrained fanaticism, or the victims of licentious and ungovernable passions, perverted into an unnatural taste by their own indulgence.'[89]

Paulding, who had earlier specialized in patriotic excoriations of Britain, incorporated into his treatise on slavery messages to Irish Catholic voters. England, he reminded them, had imposed slavery on America;[90] but now, motivated by aristocratic hatred for the American republic, deliberately incited abolitionists.[91] Slaves in the South actually were better off than most Irish under English law in Ireland.[92] Calling attention to the prominence of women in anti-slavery agitation, he inquired if the Virgin Mary had acted in such ways. 'Still less did we ever hear of her contributing her money and her influence in furtherance of a conspiracy to debase the race to which she belonged, and to scatter the land of her birth into contending fragments.'[93]

Tapping the subtreasury of American racism, Paulding had put together formulations appropriate to a particular constituency. Other Democratic politicians did likewise. Thomas Hart Benton warned Missouri voters in 1829 against the machinations of those who opposed cheap lands in the West, charging that this 'Federal' party 'in every question between the white people and the negroes or Indians, regularly, officially, impertinently and wickedly takes part with the Indians and negroes against their white fellow citizens and fellow Christians ...' All such actions tended 'to one point ... the abolition of slavery, under the clause of the Declaration of Independence which asserts the natural equality of man.'[94]

'What good man', President Jackson asked the Congress in 1830, 'would prefer a country covered with forests and ranged by a few thousand savages, to our extensive Republic, studded with towns and prosperous farms ... and filled with all the blessings of liberty, civilization and religion?'[95] Questions such as these with their liturgical responses could be expanded to meet new circumstances. 'Massive, yet most sweet and plain character!' Walt Whitman lamented on the first anniversary of President Jackson's death. ' ... Ah, there has lived among us but *one* purer!' Soon afterwards, in sharp contrast to the notion later expressed in 'Passage to India' of races marrying and being given in marriage, Whitman demanded of his Brooklyn *Eagle* readers: 'What has miserable, inefficient Mexico to do with the mission of peopling the New World with a noble race? ... Be it ours to achieve that mission.'[96]

In the two questions from Jackson and Whitman the racist component turns solely against Indians (or Indian-ness as embodied in Mexicans). This reflected the events of the 1830s and 1840s. Indian removal and westward expansion had proved spectacularly successful. Political opposition dwindled to spotty and opportunist criticisms.[97] As John Quincy Adams had foreseen, there could be no effective resistance to the Democracy on the question of expansion because a majority of Americans, Whigs included, agreed with what was being done.[98] The expansionist consensus merged the hard and soft sides of anti-Indian racism by incorporating expressions of regret over the fate of Indians into narratives that traced the inevitability of their extinction.[99] Ideologically, the effect was to exonerate individuals, parties, nations, of any moral blame for what history had decreed. The American Indian myth, marrying the soft and hard, the Whig and Democratic, owes its most enduring incarnation to James Fenimore Cooper, an enigmatic Jacksonian whose work will be discussed in a later chapter on western fictional heroes. What must be noted here is that the merger of the hard and soft sides of racism with respect to Indians paralleled the merger of the two sides with respect to blacks. Yet these parallel sequences diverged in their political consequences, since one tended to eliminate differences between the existing major parties, while the other created a new polarity that cut across both parties.

Fully as successful as Jacksonian Indian policy – at first – was the planter alliance with northern urban Democracy. More than any other factor, this alliance perpetuated Democratic dominance in the party system. But victories, in this case, opened the way for coming defeats. Farmers, frontiersmen, urban workers and the middle class had readily accepted the racist legitimation of slavery; and they accepted also the argument that plantation slavery provided the only sure means for quarantining Africans in America. What these acceptances led to, however, was a conclusion that the entry of Africans, slave or free, into the promised land of the West had to be prevented. 'I plead the rights of white labor', David Wilmot, a Democrat from Pennsylvania, explained as he introduced the proviso that triggered the crises of the 1850s. 'I would preserve to free white labor a fair country, a rich inheritance, where the sons of toil of my own race and color can live without the disgrace which association with negro slavery brings upon free labor.'[100] So vociferously did Walt Whitman endorse Wilmot's proviso that he was dismissed from the editorship of the Brooklyn *Eagle* by owners who clung to the traditional Democratic line of backing the South on slavery in the territories. Whitman continued to write occasional editorials for the *Eagle*; for example, in 1858 he celebrated Oregon's new state constitution because it excluded blacks:

> We shouldn't wonder if this sort of total prohibition of colored persons became quite a common thing in new Western, Northwestern, and even Southwestern States. If so, the whole matter of slavery agitation will assume another phase, different from any phase as yet. It will be a conflict between the totality of White Labor, on the one side, and on the other, the interference and competition of Black Labor, or of bringing in colored persons on *any* terms. Who believes that Whites and Blacks can ever amalgamate in America? Or who wishes it to happen? Nature has set an impassable seal against it. Besides, is not America for the Whites? And is it not better so?[101]

Thus the legitimizing construct pressed into service to hold together the Jacksonian coalition in the 1830s and early 1840s ended by legitimizing the defection of its northern and western constituencies.[102] Thomas Hart Benton – prince of expansionists, egalitarian defender of squatters' rights, indefatigable racist – became, appropriately, father-in-law to the first Republican candidate for president. And to the second, Abraham Lincoln, Walt Whitman transferred the emblems of transcendental nationalism ('O powerful western fallen star ... O thoughts of him I love'), previously the endowment of Andrew Jackson.[103]

Notes

1. See Chapter 2, pp. 59–60.
2. Chilton Williamson, *American Suffrage: From Property to Democracy, 1760–1860*, Princeton, N.J. 1960, especially pp. 76–78; Gary Nash, *The Urban Crucible: Social Change, Political Consciousness and the Origins of the American Revolution*, Cambridge, Mass. 1979, especially pp. *vii–xiii* and 339–84. See also Alfred Young, ed., *The American Revolution: Explorations in the History of American Radicalism*, DeKalb, Ill. 1976. I am indebted to my colleague Joyce Appleby for her lucid account of the growth of the American market economy in response to the burgeoning 'Atlantic trade world that linked the littorals of four con-

tinents.' I agree with her argument that such expansion furnished the economic dynamic for the overthrow of the politics of deference in the United States. We would be in some disagreement, however, as to the dating and immediate cause of that overthrow. Appleby, 'Capitalism and Democracy in Revolutionary America', paper presented at the 1990 Colloquium Series of the Center for Social Theory and Comparative History, UCLA.

3.   Richard Hofstadter, *The Idea of a Party System: The Rise of Legitimate Opposition in the United States, 1780–1840*, Berkeley, Calif. 1969; Richard P. McCormick, *The Second American Party System: Party Formation in the Jacksonian Era*, Chapel Hill, N.C. 1966, p. 20; Ronald P. Formisano, *The Transformation of Political Culture: Massachusetts Parties, 1790s–1840s*, New York 1983, pp. 84–127; Joel Silbey, *The Transformation of American Politics, 1840–1860*, Englewood Cliffs, N.J. 1967.

4.   Morton Borden, *Parties and Politics in the Early Republic, 1789–1815*, New York 1967; William Nisbet Chambers, *Political Parties in a New Nation: The American Experience, 1776–1809*, New York 1963; McCormick, *Second American Party System*. A useful collection of essays by historians and political scientists is William Nisbet Chambers and Walter Dean Burnham, eds, *The American Party Systems: Stages of Political Development*, New York 1967. As to whether the parties of the Jeffersonian period can properly be considered parties, see Chambers, 'Party Development and the American Mainstream', in Chambers and Burnham, eds, *Party Systems*, pp. 4–5, and Ronald P. Formisano, *The Birth of Mass Political Parties: Michigan, 1827–1861*, Princeton 1971, pp. 21–22; Formisano, *Transformation*, pp. 3–54.

5.   McCormick, *Second American Party System*, pp. 4, 14; Theodore Lowi, 'Party, Policy and Constitution in America', in Chambers and Burnham, eds, *Party Systems*, p. 256; David Feller, *The Public Lands in Jacksonian Politics*, Madison, Wis. 1984, pp. 176–77. McCormick, *Second American Party System*, pp. 4–15, 26, 294, and in his essay, 'Political Development and the Second Party System', in Chambers and Burnham, eds, *Party Systems*, pp. 94–97, 99, 111, emphasizes the role of presidential elections in party formation. So do William Nisbet Chambers, 'Party Development and the American Mainstream', and Walter Dean Burnham, 'Party Systems and the Political Process', in Chambers and Burnham, eds, *Party Systems*, pp. 11, 29–30, and 287–89.

6.   Chambers, 'Party Development' and Burnham, 'Party Systems', in Chambers and Burnham, eds, *Party Systems*, pp. 29–30, 287–89; Richard L. McCormick, *The Party Period and Public Policy: American Politics from the Age of Jackson to the Progressive Era*, New York 1986, pp. 3–140; Walter Dean Burnham, *Critical Elections and the Mainsprings of American Politics*, New York 1970, pp. 1–33; V.O. Key, Jr., 'A Theory of Critical Elections', *Journal of Politics* 18:3–18; Samuel Lubell, *The Future of American Politics*, New York 1952, pp. 210–18; Charles G. Sellers, 'The Equilibrium Cycle in Two-Party Politics', *Public Opinion Quarterly* 29 (1965). And see also Robert Kelly, *The Cultural Pattern in American Politics: The First Century*, Washington, D.C. 1979, pp. 18–19.

7.   Burnham, 'Party Systems', in Chambers and Burnham, eds, *Party Systems*, p. 292; U.S. Bureau of the Census, *Historical Statistics of the United States from Colonial Times to 1957*, Washington, D.C. 1960, p. 691; Leon Friedman and Fred L. Israel, eds, *The Justices of the United States Supreme Court, 1789–1969: Their Lives and Major Opinions*, New York 1969, vol. 4: Appendix, Chart 1; Alfred H. Kelly and Winfred Harbison, *The American Constitution: Its Origins and Development*, New York 1970, end charts.

8.   Chambers, 'Party Development', Chambers and Burnham, eds., *Party Systems*, pp. 3, 31–32.

9.   For an assertion of the significance of ideology in American party structure, Samuel P. Hays, 'Political Parties and the Community–Society Continuum', in Chambers and Burnham, eds, *Party Systems*, p. 161. Theodore Lowi, 'Party Policy and Constitution', in Chambers and Burnham, eds, *Party Systems*, p. 263, although insisting that major parties in America were not policy oriented, concedes that in a cumulative, or averaging sense, they constructed distinctive images 'on a base line of ideology, or at least traditional tendencies, supported by perceptible difference of leadership.' Eric Foner, *Politics and Ideology in the Age of the Civil War*, New York 1980, especially pp. 34–53.

10.   See, for example, McCormick, 'Political Development', in Chambers and Burnham, eds, *Party Systems*, p. 93. For a criticism of functionalist terminology and concepts in political science, see Frank J. Sorauf, 'Political Parties and Political Analysis', in Chambers and Burnham, pp. 49–52; Lowi, 'Party Policy', pp. 238–76. See also Lowi, 'Toward

Functionalism in Political Science: The Case of Innovation in Party Systems', *American Political Science Review* 57:570–83. Richard D. Brown, *Modernization: The Transformation of American Life, 1600–1865*, New York 1976, is a thoughtful, and especially in the 'Epilogue', pp. 187–201, sensitive – but, I think, unsuccessful – effort to impart some sort of explanatory cogency to the concept of modernization.

11. Joel H. Silbey, ed., *Political Ideology and Voting Behavior in the Age of Jackson*, Englewood Cliffs, N.J. 1973, pp. 9, 180. A classic statement of the case – in my opinion *over*stated by Silbey – is Lee Benson, 'Research Problems in American Political Historiography', Mirra Komarovsky, ed., *Common Frontiers of the Social Sciences*, New York 1957, pp. 123–55, 182–83, reprinted in Silbey, pp. 70–101. Benson, *The Concept of Jacksonian Democracy: New York as a Test Case*, New York 1966. It is scarcely necessary, in 1989, to engage in any extensive review of the ethnoculturalists. Their substantial contributions as well as their misperceptions are now clearly visible. For a balanced critique, Richard L. McCormick, *The Party Period*, pp. 3–25, 30–63. See Ronald P. Formisano, 'Towards a Reorientation of Jacksonian Politics: A Review of the Literature, 1959–1975', *Journal of American History*, 43 (June 1976): 42–65, especially p. 62. For Jean H. Baker in a more recent study – *Affairs of Party: The Political Culture of the Northern Democrats in the Mid-Nineteenth Century*, Ithaca, N.Y. 1983, pp. 27–176, especially 143–48 – 'political culture' is a realm totally separate from class identification. John Ashworth, by contrast, develops a persuasive argument for class as the dynamic of Jacksonian politics: *Agrarians and Aristocrats: Party Political Ideology in the United States, 1837–1846*, London 1983, pp. 177–223. See also Amy Bridges, *A City in the Republic: Antebellum New York and the Origins of Machine Politics*, New York 1984, especially pp. 61–70.

12. John R. Commons et al., *History of Labor in the United States*, New York 1921–35, 1:153–84, 335–56; George Rogers Taylor, *The Transportation Revolution, 1815–1860*, New York 1968, especially pp. 3–14, 207–300; Howard B. Rock, *Artisans of the New Republic: The Tradesmen of New York City in the Age of Jefferson*, New York 1984, esp. pp. 237–326.

13. Commons et al., *History*, 1:231–332; Walter Hugins, *Jacksonian Democracy and the Working Class*, Stanford, Calif. 1960; Sean Wilentz, *Chants Democratic: New York City and the Rise of the American Working Class, 1788–1850*, New York 1984, pp. 172–216.

14. Wilentz, pp. 326–59; Edward Pessen, *Most Uncommon Jacksonians: The Radical Leaders of the Early Labor Movement*, Albany, N.Y. 1967, pp. 3–65; Arthur M. Schlesinger, Jr., *The Age of Jackson*, Boston 1945, pp. 180–85. For a bibliography of workingmen's parties, Pessen, p. 9n; and Wilentz, pp. 172–73n. Eric Foner, *Tom Paine and Revolutionary America*, New York, pp. 264–68. William R. Waterman, *Frances Wright*, New York 1924, pp. 142–45, 176–208. A recent and perceptive biography is Celia Morris Eckhardt, *Fanny Wright: Rebel in America*, Cambridge. Mass. 1984; Helene Zahler, *Eastern Workingmen and National Land Policy*, New York 1941.

15. Benson, *Concept of Jacksonian Democracy*, especially pp. 142–50, 165–76, 179–80. Benson rejects the notion that class or economic interest group has much direct bearing on political behavior, pp. 146, 165. But he is ambiguous on this point. Thus he leaves open a backdoor with respect to New York City's working class by which it is possible to arrive at something resembling a class or economic interest group explanation by a different route – that is, that non-British immigrants, especially Irish Catholics and other Catholics, tended to be Democratic in politics. Of course they also tended to be lower-class in economic status. See also Dixon Ryan Fox, 'The Negro Vote in Old New York', *Political Science Quarterly* 32 (1917): 263–75; Formisano, *The Transformation*, pp. 222–44; Formisano, *Mass Political Parties*, especially pp. 46, 160, 341–43; Michael F. Holt, *The Political Crisis of the 1850s*, New York 1978, pp. 17–38, especially p. 33. Hugins, p. 20, quotes George Henry Evans, one of the founders of the New York Workingmen's party, that workingmen preserved 'a lurking kindness' for the Democracy 'because Jefferson first founded it.' Dixon Ryan Fox, *The Decline of Aristocracy in the Politics of New York*, [1919] New York 1965, pp. 352–62, 381–401. One of the merits of Schlesinger's *Age of Jackson* is that it stresses the importance of the urban working class to the Democratic party: see especially pp. 176–85. Edward Pessen, *Riches, Class and Power Before the Civil War*, Lexington, Mass. 1973, p. 227 wrote: ' ... the urban rich were almost invariably Whigs.' Frank Otto Gattell, 'Money and Power in Jacksonian America: A Quantitative Look at New York City's Men of Quality', *Political Science Quarterly* 81 (June 1967): 235–52.; Kelly, *Cultural Pattern*, pp. 153, 163; and

Michael F. Holt, 'The Democratic Party, 1828–1860', in Arthur M. Schlesinger, Jr., ed., *History of United States Political Parties*, New York 1973, 1:510–14; Bridges, *A City in the Republic*, pp. 98–102.

16. Memo for an essay on the 'Genius of Locofocoism' in Notebooks, vol. 5, 'An Unfinished Chapter of Autobiography', p. 17, John Pendleton Kennedy Papers. Ralph Waldo Emerson, *Journals*, 9 October 1838, in Stephen E. Whicher, ed., *Selections*, Boston 1960, p. 92.

17. Dorothy Burne Goebel, *William Henry Harrison: A Political Biography*, Indianapolis, Ind. 1926, pp. 57–58, 224, 238. See also Chapter 3, 105–9. Stephen B. Oates, *To Purge This Land with Blood: A Biography of John Brown*, New York 1970, pp. 11–71. On yeoman farmers as land speculators, Feller, *Public Lands*, pp. 29–31, 195–97.

18. William Nisbet Chambers, *Old Bullion Benton, Senator from the New West*, Boston 1956; Eric L. McKitrick, *Andrew Johnson and Reconstruction*, Chicago 1960, pp. 85–92. States moving into 'Old West' economies during the period of party formation were Ohio, Indiana, Kentucky and Tennessee. The operative distinction was that they tended to lose population when new, or cheaper, lands opened to the west: Feller, *Public Lands*, pp. 58, 79, 146–148. And see Harry L. Watson, *Jacksonian Politics and Community Conflict: The Emergence of the Second Party System in Cumberland County, North Carolina*, Baton Rouge, La. 1981, pp. 13–14, 126–50.

19. Charles Francis Adams, *Three Episodes of Massachusetts History*, Boston 1903, 2:926–53; Quotations 947, 948.

20. Ibid., p. 49.

21. In five presidential elections, 1840–1856, Alabama, Arkansas, Illinois and Mississippi turned in Democratic popular majorities each time; Indiana four times, and Michigan and Georgia three. In all cases there were substantial votes for the losing parties. U.S. Bureau of the Census, *Historical Statistics of the United States: Colonial Times to 1957*, Washington, D.C. 1960, p. 689.

22. On Crockett, see Chapter 3, pp. 78–84.

23. Bray Hammond, *Banks and Politics in America from the Revolution to the Civil War*, Princeton, N.J. 1957, p. 349.

24. Hammond, pp. 329–46.

25. Charles H. Bonner, *John Pendleton Kennedy: Gentleman from Baltimore*, Baltimore 1961, pp. 119–20; John Pendleton Kennedy Papers, Journal 1829–1839, 10, 21 December 1833, and 5 March and 23 April 1834.

26. Kenneth Stampp, *The Peculiar Institution: Slavery in the Ante-Bellum South*, New York 1956, pp. 30–38.

27. William W. Freehling, *Prelude to Civil War: The Nullification Controversy in South Carolina, 1816–1836*, New York 1965, pp. 207–10; Holt, 'Democratic Party', in Schlesinger, ed., 499–500. Feller, *Public Lands*, p. 34.

28. *Historical Statistics*, p. 693; Douglass North, *The Economic Growth of the United States, 1790–1860*, New York 1966, pp. 66–72, 122–34; Stampp, *Peculiar Institution*, p. 31–33.

29. Williamson, Virginia, pp. 225, 233–34, 239–41; Mississippi, p. 264; North Carolina, pp. 234–35, 238–39; Louisiana, pp. 104–5.

30. Ibid., p. 239.

31. Ibid., p. 240.

32. In Louisiana, for example, a Whig-controlled constitutional convention in 1852 mandated total population as the basis of representation in the state legislature: Roger W. Shugg, *Origins of Class Struggle in Louisiana*, Baton Rouge, La. 1939, 136–39. See also Shugg, 'Suffrage and Representation in Ante-Bellum Louisiana', *Louisiana Historical Quarterly* 19 (April 1936): 393–99.

33. Goebel, *Harrison*, p. 365; *Historical Statistics*, p. 685.

34. Paul Murray, *The Whig Party in Georgia, 1825–1848*, Chapel Hill, N.C. 1948, pp. 109–30. The demolition wrought in the Whig party by the Texas question and the Mexican War is traced in detail in Richard W. Sadler, 'The Impact of the Slavery Question on the Whig Party in Congress, 1843–1854', University of Utah, Ph.D. diss.; Ann Arbor, Mich.: University Microfilms, 1969, pp. 11–72. On graduation, see Feller, *Public Lands*, pp. 68, 77–78.

35. 'Missouri Compromise Letters to James Barbour, Senator of Virginia in the Con-

gress of the United States', *William and Mary Quarterly Historical Magazine* 10 (1902): 5–24; Charles D. Lowery, 'James Barbour, A Politician and Planter of Ante-Bellum Virginia', Ph.D. diss., University of Virginia, 1966, pp. 198–246; P.P. Cynn, 'Philip Pendleton Barbour', *The John P. Branch Historical Papers of Randolph–Macon College* 4 (June 1913): 66–77; William Faux, *Memorable Days in America, Being a Journal of a Tour to the United States*, London 1823, pp. 367–74.

36. *Sketches and Eccentricities of Colonel David Crockett, of West Tennessee*, New York 1833, p. 118.

37. *Proceedings and Debates of the Virginia State Convention of 1829–1830. To Which Are Subjoined the New Constitution of Virginia and the Votes of the People*, Richmond, Va. 1830, pp. 91, 98.

38. Cynn, *Branch Historical Papers, 1913*, pp. 67–77.

39. Margaret L. Coit, *John C. Calhoun, American Portrait*, Boston 1950, pp. 329–33; Robert Seager, II, *And Tyler Too: A Biography of John and Julia Gardiner Tyler*, New York 1963, pp. 162–63, 226–28, 394, 401–5; Gallatin, *Mississippian*, 28 March 1834, quoted in James Byrne Ranck, *Albert Gallatin Brown: Radical Southern Nationalist*, New York 1937, p. 4; Ranck, pp. 2–4. And see Arthur C. Cole, *The Whig Party in the South*, [1914] Gloucester, Mass. 1962.

40. Henry W. Hilliard, Whig congressman from Alabama, in *National Intelligencer*, 6 June 1857, as quoted in Cole, p. 327.

41. Pierce Butler, *Judah P. Benjamin*, Philadelphia 1907, p. 151; Eli N. Evans, *Judah P. Benjamin: The Jewish Confederate*, New York 1988, pp. 87–88; Robert Douthat Meade, *Judah P. Benjamin, Confederate Statesman*, New York 1943, pp. 95–96, 100, 103; Louis Gruss, 'Judah P. Benjamin', *Louisiana Historical Quarterly* 19 (October 1936): 964–1068.

42. Albert K. Weinberg, *Manifest Destiny: A Study of Nationalist Expansionism in American History*, Chicago 1963, especially pp. 130–90. Holt, 'Democratic Party', in Schlesinger, ed., pp. 500–502, 507; Feller, *Public Lands*, pp. 58–59, 68, 74–78.

43. Williamson, pp. 157, 239–40; Roy F. Nichols, *The Disruption of American Democracy*, New York 1948, p. 206; Eric Foner, *Politics and Ideology*, p. 57; Coit, *Calhoun*, pp. 301–3; Brooklyn *Daily Eagle*, 14 May 1846, quoted in Lorenzo D. Turner, 'Walt Whitman and the Negro', *The Chicago Jewish Forum* 15 (Fall 1956): 8.

44. *Virginia Convention, 1829–1830*, p. 97.

45. See, for example, 'The Division of Parties', New York *Evening Post*, 4 November 1834, reprinted in Silbey, ed., *Political Ideology*, pp. 81–21.

46. Freehling, *Prelude*, pp. 86–133; Holt, 'Democratic Party', in Schlesinger, ed., p. 512. Benton quoted in Feller, *Public Lands*, p. 75; see also pp. 68, 77–78, 107–8, 111, 158–59. 'Introduction', *United States Magazine and Democratic Review*, ser. 1, no. 1. (October 1837): 1–15, in Joseph L. Blau, ed., *Social Theories of Jacksonian Democracy*, Indianapolis, Ind. 1954, pp. 21–37.

47. As for example, John Pendleton Kennedy, *Quodlibet: Containing Some Annals Thereof*, ..., Philadelphia 1840, especially p. 129.

48. Jackson, 'Farewell Address', 1837, in Blau, ed., pp. 5, 6, 16.

49. Thomas Hart Benton to officers of a Democratic nominating convention in Mississippi, 1835, in Chambers, pp. 204–5.

50. Jackson, in Blau, ed., p. 17.

51. Benton, Letters signed 'La Salle', St. Louis *Beacon*, 17 October and 11 November 1829, quoted in Chambers, p. 159.

52. Jackson, in Blau, ed., p. 17.

53. See, for example, 'The Farmers' Declaration of Independence', Fred A. Shannon, ed., *American Farmers' Movements*, Princeton, N.J. 1957, pp. 136–41. Henry George exemplified this nostalgic radicalism: Saxton, *The Indispensable Enemy: Labor and the Anti-Chinese Movement in California*, Berkeley, Calif. 1971, pp. 92–103.

54. Eugene Genovese, *The Political Economy of Slavery: Studies in the Economy and Society of the Slave South*, New York 1967, pp. 243–74; Nichols, pp. 66, 231–33.

55. Zahler, *Eastern Workingmen*; Address of John Commerford to the General Trades Union, *Workingmen's Advocate*, 19 September 1835, quoted in Walter Hugins, *Jacksonian Democracy and the Working Class*, Stanford, Calif. 1960, pp. 73–74; Philip S. Foner, *History of the Labor Movement in the United States*, New York 1947, 1980, 1:187–88, 538n.

56. Major L. Wilson, 'The Concept of Time and the Political Dialogue in the United States, 1828–1848', *American Quarterly* 19 (Winter 1967): 619–44.

57. George Bancroft, *History of the United States of America, from the Discovery of the Continent*, Boston 1876, 4:521–22.

58. Russel B. Nye, *George Bancroft, Brahmin Rebel*, New York 1944, pp. 135–59; Baker, pp. 120–21; William L. Van de Burg, *Slavery and Race in American Popular Culture*, Madison, Wis. 1984, pp. 26–31; Glen W. Price, *Origins of the War with Mexico: The Polk–Stockton Intrigue*, Austin, Tex. 1967.

59. Walt Whitman, Brooklyn *Daily Eagle*, 2 December 1847, in Cleveland Rogers and John Black, eds, *The Gathering of the Forces*, New York 1920, 1:265–66.

60. John O'Sullivan, *Democratic Review*, July 1845, quoted in Weinberg, *Manifest Destiny*, p. 145.

61. Chambers, p. 353.

62. Walt Whitman, 'Passage to India'.

63. Bohner, *Kennedy*; Jon L. Wakelyn, *The Politics of a Literary Man: William Gilmore Simms*, Westport, Conn. 1973, pp. 23–30; Glyndon G. Van Deusen, *Horace Greeley: Nineteenth–Century Crusader*, New York 1964, p. 30 and *passim*; on Paulding, see below, pp. 151–52. Stanley T. Williams, *The Life of Washington Irving*, New York 1935, 2:36, 64–71, 190–93; Nye, *Bancroft*, pp. 121–22; James D. Hart, ed., *Oxford Companion to American Literature*, 4th ed. New York 1965, pp. 357–58; James Grossman, *James Fenimore Cooper: A Biographical and Critical Study*, Stanford, Calif. 1967, pp. 63–64, 92–95, 111–14, 139; Leon Howard, *Herman Melville*, Berkeley, Calif. 1951, pp. 89–97, 107, 122–24, 230–36; William Cullen Bryant, 'A Brief History of the *Evening Post*: The First Half Century', *The New York Evening Post One Hundredth Anniversary*, New York 1902, pp. 9–35; Justin Kaplan, *Walt Whitman: A Life*, New York 1980; Perry Miller, *The Raven and the Whale: The War of Words and Wits in the Era of Poe and Melville*, New York 1956: on Poe and Duyckinck, pp. 114, 116, 122, 124, 135, 145–46; on Hawthorne's political activities, pp. 14, 114–15, 312–13, 321; on Simms' relations to Duyckinck, pp. 104–9 and *passim*.

64. I am indebted to Perry Miller's marvelously intricate reconstruction of New York's literary world in the 1840s in *The Raven and the Whale*, especially 'Young America', pp. 71–117. For Duyckinck's editorial involvement with the *Democratic Review*, p. 110; Whitman and Young America, pp. 111, 161–62.

65. Ralph Waldo Emerson, 'Politics', in *Essays: Second Series*, Boston 1883, pp. 200–202.

66. William Sumner Jenkins, *Pro–Slavery Thought in the Old South*, Chapel Hill, N.C. 1935; E. N. Elliot, ed., *Cotton Is King, and Pro–Slavery Arguments Comprising Writings of Hammon, Harper, Christy, Stringfellow, Hodge, Bledsoe, and Cartwright*, Augusta, Ga. 1860; Eric L. McKitrick, ed., *Slavery Defended: The Views of the Old South*, Englewood Cliffs, N.J. 1963; Eugene Genovese, *Roll, Jordan, Roll*, New York 1974; Genovese, *Political Economy of Slavery*, especially pp. 28–35.

67. James Barbour, *Address of James Barbour, Esq., President of the Agricultural Society of Albemarle at their Meeting of 8th November 1825*, Charlottesville, Va. 1825, pp. 9–12; Charles D. Lowery, 'James Barbour, a Progressive Farmer of Ante-Bellum Virginia', in John B. Boles, ed., *America in the Middle Period: Essays in Honor of Bernard Mayo*, Charlottesville, Va. 1973, pp. 168–87.

68. See, for example, the discussion of Andrew Johnson's First Message to Congress in Chapter 11.

69. Pierre L. van den Berghe, *Race and Racism: A Comparative Perspective*, New York 1967, p. 77.

70. Ibid., pp. 27–37.

71. John Pendleton Kennedy, *Swallow Barn; or, A Sojourn in the Old Dominion*, New York 1854, pp. 308–10.

72. For example, Philip Barbour's address to the Virginia Convention of 1829–30 in *Proceedings and Debates of the Virginia Convention*, p. 91. A classic portrayal of white fantasies of the black avenger is the character of the Spanish captain's valet de chambre in Melville's 'Benito Cereno.'

73. Thomas F. Gossett, *Race: The History of an Idea in America*, New York 1965, pp. 3–84; William Stanton, *The Leopard's Spots: Scientific Attitudes Toward Race in America, 1815–1859*, Chicago 1960, pp. 1–140; Dwight W. Hoover, *The Red and the Black*, Chicago 1976,

pp. 1–140; George M. Fredrickson, *The Black Image in the White Mind: The Debate on Afro-American Character and Destiny*, New York 1971, pp. 1–164; Edmund S. Morgan, *American Slavery–American Freedom: The Ordeal of Colonial Virginia*, New York 1975; Winthrop D. Jordan, *White over Black: American Attitudes Toward the Negro, 1550–1812*, Chapel Hill, N.C. 1968.

74. See the Introduction, pp. 14–15.

75. Robert Joseph Clarke, *The Road from Monticello: A Study of the Virginia Slavery Debate of 1832*, Durham, N.C. 1941; Clement Eaton, *The Growth of Southern Civilization, 1790–1860*, New York 1961, pp. 302–3; Eaton, *Freedom of Thought Struggle in the Old South*, New York 1964.

76. Jenkins, *Pro-slavery Thought*.

77. James H. Hammond, 'Speech on the Admission of Kansas', U.S. Senate, 4 March 1858, *Selections from the Letters and Speeches of the Hon. James H. Hammond, of South Carolina*, New York 1866, pp. 317–22, as quoted in McKitrick, ed., *Slavery Defended*, pp. 121–25.

78. Benton, 'LaSalle' letters in St. Louis *Beacon*, 7, 10, 14, 17, 21, 24, and 28 October, and 4 and 11 November 1829, quoted in Chambers, p. 159; New York *Sun*, 24 March 1834 and 10 July 1837; Philadelphia *Public Ledger*, 20 October 1837; George P. Rawick, *From Sundown to Sunup: The Making of the Black Community*, Westport, Conn. 1972, p. 140.

79. See, for example, the speech of Ely Moore in Congress, *Congressional Globe*, 25th Cong., 35th Sess. Washington, 1839, Appendix, p. 241, quoted in Saxton, *Indispensable Enemy*, p. 27; Walter Hugins, 'Ely Moore: The Case History of a Jacksonian Labor Leader', *Political Science Quarterly* 65 (March 1950):105–25. Gary Nash's study, *Forging Freedom: Formation of Philadelphia's Black Community, 1720–1840*, Cambridge, Mass. 1987, is one of the few works in 'new social history' to focus on a northern urban African–American community and its relations to the white working class. His Chapters 7 and 8 trace the deterioration of those relationships in the early Jacksonian period. Leon Litwack, *North of Slavery: The Negro in the Free States, 1790–1860*, Chicago 1965, pp. 160, 165; Philip Foner, *History of the Labor Movement*, 1:266–276.

80. Amos L. Herold, *James Kirke Paulding, Versatile American*, New York 1926, pp. 1–18, 22, 52–54, 65, 73–74.

81. Ibid., pp. 114–15, 128.

82. James Kirke Paulding, *Slavery in the United States*, New York 1836, pp. 8–9.

83. Ibid., pp. 7–8.

84. Ibid., p. 42.

85. Ibid., pp. 56, 57.

86. Ibid., pp. 64–76.

87. Ibid., pp. 75–76.

88. Ibid., p. 178.

89. Ibid., pp. 61–62.

90. Paulding, *The Diverting History of John Bull and Brother Jonathan by Hector Bull–us*, New York 1835; *Slavery*, pp. 128–29.

91. Ibid., pp. 128–39.

92. Ibid., pp. 72–73, 82; 109–20, 172–73, 174–78.

93. Ibid., pp. 309–12.

94. Benton 'LaSalle' letters, quoted in Chambers, p. 159.

95. Andrew Jackson, Second Annual Message, 6 December 1830, Richardson, ed., *A Compilation of the Messages and Papers of the Presidents*, New York 1897, 3:1084.

96. Walt Whitman, 8 June 1846, Brooklyn *Daily Eagle*, in Rodgers and Black, eds, 2:179; and 7 July 1846, 1:246–47.

97. After the failure of the constitutional challenge to Cherokee removal, Whig critics focused mainly on accusations of excessive costs, misconduct, and needless brutality in conflicts with Indians: Daniel W. Howe, *The Political Culture of the American Whigs*, Chicago 1979, pp. 24, 40–42, 168, 172–74, 241, 274, 316n.

98. Lynn Parsons, '"A Perpetual Upon My Feelings": John Quincy Adams and the American Indian', *New England Quarterly* (September 1973): 339–79, especially pp. 339–40, 361–62.

99. Henry Rowe Schoolcraft, 'Fate of the Red Race in America: The Policy Pursued

Towards Them by the Government, and the Present Condition of the Tribes Who Have Been Removed West of the Mississippi', *Democratic Review*, 1844; and in Schoolcraft, *The Indian in His Wigwam, or Characteristics of the Red Race of America, from Original Notes and Manuscripts*, New York 1848, pp. 366–89; Henry Wadsworth Longfellow, *The Song of Hiawatha*, [1855] Boston 1895.

100. Eric Foner, *Free Soil, Free Labor, Free Men: The Ideology of the Republican Party Before the Civil War*, New York 1980, p. 267; Foner, *Politics and Ideology*, pp. 81–85; *Congressional Globe*, 29th Cong., 2nd Sess. Washington, 1847, Appendix, p. 317.

101. Brooklyn *Daily Eagle*, 6 May 1858, in Turner, pp. 5–11, quotation 7.

102. Theodore Clark Smith, *The Liberty and Free Soil Parties in the Northwest*, New York 1897; Foner, *Free Soil*, p. 267; Foner, *Politics and Ideology*, pp. 77–93.

103. Chambers, *Benton*, pp. 255–63, 367–68, 419–20; Whitman, 'When Lilacs Last in the Dooryard Bloomed'.

PART II

Transitions

7

Blackface Minstrelsy

For half a century minstrel shows provided a nationwide medium of mass entertainment, and at the end, far from fading away, they merged into vaudeville and the beginnings of cinema.[1] Blackface minstrelsy epitomized and concentrated the thrust of white racism. In this respect it was always political, but during its early years, from the mid-1840s through the 1860s, overt partisanship linked it to the Democratic party. The exclusiveness of its Jacksonian orientation surpassed that of the penny press, which although initially Democratic, contained no internal barriers against Whig infiltration.

For minstrelsy, by contrast, whiggish politics were precluded because the mass urban culture from which minstrelsy derived was itself an attack on the moral and economic premises of whiggery; and because, through its stylized form, it propagandized metaphorically the alliance of urban working people with the planter interest in the South. Not till after the war and well into Reconstruction could a nonpartisan or Republican minstrel company have commanded credibility. And such a combination even then would have reflected not so much any basic change in minstrelsy as the gradual success of the Republican coalition in capturing segments of the Democracy.

'If I could have the nigger show back again in its pristine purity', Mark Twain wrote in his autobiography, ' ... I should have but little further use for opera. ... I remember the first Negro musical show I ever saw. It must have been in the early forties. It was a new institution. In our village of Hannibal ... it burst upon us as a glad and stunning surprise.'[2] Twain's comparison to grand opera suggests that he perceived the minstrel show as a uniquely national expression. So did many of his contemporaries. Thus the preface to one of E.P. Christy's countless 'plantation songsters' recounted the origins of the 'new institution' in the following terms:

> After our countrymen had, by force of native genius in the arts, arms, science, philosophy and poetry, &c, &c, confuted the stale cant of our European detractors that nothing original could emanate from Americans – the next cry was, that we have no NATIVE MUSIC; ... until our countrymen found a triumphant vindicating APOLLO in the genius of E.P. Christy, who ... was the first to catch our *native airs* as they floated wildly, or hummed in the balmy breezes of the sunny south.

The verbs *floated* and *hummed* served partially to obscure the fact that 'our native airs' had been appropriated from the music and dance of African slaves by white professional entertainers, including (among many others) E.P. Christy. Later in the same preface a more realistic account of the actual relationship described the minstrels as having possessed 'science and practical skill in music to enable them to harmonize and SCORE systematically the original NEGRO SOLOS ...' Their labors had resulted in filling 'the air of our broad, blest land ... with the thousand native melodies.'[3]

This explanation, with which Twain would probably have concurred, stressed the rural, southern origins of minstrelsy; yet it seems evident that the spread of blackface minstrelsy was closely linked to the rise of the mass circulation press and the nationalization of theater. Hannibal, Missouri, for example, which in Twain's childhood was a rural slaveholding community, could hardly have found fragments of African music and caricatures of black slaves particularly surprising. What made the first minstrel show a 'glad' surprise was that it provided a window into the complex culture developing in the new cities.[4] Through that window appeared cultural identifications and hostilities, ethnic satire, and social and political commentary of a wide-ranging, sometimes radical character. In addition, the shows often transmitted sexual messages. Taken as a whole, they provided a kind of underground theater in which the blackface convention rendered permissible topics that were difficult to handle explicitly on the Victorian stage or in print. Spontaneity and ad-libbing, built into minstrelsy from its inception, favored a flexible approach to different audiences and regions, changing moods and times. This combination of adaptiveness and liberty of subject explains in part the popularity and staying power of minstrelsy as mass entertainment. Finally, the convention of blackface was by no means separate from, or neutral with regard to, social content; on the contrary, the blackface convention saturated that content. For a study of the ideology of minstrel shows, the interpenetration of form and content is at the crux of the matter.

The content of minstrelsy was shaped in part by the social experience of its founders and purveyors. Three men, Thomas Rice, Dan Emmett and E.P. Christy, are generally recognized as founders of blackface minstrelsy. To these should be added the name of Stephen Foster, the major *white* innovator of minstrel music. Where did these men come from and how did they happen to launch a new mode in mass entertainment? Rice, oldest of the four, was born in New York in 1808. He tried unsuccessfully to break into New York theater, then drifted west, working as stagehand and bit player throughout the Mississippi Valley. In 1831, imitating a shuffle he had seen performed by a black man on the Cincinnati levee, Rice for the first time 'jumped Jim Crow' – and Jim Crow made Rice's fortune. Adapting his act to various issues – eventually including a minstrel burlesque of Uncle Tom – Rice was applauded in London and became a perennial favorite at New York's famous Bowery Theatre. The second founder of minstrelsy, Dan Emmett, son of a village blacksmith in Mt. Vernon, Ohio, was born in 1815. He ran away to become a drummer in the army and served briefly at posts in Kentucky and Missouri. Dismissed for being underage, Emmett followed circuses and sideshows, occasionally singing comic songs in blackface. Early in 1843 he organized the first blackface quartet as a one-night fill-in at New York's Chatham Theatre. Emmett devoted the rest of his long career to minstrelsy.[5]

Edwin P. Christy, also born in 1815, was the son of 'respectable' Philadelphia parents who sought to launch him on a commercial career by arranging to place him in a New Orleans counting house. Christy rebelled and took to the road with traveling circuses. In 1843, he and several other young men were providing musical entertainment at a theater-saloon on the Buffalo waterfront. Apparently having heard of Emmett's success in New York, thc Buffalo entertainers called themsevles Christy's Plantation Minstrels; later, moving down to New York City, they became a permanent fixture at Mechanic's Hall on lower Broadway. It was through Christy's Minstrels that many of Stephen Foster's early songs reached the public. Foster, eleven years younger than Christy or Emmett, was born in Pittsburgh in 1826. Like Christy, he came of parents with intimations of upward mobility who tried to provide him with a proper education, thcn sent him off to work as a bookkeeper for an older brother in Cincinnati. Foster was meanwhile writing songs for minstrel shows for which he received ten or fifteen dollars apiece. His 'Old Folks at Home', according to the publisher, sold 130,000 copies in three years.[6]

The careers of these four men show several similarities. All were northerners and all except Emmett of urban origin. At least three came of old stock American families and were clearly of middle-class background. They all rejected the straight ways of the Protestant ethic and sought escape into the bohemianism of the entertainment world. Three had direct contact through their wanderings in the lower Mississippi Valley with the music and dance of black slaves, and we know from their own accounts that they consciously exploited this resource. None had achieved success in the theater or in any other pursuit prior to the venture into blackface minstrelsy; and in each case that venture brought spectacular success.[7] The pattern suggested by these summaries probably approximates the experiences of many professionals active during the first three decades of minstrelsy. A sample of forty-three men born before 1838 who achieved prominence as blackface performers in large northern cities or San Francisco yields the following information: five were born south of the Mason-Dixon line (including Baltimore); most of the rest (thirty-one) were born in the North, but of these only five were New Englanders. With respect to urban background, New York, Brooklyn, Rochester, Utica, Troy, Philadelphia, Baltimore, Providence, New Haven and Salem (Mass.) accounted for twenty-four of the forty-three (with London and Paris probably claiming three or four more). Regionally, upstate New York matched New York City and Brooklyn with nine each; Philadelphia came next with six.[8]

Typical purveyors of minstrelsy, then, were northern and urban; they were neither New Englanders nor Southerners (although their parents may have been); and if of rural or small town origin, were most likely to have come from upper New York State. Eager to break into the exclusive and inhospitable precincts of big city theater, they needed new and exciting materials. These they found during their forced marches through the Mississippi Valley South in the music and dance of slaves and in the half-horse, half-alligator braggadocio of the river and the frontier. The two separate lines had merged to some extent before the minstrels took them over:

> My mammy was a wolf, my daddy was a tiger,
> And I'm what you call de old virginia nigger;
> Half fire, half smoke, a little touch of thunder,
> I'm what dey call de eighth wonder.[9]

Ambivalent especially toward the black component of their borrowings, the minstrels coveted the power and newness of the music, yet failed to recognize its Africanness, or to perceive in it segments of an idiom distinct and separate from the European idiom. They ascribed the impact of slave music to its being close to nature. It 'floated wildly' or 'hummed … in the breezes', to repeat the metaphor of E.P. Christy's preface, and its wildness could be taken simply as part of the general crudity of frontier style. In any case the work of white entertainers with such materials was to 'turn them to shape', to Europeanize them sufficiently so that they would not offend refined ears. The dual task of exploiting and suppressing African elements thus began from the first moments of minstrelsy. But these elements possessed great vitality. It was suggested earlier that a major factor in the popularity and staying power of minstrel entertain-

ment was its freedom of subject matter; certainly another – perhaps *the*
other – major factor was the persistence of African borrowings (especially
in dance movement and sense of rhythm) throughout the entire half-century of blackface minstrelsy.[10]

Partial acceptance of these African musical elements was facilitated by
the fact that they fitted logically into a portrayal of the old South that
took on a symbolic and powerful, although derivative, meaning for many
white Americans during the nineteenth century. But before examining
that somewhat removed aspect of minstrel content, it is necessary to turn
to a set of meanings that were direct and immediate. For the minstrels,
as for the new mass audience upon which they depended, the city was the
focal experience of life. The city offered (or seemed to offer) new sorts
of work, money, movement, excitement. It offered access to liquor and
sex, to education, culture, progress. All this was ignored in the high culture of the established upper classes; Walt Whitman, almost alone among
nineteenth-century American poets, celebrated the city. The purveyors of
minstrelsy shared in this celebration; but in order to do so, they had to
impose some startling transformations upon materials the primary reference of which was to frontier and plantation. Here is one of the early
mutations:

> I'm de sole delight of yaller galls,
> > De envy ob de men,
> Observe this nigger when he turns,
> > And talk of dandies then.[11]

The Broadway dandy was in one respect a transplant of the swaggering
southwest frontier hero, already widely rendered in blackface. But the
dandy also caricatured a new social type in the United States – the urban
free black.

Possible uses of this stereotype, which expressed an enthusiasm for city
life uncloyed by nostalgia or regret, were limitless.[12] Early in 1852, one
of New York's permanent minstrel companies began performing a number
titled, 'Wake Up, Mose'. The hero appeared in the first verse as the
already familiar urban free black. 'He used to run de railroad – he was de
bulgine tender'; and it was clear from the context that 'bulgine tender'
meant a railroad fireman. The chorus then made an abrupt switch, followed up in subsequent verses, to a fireman of a different sort, and
presumably of different race:

> ... Round de corner de smoke am curling.
> Wake up, Mose! the engine's coming;
> Take de rope and keep a running![13]

The original Mose, as noted earlier, was a characterization of New York's Bowery Boy. Butcher's helper, apprentice carpenter or stonecutter, Mose the Bowery Boy was a gallant volunteer fireman, wheelhorse of city politics and invincible pugilist. As an urban culture hero he derived from, yet stood against, older rural heroes like the New England Yankee or the half-horse, half-alligator of the Mississippi Valley. Mose cared nothing for Yankees or alligators either; he breathed the fire of burning buildings; and when it came to warfare, he could tell even an old frontier fighter like Zachary Taylor how to run his campaigns. Mose transcended regionalism, however; and stood for the new urban mass culture as against the 'high' culture of the old elite.[14]

But Mose in blackface was something else. There was of course a historical logic in rendering the Broadway dandy as Mose in blackface, since both had reached the city by different routes from a common ancestry in frontier folklore. But this hardly explains *why* it was done. The value of such a characterization was that it extended minstrel show content to include class satire. As minstrelsy became more formalized, it moved from separate song-and-dance numbers to routines including spoken repartee, and finally to elaborate composites of song, dance and drama. The original foursome of undifferentiated musicians expanded into a line in which customary position corresponded roughly to class identification. The end-men, who always played tambourine and bones, were lower-class. By costume and vernacular they were 'plantation nigger', or 'Broadway dandy', often one of each. The middleman, or *interlocutor*, served as bogus mouthpiece for the high culture.[15] His dress and speech were upper-class, sometimes straight, more often burlesqued; and the plot was usually the putting down of the interlocutor by the end-men. Even after the ad-lib repartee of the original line had evolved into more formal presentations, the class character and plot remained substantially the same. Blackface could thus serve to enhance the ridicule directed against upper-class pretensions.[16] More important, it had the effect of preserving the comic mood, since otherwise social satire tended toward serious drama. The careers of real 'Bowery boys' – John Morrissey, the prize-fighter, for example, or the proletarian congressman Michael Walsh, and especially of David Broderick – acted out mortal conflicts between the new urban culture and the cultures of older elites.[17] This was too serious to be fun. Blackface defused such meanings without denying them. It did so by placing social content in the background of a conventional proscenium that permitted instantaneous escape through shifts of scene and mood and that constantly intervened to discredit serious implications.

Part of the entertainment lay in skating on thin ice. Temperance, a topic taken very seriously by many mid–nineteenth century Americans, was nearly always an object of ridicule in minstrel songs:

Nigger, but down dat jug,
Touch not a single drop, ...

Parodying the sentimental ballad, 'Woodman Spare that Tree', this song, published about 1850, went on to hint at more than the simple pleasures of alcohol:

I kiss him two three time
And den I suck him dry
Dat jug, he's none but mine
So dar you luff him lie.[18]

Minstrelsy had become mass entertainment in the decade of war against Mexico and the California gold rush. Shows were generally performed by males before largely male audiences. Both in the East and West, the male population was concentrated in factories, boardinghouses, and in construction and mining camps. Frontier settlements had few women and contemporary accounts tell of men dancing in saloons and hotel dining rooms dressed as women. Given this context, the song quoted above appears as a permissive reference to homosexuality and masturbation, veiled but not negated by the blackface convention. The point here is not the prevalence of homosexuality, but the tolerance of sexuality in general, the realism and the flexibility of standards that flourished behind the false facade of blackface presentation. A more typical sort of minstrel pornography, doubtless derived from Restoration comedy, would be a duet titled, 'Cuffee's Do-it', in which Cuffee was typed as a Broadway dandy:

He.   O Miss Fanny let me in
      for de way I lub you is a sin
She. (spoken) O no I cannot let you in ...
He.   Oh, when I set up an oyster cellar,
      You shall wait upon de feller,
      Sell hot corn and ginger pop,
      You be de lady ob de shop.
She. Oh, Sam, if dat's de trufe you tell ...
      Oh, Sam Slufheel, you may come in.
He.   Oh, Miss Fanny, I'se a comin' in ...[19]

Moral permissiveness was not accidental or idiosyncratic: it was an aspect of life-style. The life-style expressed in minstrelsy could appropriately be called *urbanity* since it had developed in middle Atlantic cities, moved west with the Erie Canal and urbanization of the Mississippi Valley and its tributaries, and west again with the acquisition of California. It was both urban and frontier. During the last two major frontier decades, the 1850s and 1860s, even the frontier had become urbanized: its new cities were the garrison towns and mining camps that sprang into existence before much in the way of a rural hinterland had developed around them. When Charles DeLong made the following entry in his diary for Christmas Eve, 1859,

> Spent the day in the office hunting up authorities ... in the evening went to the gymnasium, and the sparring school, and then called on Elida ... saw the Christmas tree and then went in and celebrated Christmas with Lide. Came downtown went to Nigger Festival [a minstrel show] and got supper and then went to the Catholic Church to high mass, and then down and got a little burden and went to bed late, raining some. ...

he might have been describing a day in the life of a moderately successful Bowery politician. Actually DeLong was working out of Marysville, some fifty miles northeast of Sacramento. A political henchman of Stephen Douglas, DeLong earned his living at the time by collecting the California foreign miners' tax from Chinese laborers. 'Started with Dick Wade and Bob Moulthrop collecting', he wrote for 23 October 1855, ' ... supper at Hesse's Crossing went down the river in the night collected all the way had a great time, Chinamen tails cut off.'[20] DeLong attended performances of many of the same minstrel troupes he would have seen had he lived in New York, because minstrelsy was invading the towns and camps of the Pacific slope. So prominent was San Francisco as a minstrel city that for several years one of New York's leading companies styled itself the 'San Francisco Minstrels'.[21]

The dual relationship of city and frontier profoundly affected the social content of minstrelsy. Blackface singers (again like Walt Whitman) were protagonists of Manifest Destiny:

> Mose he went to Mexico, and dar he saw Santa Anna;
> He sent a message to de camp, telling Zack [Zachary Taylor] not to surrender.
> Says Santa Anna, 'Who are you – you seem to be so witty?'
> Says Mose, 'Go 'long – I'm one of de boys – I'm from de Empire City.'[22]

Always the West and the westward movement were focal:

> Den I step on board de Oregon
> For de gemman say who bought her
> Dat she for sure's de fastest crab
> What lives upon de water.[23]

Stephen Foster's 'Oh! Susanna' (of which the verse above was a topical variation) was first performed in the year of Scott's conquest of Mexico City and reached the height of its popularity during the California Gold

Rush. A later cliché, perpetuated by Hollywood and television, has associated the song with westering pioneers from rural regions such as Kansas and Missouri. Kansas wagonmasters may certainly have sung 'Oh! Susanna'; but its origin was Pittsburgh, and it was first popularized in New York's minstrel halls.[24]

Underlying the sociological congruency between city and frontier was a psychological similarity between traveling to the city and traveling west. Each was a difficult journey involving a traumatic break with a previous life. In minstrelsy's complex matrix of social content, the *journey* became the central theme. It stood in contrast to the celebration of urban opportunity and permissiveness as a lament for what had been left behind and lost. This theme, I believe, entered minstrelsy in its beginnings, not in any sense as a reflection of journeys made by black slaves; but as a projection by the white performers of their own experience. The projection was then magnified because it also expressed the psychic experience of urban audiences. The notion of a symbolic journey suggests mistrelsy's powerful impact upon white viewers. At the same time it helps to place in perspective one of the most puzzling aspects of minstrel repertory: the endless evocation of the old South.

Early minstrels (as represented by the samples above) had understood slave music not as African but as close to nature. Correspondingly, they perceived slaves as *part* of nature – part of the nature of the South; and from this curiously ahistorical viewpoint undertook to 'delineate' the plantation culture of the South. City dwellers by birth or adoption, they were strangers and interlopers in plantation society. While they might observe and borrow from slave music, their social contacts were with whites, and it is scarcely surprising that their depiction of the South overlapped and duplicated the plantation myth that white southerners were then bringing to perfection as part of their defense of slavery. That myth was also ahistorical because its inspiration was to fix the black slave as an everlasting part of nature rather than as a figure in history.

When the wandering minstrels carried their fragments of African-American music back to northern and western cities, they took them encased in a mythology of the South as a region fascinatingly different, closely wedded to nature, and above all, timeless. The word *timeless* defines the relationship that would develop between the image of the South and the *anomie* experienced by men and women of rural, eastern background who lived in cities or who moved out west. The South became symbolically their old home: the place where simplicity, happiness, all the things we have left behind, exist outside of time.

> Down by the river our log hut stands
> Where father and mother once dwelt

> And the old door latch that was worn by
> our hands ...[25]

What has been left behind collectively may be a rural past, but individually it is childhood. New cities and new frontiers, attractive to conspiring and perspiring adults, have little room for children; and the South, in the legend of blackface minstrelsy, became the antithesis to both.[26]

Minstrelsy's social content keyed into its politics. When E.P. Christy organized his first entertainments in Buffalo in 1842, he brought in a younger man, George Harrington, who adopted the name Christy and eventually became more famous than his mentor. The senior Christy retired in the mid-1850s; George Christy went into partnership with a New York theatrical promoter, Henry Wood. Under their joint direction, Christy and Wood's became a metropolitan establishment and one of the best-known companies of the pre-war era. Henry Wood belonged to a remarkable family. His brother Benjamin served three terms as a Democratic congressman from the city and one term as state senator; for almost half a century he presided over the aggressively Democratic New York *Daily News*. A second brother was Fernando Wood, copperheadish mayor of New York, fighter for control of Tammany Hall, several times congressman.[27]

George Christy went to San Francisco in 1857. There he performed under the sponsorship of Tom Maguire, West Coast tycoon of minstrelsy, opera and varied theatricals. Maguire had spent his younger days on New York's Bowery as a saloon keeper, hack driver, fight promoter, volunteer fireman and Tammany stalwart. When David Broderick, a New York stonecutter from a similar background, abandoned the Bowery for the Golden Gate in 1849, he lived for several years as a boarder at Maguire's house and apparently helped Maguire to escape bankruptcy by arranging the sale of his Jenny Lind Theatre for $200,000 to an obliging (Democratic) city administration of San Francisco. Maguire was soon back in business with other theaters.[28]

After launching the nation's first minstrel quartet on the New York stage, Dan Emmett toured England with middling success, then returned to White's Minstrel Melodeon on lower Broadway. By the late 1850s, Emmett had worked out a lasting connection with Bryants' Minstrels of New York, next to Christy's the most enduring of the pre-war troupes. Composer of dozens of songs and musical farces, Emmett was especially noted for his walkarounds or group finales. One of these, which took its title from its New York premiere, 'Dixie's Land', became popular in the South, where it was appropriated by itinerant minstrels and emerged during the war as 'Dixie', the *de facto* Confederate national anthem. In post-war years, the Bryants, following the trend of theater and fashion, moved uptown to East Fourteenth Street. Emmett by this time had drifted back to the Midwest, but the Bryants commissioned a special walkaround in honor of their uptown location, and Emmett obliged with a piece called 'The Wigwam'. In May 1868, 'The Wigwam' climaxed the Bryants' opening in their new theater at Tammany Hall's recently constructed Fourteenth Street headquarters.[29]

Stephen Foster, drinking himself to death in New York during the Civil War, sometimes peddled his handwritten songs along Broadway, and at least one of the buyers was Henry Wood of Wood's Minstrels. In happier days, Foster had helped to organize the Allegheny City Buchanan-for-President Club. All ardent Democrats, the Fosters were related by marriage to President Buchanan's brother, an Episcopalian minister. In 1856 Stephen Foster contributed two songs to the Buchanan Glee Club. One was a lampoon of Abolitionism; the other was a paean to the unifying spirit of the South:

> We'll not outlaw the land that holds
> The bones of Washington,
> Where Jackson fought and Marion bled
> And the battles of the brave were won.[30]

From such fragments of evidence, several 'founding' minstrels as well as two or three of the nation's best-known minstrel companies can be placed in a scattered but consistent pattern of pro-Southern expression and intimate contact with Democratic party leaders in New York and San Francisco.[31] The pattern points to a more general typicality when considered against the background of minstrelsy's political orientation, which has already been defined – in a negative sense – by its social content. Temperance, hostility to recent European immigration, and lack of enthusiasm for, or direct opposition to, territorial expansion were frequently (not always) characteristic of the Whig, Liberty, Free Soil, Native American and Republican parties. Regardless of mutual antagonisms, these parties always opposed the Democratic party, which, in turn, was nearly always hostile to temperance, receptive to recent European immigration and strenuously in favor of territorial expansion. The positions of the Democratic party on these issues were congruent to the outlook expressed by blackface minstrelsy; the positions of anti-Democratic parties generally were not. Ministrelsy, then, appears to have been oriented towards the Democratic party. Since minstrels were usually northern, as was most of their mass audience, it would seem reasonable to pursue an inquiry into the politics of minstrelsy by investigating its responses to major problems confronting the northern wing of the Democratic party.

Chapter 6 defined the Jacksonian legitimizing construct as comprising three basic components: egalitarianism (anti-monopoly), nationalism (territorial expansion), and white supremacy. I argued that northern party leaders could be expected, both for their own career ambitions and through commitment to Democratic principle, to seek to perpetuate, or regain, control of the federal government. In the period of Democratic dominance before the Civil War it was largely a matter of perpetuating Democratic control; and at any particular moment continued control over the federal apparatus depended on unity among the party's regional branches. The price of unity, as set by southern Democrats, was defense of the institution of slavery by the national party. Consequently, a major task of northern leaders was to resist criticisms of slavery from outside the party and to prevent anti-slavery sentiment from infiltrating party ranks. This became no easy task as views hostile to slavery gained widening acceptance in the North and West.[32]

For blackface minstrelsy, slavery was an inescapable topic and its political stance was a defense of slavery. That this should seem a statement of the obvious is in itself a revealing commentary. In a broader frame of reference, artistic endeavors aimed at 'delineating' the cultural traditions of oppressed or enslaved peoples would more commonly be associated, I think, with ideologies of liberation than of oppression. Minstrelsy, however, faithfully reproduced the white slaveowners' viewpoint.

> Old Massa to us darkies am good
> Tra la la, tra la la
> For he gibs us our clothes
> and he gibs us our food ...[33]

Slaves loved the master. They dreaded freedom because, presumably, they were incapable of *self*-possession. When forced to leave the plantation they longed only to return. These themes in minstrelsy worked at several levels. On the one hand, propagating the plantation myth, they portrayed slavery as benign and desirable. On the other hand, they reinforced the image of the South as symbol of the collective rural past and of individual childhood, thus appropriating an emotional impact that was logically unrelated to their content. At the same time, the docility attributed to slaves, commendable as this might seem to a southern planter, was certain to strike northern audiences imbued with Jacksonian principles of upward mobility as ridiculous and contemptible.

Was minstrelsy monolithic in its justification of slavery? Almost, but not quite. There appeared a scattering of anti-slavery expressions that entered the genre in two different ways. First, the early borrowings of African-American music and dance carried anti-slavery connotations that sometimes persisted subliminally in traditional verses like this from 'The Raccoon Hunt':

My ole massa dead and gone,
A dose of poison help him on
De debil say he funeral song.[34]

Subversive sentiments might be negated in chorus or verses, perhaps added later. This seems to have been the case with the ballad 'De Nigga Gineral', which referred to Nat Turner's rebellion, although parts of the song were apparently of older origin. Here the anti-slavery thesis represented by a black general, 'chief of the insurgents', is carefully set at rest by antithetical verses telling of his defeat, repudiation by his own followers, and execution.

O, Johnson Ben he drove de waggon
    Ho, boys yere most done ...
And dey hung him and dey swung him
    Ho, boys, yere most done.[35]

A second and later means of entry for anti-slavery content was through the essentially white identity of romantic and nostalgic songs, European in tradition and style, which quickly became a staple of minstrel repertory. Performed in blackface, yet dealing seriously with themes of parted lovers, lost children and so forth, these songs both invited identification with the situation of the slave and suggested that slavery might have been the cause of separation or loss. But to admit such a possibility was to contradict the myth of the benign plantation and yield ground to anti-slavery propagandists. Thus, even when rendered in 'darkey' vernacular, sentimental minstrel songs seldom made direct mention of slavery. Occasional references did nonetheless break through. They were then usually softened or disguised by shifting specific griefs to the generalized sorrows of time and distance; or by emphasizing the troubles blacks were likely to encounter in the North.[36]

The two sorts of expressions described above represented the only penetration into minstrelsy of anti-slavery views. By contrast, a major trend through the 1850s and into the war years consisted of attacks against Abolitionists, who were portrayed as stupid, hypocritical, cowardly, subservient to England and practitioners of miscegenation. Minstrelsy not only conveyed explicit pro-slavery and anti-Abolitionist propaganda; it was, in and of itself, a defense of slavery because its main content stemmed from the myth of the benign plantation. Critics of slavery were well aware that the incompatibility between that myth and romantic concepts of love and family were a weak point in slavery's defense; and against this point was directed one of their main attacks – that slavery prevented marriage and broke up families. This was the central message of *Uncle Tom's Cabin*;

and anti-slavery singers (never minstrels) like the Hutchinson Family of New Hampshire had been developing similar criticisms long before Stowe's novel appeared. The counter to this attack – in which minstrelsy led the field – took the form of ridiculing the very notion of love, or any other human or humane emotion, among blacks. Within a few months after the appearance of *Uncle Tom's Cabin*, minstrels had coopted the title and main characters, while reversing the message.[37] The famous T.D. Rice 'jumped Jim Crow' in the role of Uncle Tom. Indeed all that was needed to render a serious theme ludicrous in blackface minstrelsy was to permit its dehumanizing form to overbalance the content. In an age of romantic sentiment, minstrels sang love songs like this one:

> My Susy she is handsome
>   My Susy she is young ...
> My Susy looms it bery tall
>   Wid udder like a cow
> She'd give nine quarts easy
>   But white gals don't know how.[38]

By 1860 the infiltration of anti-slavery sentiments into northern party ranks, combined with the mounting anxiety and aggressiveness of southern Democrats, had made further compromise impossible. The party split; Lincoln was elected; secession and civil war followed. Although virtually impotent at the national level, the Democracy remained locally powerful in many regions of the North. The task now facing its activists was to hold together their potentially large constituency through protestations of loyal Unionism while at the same time seeking to discredit Republican leadership. Once again slavery was at the heart of the matter. The South, Democrats argued, would fight to the bitter end, convinced that the Republicans intended to destroy slavery. But the war could be settled and the Union preserved, if – through ouster of the Republicans from control of the federal apparatus – the slavery issue were fully set at rest. This line was vigorously pushed in mass media accessible to Democratic leaders; and these were primarily newspapers and blackface minstrelsy.

Minstrels readapted the plantation myth to wartime purposes, their message being that a struggle against slavery was neither necessary to save the Union, nor desirable. Traditional blackface caricatures were politicized. The 'plantation nigger' now lamented the inexplicable 'white folks' war that was causing everyone so much trouble; while up North the 'Broadway dandy' thrived like the green bay tree. He conspired with Republican leaders, rejoiced in the war but dodged the draft; paraded in fancy uniform, but took to his heels at the first whiff of gunpowder:

Niggers dey can pick de cotton – dey'll do it very freely
But when dey smell de bullets, how dey'll run for Horace Greeley![39]

To their basic paradox of lauding the plantation system in the midst of a war against the plantation South, the minstrels added a satirical and sometimes brilliant critique of Republican war policy. They questioned the competence of particular leaders (including Lincoln). They attacked political generals, profiteers and shoddy contractors. Songs like Dan Emmett's 'How Are You, Greenbacks?' provided a framework for variations upon the class and ethnic sequences worked out during the 1850s.

We're coming Father Abram, one hundred thousand more
Five hundred presses printing us from morn til night is o'er ...
To line the fat contractor's purse, or purchase transport craft
Whose rotten hulks shall sink before the winds begin to waft.

The bearers of true patriotism, according to minstrel repertory, were honest workingmen who battled to save the Union. Outstanding among these were regiments raised from New York's volunteer fire companies ('For I belong to the Fire Zouaves that started from New York ...'); and the Irish ('Meagher is leading the Irish Brigade'); and – while nearly always treated comically – the lager-drinking Germans ('I'm Going to Fight Mit Sigel'). General McClellan became a symbol of the straightforward Union-loving soldier as opposed to the profiteering, Abolition-tainted Republican politician. Minstrelsy in 1864 mounted an extensive campaign for McClellan, whose platform as Democratic presidential candidate called for peace on any terms of reunion acceptable to the South.

We're willing, Father Abram, ten hundred thousand more
Should help our Uncle Samuel to prosecute the war;
But then we want a chieftain true, one who can lead the van,
George B. McClellan you all know he is the very man ...[40]

Thus while loyal workers and soldiers defended the nation, their efforts were sabotaged by profiteers and politicians, and worst of all, their lives needlessly expended for the benefit of the 'niggers':

Abram Linkum said to me
    Send de sojers down!
He's gwine to make de niggers free
    Send de sojers down!

At this level the entire spectrum of minstrelsy from the plantation myth through its urban repertory of ethnic humor and class satire was permeated by the blackface form:

> I wish I was a blinkin' [Abe Lincoln], a blinkin', a blinkin'
>   I wish I was a blinkin'
> I'll tell you what I'd do ...
> Oh, if I was much bigger – some bigger – great bigger,
>   Oh, if I was some bigger I tell you what I'd do:
> I'd buy up all de niggers – de niggers – de colored African American citizens,
>   I'd buy up all de niggers, and – sell 'em, wouldn't you?[41]

This 'comic-banjo' piece, as it was described, appeared in a songster published in New York in 1863. Geographically and emotionally, it was only a block or two from a song such as this to the lynching of blacks on the sidewalks of New York during the draft riots of the same year.[42]

National historians have traditionally attached major importance to the Jacksonian era. The effects of that era have been interpreted variously in terms of nationalism, politics, social status, population movement, and technological and economic growth. Each of these interpretations assumes the diffusion of new ideas and attitudes through a population, which, during the period under consideration, was moving from the Mississippi Valley to the Pacific Coast and increasing from 17 million to 50 million. Doubtless diffusion of ideas and attitudes occurred in such traditional ways as by word of mouth and written correspondence; but it occurred also through steam-powered presses and popular entertainment that brought mass audiences into the tents, town halls and theaters of new population centers.

Thus gathered together, they could rejoice in what Mark Twain had described as a 'glad and stunning surprise'. At other times a vitriolic critic of American society, Twain's uncritical approval of minstrelsy is testimony to the pervasiveness of its influence. Minstrel songs, Twain wrote, 'were a delight to me as long as the Negro show continued in existence. In the beginning the songs were rudely comic ... but a little later sentimental songs were introduced such as "The Blue Juniata", "Sweet Ellen Bayne", "Nelly Bly", "A Life on the Ocean Wave", "The Larboard Watch", etc.'[43] Two of the five songs mentioned were Stephen Foster's. What probably had gladdened Twain on his first encounter with minstrelsy was its portrait of the new urban culture. What he remembered, writing his autobiography long afterwards, was the white voice of the sentimental ballads. For Twain, as for many of his contemporaries, these songs touched a central chord of white American consciousness – the place left behind, the endless outward journey: ('O! Susannah, don't you cry for me, I'm bound for Californie. ...' This self-pityingly heroic image, cameoed in a conventional form that negated non-white humanity, epitomized the Jacksonian imagination. Here is the Free Soil hero on his passage to India, strumming blackface minstrel songs.

Notes

1. T. Allston Brown, 'The Origins of Minstrelsy', in Charles H. Day, *Fun in Black or Sketches of Minstrel Life*, New York 1874, pp. 5–10.

2. Mark Twain, *The Autobiography of Mark Twain*, New York 1961, p. 64.

3. Edwin P. Christy, *Christy's Plantation Melodies No. 4*, Philadelphia and New York 1854, pp. *v–vii*.

4. Hans Nathan, *Dan Emmett and the Rise of Early Minstrelsy*, Norman, Okla. 1962; Nathan Huggins, *Harlem Renaissance*, New York 1971, pp. 244–301; Robert G. Toll, *Blacking Up: The Minstrel Show in Nineteenth Century America*, New York 1974. Toll's study provides a nearly definitive survey. Two older but still useful works are Carl Wittke, *Tambo and Bones: A History of the American Minstrel State*, Durham, N.C. 1930, and Dailey Paskman and Sigmund Spaeth, *'Gentlemen Be Seated!' A Parade of the Old Time Minstrels*, Garden City, N.Y. 1928. An earlier version of this chapter appeared under the title 'Blackface Minstrelsy and Jacksonian Ideology', *American Quarterly*, 27 March 1975, pp. 3–28.

5. Nathan, *Dan Emmett*, pp. 98–120; Edward LeRoy Rice, *Monarchs of Minstrelsy from Daddy Rice to Date*, New York 1911, pp. 7–8.

6. *Christy's No. 4*, pp. *v–vii*; John Tasker Howard, *Stephen Foster, America's Troubadour*, New York 1934, pp. 65–201, 372–77.

7. Brown, *Origins of Minstrelsy*, pp. 5–10; *Christy's No. 4*, p. *vii*; Nathan, *Dan Emmett*, pp. 70–71, 116–22; Howard, *Stephen Foster*, pp. 202–14.

8. The biographical data comes from Rice, *Monarchs of Minstrelsy*. See also *Bryant's Essence of Old Virginny*, New York 1857, pp. *vii–viii*, and *Buckley's Melodies*, New York 1853, pp. *v–vii*.

9. Charley White, *White's New Illustrated Melodeon Song Book*, New York 1848, pp. 51–52; *Christy's Ram's Horn Nigga Songster*, New York n.d., pp. 99–100; "Twill Nebber Do to Gib It Up So', *Old Dan Emmit's Original Banjo Melodies*, Boston 1843, sheet music in 'Dan Emmett' folder, Theater Collection, Harvard Library. See also Nathan, *Dan Emmett*, pp. 50–56, and Constance Rourke, *American Humor: A Study of the National Character*, New York 1931, pp. 77–103.

10. *Christy's No. 4*, p. *v*, Nathan, *Dan Emmett*, pp. 70–97; Toll, *Blacking Up*, pp. 11–20, 25–57. Jean and Marshall Stearns, *Jazz Dance*, New York 1968, pp. 11–60; Marshall Stearns, *The Story of Jazz*, New York 1956, pp. 3–33, 109–22; LeRoi Jones, *Blues People*, New York 1963, pp. 1–59, 82–86.

11. 'The Dandy Broadway Swell', *Wood's New Plantation Melodies* New York n.d., pp. 50–51.

12. *Christy's Panorama Songster* New York n.d. (1850?), p. 93, for an example of ethnic satire in blackface.

13. M. Campbell, *Wood's Minstrels' Songs*, New York 1852, p. 25.

14. *Christy's Plantation Melodies No. 1*, Philadelphia and New York 1851, pp. 45–46. Playbills, Theater Collection, Harvard Library: Chatham Theatre, New York, 1848; Jenny Lind, San Francisco, 1851; St. Charles, New Orleans, 1857. Walter J. Meserve, *Heralds of Promise: The Drama of the American People in the Age of Jackson, 1828–1849*, Westport, Conn. 1986, pp. 120–22. See also David Grimsted, *Melodrama Unveiled: American Theater and Culture, 1800–1850*, Chicago 1968, pp. 65–75; and Alvin F. Harlow, *Old Bowery Days: Chronicles of a Famous Street*, New York 1931, p. 264.

15. Twain, *Autobiography*, pp. 65–66.

16. 'Mose he went to college, he said he was a poet ...' in *Wood's Minstrels*, p. 25. Minstrel burlesques of tragedy and grand opera exemplified this usage. See Harlow, *Old Bowery Days*, p. 265 for an account of T.D. Rice in a burlesque of *Othello*.

17. 'Michael Walsh', *Dictionary of American Biography*, New York 1936, 19:390–91; Jack Kofoed, *Brandy for Heroes: A Biography of the Honorable John Morrissey, Champion Heavyweight of America and State· Senator*, New York 1938; David A. Williams, *David C. Broderick: A Political Portrait*, San Marino, Calif. 1969.

18. *Christy's Ram's Horn*, 76–77.

19. Ibid., 109–110. Many male performers built reputations playing 'wench parts', Rich, *Monarchs of Minstrelsy*, pp. 71, 86–87. And see Frank C. Davidson, 'The Rise, Development, Decline and Influence of the American Minstrel Show', Diss. New York Univ., 1951, pp. 130–31.

20. Carl I. Wheat, ed., '"California's Bantam Cock": The Journals of Charles E. DeLong', *California Historical Society Quarterly* 8:346 and 10:185.

21. Rich, *Monarchs of Minstrelsy*, pp. 27, 68–70.

22. *Wood's Minstrels*, p. 25.

23. *George Christy and Wood's Melodies*, Philadelphia 1854, pp. 39–40.

24. Howard, *Stephen Foster*, pp. 119, 136–39, 144–45.

25. *Christy's Plantation Melodies No. 2*, Philadelphia 1853, p. 35.

26. Twain repeatedly makes these connections; see Twain, *Autobiography*, pp. 5–6.

27. Rice, p. 20; Samuel A. Pleasants, *Fernando Wood of New York*, New York 1948; Leonard Chalmers, 'Fernando Wood and Tammany Hall: The First Phase', *New York Historical Society Quarterly*, 52 (October 1968): 379–402. On Henry Wood, see Paskman and Spaeth, pp. 155–56.

28. Rice, 20; 'DeLong Journals', *California Historical Society Quarterly*, 9:385; 'Continuation of the Annals of San Francisco', *California Historical Society Quarterly* 15 (June 1936): 178–80, 184; *New York Clipper*, 23 May 1868; Kofoed, *Brandy for Heroes*, pp. 69–86; Williams, *Broderick*, pp. 29–31.

29. *Clipper*, 25 April and 30 May 1868; Nathan, *Dan Emmett*, pp. 135–42, 214–75.

30. Howard, *Stephen Foster*, pp. 27–28, 43–45, 256–64.

31. I know of no comparable linkage between any individual minstrel or minstrel group and any party opposed to the Democracy. Song books issued by such parties seem generally to have excluded songs of identifiable minstrel origin.

32. Eric Foner, *Free Soil, Free Labor, Free Men: The Idelology of the Republican Party Before the Civil War*, New York 1970, pp. 149–55; Foner, *Politics and Ideology in the Age of the Civil War*, New York 1980, pp. 57–76; Jean H. Baker, *Affairs of Party: The Political Culture of Northern Democrats in the Mid–Nineteenth Century*, Ithaca, N.Y. 1983, pp. 212–58.

33. *Christy's Panorama Songster*, p. 79. See also Toll, *Blacking Up*, pp. 72–97. I think Toll here somewhat over-emphasizes the expression of anti–slavery sentiment in minstrelsy.

34. *Christy's Ram's Horn*, p. 102.

35. Ibid., p. 200; *Christy's No. 2*, pp. 44–45.

36. Twain, *Autobiography*, p. 66; Howard, *Stephen Foster*, pp. 210–11, 246; *White's Serenaders' Song Book: No. 4*, Philadelphia 1851, p. 40.

37. *Christy's Panorama Songster*, p. 85; *Christy's Plantation Melodies No. 3*, Philadelphia and New York 1853, pp. 10–11, 40–41; *Hooley's Opera House Songster*, New York 1864, p. 5; 'Joshua' [Hutchinson], *A Brief Narrative of the Hutchinson Family: Sixteen Sons and Daughters of the 'Tribe of Jesse'*, Boston n.d.; A. B. Hutchinson, *The Granite Songster*, Boston 1847; George W. Clark, *The Liberty Minstrel*, New York 1845. On the permutations of *Uncle Tom's Cabin*, see Harry Birdoff, *The World's Greatest Hit*, New York 1912, p. 6, and Toll, *Blacking Up*, pp. 93–97.

38. *Christy's Ram's Horn*, pp. 46–47.

39. Frank Converse, '*Old Cremona' Songster*, New York 1863, pp. 9–10.

40. Dan Bryant, *How Are You Greenbacks*, New York 1863, sheet music, 'Bryant's Minstrels' folder, Theater Collection, Harvard Library. *Hooley's Opera House*, pp. 16–17; *The Little Mac Songster*, New York 1863, pp. 11–13, 29, 42–43, 53.

41. Converse, 'Old Cremona', pp. 44–45, 47–48.

42. James B. Fry, *New York and the Conscription Act of 1863: A Chapter in the History of the Civil War*, New York 1885; A Volunteer Special [William Osborn Stoddard], *The Volcano Under the City*, New York 1887.

43. Twain, *Autobiography*, p. 66.

8

Constructing a Western Hero

From Ulysses to Rambo, the construction of heroes has been at the crux of the ideological process. Bourgeois culture converted ideological expressions into commodities. Jacksonian politics immersed those commodities in urban markets that expanded and overlapped, spilling out into the national market. Mass political parties and denominational religion, the press, theater and book publishing – in about that order of chronology and importance – defined separate arenas for trying out the marketability of model heroes. Competition bridged these separations: newspapers competed with melodrama and blackface minstrelsy for consumers' nickels and dimes; entrepreneurs of melodrama sought to distance their counterparts in comedy and tragedy; story papers and book publishers wooed a newly literate audience through competitive fictional genres, and especially through the competitive promotion of heroes. Politicians alternately imitated or bought into these artifacts of mass culture. Within this network of markets, ideological construction might seem to have been self-generating, yet never ceased to display the class and interest group signatures that attest its origins.

The present chapter and its thematic sequel, Chapter 14, 'Nationalizing the Western Hero', together examine a series of vernacular characterizations from Royall Tyler's Yankee to Owen Wister's Virginian. Despite a stress on region explicit in the first and final terms of the series, its decisive elements are not regional idiosyncrasies but race and class. What most closely linked the Yankee and Virginian across a hundred-year time span was their common identification as white men and as servants, or virtually so, to upper-class masters.

The Yankee's master, as noted earlier, was Colonel Manly, a Massachusetts gentleman, late of the Continental Army.[1] Although the Colonel's Yankee servant might steal the show, there could have been no doubt in 1787 that the hero's role belonged to the Colonel. Morally exemplary action and dialogue must emanate from him, and he alone could take the lead in romantic love. Nor could there have been much ambiguity as to the Colonel's class status. He spoke for the landlord–merchant oligarchy that had led the Revolution and dominated the economic, political and social life of the new nation. Informing this characterization was the assumption that audiences, then largely of the same class as Colonel Manly, would identify with him as a vicarious experiencer of romantic love and as a mentor of political morality. Should members of the lower class happen to infiltrate the theater audience, they could be expected to experience similar identifications, since they looked habitually to their betters for moral and intellectual tutelage. Thus, at the beginning of the series, the politics of deference defined the class status of heroes. Whatever individual characterization Tyler may have achieved, his portrayal of Colonel Manly would remain stereotypical. The Colonel would be replicated by Washington's staff officers in William Dunlap's *Andre* (1794), by cloning of the same types in celebrationist drama after the War of 1812, and by their diffusion through the nation's first harvest of novels during the 1820s and 1830s.[2] Genteel protagonists of works by Cooper and his contemporaries appeared indistinguishable from Tyler's Manly. Despite their good hearts and devotional patriotism, however, these standardized romantic heroes remained flawed as spokesmen of American nationality. Lacking any distinctive American voice (because early nineteenth-century Americans of upper-class background and education still spoke the same English as their English counterparts), they emerged merely as American cousins to English ladies and gentlemen, already rather too well-known on the American stage. Moreover, the very attribute that initially had qualified them for heroic roles – their class status – took on negative reference as the Jacksonian upsurge restructured American culture and politics.

Stage Vernaculars

For reciprocally opposite reasons, vernacular characterizations moved into this space. There were two sets of vernaculars, overlapping but significantly different. The first set entered the culture by way of farce and comedy, while the second came in more circumspectly through various forms of published fiction. Since the stage vernaculars have been treated earlier in some detail, all that will be necessary for their case is to summarize distinguishing characteristics, especially those that might have tended to enhance or retard their potential as spokesmen of American nationality. Blackface minstrels, because of their racial masks, were precluded from direct participation in such spokesmanship.[3] There remained three other theatrical types: the Yankee, the southwestern frontiersman, and Mose, the urban workingman and volunteer fireman.[4]

Aside from the appeal of distinctively American speech, the runaway popularity of stage vernaculars during the three decades prior to the Civil War appears causally linked to their lower-class status (a necessary prerequisite to deviant speech), and to an egalitarian contempt for upper-class pretensions that marked stage vernaculars as 'natural' Jacksonians. Only the Yankee, eldest member of the set, had traced a gradual evolution from deference to egalitarianism. By the 1830s, as the urban masses established their presence in theaters, the Yankee had left his original politics of deference behind him. Meanwhile, the southwestern frontiersman and Mose, the urban workingman, were taking their first public bows as all-out egalitarians.

But to act out American nationality, it was not enough simply to reverse certain attributes of standard romantic heroes like Colonel Manly. Dialect in lieu of correct English could be a step toward American-ness because it differentiated Americans from the English; but because vernacular dialect had to be regional, it might, if pushed too hard, negate national identity. A parallel logic applied to class. Substitution of lower- for upper-class identity tended to enhance American-ness in a nation whose artisans and yeomen were successfully challenging the politics of deference. Yet it carried its own disqualification. How could a society weaned on leaders like George Washington and Colonel Manly find full satisfaction in spokesmen who might be told to use the servants' entrance at the homes of affluent and cultivated citizens? On the other hand, if such spokesmen failed to encounter some degree of rejection from an obviously recalcitrant upper class, how could they continue to be thought of as champions of the lower class? Here, in class terms, is the contradiction underlying the problem of marriageability, defined by Henry Nash Smith in reference to Cooper's wilderness heroes.[5]

Distinctive speech, lower-class status and egalitarian sentiment, then, enhanced popularity, yet tended, initially, to be self-limiting. One other major source of vernacular popularity contained no such limitations. This source, at the very beginning, had been pinpointed by Tyler's Yankee when he demanded, 'Sir, do you take me for a neger?' In contrast to romantic heroes, all vernaculars (including blackface minstrels) advocated white supremacy. But it is important to note, in comparing stage with fictional vernaculars, that the former proved more relentlessly racist than the latter. Perhaps this differential simply measured a wider space in fiction for the luxury of ambivalent loyalties. Or perhaps it resulted from the fact that comedians (unlike writers of fiction) were obliged to confront mass audiences in urban settings face to face. More significant than either,

I think, is that the hard side of racism generally appeared in nineteenth-century America as a corollary to egalitarianism. Stage vernaculars – likely to be enthusiastic egalitarians – tended to link the ideal of a social order without class distinctions to racial barriers that would separate the white fraternity from non-white outsiders, thus exporting class hierarchy. Fictional vernaculars, on the other hand, often accepted or even defended class hierarchy. A soft position on race, for many of these characterizations, complemented their rigor in matters of class.

Before shifting focus from stage to fictional vernaculars, certain problems of definition and conceptualization need to be clarified. The term *natural Jacksonian*, applied thus far only to stage vernaculars, offers a convenient starting point because the usefulness of that term rests on a concept of class. What I mean by *natural Jacksonian* is a vernacular character of lower-class status to whom is attributed class consciousness in the form of egalitarian values. Mose, the urban workingman, precisely fills out the definition since he exhibited both lower-class status and egalitarian response. The Yankee embodies the definition as historical process. At the outset the Yankee had been characterized as lower class in status but a conscious adherent of deference. Tyler pointed to the subliminal flaws in the Yankee's deference; and by the time of Jones's *Green Mountain Boys* (1832) the Yankee was opportunistically employing white racism to justify his shift from deference to egalitarianism.[6]

The southwestern frontiersman, finally, illustrates the vast complexity of interrelationships to which this definition gives access. David Crockett entered the public domain as a *persona* deliberately created by a local politician seeking to make the best of his lower-class base. Paulding brought that *persona* to the stage in *Lion of the West*. In both cases 'natural' Jacksonianism coincided with Jacksonian politics. The next step was the hijacking of the Crockett *persona* by whiggish ghostwriters who were obviously aware that its political value flowed from its 'natural' Jacksonianism. This level of complication was further escalated when Crockett, together with his fictional personifications, took up formal membership in the Whig party, all the while insisting on the integrity of the 'natural' Jacksonian original.[7]

Competition kept pace with increasing polemical complexity. At the simplest level, competition had resulted from treating ideological artifacts as commodities. This corresponded to a market-oriented society in which a single class monopolized ideological construction. Competition would then be likely to occur, not so much over ideological content, as over the effectiveness of packaging and marketing; and such appears roughly to have been the situation of Middle Atlantic and Northern cities after the War of 1812 but before the advent of the Workingmen's parties. As the Jacksonian era brought new class formations into mass politics, ideological competition would become multilayered, involving not only efforts to maximize audiences, but the deployment of oppositional artifacts. Plural class formations would generate rival claimants to American-ness and national spokesmanship. 'Natural' Jacksonian vernaculars on the Jacksonian side would soon be vying for popularity against counterparts under Whig management like the Crockett of the narratives and Seba Smith's Major Downing. Crockett, the man, might be expendable; but vernaculars conceived in his image set the stage for the Harrison campaign of 1840, and foreshadowed, at least, the coalition of eastern and western class formations that would take the name Free Soil.[8]

Meanwhile, America's peculiar party system structured the ideological market. Since major parties must be coalitions of class and interest groups, they could accommodate multiple, even antithetical, ideological symbols. Democrats found room at the top for planter landlords like Andrew Jackson and for tub-thumping urban workingmen like David Broderick. Whigs were able simultaneously to tolerate Hudson Valley anti-renters and Yankee textile magnates. The binary pressures of the two-party system tended to enforce a segmented ideological market. It would scarcely have been worthwhile, for example, during the 1840s and 1850s, for blackface vernaculars to seek patronage in the Whig camp; or for inspirational singers like the Hutchinson Family to peddle their temperance, pro-Indian and antislavery repertory among Democrats. At longer range, however, the strivings of a dominant party to remain dominant, and of its subordinate partner to overturn that dominance, worked to nationalize ideological competition. It was at this range that politics broadly inspired ideological construction. Thus, consolidation of Democratic control over the federal government in the 1830s coincided with popularization of theater and the pre-eminence of 'natural' Jacksonian vernaculars in comedy and farce. The long struggle to oust the Democracy from federal power then pushed Free Soil, and subsequently Republican, ideological entrepreneurs toward constructing a composite vernacular hero who, by transcending the limits of region and class, could bid for national spokesmanship. This task they carried out not primarily in theater but through the transformation of fiction into a mass medium.

Vernaculars in Fiction

Fictional vernaculars began as the progeny of nationalist authors of the 1820s and 1830s, among whom the most important to this connection were James K. Paulding, John Pendleton Kennedy, Seba Smith, William Gilmore Simms, Robert Montgomery Bird, James Fenimore Cooper, and the anonymous ghostwriters of the Crockett narratives. These writers drew their inspiration in part from the life of Daniel Boone, widely publicized during the surge of migration into the Mississippi Valley that followed the War of 1812. They were of course also influenced by the proliferation of stage vernaculars.[9]

Here again it seems appropriate to begin with the class-oriented notion of 'natural' Jacksonian, a starting point that immediately opens a major difference between stage vernaculars and those in fiction. Whereas stage vernaculars strongly favored 'natural' Jacksonianism, fictional vernaculars shied away from it. Of the authors referred to above, only Seba Smith, Paulding and the Crockett ghostwriters produced 'natural' Jacksonians as positive characters. What sort of vernaculars did the others produce. Necessarily, being vernaculars, they had to be lower class, but their consciousness was not egalitarian. On the contrary, it remained exactly the sort that members of the old merchant–landlord oligarchy would have wished to imagine in their artisans and yeomen: loyal adherence to the politics of deference.

Kennedy's Horseshoe Robinson offers a vivid example. In the novel of the same name (1835), Robinson appears as a Carolina yeoman and rural artisan speaking back country dialect. When revolution divides the gentry, he goes with the revolutionaries, to whom he manifests a devotion comparable to that of a ferocious but well-trained police dog. His class consciousness is delineated in a scene (summarized earlier in this study) in which Robinson, now sergeant, good-humoredly prepares a meal while his traveling companion – a major in the Continental Army – lounges on the grass waiting to be served.[10]

Simms, Bird and Cooper produced diverse vernacular types including some that resemble 'natural' Jacksonians; and it was from these that they recruited most of their murderers, kidnappers, renegades and traitors. They bestowed their blessings on deferential behavior. Thus, in Simms's *Woodcraft*, the aristocratic Mrs. Eveleigh's yeoman retainer, Fordham – who has used his woodcraft to defend that lady from Tory traitors on one side and frontier egalitarians on the other – is rewarded with the management of her plantation and marriage to a blooming country lass.[11] Bird, in *Nick of the Woods*, eloquently set forth the virtues of his Kentucky militia colonel, Tom Bruce. Yet it remains clear that Bruce, who speaks in an exaggerated southwestern dialect, must always remain 'a plain yeoman, endowed with those gifts which were necessary to his station.' Presumably the gifts that qualify the romantic hero, Roland Forrester, for a captain's commission in the Continental Army and hereditary membership in the James River aristocracy were of a different order. Bruce, recognizing the difference, displays an unctuous admiration for the young captain, and for the captain's uncle, Major Forrester, under whom Bruce once had served as 'copporal' against the French and Indians.[12] Cooper's Leatherstocking, throughout his multivolume career, always allied himself with whites of the gentry class (or their surrogates in officer's uniform) and always looked with contempt on the lower-class whites who crossed his orbit.[13]

This brief sample exhibits a set of fictional vernaculars in major novels published between 1823 and 1852 who replicate a state of mind that Tyler had somewhat doubtfully imputed to his prelapsarian Yankee in 1787. That indeed is a time lag. Here is a literary output that Marxian critics of a somewhat earlier era might have described as typifying false consciousness. False consciousness need not of course be false portrayal; and deferential vernaculars may have been no less accurate, in the sense of social realism, than egalitarians. The point at issue, however, is not realism in literature but ideological direction. Fictional vernaculars, by and large, seem to have been moving in a different direction from those of the stage.

Kennedy, who was a Whig, and Paulding, a militant Democrat, shared a common characteristic: their ideological constructions dovetailed neatly with their declared politics.[14] To set up a hypothesis on that basis might seem tempting, but unfortunately it would not survive any test beyond these two. At the outset, it would not work for the other 'natural' Jacksonians in the fictional set, since their authors (Seba Smith and the ghostwriters of the Crockett narratives) were Whigs. Nor does it fare much better with the deferential vernaculars, among whose authors only Bird and Kennedy were Whigs. Simms may have flirted with whiggery, but merely by way of following John C. Calhoun. The essential stations of Simms's transit were National Republican, Jacksonian Democrat, States' Rights Democrat and secessionist. This brings us, again, to the last and most renowned of the creators of deferential vernaculars – Cooper, who left his political testament under the title *American Democrat* and who supported Jackson for the presidency.[15]

The relations of ideological construction to political affiliation obviously cannot be decoded simply by one-on-one formulations. The next step is to explore class experiences that would presumably inform both ideological construction and political engagement. I will focus here on Cooper's Leatherstocking saga as the most densely complex among many works that developed vernacular characterizations. It will then remain to inquire how typical Cooper may have been of the genre. *Deerslayer* (1841), the opening installment (although the last written) of Cooper's five-part serial, reconstructs the youth of the pathfinder and scout, Natty Bumppo, who had earlier been introduced as a tragicomic vernacular already past middle age in *The Pioneers* (1823). *Deerslayer* traces the Leatherstocking's passage from adolescence to manhood, from deer hunter to hunter of men. Establishing his true calling as that of Indian killer, this transformation placed the fictional hero in historical context, inasmuch as among the nation's most revered leaders in Cooper's day were its Indian fighters.

Of course that was nothing new. In 1637, the commander of the Massachusetts Bay militia, Captain John Mason, had written in his journal:

> The Captain also said, We must burn them; and ... brought out a firebrand, and ... set the Wigwams on fire. ... Thus did the Lord judge among the Heathen, filling the place with Dead Bodies. ... And thus was their impregnable fort with themselves utterly destroyed.[16]

'What good man', President Andrew Jackson demanded (five years before publication of *The Deerslayer*) could prefer Cherokee 'savages' over the citizens of Georgia, equipped as they were with 'the blessings of liberty, civilization and religion?'[17] Jackson addressed the question to Congress in a message advocating removal of all Indians from east of the Mississippi. Jackson, a contemporary highly honored by Cooper, had been well-known as an Indian fighter before his victory over the British at New Orleans. Cooper's vernacular hero, Leatherstocking, can thus be identified as a fictional representation of a popular hero already more than two centuries old.

Considered as a depiction of social reality, however, Cooper's characterization offers puzzling contradictions. Leatherstocking's Indian killing has become selective: some of his best friends are Indians. Morever, his attitudes toward white society are ambivalent:

> As for farms, they have their uses, and there's them that likes to pass their lives on 'em; ... but where are you to find your shades and laughing springs ... and vinerable trees a thousand years old, in a clearin'? ... All is contradiction in the settlements, while all is concord in the woods. Forts and churches almost always go together, and yet they're downright contradictions.[18]

Leatherstocking delivered this opinion on his first manhunt. At the end of his long career, the aging scout was still ready to expound subversive sentiments:

> What will the Yankee choppers say when they have cut their path across from the eastern to the western waters. ... They will turn on their tracks like a fox that doubles, and then the rank smell of their own footsteps will show them the madness of their waste.[19]

Given declarations such as these, President Jackson could hardly have classified the Leatherstocking as a 'good man' without violating the logic of his own Indian-killing persuasion. Cities and farms, civilization and Christianity were desirable; forests and savages were not. This separation justified whatever the white republic might find necessary or convenient to do to Indians; and those who questioned that justification ceased by definition to be good. They became renegades, vestiges of aristocratic privilege or the spawn of artificially created monopolies, alien to the real America. White society must keep itself undifferentiated by social hierarchy in order to stand monolithically against savage and non-white enemies.[20] As Indian killing and white egalitarianism closed ranks, the Indian killer of social reality converged with the 'natural' Jacksonian of ideological construct.

By contrast with the starkly simple scenario available to 'natural' Jacksonians as Indian killers, the scenario surrounding Leatherstocking becomes vastly complicated. It contains good and bad Indians as well as virtuous and villainous whites. White characters occupy diverse geographical locations in relation to the frontier and different levels within a hierarchical class structure. There is no longer a single hero, but three different heroes and at least one heroine as well. Below is a schematic tabulation of major character types in the Leatherstocking scenario.[21]

LEATHERSTOCKING

Civilization	Wilderness
Good Whites	**Good Indians**
Romantic hero and heroine	Indian hero (Chingachgook)
Military	Relatives, fellow tribesmen of the Indian hero (Mohicans, Pawnees)
Governors, judges, senators occasional settlers, bee hunters, etc.	
Bad Whites	**Bad Indians**
Settlers; especially squatters, bounty-hunters, 'Yankee choppers', frontier rowdies	Hordes of hostile Indians – Mingoes, Hurons, Sioux – usually allied with French before the Revolution, British during and after

FRONTIER

East	West

Names may be assigned from any novel of the series, since the five form a unified whole. Within that totality, racial and class relations among the various character types remain relatively constant. Leatherstocking, the vernacular hero, is of course white. His closest tie is to the Indian hero, Chingachgook, his companion of hunt and battle. The white heroine usually suffers captivity by villains, white or Indian: Leatherstocking and his Indian comrade effect her rescue. In this action the romantic hero participates and it is clear that he will eventually marry the heroine. Leatherstocking, who is permitted no love except the love of wilderness, goes on with his Indian companion into the West.

Bad whites are lower class. Essentially they are 'natural' Jacksonians. They hunt and fight for the pleasure of killing, or for money. They carry axes and chop down the forest. They are rapacious, brutal, insensitive, like Hurry Harry in *Deerslayer* or the ominous and finally omnipotent squatters of *The Prairie*. Good whites, on the other hand, are of upper-class background. Especially must this be so with the romantic hero, usually a young officer, first in British, later in United States uniform, and his bride-to-be, the romantic heroine. Climactic confrontations of the Leatherstocking saga resemble the Indian-killing prototype in that they follow racial lines. Unlike that prototype, however, Cooper's racial divisions never coincide precisely with good and evil. At each turning point, the good whites and their good Indian allies will be found shoulder to shoulder with bad whites against hordes of bad Indians.

Virtuous character types on Cooper's frontier are always outnumbered by bad ones. The reader need have no fear for the immediate outcome, since Leatherstocking and his Indian companion are each equal to legions; but the ultimate event remains far from certain. After Leatherstocking and his comrade have pursued their westward journey, will the squatters and frontier rowdies – the 'natural' Jacksonians – be left in control? For this longer perspective, hope must rest upon the romantic hero and heroine, and on their upper-class linkages at varying distances eastward to pillars of social order and stability – generals, judges, land-owning squires, even a few congressmen and senators.

Cooper's notion of the frontier thus stands diametrically opposed to the concept later put forward by Frederick Jackson Turner.[22] For Cooper, the frontier released and brought to power the most depraved elements of white society. One might hope that as the frontier swept westward along trails opened by wilderness scouts like Leatherstocking, the institutions of law and order would move in, presided over by men of affluence, culture and authority. Yet Cooper never seemed certain of this outcome. Identifying with a landlord aristocracy that he saw as squeezed out between land-grubbing squatters and money-grubbing commercial boosters – both, on his very home turf, likely to be invading Yankees – Cooper played the role of last spokesman for an older and better order. He had scant sympathy for 'natural' Jacksonians. Nonetheless he admired and gave his political support to Andrew Jackson, perceiving him not as a huckster for the madding crowd, and never as an egalitarian, but as an old-style aristocrat whose relation to the masses was that of military authority. While Cooper's politics were, in the formal sense, Jacksonian, his social values were Old Federalist.[23] This apparent contradiction brings us to the heart of the Leatherstocking scenario: a class analysis framed in the perspective of a frustrated and powerless segment of the upper class.

What then is the class status of Cooper's Leatherstocking? Like Tyler's Yankee, he proclaims himself to be of white blood, obligated to live by white 'gifts'; and like the Yankee he has begun his career as a servant. His name and his speech attest lower-class origin, although some of his vocabulary and most of his sentiments may point to nobler connections.[24] Perhaps Cooper, struggling to conceptualize a spokesman for American nationality, intended him to span all classes, or tried to imply that because the Leatherstocking left organized society behind he had passed beyond class identification. At all events, by permitting the Leatherstocking to act out the fantasy of flight from civilization into wilderness, Cooper remodeled a conventional popular hero into an exponent of his own alienation. The aspect that most sharply distinguishes Leatherstocking from other vernaculars (including Bird's Nathan Slaughter in *Nick of the Woods*) is his penchant for holding the commercial-industrial proliferation of America in negative contrast to the purity of wilderness. But this beatification of wilderness contains socially conservative, even reactionary, implications. The thrust of Leatherstocking's critique – since wilderness in itself might furnish reprimands but never alternatives to a corrupt social order – is to reaffirm the politics of deference.

If that was the goal of the author, his construction overshot it. For some of Cooper's contemporaries, I think Leatherstocking expounded upon national destiny in terms more credible than the one-dimensional rhetoric used by Jacksonian politicians. Later, the Leatherstocking became emblematic of modern man, or at least of modern western man, in flight from his technological triumphs. Seeking redemption in the purity of wilderness, he brought the outriders of civilization – the Yankee choppers, the omnivorous squatters – relentlessly in his footsteps. He must end by destroying what he sought to preserve. The implications of this contradiction have remained central to the American experience of opening a wilderness in the midst of the age of science and industrialization. To have conceived such a hero was in itself an act of artistic inspiration. Did Cooper's inspiration have socio-economic sources? One may at least speculate that the circumstances of Cooper's class situation lent hunger and teeth to his creative imagination. So much so, perhaps, that the real bite of that imagination seems to have been largely reserved for twentieth-century readers.

Yet even during Cooper's lifetime his hero won acclaim in Jacksonian America. Then, as later, his audience appeal rested on an ability to speak to different levels of social awareness. At the popular level, the hero as 'natural' Jacksonian remained totally identified with white 'gifts'. Since the egalitarian ideal was of a racially homogenous society undifferentiated by class, the primary thrust of his actions was outward against non-white foes. Cooper deliberately caricatured this level of heroism in some of his ruffians like Hurry Harry or the sons of Ishmael Bush.[25] Leatherstocking, always an elitist, hated them more than he hated Mingoes or Hurons, and never ceased to denounce the society that created such rapacious types. Yet as a character in fiction, Leatherstocking could not divest himself of his Jacksonian brothers because the 'emblematic' aspects of his characterization stemmed from opening the wilderness and clearing out the Indians. He might regret the duties imposed by white gifts, but he could not shirk them. Even his friend Chingachgook merited classification as a good Indian simply because he joined the whites against people of his own race; and because, as the last of the Mohicans, he was himself well on the road to extinction.

The entire Leatherstocking saga abounds in massacres of Indians. Both the first and final installments conclude with ritual slaughters:

> They came upon the charge, the scarlet of the King's livery shining among the bright green foilage of the forest. ... A general yell burst from the enclosed Hurons; it was succeeded by the hearty cheers of England. ... In this scene of confusion and dismay nothing could surpass the discretion and coolness of Leatherstocking. ... The shrieks, groans and denunciations that usually accompany the use of the bayonet followed. That terrible and deadly weapon was glutted in vengeance.[26]

If in this scene we substitute frontiersmen for Redcoats, knives and hatchets for British bayonets, the final scene in Cooper's *Deerslayer* would be virtually identical with those of Bird's *Nick of the Woods* or Simms's *Yemassee*.[27] But similar scenes could also be found in the Crockett narratives or in Paulding's *Westward Ho!*, both of which offer positive portrayals of 'natural' Jacksonians.[28] Has class identification here been reduced to race? If so, salient elements in the body of each work would be left unaccounted for. I think a more appropriate conclusion could be stated, in Gramscian terms, that the artisan-yeoman upsurge against the politics of deference had already won a decisive victory: it had circumscribed the intellectual and imaginative space available to its opponents. I am not suggesting that Leatherstocking or Nathan Slaughter can be trimmed down to the simpler level of 'natural' Jacksonian Indian killing; but rather that the more complex constructions were compelled to embrace the less complex in uneasy partnership. Literary critics have often ascribed the aesthetic power of 'classic American literature' – especially Cooper's Leatherstocking Tales – to their mythic and symbolic representation.[29]

Contradictions built into the central characters then appear as archetypal aspects of the human condition rather than as perceptions historically located and filtered through social experience. The point I would settle for here is that 'literary' and ideological conceptualizations are sometimes complementary, each furnishing context to the other's abstraction.

Free Soil Heroes

By about 1845 Cooper and his fellow fictionalists had successfully amalgamated the comic vernacular with the Indian killer. The result was a mix of regional memories of old frontiers from Kentucky and Tennessee to New York and New England. Leatherstocking – and Daniel Boone, almost as thoroughly fictionalized as Leatherstocking himself – were the preeminent mixers. Their offspring remained vernacular, thus necessarily lower class, yet commanded more respect than their comic counterparts on stage. Increasingly these 'sons of Leatherstocking' assumed the burdens of westward expansion and national destiny. Charged with such responsibilities, they could devote only off-duty hours, as it were, to cultivation of the comic vein.[30]

In *Virgin Land*, Henry Nash Smith shows how the vernacular comic of the early nineteenth-century novels was remodeled on the image – or, more accurately, on one of two possible images – of Kit Carson, the Rocky Mountain trapper and Indian fighter.[31] Both Carson and Daniel Boone, in their literary incarnations, contained the same subversive potential as Leatherstocking, in that their closeness to nature, their susceptibility to natural 'sublimity', and their persistent withdrawal into the wildnerness expressed criticism of the commercial–industrial order they sought to leave behind. For Carson, this potential adhered mainly to his earlier phase as trapper and mountain man. But Carson later served as pathfinder to John C. Frémont, commander of scouts in the Mexican War and territorial governor and pacifier of Indians in the newly conquered domain.[32] To model the western hero on this later portion of Carson's career required no radical turns of conceptualization. All that was needed was to reach back behind Cooper's complex class-divided scenario to the older and simpler version wherein the Indian fighter had operated as spokesman of a presumably homogenous and undivided white fraternity. Both options remained available in the literary lineage of the western hero. But of course it was not literary taste that dictated the choice. It was the impact on literary taste of the rapid penetration of agricultural society into wilderness. The Jacksonian program of buying social harmony in exchange for territorial expansion at the expense of Indians and of Mexico tended to disqualify the more complex of the two options, temporarily at least, as subject matter for the willing suspension of disbelief. Only writers as isolated and self-sustaining as Thoreau could continue to attach artistic credence to the idea that communion with wilderness might serve to correct, or atone for, the ills of an ugly and amoral social order. Thus the western hero as modeled on the empire-building phase of Carson's career celebrated the social order rather than criticized it.

Through the politics of John C. Frémont, these identifications also served to link the western hero to the anti-slavery cause – an anticipation subsequently borne out by Carson's services to the Union during the Civil War. Yet it is worth noting that it was not Frémont who furnished the heroic model, but Carson, whose relation to Frémont replicated that of Leatherstocking to the aristocratic officers he had served in the British and American armies. In any case, the western hero moved decisively in an anti-slavery direction. Doubtless there were southern sympathizers among early writers of western romance. Theoretically, they might have developed a hero who championed the expansion of slavery . I have seen no evidence of any attempt in that direction, however, perhaps simply because of the relative absence of a literate mass audience in the South. The existence of such an audience in the North and West made possible the industrialization of serial and book publishing in northern cities (building on what already had been done by the penny press), which in turn closed off certain ideological directions that might otherwise have remained open. The outcome of these several sequences was a shift of characterization from elitism to egalitarianism that pushed forward the process begun by those whiggish authors and publishers who had wooed David Crockett in the 1820s.[33] It would seem accurate to describe the western hero as having become, by the 1850s, a frontispiece for the Free Soil movement.

Among the literary problems of western fiction examined by Smith is that of marriageability. The pressures and opportunities of literary success induced western romancers to search out ways of mating their popular heroes to straight romantic heroines.[34] Cooper himself apparently tried out every possible device to achieve this end. The simplest was to reduce the heroine's class status to make her more accessible to the hero, who, as a vernacular, must be lower class. A more complicated alternative was surreptitiously to upclass the hero by revealing him to be disguised as a veracular but to be in reality an educated, upper-class youth, who, for suitably noble and selfless reasons, has chosen to operate incognito. This was the plot of *The Pioneers*. In the last of the Leatherstocking series, *The Prairie*, and again in *Oak Openings* (1848), Cooper tried out a gradualist technique that began by doubling the vernacular hero to provide a younger companion as apprentice or neophyte. Traces of class and regional origin in the companion could then be minimized, while his speech would be allowed to soar into proper English at moments of crisis or high emotion. The effect would be gradually to distance the younger companion from the vernacular characterization, thus bringing him closer, in overt behavior, to the upper-class manners of the heroine. None of these devices, in Smith's estimate, proved effective for Cooper; and even among Cooper's successors the problem of marriageability remained unresolved until after the Civil War.[35]

If this dilemma is posed as a literary problem, possible solutions can be evaluated only in terms of fictional credibility or aesthetic satisfaction. If, however, we move outside literary frames of reference, the real impact of class in respect to marriageability comes into focus. What the Free Soil Movement, as a class-alliance-in-the-making, required for its operating myth was the story of a man of yeoman or artisan background who would win the love of an upper-class young lady and claim her, not by force or stealth, but by convincing her male guardians through his own achievement that he had the power and right to do so. The West provided ample arenas for such demonstrations. Yet it would not be enough merely to string together appropriate plot devices. What was needed was concurrence of authors and audiences upon the credibility, as well as desirability, of such an outcome. Desirability might come easily enough for mass audiences weaned on the penny press and already asserting themselves through political behavior; but the *un*willed, or spontaneous, suspension of disbelief would be likely to take shape more slowly.

Once the problem is stated in class terms, it becomes obvious why Cooper had difficulty coping with marriageability. His Old Federalist mentality could hardly have endorsed either the Free Soil alliance or cross-class marriage; he used plot devices to resist both. The first of the plot devices referred to above had the effect of negating Free Soil aspirations by mating the hero to a heroine already demoted from upper-class status. The second device, despite playing with dual identity, arrives at a similar negation through its presupposition of upper-class origin for the hero. To the aspirant Free Soiler, this would seem even more objectionable than the first, because, in addition to preserving the sanctity of intraclass marriage, it proclaims the capacity of upper-class young men to invade lower-class precincts and outdo lower-class males on their own turf.[36] In that respect it stands on a par with John Pendleton Kennedy's fiction of the planter aristocrat who overturns a Jacksonian bully at fistfighting. The third device, that of whittling away regional and vernacular peculiarities through doubling, *could* provide a way of advancing by gradual stages toward upwardly mobile marriage; and in fact *did* provide such a trail for some of Cooper's successors after the Civil War. But not for Cooper; he used it merely to install a mezzanine level between upper and lower class in which properly deferential artisans and yeomen could mimic the mating rituals of their social superiors.

Characterizations drawn from several western romances published in the later 1840s and early 1850s flesh out what has been said rather abstractly so far about Free Soil heroes. The first of these is the prodigious Ohio River boatman, Mike Fink; not the pseudo-folkloric Mike Fink of the tall stories and almanacs in which he was often paired with Davy Crockett, but Mike Fink as the fictional protagonist of a novel by Emerson Bennett, published in Cincinnati in 1852. Vernacular identity is established through Fink's southwestern jargon: 'Why, yes, I reckon as how you mought as well know my name, seeing as how you mought some time or other take a fancy for a leetle brush, for which I'm al'ays on hand. I'm nobody less nor Mike Fink, at your sarvice.'[37] Language, together with his trade as a flatboat operator and propensity for boozing, assigns Mike Fink firmly to lower-class status. Yet he carries no trace of deference in language or bearing toward other males, regardless of their class. Like David Crockett, he is already a considerable distance into Free Soil territory by contrast with Cooper's Leatherstocking or Kennedy's Horseshoe Robinson.

Fink is portrayed as attractive to women. Presumably he enjoys his girlfriends between drunken sprees; his stand toward upper-class females, however, remains impeccable. He presides like the father confessor in *Romeo and Juliet* over the aristocratic romance that blossoms on the very deck of his flatboat. Fink's author, clearly, was not unaware of tensions beneath the surface of his fiction. When the romantic hero, a gallant youth of Virginia Tidewater background, learns that his beloved Aurelia is descended from Spanish nobility and actually the heiress to a grand estate in Mexico, he declares, '"One must not love above his station."'

> Aurelia started back ... [and] gently took his hand ... : 'No station is above that of an honest and honorable man. No true woman, but that he, who possesses these virtues, may hope to win.'[38]

Aurelia's message, however, was not addressed to vernacular heroes. Not yet.

In the year after *Mike Fink*, Emerson Bennett published, also in Cincinnati, a two-part serial entitled *The Prairie Flower; or, Adventures in the Far West*. The West was now California and Mexico, the fictional time 1843. Fink's father confessor role has been taken over by none other than Kit Carson, who pops in and out saving romantic heroes and heroines (in this case, two of each) from bands of Indians and Mexicans. Carson appears as young, small, soft-spoken. Yet 'that renowned name [is] better known on the mountains and over the broad West than that of any other living being.'[39] Carson commands respect from lawless mountain men; he is terror and death to Indians. As to his language, it varies unpredictably from southwestern vernacular to what might be described as planter-genteel:

> Say what you will, comrades, thar is after all but one way of settling this affair, and that is to pitch into the varmints and lift their hair. I've had a little experience in my time ... and may safely say I've never knowed an Indian yet as wasn't a coward, when assailed in a vigorous manner by a determined paleface.[40]

Within this bifurcated language we are presumably to read both Carson's yeoman origin (like Abraham Lincoln, he had been born in a Kentucky log cabin) and his natural aristocracy, which shines through in fragments of grammatically pure diction. Young, handsome, bold though he may be, Carson remains throughout Bennett's serial totally outside the range of romantic interest.

A work heavily relied on by Henry Nash Smith in establishing the pre–Civil War orbit of the western hero was Charles Averill's *Kit Carson, Prince of the Gold Hunters*, published in Boston in the year of the Gold Rush, 1849. Here Carson not only anchors the theme and provides the title but participates centrally in Averill's melodrama; yet again he remains outside any romantic couplings. He even appears oblivious to such obvious tokens of sexuality as the heaving bosom of a young woman in a swoon. (Carson had rescued this 'youth' from Indian captivity ten years earlier, and after taking care of her all that time in the wilderness, still believes her to be a boy.)[41] In Averill, Carson approaches sanctification. The romantic hero, Eugene Lincoln (son of a *good*, though poverty-stricken Boston family) soliloquizes as follows:

> And this – this is Kit Carson ... the wonderful man whose hardihood and enterprise have made him so celebrated. And yet, how honest, how frank, how manly. And ha! I have heard that of his character which leads me to believe, that the rough manner, the uncultivated speech ... are in a degree assumed; that he in his youth received the benefits of a good education ... but that he ever loved the wild delights of a hunter's life, and, with its freedoms and pleasures, determined to adopt its plain habits and plainer speech. – Yes! and even while he has at his command the choicest ... language of polished life, he feels a sort of pride in disguising it beneath the ruder diction, known to the rough frontiersman![42]

Here is the device of disguise, already noted in Cooper, with its upper-class one-upmanship; but since Averill and many of his readers must have been aware of Carson's actual social background, the main effect would be to bring forward the notion of natural aristocracy with its presumed powers – outward and visible signs of inward grace – to purify 'uncultivated' speech.

The key, I think, is the repeated stress on male egalitarianism. When Lincoln tells 'Mr.Carson' his name, the other responds:

> Lincoln, hey? That sounds manly and honest; I like it, – none of your high-strung, windy-sounding Fortesques and Mortimers, and sich dandified non-sense. But I say, stranger, don't *mister* me anymore; I'm not used to having a handle to my name. ... I'm plain Kit Carson – all the same name to friend or foe.[43]

Given the previously noted congruence between egalitarianism and the hard side of white racism, one would anticipate increasing ferocity against Indians as the hero moves from deference to egalitarianism. While it would scarcely be possible to quantify such a shift, the books under examination suggest that to many readers ferocity did not seem abnormal or demeaning as a heroic attribute. Thus Bennett narrates a transaction, presumably characteristic, on the part of two vernaculars of southwestern style who have just survived a skirmish with Indians.

> ... 'But I say, Tom?'
> 'Well, hoss?'
> 'Didn't we throw 'em purty?'
> 'Well, we did, old coon.'
> 'I'll be dog-gone if we didn't. Come, let's lift thar hair – augh!'
> With this, both trappers drew their knives, and taking from a little bag attached to their garments a small sandstone, commenced sharpening them with as much indifference as if they were about to slice buffalo instead of dipping them into the blood of human beings. ... The first Indian they came to was not dead; and running his knife into his heart with a barbarousness that made me shudder, Black George observed,
> 'That's your meat, Tom.'[44]

Lest this be taken for moral condemnation, the author has prefixed an admonition that western Indians are even less to be admired than the bold, cunning Indians of the eastern forest. 'The present tribes have degenerated wonderfully. They are taken as a whole, a dirty, cowardly, despicable set, without one noble trait, and not worth the powder it takes to kill them'. Even the saintly Carson expresses such sentiments. Averill presents Carson as a relentless destroyer of Indians; Bennett links him specifically to scalp-hunting: 'I'll have a talk with you by-and-by', Carson says, as he shakes the hand of an eastern acquaintance, 'but now we mountain men hev got a right smart chance at scalping – arter which I'm at your sarvice.'[45]

Building on Smith and generalizing from these selected examples, it seems reasonable to conclude that by the early 1850s the western hero had moved about half-way from deference to egalitarianism; but that sexual encounters and marriage, although of enormous interest, remained screened from changing class relationships. The hero's vernacular extravagances are winding down, his regional peculiarities fading into a kind of diffused westernism. Meanwhile, ferocity against Indians remains at a high level, or has even increased by contrast to the rather muted blood lust displayed by Cooper's Leatherstocking. The Leatherstocking scenario is, in any case, recessive; in the ascendant is the 'natural' Jacksonian scenario of white brotherhood purified and consolidated through the destruction of non-whites.

Yet the Free Soil hero exhibits certain anomalies, or silences. Pushing the hard side of white racism against Indians, he keeps discreetly silent on the subject of African Americans. Although we know, retrospectively, that he must move on to anti-slavery, he seems to hold no thoughts worth expressing on the subject of slavery as a social institution. And despite all the adulation, contemporary readers would have been hard-pressed to learn from these texts that Carson had recently taken part in the war against Mexico. Carson performs as a regulator only in a West that already belongs to the United States. Doubtless these silences corresponded to fracture lines in the Free Soil alliance. The career of George Wilkes – an episode in urban artisan culture to which the next chapter is devoted – acts out approximately those silences: Wilkes, something of a Free Soil hero himself, was especially a merchandiser of Free Soil heroes.

Notes

1. Royall Tyler, *The Contrast*, in Richard Moody, ed., *Dramas from American Theatre, 1762–1909*, Cleveland 1966, p. 42. On Tyler, see Moody, pp. 27–32.

2. William Dunlap, *Andre*, in Arthur H. Quinn, ed., *Representative American Plays*, New York 1923, pp. 81–108. Representative titles in the group of novels: Robert Montgomery Bird, *Nick of the Woods; or, The Jibbenainosay, A Tale of Kentucky*, 1837; James Fenimore Cooper, *The Spy: A Tale of the Neutral Ground*, 1821, and the Leatherstocking series, beginning in 1823; John Pendleton Kennedy, *Horseshoe Robinson: A Tale of the Tory Ascendancy*, 1835; James Kirke Paulding, *Westward Ho!: A Tale*, 1832; William Gillmore Simms, *The Partisan: A Romance of the Revolution*, 1835; Seba Smith, *The Life and Writings of Major Jack Downing of Downingville, Away Down East in the State of Maine. Written by Himself*, 1833.

3. See Chapter 7, p. 166.

4. See Chapter 5, pp. 116–19.

5. Henry Nash Smith, *Virgin Land: The West as Symbol and Myth*, Cambridge, Mass. 1970, pp. 59–70.

6. See Chapter 5, 154–163. Francis Hodge, *Yankee Theater: The Image of America on the Stage, 1825–1850*, Austin, Tex. 1964, p. 171; Samuel Woodworth, *The Forest Rose*, 1825 in Moody, ed., *Dramas*, pp. 147, 159–61, 169.

7. See Chapter 5, footnote 41. James K. Paulding, *The Lion of the West*, retitled *The Kentuckian, or A Trip to New York*, James N. Tidwell, ed., Stanford, Calif. 1954.

8. See Chapter 3.

9. Henry Nash Smith, *Mark Twain: The Development of a Writer*, New York 1974, p. 4; Smith, *Virgin Land*, pp. 51–60, 94. An illuminating discussion of Daniel Boone and the

Boone 'myth' will be found in Richard Slotkin, *Regeneration Through Violence: The Mythology of the American Frontier, 1600–1860*, Middletown, Conn. 1973, pp. 268–354. For Slotkin's treatment of Simms, Bird and Cooper, ibid., pp. 484–516; and Slotkin, *The Fatal Environment: The Myth of the Frontier in the Age of Industrialization*, Middletown, Conn. 1986, pp. 81–106. Among early works glorifying Daniel Boone were John Filson, *The Discovery, Settlement and Present State of Kentucky*, 1784; Daniel Bryan, *The Adventures of Daniel Boone*, 1813; and Timothy Flint, *The Life and Adventures of Daniel Boone, the First Settler of Kentucky*, 1833.

10. See Chapter 2, pp. 70–71. John Pendleton Kennedy, *Horseshoe Robinson: A Tale of the Tory Ascendancy*, Philadelphia 1835, 1:22.

11. William Gillmore Simms, *The Partisan: A Romance of the Revolution*, [1835] Chicago and New York 1885.

12. Robert Montgomery Bird, *Nick of the Woods; or, The Jibbenainosay, A Tale of Kentucky*, [1837] New York 1928, pp. 8, 21–22.

13. James Fenimore Cooper, *The Pioneers*, 1823, *The Last of the Mohicans*, 1826, *The Prairie*, 1827, *The Pathfinder*, 1840, *The Deerslayer*, 1841. The Leatherstocking's hostility to Hurry Harry in *Deerslayer* or to Ishmael Bush and his frontier rabble sons in *The Prairie* exemplifies his characteristic antipathy to lower-class whites. His alliance with, and subservience to, the white gentry is typified by his relation to Judge Temple and family in *The Pioneers*.

14. On Kennedy, see Chapter 2, pp. 65–66. On Paulding, Amos L. Herold, *James Kirke Paulding: Versatile American*, New York 1926, pp. 18, 20, 22, 65, 73–74, 128. And see Paulding's characterizations of Nimrod Wildfire in *Lion of the West*, and of Ambrose Bushfield, especially pp. 65–68, in *Westward Ho! A Tale*, New York 1832.

15. Milton and Patricia Rickels, *Seba Smith*, Boston 1977, *passim*. On Simms, John L. Wakelyn, *The Politics of a Literary Man: William Gillmore Simms*, Westport, Conn. 1973, *passim*. On Bird, Curtis Dahl, *Robert Montgomery Bird*, New York 1963; Robert L. Bloom, 'Robert Montgomery Bird, Editor', *Pennsylvania Magazine of History and Biography* 76 (April 1952): 126–28. James Fenimore Cooper, *The American Democrat; or, Hints on the Social and Civic Relations of the United States of America*, [1838] New York 1931; Dorothy Waples, *The Whig Myth of James Fenimore Cooper*, New Haven, Conn. 1938, especially pp. 1–25 and 50.

16. Captain John Mason, 'Brief History of the Pequot War', in Charles Orr, ed., *The Pequot War*, Cleveland 1897, pp. 28–31.

17. President Andrew Jackson, 'Second Annual Message', 6 December 1830, in James D. Richardson, *A Compilation of the Messages and Papers of the Presidents*, New York 1897, 3:1084.

18. James Fenimore Cooper, *The Deerslayer*, New York 1961, p. 265.

19. Cooper, *The Prairie*, New York 1964, p. 79.

20. Andrew Jackson, 'Farewell Address', in Joseph L. Blau, ed., *Social Theories of Jacksonian Democracy*, Indianapolis, Ind. 1954, pp. 1–20, especially p. 17; Blau, 'Jacksonian Social Thought', pp. *ix–xxviii*.

21. Names in parentheses are taken from *The Prairie* or *Deerslayer*.

22. Richard Hofstadter, *The Progressive Historians: Turner, Beard and Parrington*, New York 1970, pp. 47–164.

23. Cooper, *The American Democrat*, pp. 85–91, 130, and *passim*.

24. Cooper, *Deerslayer*, p. 35; Smith, *Virgin Land*, p. 64.

25. James D. Hart, *The Popular Book: A History of America's Literary Taste*, Berkeley, Calif. 1961, pp. 80–82. *Deerslayer* and *The Prairie*, respectively: 'sons' because Ishmael Bush himself is more than a caricature; he grows into a towering figure who commands admiration and terror.

26. *Deerslayer*, pp. 538–39.

27. William Gillmore Simms, *The Yemassee*, [1835] New York 1962, pp. 396–406; Bird, *Nick of the Woods*, pp. 378–84.

28. Comparable episodes occur directly or in retrospect in Paulding's *Westward Ho!* pp. 9, 94–95, and in James A. Shackford and Stanley J. Folmsby, eds, *A Narrative of the Life of David Crockett of the State of Tennessee*, [1833] Knoxville, Tenn. 1973, pp. 88, 90.

29. D.H. Lawrence, *Studies in Classic American Literature*, Garden City, N.Y. 1951, especially pp. 72–73; Lawrence, *The Symbolic Meaning: The Uncollected Versions of Studies in Classic*

American Literature, Arnim Arnold, ed., London 1962, pp. 18–19, 30–31, 106–111; Henry Seidel Canby, *Classic Americans: A Study of Eminent Writers from Irving to Whitman*, [1939] New York 1959, pp. 136, 140–42; Carl Van Doren et al., eds, *The Cambridge History of American Literature*, New York 1917, 1:298–300, 306; Richard V. Chase, *The American Novel and Its Tradition*, Garden City, N.Y. 1957, pp. 7–12, 44–45, 52–65; Leslie Fiedler, *Love and Death in the American Novel*, New York 1966, pp. 179–82; H. Daniel Peck, *A World by Itself: The Pastoral Moment in Cooper's Fiction*, New Haven, Conn. 1977, pp. 120–45.

30. Smith, *Virgin Land*, pp. 48–120.

31. Ibid., pp. 81–89.

32. Edward S. Ellis, *The Life of Kit Carson, Hunter, Trapper, Guide, Indian Agent, and Colonel, USA*, New York 1889.

33. See Chapter 3, pp. 78–84.

34. Smith, *Virgin Land*, pp. 64–70.

35. Ibid., pp. 68–70, 96.

36. For a discussion of the reaction of urban workingmen to such intrusions on 'their' sexual turf, Christine Stansell, *City of Women: Sex and Class in New York, 1789–1860*, New York 1986, pp. 95–97.

37. Emerson Bennett, *Mike Fink: A Legend of the Ohio*, rev. ed., Cincinnati 1852, p. 14.

38. Ibid., p. 17 and *passim*; p. 100.

39. Emerson Bennett, *The Prairie Flower; or, Adventures in the Far West*, Cincinnati 1853, pp. 55–56.

40. Ibid., p. 58.

41. Charles E. Averill, *Kit Carson, The Prince of Gold Hunters; or, The Adventurers of the Sacramento, A Tale of the New Eldorado, Founded on Actual Facts*, Boston 1849, p. 104; Smith, pp. 88–89, 100.

42. Averill, p. 87.

43. Ibid., p. 88.

44. Bennett, *Prairie Flower*, p. 45.

45. Ibid., pp. 44, 58; Bennett, *Leni Leoti; or, Adventures in the Far West, A Sequel to Prairie Flower*, Cincinnati 1853, p. 45; Averill, *Kit Carson*, pp. 73–90.

9

George Wilkes:
Mutations of Artisan Radicalism

Born in New York City in 1817, George Wilkes grew up in the same urban artisan environment that nourished blackface minstrelsy as well as the penny press – to which his early ventures were closely linked. Wilkes's career traces a passage from the radical republicanism of Tom Paine and Frances Wright to the conservative Republicanism of Rutherford B. Hayes. While many diverse tendencies found their way into the Republican coalition, the one exemplified by Wilkes is important especially in terms of ideological construction because it led through Locofoco Democracy, squatters' rights, the homestead movement, Free Soil and anti-slavery. It established the connections by which white egalitarianism made the transit from Jacksonian Democracy to the Republican party.[1]

Among the friends of George Wilkes's youth were David Broderick, son of an Irish stonecutter; Mike Walsh, whose Irish immigrant father ran a mahogany yard; and Tom McGuire, an occasional saloon-keeper, promoter of entertainments and prize fights. Wilkes himself, of 'obscure origin', was 'possibly the son of ... [a] cabinet and frame-maker.'[2] Radical republicanism suited these young men like an ancestral tradition. What was new, however, was the explosion of artisan production and artisan culture into a continental market. Mass circulation newspapers, mass forms of entertainment, the dynamics of mass politics, added new connotations to familiar rhetoric. For a generation that perceived wealth and power seemingly within arm's reach, the grand abstractions set forth by earlier revolutionaries in the universal cause of humanity took on a particular and individual exuberance. Equality, in its radical republican context, had meant that craftsmen and mechanics, even saloon-keepers, ought to have the same political rights as wealthy merchants and Hudson River

205

landlords. But why should young white America rest content with political rights if access to wealth was equally part of its birthright?

Wilkes, Broderick and McGuire made substantial fortunes. Walsh died in poverty, perhaps because, as the eldest, he held a more austere sense of republican virtue, or because he was an alcoholic, or from some combination of these. Wilkes, who would achieve national reputation as a political journalist (as well as sports reporter, war correspondent and literary critic) articulated experiences typical for his class and generation. True to his background, he turned ideological products into commodities, pushing the self-evident truth that in America radical republicanism and individual opportunity were heads and tails of the same coin. Within Wilkes's lifetime the urban artisan milieu that had shaped his consciousness broke apart. One part moved upward into a new class of industrial employers. Another part, closely linked to the first, formed a cadre of skilled and frequently prosperous industrial mechanics. The third and largest merged into the industrial working class.[3] Middlemen of artisan ideology like Wilkes were then torn between the heads and tails they had once thought were aspects of the same entity. Ardently egalitarian, Wilkes never ceased to declare himself a radical republican and radical republicanism the cause of universal humanity; but his circle narrowed, step by step excluding those whom individual opportunity had neglected to humanize with wealth and power.

Wilkes and Broderick

Class conflict in New York City during the 1840s was fought out in the streets, in police courts at the fringes of the underworld, and through the politics of Tammany Hall. Walsh and Broderick, leaders of volunteer fire companies, established local constituencies. Walsh called his followers the Spartan Band, his newssheet *The Subterranean*; Broderick, after he quit the stonecutter's trade, opened a workingmen's saloon also called The Subterranean. Challenging Tammany from the left, they bulldozed its meetings in efforts to overturn official nominations. The two had entered politics by way of the Locofoco faction of Tammany, a radical wing that tried to channel the national bank war into a campaign against local bankers, some of whom were Tammany leaders. Actually Locofocoism marked the final stage of the Workingmen's movement when, after having tried out independent party tickets, the insurgents returned to Tammany, now part of the Democratic apparatus.[4]

Linking these young men to the original Workingmen's party of 1829 was Walsh's alliance with George Henry Evans, one of the founders of that party and editor of the *Workingmen's Advocate*. Evans, an associate of

Frances Wright and Robert Dale Owen, had played a pivotal role in the emergence of the first wave of mass circulation dailies, although he had not shared their success. His radical politics remained too tenacious for that. By way of the bank war and antimonopoly, Evans had moved the *Workingmen's Advocate* to a focus on speculative ownership of land as the basic cause of inequality. From the revolutionary demand for equalization through confiscation, he gradually eased off to a plan for free distribution of federal public lands to actual settlers. Evans's views eventually permeated national politics through the Free Soil party and Homestead movement. Broderick and Walsh shared these ideas. Walsh signed the opening manifesto of Evans's National Reform Association and traveled with him to the Workingmen's Convention at Boston in 1844. The *Subterranean* merged briefly with the *Workingmen's Advocate*, supporting, among other ventures, Broderick's decision to run for Congress.[5]

George Wilkes meanwhile pursued a different route into the same arena. While employed as a law clerk he experimented with police court journalism featuring stories of the lives of criminals and exposés of evil doings by the wealthy. In 1845 he joined Walsh as an editor of the *Subterranean*. Enemies charged that the profits of their journalism flowed chiefly from blackmail. Both editors served time on criminal libel convictions, which they described as honorable wounds suffered in the republican cause. Walsh's prison term, abbreviated by a pardon from Democratic Governor Silas Wright, put him in line for election to the New York State Assembly, and eventually Congress. Wilkes emerged from four weeks in the Tombs as author of a pamphlet exposing corruption in the criminal justice system. With Enoch Camp, in whose office he had worked as a law clerk, Wilkes then founded what became one of America's most enduring periodicals, *The Police Gazette*.[6]

A declaration of purpose in an early issue promised exposés of professional criminals said to be pouring into the city from such hellholes as Newgate Prison and Botany Bay. The *Gazette* would aid law enforcement by supplementing the efforts of the overburdened police. Side by side with demonstrations of civic responsibility appeared ads like the following: 'Great Anatomical Museum ... splendid MODEL VENUS showing the "foetus in uteri" and the surrounding organs.'[7] At first a belated imitation of the penny press, the *Gazette* developed an almost exclusive focus on pornography, prostitution and crime. Wilkes's pamphlet, *Mysteries of the Tombs*, was already an experiment in this literary genre. The title suggests familiarity with Eugene Sue's *Mysteries of Paris*; and Wilkes went on to exploit sex against a background of urban mystery and gothic romance in *The Lives of Helen Jewett and Richard P. Robinson*, a fictionalized version of the reportage that had helped to win mass circulation for the penny press a decade earlier. As portrayed by Wilkes, Helen Jewett, daughter of an immigrant shoemaker, was intelligent, honest when circumstances permitted – and frank in her acceptance of sexuality: 'Yes ...', said the man ... slipping his hands between hers until his muscular arms met behind her waist. ... she summoned no prudery ... but let the hot flash of passion shrivel all resisting sense. ... ' That was Helen as teenager; in full career, still gripped by hot flashes, she sought the company of actors, 'generally fellows with a fine flow of blood and thumping developments under their occiputs.' Drifting into prostitution, Helen fell in love with one of her clients, Robinson, a young man of wealthy connections, whom she pursued. He, to save his reputation, killed her with an axe in her own bed.[8]

Wilkes's account of Jewett and Robinson was a precursor of the dime novels that would soon be flooding the market. A pioneer in this field, he pursued opportunity with egalitarian enthusiasm. Yet republican virtue was not totally forgotten since his theory of the crime was that originally put forward by the New York *Sun* and the *Transcript*. Helen Jewett in death thus became a symbol of natural innocence exploited and destroyed by the aristocracy of old wealth. Wilkes repeated the suggestions of a rigged verdict, the reports of affluent males crowding the courtroom to cheer the defendant while abusing and threatening female witnesses for the prosecution.[9] 'A large class of young men', he wrote, 'who felt disposed to proclaim their adhesion, wore a fancy glazed cap. ... ' These were known as 'Robinson caps'. James O'Meara, contemporary and biographer of David Broderick, many years later described Broderick leading a delegation of New York Democrats to greet President Polk on his arrival at Perth Amboy. Broderick wore a black broadcloth suit and a 'Helen Jewett mourner' hat. His hat was a badge of political opposition to the upper-class partisans of the alleged murderer, Robinson, and his aristocratic attorney, Ogden Hoffman. O'Meara explained that the 'Helen Jewett mourner' was a 'white beaver hat with a band of crepe or bombazine half way up the crown ... caricatures of that period always put just such a hat on the head of immortal "Old Hickory". ... '[10]

From pornography, Jacksonian style, Wilkes turned to the winning of the West. In 1845 he produced a scissors-and-paste *History of Oregon* combining a resumé of United States claims to the Northwest coast with his own proposal for a transcontinental railway to Puget Sound. Here again he was paralleling a major trend in the penny dailies. To the standard rhetoric, however, Wilkes added ingredients that were by no means commonplace. Dismissing constitutional inhibitions, he advocated a publicly owned railroad. Private ownership would create 'monster monopolies and degraded labor', placing western settlers 'at the mercy of a Company ... of enormous wealth and gigantic influence.' Only through federal construction and ownership could the benefit be 'equally distributed ... among the artizans and laborers of the whole country. ... An immense mechanical and laboring population' would be drawn to the Pacific Coast. The government then need only grant a hundred-acre allotment to every man who worked a year on the railroad, and 'instead of making a few men richer ... [it] would perform the highest achievement of Republican philanthropy, by elevating Labor to its true importance in the socal scale.'[11]

Wilkes, like George Henry Evans and Broderick (and like another urban journalist, Walt Whitman), saw the West as a leveller of social inequalities. Reporting the Sacramento Valley squatters' rebellion of 1850 in the *Police Gazette*, Wilkes wrote that the 'people' did right to 'put the speculators under their feet.' Had not Americans rejoiced at 'bloody revolutions that have given freedom to nations, our own among the rest', and ought they not 'exult over the emancipation of the landless in this equally important struggle?'[12]

Broderick made his bid for Congress in 1846. He carried the Tammany nomination in what had been a solidly Democratic district, but Tammany conservatives set up a candidate against him, splitting the vote and throwing the election to a Whig. His savings exhausted in the campaign, disappointed and embittered because he believed his Locofoco constituents had not stood by him, Broderick borrowed travel expenses from Wilkes and set sail for San Francisco in the spring of 1849. There he moved in with his old friend Tom McGuire, manager of the Jenny Lind Theater and thriving as an impresario of entertainment from blackface minstrelsy to grand opera. Broderick set about perfecting New York political methods in San Francisco. By 1850 he had command of an urban machine that sent him to the California State Senate. He wrote Wilkes that the situation was wonderfully favorable. There was no limit to what he might attempt if Wilkes would come out and help him. 'If you conclude to come, you can divide with me my last dollar if you require it, for you know, George, there is no man on earth whom I respect more than I do you.'[13]

Democracy in California

Wilkes came in 1852. Here, as in New York, the battle was not so much with the opposite party as against an aristocracy of old wealth inside the Democratic party. In California, this was the so-called 'chivalry', led by trustees and spokesmen for Southern slaveholders. Back East, the young radicals had readily enough acclaimed the leadership of slaveholders at the national level – Calhoun, Jackson, Polk – because black slavery at a distance posed no threat to an egalitarianism conceived as applying only to whites. But having the brothers and cousins of plantation owners elbow to elbow was a different matter. Their wealth and political experience gave them advantages over ordinary men like those the great merchants and Hudson River landlords had enjoyed in New York. Slaveholders in California became a threat to white egalitarianism. Moreover, to Broderick and Wilkes they appeared vulnerable because, while the new state was overwhelmingly Democratic, most of its voters came from eastern cities or from non-slaveholding agricultural regions. By 1854 California was more highly urbanized than any other state between the Alleghanies and the Pacific.[14]

Wilkes served as campaign manager and ghostwriter during the early years of Broderick's rise to power, helping in 1854 to lay out the system of alliances that elected Broderick to the United States Senate two years later. Their strategy was essentially to construct a Tammany-style ward apparatus in San Francisco, stressing Workingmen's and National Reform Association issues, while seeking support in the mining districts by appeals to egalitarian and Free Soil sentiment. Broderick defended the Sacramento Valley squatters, advocated homestead legislation and a transcontinental railroad. In the United States Senate he broke with what he denounced as the proslavery policies of the Buchanan administration more decisively than did Stephen Douglas, whose follower he was sometimes said to be. But if Broderick and Wilkes were able to grasp the vulnerability of their enemies, the enemies also understood Broderick's weaknesses. They told his constituents that he had crossed over from Jacksonian egalitarianism to 'mongrel' egalitarianism. The insult that triggered Broderick's duel with the Southern fire-eater David Terry was Terry's statement that Broderick, seemingly a follower of Stephen Douglas, was actually in harness to the other Douglass, whose first name was Frederick.[15]

The duel itself, in which Broderick lost his life, was widely interpreted as a trap set for him by his aristocratic enemies. Remembrance of this drama remained alive in California and national politics for many years. Anson Burlingame in 1859 described Broderick's career as having 'shed a new dignity on the toil of man'. After the Civil War, when San Francisco stonecutters demonstrated for the eight-hour day, they carried a portrait with the words 'Broderick was one of us'. And the New York *Times* thirty years after his death wrote that he was 'idolized by the liberty-loving masses of California.'[16]

Since ghostwriters are by definition invisible, evidence of Wilkes's contribution to the Broderick orbit remains largely indirect. The most persuasive evidence is that, although Wilkes and Broderick quarrelled in 1855, Wilkes then returning to New York, they later resumed friendship; Broderick, who had no close relatives, named Wilkes the major beneficiary of his will, presumably in gratitude for service to his career. A direct glimpse emerges from a newspaper account of a banquet organized by Wilkes in 1854 to honor the newly appointed military commander on the Pacific Coast. Present were leading federal office holders, the governor and the mayor, as well as most of San Francisco's delegation to the state legislature. Among the toasts was one by Governor James Bigler to George Wilkes, 'who by his pen has contributed so largely to vindicate the true democracy of California during the recent agitations in this state.' Wilkes responded with a toast of his own:

> The American Mind – The true constitution of our government ... [which] will always present for European contemplation, a compact and terrible Republic of free thought, that cannot be dissolved or subverted, so long as this continent is peopled with our race.[17]

Yet Broderick and Wilkes had found grounds to quarrel within their republic of free thought. Why? According to Wilkes's account, he had twice tried while in California to combine devotion to Broderick's career with initiatives in his own interest. First, he had gathered promises from state legislators to enact an exclusive franchise for wharfage around the city of San Francisco. Broderick, learning of the scheme, told Wilkes that because of their close association, he, Broderick, was certain to be linked to the scheme and that it would damage his reputation. Wilkes then withdrew and the venture failed, at a personal loss to himself, he estimated, of over $100,000.[18] The second episode was one both men seem to have taken more seriously. Wilkes wrote that the only public office he had ever wanted was that of Supreme Court justice in California. When one of the incumbents died in 1854, Wilkes went directly to Governor Bigler to ask for the appointment. Bigler, assuming that the request reflected Broderick's wish, agreed. But Broderick had already promised the judgeship elsewhere. The confrontation between Wilkes and Broderick occurred at McGuire's. Rising in rage, Broderick denounced his friend as a traitor and ordered him out of the house. Wilkes left; and soon afterward left California never to return.[19]

What emerges from Wilkes's perception (the only viewpoint we have) is that neither he nor Broderick saw anything wrong in manipulating political power to personal advantage. The only question was for whose advantage. Since this reduced any moral dilemma to a balancing of personal loyalties, it implied a concept of political power not as accrued from the trust of certain groups of constituents, but as a kind of natural resource subject to private expropriation like a gravel quarry or gold mine. Despite their rhetoric about the rights of labor and the dignity of toil, they seem to have given little thought to their collective responsibility to the needs of the class from which they had both emerged. They believed, perhaps correctly, that they could enlist the admiration of Free Soil and Locofoco constituents by outdoing the aristocrats at their own styles and behavioral codes. Broderick must have walked into the trap that ended his life with some such notion of demonstrating his superiority to his class origin; he had meanwhile been salting away the rewards of political success as diligently as any old Tammany banker. Having come to California on borrowed money, Broderick left behind him an estate comprising at least 362 separate parcels of land in San Francisco valued at more than $300,000. Wilkes, due to the high cost of litigation, realized only a portion of the inheritance; but that portion enabled him to reestablish himself in New York as an independent editor and publisher.[20]

The Spirit of the Times

In 1856, Wilkes bought into an ancient, esteemed, and nearly defunct sportsmen's weekly, *Porter's Spirit of the Times: A Chronicle of the Turf, Field, Sports, Literature and the Stage*. Its previous orientation had been to horse-loving Southern gentlemen of the old type;[21] Wilkes turned it toward the Mississippi Valley and California. What he also added – and by virtue of which he launched the *Spirit* into another half-century of profitable publication – was his own involvement in urban culture. Lacking any reputation as a sportsman, he shrewdly planned his first major venture in that most urban of all American sports, prizefighting. He arranged a match between John Heenan, a native of Troy, New York who had learned the blacksmith's trade at Benicia navy yard in California, and Tom Sayers, England's 'world champion'. Wilkes followed Heenan across the Atlantic to cover the event while the *Spirit* promised a special edition of 100,000 copies within six hours of arrival of the steamer bearing his dispatches.[22] The result fulfilled Wilkes's greatest expectations. While the 'Benicia Boy' was demolishing England's champion, having knocked him down twenty-seven times, the crowd broke into the ring and the referee fled, leaving the outcome technically undecided. Wilkes then entered the fray with letters and articles flaying the hypocrisies of British sportsmanship. Eventually he negotiated a compromise in the office of *Bell's Life in London* (the English counterpart of the *Spirit of the Times*) by which the championship, although withheld from Heenan, was vacated by Sayers, who thus acknowledged defeat. Wilkes had himself presented by Ambassador George Dallas at the Court of St. James's before returning to a hero's welcome in New York.[23]

America was on the brink of war. A later biographical sketch said of Wilkes that upon turning war correspondent he wrote about battles 'as if they were a series of sporting events.'[24] Actually, it was the other way around. Despite his journalistic commitment to sports, he never shook off a vein of Puritanism that denied significance to any activity that could not somehow be linked to ultimate reality. And that reality was for Wilkes political. Horse racing, prizefights, war reportage, all had to be politicized to be legitimate. What resulted was a continuing schizophrenia between the *Spirit*'s editorial centerspread and the main body of the journal. Perhaps for this reason, Wilkes's political articles became increasingly intense. It seems unlikely that many subscribers read them, yet they were widely read elsewhere and at times extraordinarily influential.[25]

Like Broderick, Wilkes was a militant Unionist. When war began, he urged northern Democrats to supersede the Republican party through their own devotion to all-out war against the slaveholders. This proved a faint hope. Democratic leaders, leaning on the traditional southern alliance, seemed ready to promote peace on Confederate terms. Wilkes denounced them. At a time when old friends were booming McClellan for the presidency, Wilkes described the commanding general as front man of a defeatist conspiracy. His philippics, widely reprinted, were supposed to have influenced the administration especially through Secretary of War Edwin Stanton.[26] In November 1862, McClellan was relieved of top command. Wilkes credited his own exposés of 'incapacity and want of loyalty' with the result that 'this muddy incubus' had been 'virtually dismissed' from the service. Yet McClellan as Democratic presidential candidate was more dangerous than McClellan the general. 'Coldly aristocratic and "conservative"', esteemed by 'Jefferson Davis and the South', he would provide 'an eligible rallying point until the Confederacy could indicate who ultimately would be the Common President.'[27]

Wilkes blamed Democratic leaders for the New York draft riots in 1863, particularly Mayor Fernando Wood and Governor Horatio Seymour. He also charged the Irish Catholic hierarchy with complicity. As to the rioters themselves, they were a 'ferocious substratum' led by criminals and Confederate agents, yet happily lacking 'roots in the real masses of the people ... there was not an American laborer or mechanic' among them.[28] From Union Democrat, Wilkes moved to Radical Republican. Andrew Johnson he saw as captive of the Southern aristocrats. Congressional Reconstruction, including suffrage for black freedmen, seemed the only alternative. He now applauded advocates of inter-racial egalitarianism like Charles Sumner and Benjamin Butler. Avid for impeachment, Wilkes characterized General Grant as contemptible for siding with the president, admirable for breaking with him. He supported Grant in 1868.[29]

After that election, Wilkes tried for a time to minimize politics in favor of themes more directly relevant to his sporting clientele. The *Spirit* frequented resorts like Saratoga and the great racetracks at the outskirts of cities. Editorially it promoted sporting associations and standardized rules; and much as the *Police Gazette* had once exposed pimps and pickpockets, it hounded crooked gamblers who preyed on gentlemen at the tracks. Having used the prize ring to establish his own sporting credentials, Wilkes left that sport carefully behind him. With the onset of the Gilded Age, the *Spirit*, thoroughly urbanized, shifted its focus from prizefighting to trotting horses and Atlantic yacht races. The 'American Gentleman's Newspaper' flourished under his cosmopolitan touch.[30]

Theater notices became his particular pride. Underpinning this section, and marking the point at which Wilkes and many of his associates had first encountered the power of dramatic performance, was an unfailing celebration of blackface minstrelsy. From this the *Spirit* gradually cast its net across the theatrical spectrum. Wilkes obviously admired showmanship, and it would be hard to find a more illuminating guide to urban entertainment in the Reconstruction years than the weekly notices published under his direction. He moved on to interviews with actors, directors, and playwrights, and speculative pieces on the national character of American drama.[31] As one who had pushed his way up from the bottom, he felt compelled at last to settle scores with the acknowledged giant of high culture: 'Shakespeare, from an American Point of View, Including an Inquiry as to his Religious Faith, and his Knowledge of Law, with the Baconian Theory Considered' first appeared in serial form in the *Spirit* in 1875.[32]

The occasion was espousal of the 'Baconian Theory' by such erudite persons as Lord Palmerston and General Benjamin F. Butler. But Wilkes was not vitally interested in disputed authorship. His real concern was to show that the author, whatever his name, had remained captive to the time in which he lived and to the aristocratic class upon whose patronage he had depended. What emerged was an ideological critique that distinguished between poetic intuitions potentially universal in scope and moral-political judgments to which no modern republican ought to give credence. Had Shakespeare expressed 'one generous aspiration in favor of popular liberty', or 'alluded to the laboring classes without detestation or contempt'? Wilkes said he had not. Viewing the world through the eyes of kings and nobles, he had 'deliberately' misrepresented 'Jack Cade', and even Shakespeare's Brutus, often cited as a champion of liberty, was defending only 'the privileges of his own patrician class'.[33]

Moreover, Shakespeare was anti-Semitic. The world owed him no thanks for his contribution through *The Merchant of Venice* to this 'grovelling and contemptible reflection upon the Jews ... least of all should he be respected for it in America.' On the other hand, in Wilkes's critique, the world owed Shakespeare little thanks either for the portrayal of Othello, justified as it was 'by representing the black man as descended from a line of kings.' Wilkes felt that Desdemona's love for Othello was 'merely an animal fascination after all.' The Moor was 'black enough to be a shocking and repulsive contrast to the fair, confiding and unsophisticated girl whom he unworthily tempted from filial duty and Caucasian compatibilities.' Her marriage to the 'old black man' was 'revolting to modern audiences' because of 'the violence it inflicts upon the wholesome laws of breeding. ... The world must move on', Wilkes concluded, 'and Shakespeare must face the ordeal of improved ideas. ... '[34] Thus he reenacted the Benicia Boy's egalitarian triumph of twenty years earlier. The outcome, curiously, placed him in agreement, as a Shakespearean critic, with John Quincy Adams.

Egalitarian Empire

For those who successfully pushed their way up from the bottom in the age of Robber Barons, egalitarianism tended to merge into camaraderie with millionaires. In 1867 Wilkes became trustee of a project to colonize and develop Baja California. The original land grant from which this project emanated conveyed the bulk of the peninsula, almost 50,000 square miles, together with powers later described by Wilkes as 'similar to those enjoyed by the Hudson Bay and East India companies.'[35] Extracted from Benito Juarez, desperate for guns in his struggle against French intervention, as a bonus to arms agents, the grant was first subscribed by San Francisco speculators, then sold in 1866 to a New York consortium. For steering an act of incorporation through the New York legislature, Wilkes was rewarded with a seat on the board of directors and probably received a bundle of newly printed stock certificates as well.[36]

By the act of incorporation, the trustees of the Lower California Company were, in addition to Wilkes, August Belmont, New York banker, American representative of the House of Rothschild, and from 1860 to 1872 chairman of the Democratic National Committee; General Benjamin Butler, the flamboyant congressman from Massachusetts; William G. Fargo of Wells-Fargo Express, also a director of railroads, steamship owner and (during the Civil War) Democratic mayor of Buffalo; Cornelius Garrison, Gold Rush millionaire (his successes were in Panama transportation and San Francisco banking, not gold mining), later president of the Missouri Pacific Railroad and operator of steamships to South America; John A. Griswold, upstate New York iron manufacturer, Unionist Democratic congressman, and one of three contractors who built the USS *Monitor* for the United States Navy; Leonard Jerome, a principal owner of the New York *Times*, maker (and loser) of several Wall Street fortunes, and grandfather of Winston Churchill; and William Travers, briefly Jerome's partner, millionaire broker, merchant entrepreneur and leading New York Democrat.[37]

Leaving aside Wilkes and Butler, the trustees comprised a *Who's Who* of eastern Democratic wealth. In politics and life-style they resembled those bankers and monopolists whom the Locofocos had sought to drive out of Tammany thirty years earlier. To men such as these the Baja venture was merely a minor gamble in which they could afford to lose a few thousands on the long shot that some bonanza might turn up. For Wilkes and Butler there were more compelling motivations; not yet millionaires, they soon might be if the Lower California Company succeeded.

The first step as specified in the Mexican grant was to colonize two hundred families within five years. The company retained J. Ross Browne, at that time 'United States Commissioner of Mines and Mining for the Far Western States', whom Wilkes must have known in California, to conduct a survey of the peninsula.[38] Completed in the summer of 1867, Browne's report provided material for a brochure, authored by Wilkes, but with selective omissions. Among the portions left out were the comments by Browne's assistant who had traveled overland from Cabo San Lucas to San Diego. 'The grantees have been woefully deceived', the assistant wrote. Land of any value was at the northern and southern extremities, beyond the boundaries of the grant. In the central region, usable harbors gave access only to cactus desert lacking water and wood: 'To send a party of colonists here, without previous preparation of the land at great expense, would be criminal.' Records of earlier attempts foretold 'only too plainly how it would result.' These facts 'forced themselves so strongly upon me that I have considered it my duty to report them, feeling confident that the. ... Company would know how far to accept them and how much of them to disregard.'[39]

The image conveyed in Wilkes's brochure was of a second Eden awaiting the plow. 'Wine, hides, ... sugar, dried meats, figs, raisins, dates, oranges, ... gold, silver and copper ores' were already in production. From his desk flowed copy that stimulated news stories in New York and San Francisco, mass meetings of prospective colonizers, and advertisements like the following in a San Francisco daily: 'Free Land. Free Trade. No Fences Necessary. Homes for the Poor. Health for the Rich. 160 acres free to the first 1000 settlers. Plus city lot. ... ' The Mexican land grant promised citizenship, exemption from taxes and military service, and religious freedom, as well as local self-government. And to clinch it all, the company's recent appointment of General John A. Logan as 'Governor of colonization ... assured to settlers from the United States ... the immediate patronage of an experienced and vigilant authority.'[40]

What of settlers from other countries? Wilkes introduced the subject of Chinese immigration, which he linked to the 'treaty recently negotiated' in Washington under the aegis of America's former minister to China, Anson J. Burlingame, who had returned as chief of a Chinese diplomatic mission:

It would almost seem as if the grant and character of the Company had been specially devised to meet the new impulse [which] ... promises to transfer the waste millions ... from one coast of the Pacific to the other, in the interest of the United States. ... The liberal policy of the Company, in guaranteeing equal political, legal, social and religious rights to all settlers of whatever race ... not only affords ... a field where [China] may exhibit the intelligence and capacity of her people in fair competition with the European races, but ... a means ... of putting an end to the execrable Coolie trade.

For while it was well-known that Chinese immigrants had sometimes been enslaved 'as in Cuba and other parts of the West Indies', or 'denied even the poor privilege of an oath in court, as in Upper California', they would henceforth have the option of 'a land where labor is free and honorable, and where equal rights make every settler's life and property secure.'[41]

The apparent thrust of this passage was to commit the Lower California Company to an inter-racial egalitarian republicanism in the administration of its colonial empire. Such a reading was consistent with Wilkes's wartime transit to Radical Republicanism; and it was this interpretation that he stressed in approaches to Burlingame and to the Mexican minister at Washington seeking their approval of the company's colonization plans.[42] Yet Wilkes, who had seen the real conditions of Chinese contract laborers in California, knew the chances of their enjoying any rights whatever in colonies locally governed by Americans were marginal; and the possibility that the company might intervene to alter this pattern even more remote. As he himself noted in an article in the *Spirit*, the majority of his fellow trustees stood against the Fourteenth and Fifteenth Amendments.[43] Wilkes included in the appendix of his brochure – apparently with approval – material extolling the profitableness of Chinese 'tropical laborers ... under the management of capitalists.' And in a letter to J. Ross Browne, who had just been named Burlingame's successor as envoy to China, he asked Browne's aid for the company's effort to 'contract ... for ten thousand or more Chinese colonists.' Ten thousand was the number then at work on Central Pacific Railroad construction, and obviously involved indentured labor rather than individual colonization. All in all, it seems unlikely that Wilkes seriously anticipated egalitarian rights for Chinese in Lower California; and the possibility remains – despite the eloquent criticism he had once made of land grants to privately owned railroad corporations – that he now perceived no contradiction in proposing an egalitarian white colony operated by a private corporation for the exploitation of indentured non-white labor.[44]

So far as the Lower California Company was concerned, these possibilities were never put to the test, but not for lack of effort on Wilkes's

part. Schooners began taking recruits from San Francisco to Baja California during the fall of 1870. Most were back within a few months to charge
that they had been swindled. From a stalemate of charges and counter-
charges in the press, the company was rescued by a brief bonanza: moss-
like dry fibers found clinging to cactus stalks had been identified as
orchilla, a dyestuff having commercial value.[45] Again the ads, articles,
promises; from New York a ship reportedly carrying three hundred
colonists left in March, and by April the refugees were straggling up the
coast to San Diego and San Francisco having escaped the colony by begging space on passing vessels.[46]

The orchilla disaster terminated efforts at colonization from the
United States. Meanwhile, during the five years that followed signing of
the Burlingame Treaty in 1868, Chinese immigration to America had
increased three times beyond the average entries of the preceding five
years.[47] But none of those emigrants reached Baja California. Lacking
some bonanza more interesting than orchilla, the directors had apparently
vetoed further investments in an increasingly unpromising long shot.
Wilkes made one more desperate effort. He appeared at Versailles in the
summer of 1871 before the French provisional government headed by
Auguste Thiers to propose Lower California as a place to which Com-
munard prisoners might be deported in lieu of execution.[48]

The Paris Commune

This proposition apparently had not originated with Wilkes. He had made
connections in France with an old acquaintance, Charles D. Poston, once
of the San Francisco Customs House, and later a mining promoter in
southern Arizona, who had served as territorial delegate to Congress and
accompanied J. Ross Browne to China with the honorary title of United
States commissioner of agriculture. Poston had been the Lower California
Company's agent in its tentative bid for Chinese contract labor. Now a
foreign correspondent for the New York *Tribune* and still interested in
Arizona mining, Poston presented the Thiers government with an
elaborate scheme for shipment of Communist prisoners – those among
them at least who were craftsmen and mechanics – around Cape Horn to
the mouth of the Colorado. Since the government at first seemed favora-
bly disposed, Wilkes entered his own proposal as an adjunct to Poston's.
Nothing came of either one.[49]

A more important outcome of Wilkes's European travels in 1871 was
his account of the Paris Commune. Centerspreads in the *Spirit of the Times*
show him, as one would expect, sympathetic to France in the Franco-
Prussian War. Shocked and astonished at the French debacle, he first

portrayed the Paris Commune as an irresponsible betrayal of the republican cause. Probably the influence of the New York *Herald*'s romantic and daring war correspondent, Ohio-born Aloysius McGahan, suggested a different interpretation. Visiting Paris in the final days of the Commune, Wilkes was profoundly moved by his glimpse of the beleaguered revolutionary city and the austere republicanism of its defenders. From this experience stemmed a series of 'Editor's Letters' to the *Spirit*, several of which appeared also in the daily New York *Herald*.[50]

Wilkes now saw the Thiers government in the role of betrayer, plotting a restoration of monarchy. Arrayed to implement this plot stood, first, the Prussian army, next the crowns of Europe leagued with the papacy and the bishops, and behind them, the perfidious power of Great Britain. Americans had been deceived because 'under the curse of a common language [British newspapers] do the foreign thinking for America ... almost every American I meet wishes the Communists to be shot or hung. *I* pray they may succeed.' Only the Commune had tried to save France from monarchical and clerical reaction and would have succeeded if other French cities had come to its aid.[51]

Believing the Commune to have been a section of the First International, Wilkes apparently conceived the International as a vast, monolithic secret society, called into being by gallant republican gentlemen to overturn the conspiracy of kings, aristocrats and priests. If he had read the *Communist Manifesto*, nothing in his writing so indicates. The program of the International he reduced to that of the Locofocos in the 1830s: manhood suffrage, economic liberalism, religious liberty reinforced by secular education, and land reform through stringent inheritance taxes. To the International's linkage with labor, he imparted an almost mystical connotation:

> This mighty organization ... which makes Presidents as well as Monarchs tremble on their thrones, ... owes its development ... in large measure to the great industrial exhibitions and congresses of labor known as World's Fairs, the first of which was held in London in 1851. ... These great ovations to mechanical production and inventive genius, made the kings, who had so unwarily installed them, crawl about among their triumphant riches like the pygmies they were; while MAN, working man, who had constructed them, stood forward, as by one sudden flash or revelation, in his noblest laboring and creative attitude, which is God.[52]

Whatever misconceptions and wishful thinking Wilkes may have yielded to, there remained an authentic force to his defense of the Communards. He, too, saw them as storming the gates of heaven and revered them for it. This vision crystallized his own mounting anxiety over the accumulation of wealth, the corruption of republican virtue in America, where 'conspiracies of wealth and power' likewise were 'leading us on the velvet track of monarchical reaction.' The immediate danger in America was executive usurpation. 'The most corrupting form of monarchy known in the world', Wilkes wrote in 1871, 'is that which conceals itself in the Constitution of the United States, in its failure to prohibit the reeligibility of the Executive.' Yet in America also a new force had risen, counterpart to, perhaps even a subdivision of, the International. Wilkes's reference was to the National Labor Union, founded five years earlier as a federation of local unions and city central labor councils aimed at preserving the gains made by labor during the war; what particularly interested him was the union's call for a labor convention in Columbus, Ohio to frame 'a platform of principles' and nominate 'a Labor candidate for President.'[53] Wilkes published the last two letters of his series, recapitulating the entire argument, separately as a pamphlet dedicated 'to the National Labor Union'.[54]

Wilkes had turned against President Grant during the previous summer over matters of foreign policy, and had accepted a last-minute 'Union Republican' nomination for Congress obviously directed against the administration since he ran in tandem with Horace Greeley, similarly nominated from an adjoining district. Both were defeated.[55] Back from France at the end of 1871, Wilkes immediately pressed the strategy of revolt inside the Republican party to bring forward an anti-Grant candidate later to be endorsed, he hoped, both by the Democrats and by the campaign committee emanating from the Columbus labor convention.[56] The *Spirit*'s centerspreads indicted Grant for subservience to England, rigged elections, military occupation in the South and corruption of high office. Grant had 'the face of Caesar.'[57] But Wilkes had conceived the Republican revolt as led by Radicals like Benjamin Butler and Charles Sumner. Sumner, who had offered a one-term constitutional amendment in the Senate, was Wilkes's first choice; he wrote that he would have nominated Sumner at the Liberal Republican convention but Sumner refused to consider it. The nomination went instead to Greeley, whom Wilkes loyally supported despite his belief that Greeley made foolish mistakes and that his campaign was sabotaged by his own advisers.[58]

As hope faded, polemics intensified. Grant was 'the most dangerous man who ever set his foot against the will of the people.' All the evils that had swarmed upon the nation since the days of his youth, Wilkes now attributed to Grant's despotic ambition:

> The difference between the country then [and now] is as startling as that between a quiet New England village and Pompeii...with her cruelties and obscenities and wanton luxuries written in fire upon her face. ... The rapidity with which our political condition has become corrupt is appalling. ... The result of the war placed a military party in power, organized corruption took

possession of our Government, and now Grant stands forth as the candidate of the great corrupt Money Power.

Wilkes then made a distinction that to him was obviously crucial: by 'rich men' he did not mean those 'who by industry, economy and ability have acquired small fortunes as their just reward', but rather 'the chronic millionaires and speculative capitalists who, without industry, without economy, but with dangerous ability, have grown enormously rich out of the labor of others, and together have succeeded in controlling even the national finances.'[59]

1877

After the reelection of Grant, Wilkes returned to sports and Shakespeare. His defense of the Paris Commune in Gilded Age America was perhaps the finest hour of a not altogether admirable career; certainly the high-water mark of his radicalism. Yet that radicalism now no longer meshed with any practical application. From the outset, its commitment to equality as the cause of universal man had been undermined by the American reality of racial subordination. Economic growth and extension of the continental market, while furnishing a base for egalitarian politics, rested upon the expropriation of land, resources, and labor from non-white populations. Jacksonian egalitarianism had never envisioned the liberation of captive geese that laid golden eggs; at most it demanded for lower-class whites a chance at the eggs. Wilkes, who had conscientiously avoided celebrating white supremacy, could not oppose it either, so totally had it permeated the culture that shaped the politicalization of his experience. Briefly repudiating white supremacy at the end of the Civil War, he reaffirmed it not only by his criticisms of Grant and of Shakespeare, but in the ruthless pursuit of individual opportunity offered by the Lower California Company.[60]

Even within its prescribed racial boundaries, the egalitarian commitment in America served to legitimize that other commitment, individual success. If individual success flowed from radical republicanism, how could it be thought to produce socially evil results? If class conflict sharpened, the sharpening must have other causes – conspiracies of kings and priests, for example; or, in America, the usurpation of executive power. Wilkes recognized the Commune as an accusation against the social order he had himself helped to construct. The only remedy he could admit was a crusade against concentration of governmental power, as if that concentration created the class for which power was to be exercised, rather than the other way around. This was a trip into nostalgia. He was dismayed that the Columbus National Labor Union convention, after endorsing the same remedy, somehow failed to rally the multitudes of 'labor' to vote Horace Greeley into the presidency.[61]

In the past Wilkes had been sensitive to the conditions of working people. The Depression of 1873 elicited no such concern. The *Spirit* hailed the Democratic landslide of 1874 as 'Peace for the North and South' in the sense that a Democratic majority in Congress would spell the end of federal intervention in the South. There was no reference to economic conditions.[62] America's first nationwide industrial conflict, the railroad strikes of 1877, burst upon the *Spirit* as totally unprecedented, 'an alarming condition' unequalled 'since the rebellion'. Centerspread articles, after chiding the railroads for mismanagement, assured the *Spirit*'s readers that the right to refuse to work, or even to 'combine in refusal ... would not be denied in any reasonable quarter.' Despite the obvious solidarity of Republican and Democratic state officials with the federal administration of President Hayes and the railroad corporations in military suppression of the strikes, the *Spirit* insisted that 'all would concede' these basic rights of railroad workers. Such being the case, what vital issue required to be striven for? None. Yet the strikers resorted to violence. They attempted to prevent others from working in their place. The *Spirit* denounced them as renegades: 'The very right of the laboring man, of which a dignified strike is the expression, they deny to others; shattering with their hands the principles they proclaim with their mouths.' Thus there could be no alternative but to endorse 'the universal feeling among good citizens ... that they must be crushed ... they must be shot down as if they were burglars or murderers ... nothing remains but an entire surrender on their part, or their annihilation, as far as they constitute an obstruction to the business of the country.'[63]

Wilkes was sixty in 1877. His comrades Broderick and Walsh, senator and congressman respectively, self-styled champions of the 'subterraneans', were long since dead. The urban artisan ideology that lighted their beginnings with its declarations of the universal equality of mankind had now redefined itself by excluding from the human fraternity, first the non-white peoples upon whom American opportunity had been constructed, and next the newly coalescent mass of industrial workers, if they stood against the 'business of the country.' Wilkes's modest theatrical and sporting journal, *The Spirit*, wheeled into line just as the great pioneers of mass circulation – whose founders also had been fellow travelers from the old Workingmen's movement – were doing. Their editorial declarations duplicated those of the *Nation*, although the social origins of their constituencies were different. What was, from one point of view, the disintegration of a radical ideology, became, from another viewpoint, a contribution to legitimizing the still tentative Republican coalition.

Notes

1. Eric Foner, *Tom Paine and Revolutionary America*, New York 1976; Celia Morris Eckhardt, *Franny Wright, Rebel in America*, Cambridge, Mass. 1984, pp. 184–224; Alexander Saxton, 'Problems of Race and Class in the Origins of the Mass Circulation Press', *American Quarterly* 36 (Summer 1978): 211–35.

2. *Dictionary of American Biography*, New York 1936, 10:218; David A. Williams, *David C. Broderick: A Political Portrait*, San Marino, Calif. 1969; Alexander Saxton, 'Blackface Minstrelsy and Jacksonian Ideology', *American Quarterly* 27 (March 1975): 1–28; Frederick Hudson, *Journalism in the United States from 1690 to 1872*, New York 1873.

3. Robert Ernst, 'The One and Only Mike Walsh', *The New York Historical Society Quarterly*, 36 (January 1952): 43–64; *Dictionary of American Biography* 19:390–91; Sean Wilentz, *Chants Democratic: New York City and the Rise of the American Working Class, 1788–1850*, New York 1984; Howard B. Rock, *Artisans of the New Republic: The Tradesmen of New York City in the Age of Jefferson*, New York 1984, pp. 1–147; Christine Stansell, *City of Women: Sex and Class in New York, 1789–1860*, New York 1986. The output of urban working-class community studies has grown into a thriving cottage industry. Cumulatively, these works are of major importance; many are outstanding individually. In an interpretive sense, however, they tend to repetition and overkill. Wilentz provides a complete list in the footnotes to his opening chapter. Alan Dawley, *Class and Community: The Industrial Revolution in Lynn*, Cambridge, Mass. 1976, was a pioneer of the genre; and certainly Wilentz's examination of New York's artisans and laborers represents its full unfolding. Bruce Laurie, *Working People of Philadelphia, 1800–1850*, Philadelphia 1980, and Cynthia Shelton, *The Mills of Manayunk: Industrialization and Social Conflict in the Philadelphia Region, 1878–1837*, Baltimore 1986, stress the early impact of Chesapeake industrialization and its differences from the later New England textile model. The South and Trans–Appalachian West are still sparsely populated on a community study map. Steven Ross, *Workers on the Edge: Work, Leisure and Politics in Industrializing Cincinnati, 1788–1890*, New York 1985, examines class formation in the Ohio Valley's earliest smokestack city. Artisans and factory workers in the North and West at least were mostly white, and urban community studies have generally gone with the drift of things by focusing on the white working class and giving more attention to ethnocultural divisions than to racial segmentation. Jonathan McLeod, 'Black and White Workers: Atlanta during Reconstruction' Ph.D. diss., University of California, Los Angeles, 1987, provides a welcome break from this trend in his massively researched study of industrialization, Southern style.

4. Williams, *David C. Broderick*, pp. 1–28; Walter Hugins, *Jacksonian Democracy and the Working Class: A Study of the New York Workingmen's Movement*, Stanford, Calif. 1960; Edward Pessen, *Most Uncommon Jacksonians: The Radical Leaders of the Early Labor Movement*, Albany, N.Y. 1967; William O. Bourne, *History of the Public School Society of the City of New York*, New York 1870; Dixon Ryan Fox, *The Decline of Aristocracy in the Politics of New York*, New York 1919; Gustavus Myers, *The History of Tammany Hall*, New York 1917, pp. 1–17; James F. Richardson, *The New York Police: Colonial Times to 1901*, New York 1971.

5. Helen S. Zahler, *Eastern Workingmen and National Land Policy, 1829–1862* New York 1941, especially pp. 1–49; Hugins, pp. 86–87; Ernst, pp. 49–51.

6. Ernst, pp. 51–56; Edward Van Every, *Sins of New York as 'Exposed' by the Police Gazette*, New York 1930, pp. 9–13; *Dictionary of American Biography*, 10:218; obituaries of George Wilkes in New York papers: *Herald, Times, World*, 25 September 1885; *Spirit of the Times*, 26 September 1885; *Tribune*, 27 September 1885; John A. Garraty, *Silas Wright*, New York 1949, pp. 171–75, 381.

7. *National Police Gazette*, 21 September 1850.

8. George Wilkes, *The Mysteries of the Tombs. A Journal of Thirty Days Imprisonment in the New York City Prison for Libel*, New York 1844; and *The Lives of Helen Jewett and Richard P. Robinson*, New York 1849, pp. 7, 54; Oliver Carlson, *The Man Who Made News: James Gordon Bennett*, New York 1942, pp. 143–67.

9. James O'Meara, *Broderick and Gwin*, San Francisco 1881, p. 19.

10. Wilkes, *Lives*, p. 125; O'Meara, p. 19.

11. Clarence Bagley, 'George Wilkes', *Washington Historical Quarterly*, 5 (January 1914):

3–11; George Wilkes, *Proposal for a National Railroad to the Pacific Ocean, for the Purpose of Obtaining a Short Route to Oregon and the Indies*, 4th ed., New York 1847, as reprinted in *The Magazine of History with Notes and Inquiries*, 36 (1928): 39, 40, 48–49, 73.

12.   *National Police Gazette*, 21 September 1850.

13.   Broderick to Wilkes, 18 August 1852, in *People v. John A. McGlynn, et al.*, Case 9459, California Supreme Court Transcript, File No. 3494, California State Archives, Sacramento; and see also Williams, pp. 25–30, and O'Meara, pp. 17–19.

14.   Testimony of Emma Theresa McGuire, *In the Probate Court of the City and County of San Francisco, State of California in the Matter of the Last Will and Testament of David C. Broderick, Deceased. Testimony Proving the Will*, San Francisco 1860, pp. 78, 83; Williams, pp. 50–55, 70, *passim*.

15.   Williams, pp. 34–66, 174–84, 231–32; Jeremiah Lynch, *A Senator of the Fifties: David C. Broderick of California*, San Francisco 1911, pp. 168–76, 201; Broderick to a Committee of Inquiry, Sacramento, 24 January 1852, quoted in unidentified newspaper clipping in Benjamin Hayes, *Scrapbooks*, vol. 17, 'California Politics, 1851–1854', Bancroft Library, University of California, Berkeley.

16.   Williams, p. 248; *Remarks Delivered in the Senate and the House of Representatives of the United States on the Announcement of the Death of Hon. David C. Broderick of California, Late a Member of the Senate of the United States in the 35th Congress*, Washington, D.C. 1860, pp. 11–12; San Francisco *Alta*, 4 June 1867; New York *Times*, 19 June 1875.

17.   Williams, pp. 81, 85–87; New York *Times*, 17 June 1875. George Wilkes, *Affidavit Submitted in 4th Judicial District Court of California for the City and County of San Francisco, The People of the State of California vs. John A. McGlynn and Andrew L. Butler*, n.p., n.d., in Bancroft Library; O'Meara, pp. 57–58; unidentified newspaper clipping, Hayes *Scrapbooks*, vol. 17. Bancroft Library. The evidence of the will is actually less persuasive than it seems since the will was challenged by the State of California on allegations that Wilkes and others had conspired to forge Broderick's signature. The California Supreme Court ruled against the challenge because the statute of limitations had expired, leaving the question of forgery problematic. Broderick's major biographer, David A. Williams, in 'The Forgery of the Broderick Will', *California Historical Society Quarterly*, 40:203–14, concluded that the will was forged. My own belief is that Wilkes was fully capable of forgery. But I think the circumstances that the will was pushed not only by Wilkes but by several of Broderick's closest friends and associates indicate that, whether or not it was forged, it probably expressed Broderick's intent at the time of his death.

18.   Wilkes, *Affidavit*.

19.   Williams, p. 70n; O'Meara, pp. 116–22; Wilkes, *Affidavit*.

20.   Notice of Public Auction of Broderick Estate, San Francisco, 30 November 1861, in *People v. McGlynn*, California State Archives; New York *Times*, 25 September 1885.

21.   Norris W. Yates, *William T. Porter and the Spirit of the Times: A Study of the Big Bear School of Humor*, Baton Rouge, La. 1957, pp. 6–8, 190–200; *Porter's Spirit of the Times*, 6 September 1856; *Wilkes's Spirit of the Times*, 10 September 1859.

22.   *Spirit*, 17 March and 7 April 1860.

23.   *Spirit*, 21 April, 5 May, 9 June 1860; 1 November 1873; New York *Herald*, 25 September 1885.

24.   *Dictionary of American Biography*, 10:218.

25.   New York *Times*, 25 September 1885; *Spirit*, 26 September 1885; Wilkes, *McClellan: From Ball's Bluff to Antietam*, New York 1863, pp. 3–4.

26.   New York *Times*, 25 September 1885.

27.   Wilkes, *McClellan*, pp. 23, 24.

28.   Wilkes, 'The Copperhead Insurrectionists – a Miscreant Mob', New York *Times*, 23 July 1873.

29.   *Spirit*, 24 August, 7, 14 September, 9 November 1867; 18 January, 6 February 1868.

30.   *Spirit*, prizefighting: 27 September, 1, 8 November 1873; 20 January 1877; crooked gamblers: 20 September 1873–3 January 1874; sports associations: 8 November 1873, 28 February 1874; middle-class setting: 14 August 1858, 31 May 1873, 13 January 1877.

31.   *Spirit*, blackface minstrelsy: almost any issue; theater: 17 February 1872, 19 April, 13 December 1873, 7 March, 16, 30 May, 21 November 1874.

32.   New York 1877. Citations are from the London edition, 1877.

33. Wilkes, *Shakespeare*, pp. 2, 4–5, 68, 70–71.

34. Ibid., pp. 70, 363–66, 373–74, 457–58.

35. Wilkes to J. Ross Browne, 7 June 1868, enclosed with Browne to Secretary of State Seward in US Congress, House of Representatives, *Executive Documents*, 40th Congress, 3rd Session 1868–1869, US Diplomatic Correspondence, 1868, Part I, pp. 528–29.

36. Ruth E. Carlson, 'American Colonization Ventures in Lower California, 1862–1917', M.A. thesis, Berkeley, 1944, 22–25; *New York Assembly Journal* 90th Session, 1867, I: 1462, 1497; *New York Senate Journal*, 90th Session, 1867, 964, 979.

37. *Appleton's Cyclopedia of American Biography*, New York 1888; *Biographical Directory of the American Congress, 1774–1971*, Washington, D.C. 1971; *Dictionary of American Biography*; *National Cyclopedia of American Biography*, New York 1900, 1945; Hans L. Trefousse, *Ben Butler: The South Called Him Beast*, New York 1957.

38. Ruth E. Carlson, 'The Magdalena Bubble', *Pacific Historical Review*, 4:29–30. J. Ross Browne, 'Explorations in Lower California', *Harper's Monthly* 36–38, October, November, December, 1868, pp. 577–91, 740–52, 9–23, respectively; Lina Ferguson Browne, ed., *J. Ross Browne: His Letters, Journals and Writings*, Albuquerque, N.M. 1969.

39. Report of William M. Gabb, dated San Francisco, 15 June 1867, in J. Ross Browne, *A Sketch of the Settlement and Exploration of Lower California*, San Francisco 1869, pp. 82–122.

40. *Lower California: Its Geography and Characteristics with a Sketch of the Grant and Purposes of the Lower California Company*, New York 1868, pp. 11, 14, 41–42; San Francisco *Call*, 3 March 1871, in Carlson, 'American Colonization', p. 29.

41. *Lower California*, pp. 14–15.

42. Wilkes to M. Romero, 18 June 1868; Caleb Cushing to Anson Burlingame, 20 July 1868, in *Lower California*, pp. 18–21.

43. *Spirit*, 12 March 1870.

44. Wilkes to Browne, 8 June 1868, in *Lower California*, pp. 17, 39, 43.

45. Carlson, 'Magdalena Bubble', pp. 28, 31–38; 'American Colonization', pp. 29–30, 38–46; *Spirit*, 8 April, 26 August 1871; New York *Herald*, 5 March 1871.

46. Carlson, 'American Colonization', pp. 43–44; New York *Herald*, 5 March 1871; *Spirit*, 8, 22 April, 26 August 1871.

47. Alexander Saxton, *The Indispensable Enemy: Labor and the Anti–Chinese Movement in California*, Berkeley, Calif. 1971, pp. 173–74, 177–78.

48. New York *Herald*, 8 August 1871.

49. A. W. Gressinger, *Charles D. Poston, Sunland Seeker*, Globe, Ariz. 1961; *Biographical Directory of the American Congress*, p. 1560; *Dictionary of American Biography*, 8:121–22; New York *Herald*, 11, 29 July, 8, 9, 13 August, 8 September 1871.

50. *Spirit*, 16 July, 10, 17 September, 22 October 1870; condemnation of 'Red Republicans': 7 January, 4, 11 March, 1, 22 April 1871; Wilkes's letters from Paris: 24 June, 1, 22, 29 July, 23 September, 7 October, and 18, 25 November 1871; New York *Herald*, 16 September, 3 October 1871.

51. *Spirit*, 24 June, 1 July 1871. On McGlashan, *Dictionary of American Biography*, 12:45–46.

52. *Spirit*, 23 September, 18 November, 1871. Wilkes, *The Internationale: Its Principles and Purposes. Being a Sequel to the Defense of the Commune*, New York 1871, pp. 4–6, 7–14.

53. *Spirit*, 25 November 1871; Wilkes, *Internationale*, pp. 5, 16–17. David Montgomery, *Beyond Equality: Labor and the Radical Republicans, 1862–1872*, New York 1967, pp. 191–92,.

54. Wilkes, *Internationale*, title page.

55. *Spirit*, 5, 12 November 1870.

56. Ibid., 11, 25 November, 9, 23, 30 December 1871.

57. Ibid., 25 November, 23, 30 December 1871.

58. Ibid., 9, 20 December 1871, 30 January, 3 February, 23, 30 March, 11 May, 29 June, 9 November 1872.

59. Ibid., 1 June, 6 July, 28 September, 1872.

60. Ibid., 29 April, 20, 27 July, 10, 24 August 1872.

61. Ibid., 16 March, 9 November 1872.

62. Ibid., 7 November 1874.

63. Ibid., 28 July, 4 August 1877.

10

Republican Innovators

In the preceding chapter the devious enterprises of George Wilkes served to mark the transit of artisan egalitarianism from the workingmen's parties of the late 1820s to the urban radical wing of Jacksonian Democracy and thence into the Free Soil alliance, which in turn furnished essential building materials for the Republican synthesis. Perhaps in the long run it was this radical inheritance that made possible the survival of the Republican party, especially during the crisis of the 1890s. Yet the original thrust of Republican ideology had stemmed not from artisan radicals but from the conservative responses of National Republicans and Whigs. Disastrously programmed by whiggish gentry in the terminology of social heriarchy, mercantilism and counting-house ethics, the National Republican thesis had stood in contradiction to the demands of democratic electioneering during the 1840s and remained an obstacle throughout the 1850s and 1860s to the formation of any new coalition.

What finally opened the way for a successful coalition were the efforts of a cohort of innovators who matched their creative talents against the already established *virtuosi* of Jacksonianism. Certainly a principal workshop wherein Republican innovation unfolded was Horace Greeley's New York *Tribune*. One way or another associated with the *Tribune* were party builders and political strategists in a first wave stemming from the old Anti-Masonic movement, in which Thurlow Weed, William Seward, and Greeley himself were outstanding names. The first wave was followed by a second in the 1850s and 1860s composed of men more specialized, not so much organizers and party builders as intellectuals and theorists. Henry C. Carey of Philadelphia and Richard Hildreth of Boston exemplified this later type.[1]

Republican innovators spread far beyond the *Tribune*; nor were they by any means in agreement among themselves. But their writings con-

227

verged and overlapped during crucial transitions between the National Republican thesis and a Republican synthesis still in process of formation. For seriously committed people in the middle reaches of the political spectrum, such transitions posed moral challenges to intellectual endeavor.

The adjectives *moral* and *intellectual* here become indivisible. The Jacksonian position on slavery had to be wrestled with to produce a moral indictment that was intellectually persuasive. On the other hand, a tolerance for mass immigration – logically as indispensable to free settlement of the West as it was to recruiting a free industrial labor force – had to be legitimized for Republicans in lieu of a traditionally moralistic whiggish nativism. Yet to grapple with slavery and immigration would be only a beginning. A grave threat to Republican progress lay in the political instability of those economic projects carried forward from National Republicanism. Protective tariffs, centralized control over banking and currency, federal subsidies to transcontinental railroads, all remained vulnerable to the bank-monster and anti-monopoly missiles that Jacksonians had used effectively in the past; and which Andrew Johnson, when he inherited the presidency from Lincoln, would at once begin to wheel into place again. Conceptually these various issues were separable; historically they were not. Each deriving its specificity from association with the others, they confronted Republican innovators like a set of simultaneous equations.

The first chapter in the final part of this study will survey the general political program that resulted from Republican innovation. The present chapter, paralleling Chapter 9 on the career of George Wilkes, examines in some detail the work of two of those innovators.

Richard Hildreth and Harriet Beecher Stowe

Drawn from the fields of political economy and literature, the innovators were Richard Hildreth and Harriet Beecher Stowe. Others might have been chosen from the same cohort. Yet the selection is not altogether arbitrary, since it rests on a concept of typicality not as *ordinary* or *commonplace*, but as an epitomizing or filling of potential – typical in the sense sometimes applied to fictional characterization by which Balzac's Rastignac or Thackeray's Becky Sharp, for example, may be seen as typical of their class and time. Other contemporaries replicated what these two had to say about Republicanism in general; none approached them on the issues of race and slavery.[2]

The National Republican thesis had handled race, so far as the Indians were concerned, by insisting on just and benevolent treatment in accordance with Enlightenment precepts such as those enunciated by Vattel; and, as to Africans, through acknowledging the injustice of slavery (imposed, presumably, by British tyranny on reluctant colonials) and through commitment to terminate slavery at some reasonable future time.[3] These professions had cleared the way for a coalition of merchant–landlord oligarchies, North and South, in pursuit of a continental nation to be carved from lands inhabited by Indians and in which property in African slaves would be constitutionally legitimated. It was to this prospect that John Quincy Adams had dedicated his first career. If the prospect contained traces of pragmatism or even cynicism, these remained rationally subordinated to a doctrine of greater good, since enlightenment, both moral and intellectual, could be expected to flow from an educated, republican upper class. Only when the coalition succumbed to the separation of slaveowner interests from the general interests of commerce, commercial agriculture and industry had Adams begun to preach overthrow of the planter class, a goal to which he devoted the remainder of his life.

The new commitment required him to turn his back on moral problems associated with race. Indians were left to fend for themselves; and so also, in a different sense, were African slaves. Adams's accusations against the Slave Power rested on a rationalist assertion that political degeneracy must necessarily result from a social institution that defied reason and natural law. But as the tides of nineteenth-century cultural history shifted from rationalism to romanticism, this basically rationalist argument had taken on another connotation: that slaveholders had earned their own damnation through sinful union with the African heart of darkness. The Free Soil alliance could thus tap the emotional dynamism of waging war against willed evil. Surely this was one meaning for the *walpurgisnacht* at Legree's plantation in the closing chapters of *Uncle Tom's Cabin*. As late as 1858 William Seward's 'irrepressible conflict' and Lincoln's 'house divided' still invoked this composite argument. The new party's two most prominent leaders had scarcely moved beyond Adams's ideological construct of thirty years earlier.[4]

That construction, however, failed to meet the needs of the Republican party in the 1850s and 1860s because it offered no morally acceptable guidelines for coping with the African Americans themselves.[5] If released from slavery, what would be done with them? Were they to be expelled; or destroyed, as carriers of a reincarnated original sin? Romantic sentiment was perhaps capable of justifying such a solution after the fact, but scarcely of approving it beforehand as a guide to action. Republicans needed some concept of the nature of Africans, human or otherwise, in order to balance their moral repudiation of the Jacksonian compact with slavery by proposing viable alternatives. Richard Hildreth and Harriet Beecher Stowe turned their manifold talents to this ideological task. Both had experienced direct glimpses into the slaveholding South, and both produced fictional accounts of heroic slaves who escaped to freedom. Hildreth indeed had anticipated such a need long before the beginnings of the Republican party. His *Archie Moore* preceded *Uncle Tom's Cabin* by sixteen years. The first edition in 1836 probably reached only the inner circle of New England Abolitionists. An expanded version, riding on the colossal success of *Uncle Tom's Cabin*, achieved substantially wider readership. But although Stowe's novel outsold Hildreth's by many thousandfold, Hildreth was certainly correct in claiming that 'his invention ... [was] the first successful application of fictitious narrative to anti-slavery purposes.'[6]

The Education of Archie Moore

With respect to slavery, Hildreth began from approximately the same ground as did John Quincy Adams at the start of his second, or antislavery, career. This was scarcely surprising – despite forty years' difference in their ages – since they came from nearly identical social origins. Both were grandsons of eastern Massachusetts yeoman farmers, both were Harvard graduates, and their fathers had each been the first in his family to attend college. But while the Adamses had moved on to the presidency and substantial wealth, the Hildreths traced, in financial terms, a downward course. Hildreth's politics became more radical than those of Adams. In 1836, however, they shared a view of slavery as the main obstacle to national progress and a conviction that it must be terminated. Hildreth's *Despotism in America*, an essay in political economy conceived as a companion piece to *Archie Moore*, mounted an indictment of the planter class comparable to sections of Adams's diary, although more systematic than anything Adams had written on that subject.[7]

Unyielding in his condemnation of slavery, Hildreth remained tentative and uncertain in his notions of race. The novel seems to have served as a means of trying out different sets of ideas by placing them in conjunction with, and opposition to, one another. Its form is that of first-person narrative, told by the slave Archie Moore. As if taking off from Adams's embittered diary entries about Thomas Jefferson, the narrative begins with Moore's remembrance of the Virginia aristocrat and Revolutionary patriot who he learned was his father:

> Of liberty indeed, he was always a warm and energetic admirer. Among my earliest recollections of him, is the earnestness with which, among his friends and guests, he used to vindicate the cause of the French revolution, then going on. Of that revolution, throughout its whole progress, he was a most eloquent advocate and apologist; ... The *rights of man*, and the *rights of human nature*

were phrases, which, although at that time, I was quite unconscious of their meaning, I heard so often repeated, that they made an indelible impression upon my memory. ... Had I been allowed to choose my own paternity, could I possibly have selected a more desirable father? – But by the laws and customs of Virginia, it is not the father but the mother, whose rank and condition determine that of the child; – and alas! my mother was a concubine and a slave![8]

Like many other white writers who have attempted fictional recreations of African-American experience, Hildreth apparently could realize that experience only literally, as the experience of a white man turned black. He imagined both his narrator's skin and his consciousness as indistinguishable from the Euro-American. In justice to Hildreth, it ought to be said that he was among the earliest practitioners of this subsequently threadbare plot device. Perhaps he came to it pragmatically, hoping to make his story more palatable to white readers, as Harriet Beecher Stowe would do with Eliza and George Harris in *Uncle Tom's Cabin*. But Eliza and Harris were secondary characters, whereas Archie Moore – like Robinson Crusoe upon whom he certainly was modeled – carried the world on his shoulders. It seems more likely that Hildreth followed the only path accessible to his fictional imagination; and that he believed he had added moral grandeur to his hero who, although possessing the option of slipping away into the white world, would choose to assume the burden of blackness. David Brion Davis has speculated that there may have been 'a kind of unconscious collaboration even between abolitionists and their opponents in defining race as the ultimate "reality."'[9] Unconscious or not, Hildreth's characterization left readers free to believe, if they chose, that nobility and philanthropy traveled with white blood; by contrast with the cowardice and opportunism attributed to many of Archie Moore's fellow slaves. Having opened up this speculative possibility, Hildreth then attempted to close it off.

A latter-day Robinson Crusoe cast away by the accident of birth in the desert of American slavery, Moore, like Crusoe, possessed the power to recreate a social order out of moral intellect. The moral intellect favored by Hildreth, who was an admirer and translator of Jeremy Bentham, found its highest expression in a rational calculus of pleasure and pain by which institutions as well as human actions could be judged objectively, without benefit of scriptural or extraterrestrial instructions.[10] By these humanist standards, Hildreth's hero not only measured the immorality of slavery but penetrated the self-serving ideologies of such substrata as preachers, yeomen and storekeepers among whites; mulattoes, drivers, and house servants among blacks. The fiction at this level achieved impressive social realism. Archie Moore, born of a white father and light-skinned slave mother, had begun by imagining himself 'of a superior caste, and would have felt it a degradation to be put on a level with those a few shades darker.' But the educational curriculum to which he was subjected pushed him to new understandings:

> ... I no longer took sides with our oppressors by joining them in the false notion of their own natural superiority; – a notion founded only in the arrogant prejudice of conceited ignorance, and long since discarded by the liberal and enlightened; but a notion which is still the orthodox creed of all America, and the principal, I might almost say the sole, foundation, which sustains the iniquitous structure of American slavery.[11]

Armed with this realization of white racism and its functions, Archie Moore stood ready for final confrontation with the institution of slavery. Hildreth brought him to that confrontation not in the company of whites, or of other light-skinned men like himself; but in the company of a black slave of pure African descent.

In somewhat the same way that Uncle Tom became the hero of Stowe's novel, Hildreth's African slave (also named Thomas) became a second hero in *Archie Moore*. Thomas 'was of unmixed African blood. ... Nature had intended him for one of those lofty spirits who are the terror of tyrants, and the bold assertors of liberty. But under the influence of religion, he had become a passive, humble and obedient slave.' The religion – like that of Stowe's Uncle Tom – was Methodism. Thomas and Uncle Tom, however, responded differently to brutal treatment. When, soon after childbirth, Thomas's wife died from being whipped by the plantation overseer because she worked too slowly, Thomas had forsaken Methodism, returning to that for which 'nature had intended him.'[12]

He and Archie Moore escaped together into the marshes bordering the plantation. There the overseer, accidentally separated from other pursuers, fell into their hands. More ruthless than Archie Moore, Thomas insisted upon retribution:

> When I called to mind all the circumstances that had attended the death of Thomas's wife, I could not but acknowledge that Mr. Martin had been her murderer. I had sympathized with Thomas then and I sympathized with him now. ... I could not but acknowledge his death would be an act of righteous retribution.

And after the execution:

> We now resumed our flight, – not as some might perhaps suppose, with the frightened and conscience-stricken haste of murderers, but with that lofty feeling of manhood vindicated, and tyranny visited with a just retribution, ... which burned in the bosoms of Wallace and of Tell. ... [13]

It was Thomas, the African hero, who had taken the lead in combat.

Wounded, he turned back into the swamp, permitting his light-skinned comrade to escape to the North. Thomas reappeared in the closing pages of the addendum written by Hildreth after the publication of *Uncle Tom's Cabin*. Thomas had waged guerilla war against the plantations for twenty years. Captured at last in old age, he taunted his captors – while they prepared to burn him to death – with the tally of their white brethren he had slain.[14]

Before turning to an assessment of Hildreth's contribution to Republican ideology, it seems unavoidable to touch on an aspect of *Archie Moore* that makes it one of the most puzzling texts in anti-slavery literature. The aspect emerges naturally enough from the satire of sexual promiscuity on the Jeffersonian plantation. Archie Moore had fallen in love with Cassy, the daughter of a mulatto slave mother and Archie's half-sister by Colonel Moore. The colonel's wife enthusiastically endorsed this union. Colonel Moore intervened; not, however, because he objected to incestuous relationships among slaves, but because he wanted Cassy for himself. By fending off her father's attentions, Cassy preserved her chastity for Archie, who eventually became a devoted husband and father of her children. The brother–sister relationship serves no visible purpose in the plot. Was it intended as part of the satire? That seems unlikely since neither character was elsewhere treated satirically.

Understandably the sequence did not sit well with Victorian readers and certainly contributed to reducing the book's sale among church-based anti-slavery groups. Nonetheless, Lydia Maria Child loyally defended it in *The Liberator*:

> Some are shocked because Archie Moore married his half-sister; but it must be remembered that the author is not attempting to describe the beau ideal of human perfection; he is showing what a man of powerful character is likely to become under the degrading influence of slavery. It would be unnatural to suppose elevated purity of sentiment, or unimpaired moral strength, either in slaves or their masters. ...

Resting on already established ideological grounds, Child's defense could be interpreted as referring either to the rationalist argument that unreasonable institutions produce social deterioration, or to the romantic notion that African sexuality had invaded the moral fabric of the South.[15]

Hildreth, although doubtless grateful for a favorable review, could not consistently have accepted either interpretation. Clearly he was not attempting to show that African sexuality corrupted American purity. Rather, he presented sexuality throughout his novel as a potentially constructive element of the human animal. What was wrong with planter sexuality was not that it was uninhibited, or even promiscuous; but that it was coercive and exploitative. Nor was he trying to predict 'what a man of powerful character' was 'likely to become under the degrading influence of slavery.' On the contrary, he was seeking to show that persons of 'powerful character' and moral intellect could rise above unjust institutions and irrational superstitions. The marriage of Cassy and Archie represented triumph, not degradation. Hildreth must have believed he was enlisting Archie Moore among the ranks of Byronic heroes, dedicated, like Prometheus, to human liberation despite the gods. This suggests how deeply enmeshed the utilitarian and seemingly rationalist Hildreth had actually become in romanticism. Since, however, the incest taboo was scarcely an appendage of slavery, it might have been wiser for him (in what was avowedly an anti-slavery novel) to have avoided that issue.[16]

A first step in locating Hildreth in the development of Republican ideology must be to establish his relationship to John Quincy Adams. Similarities in their ideas on race have already been noted. Even at that opening level, however, there existed a significant difference, because while Adams consistently asserted the reality of non-white inferiority, Hildreth began by conceding merely the possibility. If one reads *Archie Moore* together with the introduction of the African hero, Thomas, as a sequence of deepening understandings, it seems clear that Hildreth ended by affirming the universal humanity of black and white.

Both Hildreth and Adams, from beginnings in the Enlightenment, consciously attached themselves to romanticism. Their romantic affiliations differed radically. For Adams, grieving over the lost certainties of Christianity, man's image was that of the upsidedown lighthouse, sending out signals of devotion to an ever more distant deity. Hildreth dismissed the absentee deity with angry contempt. God's tasks, for Hildreth as for Marx, could best be carried out by human heroes bent upon storming the gates of heaven.

Such a reading of Hildreth would endorse servile war against slavery and justify Harpers Ferry twenty years before the fact. Such a reading defined the nature of African Americans by predicting that real liberation would make them real equals of Euro-Americans. The possibility of such a reading explains the remarkable final sentence of Lydia Maria Child's review in *The Liberator*: 'If I were a man, I would rather be the author of that work than of anything ever published in America.' It helps also, I think, to explain the high esteem in which Hildreth was held by men like Charles Sumner, John Andrews, William Seward and even William Dean Howells. Hildreth was a pattern-maker, an ideologist's ideologist. The same qualities, of course, rendered his fiction less, rather than more, accessible to the mass of potential Republicans. Underlying the difficulty of emotional affiliation to its relentless and austere protagonists was a conceptual framework derived from rationalism and anticlerical skepticism, brought forward into the revolutionary era of romanticism, but no further.

This, however, was already out of phase with the religious, family-oriented sentimentality of the 1850s and 1860s.[17]

Uncle Tom's Crucifixion

If Hildreth was out of phase with mid-Victorian America, Stowe was not. Although of New England clerical background similar to Hildreth's and only four years younger, Stowe's intellectual heritage diverged fundamentally from his. Stowe had no taproots in the Enlightenment. She by-passed the revolutionary era of romanticism. Her soberly optimistic romanticism was more utilitarian than that of the Benthamite Hildreth. Placing herself in the heartland of middlebrow America, Stowe's heroes were neither transcendant nor threatening; their sexuality reinforced, never disrupted, family solidarity. Unlike Jefferson, Stowe found a place for constructive evil in her cosmology; unlike Hawthorne, she allowed no cross-fertilization between evil and good. The two occupied separate spaces. Evil, in *Uncle Tom's Cabin* at least, adhered only to isolates, to outcasts from family life and from society.[18] Decency and good intentions, by contrast, belonged to the normal run of human beings, and this held true even inside the partially corrupted kingdom of slavery. Consequently, the Christian obligation to resist evil pointed not so much to a revolutionary conquering of new heights as to a simple determination to find a way back to the family fireside.

All this, as part of the conventional apparatus of Victorian conservatism, dictated obvious differences between the anti-slavery writings of Hildreth and Stowe. Where Hildreth rejoiced in social satire, Stowe tended to hold aloof from it. Where Hildreth portrayed a society permeated by violence, Stowe located violence only in the underworld of slave traders, slave catchers and social outcasts. The measure of heroism for Hildreth was to use violence against slavery. Stowe's heroism was to refrain from violence except in self-defense; and her hero of heroes, the Christ-like Uncle Tom, went to his death without raising hand or voice against his executioners.[19]

Sex and violence for both authors were closely linked, although in strikingly different ways. In Hildreth's panorama, the two forces infused human relations, but their moral accounting depended on who used them and to what purposes. For Stowe, overt sexuality or sexual desire was a sure sign of evil. Most of Stowe's female characters in *Uncle Tom's Cabin*, black and white, were virtuous, and none of these virtuous females exhibited any trace of sexual desire. The only woman portrayed as sexually active was the mulatto, Cassy, who had been deceived and wronged in girlhood, then sold to the villainous Simon Legree. Not only was sexuality evil in Stowe's lexicon, it was essentially male. A proper social system would control male sexuality by surrounding it with the influences of virtuous women, sanctified in custom and institution. The fatal flaw of slavery was that by stripping slave women of their defenses, it unleashed male sexuality, which might then engulf women as sexual accomplices. Such was the fate of Cassy at the hands of Legree.

Male sexuality and violence in *Uncle Tom's Cabin* were assigned only to outcasts and lower-class males. These included slave traders, slave catchers, and of course Legree himself. Born in rural New England, Legree had eluded his mother's saving influence by running away to sea. The reader is permitted flashbacks of him in dockside working-class taverns – way stations, presumably, along his path to the abyss.[20] Stowe's Legree is in the direct lineage of Royall Tyler's vernacular Yankee. Evil thus presents a class orientation. It also presents, for Stowe, a racial orientation, but one that is indirect or derivative. I can find no reference in Stowe's anti-slavery fiction to black male sexuality as a threatening force. On the other hand, the only woman actually shown in collaboration with white male sexuality is a mulatto slave, Cassy.[21] Could Stowe have fictionalized a white woman in Cassy's situation? Since the answer, I think, is *no*, the conclusion must be that Stowe shared with John Quincy Adams the notion of a special heart of darkness that emanated from the exposure of African female sexuality to white male lust. Stowe, of course, took pains to record that Cassy desired to escape, that she was driven to madness, that she did escape when opportunity offered, and finally found her way back to domestic virtue.[22] The implication is that African women, liberated from slavery, would not choose to submit themselves to sexual degradation. Nonetheless, they seemed to Stowe more vulnerable to that subversion than white women; thence the mortal danger posed by the slave system.

A romantic optimist, Stowe kept this catastrophic vision at a distance. The immediate thrust of her novel was that slavery, by unleashing male sexuality and violence, disrupted families both black and white. Yet since civilized culture rested on family life, the outcome might be a fall into savagery like that of Legree's plantation. Such an indictment of slavery was hardly original with Stowe.[23] Her placing of it at the center of her fiction, however, was tactically brilliant because it left the Jacksonian enemy with no credible Victorian rejoinder. As a tactician, Stowe surpassed Hildreth.

She surpassed him also as a strategist, or – to return to a term employed earlier – as an ideological innovator. Stowe's major contribution to Republican racial ideology was her analogizing of gender and race. Women, for Stowe, were more perceptive, more empathic, more yielding, more loving than men. Men sought to conquer; women to nurture, to restore, to redeem. Jesus, a redeemer rather than a conqueror, embodied a feminine psyche. The closest followers of Jesus among men must also be the most womanlike. Thus Augustine St. Clare, the benevolent father of the angelic Eva, displayed as a child 'an extreme and marked sensitiveness of character, more akin to the softness of woman than the ordinary hardness of his own sex.' All the good influences of his life, St. Clare revealed to his brisk spinster cousin from New England, had come to him through his mother. The cousin thought St. Clare spoke like a '"professor of religion"; later she would say to him, half seriously, '"Augustine, sometimes I think you are not far from the kingdom."' She was right. On his deathbed, St. Clare exclaimed that he was '"coming HOME at last!" … Just before the spirit parted, he opened his eyes, with a sudden light, as of joy and recognition, and said, "Mother!" and then he was gone.'[24]

St. Clare had entertained dreams of helping to create a utopia beyond slavery, but he accomplished nothing. Men with feminine psyches, like Jesus, must prove ineffective in a world shaped by self-assertion and conquest. In one sense, such men were rightly set aside because their virtues made them ineffective within the world; yet they were the John the Baptists of future salvation. Without them, there would be no hope.

Stowe wrote mainly about women and African Americans. Of American Indians, who resisted conquest and domination from outside, she had little or nothing to say. African Americans resembled women in that both resided inside the social structure and inside the life of the family. Stowe repeatedly identified African-ness with femininity. In the preface to *Uncle Tom's Cabin*, where, presumably, she sought to summarize the intent of her fiction as concisely as possible, she spoke of Africans as an 'exotic race, whose ancestors … perpetuated to their descendants, a character so essentially unlike the hard and dominant Anglo-Saxon race, as for many years to have won from it only misunderstanding and contempt.'

Stowe's choice of a pronoun for 'Anglo-Saxon race' in the passage quoted above was the impersonal form, *it*. In a subsequent paragraph, referring to the African race – 'bound and bleeding at the foot of civilized and Christianized humanity' – she selected the feminine personal form, *her*.[25] These identifications remain consistent through the text of *Uncle Tom's Cabin*. Explaining Uncle Tom's instantaneous alliance with Eva, Stowe wrote that he 'had the soft, irrepressible nature of his kindly race, ever yearning toward the simple and childlike. … '[26] Tom also displayed an inherent taste for beauty – 'the birds, the flowers, the fountains … the silken hangings' of St. Clare's mansion. Aesthetic appreciation – feminine for Stowe – was 'a consideration to which his sensitive race is never indifferent.'

> If ever Africa shall show an elevated and cultivated race, – and it must come, sometime, her turn to figure in the great drama of human improvement, – life will awake there with a gorgeousness and splendor of which our cold western tribes faintly have conceived.

But the true beauty of physical things rested in their representation of spiritual beauty:

> ... the negro race ... will, perhaps, show forth some of the latest and most magnificent revelations of human life. Certainly they will, in their gentleness, their lowly docility of heart, their aptitude to repose on a superior mind and rest on a higher power, their childlike simplicity of affection, and facility of forgiveness. In all these they will exhibit the highest form of the peculiarly *Christian life*, and perhaps as God chasteneth whom he loveth, he hath chosen poor Africa in the furnace of affliction, to make her the highest and the noblest in that kingdom which he will set up.[27]

Uncle Tom's willing acceptance of crucifixion prophecied the kingdom. He even took with him Legree's two black slave drivers, like thieves flanking the cross. 'It is the statement of missionaries', Stowe wrote in verification, 'that, of all races on earth, none have received the Gospel with such eager docility as the African. The principle of reliance and unquestioning faith ... is more a native element in this race than any other. ... '[28]

Meanwhile, however, in preparing for the millennium, there might be need for less exalted, more practical champions, like St. Peter, with the task of building the church in present reality. To this role Stowe assigned the two Georges – the all-white George Shelby, who smashed Legree with his fist and freed the slaves on his father's plantation; and the mulatto George Harris, who shot the slave catcher with his pistol, and carried his family away to Liberia.[29] Near the end of her novel, Stowe outlined, through the reflections of George Harris, a racial division of labor in Christian progress. 'To the Anglo-Saxon race has been intrusted the destinies of the world, during its pioneer period of struggle and conflict. To that mission, its stern, inflexible, energetic elements, were well adapted.' Yet such intermediate steps would be worthless without the final vision. On the brink of embarking for Liberia, George Harris feared that the half of his blood that was white might draw him away from the 'sublime doctrine of love and forgiveness.' Fortunately, he reminded himself, he had at his side 'an eloquent preacher of the Gospel ... in the person of my beautiful wife. When I wander, her gentler spirit ever restores me, and keeps before my eyes the Christian calling and mission of our race.'[30]

It was suggested at the start of this chapter that the ideological construction of John Quincy Adams, while effective in directing political energies toward liquidation of the planter class, failed to provide any morally acceptable guidelines for coping with African Americans themselves. Hildreth and Stowe proposed solutions to this problem. One might even suppose – given the dates of their writing and the shared names and attributes of their central characters – that the authors pursued a dialogue in which Hildreth offered the opening statement, Stowe responded, and Hildreth in his 1852 addendum, rebutted Stowe's response.[31]

Hildreth's opening was that Africans were part of universal humanity. If once fully liberated, they could become equal citizens in a republican society and ought to be so dealt with. Hildreth's position was morally and logically consistent. Its difficulty lay in the fact that it took no account of the vast number of Republicans and potential Republicans – especially those reaching the new party by way of the Free Soil alliance – who had become accustomed to the use of white egalitarianism as a means of resisting upper-class domination. Such a constituency was not likely to enlist in a crusade for Free Soil if African Americans were to have equal access to the free soil.

Stowe's response was to divide political time into two segments – the real present and the sacred future. During the real present (the 'pioneer period'),[32] whites because of their masculine traits would be better qualified than Africans to advance the banners of Christian progress. Africans, blessed with the feminine (and Christlike) traits of love, humility and self-sacrifice, must march at the rear during the real present. In the sacred future they would come into their own. Stowe symbolized these two periods through Topsy's relationship to Eva and Tom's relation to Christ.

> There stood the two children, representatives of the two extremes of society. The fair, high-bred child, with her golden hair, her deep eyes, her spiritual, noble brow, and prince-like movements; and her black, keen, subtle, cringing, yet acute neighbor. They stood the representatives of their races. The Saxon, born of ages of cultivation, command, education, physical and moral eminence; the Afric, born of ages of oppression, submission, ignorance, toil, vice.[33]

That contrast might justify any sort of well-wishing intermediate status. Even colonization to Africa remained possible. Stowe's hero of the real present, George Harris, opted for colonization. Stowe, in her preface, looking to the distant future, took for granted that Africans, long since returned to Africa, would recall their American house of bondage only as the Israelites remembered the Egyptian captivity.[34]

Of Uncle Tom's slow death at the hands of Legree, Stowe wrote, 'And this, oh, Africa, latest called of nations, – called to the crown of thorns, the scourge, the bloody sweat, the cross of agony, – this is *thy* victory; by this shalt thou reign with Christ when his kingdom shall come on earth.'

Hildreth in his rebuttal portrayed the other Tom, relentless and unforgiving in warfare against white oppression. But the more effective rebuttal, of course, was delivered by the multitudes who read *Uncle Tom's Cabin* and applauded its dramatizations, whether in earnest melodrama or in the burlesques of blackface minstrelsy.[35]

What were the ideological effects of these books on the Republican coalition? They contributed, I think, to delineating a spectrum with regard to race and slavery broad enough to include divergent Republican tendencies, yet clearly marked off from the Jacksonian side. This discussion, so far, has emphasized differences between the books; here it is important to pay attention to similarities. *Archie Moore* and *Uncle Tom's Cabin* resemble one another in their tone of earnest persuasion. No real laughter breaks the surface of either one. Although Hildreth used satire, his satire is never funny and often bleakly utilitarian. Nor is there play with artistic form or the ambiguity of multiple and overlapping meanings. Neither author dallied with the notion of art for pleasure's sake. If Hildreth allowed any place for aesthetic pleasure in his calculus of pleasure and pain, it was for the pleasure conveyed by 'artistical efficiency', by rational presentations of natural and human phenomena. Stowe, after perhaps substituting *moral sensibility* for 'artistical efficiency', would have concurred. In short, these works targeted an intermediate literary taste, bounded on the high side by such emblematic writings as *Moby Dick* or *The Scarlet Letter*, on the low side by comedy or blackface minstrelsy. The territory thus encompassed corresponded roughly to the middle estate, that old home of American whiggery to which Hildreth and Stowe were legitimate heirs, and which they now endeavored to expand.[36]

The books also resemble one another in that they present alternative answers to the same crucial question of early Republicanism: How can I conscientiously advocate overthrow of the slave system without some morally acceptable plan for dealing with the slaves who will thus be set free? The question itself marked a dividing line between Republicanism and the Democracy, since on the Democratic side such a question could not even be asked. Bringing forward the hard side of white racism, Democratic doctrine portrayed African Americans as sources of contamination to free society should slavery ever weaken its grip; far from being a threat to the republic, the Slave Power became its chief salvation.[37] Clearly this way of viewing things would not satisfy a growing number of Free Soil–oriented Jacksonians, who, thanks in part to Harriet Beecher Stowe, were moving towards Republican ways of thinking.

The answer Stowe offered derived from her analogizing of gender and race. If the psyches of Africans (like those of women) were more Christlike and submissive than the psyches of white males, certain conclusions must follow: first, that slavery could be terminated without danger to the republic; second, that it ought to be terminated; and third, after slavery, and at least during the foreseeable present, Africans, like women, must occupy separate and subordinate positions in the social hierarchy. Stowe herself, through the fictional character George Harris, spoke for colonization. Lincoln, who could hardly have been a convert to Stowe's romantic feminism, likewise favored colonization. When that proved unfeasible, he shifted (or was shifting at the time of his death) to some scheme of guardianship or indenture through which African Americans might be inured gradually to the perils of competition and burdens of suffrage.[38] The point here is not whether those plans would have worked, but that during the 1850s and early 1860s the possibility of proposing such plans empowered conscientious whites to set themselves against the Slave Power.

Hildreth of course gave short shrift to romantic feminism. Yet his own work accomplished a similar result. For those who accepted the argument that Africans were equal members of universal humanity, there was nothing to be feared either in abolishing slavery or liberating African slaves. Treated equally as human beings, African Americans could be expected to respond as human beings. We have abundant evidence of the impact of *Uncle Tom's Cabin*; with *Archie Moore* we depend largely on inference. Narrower in its outreach, Hildreth's radical argument may have had greater penetrating power precisely because it was less original. His argument would have been familiar to any of his contemporaries who had, as he did, intellectual roots in the Enlightenment. Such key figures as Thaddeus Stevens, Charles Sumner and Frederick Douglass must have recognized this kinship. Sumner had tried to arrange an English edition of *Archie Moore*. We know that Frederick Douglass kept a copy of *Despotism in America* among his papers and that, with his wife, he visited Hildreth's grave in the Protestant Cemetery in Florence in 1887. Less exalted Radicals like George Wilkes and Benjamin Butler adapted parallel scripts.[39] Nor could African Americans who believed in, or hoped for, racial equality, have failed to be impressed that an argument such as Hildreth's emanated from the white Republican party. Certainly this must have been a factor in leading free blacks in the North like Douglass, and freedmen in the South like the black leaders of the Union League, to put their lives and aspirations on the line under Republican auspices.[40] It would seem fair to say, then, that the ideological effect of the two books together was to expand and solidify the Republican coalition against slavery. Once slavery was terminated, the differences between the two would begin to outweigh their similarities.

Notes

1. Hans L. Trefousse, 'The Republican Party, 1854–1864', in Arthur M. Schlesinger, Jr., ed., *History of U.S. Political Parties*, New York 1973, 2:1148; George H. Mayer, *The Republican Party, 1854–1964*, New York 1967, pp. 27, 32; Donald E. Emerson, *Richard Hildreth*, Baltimore 1946, pp. 151–57; Glyndon G. Van Deusen, *Horace Greeley, Nineteenth Century Crusader*, New York 1953, pp. 50–57, 130–32; Eric Foner, *Free Soil, Free Labor, Free Men: The Ideology of the Republican Party Before the Civil War*, New York 1970, pp. 18–23, 36–39, 51–58.

2. Henri Avron, *Marxist Esthetics*, Ithaca, N.Y. 1970, pp. 50–51; Frederic Jameson, 'Introduction', ibid., p. *xix*; Stefan Morawski, 'Introduction', Karl Marx and Frederick Engels, *On Literature and Art*, New York 1974, p. 31. On the ideological linkage between anti-slavery and the spread of wage labor and entrepreneurship in wage labor, see John Ashworth, 'The Relationship Between Capitalism and Humanitarianism', *American Historical Review* 92 (October 1987): 813–28.

3. See Chapter 1, pp. 41–42.

4. Kenneth Stampp, 'Race, Slavery and the Republican Party in the 1850s', brings into focus, especially with reference to the Lincoln–Douglas debates in 1858, the problem that confronted Republicans in formulating a politically viable concept of African-American-ness: Stampp, *The Imperiled Union: Essays on the Background of the Civil War*, New York 1980, pp. 105–35. Robert W. Johannsen, *The Lincoln–Douglas Debates of 1858*, New York 1965; Glyndon Van Deusen, *William Henry Seward*, New York 1967, pp. 193–94; Frederic Bancroft, *The Life of William H. Seward*, [1900] Gloucester, Mass. 1967, 1:454–65; William E. Gienapp, *The Origins of the Republican Party, 1852–1856*, New York 1987, p. 445.

5. A comment of Eric Foner's in 'The Causes of the American Civil War: Recent Interpretations and New Directions', in Robert P. Swierenga, ed., *Beyond the Civil War Synthesis: Political Essays of the Civil War Era*, Westport, Conn. 1975, p. 23n, is appropriate here: 'In America, by contrast [i.e., to earlier hierarchical views of the social order], where freedom implied the ability to compete for advancement, the idea of freeing the slaves inevitably raised the question of social equality.' There was a corresponding moral gap in the 'Free Soil' position on Indians, but because national attention was fixed on slavery and secession, that gap did not really confront Republican ideological innovators until after the Civil War.

6. Emerson, *Hildreth*. Martha M. Pingel, *An American Utilitarian: Richard Hildreth as Philosopher, with Selections from his Published and Unpublished Works*, New York 1948; Arthur M. Schlesinger, Jr., 'The Problem of Richard Hildreth', *New England Quarterly* 13:223–45; Louis S. Friedland, 'Richard Hildreth's Minor Works', *Papers of the Bibliographical Society of America* 40 (1946): 127–50; Richard Hildreth, *Archie Moore, the White Slave, or Memoirs of a Fugitive*, [New York and Auburn, 1856] New York 1971, p. *xxi*. On the publication history of *Archie Moore*, ibid., pp. *ix–xxii*; Schlesinger, Jr., 'Problem', p. 230n.

7. Richard Hildreth, *Despotism in America, or, an Inquiry into the Nature and Results of the Slave Holding System in the United States*, Boston 1840; Schlesinger, Jr., 'Problem', pp. 233–34; Emerson, pp. 73–84.

8. Hildreth, *Archie Moore*, 1856 ed., pp. 7–8.

9. Ibid., p. 44; Friedland, 'Minor Works', pp. 128–31; David Brion Davis, *The Problem of Slavery in the Age of Revolution*, Ithaca 1975, p. 14.

10. Jeremy Bentham, *Theory of Legislation*. Translated by Richard Hildreth, Boston 1840; Emerson, *Hildreth*, pp. 89–94. On anti-clericalism, Schlesinger, Jr., 'Problem', pp. 234–35; Hildreth, *A Letter to Andrews Norton on Miracles as the Foundation of Religious Faith*, Boston 1840, in Pingel, *American Utilitarian*, pp. 129–51; Hildreth, *Native Americanism Detected and Exposed by a Native American*, Boston 1845, in Pingel, *American Utilitarian*, pp. 177–98, especially pp. 193–96.

11. Hildreth, *Archie Moore* [1856], pp. 33, 166.

12. Ibid., pp. 173–74.

13. Ibid., pp. 203, 205, 206.

14. Ibid., pp. 291–305. The same text, published in London under the title, *The White*

Slave, 1852, carried an announcement facing the first page: 'Uniform with this work is published *Uncle Tom's Cabin* by Mrs. Harriet Beecher Stowe.'

15. Hildreth, *Archie Moore* [1856], pp. 32–48 and *passim*; Lydia Maria Child, *Liberator*, 18 May 1837, quoted in Hildreth, *Archie Moore* [1856], p. *xiv*. See also Friedland, 'Minor Works', p. 128.

16. Compare with Harriet Beecher Stowe, *Lady Byron Vindicated: A History of the Byron Controversy*, Boston 1870; and see Ann Douglas on Stowe's defense of Lady Byron in *The Feminization of American Culture*, Boston 1978, pp. 244–46.

17. Child, *Liberator*, as quoted in Hildreth, *Archie Moore* [1856], p. *xiv*. On the relation to John Andrews, Charles Sumner and William Dean Howells, Emerson, *Hildreth*, pp. 157–61; Friedland, 'Minor Works', pp. 128–35; Van Deusen, *Seward*, p. 401.

18. Harriet Beecher Stowe, *Uncle Tom's Cabin*, New York 1952; see, for examples, pp. 63, 114–31, 322–32.

19. Ibid., pp. 390–91.

20. Ibid., pp. 366–67.

21. Ibid., pp. 357, 362–63, 365, 370.

22. Ibid., pp. 390–92, 402, 425.

23. I am indebted to George Fredrickson's *The Black Image in White America: The Debate on Afro–American Character and Destiny, 1817–1914*, Middletown, Conn. 1987, especially for his chapter, 'Uncle Tom and the Anglo–Saxons: Romantic Racialism in the North', pp. 97–129.

24. Stowe, *Uncle Tom's Cabin*, pp. 150, 176, 229–30, 314.

25. Ibid., Preface, p. *i*.

26. Ibid., p. 144.

27. Ibid., p. 177.

28. Ibid., pp. 389, 408.

29. Ibid., pp. 194–96, 414, 426–27.

30. Ibid., pp. 425–28. For a perceptive reading of *Uncle Tom's Cabin* as an attack on 'male dominance' in American society, see Richard Yarborough, 'Strategies of Characterization in *Uncle Tom's Cabin* and the Early Afro-American Novel', in Eric Sundquist, ed. *New on Uncle Tom's Cabin*, New York 1986, pp. 45–84.

31. Hildreth, *Archie Moore* [1856], pp. 238–408. Evan Brandstadter, in 'Uncle Tom and Archie Moore: The Anti-Slavery Novel as Ideological Symbol', *American Quarterly* 26 (May 1974): 160–75, makes a persuasive case that Stowe must have read *Archie Moore* before writing *Uncle Tom's Cabin*.

32. Stowe, *Uncle Tom's Cabin*, p. 428.

33. Ibid., p. 243.

34. Ibid., Preface, p. *ii*.

35. Ibid., p. 391; James D. Hart, *The Popular Book: A History of America's Literary Taste*, Berkeley, Calif. 1961, pp. 110–12; Harry Birdoff, *The World's Greatest Hit*, New York 1947.

36. Richard Hildreth, 'Theory of Taste: An Inquiry into the Foundations of Criticisms, and the Origin, Progress, and Revolution of Ornamental, Imitative and Suggestive Arts', in Pingel, *American Utilitarian*, pp. 75–120, pp. 114–17; Gienapp, pp. 438–39.

37. James K. Paulding, *Slavery in the United States*, New York 1836, especially pp. 48–61.

38. Lincoln on gradual emancipation, apprenticeship and colonization: see Chapter 11, note 23.

39. I am not suggesting that Stowe invented the analogizing of race and gender. Fredrickson shows that this concept, among other ideas of 'romantic racialism', was readily available to her in Cincinnati and New England, pp. 102–110; Reginald Horsman, *Race and Manifest Destiny: The Origins of American Racial Anglo–Saxonism*, Cambridge, Mass. 1981, pp. 264–66; Ronald G. Walters, *The Anti-Slavery Appeal: American Abolitionism after 1830*, Baltimore 1976, pp. 57–60. Stowe was an 'innovator' because she gave these ideas crucial placement in the Republican critique of slavery. Her contribution was more 'original' than Hildreth's because romantic racialism was still new to American anti–slavery thought in the 1840s: Fredrickson, pp. 101, 102–10; David Donald, *Charles Sumner and the Coming of the Civil War*, New York 1960, pp. 60, 194. Hildreth corresponded with Sumner on anti-slavery politics and on the Trieste consulship, which he was granted near the end of his life: Hildreth

to Sumner, 6 April 1854, and 5, 13 January, 11 March, 18 October 1862, in the Houghton Library, Harvard University; Frederick Douglass Papers, Library of Congress Microfilm, 1974, Reel 24; Philip Foner, ed., *The Life and Writings of Frederick Douglass, Vol. 4*, New York 1955, p. 127.

40. See, for example, Howard N. Rabinowitz, ed., *Southern Black Leaders of the Reconstruction Era*, Urbana, Ill. 1982, and Michael Fitzgerald, 'The Union League Movement in Alabama and Mississippi: Politics and Agricultural Change in the Deep South during Reconstruction, Ph.D. diss., University of California, Los Angeles, 1986; W.E.B. DuBois, *Black Reconstruction in America, 1860–1880*, [1935] Cleveland 1964, especially 'Back Toward Slavery', pp. 670–710. Gerald Jaynes, *Branches and Roots: Genesis of the Black Working Class in the American South*, 1862–1882, New York 1968, pp. 282–85, 295.

PART III

Republican Synthesis

11

Republicans

If England's industrial revolution provided a 'norm' for industrializing nations, the United States was foreclosed from following that norm by the existence of a successful slave plantation economy in the South. The slave system worked in several ways to facilitate industrialization. It offered expanding markets for manufactured goods, as well as for financial services and transportation. At the cutting edge of commercial capital investment, the plantation South generated agricultural exports that dominated transatlantic commerce. Given the regional relationships fixed by the Constitution, these exports stimulated diversified enterprise in New England and Middle Atlantic cities and infrastructural expansion throughout the North and West. Both effects contributed to setting the stage for industrial take-off.[1]

From the plantation South, on the other hand, emanated the major political opposition to industrialization. By dominating the Democratic party, southern planters exercised a veto over federal policies from Jackson's inauguration in 1829 to that of Abraham Lincoln in 1861.[2] The new Republican party, as a party of industrialization, had no choice but to make the planter class its primary target. The Republicans focused on slavery in the territories in part because that issue had been given them by Jacksonian usage of white racism to defend slavery; but also because the exclusion of slavery in the territories offered a constitutional, perhaps peaceful, strategy for taking control step by step of the federal apparatus. This was the political thrust of the Free Soil alliance.[3] Innovative endeavors such as those of Hildreth and Stowe were intended to provide a moral accounting for this strategy. Yet the driving force of the Republican party was never simply antislavery or westward expansion. The driving force was industrialization.

There is of course a teleological flaw in stating this matter too bluntly.

Industrialization during the formative years of Republicanism was a process, a direction, not an achieved state. Especially was this the case in respect to class formation. Industrial workers as well as industrial capitalists still moved within a traditional class spectrum that extended from casual laborers at the lower end, through yeomen and artisans, to merchant–manufacturers and merchant princes on the upper side. Nor is there any need to suppose that ideological innovators of the pre-war decades had access to some conspiratorial tunnel vision that showed them industrial capitalism as it would be in the 1880s and 1890s. Yet having said this, it should also be said that to think about the past without admitting some element of teleology is scarcely possible. Whether we wish it or not, we know what history brought and our knowledge circumscribes the apparent randomness, or contingency, of what went before.

Richard Hildreth (to anticipate the present chapter) had, by 1837, correctly predicted the extension of Adam Smith's logic to the chartering of corporations. On the whole, Hildreth's successes in the ideological marketplace failed to match those of George Wilkes. Yet when Wilkes in 1845 transcribed his egalitarian enthusiasms into a plan for transcontinental railway construction, which, instead of grinding up small producers, would furnish them a safe Smithean workshop in the West, his proposal withered for lack of buyers. This contrast might seem to corroborate the rule of randomness; what actually happened, however, was that the two proposals traveled by different routes to similar endings. Wilkes's plan for egalitarian railroads perished of malnutrition; Hildreth's egalitarian laws of incorporation flourished, but reversed their meaning.

It would seem, then, that the ideological marketplace was magnetized, already tuned to a field of distant force. Within the producers' republic in which Hildreth and Wilkes had both been socialized, wealth in land and capital was coagulating. Certainly they perceived this trend, and their proposals at one level represented efforts to turn it back. Hildreth, distancing himself whether by intent or otherwise from the world he was helping to build, lived out his last years in exile and virtual ostracism. But Wilkes, who had begun by identifying the artisan republic with acquisitive individualism, would end by deploying acquisitive individualism in defense of the land grant railroads.

In his study of pre–Civil War Republicanism, *Free Soil, Free Labor, Free Men*, Eric Foner has argued that the concept of free labor (then nearly equivalent to self-employed labor) held a central place in Republican ideology. 'The Republicans' glorification of northern labor', Foner wrote, 'might have led them to a radical political appeal, in which the rights of workingmen were defended against the prerogatives of the rich and propertied.' If in fact it led them to no such divisive tactics, that was partly because the fission of the artisan class into industrial workers and employers was only beginning in the 1850s. '"The interests of the capitalist and the laborer [Foner's source here is Henry C. Carey] are ... in perfect harmony with each other, as each derives advantage from every measure that tends to facilitate the growth of capital."' Idealizing free labor, raising that ideal as a positive goal of Republican politics, added an affirmative side to the crusade against the Slave Power so long and bitterly advocated by John Quincy Adams. 'I am a Free Soiler', declared Richard Henry Dana, Jr., 'because I am of the stock of the old Northern gentry, and have a particular dislike to any subservience on the part of our people to the slave-holding oligarchy.'[4]

Formulations such as these, in partnership with their racist companion pieces, served to legitimate the Free Soil alliance of yeomen, artisans and established capital out of which sprang the Republican party. Old Whigs, as Foner explained, provided the pivotal element:

> The idea of combating southern political power and its economic consequences was the key to conservative support for the Republican party. Such measures as a Pacific railroad, a homestead act, a protective tariff, and government aid to internal improvements had been blocked time and again by the Democratic party, at the dictation, it seemed, of the South. The conservatives hoped to use the Republican party to wrest control of the federal government away from the slaveholders. ...

Extending this sequence to the Civil War, Foner quoted (with at least partial approval) the assertion of Raimondo Luraghi that 'war became part of the process of "building a modern, centralized nation-state based on a national market, totally and unopposedly controlled by an industrial capitalist class."' Given this understanding – which I share – of what was contained in the Republican coalition, I think it not unreasonable to begin with an assertion that the driving force of that coalition was industrialization.[5]

The Republican Economic Program

The keystone of the Republican program was the old American Plan, carried forward from the National Republican thesis. A protective tariff was to encourage domestic manufacturing and produce revenue for internal improvements. Internal improvements in the form of federally subsidized transportation would bring food and raw materials from the West to eastern manufacturing cities and open up western markets to manufactured products. Finally, a federalized banking system, somehow reincarnated from the old Banks of the United States, would govern a uniform currency and regulate credit in the interests of respectable, established and indispensable capital. These three propositions together had fired most of the political controversies of the past thirty years. The power of the plantation South was manifest in the fact that it had successfully stalemated all three.[6]

Republican innovators by the late 1850s had pushed their new party well beyond its whiggish antecedents. In terms of economic program, innovation took the form of two additions to the classic National Republican triad. One was advocacy of mass immigration; the second was a proposal to grant homesteads from the public lands; both had been borrowed from the Jacksonian enemy. Urban Democrats traditionally had championed immigration. Homesteads were first propagandized by urban artisan radicals such as George Henry Evans, David Broderick and George Wilkes; the regular Democracy under southern governance had stood against them; but to western agrarians from David Crockett through Thomas Hart Benton to Andrew Johnson, agitation for cheap lands had been stock in trade. Whigs, of course (like John Quincy Adams), had abominated homesteads; while whiggish nativists, carrying their long opposition to immigration into the Republican party, had played a significant role in the presidential nominating convention of 1860. But if nativists believed they had cut a deal by getting Abraham Lincoln instead of Seward, they must have been bitterly disappointed with Lincoln's 1863 message to Congress, which urged establishment of a 'system for the encouragement of immigration' on the ground that there was a 'great deficiency of laborers in every field of industry.'[7]

Homesteads and advocacy of European immigration, then, may be seen in part as bargaining offers for drawing Free Soilers and Jacksonian Unionists to the Republican ranks – a transit upon which rested Republican hopes of constructing a majority coalition. Even more important, mass immigration had become a crucial resource for the manufacturing sector, the emergence of which out of the matrix of commercial capital represented a major structural change differentiating the new Republican party from its Whig predecessor.

Two sets of problems confronted Republican leaders in assembling their economic program. The first, and historically the earliest, involved reconciling Old Line Whigs to the acceptance of alien doctrines. With regard to homesteads and the wooing of western agrarians, the opening gambit can be traced back to David Crockett, whose brief glory resulted largely from the efforts of the Philadelphia publisher, Henry C. Carey, then a Whig, subsequently a Republican. Harrison's log cabin campaign in 1840 served as dress rehearsal for Republican strategies in 1856 and 1860.[8] One of the outstanding architects of that campaign was Richard Hildreth, political editor of the Boston *Atlas*;[9] while the campaign itself first brought to national prominence the Whig (and Republican) voice of the Golden West, Horace Greeley of the New York *Tribune*.[10] As to immigration, certainly the leading proponent of new views for old Whigs was William Seward, whose advocacy of political alliance with Irish Catholics may have cost him the 1860 presidential nomination.[11] Henry C. Carey, already referred to in connection with the orbiting of David Crockett, was the chief exponent of the theory underlying such advocacy – the linking of tariffs to immigration as elements necessary for a prosperous manufacturing sector. Carey, aside from his publishing career, was a political economist of substantial reputation, a spokesman for Pennsylvania's coal and iron interests and an ardent proselytizer of protective tariffs and federal encouragement to immigration. By way of emphasizing the importance (and relatively small numbers) of this cohort of Republican innovators, it is worth noting also that Hildreth's ideological constructions concurred with and reinforced those of Carey in the areas of tariff, immigration and Free Soil alliance. Both men were closely associated with the New York *Tribune* during the 1850s when that paper served as a major channel for popularizing Republican economic doctrine.[12]

Republican leaders by 1860 could take Old Line Whigs more or less for granted. What they could not take for granted was that Free Soil and Unionist recruits to the new party would acquiesce in the National Republican trinity of protective tariffs, federal banking controls and internal improvements. Since most such recruits came out of Jacksonian backgrounds, they would have been educated to view that trinity in the same light as the advent of the Antichrist.[13]

Hildreth, Banking and General Incorporation

Richard Hildreth died in 1865, after three years as United States consul at Trieste, where, aging and failing in health, he had been put out to pasture. In contrast to his Jacksonian counterpart and ideological opponent, George Bancroft – who supped richly at the federal table both before and after the Civil War – Hildreth's minor consulship was his only recognition for a lifetime of service to the anti-slavery and Republican cause.[14] Lawyer, journalist, novelist, historian, political analyst, and for half a decade an editor of Greeley's *Tribune*, it was perhaps Hildreth more than any other who laid the ideological basis for justifying the Republican economic program to a mass electorate.[15] The key document in that context is his *Argument for Open Competition in Banking*, published in 1837.

Hildreth had begun this argument by siding with the Jacksonian enemy against Biddle and the Second Bank of the United States. Then he castigated Jacksonians for incorporating state banks into their federal spoils system. His remedy was a plan for 'free banking', which was in fact written into law along substantially the lines of his proposal by the Whig-controlled New York legislature in 1838. Free banking meant that, rather than cranking out individual charters, always prone to political favoritism, a state legislature would set up general rules under which any qualified applicants could enter the banking business. Hildreth argued that the natural laws of free competition would then bring the benefits of banking to every community, while at the same time eliminating abuses that flowed from monopolization and political corruption. What is important for the present context is not the economic realism of Hildreth's proposal, but its ideological impact. He was laying claim to the heritage of Adam Smith, previously the unchallenged domain of Jacksonians:[16]

> ... banks, the more numerous they become act constantly ... to check each other's operations. ... They become the most watchful guardians over each other, and while each struggles to obtain for itself the largest possible share of the circulation, none is able to engross a dangerous amount of it. ... Trade will no longer lie at the mercy ... of a few purse-proud, domineering, dictatorial bank directors. ... Instead of being subject to artificial regulations, the currency will be controlled and guided by its own necessary laws – the Law of Trade ... which does better than set things to right, – which prevents them from ever getting wrong.[17]

There is no need to claim that Hildreth invented this line of thought. We are told that general incorporation laws (restricted to Protestant churches and charitable institutions; and in Massachusetts to aqueduct companies) were already being enacted prior to 1801. The New York legislature considered the concept of general incorporation for banking as early as 1825.[18] Clearly Hildreth was unusual among Whigs in pressing such ideas as political program. For the most part, Jacksonians were the main advocates of general incorporation laws, which they believed would eliminate special privilege; whereas Whigs tended to prefer the more permissive but politically indefensible alternative of special charters. But the Republican party, following the lead piloted by Hildreth (among others), took over the championship of general incorporation at the state level and inserted that device into the National Banking acts of 1863 and 1864.[19]

'For the history not only of banking but also of corporate enterprise in general', Bray Hammond wrote many years ago, 'the New York free banking legislation of 1838 was of prime significance; for it presented a conflict of economic evolution and law from which the characteristic nineteenth century conception of the corporation as an instrumentality of individualism and laissez faire emerged. ... Before the transition from the old conception to the new, the corporation was identical with monopoly and antithetical to democracy; following the transition it lost its hateful connotations and became the guileless handmaid of free enterprise.'[20]

Since such 'guileless handmaids' proliferated through general laws at the state level, for which Jacksonian legislators often cast their votes, they could readily be justified under the egalitarian principle of equalizing opportunity; the same principle would soon be serving to sweeten the centralizing thrust of the move to federally chartered banks.

By the time of Lincoln's first election, Republican innovators had assembled ideas and concepts essential to the new party's industrializing program, and had made impressive progress in translating those ideas and concepts into the language of laissez-faire and equal opportunity – into the language, that is, of Jacksonian Democracy. But, since the central issues in the campaign of 1860 were not those of industrializing policy, but those of slavery in the territories and the Union versus secession, it remained an open question how much progress had been made toward winning a mass constituency for the Republican economic program. Lincoln himself fell short of carrying a majority of the electorate. Immediately after his inauguration, the central issue became war to save the Union, and the problems of industrialization policy were left, for the time being, to fend for themselves.[21]

The Republicans at War

War seemingly facilitated industrialization policy. Aside from pushing technical breakthroughs like the interchangeability of parts in weapons manufacture, war enabled the new party to introduce its long-range economic program not as deliberate alterations in the socio-economic structure of the nation but as expedients to meet wartime emergencies. Thus the Transcontinental Railway Act would thwart separatism in the West and help hold California for the Union; higher tariffs would aid in bringing needed revenue; the national banking laws would expedite bond sales. Temporarily at least war gave to Republican leaders manipulation of an enormous head of steam generated by American nationalism. It brought them to the difficult industrial crossing as captains of a semi-militarized ship and placed in their hands the most effective military instrument the world had yet known. All these taken together contributed to an illusion that victory in war would open the way for an almost painless transition to industrialization policy.[22]

The dream of easy transition complemented and reinforced aspirations for Republican reconciliation with the old Whig South. Lincoln, who remembered collaborating in earlier years with Southern Whigs like

Alexander Stephens and even Henry Clay, envisioned a settlement that would bring to leadership those competent, kindly gentlemen, kissing cousins to the western and northern Whigs from whom the Republican party had its beginnings. Such images of a pre-lapsarian era before slavery had separated the National Republican oligarchy survived in collective memory. Lincoln's reconstruction plan, as it took shape during the last two years of his life, aimed at just such a restoration; one of its corollaries being to bring forward the soft, rather than hard side of white racism by establishing a system of guardianship or indenture for the former slaves under benevolent whiggish tutelage.[23] To end the melodrama of civil war with familial reconciliation would have been in tune with the romantic sentimentality of Harriet Beecher Stowe's fiction. Doubtless Lincoln knew this would not work; perhaps he hoped some of it might work.

Conditions set by history – of which the most intractable was the length and bitterness of the war – limited Republican initiatives from the outset. The danger of losing the war, or fear that war might settle into endless deadlock, pushed Republicans to the Emancipation Proclamation, as well as to the enlistment and conscription of black soldiers.[24] These departures obviously ran counter to the expectation of whiggish reconciliation entertained by conservative Republicans, including Lincoln; and ran counter also to expectations held by Unionists and Free Soilers of Jacksonian background who held no quarrel with slavery *inside* the South, and took for granted a separate or subordinate status of blacks. For white males to struggle against other white males for the future of the white republic, while women and African Americans waited passively on the outcome, might fit comfortably enough inside the Stowe scenario; but for white and black soldiers together to overthrow the planter class demanded a more radical construction, such as Hildreth's.[25]

In military terms, the Union cause reached its lowest ebb early in 1863. Lincoln's leadership appeared to be faltering. There were apprehensions of Republican defeat in the presidential election of 1864. To stave off that disaster, Republican leaders leaned more heavily than ever on the Free Soil alliance. They offered the vice-presidential nomination to the western agrarian and Tennessee Unionist, Andrew Johnson, the only Southern senator who had rejected secession. Running in tandem, Lincoln and Johnson scored a victory for which hundreds of thousands of Unionist Democrats cast their ballots.[26] This electoral bargain exemplifies the extent to which Republicans had been forced to subordinate propagation of their industrialization program to the necessities of winning the war, since that was the only matter on which they could have come to any agreement with Andrew Johnson.

The Johnson Counteroffensive

The new party found itself pushed to the wall when Johnson, seizing the opening offered by Lincoln's death, attempted to reestablish the old Jacksonian majority with himself at its head. In his earlier career Johnson had spelled out the politics of Free Soil Democracy. He hated precisely that element in the South which Lincoln most revered. Johnson's wars had been waged against planter aristocrats. In Tennessee he had advocated free public education financed by taxation of land and slaves; and in national politics championed free homesteads from the public domain. He stood for westward expansion and above all for the nation, that sacred Union of states that alone could guarantee the equal rights and equal opportunities of democratic citizenship. The only real problem he perceived in African slavery was, not that it violated democratic principle, but that it enhanced the monopolizing powers of the planter aristocracy.[27] During the war, Johnson grudgingly acknowledged that the end of slavery was inevitable. 'As for the negro', he explained early in 1864, 'I am for setting him free, but at the same time I assert that this is a white man's government. ... If whites and blacks can't get along together, arrangements must be made to colonize the blacks.'[28]

Doubtless Johnson was eager to claim the presidency in his own right. Underlying personal ambition, and perhaps of greater importance, was loyalty to Jacksonian convictions. These must in the long run guide national progress. Republicans, in Johnson's view, for all their devotion to national unity, could never be relied on for principled leadership. Their party was too deeply infiltrated by the worst elements of whiggery. Banks, tariffs and government-sponsored monopolies fattening on the labor of the people – all these monsters against which Jackson had battled in the old days – now surged back into the places of power.[29] The fact that Congress was out of session when Johnson took over the presidency in April 1865 opened the way for a speedy restoration of the seceded states under presidential proclamation. To Johnson's advantage was the fact that his plan for Reconstruction remained nearly identical to that left partly in place by Lincoln. The only significant difference was the exclusion from political amnesty of persons owning property valued at over $20,000. This would have been totally unacceptable to Lincoln. Johnson apparently hoped that by excluding planter aristocrats from immediate political activities he could open the road for an upsurge of yeoman democracy. In this, certainly, he was disappointed. Southern yeomen, instead of generating a new lower-class leadership, reelected the same planter aristocrats who had led the Confederacy to defeat. Johnson might have rejected the outcome; but he opted to accept it, using the presidential pardon power to exact political loyalty. Johnson of course knew the South well enough to know that the elected planters, formally at least, must be upper-case Democrats, regardless of how aristocratic their personal politics might be.[30]

The new president's first message to Congress – drafted (although this was not publicly known at the time) by the foremost ideological innovator of Jacksonian Democracy, George Bancroft – began with a defense of presidential restoration in the South.[31] Ratification of the Thirteenth Amendment (a process virtually completed at the time the message was sent to Congress) would make the nation 'once more a united people ... bound more than ever to mutual protection and support.' All that was needed to complete the work of reunification was for the representatives chosen by the restored states to 'resume their places in the two branches of the National Legislature.'[32]

Having confronted the Republican majority with its responsibility, the message then turned to a reassertion of the Jacksonian persuasion. First with respect to race and labor:

> Slavery was essentially a monopoly of labor, and as such locked the States where it prevailed against the incoming of free industry. Where labor was the property of the capitalist, the white man was excluded from employment. ... With the destruction of the monopoly, free labor will hasten from all parts of the civilized world. ... And the future influx of population will be mainly from the North, or from the most civilized nations of Europe. ... The removal of the monopoly of slave labor is a pledge that those regions will be peopled by a numerous and enterprising population, which will vie with any in the Union in compactness, inventive genius, wealth and industry.[33]

By 'compactness' Johnson meant racial homogeneity. The message was predicting that the future labor force in the South would be made up of white migrants from the North and from northwestern Europe. What then would become of the former slaves?

> The career of free industry must be fairly opened to them, and then their future prosperity and conditions must, after all, rest mainly on themselves. If they fail, and so perish away, let us be careful that the failure shall not be attributable to any denial of justice. In all that relates to the destiny of the freedmen, we need not be too anxious to read the future; many incidents which, from a speculative point of view, might raise alarm, will quietly settle themselves.[34]

Nowhere in this lengthy message was there direct reference to the fact that blacks in the South were not yet citizens; that none had the right to vote; and that special codes hastily enacted by all the seceded states between Appomattox and the time of Johnson's message had set in place a regional legal basis for keeping the ex-slave (in the words of Kenneth Stampp) 'exactly what he was: a propertyless rural laborer under strict controls, without political rights, and with inferior legal rights.'[35]

What Johnson's recommendation came to with respect to southern blacks was that they be left to take care of themselves; and if through the workings of 'free industry', under the benevolent protection of their newly acquired legal status, they should happen to 'fail, and so perish away', that would be an outcome for which no white man need blame himself or feel regret. In any case, more urgent matters claimed the attention of Congress:

> Monopolies, perpetuities and class legislation, are contrary to the genius of free government. ... Here there is no room for favored classes or monopolies. ... Wherever monopoly attains a foothold, it is sure to be a source of danger, discord and trouble. ... [36]

In December 1865 there could have been little doubt in the mind of any reader that the presidential message referred to the main features of the Republican industrializing policy.

Since Republican leaders feared, probably with good reason, that their economic initiatives were not yet firmly enough grounded in the North and West to stand against Johnson's counteroffensive, they were forced to buy time by legislative interventions in the South far more radical than most would have been likely to choose under other circumstances. In Congress they rejected the electoral results of the Johnson restoration. They then mandated black suffrage, at that time virtually nonexistent in any part of the Union except New England and New York.[37] This tactical response to Johnson's attack had the effect of vacating the moderate, racially conservative middle ground, which – taking the popularity of Stowe's novel as an index – would probably have seemed about right to a majority of Republicans, especially those in the Free Soil contingent. The new party moved instead to a flanking position that required an inter-racial egalitarianism like that of Hildreth's for its ideological validation.

Radical Republicans such as Charles Sumner and Thaddeus Stevens stood ideologically close to Hildreth. The logical strategy, as adumbrated by Hildreth and pushed by Sumner and Stevens, would have been to base suffrage reform on a revolutionary program of land redistribution. Nor would such a strategy have entailed any contradiction to the principles of Adam Smith, but would rather have liberated liberal doctrine from the irrational restraints imposed by Jacksonian white egalitarianism.[38] Needless to say, the Republican majority with its whiggish center and Free Soil peripheries was incapable of any such demarche. The party did in fact legislate a place for black soldiers in the reorganized regular army in 1866, yet permitted exclusion of African American soldiers from the South, and abandoned land redistribution altogether. What resulted instead was a bloody sacrifice of black Republicans[39] after they had held the southern salient through the crucial presidential elections of 1868, 1872 and 1876.[40]

By 1876, the last year but one of Republican Reconstruction, federal power in most parts of the South existed in name only.[41] The so-called 'volunteer' regiments that comprised the bulk of the Union Army in 1865 (including all of its more than 100,000 black soldiers) had been rapidly demobilized following Appomattox. At the same time, 'colored troops' were being withdrawn 'from the interior of the Southern States', in order, as General Grant put it in March 1866, 'to avoid unnecessary irritation and demoralization of labor in those states.' The sort of irritation Grant referred to had been exemplified in the Memphis riots during which, according to the historian John Hope Franklin, more than a hundred 'negro men, women and chldren' had been killed or wounded. White rioters, who burned 'four churches and twelve school buildings' were presumably expressing resentment at the presence of black troops in Memphis.[42]

As the Union Army dissolved, the importance of the state militias escalated. Most southern states under Johnson's restoration had not only enacted black codes but organized white militias to enforce the codes. Congress, when it broke with Johnson, had illegalized the militia in seceded states. Subsequently, hoping that the new Radical Republican regimes in the South would prove capable of self-defense, Congress authorized reinstitution of the militia, with enlistment now open to African Americans. Much of the violence of 'redemption' centered in struggles for control over local and state militias. Redeemers first tried to capture militia companies by infiltration. Failing that, they assembled extralegal military societies (white leagues, Ku Klux Klans, the Red Shirts) which operated essentially as armed units of the Democratic party.[43]

Southern Republicans could often protect their political bases in urban areas or in regions of dense black population such as Beaufort, South Carolina, which repeatedly elected the black Unionist war hero, Robert Smalls, to Congress. But in rural regions of mixed or mainly white population – that is, throughout most of the South – black leaders and white Republicans were systematically murdered or forced into hiding, their defense cadres and militia formations overpowered and disarmed. Characteristic of this pattern, which dominated the final years of Reconstruction, was the massacre at Hamburg, South Carolina in July 1876. White Democrats, led by a former Confederate general, converged on the town, demanding that a black militia company give up its officers and surrender its weapons. Some forty black militiamen barricaded themselves in a brick building. Unable to dislodge them with small arms fire, the besiegers brought up artillery from across the state line in Georgia and began to batter down the walls. The black militiamen broke out; some escaped, and some were captured. Of the captured, several, including the company's first lieutenant, were executed by being riddled with bullets and bayonetted. Meanwhile, white vigilantes roamed through the black quarter of the town looting and killing. Hamburg perhaps received unusual attention because the black congressman, Robert Smalls, came from nearby Beaufort. 'The whole affair', an eyewitness wrote to Smalls, 'was a well and secretly planned scheme to destroy all the leading Republicans of the county of Aiken. ... '

Seeking to persuade President Grant to send adequate federal troops to South Carolina, Smalls insisted that this statement be read into the record of the 44th Congress. The reading was repeatedly interrupted, on one occasion by a Democratic congressman from Pennsylvania who demanded to know the name of the witness. 'I will say to the gentleman', Smalls replied, 'that if he is desirous that the name shall be given in order to have another Negro killed, he will not get it from me.'[44] D.H. Chamberlain, the last Republican governor of South Carolina, also begged Grant to intervene. The president, who had ignored similiar pleas from other parts of the South, was being told by political advisers that further intervention might cost the Republican party such pivotal northern states as Ohio.

> The views which you express [Grant responded] ... I fully concur in. The scene at Hamburg ... is only a repetition of the course that has been pursued in other states ... notably in Mississippi and Louisiana. Mississippi is governed today by officials chosen through fraud and violence, such as would scarcely be accredited to savages, much less to a civilized and Christian people. How long these things are to continue, or what is to be the final remedy, the great Ruler of the Universe only knows. ... [45]

Thus spake the conqueror of Vicksburg and Richmond in the summer of 1876.

Racial Ideology at the End of Reconstruction

In terms of racial ideology, the sequence of these events may be summed up as follows. The redeemers, left to pursue home rule on what they regarded as their own turf, converted black Republicanism into a monster that had to be endlessly destroyed. The whiggish, soft side of white racism went underground in the South, while the hard side furnished the ideological keystone of bourbon Democracy. This, I suppose, is what Joel Williamson meant when he wrote that by freeing the slaves, America had 'also freed racism'. The hard-side mentality, according to Williamson, rested on a belief that African Americans, once liberated from 'the restraining influences of slavery', must retrogress 'toward their natural state of bestiality'. The white man's burden, according to this hard-side view, would then consist simply in confining the black population until it could be destroyed or driven out; or – to recall Andrew Johnson's phrase – till it had time enough to 'perish away.' Williamson maintained that soft-side ideas continued to find sanctuary among southern 'conservatives', yet conceded that conservatives survived in the late nineteenth century South only by yielding place to the hard side.[46]

The Republicans had consented to, in a sense connived at, this reorientation of southern attitudes. Johnson's counteroffensive at the very beginning of Reconstruction had forced the Republican party to abandon the middle ground favored by Lincoln and corresponding approximately to Harriet Beecher Stowe's sentimental romanticism. For tactical defense, the party took possession of a flanking position represented ideologically by Hildreth and a scattering of Radicals. But to remain tenable, the flanking position – black suffrage in the South – would have had to be buttressed by the creation, on one hand, of a black landed peasantry, and on the other, of an armed black military presence. For the majority of Republicans, such new departures lacked moral commitment and were therefore opportunistic. Tactical advance triggered strategic retreat, back to Stowe, back even to John Quincy Adams. These manoeuvers protected the new party's still tenuous grip on federal power during the decade of Reconstruction.[47] Success of the party's 'northern strategy' made possible a turn away from its 'southern strategy'.[48] In both advance and retreat, the racial formulations remained negotiable; what was not negotiable was the Republican industrialization program. Certainly this was no secret agenda. As early as the first election of Lincoln, John Sherman (among many others) – the congressman and senator from Ohio and younger brother of William Tecumseh Sherman – had spelled it out clearly:

> ... those who elected Mr. Lincoln expect him ... to secure to free labor its just right to the Territories of the United States; to protect ... by wise revenue laws, the labor of our people; to secure the public lands to actual settlers ... ; to develop the internal resources of the country by opening new means of communication between the Atlantic and the Pacific.[49]

Outside the South, the soft side of racism – with respect to African Americans – became a Republican monopoly. Acknowledging their loyal assistance in saving the Union, Republicans continued to honor something resembling Hildreth's white image of the black warrior.[50] Lincoln, in fact, had made that image (stripped of the autonomy attributed to it by Hildreth) a keystone in his 1864 presidential campaign.

> Peace does not appear so distant as it did. I hope it will come soon, and come to stay; and so come as to be worth the keeping in all future time. ... And then,

there will be some black men who can remember that, with silent tongue, and clenched teeth, and steady eye, and well-poised bayonet, they have helped mankind on to this great consummation; while, I fear, there will be some white ones, unable to forget that, with malignant heart, and deceitful speech, they have strove to hinder it.[51]

If, by the end of Reconstruction, the image had outlived its usefulness for the southern salient, still, with appropriate reductions of scale, it might come to focus in the West.

The Republicans in 1865 had disbanded what was probably the largest black army ever assembled. One year later they pushed through Congress, against Democratic opposition, plans for a permanent African-American nucleus in the reorganized regular army. Recruitment, initially, was to be from veterans of the demobilized volunteer regiments.[52] Supporters of this project, and its opponents, took for granted that military units of regimental size must be either black or white; and they assumed also that the commissioned officers of black regiments would be white, since that had been the practice throughout the war. The main debate took place in the Senate, where California had the distinction of leading the opposition. '...I wish to express my thought', said James McDougall, who had served as attorney-general in Illinois and California, and as a Democratic congressman, before becoming a United States senator, 'that the people of my country are able to maintain themselves, and do not need to be maintained by an inferior race....This undertaking to place a lower, inferior, different race upon a level with the white man's race, in arms, is against the laws that lie at the foundation of republicanism.'[53]

Senator Benjamin Wade of Ohio set forth the majority position: '...because experience has shown that they are just as good troops as the whites, and because we want to make no distinction between the one kind and the other, I think there should be in each arm of the service a certain proportion of colored troops.' To Wade's declaration of egalitarian principle, his colleague from Massachusetts, Senator Henry Wilson, who had risen from back country yeoman origins to become a successful manufacturer of boots and shoes (and, later, vice president under Grant), added a more utilitarian note:

... We have some colored regiments west of the Mississippi that were raised in Kentucky, who understand the management of horses as well as any men in the country, admirable riders; and some of those regiments have been stationed in the same neighborhood with white regiments from which we have had twenty-five to thirty-five percent of desertions; and we have not had a solitary case of desertion in the colored regiments. I think that it is a great matter of economy to put some of those colored regiments into the field in the Indian country, in the mountains, and in sections of the country where white men desert largely and go to the mines. ... These men are much more under command and far less likely to desert.

The other senator from California, John Conness, a former Democrat who had turned Union Republican, then asked, 'Do you propose to send your black men to us?' To which Wilson replied, 'They are so hard upon them in that section of the country that they will not run away, while white men will.'

These exchanges worked up to a bipartisan coda predictive of the uses to which black regiments would later be put. Wilson offered an amendment to authorize temporary employment of Indian scouts at the same pay and allowances as regular cavalry. McDougall, who had been so vehement against the arming of African Americans, found the selective arming of Indians more to his taste. On the basis of his experiences among 'the Kiowas, the Arapahoes, the Comanches, the Oneidas, and other Indians', he told his colleagues, 'I can say ... that there are a body of Indians who are attached to this country; there are a great many Indians hostile to it; and the employment of a thousand Indians on the frontier by the Government would be a great economy. General Grant knows it; I know it.'[54]

Thus the reorganized army of the republic became an inter-racial army. The War Department recruited black regulars, mainly in the South, gathering them into four regiments subsequently designated the 24th and 25th Infantry and the 9th and 10th Cavalry. By 1870 they had taken up posts on the southwestern frontier. They became fixtures in the trans-Mississippi West where (except during the Spanish-American War) they remained until the early years of the twentieth century. These regiments were prestigious in black communities, especially since service in them offered one of the few escape routes from southern sharecropping.[55] Yet that service also entailed upon black soldiers a role that resembled the fictional roles of Crusoe's Friday and Leatherstocking's Last of the Mohicans: they bore arms, but seldom for their own purposes. Mostly they fought against Indians, and mostly they served outside the South.[56]

The Republican party, however, was by no means monolithic on questions of race. Two principal segments of the party – its traditional whiggish core and its more recent Free Soil adherents – pursued ideological legitimations that even as late as the 1870s remained contradictory. The party's whiggish core still favored the soft side of racism with respect both to African Americans and Indians, and tended to apply similar attitudes to Chinese immigration. Free Soil Republicans, on the other hand, stood with the Kit Carson of fact and fiction in preserving a structured silence on the subject of African Americans, while promoting the racial extermination of Indians. The chapter that follows will examine the working out of these contradictions in the new territory of Colorado.

Notes

1. The classic text is Douglass C. North, *The Economic Growth of the United States, 1790–1860*, New York 1966, supplemented by another, George Rogers Taylor, *The Transportation Revolution, 1815–1860*, [1951] New York 1968.

2. Michael F. Holt, 'The Democratic Party', 1828–1860, in Arthur M. Schlesinger, Jr., ed., *History of United States Political Parties*, New York 1973, 1:502; Hans Trefouuse, 'The Republican Party, 1854–1864', in ibid., 2:1158; Eric Foner, *Free Soil, Free Labor, Free Men: The Ideology of the Republican Party Before the Civil War*, New York 1970, p. 191.

3. Holt, 'Democratic Party', Schlesinger, ed., 1:512; Trefouuse, 'Republican Party', 2:1149–1150, 1155, 1160; Foner, *Free Soil*, pp. 54–60, 73–102, especially pp. 76–77, 79, 83; Theodore Clarke Smith, *The Liberty and Free Soil Parties in the Northwest*, New York 1897; William E. Gienapp, *The Origins of the Republican Party, 1852–1856*, New York 1987.

4. Foner, *Free Soil*, pp. 18–20, 32, 191–92; the source of the quotation from Henry C. Carey is *Principles of Political Economy*, 1:339. David Donald, *Lincoln Reconsidered: Essays on the Civil War Era*, 2d ed. New York 1956, pp. 34–35. Donald, maintaining that anti-slavery New Englanders like Dana were moved mainly by status anxieties, proposed a psychoanalytic reading of Dana's statement that converted it into a 'quite unconscious' attempt to downgrade New England cotton textile magnates by attacking the slave system from which they obtained their raw material. If, however, Dana's words are permitted to speak for themselves, what they convey is agreement with John Quincy Adams's class resentment against the 'slave-holding oligarchy'.

5. Eric Foner, 'The Causes of the American Civil War: Recent Interpretations and New Directions', in Robert P. Swierenga, ed., *Beyond the Civil War Synthesis: Political Essays on the Civil War Era*, Westport, Conn. 1975, p. 31. The quotation is from Raimondo Luraghi, 'The Civil War and the Modernization of American Society: Social Structure and Industrial Revolution in the Old South Before and During the Civil War', *Civil War History*, 18:249. Eric Foner's *Reconstruction: America's Unfinished Revolution, 1863–1877*, New York 1988, a thorough and sensitive synthesis of several decades of intense scholarship, is the best work with which to begin a study of Reconstruction. Foner's Chapter 10, 'The Reconstruction of the North', pp. 460–511, carries his argument from the earlier period, to which I have referred here, into the era of Reconstruction.

6. Holt, 'Democratic Party', Schlesinger, ed., vol. 1: *passim*, and pp. 512, 529, 531.

7. Charlotte Erickson, *American Industry and the European Immigrant*, Cambridge, Mass. 1957, pp. 1–11; George M. Stephenson, *A History of American Immigration, 1820–1924*, [1926] New York 1964, pp. 135–37; William Nisbet Chambers, *Old Bullion Benton, Senator from the New West*, Boston 1956, pp. 166, 228, 373; Kenneth Stampp, *The Era of Reconstruction, 1865–1877*, New York 1967, pp. 54–56; Glyndon Van Deusen, *William Henry Seward*, New York 1967, pp. 221, 225–26; William E. Gienapp, 'Nativism and the Creation of a Republican Majority in the North Before the Civil War', *Journal of American History* 72:529–59; Gienapp, *The Origins of the Republican Party, 1852–1856*, New York 1987, pp. 423–28, 445; Charles Granville Hamilton, 'Lincoln and the Know-Nothing Movement', *Annals of American Research*, Washington, D.C. 1954, pp. 1–20; Abraham Lincoln, 'Third Annual Message', 8 December 1863, in James D. Richardson, *A Compilation of the Messages and Papers of the Presidents*, New York 1897, 8:3383.

8. See Chapter 3, p. 82.

9. Emerson, *Hildreth*, pp. 57–62; Richard Hildreth, *My Connection with the Atlas Newspaper* ..., Boston 1839; Hildreth, *The People's Presidential Candidate; or, The Life of William Henry Harrison of Ohio*, Boston 1839; Hildreth, *The Contrast: or, William Henry Harrison versus Martin Van Buren*, Boston 1840.

10. Glyndon Van Deusen, *Horace Greeley: Nineteenth Century Crusader*, New York 1964, pp. 35–58.

11. Van Deusen, *Seward*, pp. 67–71; Frederic Bancroft, *The Life of William H. Seward*, [1900] Gloucester, Mass. 1967, 1:454–65; Michael F. Holt, 'The Antimasonic and Know-Nothing Parties', in Arthur M. Schlesinger, Jr., ed., pp. 593–620.

12. Richard Hildreth, 'Native Americanism', in Pingel, *American Utilitarian*, pp. 177–98; Hildreth, 'A Plea for Sunday Freedom: in a Letter to John Quincy Adams, President

of the Late Baltimore Lord's-Day Convention. By "One of the New Generation'", *Liberator*, 24 January 1845, p. 16; Arnold W. Green, *Henry Charles Carey: Nineteenth Century Sociologist*, Philadelphia 1951, pp. 25, 34–35, 49–57, 101, 107–9, 127, 134–43, 158–71; Joseph Dorfman, *The Economic Mind in American Civilization, 1606–1865*, New York 1946, 2:789–825; David Montgomery, *Beyond Equality: Labor and the Radical Republicans, 1862–1872*, New York 1967, pp. 86–87.

13. Holt, 'Democratic Party', in Schlesinger, ed., pp. 512–13; Leon Friedman, 'The Democratic Party, 1860–1884', in Schlesinger, ed., 2:894–95.

14. Emerson, *Hildreth*, pp. 161–63; Friedland, 'Minor Works', pp. 130–34.

15. Emerson, *Hildreth*; Pingel, *American Utilitarian*; Schlesinger, Jr., 'Problem.'

16. Richard Hildreth's *The History of Banks: To Which Is Added, A Demonstration of the Advantages and Necessity of Free Competition in the Business of Banking* was published in Boston in 1837; see Emerson, *Hildreth*, Appendix II, p. 170. Citations are from the differently titled edition of 1840, which notes, and stresses the importance of, the New York Free Banking Act of 1838: Hildreth, *Banks, Banking and Paper Currencies, in three parts. I. History of Banking and Paper Money. II. Argument for Open Competition in Banking. III. Apology for One Dollar Notes*, [Boston 1840] New York 1968. On the New York free banking law, Bray Hammond, *Banks and Politics in America from the Revolution to the Civil War*, Princeton, N.J. 1957, pp. 572–604. On the enactment of the New York banking law, pp. 583–84. Some New York Jacksonians, for example, John W. Vethake, New York *Evening Post*, 21 October 1835, had been advocating 'free banking' and general incorporation laws, but without persuading their party in the legislature. See Joseph L. Blau, ed., *Social Theories of Jacksonian Democracy*, Indianapolis, Ind. 1954, pp. 211–36.

17. Hildreth, *Banks*, pp. 147, 153.

18. Joseph Stancliffe Davis, *Essays in the Earlier History of American Corporations*, Cambridge, Mass. 1917, 2:16–17; Hammond, *Banks*, pp. 572–73, 583–84. For early general acts of incorporation, George H. Evans, Jr., *Business Incorporations in the United States, 1800–1943*, New York 1948, pp. 11, 17. See also John W. Cadman, Jr., *The Corporation in New Jersey: Business and Politics, 1791–1875*, Cambridge, Mass. 1949, p. 26.

19. In New York State the Jacksonian Regency had established a political monopoly over state banking. After the demise of the Second Bank of the United States, New York Whigs used free banking legislation as a means of breaking open that monopoly. For bank politics in New York: Lee Benson, *The Concept of Jacksonian Democracy: New York as a Test Case*, New York 1963, pp. 89–105; Dixon Ryan Fox, *The Decline of Aristocracy in the Politics of New York, 1801–1840*, [1919] New York 1965, p. 403; John A. Garraty, *Silas Wright*, New York 1949, pp. 171–73; George H. Evans, *Business Incorporations*, describes the period from 1800 to 1875 as an era of special charters. A scattering of states adopted general incorporation laws prior to the Civil War, but this did not become the dominant pattern until the 1870s. More decisive than the adoption of general incorporation laws were provisions, usually constitutional, forbidding incorporation by any other route. No states adopted such restrictions prior to 1845; 13 between 1845 and 1859; and another 31 between 1859 and 1913: Evans, *Business Incorporations*, pp. 10–11. Historians of corporations seem to concur that before the Civil War private business interests preferred special charters to general incorporation because they perceived the former as more permissive and flexible: Stuart Bruchey, 'The Historical Development of the Corporation in the United States', *Encyclopaedia Britannica*, Chicago 1972, 6:523–32; Thomas C. Cochran, 'Business Organization and the Development of Industrial Discipline', in Harold F. Williamson, ed., *The Growth of the American Economy: An Introduction to the Economic History of the United States*, New York 1944, pp. 303–18; James W. Hurst, *The Legitimacy of the Business Corporation in the Laws of the United States, 1780–1970*, Charlottesville, Va. 1970, pp. 13–57; W.C. Kessler, 'Incorporation in New England: A Statistical Study', *Journal of Economic History*, 8 (May 1948): 43–62. Ronald E. Seavoy, *The Origins of the American Business Corporation, 1784–1855*, Westport, Conn. 1982, p. 182, attributed the pressure for 'general incorporation statutes' to 'the social and political forces that democratized American society during the Age of Jackson.' Herbert Ershkovitz and William G. Shade, 'Consensus or Conflict? Political Behavior in the State Legislatures during the Jacksonian Era', *Journal of American History* 53 (December 1971): 591–621, found that on selected issues involving corporations, Whigs in state legislatures of New Hampshire, Pennsylvania, Ohio, New Jersey, Virginia and Missouri

consistently favored corporations, whereas Democrats consistently but somewhat less u-nanimously opposed them. The selected issues (granting and extension of special charters, increased capitalization, note issue, limited liability, requiring or suspending specie payment) unfortunately did not include general incorporation laws.

20. William Greenleaf, ed., *American Economic Development Since 1860*, New York 1968, p. 50; Louis M. Hacker, ed., *Major Documents in American Economic History*, Princeton, N.J. 1961, 1:108–11; Bray Hammond, 'Free Banks and Corporations: The New York Free Banking Act of 1838', *Journal of Political Economy* 44:184–85. See also Hammond, *Banks*, p. 573.

21. On the tenuousness of Republican control, see David Donald, *The Politics of Reconstruction, 1863–1867*, Cambridge, Mass. 1984, pp. 12–13.

22. Thomas C. Cochran and William Miller, *The Age of Enterprise: A Social History of Industrial America*, New York 1961, p. 110; Edward Chase Kirkland, *Industry Comes of Age: Business, Labor and Public Policy, 1860–1897*, Chicago 1967, pp. 18–20, 44–46; John F. Stover, *American Railroads*, Chicago 1961, pp. 67–69, 88.

23. Lincoln in his Second Annual Message, 1 December 1862, asked Congress to initiate a constitutional amendment which would 1) authorize federal compensation for slave owners in any slave state that adopted a gradual emancipation plan to be completed at least by 1900; and 2) authorize appropriations for colonizing freed persons 'with their own consent at any place or places without the United States.' More than a third of the 16-page message was devoted to arguments in support of this plan: Richardson, *Messages and Papers of the Presidents*, 7:3327–3343. The proposed amendment is on p. 3337. Lincoln defended apprenticeship in letters to Major General John A. McClerand, 8 January 1863, and General Nathaniel P. Banks, 5 August 1863. Roy P. Basler et al., eds, *The Collected Works of Abraham Lincoln*, New Brunswick, N.J. 1953, 6:48–49, 364–65. Lincoln's Ten Percent Plan proclamation, 8 December 1863, promised that any state plan for freed persons, which, while assuring permanent freedom and providing for education, 'may yet be consistent as a temporary arrangement with their present condition as a laboring, landless and homeless class', would 'not be objected to by the National Executive.' Richardson, 7:3415. Lincoln defended this proposal in his Third Annual Message, also 8 December 1863: Richardson, 7:3391. In his last public speech, 11 April 1865, he again defended the apprenticeship plan: Basler, 8:399–405. For convenient access, Arthur Zilversmit, ed., *Lincoln on Black and White: A Documentary History*, Belmont, Calif. 1971, pp. 140, 143, 152–56, 183–86.

24. J. G. Randall and David Donald, *The Civil War and Reconstruction*, 2d ed. rev., Lexington, Mass. 1969, pp. 355–69, 498–513, 531; James M. McPherson, *The Negro's Civil War*, New York 1967, pp. 173–74; Benjamin Quarles, *The Negro in the Civil War*, Boston 1953, pp. 201–13, 230; John Hope Franklin, *From Slavery to Freedom: A History of Negro Americans*, New York 1967, pp. 290, 292–94; W.E.B. DuBois, *Black Reconstruction*, New York 1964, pp. 55–83. On the Emancipation Proclamation and blacks in the Union Army: Basler, *Collected Works*, 5:388–89; Philip Foner, ed., *The Life and Writings of Frederick Douglass*, New York 1952, 3:273, 317–19; U.S. Bureau of the Census, *Historical Statistics of the United States from Colonial Times to 1953*, Washington, D.C. 1960, pp. 7, 9.

25. On the process by which Unionist Democrats were drawn to the Republican party, see Eric McKitrick, *Andrew Johnson and Reconstruction*, Chicago 1960, pp. 45–47.

26. Ibid., pp. 90–92.

27. Stampp, *Era of Reconstruction*, pp. 50–82, and see especially p. 55. For various interpretations of Andrew Johnson: Howard K. Beale, *The Critical Year: A Study of Andrew Johnson and Reconstruction*, New York 1930; LaWanda and John H. Cox, *Politics, Principle and Prejudice, 1865–1866: Dilemma of Reconstruction in America*, New York 1969, pp. 88–106; McKitrick, *Andrew Johnson and Reconstruction*, and McKitrick, ed., *Andrew Johnson, A Profile*, New York 1969.

28. Stampp, *Era of Reconstruction*, 56; Rovert W. Winston, *Andrew Johnson, Plebeian and Patriot*, New York 1928, p. 252.

29. LaWanda and John Cox, pp. 99–106; Stampp, pp. 57–59. Alfred D. Chandler, Jr., ed., *The Railroads: The Nation's First Big Business*, New York 1965, pp. 49–50; Taylor, *Transportation Revolution*, pp 94–96; Cochran and Miller, *The Age of Enterprise*, p. 110.

30. Stampp, *Era of Reconstruction*, pp. 61–64, 78; McKitrick, *Johnson*, pp. 142–52; William A. Dunning, *Reconstruction, Political and Economic*, New York 1962, pp. 44–45.

31. Russel Nye, *George Bancroft, Brahmin Rebel*, New York 1944, pp. 229–33; Beale,

Critical Year, p. 49n; LaWanda and John Cox, p. 131.

32. John Savage, *The Life and Public Services of Andrew Johnson, Seventeenth President of the United States, Including His State Papers, Speeches and Addresses*, New York 1866, Appendix, p. 116; Richardson, *Messages and Papers of the Presidents*, 8:3556.

33. Richardson, 8:3558, 3559.

34. Ibid.

35. John Hope Franklin, *Reconstruction After the Civil War*, Chicago 1961, pp. 48–50, 55; Stampp, *Era of Reconstruction*, pp. 79–82; Walter L. Fleming, ed., *Documentary History of Reconstruction, Political, Military, Social, Religious, Educational and Industrial, 1865–1906*, New York 1966, 1:274–75, 279–80, 281–82, 283–85, 287.

36. Richardson, 8:3559–3560.

37. Eric Foner, in his recent study, *Reconstruction: America's Unfinished Revolution, 1863–1877*, stresses, correctly, I think, the role of 'Radical Republicans, Southern Unionists, and the freedmen themselves', pp. 271–80; the 'moderate' bulk of the party from outside the South, however, was necessary for the congressional legislation that established black suffrage. See also Stampp, *Era of Reconstruction*, pp 110, 141–42; McKitrick, *Johnson*, pp. 481–85; William Gillette, *Retreat from Reconstruction, 1869–1879*, Baton Rouge, La. 1979, pp. 1–24, especially pp. 7–9.

38. For views of Stevens, Sumner, et al., similar to those of Hildreth, see Foner, *Reconstruction*, pp. 230–31, 504–5, and Stampp, *Era of Reconstruction*, pp. 87–88. On efforts to obtain land redistribution, Foner, *Reconstruction*, pp. 235–38, 245–46, 308–10, and Stampp, *Era of Reconstruction*, pp. 123–31; also, Fleming, ed., *Documentary History*, 1:151–53; Philip Foner, ed., *Frederick Douglass*, 4:31–32; Gillette, pp. 23–24. For the situation of the urban black working class, Jonathan McLeod, 'Black and White Workers: Atlanta during Reconstruction' Ph.D. diss., University of California, Los Angeles, 1987.

39. Jack D. Foner, *Blacks and the Military in American History*, New York 1974, pp. 52–71; Arlen L. Fowler, *The Black Infantry in the West, 1869–1891*, Westport, Conn. 1971, especially pp. xi–xiv, 3–15; William H. Leckie, *The Buffalo Soldiers: A Narrative of the Negro Cavalry in the West*, Norman, Okla. 1967, especially pp. 3–18; John H. Nankivell, *History of the Twenty-Fifth Regiment, United States Infantry, 1869–1926*, [Denver 1927] New York 1969, pp. 5–11; Erwin N. Thompson, 'The Negro Soldiers on the Frontier: A Fort Davis Case Study', *Journal of the West* 7:218. On the resurgence of racism in national politics, Forrest G. Wood, *Black Scare: The Racist Response to Emancipation and Reconstruction*, Berkeley, Calif. 1968, pp. 82–89. On the use of terror in the South, Allen Trelease, *The Ku Klux Klan Conspiracy and Southern Reconstruction*, New York 1971; Foner, *Reconstruction*, pp. 425–44, 553–63; Stampp, *Era of Reconstruction*, pp. 186–215; Vernon L. Wharton, *The Negro in Mississippi, 1865–1900*, New York 1965, pp. 185–88, 193–94; Herbert Aptheker, ed., *A Documentary History of the Negro People in the United States*, New York 1951, pp. 610–14; Fleming, *Documentary History*, 2:406–7; Michael Fitzgerald, 'The Union League in Alabama and Mississippi', Ph.D. diss., University of California, Los Angeles, 1986. Gillette, p. 160, quotes the Washington *National Republican*, normally supportive of the Grant administration, protesting that Republican policy, having pushed black Mississippians forward to advanced positions, 'now abandons them … to the relentless vengeance of enemies. … It is but "the beginning of the end", for with the mangled remains of these victims of false promises … fragments of a broken Constitution and … free suffrage, will be buried with them', 15–21 September 1875.

40. Grant's margin of the national popular vote in 1868 was less than the Republican votes estimated to have been cast by black freedmen: Charles H. Coleman, *The Election of 1868: The Democratic Effort to Regain Control*, New York 1933, pp. 306–7. Had there been no voting by black freedmen, Grant would have carried the electoral vote but with a minority of the popular vote. Under those hypothetical circumstances, a shift of less than 1 percent in two key states such as Pennsylvania and California would have cost Grant the presidency. In 1872, six of nine 'reconstructed' states in the South contributed 50 electoral votes and a popular majority of 124,000 to Grant's reelection. In 1876, with all eleven seceded states readmitted, three, Florida, Louisiana, and South Carolina, were still under Radical Republican governments. The Republican electoral votes cast by these states were challenged by rival Democratic returns. With all 19 electoral votes counted as Republican by the Compromise of 1877, the Republican party held on to the presidency by 1 electoral

vote. It had lost the popular vote by a quarter-million: see Stampp, pp. 209–210. For electoral statistics, Bureau of the Census, *Historical Statistics*, pp. 862, 684–85, 688; Gillette, pp. 323–26. George Rawick, *From Sundown to Sunup: The Making of the Black Community*, Westport, Conn. 1972, pp. 140–47, has shown that the political meaning of these events remained fixed in the recollections of freed persons sixty-five years later.

41. Wharton, pp. 185–86; Aberdeen, Miss., *Examiner*, 2 August 1883, in Wharton, pp. 187–88; Franklin, *Reconstruction*, pp. 119–20; Gillette, pp. 35, 315–16.

42. Morris J. MacGregor and Bernard C. Nalty, eds, *Blacks in the United States Armed Forces: Basic Documents*, Wilmington, Del. 1977, 3:3–4; U.S. Grant, Lieutenant General, to Major General G.H. Thomas, Washington, 28 March 1866, in ibid., pp 3–14; Foner, *Reconstruction*, pp. 261–64; Rembert W. Patrick, *The Reconstruction of the Nation*, New York 1967, pp. 82–84.

43. Otis A. Singletary, *Negro Militia and Reconstruction* [Austin, Tex. 1957] Westport, Conn. 1984, especially pp. 4–16, 32–33, 129–44. Charles Johnson, Jr., 'Black Soldiers in the National Guard, 1877–1949.' Ph.D. diss., Howard University, 1976, pp. 45–61.

44. *Congressional Record*, 44th Cong., 1st Sess., IV, pt. 5, pp. 4641–4642, in Aptheker, *Documentary History of the Negro People*, pp. 610–614; Foner, *Reconstruction*, pp. 570–72; Patrick, p. 253.

45. Wharton, pp. 193–94. Gillette, pp. 155–59. President Grant to Governor D.H. Chamberlain, 26 July 1876, in Fleming, *Documentary History*, 2:406–7.

46. Joel Williamson, *The Crucible of Race: Black–White Relations in the American South Since Emancipation*, New York 1984, pp. 109–329. The quotations are from pp. 109, 111.

47. See above, note 40.

48. Gillette, p. 371.

49. David Donald, *Lincoln Reconsidered: Essays on the Civil War Era*, 2d ed. New York 1956, p. 106. The problem of teleology, referred to at the start of this chapter, comes very much to the fore in the anthology of essays in 'New Political' history referred to in note 5 above. The editor claims that 'New Political Historians', p. *xii*, have escaped teleology, first, by showing that voters during the Civil War and Reconstruction were primarily moved by 'nativist ethnocultural issues such as naturalization and temperance laws, by personality factors, and by internecine party patronage squabbles' rather than by 'such national issues as tariff and land policy or the extension of slavery into the territories', p. *xiii*; and second, by applying new statistical techniques which facilitate detailed analyses of roll call voting in Congress. To readers who maintain a certain agnosticism as to the newness of 'New Political' history, it may seem curious that voters allegedly fixed on ethnocultural, religious and factional identifications should have sent to Washington so many congressmen and senators who went down the line in virtually undented blocs for the positions of their respective parties on precisely 'such national issues as tariff and land policy or the extension of slavery into the territories.' This, essentially, is what the roll call voting analyses demonstrate. They show that the concept of factionalism as, for example, Radicals versus Moderates, has little relevance to Republican congressional voting in this period; and that during the crucial last two Reconstruction congresses, 1873–1877, Republican congressmen and senators agreed massively on major economic issues and almost unanimously on the various measures of southern Reconstruction: Swierenga, ed., pp. 165–242. David Donald again, whose Fleming Lectures published by Louisiana State University Press in 1965 under the title, *The Politics of Reconstruction, 1863–1867*, were partly instrumental in directing the attention of 'new political historians' to problems of the Civil War and Reconstruction, summed up the findings of these historians in a second edition of his lectures (Harvard University Press, 1984): '...we are unable clearly to identify the membership of either Moderate or Radical factions or to attribute to either distinctive views on the conduct of the war, or the rehabilitation of the South, or on general economic policies', pp. 8–9. I think it might be concluded from all this that Republicans – or at least Republican political leaders who made it to Congress – were thinking collectively in much the same way that Richard Henry Dana, Jr., had thought in the 1850s and that John Sherman was thinking in 1861.

50. See, for example, Senator Henry Wilson's advocacy of black troops in the Union Army: Richard H. Abbott, *Cobbler in Congress: The Life of Henry Wilson, 1812–1875*, Lexington, Ky. 1972, pp. 135–40, 160.

268 The Rise and Fall of the White Republic

51. Zilversmit, ed., pp. 148–151; James M. McPherson, *Ordeal by Fire: The Civil War and Reconstruction*, New York 1982, p. 361.

52. Franklin, *Reconstruction*, pp. 35–36; Patrick, p. 27; Jack Foner, *Blacks and the Military*, pp. 52–54; Nankivell, pp. 5–11; MacGregor and Nalty, *Basic Documents*, 3:16–28. For a resumé of military service of the black regiments in the West, pp. 29–86.

53. *Congressional Globe*, 39th Cong., 1st Sess., 2:1378–1386. On MacDougall, see pp. 1379–1380.

54. Ibid., p. 1385; *Biographical Directory of the American Congress, 1774–1961*, Washington, D.C. 1961, *passim*. On Henry Wilson, see Abbott, *Cobbler in Congress*; and Elias Nason, *The Life and Public Services of Henry Wilson*, Boston 1881, p. 375.

55. T.G. Steward, Chaplain, 25th U.S. Infantry, *The Colored Regulars in the United States Army*, Philadelphia 1904, p. 18, described the Army Reorganization Act of 1866 as a 'Magna Carta' for 'American Negroes.' See also Jack Foner, *Blacks and the Military*, pp. 52–71; and John M. Carroll, ed., *The Black Military Experience in the American West*, New York 1971, *passim*.

56. Jack Foner, *Blacks and the Military*, pp. 52–132; Fowler, *Black Infantry*; Leckie, *Buffalo Soldiers*; MacGregor and Nalty, *Basic Documents*, vol. 3, *passim*.

12

Organizing the West

Colorado, entering the territorial family in 1861 as a result of gold discoveries near Pike's Peak, became the most eminently Republican of western territories. During the next thirty years it provided a working model of Republican economic program. Its scattering of frontier settlements coalesced into an industrial oligarchy, affluent in mining, agriculture, railroad construction and the manufacture of sophisticated mining machinery. With its extractive industries still in boom phase through the postwar decade, the territory rode out the Depression of 1873 relatively unscathed. Capital and labor flowed in. Denver by 1900 had more than 100,000 inhabitants. From statehood in 1876 to the turn of the century, Colorado sent only Republican senators to Washington, chose Republican representatives in eleven out of seventeen elections and kept Republicans in the governor's office during fifteen out of twenty-four years.[1]

Opening the road for this spectacular performance had been a series of military operations against Confederates in New Mexico and against the Great Plains Indians. Colorado's first and second territorial governors – William Gilpin and John Evans, both Lincoln appointees and ardent Unionists – had based their administrations on a cohort of pioneer entrepreneurs, many of whom had crossed the Mississippi to fight for Free Soil in Kansas. Spearheaded by this elite, volunteers recruited from the mine camps not only secured Colorado but carried off winter marches and shootouts that helped save the Southwest – New Mexico and Arizona, perhaps Southern California as well – for the Union.[2] Territorial leaders then turned their military apparatus against the Cheyenne and Arapahoe who still controlled sections of the plains between Denver and Kansas. An immediate result was the battle, or massacre, at Sand Creek in November 1864, which helped initiate the final round of Indian wars in North America.[3] Sand Creek also touched off a split within Republican ranks over Indian policies. At issue were the Jacksonian and whiggish versions of white racism. Colorado thus provides a circumscribed but dramatically visible stage on which to follow the adjustment and modification of ideological components in the legitimation of Republican economic policies in the West. Insofar as these were new policies designed to meet new circumstances, traditional ideological constructions failed to support them. What had united the whiggish, Jacksonian and Free Soil components of Republicanism in 1861 had been concurrence on saving the Union and excluding slavery from the territories. To extend this alliance – doubtless essential to the survival of the Republican coalition – proved difficult because of the divergent political commitments of former Whigs, Jacksonians and Free Soilers; and especially these stood at loggerheads on issues involving race and class.

Throughout the territorial years in Colorado, Republican leaders necessarily exemplified in their careers the major tendencies within the party. Most such leaders were deeply involved in Sand Creek, either as organizers and defenders or as opponents and critics. Two sections of the chapter that follows focus on conflict and compromise among selected Republican leaders in conection with the massacre at Sand Creek. A third section examines Sand Creek as a stage in constructing the racial component of the Republican legitimizing synthesis.

John Chivington and John Evans

John Chivington, commanding officer of the Sand Creek expedition, was born in 1821 near Cincinnati, Ohio, the child of hardscrabble frontier farmers. His father, who presumably fought under Harrison at the battle of the Thames, died in 1826. The son, with occasional schooling from itinerant preachers, worked at woodcutting and rafting logs downriver to Cincinnati. He may have earned extra money as a 'purse fighter' along the riverfront. At twenty he married a young woman from Virginia, a house servant but with some schooling and staunchly Presbyterian. Chivington learned the carpenter's trade, entered the Masonic Order, participated in a rifle society or militia company, and studied for the ministry. Since there were few Presbyterians within reach, he joined the Methodists and was ordained in 1844. According to Chivington's only biographer, the young couple, now with three children, set up Methodist churches and Masonic lodges in various frontier communities. With respect to slavery, Chivington at first favored gradualism and nonintervention. A change came after he was dispatched to circuits in Missouri. One account has it that he defended an escaped slave woman whose master intended leasing her out as a prostitute. However this may be, encounters with slavery and slaveowners apparently converted him to Free Soil doctrine. Protests and threats from his congregations then induced the Methodist Conference to transfer him to Nebraska.[4]

In the spring of 1860, Chivington arrived at Denver as Presiding Elder of the Methodist Episcopal Church, North, for the Rocky Mountain District. He toured the mining camps preaching in saloons and outdoor meetings, organizing churches and Masonic lodges.[5] Retrospectively at least, Chivington viewed his trajectory as part of a divinely inspired mission. On the wagon road to Denver it had seemed to him that the prairies had once been 'a great reservoir of water', surging westward 'until it culminated in the lofty hights of Long's and Pike's Peak ... God had Smiled upon the multitudinous waters, they Smiled in return, hardened into solid earth and so remained smiling and all my thoughts of this mighty Empire have been of it as the smiling relm.' But while hard-working pioneers labored to lay 'the foundations of civilization' in Colorado, 'there was a storm gathering in the East. ... ' 'Maddened to desperation', the slaveowners had often threatened and were as often 'placated by humiliating concessions until they really believed themselves the ruling class, and all others only mudsills.' Under cover of Buchanan's 'weak and undecided' administration, the slave owners attempted to destroy the republic.[6]

Chivington saw Confederate flags flying over private mercantile houses in Denver. When young miners enlisted in the territory's First Regiment, one of the new recruits had been shot by a saloon keeper who refused service to Unionists. Chivington preached the funeral sermon. For any man who gave his life 'to cement ... the Union in one *Nation* [of] states', Chivington declared, God surely 'would see to it that he had a good place and time in the hereafter.'[7] Chivington supported Governor William Gilpin's vigorous (although perhaps dubiously legal) actions in raising the First Colorado Regiment. To the governor's offer of a post as chaplain, Chivington replied that his intense feelings would require him to take a hand in the fighting. He accepted a commission as major.[8]

The First marched from Denver to the aid of hard-pressed Unionists in New Mexico. Chivington recalled a battle (actually the turning point in the New Mexico campaign) in which he had led four hundred men over a mountain trail to take the enemy in the rear. Looking down, they saw the camp far below them, strongly set up, with artillery, on a promontory of the canyon. 'Singing "On Jordan's Stormy Bank I stand, etc."', they plunged down and up the opposite slope. During another battle in the same campaign, he had ordered a head-on attack by his cavalry. 'It was one of these things I had wanted to see when I was a boy, a dashing cavalry charge. I never saw a more gallant thing in my life. ... The men charged through and through the ranks as many as four times, shooting them with their revolvers, clubbing them, sabering them and slaughtering them generally. ... ' Chivington took over command of the regiment in New Mexico – apparently as the result of a petition by the men – when the original commanding officer resigned.[9]

So far as the Colorado Territory was concerned, the military phase of war against the Confederacy ended with the New Mexico campaign. But a new war was shaping up against the Plains Indians. Returning to Denver in 1862, Chivington, now colonel, was assigned command of the Colorado District.[10] He and John Evans, the newly appointed territorial governor, believed that agents of the Sioux were building a general confederation.[11] They feared (by no means unreasonably) that Denver might be vulnerable to Indian attack since it depended on the Kansas wagon road for supplies, while the territory had been stripped of soldiers to reinforce Union armies in the Mississippi Valley. In spring of 1864, Governor Evans called on friendly Indians to separate themselves from hostiles by coming in to designated forts and agencies where, presumably, they would receive protection and provisions. When there was no immediate response, Evans requested authority to recruit more volunteers. Early in August he warned the Commissioner of Indian Affairs that 'the largest Indian war this country has ever had, extending from Texas to the British lines' had broken out. Declaring a state of emergency, he summoned Colorado citizens 'to kill and destroy ... all hostile Indians on the Plains', offering as incentive that they should 'hold for their own use and benefit' any properties that might thus fall into their hands. As soon as authority for new recruitment reached them, Evans and Chivington organized the Third Volunteer Regiment for one hundred days' service.[12]

Evans, Colorado's second territorial governor, was born of Quaker parents at Waynesville, Ohio in 1814. His paternal grandfather, having converted from Presbyterianism to marry into a South Carolina Quaker family, had joined his wife's kinfolk in bearing witness against slavery by selling their Carolina farms and moving north of the Ohio. During Evans's childhood the family was at least two generations into prosperous frontier entrepreneurship. The grandfather, reputed to have invented a screw augur, had been manufacturing tools before he left the South. In Waynesville, properties of the immediate family included the Evans augur shop, a general store, a brick mill, partnership in a flour mill, and several farms.[13] Young Evans, despite paternal admonitions to pursue the family enterprises at Waynesville, determined to become a doctor. ('Only think of following a trade for no other purpose than my own pecuniary advantage!' he had written his cousin. 'It is the imperative voice of the Almighty that we shall do all the good we can. ... ')[14]

After working his way through medical college in Cincinnati, Evans married the daughter of a country physician (a Quaker turned Swedenborgian) and began practice in rural communities in Illinois and Indiana. Since his patients had little cash, they paid in kind and the young doctor accumulated a barn full of corn; he built a flatboat in 1842 and set off downriver to market his fees at New Orleans. Writing his wife en route, he described seeing a slave whipped by a drunken overseer for stealing a turkey, which soon afterwards turned up 'running at large'. Evans added that the overseer seemed only to regret having lost several days' labor. 'Slavery can only be maintained by the most inhuman barbarity. ... ' Slaveowners 'revel in luxury' by 'tasking under the whip their fellow beings.'[15]

Evans joined the Masonic Order. In 1842 or 1843 he and his wife converted to Methodism through the influence of a young minister, Mathew Simpson, then president of the newly established Indiana Asbury University. Simpson, an eloquent advocate of higher education for the common man, was taking the lead against Presbyterian domination of Indiana's governmental institutions, including the state university and public school system. Methodists by the early 1840s outnumbered Presbyterians in Indiana by four to one. Most Indiana Presbyterians were Whigs. So were many Methodists, Evans among them. In 1845 a Methodist–Democratic coalition around a Methodist gubernatorial candidate, James Whitcomb, finally overturned Whig dominance. Evans now stepped forward as the state's foremost advocate of a hospital for the insane. He visited such institutions in the East and became a partisan of Dorothea Dix. Adopting his recommendations, the legislature put him in charge of construction and later appointed him superintendent of the hospital.[16]

Meanwhile, Evans was shifting his enterprises to Chicago. He accepted a chair at the new Rush Medical College and in 1848 moved his family and practice to Chicago. During the next thirteen years Evans made a fortune in real estate and railroad promotion. He became director of the Chicago and Fort Wayne Railroad, later part of the Pennsylvania system. He served on Chicago's city council, reorganized its public schools, edited the *Rush Medical and Surgical Journal*, helped set up the Chicago Medical Society and the first general hospital in Illinois; and he took the lead in founding Northwestern University and Garrett Bible Institute. Armed with inside information on the route of the Milwaukee Railroad, he and his Methodist associates bought up farmland along the lakeshore that furnished locations and endowments for the two institutions, as well as the site of the town of Evanston. Evans remained president of Northwestern's Board of Governors until 1894. According to a history of the university, his gifts, including two professorial chairs funded at $50,000 apiece, exceeded $180,000.[17]

Rush Medical College, while Evans was on the faculty, admitted but apparently refused to graduate a black medical student. Evans publicly criticized such discrimination.[18] On a militantly anti-slavery platform he ran (unsuccessfully) as an 'Independent Democratic' candidate for Congress in 1854.[19] He labored through the 1850s to construct the Republican party in Illinois, and after Lincoln's election became one of the earliest advocates of emancipating and arming the slaves. During that first summer of the Civil War, Evans arranged for an 'immense' rally at which his old friend Mathew Simpson, now bishop, 'electrified the Audience' with a declaration that Christian duty required defense of the Union by force of arms. 'One of the historic events of the war', in Evans's recollection, Simpson's speech, 'or sermon', set the 'keynote to the enlistment of religious people all over the country.'[20]

John Evans's career exhibits an almost miraculous convergence of religious obligation and capital accumulation. Bishop Simpson happened to be in Chicago in the summer of 1861 because Evans had persuaded him to transfer his seat from Pittsburgh to Evanston. The rising value of lots in Evanston not only augmented educational endowments but multiplied investments made by Evans and other backers who had laid out and purchased large blocs of the town. These investments rested not so much on what Henry George termed the unearned increment of accelerating land values as upon fertility rates, conversion potentials, westward movement and upward mobility among the Methodist Episcopal denomination. So successful was the Evanston venture that Evans had attempted to repeat it on a larger scale at Oreopolis near the mouth of the Platte River in the Nebraska Territory.[21] This was the point at which the Burlington Railroad, a pre–Civil War land grant company, was expected to cross the Missouri. A consortium led by Evans acquired two sections for a town. In 1858 Evans had lobbied the Nebraska territorial legislature for the charter of a Methodist seminary and university to which the Oreopolis land company deeded building sites, while the Kansas–Nebraska Methodist Episcopal Conference gave its endorsement to the project.[22]

The Oreopolis project collapsed because the railroad opted for an alternate route. Evans, however, had become widely acquainted among Nebraskans, especially perhaps among Methodist political leaders in Nebraska. One of these, Samuel Elbert, later Evans's son-in-law, served as a delegate to the Republican national convention that nominated Lincoln, and in December letters to the president-elect from the Nebraska Council and Legislative Assembly proposed Evans for the territorial governorship. Bishop Simpson wrote in Evans's behalf. When the Nebraska appointment did not fall to Evans, the bishop complained to Lincoln that he was neglecting midwestern Methodists despite their loyal contributions to his administration. Early in 1862 Lincoln offered Evans the governorship of Colorado, which Evans accepted – conditional upon the designation of Samuel Elbert as territorial secretary.[23]

In Colorado, Evans pursued many of the same commitments that had distinguished his earlier career. His first speech, stressing the territory's need for railroads, predicted that the Republican-sponsored Pacific Railway Act would furnish the means for meeting this need. He used every resource of his political position to route the transcontinental through Denver; and had he succeeded in winning statehood for Colorado in 1864 or 1865 he might have succeeded in his efforts to determine railroad routes as well. Statehood for Colorado was urgently on the agenda of the national administration to strengthen Lincoln's prospects for November 1864. When Congress set up enabling legislation for Colorado, Nebraska and Nevada, Evans immediately summoned a constitutional convention. Taking for granted that statehood would be approved, Colorado's Republican party then nominated Evans and Henry M. Teller, a lawyer-businessman and booster of the city of Golden, as senatorial candidates, and Chivington for the House of Representatives. These events set the political context within which Evans and Chivington pushed their military preparations to defend Denver and the territory's scattered mining camps from anticipated Indian attacks.[24]

In mid-September came a message from Major Edward Wynkoop, commanding Fort Lyon on the upper Arkansas, that he was bringing in leaders of bands of Cheyenne and Arapahoe who had evidenced their desire for peace by surrendering four white captives they had been holding as hostages. Governor Evans, apparently embarrassed by the actual response to his earlier invitation, at first refused to meet. He did meet, however, on 28 September 1864, in a conference attended by Denver civilians, by United States Indian agent Simeon Whiteley, by Chivington; and by Major Wynkoop, Captain Silas Soule and Lieutenant Joseph Cramer from Fort Lyon, all three officers in the Colorado First and, like Chivington, veterans of the New Mexico campaign. The Indian leaders said their people were helpless and hungry, desperate for provisions since they were now cut off from the buffalo range, and fearing attack both from soldiers and settlers. Evans, blaming hostilities on the Indians, said the matter was in the hands of higher military authorities.[25] Chivington, who had telegraphed Major General Samuel B. Curtis, commander of the Department of Kansas, to inform him of Wynkoop's initiative, had that morning received Curtis's answer, warning against any peace 'until the Indians suffer more.'[26] Chivington said little until the end of the conference. Then, according to the transcript by Simeon Whiteley, he spoke briefly to the following conclusion: 'My rule of fighting white men or Indians is to fight them until they lay down their arms and submit to military authority. They are nearer Major Wynkoop than anyone else and they can go to him when they get ready to do that.'[27] This was the note on which the Denver conference ended. Major Wynkoop returned with the Indian leaders to Fort Lyon, where he assigned places to camp and distributed provisions. He also forwarded a report of his activities to Major General Curtis.

Early in November, Curtis relieved Wynkoop of the Fort Lyon command, replacing him with Major Scott Anthony, another First Colorado officer and veteran of the New Mexico campaign. Anthony, under orders to keep all Indians at a distance and to issue no more rations, sent the bands of Cheyenne and Arapahoe from the vicinity of the fort to camp at Sand Creek, forty miles away. Evans, meanwhile, had departed for Washington, hoping to reactivate the movement for statehood, which had just been voted down in a September territorial referendum. This reversal seems to have resulted not so much from escalating border warfare as from rivalries among territorial leaders over designation of the state capital and control of as-yet-to-be-built railroads. In Washington, Evans demanded that Lincoln replace territorial officials who bucked his leadership. He received assurances that the president was willing to comply.[28]

Toward the end of November Chivington consolidated the scattered companies of his new Third Regiment. It was generally known that the most hostile bands of Cheyenne were based along the Smoky Hill route east of Denver, but Chivington moved southeast to Fort Lyon. He stationed pickets around neighboring ranches and the fort itself to prevent anyone leaving, then announced a night march to Sand Creek. Major Anthony, by Chivington's later account, concurred enthusiastically in this project; but other officers of the garrison, led by Captain Soule and Lieutenant Cramer, who were deeply suspicious of Chivington's intentions, protested. Anthony assured them that the plan for Sand Creek was merely to round up certain hostiles thought to be hiding among the peaceful Indians; that the real thrust would be northward to the Smoky Hill region. In any case, they obeyed orders.[29]

The expedition reached Sand Creek between daybreak and sunrise. Chivington reported that the Indians fired the first shots and drew the first blood; that the men under his command 'like white men and true soldiers accepted the wager of battle. ... ' According to the estimate of his officers, the outcome was five or six hundred Indian dead, mostly warriors, with only about as many women and children as might have been slain in a white village under comparable circumstances.[30] Immediately after Sand Creek, Chivington notified Denver that he was on his way north to Smoky Hill, 'so look out for more fighting.' Instead he marched briefly southward, then hurried back to Denver for the alleged reason that his soldiers and their mounts were worn out from winter campaigning. Loaded with buffalo robes, driving captured Indian ponies, Chivington's hundred-day volunteers returned to a heroes' welcome. The *Rocky Mountain News*, closely linked to Governor Evans, placed Sand Creek 'among the brilliant feats of arms of Indian warfare.'[31]

Sand Creek, however, outraged many Republicans, including eastern editors and congressmen. On one hand, the massacre violated moral and ideological scruples against the deliberate extermination of Indians; on the other, it disrupted transportation to Colorado as the Cheyenne and Arapahoe mounted desperate reprisals along the wagon road from Kansas. The frustration of western entrepreneurs was cogently expressed by Jerome Chaffee, an upwardly mobile Michigan schoolteacher who, by virtue of successful banking and smelting ventures in Central City, later became one of Colorado's first United States senators. 'You cannot be too urgent with the Secretary of War or the President', Chaffee wrote the territorial delegate in Washington in January, 1865. 'You can hardly realize, without seeing it, the large amount of machinery en route for our Territory to work the mines with. Everything in the way of supplies is exhorbitantly high, all on account of the hazard of transportation. ... It is peculiarly disastrous to us now because so many eastern capitalists have been and are investing in our mines, and preparing to open and develop them.' If one implication of Chaffee's appeal was to rebuke Evans and Chivington for having provoked Indian counterattacks, the other certainly was to criticize the federal military for its failure to repress those attacks. Lofted by such ambivalent anxieties, repercussions at the War Department and in Congress caused Sand Creek to become one of the most thoroughly investigated episodes of the Great Plains wars.[32]

Edward Wynkoop and Silas Soule

Edward W. Wynkoop, born in 1836 in Philadelphia, came of an old Pennsylvania family of Dutch background. At twenty he went to Kansas to serve in the LeCompton land office, then headed by his brother-in-law, General William Brindle. In 1858, as provisional sheriff of Arapahoe County, he was one of a party sent by Governor James Denver of Kansas Territory to extend territorial administration to the new gold camps in Colorado. His party founded Denver City. Wynkoop worked a placer mine with moderate success at Clear Creek and won by election the post of county sheriff, which he held until Colorado's territorial organization in 1861. Like Chivington, he supported Governor Gilpin's emergency measures to hold Colorado for the Union. Gilpin appointed him captain of Company A in the First Colorado Regiment. When Chivington took command of the regiment in New Mexico Wynkoop was promoted to major.[33] In an autobiographical account written several years after Sand

Creek, Wynkoop recalled that he had been neutral with respect to slavery and the status of blacks when he first came to Kansas but later placed himself on the anti-slavery side. He traced a similar shift in his ideas about Indians.

> ... hearing at times of outrages committed by the Red Man I naturally at one time belonged to the exterminators, my youthful experience had not taught me the why and wherefor of these outrages, I did not stop to inquire whether an Indian when he killed a white man or run off cattle was justifiable or not. ... The conviction of having been unjust in my opinion in regard to the Indian character was caused by the following incident, and my subsequent experience enabled me to see the injustice often practiced toward a race which I have known in many instances to exhibit nobler traits than their oppressors.[34]

Wynkoop then narrated the events immediately preceding the Denver conference of September 1864. In command of the small garrison at Fort Lyon, surrounded by 'five of the hostile tribes', he had given orders 'to kill all Indians that could be reached.' When a sergeant brought in two Indian prisoners, Wynkoop reprimanded him for failure to obey orders; the sergeant explained that 'in the act of firing he observed one of the Indians hold up a paper and make signs of peace. ... '

The paper turned out to be a letter written by a half-breed in the Cheyenne band stating that the Indians were anxious for peace; that they had been forced to war by the whites; that in all their efforts to communicate with the fort they had been driven off; and that they held white captives 'whom they wished to deliver up'. Wynkoop asked the two messengers if they had not known they would be fired on when they approached the fort. The older replied that he had taken the chance hoping that even if he were killed the letter would be found and 'might give peace' to his people once more. The younger said he came because he 'would not let old One Eye come alone. ... I was bewildered with an exhibition of such patriotism' Wynkoop wrote in his memoir; '... and these were the representatives of a race that I had heretofore looked upon without exception as being cruel, treacherous, and blood-thirsty without feeling or affection for friend or kindred.'[35]

This altered perception set him at a distance from Chivington, with whom on questions of slavery and Unionism he had had no previous disagreement. After his removal virtually in disgrace from Fort Lyon, Wynkoop experienced a rapid reversal of fortune. By January 1865, he was back in command at Fort Lyon charged with preparing an official report on Sand Creek. What Wynkoop reported – in contrast to Chivington's account – was that the Cheyenne and Arapahoe at Sand Creek had believed themselves under government protection. They were not a war party. The attack was without justification. Two-thirds of the sixty or seventy dead Wynkoop claimed to have found at the encampment were women and children.[36] An unknown number, perhaps several hundred, must have fled to face the Great Plains winter without horses, food or buffalo robes. Of Chivington himself, Wynkoop wrote,

> ... eye-witnesses have described scenes to me, coming under the eye of Colonel Chivington, of the most disgusting and horrible character; the dead bodies of females profaned. ... Colonel J. M. Chivington all the time inciting his troops to these diabolical outrages. Previous to the slaughter commencing he addressed his command, arousing in them, by his language all their worst passions, urging them on to the work of committing all these atrocities.[37]

Next to Wynkoop's testimony, that of his two subordinates at Fort Lyon, Captain Silas Soule and Lieutenant Joseph Cramer, weighed most heavily against Chivington. Soule, born in Massachusetts, had come to Kansas in 1854 with his father, an agent for Boston's Emigrant Aid Society who had established the first underground railroad station in Kansas. The son became a Jayhawker and member of the Dow band, partisans of John Brown. Soule was said to have played a principal role in an almost suicidal scheme to rescue the Harpers Ferry prisoners. Brown and his companions refused to make the attempt, probably to avoid sacrificing the lives of their would-be rescuers. Soule then enlisted in the army, saw service scouting under Kit Carson, rose rapidly and entered the First Colorado Regiment as captain.[38] When the War Department ordered a military commission to investigate Sand Creek, Soule appeared as first witness. After corroborating Wynkoop's account, Soule accused Chivington of having deceived the Fort Lyon officers as to the purpose of the Sand Creek expedition. Obeying Chivington's orders on the basis of assurances relayed to him through Major Anthony, Soule said, he had not believed a general assault was intended until the command to open fire. Cramer testified that Chivington in the presence of other officers had shouted at him, "'Damn any man that was in sympathy with Indians", and such men as Major Wynkoop and myself had better get out of the United States' service.' He had seen 175 bodies at Sand Creek, Cramer said, mostly women and children and almost all had been scalped or mutilated.[39]

Midway in the investigation, Soule, on duty as provost marshal, was shot to death on a Denver street. Colonel Tappan, presiding officer of the commission (and like most of the others a veteran of the New Mexico campaign) described the killing as an assassination in revenge for Soule's testimony. The alleged assailant was a soldier in Colorado's Second Regiment. Captured in New Mexico, he was sent back in irons. He then escaped – or was allowed to escape – from Denver's military prison and vanished from the record. Wynkoop later charged that he had been hired by Chivington.[40]

Critics and Defenders of Sand Creek

In the hundreds of pages of testimony gathered by the military commission and by two congressional investigations, the bulk of evidence, I think, sustains Wynkoop and Soule; but that of course may be a partial reading. A century afterwards historians still disagree in their interpretations of Sand Creek.[41] The problem is that the evidence itself is polarized. Witnesses testified as friends or enemies of Chivington. Their partisanship tolerated no middle space. Yet these same men had risked their lives together in defense of the Union and most of them must have shared the basic Euro-American assumptions of white superiority. How could a massacre of Indians in those days have generated such lethal hostilities among them?

The literature on Sand Creek has brought forward two types of responses to this question. One type, generally developed by admirers of Wynkoop and Soule, asserts that some men possess the moral fiber to stand against injustice and brutality while others do not. The second type, often advanced by sympathizers with Chivington (and especially with Evans), noting that Sand Creek was only one of many exchanges in a long conflict, insists that it was blown out of proportion on the one hand by the agitation of Indian traders defending their profitable enterprises; and on the other by outcries from visionary reformers incapable of facing up to western reality.[42] The first type of response seems to me to bypass the historical question. The second type lacks persuasive power both because it tends to minimize the seriousness of Republican reactions to Sand Creek, and because it underrates men like Wynkoop, Soule, Cramer and Tappan, who in fact spent most of their adult lives immersed in western reality. I would think it more defensible to argue that men aligned themselves as friends or foes not because they agreed or disagreed over Sand Creek; but rather that their judgments of Sand Creek were shaped by differing class backgrounds and social experiences which already had disposed them, potentially at least, to collaboration or hostility. Chivington's military career prior to Sand Creek illustrates such a connection.

The original commander of Colorado's First Regiment had been Colonel John P. Slough, a 'Denver lawyer' formerly prominent in Ohio politics. Next in rank to Slough was Samuel Tappan, subsequently to preside over the military investigation of Sand Creek. Massachusetts-born and, like Silas Soule, reared in an anti-slavery milieu, Tappan had come to Kansas as a reporter for the New York *Tribune*. He continued west to cover the Colorado gold rush, settling at Black Hawk, where he pursued mining and local politics. In 1861 appointed lieutenant colonel of the First Regiment, he outranked Chivington, then a major. When Slough resigned in New Mexico, Tappan apparently made no effort to secure the top post for himself, and it was he who presented a petition from the enlisted men to General E.R.S. Canby requesting that command be given to Chivington. Tappan, however, had also supported Slough in efforts to persuade General Canby to remove Chivington and send him back to Denver. Tappan later informed Slough of attempts made against Slough's life at Raton Pass. Slough replied that he had been unaware of those attempts but knew he had been fired on during the battle of Pigeon's Creek by men in a company that sided with Chivington. He had decided to resign, he explained, because he felt certain he would be murdered if he did not, and that those now 'in command were at the bottom of this thing.'[43]

Chivington obviously despised Slough. Describing the First Regiment's forced march from Raton Pass to the relief of Fort Union, Chivington recalled that the 'Colonel who had gone ahead by coach' met them, resumed command, 'and marching the poor, tired and footsore fellows God only knows where and all and then we had to stand on our pins and let the Regular Officers talk at us for two hours and more, when we were allowed to pitch tent, eat a morsel and lay down to rest half the night.'[44] Chivington's identification with 'footsore' soldiers and against the 'Colonel' and 'Regular Officers' suggests – although by no means confirms, since this account was written twenty years after the fact – that he had been using egalitarian appeals to the enlisted men to discredit aristocratic modes (such as riding in coaches) among the officers. His own observation that he had been 'made a major' because his work as Methodist elder caused him to be 'better acquainted in the territory than any other man' points in the same direction. There is abundant testimony from the investigations that Chivington – like Evans – was politically ambitious; that he endeavored to use the Indian wars to further his career and that he appealed especially to segments of the territorial population eager for the destruction of Indians.[45]

The last point was stressed both in Chivington's favor and to his detriment. Thus on the one hand Captain S.M. Robbins of the First Colorado concluded a sworn statement as follows:

> I should like to say a friendly word ... in the Chivington interest. ... The point I wish to make is, that perhaps Colonel Chivington may have been forced into this by the sentiment of the people.
>
> *Question.* Would the sentiment of the people lead a man to attack Indians who were known to be friendly, and who were known to be trying to avert hostilities?
>
> *Answer.* I should say it would. They wanted some Indians killed; whether friendly or not they did not stop to inquire.[46]

On the other hand, John S. Smith, United States Indian interpreter and special agent at Fort Lyon, attributed the massacre to the fact that 'Colonel Chivington was running for Congress ... and I understand he had this Indian war in view to retain himself and his troops in that country, to carry out his electioneering purposes.'[47] Alexander C. Hunt, United States marshall for the district of Colorado, after observing that Chivington's effort 'to exterminate the Indians' seemed 'quite a popular notion', testified that chiefs of the Indian bands at Sand Creek had been regarded 'as the special friends of the white man ever since I have been in this country.' As to Chivington's motive for the attack:

> It may be invidious in me to give my idea of his motive. I was entirely satisfied that his motive was not a good and virtuous one. ... I think it was hope of promotion. He had read of Kit Carson, General Harney and others, who had become noted for their Indian fighting. I have no objection to state that.[48]

It is worth noting that Hunt, later a territorial governor of Colorado himself, was one of several federal appointees Evans had tried to persuade Lincoln to remove.[49]

Chivington – unlike other Republican leaders under discussion here for whom biographical data is available – was of lower-class origin. Whatever his political affiliations during the 1840s and 1850s in Ohio and Missouri, he was by virtue of his background – like David Crockett or Major Jack Downing – a 'natural' Jacksonian. White egalitarian resentment against aristocratic pretensions came as naturally to men like Chivington as the whiggish soft side of racism came to men like Soule and Tappan. Wynkoop is more difficult to decipher. Owing his Western apprenticeship to family connections with the upper echelons of the Pennsylvania Democracy, he had moved to the soft side of racism by way of a sort of conversion experience. Although uncertain in Wynkoop's case, class background thus appears to have been a significant factor in these cleavages. Some of the most vociferous testimony against Chivington came, however, not so much from class antagonists as from an interest group of Indian agents and their associated traders.[50] Generally the Indian trader interest has carried a bad name in American history; doubtless because of mercenary or corrupt individual behavior; also, and perhaps mainly, because it stood opposed to 'progress' understood as the rapid expansion of white settlement. This interest approximated a monopoly dependent upon the partial autonomy of Indian tribes and federal protection for privileged trade access. Its thrust was whiggish in the sense that opposition to uncontrolled settlement of the West had been whiggish. Howard Lamar, historian of the Southwest territories, draws an illuminating contrast between the old West of traders and peacemakers like the Bents and St. Vrains and the new West created by industrial warriors like Evans and Chivington. The traders, significantly, were racial amalgamators; the industrial warriors racial exterminators.[51]

In his 1865 apologia, *To the People of Colorado*, Chivington built his
defense upon two accusations, both populistic in their class orientation.
The first was that a corrupt inner circle of Indian agents and traders –
whose profiteering he had interrupted by the attack on Sand Creek – bore
false witness against him, playing on the ignorance and credulity of 'the
unsophisticated people of New England, the people generally of the
States', and especially 'the billious old maids in the United States Senate
and the House of Representatives.' The second was that persons 'wearing
the uniform of officers, without the courage to perform a brave deed
themselves, are the loudest to condemn the conduct of a brother soldier
who wins a single laurel that they cannot steal. Such men ... venemous as
reptiles and cowardly as curs' vilified Colorado's real soldiers as murderers. At the same time they pandered to the Indians:

> It is not surprising that the Indian believes himself to be the white man's
> superior. White men of the frontiers, do you desire to become the servile dogs
> of a brutal savage? If you do, this policy will suit you, though I thought dif-
> ferently and acted accordingly.[52]

There remains the problem of John Evans, Chivington's collaborator
and political ally: if Chivington came of lower-class frontier origin, Evans
clearly was from the upper class. Not only had Evans moved successfully
among wealthy men throughout his own career; both his parents and
grandparents had prospered as 'frontier capitalists'.[53] His education,
which had taken him through Quaker school in Philadelphia and medical
college at Cincinnati, stood a world apart from Chivington's. 'My father
was a Whig', Evans recalled in the late 1880s, 'and my sympathies were
all that way, though I was not active in politics until the Whig party was
dissolved, when I became a Republican and have been one ever since.'[54]
Certain details apparently eluded Evans's recollection. He had won his
first public office by virtue of leadership in a Methodist–Jacksonian coalition in Indiana; he had solicited an independent Democratic nomination
for congress in 1854; and had received the Colorado governorship not
simply as a western Republican, but as a spokesman of western Methodists.[55]

These lapses of memory tell us that Evans in later years was embarrassed at having once dabbled with the prewar Democracy. More important, they indicate that Methodism had furnished him a solution to the
classic Whig dilemma of how to exert upper-class leadership within a mass
democratic society. When he converted from Quakerism to Methodism
Evans had taken a downward step in class status. Yet he had stepped also
into a constituency eager to follow, and emulate, affluent, educated men.
An aggressively egalitarian religion minimized class distance, brought the

pursuits of politics and entrepreneurship within that ethic of doing good to which Evans had obligated himself as a youth. It thus served to wash away the taint of hypocrisy habitually charged by Jacksonians against Whigs. Only regionally, of course, could Methodism or any other denomination achieve such results; and at one further remove it seems obvious that the results themselves were conditioned by the historical time period. They rested on the vast bonanzas of land and resources opened up for Euro-Americans by the War of 1812. These, basically, more than any particular religion, reduced the need for hypocrisy. Even a wealthy man of egalitarian proclivity might now be substantially what his ideological construct advocated. The potential for integrity opened new reserves of political influence.

Methodism, then, appears through Evans's experience as one of several socio-political networks within which individual careers and fortunes could be built upon the upward mobility of mass constituencies. Men of upper-class origin and education like Evans might be heavily advantaged; yet since the upward mobility was real there remained elbow room for men of lower-class origin as well. Evans and Chivington could become collaborators, fellow builders of institutions, even friends. From these beginnings emerged the Free Soil movement and major segments of the class coalition that became the Republican party.

Divergent class routes into Republicanism necessarily corresponded to different ideological mixes and varying degrees of conflict over previous convictions. For Chivington there was no difficulty in becoming an Indian exterminator. For Silas Soule and Samuel Tappan, and even for Wynkoop, there was no great difficulty in becoming an Indian sympathizer. For Evans, however, real tensions persisted between received values with respect to the treatment of Indians and his belief that Christian progress flowed from entrepreneurship and capital accumulation. What was needed was to justify Indian removal, not in the familiar lower-class rhetoric of white egalitarianism, but in terms that could invite upper-class acceptance because derived from whiggish precedent and from Protestant traditions of individual calling and moral perfectionism.

It can hardly come as a surprise, then, to find Evans in later years mulling over arguments already well used in the days of Jefferson and Adams. Rightful possession of land must rest on effective agricultural practice in supporting a population. Thus justified, Evans could ridicule 'the proposition that a country a thousand miles long and five hundred miles wide, one of the most fertile in the world, should belong to a few bands of roving Indians, nomadic tribes in fee as their property.'[56] Given the self-evident absurdity of such a proposition, was it not perverse to reinforce it by negotiating treaties of purchase with Indians? National sovereignty should have no truck with purchase. Burned clean by the struggle against secession, the nation, for Evans, had become the only source of right. Knowing his Quaker heritage must cry out against such a doctrine, he found himself obligated to settle accounts with that heritage. William Penn, he told an interviewer in 1888, had been mistaken to teach that Indians owned the land they lived on:

> ... nearly all the Indian wars have resulted from the fact that the Indians took in that doctrine, which was acknowledged by the U.S. government ... and that we had to buy it of them by treaty or purchase, instead of teaching them ... that they had a right to hunt on the land, but that right must be subject to the higher occupation of the land, for a larger population and for civilization. Their wildness should have been impressed upon them from the beginning. ... [57]

Evans's shining example of civilization among Indians was the case of the Tabeguache Utes. During his years as governor (and, *ex officio* territorial superintendent of Indian affairs), they had ceded to the United States 'nearly all the important settlements thus far made in Colorado and all the valuable mining districts discovered up to this time.'[58] Evans, with the backing of 'the great Ute chief', Ouray, had used their tribal allotment to buy and distribute individually 'an immense herd of sheep.' This was intended to teach the benefits of private enterprise. Ouray at least proved an apt pupil. By paying him the salary of a government interpreter, Evans made him 'a kind of king among them.'

> He kept and bought from some of the other Indians their sheep. ... [H]e hired a Mexican herder to take care of the flock on shares, and he became quite wealthy, and he built him a fine house over near Ouray, the town named after him, which is a very wealthy mining camp now, and he lived there and he had a little squaw, Chepcti, who was quite a nice little Indian, and he had a great many noble traits of character.[59]

But Evans enjoyed no such successes with the Cheyenne and Arapahoe. They even had mocked his efforts to induce them to 'settle down in houses and live like white people.'[60]

Yet he had always recognized the injustices Indians suffered, Evans recalled. 'At the same time when we come to be butchered by them, it is right to defend ourselves and there my Quaker sentiments desert me.'[61] Perhaps Evans also remembered his proclamation of emergency in the summer of 1864; and that his official letter book contained the transcript of an appeal sent to Brigadier General Patrick Connor at Salt Lake, approximately a month before Sand Creek: 'Bring all the forces you can; then, pursue, kill and destroy them, until which we will have no permanent peace on the plain.'[62]

Critics of Sand Creek, led in the West by men like Wynkoop and

Samuel Tappan, stood their ground effectively at first. Tappan served with General William Tecumseh Sherman (whose views of Indians he opposed) on the United States Indian Commission, authorized by Congress and appointed by President Johnson in 1867. Wynkoop, promoted to lieutenant colonel, commanded a military escort for peace negotiations with the Cheyenne and Arapahoe in the fall of 1865. That settlement was also a reservation treaty; and over its implementation Wynkoop – *persona grata* among the Indians because of his role at Fort Lyon – presided as Indian agent. But he was dismayed at changes imposed during Senate ratification of the treaty; and a far western Indian agency may have been scarcely enough to satisfy an ambitious young man in the opening years of the Gilded Age. Wynkoop resigned to enter the iron business in Pennsylvania, failed during the depression of 1873, and returned, destitute, to the West. By 1874 he was seeking to recoup his fortune in the Black Hills gold rush, where his military experience made him a natural leader of the miners against the Sioux.[63] This vignette of an earnest man whose (unsuccessful) attempts at acquisitive behavior ran counter to his belief system suffices to make clear that when Republicans organized the West after the Civil War, the political economy of Free Soil was already eroding the foundations of the whiggish Indian sympathizer tradition. Yet if only through the stubbornness of ideological inertia (sometimes harnessed in tandem with Indian agent and trader interests) this tradition continued to be widely and deeply held. It evoked, as William McFeeley has it in his biography of Grant, a 'cry from the heart' in response to Sand Creek, and it furnished the political viability of Grant's so-called 'peace policy' during the early 1870s.[64]

How, then, fared the defenders of Sand Creek? Chivington, facing court martial, resigned from the military. He never resumed the ministry, but engaged with less than middling success in business ventures throughout the West, returning finally to Denver to live out his old age as a hero of the pioneer days.[65] For Evans, Sand Creek presumably terminated a promising political career. In reality, however, the Indian massacre, endorsed by Colorado Republicans, even by the opposition press, could only have strengthened Evans within the factionally divided territory. As to the situation in Washington, Lincoln continued to support Evans after Sand Creek, in part certainly because of the political advantage the administration would derive from Colorado statehood.[66] Andrew Johnson, on the other hand, vetoed statehood bills precisely because statehood for Colorado would have worked to his disadvantage. With Sand Creek as pretext, Johnson forced Evans's resignation from the governorship in order to replace him with an anti-statehood man. The conclusion appears to be that Evans's political career was ended not by Sand Creek but by the assassination of Lincoln.[67]

We have not quite reached the end of the argument, however. In the territory – despite Sand Creek or more likely because of it – Evans was again nominated to the United States Senate, this time with Jerome Chaffee, the Central City banker and smelter operator, as running mate. 'Vitriolic' criticisms of Sand Creek contained in the report of the Joint Committee on Conduct of the War (1865) had weighed heavily in Congress against Evans and statehood. During the spring of 1866, the signer of that report, Senator Benjamin Wade, not only reversed his earlier opposition to statehood but explained his signature as a mistake due to misinformation. Wade's turnabout may have resulted less from second thoughts about Sand Creek than from a perception of the increasingly urgent need for Colorado's senatorial votes in the Republican struggle against Andrew Johnson. In any case, Johnson's veto blocked statehood; yet Chaffee continued to press the issue until final success in 1876, again a presidential year in which Republican electoral votes would be desperately needed.[68] Colorado's importance to the Republican scheme is indicated by the facts that Chaffee, after his term in the Senate, served as chairman of the national executive committee of the party; and that his daughter married the son of Ulysses S. Grant.[69] Evans, had he held on in politics as tenaciously as Chaffee, might well have followed a parallel course.

Doubtless Evans found himself morally perturbed, even exhausted, by the conflict of values that Sand Creek imposed; but that would have been a psychic cost of ideological readjustment, not any external political necessity. Opting to withdraw from public politics in 1867, he resumed the pursuits of capital accumulation and railroad promotion begun before the war.[70] Twenty years afterward the Denver Chamber of Commerce and Board of Trade summed up his achievement in a resolution of gratitude: '[H]e has set the keystone in a great series of iron roads to Denver, embracing the Denver Pacific, the Kansas Pacific, Boulder Valley and South Park, all largely the result of his indefatigable energy and skill, and which have made the city of his adoption the commercial metropolis of the Rocky Mountain Region.'[71] Through Evans's latest career could now be realized the implications of the political coalition he had earlier helped to construct. Even Wynkoop must have understood this when, in his brief autobiographical venture, he quoted an 'Official letter' from William Tecumseh Sherman to General Grant as exemplifying the 'exterminators' from whom he had wished to separate himself. Two years after Sand Creek, according to Wynkoop, Sherman advocated 'vindictive earnestness' even to the 'extermination' of 'men women and children.' Whether or not his quotations were accurate, Wynkoop was hardly mistaken as to the policies Sherman as General of the Army under Grant would institute.[72] It seems reasonable to conclude that Sand Creek, far from being an aberration or throwback to premodern styles, represented the norm that would be pursued for the next thirty years both by the regular army in the West and by congresses and presidential administrations. Yet the conflict among Colorado Republicans in which men risked (and lost) not only careers but lives would remain incomprehensible without recognition of the discordant ideological components of Republicanism. The alliance of Chivington and Evans, prevailing over other commitments, announced a legitimizing synthesis for the western program of the new governing coalition.

Notes

1. Howard R. Lamar, *The Far Southwest, 1846–1912: A Territorial History*, New Haven, Conn. 1966, pp. 205–301; James Edward Wright, *The Politics of Populism: Dissent in Colorado*, New Haven, Conn. 1974; David Brundage, 'The Making of Working Class Radicalism in the Mountain West: Denver, 1880–1893', Ph.D. diss., University of California, Los Angeles, 1982; Jerome C. Smiley, *History of Denver; with the Outlines of the Earlier History of the Rocky Mountain Country*, Denver, Colo. 1901; Smiley, *Semi–Centennial History of the State of Colorado*, Chicago 1913, vol. 1; Percy Stanley Fritz, *Colorado, the Centennial State*, New York 1941, pp. 493–95.

2. Lamar, pp. 110–20, 220–35; Arthur A. Wright, 'Colonel John P. Slough and the New Mexico Campaign', *Colorado Magazine* 39 (April 1962): 89–105, and editors' introduction, pp. 81–88; Ovando J. Hollister, *Boldly They Rode: A History of the First Colorado Regiment of Volunteers*, [1863] Lakewood, Colo. 1949.

3. Stan Hoig, *The Sand Creek Massacre*, Norman, Okla. 1961; Janet LeCompte, 'Sand Creek', *Colorado Magazine* 41 (Fall 1964): 315–35; Harry Kelsey, 'Background to Sand Creek', *Colorado Magazine* 45 (Fall 1968): 279–99; Raymond G. Carey, 'The "Bloodless Third" Regiment, Colorado Volunteer Cavalry', *Colorado Magazine* 38 (October 1961): 275–300; 'The Puzzle of Sand Creek', *Colorado Magazine* 41 (Fall 1964): 279–98; Michael A. Sievers, 'Sands of Sand Creek Historiography', *Colorado Magazine* 49 (Spring 1972): 116–41. See also the historical novel by Michael Straight, *A Very Small Remnant*, New York 1963, reprinted by University of New Mexico Press, Albuquerque, 1976. I am indebted to Michael Straight both for his well-researched and perceptive account and for his generosity in sharing sources.

4. Reginald S. Craig, *The Fighting Parson: the Biography of Colonel John M. Chivington*, Los Angeles 1959, pp. 21–48; John T. Dormois, 'The Chivingtons', Kansas City *Masonic News Digest*, 28 June 1957; and Raymond G. Carey, 'The Tragic Trustee', *University of Denver Magazine*, June 1965, both in the Chivington Biographical File, Historical Society of Colorado.

5. Craig, pp. 43–52; Dormois, 'The Chivingtons'; John M. Chivington, 'The First Colorado Regiment' typescript, Bancroft Library, October 18, 1884, pp. 1–2; 'The Prospective' manuscript, Bancroft Library, 1884, p. 20.

6. Ibid., pp. 1–2, 12–13.

7. Ibid., pp. 18–19.

8. Lamar, pp. 221–24, 228–29; Chivington, 'First Colorado', p. 2; 'Prospective', p. 20.

9. 'Prospective', p. 32; Chivington, 'First Colorado', pp. 8–9.

10. Harry E. Kelsey, Jr., *Frontier Capitalist: The Life of John Evans*, Denver 1969, pp. 126, 137–53; Lamar, pp. 109–22, 226–32.

11. Kelsey, *Evans*, pp. 134–36. United States Congress, Senate, Report of the Joint Committee on the Conduct of the War, 'Massacre of the Cheyenne Indians'. 38th Cong., 2nd Sess., *Senate Report* 142 Serial 1241: testimony of S. G. Colley, p. 30; John Evans, p.

43; Chivington, p. 104. Convenient access to this and two other major investigations may be had in *The Sand Creek Massacre: A Documentary History*, New York 1973, which preserves the original pagination.

12. Kelsey, *Evans*, pp. 141–46; Hoig, pp. 67, 69–70; John Evans's Letterbook, 'Executive Papers, 1861–1870', Governor's Office, Executive Record, 1:174–77, Colorado State Archives.

13. Kelsey, *Evans*, pp. 1–113; Edgar Carlisle MacMechen, *Life of Governor Evans, Second Territorial Governor of Colorado*, Denver 1924, pp. 3–91; John Evans interview, PL–329 typescript, Bancroft Library, folder 1:1–4, folder 5:10–11; Biographical sketch of John Evans [1888?], 'in the handwriting of Lionel A. Sheldon', in Evans Interview, PL–329, folder 5.

14. Quoted in Walter Dill Scott, *John Evans, 1814–1897: An Appreciation*, Evanston, Ill. 1939, p. 8.

15. Kelsey, *Evans*, pp. 27–29; MacMechen, pp. 24–29. Evans Interview, PL–329, folder 1:3; John Evans to Hannah Evans, 28 May 1842, quoted in Kelsey, *Evans*, p. 31.

16. Kelsey, *Evans*, pp. 32–34, 35–41; MacMechen, pp. 36–45; 'President Simpson's Inaugural Address' Greencastle, Indiana, 1840, folio 82; letters. N. S. Haines to John Evans, 3 and 7 April, 29 June 1837 and 22 May 1838, folios 4 and 6, John Evans Papers, Colorado Historical Society. See also Sheldon biographical sketch, Evans Interview, PL–329, folder 5: 23–24. On Dorothea Dix, folder 5:13–14, ibid.

17. Kelsey, *Evans*, pp. 46–100; Evans Interview, PL–329, folder 1:9–10. MacMechen, p. 70, quoting Arthur Herbert Wilde, *Northwestern University: A History*.

18. Kelsey, *Evans*, p. 55; MacMechen, p. 51; Scott, *Evans Appreciation*, pp. 10–13; John Evans to W.B. Plato, 4 September 1854, John Evans Papers, folder 4, Colorado Historical Society.

19. Kelsey, *Evans*, pp. 101–5; MacMechen, pp. 81–91.

20. Evans Interview, PL–329, folder 1:7; Sheldon biographical sketch in ibid., folder 5:25–26.

21. Kelsey, *Evans*, pp. 105–6; John Evans Interview, PL–23 typescript, Bancroft Library, pp. 2–3.

22. Kelsey, *Evans*, pp. 106–9; MacMechen, pp. 84–87; Sheldon biographical sketch, Evans Interview, PL–329, folder 5:25.

23. Kelsey, *Evans*, pp. 109–113, 115; MacMechen, pp. 87–89, 106.

24. Kelsey, *Evans*, pp. 155–60; Lamar, p. 241. Chivington, 'First Colorado', p. 13.

25. Hoig, pp. 109–12; Kelsey, *Evans*, pp. 146–50; Testimony of Edward W. Wynkoop, *Massacre of Cheyenne Indians*, pp. 81–84; see note 11, above; and in U.S. Congress, Senate, *Condition of the Indian Tribes: Report of the Joint Special Committee Appointed Under Joint Resolution of March 3, 1865*, 39th Cong., 2nd Sess., 1867, *Senate Report No. 156*, hereafter referred to as *Condition of Indian Tribes*, pp. 76–77; and in 'Report of the Secretary of War, communicating, in compliance with a resolution of the Senate of February 4, 1867, a copy of the evidence taken at Denver and Fort Lyon, Colorado Territory, by a military commission, ordered to inquire into the Sand Creek massacre, November, 1864', 39th Cong., 2nd Sess., 1867, Ex. Doc. No. 26, referred to hereafter as Military Commission, pp. 90–91. Testimony of Joseph A. Cramer in ibid., pp. 45–46.

26. Curtis to Chivington, 28 September 1864, in Military Commission, p. 173.

27. Simeon Whiteley's report of the Denver conference is in John Evans, *Reply of Governor Evans of the Territory of Colorado to that Part Referring to Him, of the Report of the 'Committee on the Conduct of the War'*, headed '*Massacre of Cheyenne Indians*', in *Condition of Indian Tribes*, pp. 87–90.

28. Hoig, pp. 121–27; Kelsey, *Evans*, pp. 151–52, 161; MacMechen, p. 106.

29. Hoig, pp. 144, 135–45; LeCompte, 'Sand Creek', pp. 327–28; Testimony of George L. Shoup, pp. 175–79, Silas Soule, pp. 10–14, Joseph A. Cramer, pp. 46–47, Military Commission.

30. Hoig, pp. 138–39, 144. Chivington testimony, *Massacre of Cheyenne Indians*, pp. 102–6; Chivington's First and Second Reports on Sand Creek, ibid., pp. 48–50; Chivington, *To the People of Colorado. Synopsis of the Sand Creek Investigation*, Denver 1865, pp. 5–7; Carey, 'Puzzle of Sand Creek', *Colorado Magazine* 41:296–97.

31. Chivington reports, *Massacre of Cheyenne Indians*, pp. 48–50; John W. Wright, *Chivington Massacre of the Cheyenne Indians*, [Washington 1865], microcard, Louisville, Ky.

1960, p. 3; *Rocky Mountain News*, undated excerpt in *Massacre of Cheyenne Indians*, pp. 56–58.

32. Chivington testimony, *Massacre of Cheyenne Indians*, p. 108; *Rocky Mountain News*, undated excerpt in ibid., p. 58. J.B. Chaffee to H.P. Bennett, New York, 10 January 1865, in ibid., pp. 73–74. The pamphlet by John W. Wright note 31 above is a public expression of protest addressed to Senator S.S. Pomeroy: 'I know you well, and in days past we have mourned over the wrongs heaped upon the Africans. But, my dear sir, when or where did the Southern governor issue such a proclamation [as that of Governor Evans]? ... ' See also, on the reaction of James Doolittle, Wisconsin senator and Chair of the Joint Special Committee on the Condition of Indian Tribes, to what he saw at Sand Creek and heard at Denver, LeCompte, 'Sand Creek', *Colorado Magazine* 41:333–34; and letters of Sen. James R. Doolittle to Mrs. L.F.S. Foster, 'Notes and Documents', *New Mexico Historical Review* 26 (1951): 156–57.

33. Hoig, p. 82; Edward W. Wynkoop, 'Wynkoop's Unfinished Colorado History 1870', typescript, Colorado Historical Society, pp. 1–20. *Daily Rocky Mountain News*, 13 February 1882, in Wynkoop biographical file, Colorado Historical Society. Edward E. Wynkoop, 'Edward Wanshear Wynkoop', Kansas State Historical Society, *Collections*, 13 (1913–14): 71–79.

34. 'Wynkoop's Unfinished History', p. 28.

35. Ibid., pp. 29, 30.

36. Wynkoop's report, 15 January 1865, in *Massacre of Cheyenne Indians*, pp. 81–84; 'Wynkoop's Unfinished History', pp. 38–39; Carey, 'Puzzle of Sand Creek', *Colorado Magazine* 41:296–97.

37. Wynkoop's report, *Massacre of Cheyenne Indians*, pp. 82–83; Testimony of John Smith, ibid., pp. 7–11, and 'Condition of Indian Tribes', pp. 87–88; Testimony of James P. Beckwith, pp. 68–76, and James D. Cannon, p. 110, in Military Commission.

38. C.A. Prentice, 'Captain Silas S. Soule, a Pioneer Martyr', *Colorado Magazine* 12 (November 1935): 224–28; Hoig, pp. 138–39; Veterans' Records, pension, Silas S. Soule, Captain, First Colorado Regiment: National Archives Trust Fund Board, WC 72–533.

39. Testimony of Soule, pp. 8–34, and of Joseph Cramer, pp. 44–68, Military Commission. Quotation, p. 47.

40. Military Commission, pp. 159, 188–89. Edward E. Wynkoop, 'Edward Wanshear Wynkoop', p. 77. 'Wynkoop's Unfinished History', p. 39. *Rocky Mountain News*, 24–27 April, 29–30 May, 5, 13 June, 12, 15 July, 3 August 1865. Black Hawk *Mining Journal*, 24–26, 29 April, 1, 11, 31 May, 14 June, 13, 16 July 1865. LeCompte, 'Sand Creek', *Colorado Magazine* 41:330–32.

41. For an example of opposite interpretations of Chivington, see Craig and Hoig.

42. Hoig, LeCompte and C. A. Prentice exemplify the first type, as does the historical novel by Michael Straight, *A Very Small Remnant*. The second type is well represented by Kelsey and Carey.

43. James C. Enochs, 'A Clash of Ambition: The Tappan–Chivington Feud', *Montana: The Magazine of Western History* 15 (July 1965): 58–67. Samuel F. Tappan to J. P. Slough, 28 December 1862 and Slough to Tappan, 6 July 1863, letters 12 and 13, FFP1, Samuel F. Tappan Collection 617, Colorado Historical Society. Obituary of Samuel F. Tappan, Boston *Evening Transcript*, 8 January 1913.

44. Chivington, 'The Prospective', p. 25.

45. Chivington, 'First Colorado', p. 2; Testimony of Jesse H. Leavenworth, pp. 3–4, John S. Smith, p. 6, D.D. Colley, p. 15, and A.C. Hunt, p. 46, in *Massacre of Cheyenne Indians*.

46. Testimony of S.M. Robbins, ibid., p. 14.

47. Testimony of John S. Smith, ibid., p. 6.

48. Testimony of A.C. Hunt, ibid., p. 46.

49. Kelsey, *Evans*, 159, 161. Lamar, p. 263.

50. Gene Ronald Marlatt, 'Edward W. Wynkoop: An Investigation of His Role in the Sand Creek Controversy and in Other Indian Affairs, 1863–1868', M.A. thesis, University of Denver, 1961, pp. 4–8; 'Wynkoop's Unfinished History', pp. 1–10. Obituaries of Edward W. Wynkoop, Raton, New Mexico *Range*, 25 September 1891, and Santa Fe *Daily New Mexican*, 12 September 1891, in Wynkoop Collection, Museum of New Mexico, Santa Fe. Edward E. Wynkoop, *Collections*, pp. 71–79. 'Commemoration of Mrs. Edward W. Wynkoop

... written in 1938 by Frank Francis Murray Wynkoop, a son. ... ' typescript; and 'Intimate Notes Relative to the Career of Colonel Edward Wynkoop Which Are Not at All or Incompletely Included in This Scrapbook' by one of his sons, probably Francis, both typescripts accompanying Wynkoop Scrapbook, Museum of New Mexico, Santa Fe. 'James William Denver', *Dictionary of American Biography*, New York 1964, 3:242–43. Testimony of Jesse H. Leavenworth, pp. 3–4, John S. Smith, pp. 4–12, D.D. Colley, pp. 14–16, S.G. Colley, pp. 29–32, in *Massacre of Cheyenne Indians*; of John T. Dodds, p. 65, William Bent, pp. 93–95, Robert Bent, pp. 95–96, in *Condition of Indian Tribes*; of James P. Beckwith, pp. 68–76, and John W. Prowers, pp. 103–9, in Military Commission, is all more or less hostile to Chivington and Evans. The nine men were, or had been, Indian traders or agents. For Chivington's comments on the Indian trader interest, testimony, *Massacre of Cheyenne Indians*, p. 108, and *To the People of Colorado*, pp. 6–8. See also Kelsey, *Evans*, pp. 150–51, and William Unrau, 'A Prelude to War', *Colorado Magazine* 41 (Fall 1964): 299–313, on Indian traders and agents.

51. Lamar, pp. 45–47, 250–51.
52. Chivington, *To the People of Colorado*, pp. 4–8.
53. Kelsey has appropriately titled his biography of Evans, *Frontier Capitalist*.
54. Evans Interview, PL–329, folder 2:6.
55. Kelsey, *Evans*, pp. 38–41, 101–3, 110–21.
56. Evans Interview, PL–329, folder 2:19.
57. Ibid., pp. 19–20.
58. Kelsey, *Evans*, p. 133, quoting William P. Dole, *Report of the Commissioner of Indian Affairs for the Year 1863*, p. 17.
59. Kelsey, *Evans*, 132–134; Evans Interview, PL–329, folder 2:11–14; Evans Interview, PL–23: 11–14.
60. Ibid., pp. 10–11; Kelsey, *Evans*, pp. 131–57.
61. Evans Interview, PL–329, folder 2:20.
62. Evans, 'Indian Letterbook', Colorado State Archives.
63. Robert G. Athearn, *William Tecumseh Sherman and the Settlement of the West*, Norman, Okla. 1956, pp. 172–274; Obituary of Samuel F. Tappan, Boston *Evening Transcript*, 8 January 1913; 'Wynkoop's Unfinished History', pp. 46–50; *Rocky Mountain News*, 13 February 1882; Edward E. Wynkoop, 'Edward Wanshear Wynkoop', pp. 77–79.
64. William S. McFeeley, *Grant: A Biography*, New York 1982, p. 307. On Indian policies of the Grant administration, pp. 305–18. On the continuing effectiveness of the Indian sympathizer tradition, Chicago *Tribune*, 21 May 1870, reporting a conference on Indian policy attended by Samuel Tappan at Cooper Union in New York.
65. Denver *Republican*, 24 April, 27 April, 4 May, 11 May, 18 May 1890. Craig, pp. 232–38.
66. Kelsey, *Evans*, p. 161. Black Hawk *Mining Journal*, 9, 10 December 1864, 11 September 1865.
67. Lamar, pp. 258–61.
68. Ibid., pp. 262, 272–73; Kelsey, *Evans*, pp. 164–68; MacMechen, pp. 149–50; Smiley, *Semi-Centennial History*, 1:478–79; Carey, 'Puzzle of Sand Creek', *Colorado Magazine* 41:297–98; *Massacre of Cheyenne Indians*, pp. i–vi. Without statehood for Colorado in 1876, the Republicans would have lost the presidency by two electoral votes.
69. *Dictionary of American Biography*, New York 1985, 2:590.
70. Lamar, pp. 273–77; Kelsey, *Evans*, pp. 169–207; MacMechen, pp. 159–98; Evans Interviews, PL–23: 5–8 and PL–329, folder 3.
71. Resolution, Denver Chamber of Commerce and Board of Trade, 9 April 1887, in Evans Interview, PL–329, folder 1.
72. Letter, 28 December 1866, as quoted in Wynkoop's Unfinished History, p. 28. On Sherman's views of Indians, *Memoirs of William Tecumseh Sherman, Written by Himself*, New York 1891, 2:413; Sherman to John Sherman, 23 September 1868, quoted in Athearn, *Sherman and the West*, p. 273.

13

Class Organization in a Racially Segmented Labor Force

The preceding investigation of Colorado may now serve a dual purpose. That investigation emphasized the adoption by Republican leaders of elements of hardline racism previously associated with Jacksonian politics. Specifically, the Republican leaders sought to persuade former Whigs to agree to Indian extermination, and former Free Soilers to accept, as a means of opening up individual opportunity, the promotion of industrial growth through federal encouragement of corporate investment and economic consolidation. But the Colorado episode also illuminates the relationship of working-class organizations to racial discrimination. This chapter seeks to show that within the constraints imposed by Republican economic policies, wage earners developed a uniquely American organizational apparatus that depended on, and maximized, racial exclusion. Such an argument points in two divergent and perhaps contradictory directions. On the one hand, a labor movement so constructed could be expected to inhibit working-class challenges to industrial capitalism; and such a finding about nineteenth century labor organizations, by showing that racist ideology worked to legitimize capitalism, would tend to confirm the propositions set out in the Introduction. On the other hand, to find that working-class organizations independently generated racism would seem to run counter to at least one of those propositions. I will return to this dilemma in the concluding chapter.

Here, the opening step is to sketch the contours of an interrelationship between race and labor organization. To do so requires shifting back and forth between western and national perspectives. Colorado will figure as one of two types of western labor development – the extractive industrial type; while California will represent the urban manufacturing type. Both are convenient abstractions since Denver became a machine manufacturing center and California contained mines and lumber mills. The point, however, is not regional comparison but the reciprocal interplay between a unionism that took shape in western extractive industries and a unionism that arose in western manufacturing cities. Regional comparisons will be directed mainly to similarities and differences between the 'old' East and the 'new' West. In what follows, the focus will be, first, on working-class sponsorship of racial hostilities in California and Colorado; next, on a comparison of racial patterns, East and West; third, on the organizational dynamics of industrial conflict; and finally on the impact these developments had upon the strategies and structures of organized labor.

Racial Politics in California and Colorado

California voters before the Civil War, like the rest of the national electorate, were predominantly Democratic. The majority, from northern cities and nonslave agricultural regions, stood for Unionism, opposed extension of slavery and resisted entry by blacks, slave or free, into California. Their politics carried forward the politics of Free Soil Democrats like Broderick and George Wilkes. During the war they had favored Union Republican candidates but without much enthusiasm for entrepreneurial types like Leland Stanford and the Crocker brothers. Within two years of the war's end they voted Democrats back into control of the state government. This reversal – confirming the far-western potential of Andrew Johnson's neo-Jacksonian revival – hinged upon political activation of workingmen in San Francisco, which then contained more than one-third of the state's population. Trade unionism, in San Francisco as in other cities, had prospered during wartime; and trade unionists hoped that wartime wages and working conditions could be made permanent through the mediations of a Democratic and presumably pro-labor state administration.[1]

There was one other issue that Democratic politicians wooing the labor vote pushed hard: the Chinese. Not illogically, Democrats blamed Chinese immigration on their opponents, since Republicans were founders of the Central Pacific Railroad; and the railroad, importing labor gangs from South China, had already hired thousands of Chinese for its construction crews.[2] At this juncture the implications of Chinese immigration became important beyond its immediate economic effect, substantial though that clearly was. National politics in 1867 deadlocked over the status of black freedmen. But civil war still dominated collective memory; the Slave Power, by official designation, remained a threat to the Union; and so long as such fears retained credibility, they furnished a measure of protection for freed blacks whom history had cast as an antithesis to the Slave Power conspiracy. No such protection shielded the Chinese. Thus the Chinese issue, while directly stating racist hostilities in California, referred metaphorically to nationwide anxieties over the potential power of free blacks.[3]

The metaphor itself could approach direct statement since, from their earliest appearance in the West, the Chinese had been likened to Africans as a non-white, hence inferior race, occupying a semi-servile status. How can that negative comparison be accounted for? Probably the commonest explanation traces anti-Chinese hostility to economic competition. Here, essentially, is the direct economic argument whose logical difficulties were examined in the introductory essay. And there is a further difficulty specific to California: while competition with Chinese certainly presented an economic problem for white workingmen, such competition failed to occur on any large scale until after completion of the transcontinental railroad in 1869; whereas expressions of anti-Chinese hostility began at an earlier date.[4] Before 1869, the characteristic situation of California was one of labor shortage. White workingmen had not yet come to the Pacific Coast in large numbers, and those who did found attractive opportunities in mining and farming. Pay scales for whites were substantially higher than in the East. The presence of the Chinese tended to enhance opportunities for whites, since Chinese labor made possible infrastructure enterprises such as railroads, and by taking over low-paid and menial tasks left the skilled and prestigious positions for whites. This relationship changed when completion of the railroad enabled white workingmen to migrate in large numbers. Job competition would then become significant. Yet racial hostility in words and actions preceded that development by twenty years.[5]

The time lag suggests that anti-Chinese sentiment could hardly have originated from encounters in California, but must have been contained in Euro-American culture before the first contacts with Chinese. An alternative theory has been proposed to the effect that negative attitudes were shaped in an earlier period through reports of China brought back by merchants and missionaries. The thrust of this explanation would be to locate the hard side, the cutting edge, of racism within the upper class, especially among Whigs of northeastern origin; whereas evidence for California (and later for Colorado) places that hard side lower in the class hierarchy and most commonly among groups of Jacksonian or Free Soil background. Rather than attributing anti-Chinese hostility in the West to Eastern merchants and missionaries, it would seem more realistic to link it to the general hatred and contempt for people of color propagated by the politics of slavery and anti-slavery, by wars against Indians, and war against Mexico. A corollary to this argument would be to explain the

behavior of European immigrants as resulting from ideological precon-
ceptions carried over from Europe and sharpened into operative racism
by social, political and economic experiences in America.[6]

By 1867, at all events, hostility toward the Chinese was firmly established in California as part of a prevailing white supremacist outlook. The
linkage of the Chinese to African Americans could hardly have been more
cogently expressed than in the victory speech of Governor Henry Haight
after the Democratic resurgence of that year: 'I will simply say that in this
result we protest ... against populating this fair state with a race of Asiatics
– against sharing with inferior races the Government of our country ...
and this protest of ours will be re-echoed in thunder tones by the great
central states until the Southern States are emancipated from negro
domination, and restored to their proper place as equals and sisters in the
great Federal family.'[7] Haight obviously anticipated national repercussions, and he was right; with its winning combination of racial and
economic rhetoric, the California campaign reinforced Andrew Johnson's
counter-offensive and helped prepare the downfall of inter-racial politics
in the South. For California, it demonstrated the effectiveness of race
identification in unifying the working-class constituency, deeply fragmented though it was by differences of ethnicity, religion and national
origin.[8]

Politics in Colorado differed significantly from politics in California.
Whereas California had experienced no territorial stage, Colorado
lingered in territorial status for a quarter-century. Colorado's gold rush
came not at the apex of Jacksonian Democracy, as did California's, but on
the eve of the Civil War and in the ascendancy of Republicanism; and
Colorado remained solidly Republican for almost three decades after
California had returned to a two-party system. Racial conflict in Colorado
had taken the form mainly of wars of expropriation against Indians. In
California, where the Indians already had been reduced by two hundred
years of Spanish and Mexican domination to virtual powerlessness, overt
racial conflict targeted Chinese immigration. In Colorado, by contrast,
the Chinese issue raised no serious controversy until the election of 1880.

These differences informed the divergent responses of California and
Colorado to the depression in the mid-1870s and the national railroad
strikes in 1877. Like most of the rest of the nation, California suffered
heavily in the depression, which affected agriculture as severely as
manufacturing and transportation. Completion of the transcontinental
railroad four years earlier had multiplied the Euro-American labor force,
and unemployed workers – white and Chinese – accumulated in San Francisco. Racial and political tensions escalated. The railroad strikes brought
them to the flash point. Originating on the eastern seaboard in the early
summer of 1877, the strikes had been directed against efforts of the rail-

roads to recoup their losses through wage cuts and increased work loads. They erupted into mass insurgency against a government seemingly favorable to the interests of industrial entrepreneurs at the expense of working people. Uprisings across the continent involved workers in industrial cities, including Baltimore, Pittsburgh, St. Louis, Chicago and San Francisco, in armed conflict with the police and military. In San Francisco, demonstrations supporting the railroad strikes were taken over by anti-Chinese agitators. Fighting continued for four days. Mobs killed Chinese in the streets and tried to burn the Pacific Mail Company docks, where Chinese immigrants frequently came ashore. Anger at the Central Pacific Railroad was transposed into violence against Chinese, of whom the railroad was reputedly the largest employer. Temporarily at least these events shattered the balance of California politics.[9]

No such disruptions occurred in Colorado. Still in its bonanza phase during the 1870s, the territory suffered less than California in the depression of 1873. Nor were there direct repercussions from the railroad strikes. Doubtless this was due in part to the failure of John Evans and his associates to route the transcontinental main line through Denver. But more fundamentally it was due to the newness of mining in Colorado. Successful miners were still local men and capital investment appeared to flow from their accumulations. Republican leaders, whose experience with capitalism had been that of individual achievement, could speak persuasively as producers – men who had labored with their own hands – and as champions of the local interest against intrusions from outside. Local interests of course depended on uninterrupted rail transportation; yet assessments of who was to be blamed for the strikes and what ought to be done about them tended, initially, to unite Coloradans across class lines. Colorado's leading Republican newspaper, the *Rocky Mountain News*, expressed this ideological stance by blaming railroad problems on overcapitalization and mismanagement of the great transcontinental lines. Railroad managers were accused of seeking to make up for 'the "watering" process' and 'the thousand and one ways by which railway lines have been made to represent fictitious values' by a 'blackmail tax of ten percent on their helpless employees.' But they must be made to understand 'that the men who work their roads for them are not responsible for the bond issues or the mismanagement, and that public sympathy is always with the oppressed and against the oppressor.'[10]

Meanwhile the new administration of President Hayes – whom Colorado's first electoral votes had helped save from defeat – responded to the early successes of the strikers by an alliance with the railroad corporations. Ruthlessly and effectively, the alliance deployed private guards, police, state militia and the United States Army to suppress the strikes.[11] Editors of the *Rocky Mountain News*, perceiving (thanks apparently to close perusal of the New York *Nation*) that they had let regional enthusiasm obscure more basic allegiances, abruptly reversed course:

> 'What is most to be feared', says the Nation, 'is that through some weakness on the part of the companies the strikers may come out of the struggle with an appearance of victory ... which would be a national calamity.' ... [I]f our railways could be arrested by a band of strikers with impunity it would not be long before all labor would strike against all capital. ... The right to stop a railroad train is no more vested in a band of strikers than is the right to rob a stage coach in a band of highwaymen, and upon reflection it will be hard to determine which is the greater crime against society and good government. ... [12]

As this episode of journalistic truth-seeking suggests, Colorado was shuffling off aspects of the frontier condition that California had left behind twenty years earlier. The process of economic development was one also of homogenization. Beneath frontier idiosyncrasies that had distinguished the eminently Republican territory of Colorado lay similarities in demography and ideology that linked it to other western regions. Colorado's population resembled that of California in composition and origin, and a significant portion of it had reached Colorado by way of California.[13] Political divisions tended to follow the old cleavages of Jacksonian versus Whig, although in California these appeared as interparty contests while in Colorado they surfaced as Republican factionalism. In both regions, the primary sequence of racial conflict operated against a backdrop of struggle over slavery and the status of blacks, together with hostilities against Mexican-Americans carried forward from the Mexican War. Finally and crucially, disputes about race – regardless of the racial objects of those disputes – pitted white egalitarians (characterized by the hardest side of racism) against white elitists (necessarily characterized by a degree of racial tolerance) who sought to use non-white populations as bulwarks of class privilege. Meanwhile, the increasing flow of European immigrants, most of them wage-workers, was drawn to the egalitarian side. Whiteness then came to symbolize the solidarity of producers against those who prospered at the producers' expense by conniving with and manipulating racially subordinated populations. These categories, derived from the Jacksonian background, took on new meanings from the memories of Civil War and Reconstruction.[14]

Racial Patterns, East and West

The gubernatorial campaign of 1867 had institutionalized anti-Chinese tactics in California. Ten years later the railroad strikes transferred those tactics to working-class leadership. From the angry crowds in San Francisco emanated a new political movement, the Workingmen's Party of California, whose rise to power focused national attention on the demand for exclusion of Chinese laborers from the United States. The Workingmen briefly usurped the place of the Democracy, which had first raised the Chinese question, then were absorbed back into the major party.[15]

A similar sequence unfolded somewhat belatedly in Colorado. When Chinese began trickling into the territory about 1869, the Republican-controlled legislature had welcomed them as 'eminently calculated to hasten the development and early prosperity of the Territory.' The Census of 1880 reported about 600 Chinese in Colorado, 238 of them in Denver.[16] In 1880 for the first time the Democratic party mounted a major presidential campaign. The *Rocky Mountain News*, recently purchased by wealthy Democrats, worked up anti-Chinese sentiment in the fall of that year. Shortly before the election, a Democratic parade spilled over into attacks on Chinese and the following day, Sunday, erupted into citywide rioting that smashed Chinese wash houses and gutted Denver's small Chinatown. One Chinese was kicked to death on the street while several hundred took refuge in the jailhouse.[17]

Afterwards, Republican newspapers blamed Democrats, and the Democratic *Rocky Mountain News* maintained that the rioting had done a service by cleaning up the city. In Colorado, as earlier in California, Democratic electioneering was clearly directed to white workingmen. That white workingmen were by no means unresponsive to such appeals is suggested by evidence that similar although less publicized violence was common in Colorado's mining camps. Joseph Buchanan, a spectacularly successful organizer of southwestern railroad workers for the Knights of Labor and editor, in 1883, of the Denver *Labor Inquirer*, after calling upon 'workingmen of all countries' to 'unite', described Chinese workers as 'vermin', 'like so many leeches sucking our blood', and declared editorially, '... [W]e feel like going forth and inciting people to butcher every thieving infernal Chinaman in the country.'[18]

Chinese exclusion took control of far western politics. Since 1860, Republicans had preempted the traditional Democratic hospitality to European immigrants; and in the interest of rapid economic development of the West, had extended a similar hospitality, through the Burlingame Treaty of 1868, to Chinese. The railroad strikes and effective uses of racist politics like those in California and Colorado now compelled Republican administrations in Washington to yield ground on Chinese immigration. Republican legislators joined their Democratic colleagues in voting to alter the nation's traditionally open immigration policy by imposing a racially determined restriction upon one group only – Chinese laborers.[19]

This exclusionist sweep, however, did not greatly diminish the effectiveness of anti-Asian agitation. Departure of Chinese already in the

United States had not been mandated; the act, dependent on ten-year renewals and silent as to possible entry of other Asian migrants, guaranteed periodic reopening of the debate. A relative labor shortage, which had made importation of a non-white, politically powerless and therefore controllable labor supply economically attractive to railroad contractors, offered similar inducements to manufacturers of consumer goods and to entrepreneurs in that typically far-western form of agriculture, 'factories in the fields'. Japanese and Mexican migration first began to reach significant volume in the 1890s. Preserving the West as a white man's country would thus remain for another seventy-five years central to labor oganization and working-class politics. Moreover, that issue now carried the prestige of success, endorsement by popular majorities in western states, and the blessing of bipartisan approval.[20]

In the East, racial segmentation of the labor force lacked the monolithic simplicity of the western model. This resulted not from any weakening of racial consciousness among whites, but from demographic facts and from problems posed by the politics of Civil War and Reconstruction. A movement to preserve wartime gains of the urban working class – parallel to that of the San Francisco trade unionists but on a broader scale – culminated in a delegated national convention, the National Labor Union (NLU), which held its first meeting in Baltimore in 1866. Immediately enmeshed in convention deliberations was the dilemma of a racially divided labor force. Already in the North, black workers, some of them skilled and many of them veterans of the war, were seeking admission to labor unions. In the South, slaves equal in number to about one-eighth of the US population had been set free by the Thirteenth Amendment. While most were agricultural laborers, some were skilled or semi-skilled artisans. It was well-known that slaves had worked as shipwrights, house carpenters, stevedores, railroad brakemen and firemen, miners and iron founders. Given the apparent direction of Republican policies in the early years of Reconstruction, it would have seemed that ex-slaves were about to become free wage laborers with the same rights, presumably including suffrage and geographical mobility, as white workers.[21]

Debates in the National Labor Union framed a set of opposite alternatives: inclusion or exclusion. Advocates of the first based themselves on the tradition of the Jacksonian workingmen's parties, that milieu in which radical artisan ideology had been shaped into the producer ethic. Suffrage, already widely extended by 1830, had appeared the shortest route to economic and social reforms since producers comprised, potentially, a national majority. Jacksonian egalitarianism had applied to white men only; yet if several million black producers were to be added to the ranks of the whites, the rational self-interest of white working people required the inclusion of black workers in labor organizations. That was the position, certainly, of Ira Steward, New England pioneer of the eight-hour movement. And that was the message transmitted from the Enlightenment through such earlier champions as Frances Wright and Robert Dale Owen and fixed in the consciousness of men who remembered the beginnings of the Workingmen's movement.[22]

Advocates of the opposite alternative were probably for the most part younger men. They emphasized the racial exclusions of Jacksonianism while modifying its Producer Ethic. Keenly aware of the development of factories and steam power, sensitive to diverging interests within the phalanx of producers, their outlook tended to be economistic and trade unionist rather than political reformist. They were accustomed to thinking in restrictive terms: how to check the influx of green hands, how to use the strength of associations to prevent newcomers from undermining the bargaining power of skilled workers. Alarmed by the Republican-sponsored Contract Labor Law of 1864, such unionists pushed for repeal of the act and demanded a ban on any sort of overseas labor contracting. Considered as an economic problem, the entrance of black freedmen into the labor market was comparable to immigration from abroad. Blacks, like recent immigrants, would be compelled by economic necessity to work for any wages offered. The same reasoning that counseled limitations on apprenticeship and opposition to recruitment and indenture of foreign workers pointed also to exclusion of non-whites. This outlook prevailed sufficiently to defeat the advocates of inclusion, so forestalling any positive action by the National Labor Union toward black workers.[23]

At that time, of course, the exclusionist argument was not followed to its logical conclusion with respect to European immigration. A large proportion of the white labor force was composed of European natives or their children. Immigration from Europe was more broadly accepted across class lines than before the war, since the Republican party had repudiated nativist tendencies in order to promote immigration as an ingredient essential to economic growth. For white working people to advocate closure of European immigration would have been to deny their own origins. No such proposals were seriously put forward by organized labor until after the Depression of 1893. This inconsistency points to the fact that neither trade unionists nor anyone else in nineteenth-century America arrived at conclusions involving matters of race simply through processes of economic reasoning.[24]

Meanwhile the operative decisions were being made at the local level. Black applicants, even those who had become skilled craftsmen, were generally rejected. The Union of Carpenters and Joiners summed up the situation in 1869 when it declared its willingness to 'extend the hand of friendship to every laboring man', but added: 'We believe that the prejudice of our members against the colored people are of such a nature that it is not expedient at present to admit them as members or to organize them.' In the same year, Lewis Douglass, son of the Abolitionist leader Frederick Douglass, was driven from a job in the Government Printing Office by the Typographical Union, which refused membership to African Americans while insisting that only union members could work at the federal printing plant.[25]

In cities with concentrations of black industrial workers such as Baltimore and Philadelphia, blacks began to organize their own unions, and these converged briefly into a black National Labor Union similar in structure to the white NLU. National conventions of the two unions exchanged speakers and delegates in 1869 and 1870. This limited cooperation was supported, among the whites, by the same groups of political reformers who had first proposed inter-racial organization. Basically Democratic in orientation (although many had been Union Republicans during the war), they were moving by the early 1870s to a concept of an independent labor party that would press the Democrats from the left. Like George Wilkes, who was sending them smoke signals about the Paris Commune, they saw Republican power, consolidated in the Grant administrations, as the main danger to America. Unmoved by the situation of black freedmen in the South, their political stance amounted to an endorsement of the Democratic party's campaigns for white supremacy. To black workers, on the other hand, the Republican party and Radical Reconstruction offered the only hopes of black liberation. This fundamental cleavage of perspective doomed any initiatives toward cooperation between the black and white labor conventions. In any case, both unions were destroyed by the depression of 1873.[26]

These events had narrowed differences between the patterns of racial segmentation prevailing in the East and West almost to the vanishing point, but did not quite eliminate them. In the West, exclusion of the non-white minority from organized labor was total; there were no exceptions, no support for alternative policies within the labor movement, and virtually no criticism of labor's racial exclusiveness from outside. The white community, including leaders of the major parties, encouraged and applauded labor's intransigence. In the East, racial exclusion remained piecemeal, *de facto*, and operated largely at local levels. A coherent alternative policy, first voiced within the National Labor Union, continued to find advocates in local and national unions and city central labor. Inthe society at large, and among working people, favorable wartime images of the African American continued to be operative, acceptance or rejection of such images being roughly characteristic of major party orientation.[27]

The concept of exclusion took on different regional connotations. In the West, where the non-white minority consisted of immigrants denied naturalization, without voting power, and – since most were males who would have no children in America – outside the scope of the Fourteenth and Fifteenth amendments, exclusion meant physical removal by act of the federal government. If federal law remained less than totally satisfactory, it could be supposed that continuing pressure would bring it around. At a second level, simply taken for granted in the West, exclusion meant rejection as potential members of labor organizations. But in the East African Americans by the 1870s were citizens, actual or potential voters. White supremacists might still dream of deportation or exclusion by local or state law, yet even in the South such projects were becoming increasingly tenuous. Exclusion therefore narrowed to the second meaning: exclusion from the ranks of organized labor.[28]

Strategy must bear some relation to tactical feasibility. Although eastern whites doubtless adhered as generally to white supremacist attitudes as did their western counterparts, consensus on the desirability of total exclusion was impossible to attain. An index to this difference was the greater use of black strikebreakers through the East and Midwest than of Chinese strikebreakers in the Far West. Within eastern labor organizations the result of these factors was that exclusionists tended to pragmatism rather than principle in their arguments. As the New York carpenters had put it, 'the prejudice of our members' made it 'not expedient' to admit them 'at present'. Prejudice might diminish at some future time. Workers in other industries (iron workers and coalminers, for example) might decide for equally pragmatic reasons that it was expedient to admit black workers to their unions. Neither the National Labor Union, nor subsequent national confederations like the Knights of Labor or the American Federation of Labor, gave principled approval to the exclusion of African Americans. On the contrary, they advocated organizing black workers; yet all three endorsed Chinese exclusion.[29]

A sociological survey of labor force segmentation in the mid-1880s would have reported substantially similar patterns for the East and Far West, the major difference being that while in one region exclusion was a dominant pattern, in the other it was the only pattern. Ideological justifications of this social reality varied widely, however: defensive and contingent in the East, assured and absolute in the West.

Craft and Industrial Unionism

In US labor history, the railroad strikes of 1877 present a watershed almost as sharply defined as the great divide of the Civil War in social and political history. Before 1877, wage earners had tended to perceive themselves as *producers*, closely linked to their employers, who were producers also, both together being respected members of an egalitarian community. After 1877 they increasingly saw themselves as an exploited class. Until 1877, no systematic use had been made of military force to suppress strikes. Afterwards, strike suppression became as much a part of normal routine for federal and state troops as Fourth of July parades or pursuit and destruction of Indians. The year that marked formal termination of Republican Reconstruction in the South opened a quarter-century of bitter and often violent class conflict. Flourishing and withering with alternate cycles of bonanza and depression, the labor movement developed two distinct organizational types, industrial unionism and craft unionism, which responded in divergent ways to the environmental factor of a racially segmented labor force.[30]

The Order of the Knights of Labor, founded inconspicuously at Philadelphia three years after the first National Labor Union convention, is customarily cited as a prototype of industrial unionism. Actually embracing a variety of forms, among which were local and national bodies of skilled craftsmen, industrial unions, cooperatives, mixed assemblies of wage earners, farmers, professionals and small proprietors, this organization spanned the dividing line between preindustrial and industrial experience.[31] What most distinctly characterized the Knights of Labor was its inclusive membership policy and emphasis on producer rather than craft loyalty. In this respect it was linked to the Jacksonian past, and its collective outlook remained similar to that of the political reformist contingent in the National Labor Union. Its declared aim was to unite all those who labored regardless of skill differentials, sex or race. The Knights recruited women and blacks. They tried, sometimes successfully, to organize black workers in the redeemed South despite legal harassment and murderous opposition. Rapid growth of the Order in the 1880s was, however, not due to the recruitment of women or African Americans. It resulted from an influx of unskilled and semi-skilled white workingmen. In 1877, apparently, the Knights had few members among railroad workers, yet early in the 1880s railroaders joined by the tens of thousands. Strikes along southwestern rail lines based in Kansas City and Denver brought a dramatic victory over Jay Gould, one of the most popularly hated robber barons in the nation. The Knights then became symbolic champions of the producers' fraternity against the power of industrial concentration. From a membership of less than 20,000, the Order leaped to 100,000 in 1885, and during the following year added another half-million to the roster. New members without organizational experience and new local unions without treasuries plunged into mass strikes, most of which were lost. By the end of the decade, the hopes roused by the upsurge of the Knights had faded, and membership, after peaking at three-quarters of a million, dispersed as rapidly as it had come together.[32]

Meanwhile, another organizational type, the skilled craft union, was growing slowly but more steadily. Several of the national craft unions founded before the Civil War had participated in the National Labor Union and had survived the depression of 1873. Through the 1880s craft organizations expanded modestly in settings that provided shelter from mechanization and the factory system. Such labor unions were controlled by, and increasingly restricted their membership to, the skilled craftsmen of each trade. Exclusiveness limited growth. Yet the uncontrolled expansion and collapse of the Knights seemed to many skilled workers proof of the inherent weakness of an inclusive membership policy. They constructed a rationale for their own organizational form upon the premise that unskilled workers, crippled by meager earnings and uncertain job tenure, could never provide a stable base for trade unionism. Unable to support union organizers or accumulate strike funds, the unskilled would remain helpless in disputes with employers, especially since they were always easy to replace. The employer could simply renew his unskilled hands from the unemployed while encouraging migration from the rural hinterland or overseas. Nor could the difficulty be solved, craft unionists argued, by combining skilled and unskilled into mixed locals, as the Knights of Labor had tried to do, since a minority of skilled workers would then be taxed in futile efforts to sustain the unskilled majority. Sooner or later the crafts workers would have no choice but to protect their own interests by splitting off and bargaining for themselves alone. If the conclusion seemed harsh, craft unionists could point out that the industrial system was not their fault; and trade unionism, once planted where it had some chance for growth, might eventually extend its benefits to workers of lesser skill.[33]

In pursuance of this line of reasoning, craft union delegates in the early 1880s formed a separate national convention, subsequently the American Federation of Labor (AFL). The Federation and the Knights were at first conceived as parallel and complementary, rather than competitive. Massive support rallied from both to the eight-hour day campaign of 1886, a movement actually initiated by the AFL. Yet afterwards, when the Haymarket bombing and subsequent arrests, convictions, and executions provided the setting for an employer counteroffensive against all organized labor, it was not the craft unions that suffered most heavily but rather the Knights of Labor. In one sense this outcome confirmed the craft unionist argument: assemblies of unskilled workers proved least able to withstand employer attacks. But it also pointed to a less obvious implication of craft unionism. Employer attacks fell more heavily on the Knights not only because their organizations were weaker, but because employers perceived them as more dangerous – precisely because they reasserted the inclusive strategy of the Jacksonian Producer Ethic. During the Jacksonian period this ethic had negated class division, but in the postwar era of industrial consolidation it took on a new meaning. Inclusiveness on Jay Gould's southwestern railroads, or at the McCormick Reaper Works, or in Frick and Carnegie's steel mills could only mean industrial inclusiveness. The mixed assemblies of the Knights of Labor foreshadowed the industrial union movement.[34]

An industrially inclusive membership strategy must make demands not only for small groups of skilled craftsmen but also for masses of unskilled and semi-skilled workers. The potential costs to employers would exceed those of meeting the demands of skilled craftsmen. Moreover, industrial inclusiveness contained political as well as economic implications. When unskilled workers organized, they were obliged because of their replaceability to protect themselves by mobilizing mass support. The tactic characteristic of industrial unionism, as exemplified in the 1877 railroad strikes and the McCormick strike that set the stage for the Haymarket bombing, was the mass picket line. If police or soldiers broke up picket lines, workers could only appeal to the public at large, especially the working class. This reversed the original thrust of the Producer Ethic; yet the reversal was logical, given the shift from the small-scale individual production of the prewar era to concentrated industrial capital. In a maturing industrial society, producer inclusiveness led toward working-class consciousness and working-class politics. Employer collisions with industrial organizations or with alliances of skilled and unskilled workers were likely to become exercises in overt class warfare, as the Homestead and Pullman strikes and Colorado's labor wars of the 1890s abundantly demonstrated.[35]

This is not to suggest that American employers accepted any form of unionism willingly. They resisted craft unions and destroyed them whenever they were conveniently able to do so. Although vulnerable in industries open to rapid technological change such as steel and farm equipment, craft unions could muster impressive survival power in industries like construction, shipbuilding, metal trades and printing which remained relatively inaccessible to mass production methods and in which the skills transmitted through apprenticeship continued to be crucial. Within these rather special environments, craft unionists perfected their techniques of self-defense. Local organization of a skill group gave bargaining advantages that could be used to improve wages and working conditions for that skill. Membership solidarity was then enlisted on the basis of craft identification rather than by virtue of the old producer ethic or a generalized working-class consciousness.[36]

Local groups coalesced into national organizations that could centralize the supervision of membership. This was done by defining the jurisdiction; seeking to include all skilled workers and exclude all others;

resisting subdivisions of the craft; asserting control over training and apprenticeship; pressing for the closed shop whenever possible; and using
the traveling card system and widely circulated rat lists to hinder
employers from exploiting the mobility of skilled craftsmen in a national
market. Since all these endeavors rested on the capability of the national
union to sustain a strike anywhere in its jurisdiction at least long enough
to inflict damage on an employer, power inside the union tended to
gravitate from the local to the national. Conventions and national executive councils progressively took over such matters as membership discipline, management of strike and benefit funds, and final authority in
approving or terminating strikes. To provide staffing for these activities,
a professional, full-time leadership appeared, mainly at the national level.
Local and regional leadership was subordinated to the national executive.
Under the pressure of economic expansion and industrial conflict, the
centralized, bureaucratic structure characteristic of American craft
unionism was beginning to take shape.[37]

Confronting such organizations of skilled workers, employers sometimes found it more convenient to negotiate than to fight. They discovered that contracts offered advantages, not least among them being
stabilization of the labor supply. Since the unions were eager to control
the labor supply, they gladly shared in tasks of apprenticeship training and
assumed responsibility for steady and reliable replacements. Work discipline might be another advantage. Whenever unionists could count on
wages and working conditions superior to those of non-union workers,
their interest would point toward outlawing incompetence and protecting
the contract from individual work stoppages or breaches of discipline.
The skilled craft union then became less an adversary and more a sort of
junior partner in the industrial apparatus.[38]

There was no such sanctuary for organizations that opened their doors
to unskilled workers. Throughout the depressions and industrial struggles
of the late nineteenth century, it was the inclusive organizations like the
mixed assemblies of the Knights and Eugene Debs's American Railway
Union that were smashed; craft unions were more likely to survive. By
1900, when the Knights of Labor had dwindled to only a few thousand
members, the craft unions of the AFL – clearly the dominant force of the
labor movement – had reached a membership of half a million. This was
one side of the coin. But the same figure reveals how narrow the craft
unions actually were: their members represented less than 10 percent of
the industrial labor force.[39]

The niche occupied by this fraction of skilled unionists was at best a
tenuous one, threatened from above and from below. The threat from
above consisted in the hair-trigger balance of profit margins upon which
contractual relations rested. In times of stringency an employer's first

cost-cutting maneuvers were always directed against labor. At any moment the friendly welcome the business agent had been learning to expect at the main office might explode into bloody struggle. The threat from below bore a different aspect. It stemmed from the divergence between the interests of the skilled craft workers and those of the masses of unskilled. Unskilled workers also coveted the benefits of unionization, and their attempts to organize often involved mass picket lines and appeals to class solidarity. They were likely to provoke employer counteroffensives in the form of anti-labor campaigns, court actions and use of state or federal power against labor. Craft unions could easily be wrecked in the process. To the extent that craft unions functioned as an accepted part of the industrial apparatus, any radical attack upon the establishment disrupted their situation. Skilled craft unionism had acquired a vested interest in the status quo that prescribed avoidance of entanglement in organizational activities of the unskilled, and intervention when possible to limit or forestall such activities.[40]

This divergence of interest underlay the gradual separation of craft unions from the Knights of Labor and dictated the explicit hostility of craft unionism to subsequent efforts at industrial organization such as the American Railway Union and the Industrial Workers of the World. It also shaped the AFL's political alliances. The political stance of craft unions frequently has been misunderstood. Far from avoiding partisan politics, they were likely to be immersed in them at the local level while campaigning statewide or nationally for the exclusion of Asian immigrant labor, and for particular reforms, especially bureaus of labor statistics, abolition of prison labor contracting and the federal Seamen's Act of the early twentieth century. They tended to avoid commitment to mass campaigns like those of Socialism or the Populist movement.[41]

Adjustments as delicate as these required a degree of *realpolitik* that led to conflicts within the craft unions themselves. The dividing line between skilled and unskilled, especially with the increasing numbers of 'semi-skilled' factory operatives, was often fluid; skilled and unskilled were likely to be linked by ties of kinship or neighborhood, more often by common values and traditions. The Jacksonian Producer Ethic remained the heritage of the entire white working class. Moreover, the later developing sense of class that linked workers in a shared identity was inclusive rather than exclusive. It spoke more clearly for industrial forms of organization than for craft unionism. Ties of class solidarity remained stronger among rank and file and local leaders than within the emergent national leadership since the new professionals, sensitive to the precariousness of the craft union situation (and of their own careers), were more closely tied to their management counterparts, with whom they regularly did business, than to the working-class milieux from which most of them came. They promoted a policy of cautious realism. The soft rhetoric of the Producer Ethic and the tougher language of class consciousness were by no means abandoned; they simply ceased to govern choices of goals.

Highly visible at the summit of the craft union edifice was the central staff of the American Federation of Labor, headed by Samuel Gompers. Actually Gompers's office was totally dependent upon the national craft unions, since power, in the form of financial controls, resided in their national executives. The real location of power in the craft union hierarchy was made clear by the long struggle over the role of central labor councils, or city centrals. Historically, city centrals had developed as standard organizational forms at least as early as the 1820s, long before the origin of national unions. Composed of delegates from whatever labor, educational or reform groups happened to be active in the community, they were particularly effective in rallying mass participation either in political campaigns or in support of strikes. Appealing to producer or class solidarity through neighborhood ties and shared values and traditions, they provided a natural organizational form for the inclusive strategy of the Producer Ethic and of industrial unionism. Labor radicals and industrial unionists usually sought leadership in city central labor councils. By contrast, city centrals proved dysfunctional for the exclusive strategy of skilled craft unionism. National officers of craft unions frequently came into conflict with their own rank and file and local leadership over the issue of participation in city centrals. The problem was widely debated and eventually disposed of by two sets of decisions. One set, arrived at within the national craft unions, prohibited locals under pain of expulsion from entering into binding commitments of strike support or contributions through city centrals to which they might be affiliated. The other set, adopted at national conventions of the American Federation of Labor (the legitimate source of charters for all city centrals), restricted the activity of the centrals to implementing policies already determined by the national unions or by the Federation itself. The cumulative result of these decisions was to circumscribe the autonomy of city centrals and to complete the concentration of power at the national level.[42]

The American Federation of Labor, then, existed to serve the needs of the national craft unions. For the most part its services consisted of mediating disputes among craft unions and representing them in dealings with government and the general public. A special and sometimes more urgent task was that of justifying the goals of craft unionism to the working class as a whole. Justification could only be in reference to inclusive identifications – the Producer Ethic or class consciousness – both increasingly irrelevant to the priorities of craft unionism. This ideological gap corresponded to an organizational structure that set 90 percent or more of the labor force outside its perimeters.[43]

Convergence on a National Pattern

Throughout this period, racial conflicts repeatedly broke the surface, reproducing and intensifying patterns earlier spelled out in the National Labor Union debates and acted out in California and Colorado. 1885 was the year of the victory of the Knights of Labor over Jay Gould. The Knights quickly won a following on the western railroads and among miners and lumber workers in the Rocky Mountains and along the Pacific slope. In sharp contrast to efforts in the East to bring black workers into the organization, Knights in the Far West excluded Chinese and engaged in violence against them. The most widely publicized of such episodes occurred at Rock Springs, Wyoming Territory, where the Union Pacific Railroad had brought Chinese during the depression of 1873 to break a strike in its coal mines. In 1885, white miners gathered at the Knights of Labor hall, then set fire to the barracks of the Chinese and shot them as they ran out, killing twenty-eight and wounding fifteen. No one was ever brought to trial because the local grand jury declined to bring indictments. For the same reason it remains impossible to identify the attackers, except that, like their victims, most were probably aliens. Contemporary observers described the white labor force at Rock Springs as composed of Welsh, Irish and Cornish immigrants. In the course of that same year, Knights of Labor assemblies participated in violent expulsions of Chinese from mines and lumber camps across Oregon and the Washington Territory.[44]

In California approximately one-quarter of wage workers were Chinese, a proportion that remained constant until the mid-1880s, then declined through the last fifteen years of the century. On the other hand, about one-third of all white wage workers were old stock Americans, the other two-thirds being immigrants or the children of immigrants, with Irish and Germans forming the largest subgroups. Among white workers, one of the few characteristics held in common was that of not being Chinese. State politics had proved the effectiveness of appeals to this common characteristic, and after 1877 trade unionists made systematic use of racial identification. During the organizational upsurge inspired by the Workingmen's party, a regional labor center had finally been established at San Francisco. Union leaders expanded its membership base by tying it to a project known as the League of Deliverance, which undertook to boycott firms employing Chinese or handling products of Chinese labor. Both the League and the assembly disintegrated following the enactment of Chinese exclusion in 1882; but three years later, as news of the massacre at Rock Springs and expulsions of Chinese from lumber and mining towns in the Northwest reached San Francisco's craft union leaders, they summoned a coastwide anti-Chinese convention. From this gathering emanated not only demands for removal of the remaining Chinese by force, but also a new regional assembly, later permanently reorganized as the San Francisco Labor Council.[45]

By the turn of the century, both San Francisco and Denver had come to be known as solid union towns. Many of their major unions, no longer regional, were affiliated to AFL craft unions with national headquarters in the East. Organizational success had resulted in part from the unifying influence of anti-Chinese hostility, supplemented, in Colorado, by surges of violence against Indians and Mexicans. The long anti-Chinese campaign gradually tapered off as federal exclusion took effect, but a more far-reaching crusade, the Asiatic Exclusion League, was initiated and led by California trade unions. The League served as focal point for political activities of the expanding labor movement. Agitation against the employment of Asians and successful pressure for state constitutional prohibitions of land ownership by 'unassimilable aliens' opened the way for the total exclusion of Asian immigration that was eventually enacted by Congress after the First World War.[46]

These events in the West acquired increasing national significance. As the anti-Chinese stance of West Coast workingmen became widely known, trade unionists in the East joined the attack. Their hostility was sharpened by instances during the late 1860s of importation of Chinese laborers to eastern factories as strikebreakers. Knights of Labor conventions advocated Chinese exclusion, voicing little or no criticism for the violent acts of the western assemblies; and the American Federation of Labor likewise supported the California position. In approving Chinese expulsion, the national labor movement assented to the racist arguments used in support of that undertaking.[47]

Patterns of thought derived from anti-Asian agitation affected American working-class attitudes toward general restriction of immigration. This issue first came up for serious discussion as a result of widespread unemployment during the 1890s. It was divisive because the notion of excluding European immigrants violated traditional concepts of white egalitarianism and producer loyalties. Moreover, for a working class so largely composed of immigrants or the children of immigrants, the proposal seemed a betrayal of ethnic and familial obligation. By 1890, however, the main sources of immigration had shifted from Western Europe to Southern and Eastern Europe. It therefore became possible to argue that the more recent immigrants – darker skinned and culturally more remote from Anglo-Irish-American norms – were, like the Asians, racially unassimilable. AFL president Samuel Gompers, himself a Jewish immigrant born in England, leaned heavily on this argument in his efforts to persuade the Federation to endorse general immigration restriction.[48]

From coast to coast organized labor presented a united front on the

Asian question. Yet until almost the end of the century, it maintained its earlier ambivalence with respect to blacks. Like the Knights of Labor, the Federation had endeavored to organize black workers and had tried, especially in the South, to find some formula for economic cooperation between black and white contingents of the labor force. Both the New Orleans dock strike of 1892 and the long-sustained efforts of coalminers and ironworkers in Alabama provided impressive demonstrations of the possibility of inter-racial solidarity. Annual conventions of the Federation proclaimed the need for union 'irrespective of creed, color, sex, nationality or politics.' When Gompers was not excoriating Asians, he eloquently denounced racial exclusiveness. The reality behind this rhetoric, however, was the gradual ascendancy of a craft unionism that validated exclusiveness; racial exclusion merged into economic exclusion.[49]

Ira Berlin and Herbert Gutman have shown how the once-extensive participation of black workers, slave and free, in the artisan crafts of southern cities was already being undermined before the Civil War by the transfer of slave craftsmen to newly opened cotton lands in the trans-Mississippi West; and was further reduced by the movement of northern and foreign-born white skilled workers to southern cities both before and after the war. As trades such as ship-repair, longshore, construction and railroading became unionized, the unions invoked the rule of jobs-for-members-only while excluding African Americans from union membership. Of the scattering of black craftsmen who belonged to AFL unions, most were in all-black locals in the South, usually earning lower wages than whites doing the same work. The United States Bureau of Labor Statistics in 1900 listed eighty-two affiliated organizations of the American Federation of Labor. Thirty-nine of these had no black membership, according to a survey by W.E.B. Du Bois, while another twenty-seven contained only a token few. Gompers and the Federation's executive sometimes issued charters for special segregated unions (federal locals) if the appropriate national organizations were unwilling to admit black applicants. While it might be claimed that federal locals brought black workers into the labor movement, such locals also served to limit competition in the interest of whites, and denied black representation in the national unions which held jurisdiction over the trades in which they worked.[50]

Exclusion came to be blamed on black workers themselves, as in the West it was blamed on Chinese. The repetition suggests a pattern of cyclical transfer from one region to the other. The first cycle was slavery and defense of slavery, expropriation of Indians and its racist justification. Transported west, these justifications served as preconditions for hatred and exclusion of Chinese, at once identified as members of an inferior race. During the second cycle, the result flowed back as a causal factor in undermining the situation of African Americans after the Civil War despite the role they had played in the war and despite their seemingly positive linkage to the Union victory. From this viewpoint, the anti-Chinese campaigns in the Far West worked as a kind of feedback loop through which white supremacist ideology moved from its pre-war matrix of producer egalitarianism and continental expansion to its postwar matrix of class consciousness and industrial conflict.

Organizational Functions of Racial Subordination

An important question remains: Was there a structural relationship between racial exclusion and the dominance of nationally centralized craft unions, or were these merely contingent sequences? The question highlights the organizational functions of racial subordination. Problems of race have been a continuing source of tension within American working-class organizations. The goal of uniting workers across racial lines in defense of common interests has often been advocated, but until at least the middle of the twentieth century the dominant, white portion of the working class adhered to the prevailing racist attitudes of the society at large. This placed white workers in the ambivalent stance of protesting their exploitation as wage earners, while simultaneously claiming a share of the benefits accruing to the white society from exploitation of non-whites.

The ideological inheritance of organized labor in the United States was the Producer Ethic. Expressing the aspirations of small, pre-industrial producers, this outlook emphasized an egalitarianism reserved for whites and rejected the notion of class. Industrial experience after the Civil War, however, imposed a recognition of the permanence of wage-earner status. That recognition assumed two major forms. The first was working-class consciousness, which pointed toward industrial unionism and an inclusive membership strategy. The other was job or craft consciousness, which pointed towards the organization of skilled craft unions with exclusive membership strategies. Expressions of hostility toward non-whites occurred in both types of organization, but the logic of the industrial or inclusive type worked in the long run against racial exclusiveness because the industrial form maximizes potential bargaining power when it includes all workers in an industry regardless of wage or skill differentials, differences of sex, ethnicity or race. By contrast, the economically exclusive policy characteristic of skilled craft unions could readily accommodate itself to racial exclusiveness, especially since most non-white workers remained at unskilled levels.

To put the matter in slightly different terms, a white-only craft union could coexist with a racially mixed unskilled labor force, whereas an all-white industrial union could not. The industrial union must push for total exclusion or else integrated membership. For this reason episodes of extreme violence (as at Rock Springs, Wyoming) were more likely to be associated with industrial than with craft unionism. But while mass killing might remain a viable solution for problems involving Indians in late nineteenth-century America, it was ceasing to be viable with respect to non-white industrial workers, if only because their employers, certain to be backed by state and federal power, would intervene. The alternative was inter-racial membership. Thus the logistics of self-defense – in race relations as in strike tactics – pushed industrial unions to more radical responses than craft unions.

Both types were forced to struggle for existence in the class warfare of the late nineteenth century. Industrial unions generally failed to survive. Skilled craft unions proved able within certain restricted economic environments to grow slowly and steadily. The importance of this fact with respect to racial discrimination can be pinpointed by noting that the type of union best able to survive during this period was the least conducive to the inclusion of non-white workers.

Before the First World War, the American labor force was constantly replenished both by recruits from rural areas and by immigrants from abroad. Since few of these newcomers possessed industrial skills, one would not expect to find them among the membership of skilled craft unions. The point appears obvious but leads to a corollary not so obvious. The United States accepted immigration as desirable, but ascribed positive values to whiteness and negative values to non-whiteness. Whites, both immigrant and native-born, would be assimilated more rapidly into the industrial hierarchy than non-whites, whether foreign-born or native. Recent immigrants, if white, could expect some of their children to become skilled workers and members of craft unions. No such expectation was open to non-white immigrants, or to native-born non-whites even if their ancestors had lived in America before the Revolution.

Skilled craft unionism in one sense received its white supremacist outlook, as did white society at large, from the prior history of racial exploitation in America. That outlook, however, was constantly reinforced because the diffusion of racist attitudes among white workers proved conducive to craft unionism. This held true for several interconnected reasons. One of the weaknesses of craft unionism had been the narrow and self-serving quality of its ethic, in contrast with the Producer Ethic on one hand, or with working-class consciousness on the other. The weakness became acute whenever a craft union encountered employer efforts to fragment the skill by transferring particular operations to unskilled or semi-skilled hands. Historically this was a common form of conflict, and craft unions were continuously engaged in protecting their boundaries against such infiltration. Their main reliance was upon discipline, which required members to refuse to work with non-union intruders and to ostracize them socially. Because this defense ran counter to the inclinations of working-class loyalty it was often tenuous and difficult to maintain. No such inhibitions stood in the way of ostracizing non-white workers since racist attitudes, reinforcing the prestige of the skilled trades, outweighed class identification and served therefore to enhance the ability of the craft unions to protect the boundaries of their skills.

Lessons garnered from struggles of the past showed the most dangerous situations for craft unionism to be those involving alliances with organizations of unskilled workers. While the shared values and traditions of the white working class constantly set the stage for the recurrence of such situations, the structure and strategy of craft unionism sought their avoidance. White supremacist attitudes aided this strategy by impeding the organization of unskilled workers. The effect was to reduce the organizational potential of the unskilled nine-tenths of the labor force and to minimize the likelihood that unions of the unskilled would be in a position to make demands upon skilled craftsmen.

By the turn of the century, craft unions, if they were tightly organized and fortunately situated, were capable of vigorous self-defense. Yet they were never able to achieve total security. They might at any moment face employer attack in the industrial sphere, or court action, or hostile legislation at local, state or national levels. They might then be obliged to appeal for support from sympathizers outside their own ranks. Sometimes the American Federation of Labor broadcast such appeals.[51] Support would be most likely to come from the white working class as a whole if the attention of that class was not too firmly riveted on the fact that fewer than one in ten workers enjoyed the benefits of craft unionism. A high level of racial hostility centered attention on racial differences between white and non-white rather than on cultural differences among immigrants, between immigrants and native born, or on economic differences between skilled and unskilled. It tended for this reason to unite the white labor force across differences of ethnic background and across inequalities of wages and working conditions. To this extent, the white supremacist commitment – part of the American heritage of artisan egalitarianism – worked to the advantage of skilled craft unionism by enabling it to draw upon the political and economic resources of the white working class without assuming responsibility to defend the interests and needs of the class as a whole.

Undoubtedly in the long run this commitment inhibited development of the sort of working-class consciousness in the United States that in other industrializing nations was becoming an effective political force. Here again the process followed a cyclical pattern. The prevalence of white racism in the society at large, and within the white labor force, contributed to the dominance of skilled craft unionism. But craft unionism in turn, defending its dominance, worked to extend and perpetuate the influence of white racism.[52]

Notes

1. Ira Cross, *A History of the Labor Movement in California*, Berkeley, Calif. 1935, is still the best general history of labor in nineteenth–century California; see pp. 29–44; Alexander Saxton, *The Indispensable Enemy: Labor and the Anti–Chinese Movement in California*, Berkeley, Calif. 1970, pp. 68–90; Philip Foner, *History of the Labor Movement in the United States*, New York 1947, 1:469; Foster Rhea Dulles and Melvyn Dubofsky, *Labor in America: A History*, 4th ed., Arlington Heights, Ill. 1984, pp. 87–89.

2. Alexander Saxton, 'The Army of Canton in the High Sierra', *Pacific Historical Review* 25:141–52; Lucie Cheng and Edna Bonacich, eds, *Labor Immigration under Capitalism: Asian Workers in the United States before World War II*, Berkeley, Calif. 1984; see pp. 1–56 for an overview of the relations between industrializing capitalism and labor migration.

3. Saxton, *Indispensable Enemy*, pp. 17–20; Saxton, 'Race and the House of Labor', in Gary Nash and Richard Weiss, eds, *The Great Fear: Race in the Mind of America*, New York 1970, pp. 102–3, 107–11; David Montgomery, 'Gutman's Agenda for Future Historical Research', *Labor History* 29 (Summer 1988): 300–305.

4. Philip Taft, *Organized Labor in American History*, New York 1964, p. 301. For examples of early expressions of anti-Chinese hostility, see Hinton Halper, *The Land of Gold: Reality vs. Fiction*, Baltimore 1855, pp. 94–96; Samuel Colville, *San Francisco Directory and Gazeteer, 1856–1857*, San Francisco 1856, pp. *xxv*; resolution of the Miners' Union of Virginia City, Nevada, San Francisco *Alta California*, 17 June 1869; and Saxton, *Indispensable Enemy*, pp. 46–66.

5. Rodman Paul, *California Gold: The Beginning of Mining in the Far West*, Cambridge, Mass. 1947, pp. 349–50.

6. Stuart C. Miller, *The Unwelcome Immigrant: The American Image of the Chinese, 1785–1882*, Berkeley, Calif. 1974, pp. 3–141; Saxton, 'Historical Explanations of Racial Inequality', *Marxist Perspectives* (Summer 1979): 146–68.

7. San Francisco *Alta*, 6 September 1867.

8. Saxton, *Indispensable Enemy*, pp. 151–78.

9. Howard R. Lamar, *The Far Southwest, 1846–1912: A Territorial History*, New Haven, Conn. 1966, pp. 205–301; James Edward Wright, *The Politics of Populism: Dissent in Colorado*, New Haven, Conn. 1974; David Brundage, 'The Making of Working Class Radicalism in the West: Denver, 1880–1893', Ph.D. diss., University of California, Los Angeles, 1982; Sherburne F. Cook, *The Population of the California Indians*, Berkeley, Calif. 1976, pp. *xv–xvii*, 1–43; Robert F. Heizer and Alan F. Almquist, *The Other Californians: Prejudice and Discrimination under Spain, Mexico and the United States to 1920*, Berkeley, Calif. 1971, pp. 1–64; Woodrow W. Borah, 'The California Mission', and Sherburne F. Cook, 'The California Indian and Anglo–American Culture', in Charles Wollenberg, ed., *Ethnic Conflict in California History*, Los Angeles 1970, pp. 1–42; Robert V. Bruce, *1877, Year of Violence*, Indianapolis, Ind. 1959, pp. 220–23; Philip Foner, *The Great Labor Uprising of 1877*, New York 1977; John R. Commons et al., *History of Labor in the United States*, [1918–35] New York 1958, 2:185–91; Saxton, *Indispensable Enemy*, pp. 112–21.

10. Denver *Weekly Rocky Mountain News*, 25 July 1877, 1 August 1877.

11. P. Foner, *Labor Uprising*, pp. 192–201. William Gillette, *Retreat from Reconstruction, 1869–1879*, Baton Rouge, La. 1979, p. 348, quotes ex-President Grant, who, after recalling the outrage that had greeted every use of federal troops to protect blacks in the South, added: 'Now, however, there is no hesitation about exhausting the whole power of government to suppress a strike on the slightest intimation that danger threatens' [Grant to Daniel Ammen, 28 August 1877, in Ammen, *The Old Navy and the New*, Philadelphia 1891, pp.

537–38].

12. *Weekly Rocky Mountain News*, 'Sober Second Thoughts', 8 August 1877. On *The Nation* as mentor of Republican ideological adjustments to the railroad strikes of 1877 (and to the battle of Little Big Horn a year earlier), Richard Slotkin, *The Fatal Environment: The Myth of the Frontier in the Age of Industrialization, 1800–1890*, Middletown, Conn. 1985, pp. 477–98.

13. Wright, pp. 11–50; Brundage, 'Working Class Radicalism', pp. 14–49.

14. Wright, pp. 15–25; Brundage, 'Working Class Radicalism', pp. 20–43.

15. Saxton, *Indispensable Enemy*, pp. 113–37, 151–52; Ronald Takaki, *Strangers from a Different Shore*, Boston 1989, pp. 272–91.

16. Roy T. Wortman, 'Denver's Anti-Chinese Riot, 1880', *Colorado Magazine* 42 (Fall 1965): 275–76.

17. Jerome C. Smiley, *History of Denver: With Outlines of the Earlier History of the Rocky Mountain Country*, Denver 1901, p. 665; Wortman, 'Anti-Chinese Riot', pp. 275–91.

18. Wright, pp. 26–27; Denver *Labor Enquirer*, 21 April, and 5, 12 May 1883, quoted in Wright, p. 26.

19. Saxton, *Indispensable Enemy*, pp. 177–78.

20. Carey McWilliams, *North From Mexico*, [1948] Westport, Conn. 1968, pp. 162–88; Roger Daniels, *The Politics of Prejudice: The Anti-Japanese Movement in California and the Struggle for Japanese Exclusion*, New York 1968.

21. Gerald Jaynes, *Branches without Roots: Genesis of the Black Working Class in the American South, 1862–1882*, New York 1986, pp. 253–79; P. Foner, *History of the Labor Movement*, 1:338–48, 355–75; Philip Taft, *Organized Labor in American History*, New York 1964, pp. 52–67; Robert S. Starobin, *Industrial Slavery in the Old South*, New York 1970; David Montgomery, *Beyond Equality: Labor and the Radical Republicans, 1862–1872*, New York 1967, pp. 90–196, especially pp. 176–96.

22. Andrew C. Cameron, *The Address of the National Labor Congress to the Workmen of the United States*, Chicago 1867, in John R. Commons, ed., *A Documentary History of American Industrial Society*, New York 1958, 9:185–90; Commons, *History of Labor*, 2:29, 129–31; David Roediger, 'Ira Steward and the Anti-Slavery Origins of American Eight-Hour Theory', *Labor History* 27 (Summer 1986): 410–26; Eric Foner, *Politics and Ideology in the Age of the Civil War*, New York 1980, pp. 61–62; Celia Morris Eckhardt, *Fanny Wright: Rebel in America*, Cambridge, Mass. 1984, pp. 2, 88, 100–102. Henry Irving Tragle, ed., *The Southampton Slave Revolt of 1831: A Compilation of Source Material*, Amherst, Mass. 1971, pp. 104–14.

23. Charlotte Erickson, *American Industry and the European Immigrant, 1860–1885*, Cambridge, Mass. 1957, pp. 52–54, 126–27; Commons, ed., *Documentary History*, 9:185–87; P. Foner, *History of the Labor Movement*, 1:370–77, 396–97; Joseph Rayback, *A History of American Labor*, New York 1966, p. 116; Montgomery, *Beyond Equality*, pp. 21–24.

24. Saxton, *Indispensable Enemy*, pp. 273–278; John Higham, *Strangers in the Land*, New York 1963, pp. 12–157; Thomas F. Gossett, *Race: The History of an Idea in America*, New York 1965, pp. 287–309.

25. Jaynes, pp. 262–64; Philip Foner, *Organized Labor and the Black Worker, 1619–1973*, New York 1974, pp. 27–29.

26. Commons, ed., *Documentary History*, 9:250; P. Foner, *Organized Labor and the Black Worker*, pp. 30–46; Montgomery, *Beyond Equality*, pp. 191–92.

27. Forrest G. Wood, *Black Scare: The Racist Response to Emancipation and Reconstruction*, Berkeley, Calif. 1968, pp. 74–82; Sidney H. Kessler, 'The Organization of Negroes in the Knights of Labor', *Journal of Negro History* 37 (July 1952): 248–76, especially p. 250; Herbert Gutman, *Work, Culture and Society in Industrializing America: Essays in Working Class and Social History*, New York 1976, pp. 121–208.

28. Jacobus ten Broeck et al., *Prejudice, War and the Constitution: Causes and Consequences of the Evacuation of Japanese Americans in World War II*, Berkeley, Calif. 1968, Chapter 1; Rose Hum Lee, *The Chinese in the United States of America*, Hong Kong 1960, pp. 76–78, and references under 'Exclusion Acts', p. 453; Milton R. Konitz, *The Alien and the Asiatic in American Law*, Ithaca, N.Y. 1946, pp. 4, 11–12, 80–88; Ira B. Cross, ed., *Frank Roney, Irish Rebel and California Labor Leader*, Berkeley, Calif. 1931, pp. 226–67, 286–87; Melton A. McLaurin, 'The Racial Policies of the Knights of Labor and the Organization of Black

Workers', *Labor History* 17 (Fall 1976): 568–85.

29. P. Foner, *Organized Labor and the Black Worker*, pp. 27–29; John Swinton, *The New Issue: The Chinese American Question*, New York 1870; Gunther Barth, *Bitter Strength: A History of the Chinese in the United States*, Cambridge, Mass. 1964, pp. 197–208; Miller, *Unwelcome Immigrant*, pp. 175–90; P. Foner, *History of the Labor Movement*, 2:58–60, 204–5; David Montgomery, *The Fall of the House of Labor: The Workplace, the State and American Labor Activism, 1865–1925*, New York 1987, pp. 26–27, 107–9; Herbert Hill, 'Myth-Making as Labor History: Herbert Gutman and the United Mine Workers of America', *International Journal of Politics, Culture and Society* 2 (Winter 1988): 132–300, especially pp. 135–36, 147–68.

30. P. Foner, *Labor Uprising*; Taft, *Organized Labor*, pp. 68–83; Paul Avrich, *The Haymarket Tragedy*, Princeton, N.J. 1984, pp. 26–35.

31. Michael Rogin in John H.M. Laslett and Seymour M. Lipsett, eds, *Failure of a Dream? Essays in the History of American Socialism*, Garden City, N.Y. 1974, p. 148: 'The traditions of native American workers were agrarian and communal too. The American labor movement had historically aimed at independent producership, even land, for laborers. … This American working-class tradition culminated in the Knights of Labor.' On the Knights of Labor, Norman J. Ware, *The Labor Movement in the United States, 1860–1895: A Study in Democracy*, [1929] New York n.d.; P. Foner, *History of the Labor Movement*, 1:504–24; 2:47–170; Leon Fink, *Workingmen's Democracy: The Knights of Labor and American Politics*, Urbana, Ill. 1984; Montgomery, *Fall*, p. 199.

32. P. Foner, *1877*, p. 229; P. Foner, *Organized Labor and the Black Worker*, pp. 47–63; P. Foner, *History of the Labor Movement*, 1:433–38, 504–12; 2:47–55, 157, 166–68; Taft, *Organized Labor*, pp. 84–92, 97–106; Melton A. McLaurin, *The Knights of Labor in the South*, Westport, Conn. 1978; Peter J. Rachleff, *Black Labor in the South: Richmond, Virginia, 1865–1900*, Philadelphia 1984.

33. Lloyd Ulman, *The Rise of the National Trade Union*, Cambridge 1966, especially pp. 3–22, 308–26, 348–77; Philip Taft, *The AFL in the Time of Gompers*, New York 1957; Montgomery, *Fall*, pp. 44–57, 172.

34. Henry David, *The History of the Haymarket Affair*, New York 1963, especially pp. 139–60; Avrich, *Haymarket*, pp. 182–89, 402, 429–32; Ware, pp. 70–72, 285; P. Foner, *History of the Labor Movement*, 2:105, 187; Robert Ozanne, *A Century of Labor Management Relations at McCormick and International Harvester*, Madison, Wis. 1967, pp. 10–26.

35. Ulman, especially pp. 334–41; Maurice Neufeld, 'Realms of Thought and Organized Labor in the Age of Jackson', *Labor History* 10:5–43; Ozanne, pp. 15–23; David Brody, *The Steelworkers in America: The Non-Union Era*, Cambridge, Mass. 1960, pp. 53–59, 126, 134; Arthur G. Burgoyne, *The Homestead Strike of 1892*, [1893] Pittsburgh, Pa. 1979, pp. 41–132; Montgomery, *Fall*, pp. 36–41; Wright, *Politics of Populism*, pp. 178–80, 231–45.

36. Ulman, especially pp. 32–37, 375–76, 554–61.

37. Ibid., pp. 49–107, 155–73, 425–29; Saxton, *Indispensable Enemy*, pp. 238–40; Montgomery, on the rise of the International Association of Machinists, *Fall*, pp. 198–203, 210–11.

38. Ulman, pp. 118–24, 308–14, 484–85.

39. P. Foner, *History of the Labor Movement*, 2:168; Ulman, p. 19; Nick Salvatore, *Eugene V. Debs, Citizen and Socialist*, Urbana, Ill. 1982, pp. 132–40.

40. A famous example is the distance maintained by Gompers and leaders of the AFL and railroad brotherhoods from the American Railway Union during the Pullman strike: Salvatore, *Debs*, pp. 132–37.

41. Taft, *Organized Labor*, pp. 230, 606; Arthur Link, *Woodrow Wilson and the Progressive Era*, New York 1963, pp. 61, 63; Michael Rogin, 'Voluntarism: The Political Functions of an Anti-Political Doctrine', *Industrial and Labor Relations Review* 15:521–35; Marc Karson, *American Labor Unions and Politics, 1900–1918*, Boston 1958, pp. 19–21; Gwendolyn Mink, *Old Labor and New Immigrants in American Political Development: Union, Party and State, 1875–1920*, Ithaca, N.Y. 1986, pp. 51, 67, 95–96, 111–12.

42. Ulman, pp. 203–301, 341–48; Montgomery, *Fall*, for a discussion of 'operatives', pp. 112–70; and see pp. 105, 120, 156, 195.

43. Ulman, pp. 378–422.

44. Paul Crane and Alfred Larson, 'The Chinese Massacres', *Annals of Wyoming* 12:47–

55, 153–60; Union Pacific Coal Company, *History of the Union Pacific Coal Mines, 1868–1940*, Omaha, Neb. n.d., pp. 75–86; [Isaac H. Bromley], *The Chinese Massacre at Rock Springs, Wyoming Territory, September 2, 1885*, Boston 1885; Saxton, *Indispensable Enemy*, pp. 205–13.

45. Ibid., pp. 11, 18, 212–25; Montgomery, *Fall*, pp. 85–86.

46. Daniels, pp. 92–105; Saxton, *Indispensable Enemy*, pp. 226–228, 238–41, 249–53, 257, 265. For examples of anti-Mexican hostility as viewed from Denver: *Weekly Rocky Mountain News*, 25 July, 2, 15 August, 5 September 1877. In the autumn of 1880, the *Rocky Mountain Daily News* mounted a three-way campaign of invective against Chinese, Indians and African Americans: see 6–31 October 1880. On San Francisco as a union stronghold, see Michael Kazin, *Barons of Labor: The San Francisco Building Trades and Union Power in the Progressive Era*, Urbana, Ill. 1987, pp. 13–63.

47. Hill, 'Myth-Making', pp. 172–83; Montgomery, *Fall*, pp. 84–87; Takaki, *Strangers*, pp. 88–92.

48. Saxton, *Indispensable Enemy*, pp. 273–78; Mink, pp. 52, 67, 71–73, 97–100, 123–29.

49. American Federation of Labor, *Proceedings*, 1893, p. 73; 1894, p. 25; 1901, p. 22; P. Foner, *Organized Labor and the Black Worker*, pp. 66–69; Robert David Ward and William Warren Rogers, *Labor Revolt in Alabama: The Great Strike of 1894*, University, Ala. 1965, especially pp. 75–89; Hill, 'Myth–Making', p. 182.

50. P. Foner, *Organized Labor and the Black Worker*, pp. 64–102; Ira Berlin and Herbert Gutman, 'Natives and Immigrants, Free Men and Slaves: Urban Workingmen in the Antebellum American South', *American Historical Review* 88:1175–1200; Jaynes, pp. 255, 267–78; Marc Karson and Ronald Radosh, 'The American Federation of Labor and the Negro Worker, 1894–1949', in Julius Jacobson, ed., *The Negro and the Labor Movement*, Garden City, N.Y. 1968, pp. 155–87; Bernard Mandel, 'Samuel Gompers and the Negro Workers, 1886–1914', *Journal of Negro History* 40:34–60; Arthur Mann, 'Gompers and the Irony of Racism', *Antioch Review* 13:203–14; Montgomery, *Fall*, on exclusion of black workers from the AFL Machinists, pp. 198–201; Hill, 'Myth-Making', pp. 168–72; William Julius Wilson, *The Declining Significance of Race: Blacks and Changing American Institutions*, Chicago 1978, pp. 71–76.

51. As in the Danbury Hatters' and Buck's Stove Company cases, for example. See Dulles and Dubofsky, pp. 188–90.

52. Montgomery, *Fall*, p. 46; Mink, especially pp. 34–35, 40–42; Nell Irvin Painter, 'One or Two More Things About *The Fall of the House of Labor*', *Labor History* 30 (Winter 1989): 117–21.

14

Nationalizing the Western Hero

The construction of heroes is at the crux of the ideological process because fictional heroes act out, or *realize*, class relationships. One person's hero, in a divided society, is likely to be another's villain. And because class relationships change, both heroes and villains offer unstable images. They display something akin to a Doppler effect, depending on whether observers are moving toward them out of the past or away from them into the present or future. Thus the bourgeois revolutionary hero, wearing the promethean garb of a Colonel Manly in the prospect of 1787, may look more like Captain Ahab, or even Captain Bly, in the retrospect of 1877. Free Soil heroes, from their beginnings as yeoman or artisan understudies to bourgeois revolutionary heroes, may be no less ambiguous. While from the viewpoint of rebelling against a politics of deference, or that of over-throwing the Slave Power, they appear as liberators, their role with respect to Indians (and those empathetic to Indians) will be exactly opposite. Members of the newly forming industrial labor force, on the other hand, many of whom doubtless concurred in massacres of Indians, would increasingly perceive Free Soil heroes (the Indian killers John Chivington and John Evans, for example) as betrayers in the sense of defending class exploitation and special privilege. So long as such divergent views remain in flux, the class commitments of heroes must be debatable; and their identification and appraisal will correspond to political acts. To this extent, literature and popular culture comprise arenas of class conflict, within which the roles of class actors are not only adumbrated, but tried out and realized.

By the mid-1850s, certainly, Free Soil heroes had acquired an aura of historic achievement. Since heroic traits such as courage and grace under pressure are to some extent exportable across class lines, Free Soil heroes could transcend the mere acting out of class situations. They became

321

powerful advocates of particular values and understandings, seemingly autonomous contenders in the arena. Their autonomy was, of course, illusory; yet the illusion furnished a property to be contended for.

The Empire of Story Papers and Dime Novels

With the outbreak of the Civil War, the Free Soil hero graduated from artisan modes to become the chief commodity of a new industry geared to mass production and distribution of inexpensive reading matter, mostly fiction. Its leading entrepreneurs were not only successful business organizers, but highly political operators. They maintained a linkage to the Republican party comparable to that of the impresarios of blackface minstrelsy to the Jacksonian party.[1] That much is demonstrable from the evidence. More speculatively, I will go on to argue that, like the minstrels, they propagated themes that almost never opposed and often supported the ideological strategies of their favored party.

The industry referred to has usually been identified by its most famous product, the dime novel. This is misleading in two respects. Not all 'dime novels' sold for ten cents. And more important, the identification leaves out a major aspect of the industry, the story paper, which both preceded and outlived dime novels. The great firm of Beadle and Adams, traditionally viewed as the inventor of the dime novel, actually began as a periodical publisher and constantly experimented with story papers. During twenty-seven of the firm's forty-two years, it kept story papers in circulation that both reprinted old dime novels and tried out new ones prior to book publication.[2]

Story papers had their origin in the early 1840s. Copying the mass circulation technology of the penny press, they relied at first on English and European works, for which they paid no royalties. Rising enthusiasm for national literature, enhanced by the Texas and Oregon crises and the war against Mexico, probably reduced the profitability of imported literary products while widening the market for American writing, especially writing about the West. Travel accounts, biographies and frontier romances proliferated. The *Flag of Our Union*, founded at Boston in the first year of the Mexican War, and one of the two most popular pre–Civil War papers, reached an estimated circulation of 80,000 in the 1850s. Its principal competitor, the *New York Ledger*, surpassed it by the end of the decade. Such was the milieu in which the Free Soil hero spent his adolescence. By 1860 he was ready for Beadle and Adams and the dime novel.[3]

Erastus and Irwin Beadle grew up, appropriately, on the shores of Cooper's Lake Otsego. Their family background resembled that of the first wave of penny daily founders a generation and a half earlier. Artisans and yeomen, the Beadle forebearers had lived in the Massachusetts Bay colony in the seventeenth century and in the Connecticut Valley during the eighteenth. The grandfather, after fighting in the Revolution, migrated to upper New York state. That the father of Erastus and Irwin tried farming at several locations in New York and Michigan before settling at Cooperstown suggests that this branch of the family may have been more on the hardscrabble than the affluent side of yeomanry. Erastus served his apprenticeship as printer and stereotyper in Cooperstown, then moved with his younger brother Irwin, an apprentice bookbinder, to Buffalo, where they worked at their trades, opened a stationery store, and experimented with publishing books and periodicals. In Buffalo they teamed up with the Adams brothers, all three born in northern Ireland; the oldest, Robert, was a stereotyper.[4]

In 1856 the Beadle and Adams brothers transferred their as yet not very promising ventures to New York City. While they continued trying to get some sort of periodical into orbit, Irwin began printing paste-and-scissors songbooks, for which, at ten cents a copy, there appeared to be a lively market. In June 1860 came the first dime novel. This was Ann Stephens's *Malaeska: The Indian Wife of the White Hunter*, a romance serialized several years earlier in *The Ladies' Companion*. Stephens was by 1860 well-known as a story paper author and editor of women's periodicals. Apparently reinvigorated by its dime novel format, her novel took off to sales that eventually reached half a million. Soon after *Malaeska*, the Beadles made a second and decisive breakthrough. Their dime novel number 8, *Seth Jones; or, Captives of the Frontier* – in which a Yankee vernacular comic carries the prototypical Free Soil role backwards into the Revolutionary era – sold 40,000 copies within a few weeks of publication. Borrowing a technique already developed by story papers, Beadle and Adams bought up saturation advertising in the New York daily press. But story papers usually had well-known authors to advertise, whereas Edward S. Ellis, at the time of *Seth Jones*, was an unknown nineteen-year-old, Ohio-born schoolteacher. This impressively risky gamble paid off, and Ellis went on to write 150 novels for Beadle and Adams, as well as biographies of American heroes from Daniel Boone to Theodore Roosevelt.[5]

Shortly before these two bonanzas, the firm had established contact with a remarkable couple, also from Ohio, Metta and Orville Victor. Metta, a product of the Wooster (Ohio) Female Seminary, aspired to be a poet and novelist. Her husband, a graduate of the Norwalk (Ohio) Seminary and Theological Institute, had dabbled in journalism and the law. When they moved to New York, Metta took on part-time editing for Beadle and Adams, and Orville joined the firm as an editor in 1861. In that same year, Metta's novel, *Maum Guinea and Her Plantation 'Children'*;

or, Holiday Week on a Louisiana Estate. A Slave Romance, became something of a second *Uncle Tom's Cabin* and is said to have achieved sales of over 100,000 copies. *Maum Guinea* was the first of 105 assorted works produced by Metta Victor for Beadle and Adams. Her husband, Orville – described by Henry Nash Smith as displaying 'an almost seismographic intuition of the nature, degree, and direction of changes in popular taste' – presided as chief editor from 1861 until the firm closed its doors in 1897.[6]

Sales for the war years (a period not likely to be thought of as optimum for literary undertakings) totalled about 5 million. 'An audience for fiction had been discovered', according to Henry Nash Smith, 'that had not previously been known to exist. Beadle has some claim to rank among the industrial giants of his day. In his field, as an organizer and promoter of a basic discovery made by his predecessors, he was a figure comparable to Rockefeller or Carnegie.' During the last year of the war, apparently in some sort of trade-off with the nation's largest story paper, the *New York Ledger*, Beadle and Adams created a distribution apparatus, the American News Company, which not only maintained outlets in major cities but specialized in sales at railroad terminals and on the trains. American News reputedly placed a standing order of 60,000 for every Beadle and Adams title. Albert Johannsen, in his monumental study, *The House of Beadle and Adams*, lists 5,642 titles of novels and serials (not including an assortment of manuals, guides, cookbooks, anthologies, as well as songsters, political tracts and biographies). If we reduce the News Company's 60,000 by a perhaps realistic one-quarter, we arrive at a figure of approximately 254 million copies of fictional works published in thirty-eight years, roughly corroborating Smith's comparison.[7]

Writers on Beadle and Adams have remarkably little to say about the politics of the firm. Johannsen reports that Erastus Beadle was once a Democrat; that he had been an Abolitionist and had voted for James Birney of the Liberty party; and that later he supported the Republicans. After retirement, he returned to Cooperstown, built a house, and in 1892 ran (unsuccessfully) for Congress on the Republican ticket. If Erastus Beadle was ever a Democrat it must have been early in his career. Turning twenty-one in 1842, he could have voted for Birney only in 1844. Given the context of upper New York state in those decades, it seems improbable that he would have switched to the Democratic side *after* voting for Birney. What seems more likely is that, following a burst of adolescent enthusiasm for the Jacksonians, he converted to Abolitionism, used his first presidential vote for Birney, and then moved, perhaps by way of Free Soil, to the Republican party in 1856 or 1860. That much seems reasonably decisive.[8]

But it tells us nothing about the political orientation of the business firm. Nonetheless, there is sufficient indirect evidence to bring that orientation into focus. Beadle and Adams's first successful publishing venture was the series of *Dime Song Books* initiated by the younger brother, Irwin. The firm is known to have published 118 such books between 1858 and 1879. From these, Johannsen lists by title 6,600 songs, of which some 2,812 were duplicates, leaving a net publication of 3,788. Unionist- and Republican-oriented titles are strikingly evident. Songster number 15, for example – issued early in 1861 – contains 'America', 'American Boy', 'American Flag', 'American Volunteer', 'Battle Hymn', 'Flag of Our Union', 'Origin of Yankee Doodle', 'Our Flag', 'Star Spangled Banner', 'Unfurl the Glorious Banner', 'War Song', and 'Yankee Doodle'. Between 1861 and 1865 appear such titles as 'All Hail to Ulysses', 'John Brown Song', 'Dixie for the Union', 'It's All Up in Dixie', 'Jeff in Petticoats', 'Sherman's March to the Sea'; and in 1868, 'U.S. Grant', and 'U.S. Grant Is the Man'. Through the entire series patriotic favorites are frequently repeated. Thus, 'The Star Spangled Banner' appears in twelve songsters, 'America' and 'Unfurl the Glorious Banner' in eleven, 'Yankee Doodle' in nine, 'John Brown Song' (various versions), 'E Pluribus Unum', and 'Flag of Our Union' in six. What these titles convey is not merely an expression of unionism, but a partisan identification with Republican unionism that would have stirred negative vibrations in many unionists of Jacksonian background.[9]

Popular music during these decades formed a central part of family and small group entertainment (as distinct from commercial entertainment). In an earlier discussion of blackface minstrelsy I noted that the minstrel repertory (which was also mass-distributed in inexpensive pamphlets similar to the Beadle songsters) carried Democratic connotations so politically polarized that songs identified with minstrelsy would have been offensive to anti-slavery and especially to Republican audiences.[10] The relative absence of minstrel-identified songs, then, would serve as an additional test of Republican orientation.

Examination of the 3,788 song titles shows 111, or 2.9 percent, to have some minstrel association. The basis for identification is the presence of black vernacular in the title, or direct knowledge of the song's minstrel ambience. Among the 111, however, are several types that would have been exempted from anti-slavery and Republican hostility. These would include romantic songs in straight English ('Loch Lomond', Stephen Foster non-dialect ballads); vernacular songs sentimentally sympathetic to blacks ('Old Black Joe'); Negro hymns or spirituals; and finally and most important, minstrel vernacular songs in which the original meaning is negated or ridiculed. 'Cuffee's War Song', 'Freedom on the Old Plantation', ''Telligent Contraband', 'We's a Gwine to Fight' are titles suggesting the ideological thrust of such songs. I have not attempted to cull out these exempted categories because to do so accurately would require working from the lyrics rather than the titles, a task likely to take more time than it could be worth. What the evidence here can show, then, is that the musical repertory of minstrelsy – despite its enthusiastic reception by an enormous audience in America – has been largely excluded from the Beadle and Adams songbooks.[11]

I turn finally to a scattering of more direct evidence. The songster number 15 referred to above, in contrast to fourteen preceding dime songsters, carried the title *Dime Military Song Book*. A publication date of January 1861 places its appearance at least one month before Lincoln's inauguration and three months before Fort Sumter. To insert the word *military*, hinting at a likely necessity of war to defend the Union, would have tended at that early date to identify the publishers (and their prospective audience) with the more radical wing of the Republican party. The speed with which the firm converted its non-fiction list to the coming war conveys a similar impression. Already in 1860, *Victor Hugo's Letter on John Brown with Mrs. Ann S. Stephen's Reply* had come off the press, and by 1861 Beadle and Adams was marketing a drill book for squad and company together with soldiers' manuals and directories. Accounts of campaigns and reports by commanders followed; while a series of biographies of embattled Republicans (both capital *R* and small *r*) was rushed to publication.[12]

Orville Victor, who had become chief editor in 1861, found time to compose works on Garibaldi, Mad Anthony Wayne, Winfield Scott, George B. McClellan and Abraham Lincoln. Other authors, including the Ohio schoolteacher, Edward Ellis, produced lives of Kit Carson, John C. Frémont, Lafayette, Parson Brownlow 'and the Unionists of Tennessee', and Ulysses S. Grant. Victor also put together three volumes titled *Men of the Time*, comprising biographical sketches of loyal generals such as Halleck, Pope, Siegel, Kearney, Butler, Banks, and Burnside. Metta Victor had written *Maum Guinea*, and in 1861 Beadle and Adams's London branch published Orville Victor's book-length essay, *The American Rebellion: Some Facts and Reflections for Consideration of the English People*. Henry Ward Beecher, sent by Lincoln in 1863 to woo the Palmerston cabinet, reportedly told Victor afterwards that his 'little book and Mrs. Victor's novel were a telling series of shots in the right spot.'[13] Going far beyond what would have been necessary to establish a decent Unionism, these activities and enterprises place Beadle and Adams conspicuously on the Republican side.

Before turning to the more speculative problem of classifying themes, it may be helpful to examine Johannsen's biographical listing of Beadle and Adams authors. By eliminating pseudonyms and by culling out authors deceased before the advent of story papers, or living abroad, or contributing only one title to Beadle and Adams publications, I have narrowed the list to a working group of 92. Collectively, they contributed 4,980 titles, averaging 54 per author. These were the creators of story paper and dime novel literature. Fourteen were women. Seventy-two percent were natives of New England, New York state and the Old Northwest, 8 percent came from Middle Atlantic states and 10 percent from the South. Exactly half had been born during the two decades 1830–1849, with another 23 percent born before 1830. Ninety-four percent of these contributors pursued middle-class professional occupations (writer, editor, teacher, lawyer, doctor, clergyman) while about 4 percent were in various businesses. At least two-thirds appear to have been full-time writers or writer-editors. Sixty percent came from professional or business families, 23 percent from farmer or worker-artisan families.[14]

Because Johannsen's list shows a wide variation in the numbers of credited titles, a separation of the ninety-two was made at 50 titles. This resulted in two subgroups: one of 23 'Regular Contributors', accounting for 83 percent of all titles and averaging 179 titles apiece; and the other of 69 'Occasional Contributors', who averaged 12.5 titles and accounted for 17 percent of all titles. Both subgroups exhibit patterns of regional nativity and professional occupations almost identical to those of the original 92 authors. Beyond these similarities are several striking differences. Only one woman appears among 'Regular Contributors'. Seventy percent of 'Regulars', compared with only 44 percent of the the 'Occasionals', were born during the decades 1830–1849. Among 'Regulars', 87 percent appear to have been full-time writers or writer-editors, among 'Occasional Contributors' only 59 percent. As to family background, 57 percent of the 'Regulars' came from business-professional families, 30 percent from farmer or worker-artisan families. Comparable ratings for the 'Occasional Contributors' were 61 and 20 percent.[15]

The relative absence of women among 'Regular Contributors' probably indicates that since women were more likely to write in the 'domestic/melodrama' category, they were less likely to be published by Beadle and Adams with its heavy emphasis on 'masculine' themes.[16] The chief importance of decades of nativity is that for those born between 1830 and 1849, the height of their careers would have coincided with the heyday of Beadle and Adams (1861–85); and it may also be significant that such writers would have spent the formative years of childhood and adolescence during the ascendancy of the Jacksonian party. That a high percentage of 'Regulars' should be described as 'full-time writers or writer-editors' needs no explanation; it may seem surprising, however, that the same description reaches as high as 59 percent among 'Occasional Contributors'. What this statistic most clearly signals is that many 'Occasional Contributors' to Beadle and Adams were frequent contributors to other publishing houses. The 41 percent remainder suggests that a significant number of professional people (teachers, lawyers, doctors, actors) wrote serials and dime novels on the side, whereas few farmers or worker-artisans did likewise.

To sum up: the crucial perception that emerges from these statistics is that the story paper-dime novel industry had called into existence a new specialization and that full-timers within this specialization produced the vast majority of work published by the industry. Regionally, these full-timers came almost entirely from north of the Mason-Dixon line with a heavy concentration from New England, upper New York state and the Old Northwest. They were totally professionalized into the middle class. A majority had grown up in business-professional families; but for a substantial minority (30 percent among 'Regulars') story paper and dime novel writing had provided a route from farmer-artisan backgrounds into the professional middle class. Merle Curti many years ago described dime novels as the only genuine 'proletarian' literature. He was certainly correct that story papers and dime novels were aimed at, and extensively read by, the lower classes of post–Civil War America. Among authors of this literature, the upwardly mobile 30 percent were like the first wave of penny daily editors, whose egalitarian rhetoric directly expressed their own class antagonisms and aspirations. The remaining 70 percent must increasingly have resembled later mass circulation daily editors in that they would be obliged to dissemble their actual class status in the interest of egalitarian discourse.[17]

If, as suggested at the outset of this section, the Free Soil hero became the chief commodity of the story paper-dime novel industry, it would follow that egalitarian discourse and Indian killing would furnish central themes for that literature. Thanks to the groundwork laid down by Albert Johannsen, this proposition can be tested quantitatively. The attached table shows percentages of Beadle and Adams serials and dime novels arranged under ten thematic classifications by publication date, within half decades. The bottom line sets out corresponding percentages of the firm's total output. Classifications 1, 2 and 4 (*Colonial; Revolution, Indian-Related; Western Adventure, Indian-Related*) include all works dealing directly with Indian conflict. Together these headings account for 26 percent of total output, exceeding any other single classification except 5 (*Western Adventure Other than Indian-Related*), which it equals. This latter, dealing mainly with conflict among whites in the West, represents the major locus of egalitarian discourse. Thus the themes of Indian killing and egalitarianism outweigh all other themes and collectively make up 52 percent of the entire product – and the reach of these themes goes far beyond this limited statistic.[18]

Comparison of percentages by half-decades shows that classification 4

BEADLE AND ADAMS BOOKS AND SERIALS: THEMES BY HALF-DECADES, 1859–1900

| Half-Decades Ending | Colonial pre–1775 | Revolution 1775–1790 | | Frontier & Western Post–1790 | | Mexican War | Civil War & Slavery | Sea | Domestic & Melodrama | Detective | Totals |
	1	2 (Indian-Related)	3 (Other)	4 (Indian-Related)	5 (Other)	6	7	8	9	10	
I 1860	2	1	3	1	3	3	0	0	11	0	24
II 1865	18	2	16	32	14	4	20	7	13	0	125
III 1870	38	11	25	119	32	4	2	27	45	0	303
IV 1875	29	12	19	227	59	11	1	29	97	5	489
V 1880	25	10	25	226	175	11	23	69	310	22	896
VI 1885	39	10	30	312	390	15	2	140	499	116	1553
VII 1890	13	3	19	209	385	7	2	107	132	271	1148
VIII 1895	4	1	3	91	298	2	3	44	75	316	837
IX 1900	0	0	1	22	116	1	2	26	21	78	267
Totals	168	50	141	1238	1472	58	55	449	1203	808	5642
Percent	3	1	3	22	26	1	1	8	21	14	100

SOURCE: Compiled from Albert Johannsen, *The House of Beadle and Adams and Its Dime and Nickle Novels: The Story of a Vanished Literature*, Norman, Okla. 1950–62, vol. 1.

(*Western Adventure, Indian-Related*) predominated from 1861 through 1880. During the next half decade, classification 5 (*Western Adventure Other than Indian-Related*) moved ahead and subsequently increased its lead until termination of the firm in 1897. This shift, perceived by dime novel readers as well as literary historians, has usually been explained as reflecting the recession of Indian warfare into a historical past.[19] Yet since both historically and fictionally, Indian warfare had set the stage for what followed, it tended to be incorporated into the given *present* of fictions. Most commonly this was done by identifying heroes in post-Indian adventure as former Indian fighters. Their adversaries – like fictional Indians – would then become enemies of civilization; while a presumed continuity might be underlined by providing villains with south-of-the-border complexions and Spanish surnames.[20]

Even more than Indian killing, the egalitarian theme overlaps classifications. When Merle Curti, in the same essay in which he characterized dime novels as 'proletarian', argued that the spirit of those novels was best expressed by their understanding of the American Revolution as a 'social struggle' against the 'overlordship of feudal masters',[21] he might more accurately have proposed that dime novel authors themselves tended to reduce most of their fictions to the ideological dimensions of the 1830s and 1840s. Not only the colonial period and the Revolution, but the Republican era and the organizing of the West were repeatedly conceptualized in dime novels in terms of conflicts between fraternal egalitarianism on one hand and social hierarchy and deference on the other. Since classlessness was perceived, Jacksonian style, as the American norm, deviations from that norm would have to be attributed to vestiges of the feudal past or to alien intrusions. The pervasiveness of metaphors from the 1830s and 1840s thus helped to obscure class divisions arising out of industrialization, for which perhaps both authors and publishers of dime novels were not eager to find vivid fictional expression.[22]

The table indicates that Beadle and Adams, successful though they certainly were in raising productivity, favored repetition over ideological innovation. The thematic classifications were arrived at descriptively from summaries of early novels. To the original nine classifications a tenth was added to provide separate housing for detective stories, which appear only after 1875 but make no significant entry until the last half of the 1880s. Not only do these ten classifications accommodate the entire output across four decades, but their percentages of distribution remain relatively constant. War, for example (except wars against Indians), never commanded much interest. Most popular of wars was the Revolution, which takes in at most 4 percent of total output, and drops from a high of 17 percent in the first half decade (when total output was only 24) to a vanishing point in later half decades. One might have supposed that the

Mexican and Civil wars would have drawn exceptional attention. Taken together – and even with the topics of slavery and anti-slavery thrown in – they account for less than 2 percent of total output. In this case they begin with a high of 21 percent for the first half decade (1861–1865) when Beadle and Adams's list of titles was at its shortest and war interest presumably maximized. In the next five years they dropped below 2 percent and never subsequently climbed as high as 4 percent. Great silences – like those earlier noted as characteristic of the Free Soil hero – appear to have attained the rigidity of taboo in dime novels and serials. Not only were there few novels about wars; almost none dealt with slavery or its aftermath. Metta Victor's 1861 best-seller, *Maum Guinea*, unlike the Leatherstocking-Daniel Boone combination, generated no progeny.

The ninth classification, *Domestic Romance and Melodrama*, becomes something of a catch-all in that it provides space for adventures elsewhere than on the American continents or at sea; however, these are not very numerous. For the most part, classification 9 contains stories of love, sex and family life, many authored by women. Such topics provided profitable enterprise for other publishers. Beadle and Adams made serious efforts to break into this market, especially during the decade 1876–1885, which accounts for an abrupt rise and fall in the percentages. Perhaps the statistic marks an effort at innovation that failed because the firm was already typecast in the minds of authors and readers by its previous successes.

Aside from the short-lived flurry of domestic romances, there are only two large deviations from the pattern of stable percentage distributions. The first is the shift from *Western Adventure, Indian-Related* to *Western Adventure Other than Indian-Related*. The second is the proliferation of detective stories after 1885. These two trends are interconnected. Detectives seldom penetrated into western adventure that involved Indians, but they swarmed into post-Indian adventures. The *Western* and *Detective* classifications for this reason overlap through the 1880s and 1890s, many detective stories being simultaneously westerns.

The detective has puzzled students of dime novels. Sometimes this puzzlement conveys a note of resentment as if detectives were to be blamed for bringing an end to the golden age of the genre.[23] Coping with the detective may be especially troublesome in connection with efforts to track the course of the western hero. In dime novels about the West, the detective appears as an intruder, an importation from the urban East, suggesting mechanical imitation rather than spontaneity. Unlike the earlier Kit Carson heroic types, the detective has no intrinsic or necessary connection with western history. His function is anomalous. His presence seems even to deny the concept of ideological innovation. My purpose in stating these problems is to set them in place for the next section. Here it will be sufficient to point out that the advent of the detective helped to dissipate a flaw entailed by history upon the western hero – his lower-class origin. Detectives are expert in disguise. Seth Jones, earliest of dime novel heroes, also practiced disguise. But disguise for Seth Jones served the same purpose it had for James Fenimore Cooper, that of an upper-class ploy to preserve aristocratic privilege while shuffling off its disabilities in an increasingly egalitarian society. Detective disguises may serve an opposite purpose. It is the detective's ability to manipulate disguises that enables him to instill respect and fear in upper-class associates. To be able to assume a class role is to be able to wield the authority of that class. The same ability precludes inquiry into the class origin of the detective. When class origin becomes unknowable it ceases to be worth investigating. Whereas Seth Jones's (and Cooper's) disguise reaffirmed class power, the disguises of the detective seem to short-circuit it. Thus the detective acts out a dream of Jacksonian yeomen and artisans: the dream of being self-made.

I am not pretending to exhaust the ideological significance of the detective within a discussion of western heroes. A symbolic figure somehow churned up from the mass cultures of nineteenth-century industrializing societies, the detective carries multiple meanings as well as disguises.[24] He had established himself in European and urban American literature before he moved west. Yet it should not be necessary to defend his legitimacy in dime novels. Certainly he had as much right to ply his trade in the American West as anywhere else.

From Seth Jones to the Virginian

'Howsumever, that don't make no difference, whether it's the Mohawks, Oneidas, or any of them blasted Five Nations niggers. They are all a set of skunks. ... There ain't any difference atwixt 'em.' This is Edward Ellis's Seth Jones speaking in his overt role as Yankee vernacular and frontier Indian hunter. But Jones (more than Leatherstocking) is also a master of men. He knows how to read the motives of others without revealing his own: '... a countenance ... made expressly to vail his soul, his very looks were deceptive; and when he chose to play a certain *role*, he could do it to perfection.' Later, Jones chooses to unveil the source of his mastery. Far from being an ignorant frontiersman, he is a man of established property, able to use language 'such as none but a scholar and polished gentleman would use.'[25]

Why would Ellis in 1860 construct his first novel around this antiquated plot device? A not unreasonable answer might be that it expressed the same class values for Ellis that it had for Cooper. There are clues (not exactly evidence) pointing in this direction. Among many pseudonyms of his prolific authorship, Ellis sometimes used the name 'James Fenimore Cooper Adams'. He returned in one of his last books to the notion of an upper-class hero disguised in frontier garb. That book was a biography of Theodore Roosevelt published in 1906.[26]

Cooper probably could never have tolerated the Free Soil alliance. Ellis, born half a century after Cooper, devoted much of his career to the ideological legitimation of the alliance, and of the Republican party which grew out of it. That the plot device used in his first novel negated Free Soil aspirations may not have been apparent either to Ellis or his readers, since the novel contained ample resources of narrative and vivid dialogue to account for its popular success with or without the plot device. Nonetheless, Ellis afterwards labored, systematically it would seem, at constructing a hero whose mastery of men could be attributed to causes other than surreptitious upper-class origin.[27]

The implications of this problem already have been examined under the aspects of fictional credibility and class relationship. It may be helpful here to review them in their political context. Whigs struggling against ascendant Jacksonians in the early 1830s had toyed with the project of a western lower-class alliance through the *persona* of David Crockett, which they had partially created; but bona fide Whigs were obviously incapable of carrying through such a stratagem. Instead, they brought forward William Henry Harrison, an upper-class hero in frontier disguise. The odor of hypocrisy attaching to that campaign helped destroy the Whig party. Crockett's story ran counter to Harrison's in the sense that Crockett had been born in a log cabin rather than simply pretending to live in one; and so in the same sense did Abraham Lincoln's. The transit of Free Soil and early Republicanism, then, might be summarized as a shift from reliance on upper-class leaders in disguise to the acceptance of leaders born in real log cabins whose western and lower-class origins gave them the necessary credentials for cementing cross-class cooperation against the planter class in the South.

In real history, Lincoln had acted out this role to the ultimate detail. Studying surveyors' geometry and Blackstone by the light of the log cabin fireplace, he remade himself from a frontier squatter into a Whig lawyer. He wooed and won an upper-class wife. He evoked acceptance and confidence that brought him to the head of a coalition of frontiersmen, farmers, artisans, merchants, industrialists. Yet Lincoln never became a saleable commodity for the story paper–dime novel industry. After Orville Victor's biography in 1864, Lincoln's name vanishes from Beadle and Adams title lists. It might be said that assassination, raising Lincoln's story to the realm of the sacred, rendered it inappropriate as mass entertainment. Yet in view of the sanctifying roles often assigned in dime novels to Revolutionary leaders or to pioneers like Daniel Boone and Kit Carson, this argument seems not altogether persuasive. The real reasons, I think, were more directly political. When he studied to be a Whig lawyer, Lincoln turned backward and eastward. The apex of his early career had been opposition to the war against Mexico. Although as president he signed into law the Homestead and Transcontinental Railway acts, he remained more closely linked to the whiggish eastern past of his new party than to its western and empire-building future. Perhaps most detrimental of all – since Indian killing was a definitive (one might almost say *guaranteeing*) characteristic of the Free Soil hero – Lincoln had shirked his opportunity in the Blackhawk War to become an Indian killer himself.[28]

Edward Ellis's legitimizing efforts took the form of hundreds of fictional projections and a smaller number of biographies, presumably direct statements of his theme. His selection of biographical subjects – reflecting the silences and taboos that governed the story paper–dime novel industry as a whole – included Daniel Boone, David Crockett and Kit Carson; but not Lincoln.[29] Like Lincoln, these three had all been born in log cabins and studied assiduously to make themselves masters of men. There the similarities ended. Giving short shrift to books, the three pursued their studies by absorbing the lessons of nature; mastery they studied through hunting animals and men. Since Ellis scarcely touched their sexual relations, it remains unclear whether or not he attributed to them upward mobility in marriage. What is clear, however, is that they had achieved self-educations presumably as good as any to be had in academies and colleges. The lives they chose in the West permitted them to become what nature intended them to be – natural aristocrats. As Ellis wrote of Boone,

> ... in the grand school of nature was the great pioneer trained. While yet a boy, he became noted for his unerring aim with the rifle, and the skill with which he read the 'signs' among the trees that were as closed volumes to others. ... It is in just such nurseries as this that the great explorers and pioneers of the world are educated.[30]

Ellis also makes clear that Leatherstocking's exasperating habit of finding in the perfection of the wilderness an accusation against the imperfections of society has long since been extirpated. Ellis's 'grand school of nature' teaches the course of empire. When Crockett, rejected by a political system not yet ready for him, returns to the West to aid his fellow countrymen in Texas, he is going to a destiny for which the school of nature had prepared him. Mexicans, in Ellis's Texas, are cruel and perfidious. And again the studied silences: there is no reference to slavery in the long chapter on Texas and the Alamo. Thus Ellis can end his biography of Crockett (published in 1884) on a note approaching cosmic optimism:

Today Texas is one of the most brilliant stars in the grand constellation of the Union … with a steady stream of immigration converging from all parts of the world, with her vast prairies, her rivers, her streams, her enterprises, her history, her sacred memories and her teeming future, Texas is indeed the *Coming Empire*.[31]

Beadle and Adams's best five years were 1881–1885. Already by the 1880s the old calling of scout and Indian fighter had become largely a matter of role playing. This was the historical context within which miners, detectives and cowboys encroached on Indian fighters in the story paper–dime novel literature. Certainly miners and cowboys had a historical base in the real world. Miners had been conspicuous in the West since the California Gold Rush. They entered western romance in the early 1850s as prospectors and gold panners. By the 1880s, perhaps more in fact than in fiction but to a substantial degree in both, miners were laboring in deep quartz mines as industrial wage earners. Cowboys likewise had an industrial connection. Spreading north from Texas in the wake of the Great Plains wars and destruction of the buffalo herds, the cattle industry had reached Montana and the Dakotas by the late 1880s. The earliest dime novel cowboy hero dates from 1887, but cowboys had played lesser roles long before that.[32]

Detectives preceded cowboys in story papers and dime novels by about a decade. Their real prototypes seem to have been investigators for the Treasury and the military. Fictionally they might be identified simply as 'Government Agents', although their official duties, however those may have been described, seldom impinged on their fictional tasks. Historically, of course, detectives, like miners and cowboys, had industrial connections. Railroads hired detectives; and by the 1880s it was no secret that Pinkertons and others like them were widely employed by private corporations.[33]

Yet detectives, in the West at least, could not have been nearly as visible as miners and cowboys. Why did they cut such a swathe in dime novels? 'The introduction of characters described as cowboys', Henry Nash Smith wrote in *Virgin Land*, 'is little more than an effort to achieve an air of contemporaneity. It does not change the shape of Wild Western fiction.'[34] The same observation would apply as well to miners, but not to detectives. Detectives, then, must have served a different literary purpose from miners and cowboys. An argument was put forward in the preceding section that the 'shape of Wild Western ficton' – taken roughly to mean the western adventure segment of story paper–dime novel publication – was determined by the ideological characteristics of the Free Soil hero. Because Indian killing was the definitive characteristic, heroes had generally been portrayed as scouts and Indian fighters. With the recession of Indian warfare, and partial replacement of Indian fighters by miners and cowboys, a credibility gap opened between the occupational activities of such characters and the tasks that western heroes were expected to perform.

If Indians were in short supply, it might be possible, temporarily at least, for Mexicans or very bad white men to be cast as the enemies of civilization; but whose business was it, in the laissez-faire society of the new West, to pursue and destroy such enemies? The notion of detective, if left sufficiently fuzzy, could meet this need; whence, I think, both the profusion of western detectives and their interbreeding with miners and cowboys – sometimes even with former Indian fighters. Two classic dime-novel characterizations, Deadwood Dick and Buffalo Bill, illustrate these sequences. Deadwood Dick, embittered by betrayal in love, becomes the leader of a band of Robin Hood–like outlaws; however he also pursues mining with such success as to be able to live on income from his claims, while devoting full time to the adventurous and demanding masquerades of a detective. Buffalo Bill Cody began in the old style as scout, pony express rider, Indian fighter and professional buffalo hunter. Then came a bifurcation of the real from the fictional. While Buffalo Bill himself went on to become a rancher and impresario of Indian-shooting and cow-boy-riding wild west shows, his fictional counterpart enacts the hero's role in countless cowboy, detective and Indian-fighting serials and dime novels.[35]

Buffalo Bill's fictional *persona* was put in orbit by one of the greatest of story paper–dime novel authors, E.Z.C. Judson ('Ned Buntline'), whose pseudobiography, *Buffalo Bill: The King of the Border Men*, brilliantly epitomizes the ideological messages of Free Soil heroes in post–Civil War western romance. Buntline's account opens with the Cody family at evening prayer in their Kansas frontier log cabin. Shouts are heard outside, the father steps to the door to be shot down by Missouri border ruffians who curse him for a 'black-hearted nigger worshipper'. His son Bill, twelve years old, vows vengeance against the killers. With the outbreak of the Civil War, Bill enlists in the Union Army as a scout, and the border ruffians go with the southern side. Most of the action consists in captures and rescues of female members of the Cody household – the widowed mother, the two beautiful sisters and Kate Muldoon, their loyal Irish servant girl. Since the border ruffians are not only Confederates but allies of Indians, their carrying off of females is equivalent to Indian captivity. Buffalo Bill and his fellow scouts travel all the way to Montana to liberate their women from the Sioux. Indians, slaughtered in vast numbers, appear numerically as the main enemy; but the most dangerous, of course, are the white renegades who mastermind these Indian depredations.[36]

Literary antecedents of the Free Soil hero have been solidly anchored by the log cabin opener. Subsequently, Buntline permits the cabin to become a white farm house, presided over rather elegantly by the widowed mother. The addition of the Irish housemaid and of equally loyal hired hands (one white, three black) whose duties appear to be those of cowboys, tends to obscure the class status of the household.[37] Buffalo Bill meanwhile is presented as a straight hero – he is young, handsome, and speaks correct English; yet he points back to vernacular beginnings by occasional turns of speech such as those contained in his description of his horse, Powder Face: 'Isn't he a rare insect? He can run ten hours and never flag, swim any current this side of the big hills, and he knows as much as I do about hide and seek.'[38]

Early vernaculars, on stage and in fiction, had emphasized regional differences. One of the effects of their work, however, when disseminated through mass media of entertainment like the penny press, blackface minstrelsy and story paper–dime novel publications, was to homogenize and nationalize vernacular speech. Each idiosyncrasy became common property. Given the spread of public education, upon which the mass media rested, it would then be possible to select vernacular phrases in the same way that similes or metaphors might be selected. Language became a matter of choice rather than necessity and could be used for disguise as well as self-revelation. In western adventure fiction this process reached a culmination with the detective and cowboy heroes. Buffalo Bill's language thus prepares the way for the obligatory scene that has been flickering in and out of the genre since its beginnings in the 1840s.

The young scout's military duties have taken him to St. Louis, where he rescues a pretty teenage girl from drunken soldiers. The girl's father turns out to be a Unionist banker and former acquaintance of Bill's father. In his gratitude the banker invites Bill into the family home:

> 'I dare not, sir', said Bill and his voice trembled as he spoke.
> 'Dare not ... ?'
> 'If I see *her* any more, I shall love her, and love above my station would be madness and folly', said Bill bluntly, and with that sense of honor which was part of his nature.[39]

When the banker offers to procure an officer's commission from General Frémont, Bill replies that he had rather remain an ordinary soldier with his group of scouts. Nonetheless, it is clear that the banker has accepted Bill's right to woo a young woman of the upper class; the two are betrothed and marry at the end of the war.[40]

This scene, so many times repeated, marks the triumph of the western hero. He has evolved from *regional* to *western* to *national*. Nationalization, the last step, expresses not so much a final de-regionalizing of the hero as the *westernizing* of national identity. Meanwhile, a parallel sequence has liberated the hero from the disabilities attached to class. It is not that lower-class origin has been denied, but that equal access to privileges of the upper class, including acquisition of wealth and marriageability, has been triumphantly vindicated. Both regional and class transformations appear most clearly through language. Regional peculiarities of the early vernacular comics have coalesced into a standard western speech which still retains certain vernacular turns of phrase. Regionally, these are no longer parochialisms; and in terms of class, they now serve, not invidiously as indices of lower-class origin, but affirmatively as declarations of the inconsequentiality of class in America.

The western hero, having begun his journey as a yeoman or artisan, has arrived at a destination from which class origin can appear inconsequential. Yet this symbolic journey now stands in contradiction to the actual experience of a segment of the labor force, since, after 1877, class could hardly have seemed inconsequential to most industrial workers. Industrial conflict introduced a temporary faltering or loss of nerve to the western hero's commitments. Deadwood Dick, most famous of dime novel western heroes, exemplifies this ambiguity in several of his adventures. In *Deadwood Dick on Deck* (1878), he brings his burgeoning talents for disguise to the aid of a vernacular hero, Colonel Tubbs, hard-pressed by the machinations of a Jay Gould–like capitalist. Eventually the eastern intruder is brought to account for various crimes such as forgery, embezzlement, arson and murder. These can be dealt with simply enough; but the capitalist has tempted Colonel Tubbs with hints that he might triple his mining profits by incorporation, squeezing out leaseholders and paying his hired labor at the lowest possible rates. To which the Colonel replies:

> '... Mebbe you cum from out in Pennsylvania whar they do thet kind o' playin', stranger, but et's most orful sure that ye kent play sech a trick out hyar among the horny-fisted galoots o' this delectable Black Hills kentry. ... '[41]

Tubbs's egalitarian rhetoric, which Deadwood Dick apparently endorses, serves to emphasize the fact that the capitalist's proposals – far from being criminal – are precisely those that upwardly mobile Free Soil heroes like Tubbs and Deadwood Dick ought to be demanding the right to engage in. 'Ha! ha! you are quite a workingman's enthusiast, I see, Colonel Tubbs [says the villainous easterner], but that is because you are unsophisticated yet. ... '[42]

That was in 1878. Ten years later, in an adventure subtitled *The Anarchist's Daughter*, Deadwood Dick arrives in Chicago as a successful western detective assigned to help Chicago's police chief during the difficult days that followed the Haymarket bombing. Dick infiltrates a working-class saloon thought to be the anarchists' headquarters. His blunt western speech rouses their suspicions. Questioned as to whether he believes in defending the rights of labor, he responds:

> Not insofar as committing murder is concerned! ... We Americans don't believe in that sort of cowardly and barbarous thing. It is only the foreign element, who can't get along in their own country, that come over here with the idea that they can run and regulate matters pretty much as they please.[43]

Slugged from behind, the detective is imprisoned in a backroom of the saloon. The 'anarchist's daughter' (who turns out of course not to be an anarchist's daughter at all) sets him free. She complains to Dick that her supposed father has forced her to work in a garment factory; and bitterly complains of the exploitation of factory workers. 'I do see that the rich are made so by the incessant toil, small wages, great privation ... of the workers; ... it is utterly impossible for the workers to educate their children, who, like themselves, must therefore remain the slaves of toil – the serfs of the men of money.'[44] Dick lends credence to this accusation by giving it sympathetic attention; just as, in the earlier adventure, he had identified with the egalitarian viewpoint set forth by Colonel Tubbs. This drift toward social criticism is quickly closed off, however; and through the remainder of the novel the detective unravels a gothic plot in which master criminals use the radicals and anarchists as foils or dupes in their effort to steal the fortune of a benevolent industrialist. At this level, Haymarket and its aftermath simply provide an opportunistic setting for conventional melodrama. Yet the setting cannot remain totally negligible given the admission into the text of accusations like the one above.

The problem of labor exploitation in a land of equal rights also claimed the attention of Frederick Whittaker, among Beadle and Adams authors probably the closest to Merle Curti's ideal of the 'proletarian' dime novelist. Whittaker specialized in rags-to-riches stories of artisans moving upward, through their own ability and courage, into management, or even entrepreneurship. Whittaker's heroes are quick to defend the dignity of manual toil, and one at least – Larry Locke the ironworker – proudly proclaims membership in the Knights of Labor.[45] Like the Deadwood Dick episodes, these fictions seem to be asserting that although labor exploitation does exist in America, the free play of competitive egalitarianism can be relied on to set it right. Thus Whittaker's 'Journeyman John', carpenter and woodcarver, treasures the gospel received in childhood from an Irish-immigrant school teacher:

> In the Old World ... a man may fail through no fault of his own. They have classes there. In America it is different. One man is as good as another. ... Learn all you can and then make up your mind to aim high. There is nothing a man cannot do in this country if he tries hard enough.[46]

True Americans, grasping this truth, would rise above doctrines of class antagonism.

Yet traces of class resentment break the surface. When Deadwood Dick attempts to bring the 'anarchist's daughter' around to a proper American viewpoint, she tells him, 'I might be a poor working girl, but I think my industry and service ought to receive better pay than it has received.' The author comments: 'For a moment Dick felt lost; he hardly expected this kind of retort.'[47] Describing 'Journeyman John's' employer (a Chicago manufacturer whose daughter will subsequently become John's wife), Whittaker wrote: 'There was something in the old man's face now as insincere in its bland smoothness as it had been disagreeable when he had last seen it in anger. Then it wore the hard, pitiless selfishness of the millionaire; ... Now it was covered with the mask of courtesy, a smile on the close-shaven lips, stretching out to the mutton-chop whiskers ... over which the cold gray eyes looked like wells of selfishness. ... '[48]

Whittaker, like Edward Wheeler, was an easterner who mythologized the West. Both were among the twenty-three 'Regular Contributors' in the tabulation of Beadle and Adams authors. Available biographical information places Wheeler among that one-third of 'Regular Contributors' who came of 'farmer/worker artisan' background. Whittaker, English-born, was the son of a law clerk (Melville's 'scrivener' comes to mind) who had migrated to New York in 1850 to escape debtor's prison. Perhaps these two authors were unusually sensitive to the experiences of working men.[49] This could be understood, on one hand, as distancing them from 'typical' dime novel authors; or, on the other, as opening their work to perceptions of the subject matter that would be less readily available to their colleagues.

Chicago, new industrial metropolis and railroad gateway to the West, provided a battleground of the imagination for the rites of passage of western heroes. In 1894 Frederic Remington covered the Pullman strike in Chicago for *Harper's Weekly*. Remington, from Ogdensburg, New York, was a connoisseur of western heroes. Finding Chicago 'under the mob', he rejoiced to see the clean young soldiers from the West making camp along the lakeshore. Remington sketched them as they patrolled the railroad yards and pushed back the 'malodorous crowd of anarchistic foreign trash. ... The soldier mind doesn't understand this Hungarian, or Pollack, or whatever the stuff is', Remington wrote; and by way of caption to his drawing of a striker downed by a soldier's rifle butt, he wrote, 'He dropped like a beef and the blood came plenty. ... These vermin are gradually coming to understand certain phases of the military profession.'[50]

But while midwestern industrial cities like Chicago (at least until 1898) might serve as tilting fields for western heroes, only the West itself could nurture and train such heroes. Remington and his close friend Owen

Wister, and their mutual friend Theodore Roosevelt, all sought therapy for psychic crises of adolescence and young manhood by journeys in the West. Remington had left the Yale art school before completing a degree, but Wister and Roosevelt were both graduates of Harvard College. The three friends applauded one another's achievements. Remington, with his action sketches and tough, Hemingwayesque prose, brought cowboys and Indian-hunting soldiers into journals of national circulation; Roosevelt celebrated them in politics; Wister raised their literary image from the not-altogether-dignified ambience of dime novels to the heights of middle-brow fiction.[51]

The Level Gaze of the Frontier

We come now to *The Virginian*, dedicated by its author to Theodore Roosevelt. Wister, like John Pendleton Kennedy before him, was a whiggish Middle Atlantic urbanite who admired the plantation culture and deferential yeomanry of the pre–Civil War Upper South. Wister's fictional hero, the hired hand of a Wyoming cattle baron, is named only 'the Virginian'. Combining the police dog ferocity of Kennedy's Horseshoe Robinson with the love of the wilderness that characterized Cooper's Leatherstocking, the Virginian has brought his white gifts to a latter-day West of miners, detectives and cowboys – not the West of Indians. Nonetheless, he has survived a symbolic encounter with renegade Indians that nearly cost him his life, and which sets the stage for his wooing of the upper-class heroine. In Wister's novel, however, negative roles are usually carried not by Indians but by lower-class whites in lineal descent from Cooper's squatters and border ruffians. Chief among these is a villainous adversary whom the Virginian puts down, first in moral confrontations, then in the field of cowboy skills, next in a trial of wit, and finally in single combat. Described by Wister as 'sullen, but tricky rather than courageous', the adversary bears the name *Trampas*, which in Spanish means 'deceits' or 'traps.' The name, combined with the adjectives *sullen* and *tricky*, would certainly have suggested to readers at the turn of the century – whether they understood Spanish or not – the notion of *mestizo* or *halfbreed*.[52]

As to the Virginian himself, he recapitulates the history of a fictional genre. Like Cooper's Leatherstocking, the Virginian feels himself to be in harmony with wilderness. Thus, at his moment of self-revelation to the heroine, he tells her of a remembered place in the mountains: 'Often when I have camped here, it made me want to become the ground, become the water, become the trees, mix with the whole thing. Not know myself from it. Why is that? … ' Such yieldings to the sublimity of nature had long been recognized as tokens of natural aristocracy. Wister, in his authorial voice, wrote of the Virginian: 'Here in flesh and blood was a truth which I had long believed in words, but never met before. The creature we call a *gentleman* lies deep in the hearts of thousands that are born without chance to master the outward graces of the type.' Natural aristocracy, both for Leatherstocking and for the Virginian, furnishes an inward grace from which flows their outer deference to social superiors.[53]

Deference had been in short supply among Free Soil vernaculars, those 'Sons of Leatherstocking' who were likely to pursue the more aggressive traits of egalitarianism and upward mobility. The Virginian, despite his many resemblances to the Leatherstocking, also reproduces unmistakable traces of Free Soil heroes. His language, evolving from the vernacular, has arrived at genteel diction. He marries above his station. With respect to upwardly mobile marriage, Wister employed literary devices not unlike those used by Cooper. The heroine comes of distinguished lineage, her ancestors, male and female, having played exemplary roles in the Revolution. But her family's fortunes are declining, her status in Wyoming being that of a schoolmarm on the cattle baron's domain: not quite at the same social level as that of a cowboy, yet by no means beyond the reach of a *deferential* cowboy who is moving from hired hand to manager. Deference, in which the Virginian most closely resembles the Leatherstocking, leads to his most decisive break from that earlier pattern. Instead of pursuing the vanishing American wilderness, he will settle down under the auspices of his employer and patron on a homestead that contains not only an upper-class wife but coal deposits for the coming railroad. All this suggests a harmonious community in which the Virginian, having left lower-class origins behind him, may become one of ours. Wister, of course, has introduced certain new ingredients into the ideological sequence that began with the vernacular Yankee a century earlier.

Social Darwinism in the late nineteenth century substituted a scientific frame of reference for the religious frame within which racism had originally taken shape. Wister, Theodore Roosevelt, Frederic Remington – together with many of their contemporaries – would perceive the 'science' in Social Darwinism as permeating their inherited social construction of reality. At the start of this study, I disclaimed any intention of producing 'another intellectual history of racial thought.' With respect to Social Darwinism, certainly, that task has already been accomplished.[54] What is required here is not the tracing back of ideas, but simply an indication of the ways in which Social Darwinism impinged upon legitimations of power.

Social Darwinian innovators, in their efforts to legitimize *hierarchy*, used the notion of a natural law of competition progressively selecting out those 'organisms' best qualified for survival and reproduction. What sort of hierarchy, however, was not predetermined by the logic of their system. That logic could rationalize the gentrification of individuals presumed to be genetically advantaged as readily as it justified the supremacy of biological groups similarly so presumed. Mainly, Social Darwinism has worked to legitimate *either* class *or* racial hierarchy. Perhaps it could just as well have legitimated both types of hierarchies at the same time, but for the most part did not do so, because the social purposes of legitimizers were usually working in opposite directions.

Andrew Carnegie in his 'Gospel of Wealth' charted one of these directions:

> Under the law of competition, the employer of thousands is forced into the strictest economies, among which the rates paid to labor figure prominently, and often there is friction between the employer and the employed, between capital and labor, between rich and poor. ... We accept and welcome, therefore, as conditions to which we must accomodate ourselves, great inequality of environment; the concentration of business, industrial and commercial, in the hands of a few; ... It is a law, as certain as any of the others named, that men possessed of this peculiar talent for affairs, under the free play of economic forces must, of necessity, soon be in receipt of more revenue than can be judiciously expended upon themselves and this law is as beneficial for the race as the others.[55]

Carnegie, in this context at least, used the term race to signify human race. Josiah Strong – to whom we can turn for an account of the other main tendency in Social Darwinism – used race more narrowly:

> Then will the world enter upon a new stage of its history – the final competition of races, for which the Anglo-Saxon is being schooled ... the mighty centrifugal tendency, inherent in this stock, and strengthened in the United States, will assert itself. Then this race of unequalled energy, with all the majesty of numbers and the might of wealth behind it – the representative, let us hope, of the largest liberty, the purest Christianity, the highest civilization – having developed peculiarly aggressive traits calculated to impress its institutions upon mankind – will spread itself over the earth. ... And can one doubt that the result of this competition of races will be the 'survival of the fittest'?[56]

The ideological tendency described by Carnegie celebrates competition among individual members of the society, or nation. Justifying class exploitation without reserve, it denies sanctuary to racially privileged segments of the lower classes. Such a social vista – like the whiggish ideal that preceded it or the old guard Republicanism that came afterwards – would be soft on race, hard on class. By contrast, Josiah Strong's ideological projection works to unite the dominant racial group across class lines. Soft on class but hard on race, it tends to deny (or denigrate) economic exploitation within the fraternity of the racially elite. Defining nationality in terms of race, it extrudes, or marginalizes, racial minorities found inside the national boundaries, while at the same time pressing an aggressive external expansionism at the expense of the world's non-white populations. '... I've got some Winchesters and when the massacreing begins, I can get my share of 'em and what's more, I will', Frederic Remington had written in 1893 to his former Yale classmate, Poultney Bigelow. 'Jews, Injuns, Chinamen, Italians, Huns – the rubbish of the Earth – I hate.'[57] For this racially oriented sector of Social Darwinism, the historical linkages – looking backward – stretched to the Free Soil movement and Jacksonian Democracy. Looking forward, they pointed to Progressivism as it later developed during the presidencies of Theodore Roosevelt and Woodrow Wilson.

The *Virginian's* most immediate literary antecedent may be found in a short story of Remington's published in 1897 in *Harper's Monthly*, which recounted the exploits of a tough sergeant (referred to as 'our Virginian') during a long, bloody shoot-out with the Cheyennes.[58] Wister's Virginian represents a composite of many heroes, new only in the sense of having been renovated to fit the industrial era and the explanatory apparatus of Social Darwinism. Near the end of the novel, Wister re-visualized his hero as Remington might have sketched him, 'looking gravely into the distance with the level gaze of the frontier.'[59] What other frontiers that distance might contain would stir the imaginations not only of Wister and Remington, but of their friend Theodore Roosevelt.

Notes

1. See Chapter 7.

2. Albert Johannsen, *The House of Beadle and Adams and its Dime and Nickel Novels: A Story of a Vanished Literature*, Norman, Okla. 1950–62, 1:22–29, 57, 61, 64, 414.

3. Henry Nash Smith, *Virgin Land: The American West as Symbol and Myth*, Cambridge, Mass. 1970, p. 87. See also Ralph Admari, 'Ballou, The Father of the Dime Novel', *The American Book Collector*, 4:121–29; and 'Bonner and *The Ledger*', *The American Book Collector* 6:176–93. An excellent recent study is Michael J. Denning, 'Dime Novels: Popular Fiction and Working-Class Culture in Nineteenth-Century America', Ph.D. diss., Yale, 1984, which begins with a detailed history of story papers and dime novels, pp. 8–128. Smith, p. 87, and Denning, pp. 9–10, link story papers to the penny press.

4. Johannsen, 1:20–29; Ralph Admari, 'The House that Beadle Built', *American Book Collector*, 4:221–26.

5. Johannsen, 1:23–29, 30–37, 364–72, 380–95, 2:262–63; Smith, *Virgin Land*, pp. 92–93; James D. Hart, *The Popular Book: A History of America's Literary Taste*, New York 1950, pp. 153–54; Philip Durham, 'Dime Novels: An American Heritage', *Western Humanities Review*, 9:34, 36–37; Durham, ed., *Seth Jones by Edward S. Ellis and Deadwood Dick on Deck by Edward L. Wheeler*, New York 1966, 'Introduction', pp. *v–vi, x–xi*; George C. Jenks, 'Dime Novel Makers', *Bookman*, 20:108–14; Edmund Pearson, *Dime Novels; or, Following an Old Trail in Popular Literature*, Boston 1929, pp. 1–13, 33–35.

6. Smith, *Virgin Land*, p. 91; Johannsen, 1:40–41, 49; 2:278–80, 285–87; Jenks, pp.

109–10. Admari, 'House that Beadle Built', p. 225.

7. Smith, *Virgin Land*, p. 91; Johannsen, 1:47–48, 53, 113. Johannsen's listing of titles appears on 1:81–443; 5,642 is my own tally from Johannsen's listing. I have made no effort to allow for reprinting of previously published works, often with changed titles or authors, since my interest here is in the total output of novels and serials. Durham, in his introduction to two Beadle and Adams classics republished in 1966, estimated a total list of over 5,000 with 3,158 of these being first printings: Durham, ed., pp. *v–vi*. Most Beadle and Adams statistics depend on hearsay, since the company's records were destroyed in the early twentieth century: Johannsen, 1:33. An article published in *Atlantic Monthly* at the height of dime novel output corroborates the scope of the enterprise: '... It is an enormous field of mental activity, the greatest literary movement, in bulk, of the age, and worthy of very serious consideration for itself. Disdained as it may be by the highly cultivated for its character, the phenomenon of its existence cannot be overlooked.' W.H. Bishop, 'Story Paper Literature', *Atlantic Monthly* 44 (September 1879): 383.

8. Johannsen, 1:69.

9. The songbooks are described in Johannsen, 1:380–95. Volume 3, pp. 55–95, lists the song titles in 118 existing Beadle and Adams songbooks.

10. See Chapter 7.

11. Johannsen, 3:63; 67, 88, 93–95.

12. Johannsen, 1:361–79, 395–412. Songbook titles are listed chronologically, 1:380–95.

13. Johannsen, 1:364–72, 410–12. Jenks, 'Dime Novel Makers', pp. 109–110. The statement attributed to Henry Ward Beecher is quoted in Johannsen, 1:40, from Charles M. Harvey, 'The Dime Novel in American Life', *Atlantic Monthly* 100 (July 1907): 39, 43. If McClellan seems miscast in the list of Beadle and Adams republican heroes, it should be noted that the publication date was 1862 when McClellan was still a promising commander-in-chief, not yet a Democratic and presidential candidate.

14. Compiled from Johannsen, 2:6–311.

15. The lower percentage of farmer and worker–artisan backgrounds for 'Occasional Contributors' probably results from sketchy biographical information. 'Unknowns' here totalled 13.

16. Table, p. 419, Column 9. And see Denning, pp. 353–82.

17. Merle Curti, 'Dime Novels and the American Tradition', *Yale Review* 26 (1937): 761–78. On comparison to 'proletarian' literature, p. 761, Bishop, *Atlantic Monthly* (1879):389, had a rather different view: 'Though written almost exclusively for the use of the lower classes of society, the story papers are not accurate pictures of their life. They are not a mass of evidence from which, though rude, a valuable insight into their thoughts, feelings and doings can be obtained by others who do not know them.'

18. Compiled from Johannsen, 1:81–433. Works under *Colonial*, almost by definition, involve Indian conflict. The year 1790, with respect to fictional time, separates the two classifications under *Revolution* from the two under *Western Adventure*. *Sea* includes sea stories of both the colonial and revolutionary periods. On egalitarian discourse, see Chapter 8.

19. Smith, p. 95; Jenks, p. 110.

20. Owen Wister's *The Virginian*, 1902, exemplifies the longevity of this tradition.

21. Curti, pp. 766, 767. See pp. 761, 766–67, 768 for a similar point about Civil War dime novels. It may be that Curti was using his survey of dime novels as a means of chastising certain historians of the Revolution, whose work he believed needed revising.

22. See, for example, Frederick Whittaker, *Journeyman John, the Champion; or, The Winning Hand*, New York 1887, for a story of industrial conflict in which a solution is found through the triumph of egalitarianism over aristocratic wealth. For a more extended examination of Whittaker's industrial conflict dime novels, see Denning, pp. 323–47. With respect to the table on p. 419, both the defining of classifications and the assignment of individual works to classifications rested partly on titles, partly on Johannsen's plot summaries, some of which consist of no more than a phrase or sentence. Johannsen and his assistants doubtless also held ideological viewpoints that scarcely led them to stress industrial conflict in their plot summaries. Fortunately that theme is central in Michael Denning's recent study. While making no claim to have combed the entire dime novel and story paper

output, p. 224, Denning has identified and pieced together (some existed only in serial form) 27 such novels, of which 8 were published by Beadle and Adams. Twenty-seven is more than I would have expected. Thematically, Denning's close readings are of great interest. Statistically, however, since Beadle and Adams alone published over 3,000 new titles [Durham, ed., pp. *v–vi*], the number remains small.

23. Johannsen, 1:59; Smith, pp. 102, 111, 119; Jenks, p. 110. Pearson, pp. 138ff.

24. The best treatment of detective fiction I have found is Ernest Mandel, *Delightful Murder: A Social History of the Crime Story*, Minneapolis, Minn. 1984. Some other useful histories of the detective genre are Howard Haycraft, *Murder for Pleasure: The Life and Times of the Detective Story*, New York 1941; Julian Symons, *Mortal Consequences: A History – From the Detective Story to the Crime Novel*, New York 1972. See also Gary Hoppenstand, ed., *The Dime Novel Detective*, Bowling Green, Ohio 1982.

25. Edward S. Ellis, *Seth Jones, or, The Captives of the Frontier*, New York 1860; Philip Durham, ed., New York 1966, pp. 19, 29, 72.

26. Johannsen, 2:6–7, 93–97. Ellis, *From the Ranch to the White House: Life of Roosevelt*, New York 1906. The title page places Ellis's biography in the 'Log Cabin to White House Series'.

27. Johannsen, 2:93–100.

28. Johannsen, 1:364–72.

29. Ellis, *The Life and Times of Colonel Daniel Boone, the Hunter of Kentucky*, New York 1861; *The Life and Adventures of Colonel David Crockett; The Life and Times of Christopher Carson, the Rocky Mountain Scout and Guide. With Reminiscences of Fremont's Exploring Expeditions and Notes on Life in New Mexico*. All three biographies, first published by Beadle and Adams in 1861, were expanded and republished by other publishing houses in the 1880s.

30. Ellis, *Life of Boone*, Philadelphia 1884, p. 3.

31. Ellis, *Life of David Crockett*, Philadelphia 1884, pp. 270–27.

32. Rodman Paul, *California Gold: The Beginning of Mining in the Far West*, Cambridge, Mass. 1947, and Paul, *Mining Frontiers of the Far West, 1848–1880*, New York 1963; Alexander Saxton, *The Indispensable Enemy: Labor and the Anti–Chinese Movement in California*, Berkeley, Calif. 1971, pp. 46–60; Smith, pp. 109–110; Richard E. Lingenfelder, *The Hardrock Miners: A History of the Mining Labor Movement in the American West, 1863–1893*, Berkeley, Calif. 1974; Mark Wyman, *Hard Rock Epic: Western Miners and the Industrial Revolution, 1860–1910*, Berkeley, Calif. 1979; Robert Dykstra, *The Cattle Towns*, New York 1971, especially pp. 74–111; Maurice Frink, W. Turrentine Jackson, Agnes Wright Spring, *When Grass Was King: Contributions to the Western Cattle Industry Study*, Boulder, Colo. 1956, pp. *vii*, 26, 33–123.

33. Smith, p. 119. Denning on post–Civil War industrial uses of detectives and entry of detectives into dime novels and story papers, pp. 229–287. Allan Pinkerton's *The Molly Maguires and the Detectives*, New York, was published in 1877: Denning, p. 390.

34. Smith, p. 111.

35. Edward L. Wheeler, *Deadwood Dick, the Prince of the Road; or, The Black Rider of the Black Hills*, New York 1877; *Deadwood Dick on Deck; or, Calamity Jane, the Heroine of Whoop-Up*, New York 1878; Smith on Deadwood Dick, pp. 100–102; on Buffalo Bill, pp. 102–11.

36. Ned Buntline [E.Z.C. Judson], *Buffalo Bill: The King of the Border Men*, New York 1881. This was first published in Street and Smith's *New York Weekly*, 1869. The edition used here for citation is titled, *Buffalo Bill and His Adventures in the West*, New York 1886, pp. 3–21, 60. On Buntline/Judson, see Jay Monaghan, *The Great Rascal: The Life and Adventures of Ned Buntline*, Boston 1952.

37. Buntline, *Buffalo Bill*, 1886 ed., pp. 9, 12. The reference to the white and black hired hands is in a slightly different version – same title, same publisher, but undated, pp. 12–16, 17–20.

38. Buntline, *Buffalo Bill*, 1886 ed. , p. 31.

39. Ibid., 181–83. Smith, pp. 104–5.

40. Buntline, *Buffalo Bill*, 1886 ed., pp. 185–87, 299.

41. Edward S. Ellis, *Deadwood Dick on Deck; or, Calamity Jane, the Heroine of Whoop-Up*, New York 1878, in Philip Durham, ed., pp. 109–110.

42. Ibid., p. 110.

43. Edward L. Wheeler, *Deadwood Dick, Jr. in Chicago; or, The Anarchist's Daughter*,

New York 1887, p. 2.

44. Ibid., p. 5.

45. Frederick Whittaker, *Larry Locke, Man of Iron, or A Fight for Fortune: A Story of Labor and Capital*, in Mary C. Grimes, ed., *The Knights in Fiction: Two Labor Novels of the 1880s*, Urbana, Ill. 1986, p. 325. Denning, p. 391, lists this novel as first serialized in *Beadle's Weekly*, October 1883–January 1884.

46. Whittaker, *Journeyman John, the Champion; or, The Winning Hand*, New York 1887, p. 6. For a discussion of Whittaker's other labor novels, see Denning, pp. 323–47.

47. Wheeler, *Deadwood Dick in Chicago*, p. 9.

48. Whittaker, *Journeyman John*, p. 8.

49. Johannsen, 2:293–96, 300–302. Also on Whittaker, see Grimes, *The Knights in Fiction*, p. 11; and Denning, p. 32.

50. Peggy and Harold Samuels, eds, *The Collected Writings of Frederic Remington*. Illustrated by Frederic Remington. Garden City, N.Y. 1979, pp. 152–54, 156, 152–54, 156. The piece quoted originally appeared in *Harper's Weekly*, 14 July 1894. On Remington, see pp. *xvii–xx*. Also Fred Erisman, *Frederic Remington*, Boise, Idaho 1975.

51. Ben Merchant Vorpahl, *My Dear Wister – The Frederic Remington–Owen Wister Letters*, Palo Alto, Calif. 1972; Richard Etulain, *Owen Wister*, Boise, Idaho 1973; G. Edward White, *The Eastern Establishment and the Western Experience: The West of Frederic Remington, Theodore Roosevelt and Owen Wister*, New Haven, Conn. 1968, especially pp. 52–74, 122–44; Owen Wister, *Roosevelt: The Story of a Friendship*, New York 1930, pp. 6, 30–32, 39–42, 106–7.

52. Owen Wister, *The Virginian: A Horseman of the Plains*, [1902] New York 1964, pp. 29, 185–205.

53. Ibid., pp. 18–19, 280.

54. See Introduction, note 1.

55. Andrew Carnegie, *The Gospel of Wealth and Other Timely Essays*, ed., Edward C. Kirkland, Cambridge, Mass. 1962, pp. 16–17.

56. Josiah Strong, *Our Country: Its Possible Future and Its Present Crisis*, New York 1885, pp. 174–75.

57. Poultney Bigelow, 'Frederic Remington: with Extracts from Unpublished Letters', New York State Historical Association, *Quarterly Journal* 10:45–52. Roosevelt had made a similar identification in his reaction to Haymarket in 1886: Richard Drinnon, '"My Men Shoot Well": Theodore Roosevelt and the Urban Frontier', David Roediger and Franklin Rosemont, eds, *Haymarket Scrapbook*, Chicago 1986, pp. 129–30.

58. *Harper's New Monthly Magazine* 95 (August 1897): 327–36. For Wister, Remington's graphic account of pursuit and slaughter, on the scale of the ritual massacres in Cooper and Robert Montgomery Bird, provided a 'thick' content to the Virginian's Indian encounter, which enters Wister's novel indirectly and rather thinly.

59. Wister, *The Virginian*, p. 258.

15

In Search of a New Antithesis

In an earlier discussion of terms I noted that *thesis*, *synthesis* and *antithesis* are used in this study descriptively but not rigorously. Rigorous usage would require that each thesis contain, or generate from its own necessity, the seeds of an antithesis. Whether or not this sort of self-sufficiency belongs to the grand Hegelian or Marxian designs from which the terms are borrowed, clearly no such internal economy governs their application to the formation of political parties in the United States. It is, I believe, illuminating to speak of a National Republican thesis, Jacksonian antithesis and Republican synthesis because the politics of deference did in fact call forth a negation in the form of egalitarian democracy, while the conflict between these two led on to the Republican coalition. In no sense, however, do any of these terms totally contain those that follow. The three-term sequence developed not autonomously but within a shaping matrix of historical continuities (plantation slavery, access to a continental domain, and so forth), which remained contingent to, yet prior to and independent of, that sequence.

One further qualification: the nodal points of this study are way stations within a single stage – that of bourgeois dominance in the Marxian dialectic. The American Revolution, the ascendancy of National Republicanism after the War of 1812, the Jacksonian coalition, the overthrow of the planter class, the installation of the Republican economic program – all represent rearrangements or transfers of power within the ongoing capitalist revolution. Like the Jacksonian party system before it, the Republican party system sustained peripheral or obsolescent class interests that entered the political arena usually by adhering to whichever of the major parties seemed most favorable to their prospects. Thus artisan producers in the early Republic vacillated politically as their faith in tariff protection or their wage earner-versus-employer identification

349

varied; while among New York City's patricians, on the other hand, those most clearly linked to overseas commerce and cosmopolitan culture maintained a Democratic allegiance despite the general swing of established property in the Northeast to Republicanism. Circumstances such as these made class coalition a basic, albeit intricate, element in the party-building process. The advent of a class interest that was neither obsolescent nor governed by bourgeois property codes, then, could be expected to make a qualitative difference in that process.

To extrapolate from the case history of George Wilkes, the urban artisan class proliferated in the 1830s and 1840s, moving west with the urban frontier, then diverged into separate segments. One segment merged with previously commercial capital to become the manufacturing interest; another maintained itself in artisanal enclaves of industry such as construction, shipbuilding, metal fabrication and printing. Evidence from the preceding chapter, for example, would justify placing the publishers and some authors of dime novels in the first segment, while identifying the class loyalties expressed in their literary output with the second segment. And of course there was also a third segment, which moved downward economically to become part of the newly forming industrial working class. Only with the railroad strikes of 1877 do we catch a persuasive glimpse of that class in action. From that point forward, subversion of the credibility of bourgeois values would become at least a potential aspect of any class alignment substantial enough to challenge the ongoing party system. It is in this sense that I refer to the 1890s as a decade of hegemonic crisis. Bringing this study to a close, I will offer two vistas of that crisis: one derived from conflicting literary constructions, the other arrived at more conventionally by way of argument in political economy. Since, however, it is conceptually possible to describe almost any ten years of United States history as a critical period, I will begin by establishing the credentials, in this respect, of the 1890s.

The Hegemonic Crisis of the 1890s

American cultural and political historians, although interpreting the 1890s in diverse ways, have concurred in stressing a high level of moral and political tension. Frederick Jackson Turner, near the end of the essay which he had begun by noting the closure of the frontier in 1890, wrote that America 'since the days when the fleet of Columbus sailed into the waters of the New World' had been 'another name for opportunity. ... But never again will such gifts of free land offer themselves.'[1] 'What was more natural', John D. Hicks inquired in 1931, than to blame 'the "heartbreaking nineties" ... upon the manufacturers, the railroads, the moneylenders, the middlemen – plutocrats all?'[2] An American born in the year of Andrew Jackson's first election, according to Richard Hofstadter, would have grown up 'in a society in which the old small-enterprise economy ... had kept its fundamental pattern more or less intact. But in his mature years he would have seen that economy fast becoming obsolete. ... This economic transformation happened so fast that the mind could not easily absorb it.'[3] Hofstadter observed that two major studies of imperialism – one by Walter LaFeber, the other by Ernest R. May – neither 'entirely in accord' with his own analysis, nonetheless agreed in viewing the 1890s as a period of 'upset' for which the depression of 1893 had served as a 'catalyst'.[4] Lawrence Goodwyn justified his 1978 reexamination of Populism by stressing that 'an important juncture in the political consolidation of the industrial culture came ... at the culmination of the Populist moment in the 1890s.' Martin Sklar and Richard Slotkin – to conclude this opinion survey with two more recent examples – both treat the decade of the 1890s as a watershed between the citizens' lowercase *r* republicanism of the older America and the new capitalized Republicanism that was ushered in by the 'incorporation of America'.[5]

It was Richard Hofstadter who applied the term 'psychic crisis' to that decade.[6] Historians in one sense simply recorded the anxieties expressed by contemporary witnesses. 'A nation that had gone so fast from competitive small enterprise to corporate giantism', Hofstadter explained, 'might readily go with equal speed from corporate giantism to a system of monopolistic tyranny. Hence discussions of big business ... are full of dark prognostications. ... '[7] In the last decade before the Civil War, Rebecca Harding [Davis] already was portraying 'life in the iron mills' as a Dante's inferno lodged along the riverside of her hometown, Wheeling, where the middle class to which she belonged lived comfortably on the upper slopes. Henry George summed up the dichotomy in the title of his famous work, *Progress and Poverty*. Clearly the sense of crisis had spread across the social spectrum.[8] A contributor to the *American Federationist* in 1895 demanded 'living, breathing Christianity' that would go 'into the poverty-stricken alleys of the robbed industrial slaves' and raise 'up its victims'. Stephen Crane's Magdalen of the New York slums succumbed to damnation and death not because of her own sinfulness but because the Christian church that might have saved her had abandoned Christ's teachings. For Charles Sheldon, a New England Social Gospel Congregationalist in a midwestern industrial city, the recovery of Christian doctrine became the essential step toward national redemption. In a society that lived by grinding the faces of its poor, 'What would Jesus do?'[9]

Rhetorical styles varied from Grangers to industrial workers, primitives to bohemian sophisticates, free thinkers to evangelists, yet the central image of a social order bereft of moral control remained substantially the same. 'Was there, then, no way of commanding the services of the mighty wealth-producing principle of consolidated capital', Edward Bellamy asked in 1887, 'without bowing down to a plutocracy like that of Carthage? ... Just there you will find the explanation of the profound pessimism of the literature of the last quarter of the nineteenth century the note of melancholy in its poetry, and the cynicism of its humor.'[10]

'The popular mind is agitated with problems that may disturb the social order', Senator John Sherman of Illinois warned his colleagues during debate over the antitrust legislation that bears his name. 'Society is now disturbed by forces never before felt.'[11] In that same year, the Minnesota Populist Ignatius Donnelly prefaced his 1890s apocalypse of twentieth-century social catastrophe, *Caesar's Column*, with a declaration that for 'the great mass of mankind' industrial society was proving a 'wretched failure'. 'The rich, as a rule, hate the poor; and the poor are coming to hate the rich ... society divides itself into two hostile camps. ... They wait only for the drum beat and the trumpet to summon them to armed conflict.'[12] Widespread evidence from the 1890s of such dark visions suggests, in Gramscian terms, a breakdown of ruling-class hegemony: the moral and cultural authority of the ruling class appeared to have become too selective, too self-serving, to justify a broad social order.

Contests of Heroes

In the midst of crisis, it might have been expected that the western hero, with his subversive origins in artisan and yeoman radicalism, would be claimed by the oppositionists. Ambivalences, falterings of moral commitment, noted earlier in certain dime novels like Wheeler's *Deadwood Dick* or Whittaker's portrayals of promethean mechanics, suggest that such a claim was contemplated and experimented with.[13] That no such project got off the ground is now rather easily explicable. First, to have brought class loyalty into the make-up of the artisan hero ran counter to the historical logic of his construction. Second, neither authors nor publishers of the story papers and dime novels, based as they were in the upwardly mobile segment of the old artisan yeoman grouping, would have tolerated such departures. In any case, we can leave these explicatons at the hypothetical level, since empirical evidence shows that no subversive claims were in fact staked out on the western hero's home turf of dime novels and story papers. On the contrary, that hero was about to be coopted and *nationalized* by boosters of the 'New Nationalism' like Theodore Roosevelt who would lead American industrial capitalism into its twentieth-century global undertakings.[14]

What of other literary territories? Among the best-known literary critiques of late nineteenth-century industrial capitalism are Edward Bellamy's *Looking Backward*, William Dean Howells's *Letters of an Altrurian Traveller*, *Caesar's Column* by Ignatius Donnelly and Mark Twain's *A Connecticut Yankee in King Arthur's Court*. The first three have usually been classified as utopian; Twain's novel could more accurately be described as anti-utopian; in any case, it requires separate treatment.[15]

All three utopian novels, despite their many differences, share a common rejection of the western hero. Bellamy's protagonist is a Boston Brahmin; Howells's a Brahmin-like stranger from the planet Altruria, where the educated elite had recently shepherded a peaceful transition from industrial capitalism to something like Christian Socialism. Since neither of these authors intended to celebrate what *is*, the *arrived* western hero failed to meet their needs. Equally unattractive for them were such earlier incarnations as David Crockett and Kit Carson, reared in the empire-building 'school of nature'. Going back even further, Leatherstocking had criticized the social order; but Leatherstocking's dependence on the purity of wilderness for his critical vantage point must have seemed anachronistic to writers who criticized contemporary society by projecting scientific and technological wonderlands in the future. It was, after all, the Chicago World's Fair of 1893 that Howells's interplanetary guest came to visit, not the vanishing frontier in the West.

Ignatius Donnelly, although Philadelphia-born, was more western-minded than either Bellamy or Howells. His careers as Free Soiler, Radical Republican and Minnesota Populist had made him a master of egalitarian rhetoric.[16] The language, for example, of his famous preamble to the Omaha Populist platform resembles that of Colonel Tubbs in *Deadwood Dick on Deck*. Donnelly went beyond Tubbs, of course, both in the stringency of his indictment and the radicalism of his proposed remedies. Since we know that Populism flourished among western miners, it is tempting to wonder why Donnelly did not recruit a western hero from one of the mining camps for his protagonist in *Caesar's Column*. As a Populist leader, however, Donnelly's outlook remained basically agrarian. What he needed was an agrarian champion; but the pantheon of western heroes, as far back at least as the Mexican War, contained no such figure. Western heroes had provided the cutting edge for Indian fighting, mining, railroad building and cattle-ranching frontiers. Because agriculture necessarily followed those frontiers, its conflict with industrialization reached a crisis only after the frontiers ceased to open up new agricultural lands. Western heroes could therefore seem as obsolete to agrarian utopians like Donnelly as to scientific and technological utopians like Bellamy and Howells. In *Caesar's Column* Donnelly chose to counterpose early republican virtue against the consolidating industrial capitalism of the 1890s. He found himself obliged to search back to planter heroes like

George Washington and even to embattled heroes of the Swiss cantons, in order to find models for his agrarian champions.[17] These were desperate devices for a Populist as ferocious as Donnelly. They underscore both the seriousness with which he sought some viable social base for his protagonist and the meagerness of available resources.

Between Donnelly, the Populist, and Bellamy and Howells, the technological utopians, there were fundamental differences of political direction. Donnelly would have used the federal government to transfer control over economic decision-making from industrial capitalists to commercial farmers. Bellamy and Howells, on the other hand, accepting industrial consolidation as necessary and potentially beneficial, proposed carrying it to what seemed its logical outcome – the incorporation of corporations, or total monopoly, no longer for private profit, but for the commonweal.[18]

Mark Twain, a close friend of Howells, stood closer to Donnelly in social thought. Yet Twain differed from Donnelly in that he was not an agrarian. An admirer of technological progress, he believed (or wished to believe) that the industrial revolution offered an agenda for improving the human condition. That agenda had been thwarted by manipulators and monopolists operating through pools, trusts and tariff systems. For Twain, however, these evils were not inherent in technological progress, nor even in industrial capitalism. Rather they were to be seen as recurrences of mankind's ancient subservience to evil tricksters and self-serving imposters. Human history, prior to the modern era, had belonged to magicians and kings, high priests and feudal aristocrats. Growing up in small town Missouri during the heyday of Jacksonian egalitarianism, he had perceived in America's political democracy and industrial virtuosity a potential liberator of humanity from its long thrall of ignorance and tyranny. Twain was a stepchild, at least, of the Enlightenment.[19]

This was the story he intended to tell, apparently, in his 'comic' novel *A Connecticut Yankee in King Arthur's Court*. Because Twain could seldom resist targets of opportunity – especially when they could be played for laughs, such as developing an anti-tariff polemic from the simplified economics of Arthurian England, or presenting the Knights of the Round Table as commercial drummers for patent medicines – his novel bears superficial resemblance to the anti-monopoly literature of the period, including the utopian novels discussed above. But Twain's purposes were not those of the utopians. If American industrial society was a potentially liberating force, then it would be logical to characterize the western hero as a modern Prometheus. Such certainly was not the view of the utopians, who kept their distance from that hero. Twain, on the contrary, was enticed by him. *Roughing It, Life on the Mississippi, Tom Sawyer*, and *Huckleberry Finn*, can be read as admiring, nostalgic, ironic variations on the western hero theme. In *The Connecticut Yankee*, Twain attempted a full-dress presentation.[20]

His protagonist, combining the 'cuteness' of early Yankees with the occupational and class versatility of western heroes in the guise of miners, detectives and cowboys, recapitulates the historical stages of vernacular characterization. But to qualify as a western hero, the protagonist, instead of going west, has turned back in space and time to a more ancient frontier, thus contrasting the accomplishments of industrial America with the backwardness of earlier human conditions.[21] All this, again, furnished easy targets of opportunity. Yet Twain was not satisfied simply to rejoice in American technological superiority. What must be shown to achieve his purpose was *value*.

A principal measure of value for Mark Twain was the nostalgic recollection of childhood in a rural past.[22] This sets him apart, again, from scientific utopians like Bellamy and Howells, whose standards were the imagined perfections of a future society. On the other hand, it links Twain to agrarian utopians like Donnelly, and more profoundly to James Fenimore Cooper, who was no utopian at all. Donnelly and Cooper both located their measures of value in the past, as did Twain, who in this respect, stands between the two. Twain's value system diverged from Donnelly's agrarianism by emphasizing the pure and uncomplicated affections of childhood rather than adult public virtues ascribed to citizen-farmers. It differed from Cooper's valuation of wilderness in that purity, for Twain, was not a property of nature presumed to be unspoiled because still untouched by human contact, but something that resided in remembered human connections. Obviously the three measures of value are closely linked, Twain's being the least abstract; and the most individual, romantic and sentimental. Each measure pointed to its appropriate hero.

What Twain's hero had to carry through, then, was to show under the most primitive conditions how things can be done – how they *are* done – in free, westernized, secular America. By the self-evidentness of truth thus demonstrated, a superstitious, ignorant, class-bound social order would be transformed into one that permitted the values esteemed by Twain as essentially human to flourish. *The Connecticut Yankee*, as we all know, failed in this task. Or, since we are speaking of fictional construction, it would be more in keeping to say that Twain failed to muster the willing suspension of disbelief requisite to the hero's success. Having played at being a western hero himself, Twain may already have formed an opinion, down under, of the sort of values and aspirations likely to coexist with egalitarian upward mobility and acquisitive individualism. In any case, the onset of disbelief could not have been instantaneous. Under the stress of literary composition, he must have been forced to confront erosions long since partially acknowledged and set aside. What resulted from these confrontations was a reversal of fictional meaning. Instead of showing that industrial technology could raise the human condition, the Yankee shows how such technology can be used to reduce it. With his band of technicians united by their high-tech weaponry, he presides over a ritual slaughter similar to hundreds depicted in western adventure fiction from Cooper to Buffalo Bill.[23]

One of Twain's favorite targets of opportunity had been lower-class deference. His protagonist in *The Connecticut Yankee* preaches egalitarianism. Twain himself seems to have been sympathetic, although slightly patronizing, to African Americans and to the Chinese in California; conforming to his Free Soil origins, he was hostile to Indians. White racist expressions seldom broke the surface of his writings, and none appears in *The Connecticut Yankee*. Yet the effect of the reversal of fictional meaning is to place the hero at a vast distance from the slaughtered. If the hero and his fraternity of technicians are human, the others can scarcely be. Struggling against psychic depression to finish his novel, Twain at first may have missed this aspect. He could hardly have missed it later when he was protesting the slaughter of Africans and Filipinos.[24] Merlin the charlatan, as Twain himself put it, had won out in the end. Consequently, there could be no real historical location for human value, but only fragmentary individual awakenings into remembered childhood. Literary historians, especially Bernard DeVoto and Henry Nash Smith, have traced the impact of this apocalypse on Twain.[25] Its impact on his western hero was even more abrupt. The hero disintegrates and drops from orbit. His fall disrupts the novel's aesthetic coherence, since the novel seems to have been initially intended to celebrate the hero's triumph.

Certainly Twain, Howells, Bellamy and Donnelly were the main spokesmen of this brief anti-hegemonic episode in American literature. Their works excelled in vivid images of the road to catastrophe, but each author failed to create a protagonist capable of imparting credibility to any alternative route. Twain's Yankee was himself a chief architect of catastrophe; for the others, alternative directions faded off into dreams, or faraway times and places. Thus catastrophe came to appear not as one possible result of economic and political decision making, but as the human condition itself. The 'damned human race' always achieved what it deserved.[26]

Populism and the Industrial Working Class

I turn now from literary constructions to an argument in political economy. What marks the crisis of the 1890s as a hegemonic crisis is that the moral and cultural authority of the ruling class had been stretched thin; if I may borrow a phrase from the preceding literary discussion, it was ceasing to induce the willing suspension of disbelief.

Since the political embodiment of that authority was the Republican party, the dialectics of party systems pointed to the assembling of a new antithesis. By whom was the task to be undertaken? There is no need to invoke myths of history without a subject. The subjects in this particular history were individuals who for a variety of reasons lost confidence in the guidance of the Republican party at the same time that they doubted the capacity of its binary partner to replace it. Still, they continued to rely on traditional politics, or at least perceived no other channel of effective collective activity. Whatever theoretical alternatives may or may not have existed, historical hindsight tells us that in fact only one materialized: Populism. The problem then can be placed as a single question: why did Populism fail to provide a new antithesis in the form of a class coalition substantial enough to disrupt the existing party system?

Constructing an answer to this question requires a survey of class formations potentially available as participants in such a coalition. Since the advent of a class interest 'neither obsolescent nor governed by bourgeois property codes' might be expected to alter the party-building process qualitatively, the most promising place to begin that survey will be with the industrial working class.[27]

A preceding chapter examined the composition and organizational structure of the industrial working class. Here it will be necessary to focus on an aspect central to the concept of hegemony: the development of class consciousness, as distinct from objective class formation. For urban artisans, objective class formation was a gradual process spanning several centuries. In America, it kept pace with the slow growth of cities during the eighteenth century and with their rapid proliferation in the nineteenth. Class consciousness embodied in an identifiable urban artisan culture appears throughout this process as a necessary result of class formation. With the advent of mass politics and mass media in the 1830s and 1840s, artisan ideology installed its egalitarian producer ethic at the center of the Jacksonian legitimizing synthesis. By the 1880s, when artisans were beginning to fade from view as an objective class, urban artisan culture had become synonomous with national culture, a turning point recorded in literature by the nationalizing of the western vernacular hero.[28]

Meanwhile, diverse class groupings were being transformed, objectively, into an industrial working class. But although this transformation seems to have occurred more rapidly and more massively than in England or any of the European industrializing nations, the prior artisanization of American national culture and its resultant stress on egalitarianism made for a situation with respect to class consciousness that differed significantly from that in England and Continental Europe. Despite rapid class formation, industrial working-class consciousness in America developed only deviously and haltingly.

The historic transition for industrial working classes has been from agrarian pre-industrial modes to urban postartisan modes. In England, a rural labor force, already keenly apprised of its low social status, moved to industrializing towns, where its status remained as low or lower than before. There was much that was new to be learned, but not many illusions to be unlearned. In America, if we leave aside the relatively small number of urban artisans who gravitated into the industrial working class, the major components of that class during the nineteenth century were old stock Anglo-Americans from agricultural regions and European immigrants from rural areas.[29]

Old stock Euro-Americans were already immersed in artisan culture and white egalitarian ideology. As noted earlier, they carried this consciousness into the National Labor Union, the Knights of Labor, even into some of the early trade unions. Recent European immigrants, on the other hand, painfully aware of having come from the lower levels of hierarchical societies, found themselves in America adopted into an apparently viable artisan culture that, by rejecting class hierarchy, promised to transcend ethnic subordination. To the extent these immigrants entered industrial employment (as generally they did), American artisan ideology represented for them, in its most classic sense, a false consciousness. Yet because it was so pervasive, and because it expressed so precisely their aspirations in coming to America, it was a consciousness that 'worked' for a few, and became for most desperately difficult to outdistance.[30]

Industrial class formation in America, as Herbert Gutman has made clear, differed in another respect also from the English, or European, model.[31] The process in the East and Midwest of the United States comprised a series of great waves of entry. Beginning with old stock Anglo-Americans in the 1850s, moving to Irish and Germans in the 1870s and 1880s, then to Southern and Eastern Europeans in the 1890s and twentieth century, the transition from rural to urban-industrial was repeated at intervals of about one generation across a 75-year time span. Class formation might be abrupt and traumatic for each of these waves; but the development of class consciousness was continually disrupted and set back by the infusions of pre-industrial recruits.[32]

To this must be added one further element unique to the United States – the now massively studied phenomenon of ethnocultural, linguistic and religious diversity. Each successive wave moved further, culturally, from the old stock; and each showed greater differentiation within itself than the preceding wave. The unifying tendencies of shared class experience yielded to other identities that congealed into the miniscule patterns of towns, neighborhoods, occupations, factories, workshops. Not only did these identities in themselves take priority over class identification, they embodied and perpetuated different stages of transition from pre-industrial to urban–industrial. Thus in the Chicago of the 1890s to cross from a brewery or cabinet shop to a nearby construction site might be to move from a German Marxist circle to a scene out of medieval Sicily. While ethnocultural fragmentation (with certain important exceptions) inhibited class identification, it opened up all these circles, shut off one from another, to the common urgings of Americanization couched in the now almost mystic terms of artisan egalitarianism. Through this proclivity, the vast expansion of media into Sunday supplements, saturation advertising, motion pictures and radio, fastened early in the twentieth century upon its mass audience. A long-range outcome is that the industrial working class of the United States can scarcely be said to have arrived at any general consciousness of class 'for itself' prior to about 1930; and even then only meagerly by contrast to industrial classes of Europe.[33]

At shorter range, however, there is evidence of a slow rise of working-class consciousness towards a peak in the 1890s. The organizational record, summarized in the preceding chapter, shows the Knights of Labor still in existence; the American Railway Union gaining nationwide support; the craft unions not yet irrevocably severed from the rest of labor. Central labor councils functioned in many cities. A contemporary observer might have concluded not unreasonably that these councils would prove a more potent force in the labor movement than national craft unions. City centrals entered politics, assumed leadership in strikes and organizing drives, often sponsored labor newspapers, cultural events and entertainment. Although the actual membership of labor unions totaled barely 10 percent of the industrial labor force, union influence spread far more widely through kinship and associational networks. Moreover, trade unions were not the only type of working-class organizations. Urban communities had their ward clubs, their favorite saloons, their picnic groves. Ethnicity, that fragmenter of class identity, served also under certain circumstances, to reinforce it. The *turnverein*, the Fenian society, the Yiddish theater, Finnish choral singers, Polish meeting halls, Italian church festivals, all, within their ethnic boundaries, tightened the cohesiveness of working-class interdependence. Although politics at national and state levels favored a conventional producer rhetoric, urban politicians often specialized in the proletarian style. To their middle-class counterparts such functionaries might seem to be tools of corrupt machines; but for their constituents they were likely to appear as men putting first things first, and who viewed upper-class morality with the cynicism it deserved. In American cities of the 1890s an autonomous working-class culture –

or, more accurately, a multiplicity of working-class cultures, fragmented and discontinuous but not altogether incoherent – was beginning to show itself.[34]

With reference to the historical elements that entered into it, the collective consciousness of industrial workers in the 1890s may be divided into four ideal types: 1) Peasant-Traditional; 2) Producer Ethic; 3) Job or Craft Consciousness; and 4) Class Consciousness. No type, except possibly the first, could have existed in pure form; yet because each type has identifiable antecedents and consequences, a comparison of the four offers a vantage point from which to survey the relationship between consciousness and behavior. Doubtless for some industrial workers, the four types represented a sequential process. Not for most: the vast majority in the 1890s remained within Types 1 and 2; whereas either Types 3 or 4 might have been arrived at without passing through any of the others. In the discussion that follows each of the four types will be characterized separately, and their political consequences then compared and contrasted.

1. In America, industrial workers of the Peasant-Traditional mentality would be those recently arrived from rural regions in Europe. They imported their sense of class subordination, transposing deference from Old World landlord elites to New World labor contractors, industrial employers and ward bosses. Their extra-class connections were primarily those of clientship. Crowded into urban slums, integrated economically into industrial America, they remained for the time being socially and culturally outside its perimeters.[35]

2. Adherents of the Producer Ethic in the 1890s probably comprised the most numerous type. Both skilled and unskilled, this type would have been strongly represented among workers living in small towns; and among those in industries of non-urban ambience such as railroads, lumbering, mining. Deadwood Dick's egalitarian mine partner was one of these. But they were by no means absent from the cities, as Frederick Whittaker's dime novel craftsmen testify. The type would have been most prevalent among native-born Anglo-Americans; yet first- and second-generation immigrants striving to break away from Peasant-Traditional enclaves would have been likely to grasp some version of the Producer Ethic.[36]

3. Skilled workers in 1890 were a small minority of the industrial labor force and most, native-born or immigrant, probably adhered to Type 3, Craft or Job Consciousness. So did many of their union spokesmen. Craft or Job Consciousness presupposed a perception that wage labor had

become permanent; consequently an awareness of class hierarchy as inherent in industrial capitalism. But within Type 3 these phenomena could be viewed positively since skilled workers, and trade unionists most of all, held advantaged positions that promised continuing benefits. Craft or Job Consciousness almost by definition excluded the unskilled.[37] Yet many unskilled, native and immigrant, accepted the leadership of skilled craft unions and might even internalize craft consciousness in the sense of hoping to acquire a skill, or anticipating that their sons might do so. For these reasons, and because of the organizational power of skilled craft unions, Craft or Job Consciousness in the 1890s was becoming the dominant type, not in numbers but in prestige and influence.[38]

4. Type 4, Class Consciousness, must have been confined to a relatively small segment of industrial workers. These included skilled and unskilled, native born and recent immigrants, along with scatterings of trade union activists and leaders. Class Consciousness, like Craft or Job Consciousness, accepted the advent of wage labor as irreversible and perceived class hierarchy as inherent in capitalist industrialization. It diverged from Craft Consciousness by denouncing wage labor status as unjustly exploitative. In this respect it resembled Type 2, the Producer Ethic; but whereas the Producer Ethic understood the exploitative aspects of industrialization to result from individual derelictions that could be corrected by moral suasion or government policies aimed at restoring producer egalitarianism, Class Consciousness understood these same aspects as the necessary results of capitalism, capable of remedy only through revolutionizing the industrial system.[39]

If the hegemonic crisis of the 1890s resulted from the non-conformance of industrialization-as-experienced to egalitarian-values-as-inherited, it follows that those segments of the working class most strongly committed to egalitarian values would be most intensely affected by the crisis. Political initiatives would not be likely to emanate from Type 1 (Peasant-Traditional) nor from Type 3 (Craft or Job Consciousness), since the former had not yet arrived at a Producer Ethic mentality and the latter had rejected it. If any efforts toward revising the party system were to originate within the industrial working class, one would expect to find them in Type 2 (Producer Ethic). Even within this type, however, workers of immigrant background recently separated from Peasant-Traditional enclaves would have been more likely to glorify the existing party system than to seek to disrupt it. Type 4 (Class Consciousness) presents a more complex picture. Its adherents would welcome the crisis as foreshadowing eventual collapse of the ruling class. Some might favor a new class coalition founded on that expectation. Yet since the more influential among them were skilled workers and craft unionists, these would tend to divert their energies (and their followers) into discrediting Producer Ethic politics as distorted by nostalgic misconceptions, and therefore inconsequential and unreliable. Others of Type 4 who were unskilled workers, middle-class radicals (or both), would be prone to place impossible demands upon their Producer Ethic allies, and then, finding themselves isolated, move to apocalyptic stances. Such were the windows of collective consciousness available to the industrial working class for evaluating the Populist insurgency.

The Rural Bases of Populism

Populism's major bases of agrarian support were in the Great Plains states, recently opened, thanks to the Republican economic program, as suppliers of grain for the world market; and in the South, tied as it long had been to production of cotton for the world market. Both regions in the 1880s and 1890s were more than proportionately burdened by mortgage and tenancy; the South by sharecropping and debt peonage as well. Populism in the Great Plains and Rocky Mountains probably actualized, or nearly so, its potential strength. But such certainly was not the case in the South nor in other agricultural regions of Populist activity such as California and the Old Northwest.[40]

Expansion of the mass base of the southern Populist coalition required alliances across race lines. While this strategy had been held to be unthinkable since the end of Reconstruction, in fact a good many people thought seriously about it during the 1890s. One was Ignatius Donnelly, sturdy radical of northwestern Populism, author of *Caesar's Column* as well as the party's most famous political manifesto. Turning his attention to racial problems, Donnelly in 1891 constructed the story of a southern aristocrat, Dr. Huguet (of Huguenot ancestry), who found himself magically turned into a black man and thus learned at firsthand what the situation of black men really was. Although by no means separating himself from racist assumptions, Donnelly endeavored to reach beyond them and the immediate political message of his book was clear: white and black must work together to defend the virtues of the old republic.[41] Whether or not they had read his book, some of Donnelly's party colleagues in the South pursued the same political logic he set forth in *Dr. Huguet*.

The Mississippi constitutional convention of 1890, held avowedly for the purpose of removing blacks 'from the sphere of politics', had testified to a prevalent belief that black political involvement might be increasing rather than diminishing. Actually black voters had taken continuous part since Reconstruction in politics not only in Mississippi but in other southern states. Normally, after 1877, such participation had been limited to bargaining for minor offices with conservative Bourbon leadership in the Black Belt counties. Yet there were hints of a different possibility. Scatterings of black voters had supported the Granger movement as well as the short-lived Greenback party. During the heyday of the Southern Farmers' Alliance, black farmers were accepted into Alliance membership, although generally in segregated chapters.[42]

The Farmers' Alliance became the matrix of Populism, and the Populist party in the South launched a bitter, often violent, revolt against landlord domination. Many white farmers bolted the old Democracy. In some regions – most dramatically in North Carolina, Alabama and Georgia – they built inter-racial coalitions. This situation confronted white voters with a choice roughly analagous to that faced by northern workingmen at conventions of the National Labor Union twenty-five years earlier: should the egalitarianism of the producer ethic include all who toiled productively; or should it exclude those deemed racially unfit for participation? As in the case of the northern workingmen, the fact that whites divided on this question did not mean that their views on race diverged. Probably almost all southern whites in the 1890s accepted as an eternal fact the superiority of the white race. What was at issue for them, simply, was whether white farmers could best improve their situations through class solidarity across racial lines, or by working within the racially exclusive boundaries of the Democratic party.[43]

Most widely known, although certainly not the greatest, of southern Populists was Tom Watson of Georgia. Elected to Congress as agrarian Democrat from a back country district, Watson became convinced of 'an irrepressible conflict between the farming interests and Democracy [that is, the Democratic party] ... between the laboring classes and the old party.'[44] Staking his career on the Populist insurgency, he not only spoke but campaigned for inter-racial cooperation. 'You are kept apart that you may be separately fleeced of your earnings', he told black and white voters. 'You are made to hate each other because upon that hatred is rested the keystone of the arch of financial despotism which enslaves you both. You are deceived and blinded that you may not see how this race antagonism perpetuates a monetary system which beggars both.'[45] Watson was not alone. Insurgency seemed to be riding an upward swell of mass support. Populists carried 45 percent of the vote in Georgia, 40 percent in Mississippi; a Populist-Republican fusion of white and black in North Carolina won control of the legislature. Yet the outcome was the same in all cases. Methods earlier employed against Radical Reconstruction were now used to break the Populist party. Its candidates were charged with conspiracy against the white race. Leaders were murdered, and its voters were bulldozed from the polls at gunpoint. In areas of heavy black population, black sharecroppers were coerced or bribed by their landlords, or by local officials, into voting against the Populist ticket. Ironically, black voters provided the margin to defeat Watson in his home county.[46]

Still, the Bourbon Democracy had been hard-pressed. The old elite began to call for revisions in the electoral laws on the Mississippi model.[47] White Populists at first rejected disfranchisement.[48] Perhaps they might have clung even more tenaciously to inter-racial alliance had the party been winning in other regions. But as defeat followed defeat locally and nationally, they yielded ground. Convinced that the race issue had overwhelmed them, they began to accuse blacks of betrayal. Leaders like Watson turned from class solidarity to white supremacy.[49] One after another, states south of the Chesapeake and as far west as Oklahoma adopted variations of Mississippi's disfranchisement plan.[50] White racism had thwarted Populist efforts to overturn the existing party system.

In agricultural regions outside the Great Plains, Populists fared no better than in the South. The Old Northwest, once a major grain exporter, had moved by 1890 to diversified farming for urban markets. California was shifting from grain to fruit. Previously supportive of Granger enterprises, these regions gave only meager backing to Populism. The basic Populist texts of railroad regulation, expanded currency, easy credit based on government storage of world market staples (cotton, wheat), said relatively little to farmers who specialized in perishables for domestic markets. Conceivably an argument stressing the relation of industrial wage rates to farm prices might have reached them had there been time to deploy and popularize such arguments. Indeed, Populism could doubtless have worked out many advantageous local alliances if victories elsewhere had been sending reliable men to push the party program in state legislatures and in Washington. Half a century earlier, when Republicans pioneered the third party route, they had inherited older Whig constituencies through which they set forth the bargains and persuasions that eventually brought artisans and entrepreneurs, nativists and immigrationists, expansionists and antislavery militants into their coalition. Lack of such well-founded progenitors denied to Populism the advantage of multistage development.[51]

Populism in the Cities

What sort of allies might Populism have discovered in the cities? Conventional wisdom says none. Yet agitation for antitrust laws, suspicion of boss-controlled machines, willingness by local elites to support wage earners against outside capital, dialogues of utopia and catastrophe in popular fiction, as well as the Social Gospel movement itself, totally an urban Protestant phenomenon – all point to the involvement of middle-class city dwellers in the crisis of the 1890s.[52] Historical hindsight indicates that in each case the actual movement was away from radical alternatives. By the end of the decade, these urban middle-class formations had coalesced into the social base of Progressivism, which, having briefly disrupted the existing party system in 1912, reestablished that system in its most conservative phase after the First World War.[53]

If, however, we hold off temporarily the gift of hindsight and stay with a notion of hegemonic crisis working across class and regional boundaries, the eventual outcomes cease to appear predetermined. The antitrust movement, for example, *might* have reasserted Jacksonian egalitarianism in the new industrial context instead of exalting bigness and efficiency. The crusade against corrupt city machines *might* have brought forward participatory democracy rather than commission or city manager models borrowed from corporate structure. Local elites in industrializing towns *might* have fought for autonomy rather than choosing to serve as comprador deputies for outside capital. The Social Gospel movement *might* have favored its activist and Christian Socialist cadres over its institution builders and imperialists.

All, or any, of these beginnings in the 1890s would have reinforced the Populist insurgency. Had they led to alliances in the cities they could have strengthened the hard-pressed rural bases of Populism. It seems that each of the beginnings referred to above in one way or another implicated the industrial working class. Antitrust agitation was in part directed against the corporate employers of unskilled immigrant labor. Corruption of city government involved collusion between such employers and political machines sustained by working-class votes. The relationship between local elites in industrializing towns and outside capital would have balanced differently had local wage earners been organized into industrial rather than craft unions. And as to the Social Gospel movement, its radical cadres generally operated as missionaries or colonizers in working-class slums where the unskilled, and consequently the unorganized, were most heavily concentrated. In each instance, working-class responses or an absence of responses to the crisis of the 1890s partially conditioned middle-class behavior. I am not arguing that urban workers could have converted the middle class to Populism. It seems more likely that greater working-class political activity would have polarized and split the middle class. Yet that result would have served Populist politics better than simple indifference. Had middle-class polarization accompanied or resulted from initiatives aimed at building a new class coalition, the contours of the 1890s might have been substantially altered. Was any sort of alliance with segments of the industrial working class potentially available to the Populist insurgency?

There is no question that some Populists strove for an alliance with industrial labor. Certainly they must have perceived the trend toward working-class cultural autonomy, perhaps even exaggerated its unifying effects, as Edward Bellamy did when he wrote in 1887, 'However chimerical the aspirations of the laboring classes might be deemed, the devotion with which they supported one another in the strikes, which were their chief weapon, and the sacrifices which they underwent to carry them out left no doubt of their dead earnestness'.[54]

Populist programs included issues upon which agrarian and industrial producers could make common cause. Party leaders cultivated close ties with the Knights of Labor, with whom they shared the ideological concepts of the Producer Ethic. When the Pullman strike broke out in 1894, agrarian activists in many regions hastened to the aid of the embattled industrial workers.[55] Neither of these initiatives led very far. The Knights of Labor, crushed by employer attacks and by the ascendant craft unions, was already nearing its end. Meanwhile, Eugene Debs's marvelously promising industrial organization, the American Railway Union, had been destroyed by the same forces. Debs himself was seeking a political home, which he found at last in the Socialist party; during the 1890s he traveled briefly with the Populists and was even considered as a presidential candidate in 1896. The vision of an alliance between agrarian radicals and militant industrial unionists certainly stirred some Populist imaginations. But Debs's organized following had been scattered by the smashing of his union, and he could offer no effective entré to the industrial working class.[56]

From the Populist viewpoint, the American Federation of Labor had to be the key to the situation. Samuel Gompers, as national spokesman for skilled craft unionism, stood against any sort of alliance with the Populist party. Craft union leaders were generally suspicious of Populism. Having themselves only recently turned away from the Producer Ethic, which they considered detrimental to their craft interests, they feared being drawn back into its network. Ideological incompatibility reflected economic and political cleavages. These are vividly exemplified in the divergent positions of the AFL and the Populists with respect to the eight-hour day. The Federation, after the disasters of 1886, had shifted from broad-gauge campaigns for the shorter workday to negotiations in selected shops and industries. The eight-hour day was to be arrived at piece-meal, wherever workers mustered sufficient strength to make it stick. This meant, in the 1890s, that only members of skilled craft unions, and not many of those, would enjoy the eight-hour day.[57]

Populists, by contrast, proposed nationwide political agitation for an act of Congress. Characteristically, they sought to push the federal government into the role of champion of the nation's producers; which, had it occurred, would have eliminated both the need for craft unionism and the privileged status of the skilled trades. Moreover, their proposal assumed the desirability of mass political action by agrarian and industrial producers directed against the industrial system. Such an assumption was of course intolerable to Federation leaders, who by this time had accepted capitalist-controlled industrialization and were seeking to survive within its interstices. They opposed mass politics as vehemently as they did industrial organization of the unskilled, and for essentially the same reasons.[58]

The Federation, however, accounted for less than 10 percent of the industrial labor force. Might not the Populists have appealed directly to the unskilled and unorganized 90 percent? Their ideological sympathy with industrial unionism pointed in that direction. So did their project of enlisting the federal government on behalf of the nation's producers. In western cities such as Denver and San Francisco, Populist labor politics sometimes proved impressively successful. Partly this reflected the strength of industrial unionism, which still overshadowed craft unionism west of the Rockies. By contrast, Populist politics never got off the ground in eastern industrial cities. While the American Federation of Labor might flourish in such cities, the vast bulk of the working class, recruited from the 'new' immigration of southern and eastern Europe, labored unorganized in the mills and factories. More than any other segment of the labor force, these 'new' immigrants perpetuated a Peasant-Traditional mentality as yet unleavened by radicalizing influences of the Producer Ethic.[59]

Equally foreign to them was the Job or Craft Consciousness of the skilled men. Although skilled and unskilled often worked inside the same plants, they existed in separate worlds, held apart by religion, language, life-style. Skilled workers were mostly old stock Americans or Irish and Germans of the 'old' immigration. 'Old' immigrants, like old stock Americans, viewed the 'new' with anxiety and often contempt. Following the depression of 1893 their craft unions, led by the Federation, began to expand the victorious war against the Chinese into a demand for general restriction of immigration. To 'new' immigrants, who doubtless applauded Chinese exclusion, this shift came as an assault on their cultural identity, a negation of familial obligations.[60]

What had Populists to say to these workers? Potentially a great deal; yet to realize that potential would have required emphasizing the issues of industrial organization and the role of the federal government, which separated Populists from craft unionists. Eager for rapprochement with organized labor, the Populists tended to do exactly the opposite. They echoed craft union criticisms and focused on grievances like injunctions and the use of Pinkertons, crucial certainly to unionists, but irrelevant to the unorganized. They advocated 'the further restriction of undesirable immigration.' Eastern factory and mill hands, if they had encountered any Populists, would have found them indistinguishable from craft unionists.[61]

There existed within the American working class a scattering of radicals who might have acted as mediators between West and East, between the Populists and the industrial labor force. For the most part these were Marxists, at the hard core of the Class Consciousness mentality. In an economic sense they were more radical than the Populists. Many, as advocates of industrial unionism, struggled against the conservative leadership of skilled craft unions; yet despite this fact – or because of it – they remained locked into the gravitational field of craft unionism. American Marxists, whether native or foreign-born, had acquired their radicalism in the European tradition from which Jacksonian egalitarianism on the one hand, and the problems of a racially and ethnically divided labor force on the other, were conspicuously absent. Perceiving the Producer Ethic mentality as naive or hypocritical, they gave short shrift to the notion of common interests shared by industrial workers and agricultural producers. Far from serving as mediators, they seem to have used their Marxism to show that collaboration with Populism would prove detrimental to working-class interests.[62] To this extent, at least, Marxian radicalism reinforced the conservative trade union leadership. Thus the craft unions, especially those of the American Federation of Labor, not only rejected any alliance with Populism on their own account, but stood as roadblocks against Populist penetration of the urban working class.

Into this gap moved the Republican party in 1896 with its dramatic shift to cultural pluralism and its promise of rising wages – even for Hungarian and Italian mill hands – to be buoyed by rising tariffs. The proclivity of Peasant-Traditional mentalities to reproduce client-patron models in cross-class relationships dovetailed with this Republican initiative. What resulted was a political separation of the American working class by which the trade union sector adhered to the Democratic party while unskilled and unorganized 'new' immigrants slipped into a kind of gigantic rotten borough presided over by industrial patrons in midwestern and northeastern smokestack cities. In this way the Republican coalition acquired a brand new constituency that would help preserve its grip on federal power until the Great Depression of the 1930s.[63]

In the hegemonic crisis of the 1890s, Populism mounted the only significant challenge to Republican dominance. There were many reasons why the Populist party failed to sustain that challenge: two suffice to complete the present argument. The first is that Populism proved ineffectual in the South because the white supremacist commitment of white southerners precluded political cooperation between whites and blacks.

The second fits into a more extended sequence. In northeastern and midwestern cities, Populism failed to establish alliances with industrial workers in part because skilled craft unions stood against mass politicization of the working class. It was of course impossible to bring together an antithesis from which the industrial working class absented itself. I am not here entering a debate as to whether labor organization helps or hinders the movement of a working class toward socialism. Obviously it has done both; and does mainly one or the other under particular historical circumstances. In the circumstances of the 1890s, American craft union leaders defended what they understood to be the interests of their membership as well as their own career ambitions. The result was to inhibit working-class political initiatives. Had craft union leaders been obliged to share labor's top bench with a set of industrial unionists like Debs or like Bill Haywood of the Western Federation of Miners, the outcome would necessarily have been different.

In a preceding chapter I tried to show that a racially divided labor force, together with racial exclusion and purposefully racist practices, were factors favoring dominance of a particular type of labor organization — skilled craft unionism. If that demonstration was persuasive, it follows that white racism both in the agrarian South and industrializing North tended to stabilize industrial capitalism, thus enhancing its capabiilty to ride out the crisis of the 1890s. The foregoing by no means exhausts the workings of white racism in the political economy of late nineteenth-century industrialization, since the focus has been narrowed to trade union and agricultural organizations that contained only fractions of the total labor force. White racism of course 'worked' throughout the entire range of the Euro-American population. Nevertheless, a focus restricted to Populism and craft unionism serves to point up basic relationships because, on issues of racial politics, the organizations in question placed themselves at the cutting edge for the class formations they partially represented.

The Two Thrusts of Social Darwinism

The election of 1896, returning the Republican party to power with a wider margin of the popular vote than any previous election except the one in which Grant defeated Greeley, opened the way for overseas expansion and world empire. That Social Darwinism provided a world view corresponding to and rationalizing world empire has become orthodox doctrine. Yet for this ideological connection to make sense, a distinction must be drawn between the two separate thrusts of Social Darwinism.[64] In the United States, at least, the class-oriented thrust could not work as a legitimizer of imperialist policies. Only the racially oriented thrust served that purpose. What the Republican party required, then, was a shift of emphasis from Andrew Carnegie's Gospel of Wealth to Josiah Strong's Social Gospel. Precisely this shift was to be acted out as a parable for the mass media in Theodore Roosevelt's journey from the Dakota Badlands to San Juan Hill in Cuba.[65]

As a North Dakota cattle rancher in the 1880s, Roosevelt had linked himself to western images and associations. When he resigned from his post as assistant secretary of the Navy in 1898, he threw himself into organizing a western volunteer regiment, of which he became lieutenant colonel under Leonard Wood and which he actually commanded through the Cuba campaign.[66] Congress had specified that the First Volunteer Regiment (later nicknamed Rough Riders) was to be recruited from the 'four territories which yet remained within the boundaries of the United States.'[67] Roosevelt added a scattering of easterners, mostly athletes from Ivy League colleges, about whom he wrote ecstatically:

> What particularly pleased me ... was that they did not ask for commissions. ... So it was with Dudley Dean, perhaps the best quarterback who ever played on a Harvard eleven; ... with Yale men like Waller, the high jumper, ... with Princeton men like Devereux and Channing, the football players; ... with Joe Stevens, the crack polo player; and with Hamilton Fish, the ex-captain of the Columbia crew. ...

Since in 1898 the only sports yet professionalized were boxing and baseball, it seems likely that all these athletes were gentlemen amateurs.

The majority of Rough Riders, however, followed the callings of cowboys, miners, cattlemen, ranchers, and cattle-related trades such as blacksmiths, farriers, saddle-makers, cooks, railroad workers. Roosevelt apparently believed them all to be hunters as well, despite the fact that none laid claim to that pursuit. 'They were a splendid set of men, these southwesterners – ... with ... eyes that looked a man straight in the face without flinching ... the three types were those of the cowboy, the hunter, and the mining prospector – the man who wandered hither and thither, killing game for a living and spending his life in the quest for metal wealth. In all the world there could be no better material for soldiers than that afforded by these grim hunters of the mountains, these wild rough riders of the plains.'[69]

Roosevelt's roster included only one detective, although some of the lower commissioned officers had served as marshals or deputy sheriffs. The top officers were regular army men like Colonel Leonard Wood; and Roosevelt himself, who assessed his qualifications as follows:

> I had served three years as captain in the National Guard; I had been deputy sheriff in the cow country ... I was accustomed to big game hunting and to

work on a cow ranch, so that I was thoroughly familiar with the use of both horse and rifle, and knew how to handle cowboys, hunters and miners. ... [70]

Roosevelt's choice of words carries forward to Wister's Virginian, 'the horseman of the plains.' If, as I suggested earlier, *The Virginian's* most immediate literary antecedent was Remington's sketch of soldiers destroying a band of Cheyennes, certainly its social and political inspiration is to be found in Roosevelt's *Rough Riders*. Here was an entire regiment of Virginians controlled by gentlemanly officers who replicated the qualities of Judge Henry, the Virginian's patron and employer. Constructed from upper-class viewpoints, both works celebrated the transcendance of class separations. Thus, while on the one hand Roosevelt's genteel amateurs 'entered upon their duties ... endeavoring to show that no work could be too hard, too disagreeable, or too dangerous for them to perform', on the other hand his 'grim hunters' and 'riders of the plain' – the bulk of the regiment – submitted willingly to civilized restraints.[71]

'Any weakness in the commander would have ruined it', Roosevelt explained. 'The men were singularly quick to respond to any appeal to their intelligence and patriotism.' And again: '... we buried seven dead Rough Riders in a grave on the summit of the trail ... vultures were wheeling ... in great circles through the blue sky overhead. There could be no more honorable burial than that of these men in a common grave – Indian and cowboy, miner, packer and college athlete – the man of unknown ancestry from the lonely Western plains, and the man who carried on his watch the crests of the Stuyvesants and the Fishes, one in the way they had met death, just as during their life they had been one in their daring and loyalty.'[72]

An Indian among the first dead reflected the historical fact that Indians had volunteered from Oklahoma and Indian Territory and that Roosevelt had permitted some to enroll. His reference to them in *Rough Riders* corresponded to the difference between Remington's slaughter of Cheyennes in his 1897 sketch and Wister's abstracted and symbolic treatment of Indian killing in *The Virginian*. For Roosevelt – Wounded Knee being now eight years gone – Indians could be spoken of tolerantly provided they came in the garb of vanishing Americans, and, like Cooper's Mohican, earned their acceptance by aiding the white hunter against his national enemies. Yet their presence (and public acknowledgement of it) marked a deviation from the classic Free Soil scenario, which in other respects remained the underlying text of *Rough Riders*. This alteration provides a key to Roosevelt's racial ideology – one to which we will need to return after completing the cast of characters at San Juan Hill.[73]

The national enemy in the early summer of 1898 was the Spanish, who retreated as the Americans advanced and who surrendered by mid-July.

Roosevelt regretted that the exigencies of modern warfare left little room for hand-to-hand combat in the style of the old West; but he was able partially to fill this gap by his own dedication:

> ... we were all in the spirit of the thing and greatly excited by the charge. ... I was with Henry Bardshar, ... [when] two Spaniards leaped from the trenches and fired at us, not ten yards away. ... I closed in ... missing the first and killing the second. My revolver was from the sunken battleship *Maine*, and had been given to me by my brother-in-law, Captain W. S. Cowles, of the navy.[74]

Engrossed in political ambitions, Roosevelt searched for symbolic meanings. Cuba in 1898 furnished rich sources, since it summoned into retrospect five hundred years of North American history.

The invasion from the United States had brought together on San Juan Hill not only the Spanish, the Euro-Americans and a scattering of American Indians; but African Americans as well – members of the four black regiments that had been fighting Indians in the Far West since the 1870s:

> Having a great desire for adventure and to see the Wild West, I enlisted in the United States army, November 7, 1887, at Washington, D.C. ... I joined my troop at Fort Grant, Arizona Territory ... Churchana, an Indian chief, had established his headquarters near Benson's Camp ... with three troops and sixty Indian scouts [we] surrounded the hostile camp ... at daybreak planted two Hotchkiss guns. ... These same guns helped to form our battery before Santiago and of which I was a gunner.

The writer of these journal entries, Horace W. Bivins, was a African American, born in Virginia during the Civil War, educated briefly at Hampton Institute, and subsequently a sergeant in the Tenth Cavalry. In the spring of 1898, Bivins with his troop was patrolling the Blackfoot Reservation, 'which the government had announced would be thrown open for settlement.' Patrol duty was interrupted by orders to entrain for Tampa, Florida.[75]

'We received great ovations all along the line', Bivins recalled. '... as we neared the South the great demonstrations became less fervent. ... The signs over the waiting room door ... were a revelation to us. Some read thus: "White waiting room only." On the door of a lunch room we read: "niggers are not allowed inside."' What Sergeant Bivins felt about his eleven years' service against Indians he did not record in his journal; but he left no doubt as to his feelings for the cause of Cuban independence. Just before the landing he had written to a friend at home:

> Oh, God! at last we have taken up the sword to enforce the divine rights of a people who have been unjustly treated ... There is no people on earth more

loyal and devoted to their country than the Negro. ... I am sorry to say that we were not treated with much courtesy while coming through the South. God grant the time will soon come when this country will have the power to enforce the ... heavenly doctrine that all men are created free and equal.

The battery to which Bivins was attached took a central part in the fighting at San Juan Hill.[76] All this – including Bivins's perception of it – was in keeping with the black regulars' emblematic role in Republican tradition.

Roosevelt, clearly, had been socialized into the same tradition. When, at the end of the Cuba campaign he bade farewell to his regiment in order to return to politics, he admonished the Rough Riders as follows:

Now I want to say just a word more. ... I refer to the colored regiments, who occupied the right and left flanks of us at Guasimas, the Ninth and Tenth Cavalry regiments. The Spaniards called them 'Smoked Yankees', but we found them to be an excellent breed of Yankees. I am sure that I speak the sentiments of officers and men ... when I say that between you and the other cavalry regiments there exists a tie which we trust will never be broken.[77]

In the Battle of San Juan Hill, however (and in his own accounts of that battle first published in magazines in the spring of 1899), Roosevelt had taken a harder racial line:

... they are, of course, peculiarly dependent upon their white officers. ... None of the white regulars or Rough Riders showed the slightest sign of weakening; but under the strain the colored infantrymen (who had none of their own officers) began to get a little uneasy and to drift to the rear. ... This I could not allow, as it was depleting my line, so I jumped up, ... drew ... and called out to them that I appreciated the gallantry with which they had fought ... but that I would shoot the first man who ... went to the rear. ... 'You don't know whether or not I will keep my word, but my men can tell you that I always do'; whereupon my cowpunchers, hunters and miners solemnly nodded their heads and commented in chorus, exactly as if in a comic opera, 'He always does; he always does!' This was the end of the trouble for the 'smoked Yankees' – as the Spaniards called the colored soldiers – flashed their white teeth at one another, as they broke into broad grins. ...

Roosevelt concluded this episode by attributing the good behavior of black soldiers (when they did behave well) to their white officers, under whose leadership they had done 'as well as any soldiers could possibly do.'[79]

From Bivins's Tenth Regiment another black sergeant, Presley Holliday, replied in a public letter that the men Roosevelt threatened with his revolver had been sent by their own commanding officer to bring up ammunition and entrenching tools; that the officer explained the misunderstanding to Roosevelt, who, on the following day, had apologized to the men of the Tenth for his mistake. 'I thought he was sufficiently conscious of his error', Holliday wrote, 'not to make a so ungrateful statement about us at a time when the Nation is about to forget our past service.'[80]

What actually occurred during the battle is perhaps less relevant to the present argument than an explanation for Roosevelt's shifting and sometimes contradictory references to African Americans and Indians. It seems clear, first, that Roosevelt's political consciousness derived from early whiggish Republicanism with its stress on class hierarchy and its tendency to use racial liberalism as a means of reducing the status of lower-class whites. This original stance had been overlaid by the Free Soil alliance, which bid for the support of yeomen and artisans against southern slaveowners by consenting to white egalitarianism in politics and organizing Indian extermination in the West. African Americans – at least as perceived by the whiggish contingents of Republicanism – occupied a somewhat more favored situation than American Indians, both because they proved indispensable in defeating the South and because they had held the southern salient during Reconstruction. Roosevelt would thus have inherited a patronizing kindliness toward blacks, which, as a westerner by adoption in the 1880s, he found institutionalized in the black regiments of the regular army. At the same time he accepted western lore uncritically, writing, for example, that Sand Creek – despite 'certain most objectionable details' – had been 'on the whole as righteous and beneficial a deed as ever took place on the frontier.'[81]

Rapid industrialization after the Civil War brought class commitments back into dominance. Conflict then superceded the collaboration of the Free Soil alliance, although that alliance itself was by no means repudiated. Its white egalitarianism continued to shape the rhetoric of party politics even as the new industrial struggles were being fought out, by altered class formations, and largely outside the boundaries of the old alliance. Roosevelt, nineteen in 1877, would have discovered in the opening thrust of Social Darwinism both a historical explanation and a class strategy for the labor wars that shaped the social milieu of his adolescence. But explanations and strategies that worked during the period of forced-draft industrialization were tending by the 1890s to undermine Republican credibility. As leaders in a new cohort of ideological innovators, Roosevelt and many of his peers then moved to the later, racially oriented, thrust of Social Darwinism. For such a shift they had been well prepared by their political tradition, since the racial thrust of Social Darwinism replicated central aspects of the Free Soil alliance – that is, it appealed for class harmony by emphasizing racial divisions: like the Free Soil alliance, it was hard on race, soft on class.[82]

Raising pragmatism to the level of principle, Roosevelt and his colleagues believed that *noblesse oblige* imposed a duty of effective leadership in the arena of mass politics. They celebrated common sense and strenuousness. Roosevelt boasted that he 'knew how to handle cowboys, hunters and miners.'[83] Had he not gone to live among them and study their language? That of course was for their own good. Pragmatism must remain at the service of progress, while progress itself would be defined by the values and aspirations of that middle estate in which the whiggish Republican tradition found its base. Consequently, there need be no problem in readjusting the relative positions of lower races.

Indians had necessarily been targeted during the Free Soil period, when land in the West was at the heart of the matter. But with continental expansion completed, Indian killing became an embarrassment from which, in *Rough Riders*, Roosevelt cautiously disassociated himself. 'Only a few were of pure blood', he wrote of Indian soldiers in the regiment. 'The others shaded off until they were absolutely indistinguishable from their white comrades, with whom, it may be mentioned, they all lived on terms of complete equality.' Describing 'one of the gamest fighters and best soldiers', Roosevelt commented that 'like most of the other Indians', this 'full blooded Pawnee' had attended 'one of those admirable Indian schools which have added so much to the total of the small credit account with which the white race balances the very unpleasant debit account of its dealings with the red.' As would be expected, Roosevelt endorsed the main features of the Dawes Act. What had to be done was to 'break up the great Indian reservations, disregard the tribal governments, allot the land in severalty.' Like his predecessor, James Barbour, three-quarters of a century earlier, he now looked to benevolent extinction through amalgamation.[84]

Roosevelt's sequence with respect to African Americans was approximately opposite. Neither extinction nor amalgamation seemed likely to him. By 1899 he had moved from the benign Republican view of black soldiers as loyal helpers in saving the Union and winning the West to an accusation that African Americans alone among all the American military in Cuba had lost their nerve under fire. This amounted to excluding them from the national family – a sharp change from earlier Republican constructions. Why?

Short-range answers to this question are obvious. The war against Spain had elicited broad support, especially in the South and West. To American blacks, the Cuban cause had appeared doubly compelling because, as Sergeant Bivins of the Tenth Cavalry expressed it, the nation at last had taken up the sword 'to enforce the divine rights of a people who have been unjustly treated.'[85] Volunteers, white and black, flocked to the colors. Southern state recruitment officers generally rejected black volunteers, but these were enrolled into federal regiments specially authorized by Congress. In the white South, after its first enthusiasm for the war, a reaction set in against arming African Americans. This in turn reinforced the drive for suffrage restriction set in motion by the defeat of Populism. Together, these factors invaded national politics. 'The President cannot ... plead ignorance of what his act in mustering negro troops would lead to', the editor of the New Orleans *Times Democrat* wrote in the spring of 1899. 'Every one of these men will come back filled with the idea that he can play this social equality racket here, as well as in Santiago;. ... The man who ... arouses the lower race against the governing one ... must assume the responsibility for every drop of blood shed in race riots. ... '[86] With mounting urgency from the South, such warnings had the effect of damping down positive appraisals of black soldiers, especially among men with national political aspirations.[87]

Longer range answers must be more speculative. I have argued that the racially oriented thrust of Social Darwinism partially replicated the Free Soil alliance. Class structure in America, however, had changed profoundly between the 1840s and 1890s. The potentially dissident class groups that had to be wooed in the earlier period were artisans and yeomen. Since the political fix of these classes was on western expansion, their relevant racial enemy had to be Indians. But Indians in 1890 had ceased to be much of an obstacle to continental expansion, which in any case was virtually complete. The potentially dissident class had now become industrial workers – among whose political fixations was the fear of being undercut by immigration and by competition from 'lower' and 'cheaper' races.

If we think of the Cuba campaign as directed to the 'large policy'[88] of establishing United States dominance in the Caribbean, setting the stage for the Panama Canal, and securing Pacific bases for commercial and military ventures in Asia, Roosevelt's regiment provides an almost perfect scale model for the politics of Social Darwinism during its later, racially oriented phase. Immigration restriction – already in place against Asians – was logically necessary to this model, since it could hardly have seemed feasible to win white working-class assent to overseas empire unless that working class was protected from drowning in the ocean of world labor. Thus, implicitly or explicitly, major policy decisions of American industrial capitalism (at least until the onset of the Great Depression) were predicted in the Rough Rider model.

Affinities between Roosevelt and Wister point to the link between class control and ideological construction. Inspired by *Rough Riders*, Wister remodeled the western hero in a form that dominated American popular culture for the next half century. That hero's mix of white egalitarianism with imperial authority and Christian mission – the hallmark of Progressivism – swept the heights of American national consciousness. The search for a new antithesis was temporarily driven down into the nooks and crannies.

Notes

1. Frederick Jackson Turner, *Frontier and Section: Selected Essays of Frederick Jackson Turner*, ed. Ray Allan Billington, Englewood Cliffs, N.J. 1961, p. 61.
2. John A. Hicks, *The Populist Revolt: A History of the Farmers' Alliance and the People's Party*, [1931] Lincoln, Nebr. 1961, p. 405.
3. Richard Hofstadter, *The Paranoid Style in American Politics and Other Essays*, New York 1967, p. 196.
4. Ibid., p. 147.
5. Lawrence Goodwyn, *The Populist Moment: A Short History of the Agrarian Revolt in America*, New York 1978, p. *xiii*; Martin Sklar, *The Corporate Reconstruction of American Capitalism, 1890–1916: The Market, the Law and Politics*, New York 1988, especially pp. 20–33. Richard Slotkin's *The Fatal Environment: The Myth of the Frontier in the Age of Industrialization, 1800–1890*, Middletown, Conn. 1985, is entirely devoted to establishing the cultural-historical context for changes that would be finalized in the 1890s. See 'Morgan's Last Stand', pp. 499–532 – the Morgan referred to being Twain's Connecticut Yankee. Alan Trachtenberg, *The Incorporation of America*, New York 1982, and Leon Fink and Jackson Lears attach similar weight to the last decade of the century in their contributions to a roundtable, 'The New Labor History', in *Journal of American History* 75:115–140.
6. Hofstadter, *Paranoid Style*, p. 148.
7. Ibid., p. 197.
8. Rebeca Harding Davis, *Life in the Iron Mills*, ed. Tillie Olsen, Stony Brook, N.Y. 1972; Henry George, *Progress and Poverty: An Inquiry into the Cause of Industrial Depressions, and of Increase of Want with Increase of Wealth. The Remedy*, New York 1880.
9. Louis Nash, 'Is This a Christian Civilization?' *American Federationist* 1 (January 1895): 252, quoted in Herbert Gutman, *Work, Culture and Society in Industrializing America*, New York 1977, p. 93; Charles Sheldon, *In His Steps*, [1896] New York 1935.
10. Edward Bellamy, *Looking Backward, 2000–1887*, Garden City, N.Y. [1888], pp. 42, 198.
11. Senator John Sherman, *Congressional Record*, 51 Cong., 1st Sess. 21 March 1890, quoted in Hofstadter, *Paranoid Style*, pp. 197–98.
12. Ignatius Donnelly, *Caesar's Column: A Story of the Twentieth Century*, [1890] Cambridge, Mass. 1960, p. 4.
13. See Chapter 14.
14. That dime novels and story papers were regarded by the genteel culture as ideologically safe is confirmed by an article in the *Atlantic Monthly* [W.H. Bishop, 'Story-Paper Literature', 44 (September 1879): 383–93]. Humorously condescending, the article sets out to discover if story papers and dime novels are responsible as often charged for delinquency among youth. The conclusion is that despite their low literary level, their moral influence is positive. In regard to class conflict, the author, after noting that 'the capitalist is occasionally abused, showing that an eye is kept on the popular movements of the day', concludes that such stories offer little if any incitement to class hostility. Since this section occupies only a few lines in a long essay, it suggests that the *Atlantic Monthly*'s author, writing two years after the 1877 railroad strikes, found little to be alarmed at in the story-paper and dime novel literature.
15. Mark Twain [Samuel Clemens], *A Connecticut Yankee in King Arthur's Court*, [1889] San Francisco 1963; Edward Bellamy, *Looking Backward*; Ignatius Donnelly, *Caesar's Column*; William Dean Howells, *Letters of an Altrurian Traveller*, [1894], Clara M. Kirk and Rudolph King, eds, Gainesville, Fla. 1961.

16. Martin Ridge, *Ignatius Donnelly: The Portrait of a Politician*, Chicago 1962; Walter Rideout, 'Introduction', Donnelly, *Caesar's Column*, pp. *xii–xxxiii*.

17. Donnelly, *Caesar's Column*, 1:48–49, 299–313.

18. 'Omaha Platform', July 1892, in Hicks, pp. 439–44.

19. See, for example, Twain, *Connecticut Yankee*, pp. 20–21 or pp. 83–91, or *Roughing It*, 1869, or the first section of *Life on the Mississippi*, 1883; Henry Nash Smith, *Mark Twain: The Development of a Writer*, Cambridge, Mass. 1962, pp. 150–54; Smith, *Mark Twain's Fable of Progress*, New Brunswick, N.J. 1964, pp. 81–86.

20. Smith, *Fable*, pp. 67–69.

21. Twain, *Connecticut Yankee*, pp. 21–22, 39; Smith, *Fable*, pp. 81, 84.

22. Twain, *Connecticut Yankee*, among many examples, see pp. 27, 526, 573–74; *Autobiography of Mark Twain*, New York 1961, pp. 1–8, 13–16, 27–30; Smith, *Development*, pp. 71–75, 156; Smith, *Fable*, p. 106.

23. Twain, *Connecticut Yankee*, pp. 554–65.

24. Ibid., pp. 559–65; Twain, *Roughing It*, [1872] New York 1953, pp. 98–101, 290–95; Twain, 'Huck Finn and Tom Sawyer Among the Indians', described as 'an unpublished manuscript by Mark Twain', *Life*, 20 December 1968. For a different reading of Hank Morgan, see Slotkin, *Fatal Environment*, pp. 499–532. Having several times cited Richard Slotkin, I should comment here on the relation of his work to my own. Anticipating some parallel treatments and overlaps, I delayed reading his books until I had substantially completed this one. When I did read them I was impressed at their clarity of literary interpretation and the richness and scope of research reflected in them. I realized also that we were operating from different conceptual starting points. His was the traditional American Studies notion of myth – mystically constructed in replication of ancient archetypes and expressing across class lines the unifying inner consciousness or character of a society or nation. This approach served in my opinion to muddy the often brilliant perceptiveness of his readings, and to hamper the argument.

Slotkin, however, appears to be moving away from the American Studies tradition. In the preface to his second book, *Fatal Environment*, pp. *xii*, he suggests that his movement has been from 'literary' to 'historical', and attributes the shift not to any change in his own conceptualizations, but to differences in time period and materials under examination. I say that he has become less mythic and more ideological. 'Ideology' – totally absent from the index of *Regeneration Through Violence: The Mythology of the American Frontier, 1600–1860*, Middletown, Conn. 1973, and mentioned scarcely, if at all, in the text – requires in the later work sixteen index entries, which collectively designate fifty–two pages of reference or discussion. *Ideology*, or its adjectival form, appears in the titles of Chapters 1, 5, 11, 13 and in the title of the concluding section, Part 8, as well as in two chapter subheads within that final section. Whereas in the earlier work, myth merged into archetype, in the latter myth tends to merge into ideology – archetypes having been largely repudiated on account of their reductibility and amorphousness, pp. 27–28. The two words are now used in tandem 'myth/ideology', pp. 15, 29, 490, as if neither by itself adequately conveyed the author's meaning. This new emphasis requires a definition. 'In contemporary anthropology and social history', Slotkin writes, p. 22, 'the term "ideology" is used to describe the system of belief, values and relationships that constitute a culture or society.' Clifford Geertz among others is cited here, especially the famous essay, 'Ideology as a Cultural System', and Geertz figures prominently in the ensuing explanation of how ideology differs from myth. Yet the 'cultural system' definition has not quite provided Slotkin with an intellectual resting place. His usage sometimes seems closer to the class–conscious usage of a Karl Mannheim, for example, than to the rather class-neutral usages of 'contemporary anthropology and social history'. Before he has even finished with the differences between myth and ideology, Slotkin has committed himself to a thorough-going Gramscian formulation: ' ... ideology in the hands of a class seeking to establish and justify its hegemony reaches out to coopt myth', p. 25; 'Thus the ideology of a class striving for ascendancy will seek to appropriate the authority of myth', p. 26. I naturally applaud these renovations in the conceptual apparatus as enhancing the value and relevance of an already splendid body of work.

25. Smith, *Development*, p. 172; *Fable*, pp. 106–7; Van Wyck Brooks, *The Ordeal of Mark Twain*, New York 1920; Bernard DeVoto, *Mark Twain's America*, Cambridge, Mass. 1932.

26. Janet Smith, ed., *Mark Twain on the Damned Human Race*, New York 1962.

27. See Chapter 13; C.B. McPherson, *The Political Theory of Possessive Individualism: From Hobbes to Locke*, New York 1964, pp. 271–77.

28. E.P. Thompson, *The Making of the English Working Class*, New York 1966; Sean Wilentz, *Chants Democratic: New York City and the Rise of the American Working Class, 1788–1850*, New York 1984; Eric Foner, *Tom Paine and Revolutionary America*, New York 1976; Howard R. Rock, *Artisans of the New Republic: The Tradesmen of New York City in the Age of Jefferson*, New York 1984, pp. 19–147; Paul G. Faler, *Mechanics and Manufacturers in the Early Industrial Revolution: Lynn, Massachusetts, 1780–1860*, Albany, N.Y. 1981, pp. 28–57, 164–88; Susan E. Hirsch, *The Roots of the American Working Class: The Industrialization of Crafts in Newark, 1800–1860*, Philadelphia 1978, pp. 3–13; Bruce Laurie, *Working People of Philadelphia, 1800–1850*, Philadelphia 1980, pp. 33–104; Amy Bridges, 'Becoming American: The Working Classes in the United States before the Civil War', in Ira Katznelson and Aristide R. Zolberg, eds, *Working-Class Formation: Nineteenth-Century Patterns in Western Europe and the United States*, Princeton, N.J. 1986, pp. 157–96, especially pp. 194–96; Lisa Lubow, 'Artisans in Transition: Early Capitalist Development and the Carpenters of Boston, 1787–1837.' Ph.D. diss., University of California, Los Angeles, 1987.

29. Ira Katznelson, 'Working Class Formation: Constructing Cases and Comparisons', pp. 3–41 in Katznelson and Zolberg, p. 35; Gutman, *Work, Culture and Society*, pp. 13–19; Martin Shefter, 'Trade Unions and Political Machines: The Organization and Disorganization of the American Working Class in the Late Nineteenth Century', pp. 197–276 in Katznelson and Zolberg, especially p. 229; David Montgomery, *The Fall of the House of Labor*, New York 1987, pp. 48–51, 58–96.

30. Alexander Saxton, *The Indispensable Enemy: Labor and the Anti-Chinese Movement in California*, Berkeley, Calif. 1971, pp. 37–44; Shefter in Katznelson and Zolberg, pp. 252–5; Montgomery, *Fall*, pp. 46, 52–53.

31. Gutman, *Work, Culture and Society*, pp. 3–78.

32. Ibid., pp. 74–76.

33. Montgomery, *Fall*, pp. 370–464; Shefter in Katznelson and Zolberg, pp. 252–76; Melvyn Dubofsky, *Industrialism and the American Worker, 1865–1920*, Arlington Heights, Ill. 1985, pp. 7–16, 139–41; Dubofsky, *We Shall Be All: A History of the Industrial Workers of the World*, Chicago 1969, pp. 471–84.

34. Objective indices are that the AFL quadrupled its membership between 1897 and 1903: Montgomery, *Fall*, pp. 6, 169–70, 172; that the new Socialist Party, increasingly based in its urban foreign language federations, recorded its largest growth in the early twentieth century: James Weinstein, *The Decline of Socialism in America, 1912–1925*, New York 1967, pp. 1–26; Weinstein, 'The Problems of Socialism Before World War One', in John H. Laslett and Seymour M. Lipset, eds, *Failure of a Dream? Essays in the History of American Socialism*, Garden City, N.Y. 1974, pp. 300–40; Daniel Bell, *Marxian Socialism in the United States*, Princeton, N.J. 1967, pp. 55–81; David A. Shannon, *The Socialist Party of America*, Chicago 1967, pp. 1–61, especially pp. 43–47 on language federations; Elizabeth Gurley Flynn, *The Rebel Girl: An Autobiography, My First Life 1906–1926*, New York 1973, pp. 21–70; and that the IWW was able to carry the message of industrial unionism to mid-western and eastern industrial cities in the same years: Dubofsky, *We Shall Be All*, pp. 13–56, 227–90; Flynn, pp. 127–73; Michael Kazin, *Barons of Labor: The San Francisco Building Trades and Union Power in the Progressive Era*, Urbana, Ill. 1987, pp. 13–63; and Jules F. Tygiel, 'Workmen in San Francisco, 1880–1901', Ph.D. diss., University of California, Los Angeles, 1977, pp. 153–64, 294–381, on San Francisco in the 1890s. On Denver, David Brundage, 'The Making of Working Class Radicalism in the West: Denver, 1880–1892', Ph.D. diss., University of California, Los Angeles, 1982. The extensive literature on immigrant communities yields supporting evidence: see, for example, Moses Rischin, *The Promised City*, New York 1970, pp. 144–94, or Michael G. Karni and Douglas J. Ollila, Jr., eds, *For the Common Good: Finnish Immigrants and the Radical Response to Industrial America*, Superior, Wis. 1977. Works discussed earlier in this chapter on the crisis of the 1890s bear directly or indirectly on working-class consciousness. Fiction, whether hostile or sympathetic to labor, provides a rich source: William Dean Howells, *A Hazard of New Fortunes*, New York 1890; Upton Sinclair, *The Jungle*, [1906] Urbana 1988; John Hay, *The Breadwinners: A Social Study*, New York 1884; Jack London, 'South of the Slot' and the 'Dream of Debs', both 1909, in Philip S. Foner, ed., *Jack London: American Rebel*, New York 1947, pp. 240–72;

London, *Valley of the Moon*, New York 1913; *Martin Eden*, New York 1908; *The Iron Heel*, [1907] New York 1957. For expressions in dime novels, see Chapter 14 and Michael J. Denning, *Mechanic Accents: Dime Novels and Working-Class Culture*, London 1987.

35.   Gutman, *Work, Culture and Society*, pp. 24–32, 55–78, 326–31; Gwendolyn Mink, *Old Labor and New Immigrants in American Political Development: Union, Party and State, 1875–1920*, Ithaca, N.Y. 1986, pp. 61–67, 205; Montgomery, *Fall*, pp. 4, 49.

36.   Shefter in Katznelson and Zolberg, eds, pp. 238–39. On Whittaker's dime novels and Deadwood Dick, see Chapter 14. Walter Licht, *Working for the Railroad: The Organization of Work in the Nineteenth Century*, Princeton, N.J. 1983, pp. 221–25, 231, 244–45, 249–56; Michael Rogin, 'Comment', in Laslett and Lipset, eds, pp. 147–56.

37.   Rogin, pp. 147–54; Lloyd Ulman, *The Rise of the National Trade Union*, Cambridge, Mass. 1966, pp. 4, 19, 49–152. As Selig Perlman wrote in John R. Commons et al., *History of Labor in the United States*, New York 1918, 2:354, the craft unions, having inherited 'the wage consciousness of Marx and the International, purged of its socialist ingredients ... restricted their appeal to the skilled mechanics.'

38.   Mink, pp. 40–41; Saxton, *Indispensable Enemy*, pp. 238–41, 270; Montgomery, *Fall*, pp. 4, 46.

39.   Shefter in Katznelson and Zolberg, eds, pp. 224–26; Mink, 200–202; Montgomery, *Fall*, pp. 197–201; Saxton, *Indispensable Enemy*, pp. 194–200, 220–23.

40.   Hicks, pp. 1–300; Goodwyn, pp. 97–212, 230–63; Richard Hofstadter, *The Age of Reform: From Bryan to FDR*, New York 1955, pp. 46–59, 421–38; Saxton, 'San Francisco Labor and the Populist and Progressive Insurgencies', *Pacific Historical Review* 34 (November 1965): 421–38; James Edward Wright, *The Politics of Populism: Dissent in Colorado*, New Haven, Conn. 1974, pp. 43, 120–82; John R. Morris, *Davis H. Waite: The Ideology of a Western Populist*, Washington, D.C. 1982, pp. 73–94; Stephen Hahn, *The Roots of Populism: Yeoman Farmers and the Transformation of the Georgia Upcountry, 1850–1890*, New York 1983, pp. 147–69, 269–89; Richard Jensen, *The Winning of the Midwest: Social and Political Conflict, 1888–1896*, Chicago 1971, p. xvi.

41.   Ignatius Donnelly, *Dr. Huguet*, Chicago 1891; Nell Irvin Painter, *Standing at Armageddon: The United States, 1877–1919*, New York 1987, p. 101.

42.   Gerald Jaynes, *Branches without Roots: Genesis of the Black Working Class in the American South, 1862–1882*, New York 1986, pp. 265–66; Vernon Lane Wharton, *The Negro in Mississippi, 1865–1890*, New York 1965, pp. 201, 204–5; Hicks, pp. 97, 114–15, 252–54; Goodwyn, pp. 118–23, 187–200, 327–29; Hahn, pp. 283–84.

43.   Albert D. Kirwan, *The Revolt of the Rednecks: Mississippi Politics, 1876–1925*, New York 1965, pp. 85–102; C. Vann Woodward, *Tom Watson: Agrarian Rebel*, New York 1963, pp. 135–45, 196–98; Robert D. Ward and William W. Rogers, *Labor Revolt in Alabama: The Great Strike of 1894*, University, Ala. 1965, pp. 39–45, 118–21; Hugh Talmadge Lefler and Albert Ray Newsome, *The History of a Southern State: North Carolina*, Chapel Hill, N.C. 1973, pp. 546–50. On the issue of race in the National Labor Union, Saxton, *Indispensable Enemy*, pp. 40–43.

44.   *People's Party Paper*, 2, 9, 23 September 1892, cited in Woodward, *Tom Watson*, p. 234; Painter, pp. 101–3.

45.   Tom Watson, 'The Negro Question in the South', *Arena* 6 (1892): 584; *People's Party Paper*, 26 October 1892, cited in Woodward, *Tom Watson*, pp. 220, 240.

46.   Woodward, *Tom Watson*, pp. 241, 269–71, 273–77; Ward and Rogers, pp. 118, 128; Wharton, pp. 199–206. On Populist percentages, Woodward, *Tom Watson*, p. 269; Kirwan, p. 101. On the North Carolina coalition, Lefler and Newsome, pp. 549–562; Jack Abramowitz, 'The Negro in the Populist Movement', *Journal of Negro History* 388 (July 1953): 257–89.

47.   Kirby, pp. 14–15.

48.   *People's Party Paper*, 8 November 1895, cited in Woodward, *Tom Watson*, p. 371; Kirby, p. 15.

49.   Jackson, Miss., *Clarion–Ledger*, 10 September 1903, quoted in Kirwan, p. 160; *Tom Watson's Magazine*, 1 (June 1905): 298, and 4 (April 1906): 165–74, quoted in Woodward, *Tom Watson*, p. 380, and pp. 370–72, on disfranchisement in Georgia; Painter, p. 220.

50.   Kirwan, pp. 122–35; Kirby, pp. 7–25.

51.   Eric Foner, *Free Soil, Free Labor, Free Men: The Ideology of the Republican Party before*

the Civil War, New York 1970, pp. 193–225; Walter Dean Burnham, *Critical Elections and the Mainsprings of American Politics*, New York 1970, pp. 34–36.

52. Shefter, in Katznelson and Zolberg, p. 209; Herbert Gutman, 'The Workers' Search for Power: Labor in the Gilded Age', in H. Wayne Morgan, ed., *The Gilded Age: A Reappraisal*, Syracuse, N.Y. 1963, pp. 38–68. Gutman overstated his case in this essay, but the point that local business in small or isolated industrial towns initially tended, sometimes, to support local labor against outside capital remains valid. The *Rocky Mountain News* editorial quoted in Chapter 13 catches Denver employers at the moment of reversing just such a tendency. And see Nick Salvatore, *Eugene V. Debs, Citizen and Socialist*, Urbana, Ill. 1982, pp. 31–35.

53. Montgomery, *Fall*, pp. 370–410; Gabriel Kolko, *The Triumph of Conservatism*, New York 1963; Kolko, *Railroads and Regulation, 1877–1916*, New York 1970; James Weinstein, *The Corporate Ideal in the Liberal State, 1900–1918*, Boston 1968; Sklar, *Corporate Reconstruction*. On the Social Gospel, Henry F. May, *Protestant Churches and Industrial America*, New York 1967, *passim*.

54. Bellamy, p. 15.

55. Saxton, 'San Francisco Labor'; Michael Rogin, 'Comment', in Laslett and Lipset, eds, pp. 148–50; Ward and Rogers, especially pp. 118–29, 137–38; Ray Ginger, *Eugene Debs: A Biography*, New York 1962, pp. 130–31, 178–80, 203–6; Hahn, p. 272. On Populist support by midwestern coal miners, Jensen, pp. 258–59.

56. Ginger, *Debs*, pp. 203–6; Salvatore, *Debs*, pp. 114–61; Theodore Saloutos, 'Radicalism and the Agrarian Tradition', in Laslett and Lipset, eds, 134–46.

57. Philip Foner, *History of the Labor Movement in the United States*, New York 1947–80, 2:180–85; Lloyd Ulman, *The Rise of the National Trade Union*, Cambridge, Mass. 1966, p. 401; Philip Taft, *Organized Labor in American History*, New York 1964, p. 135; Foster Rhea Dulles and Melvyn Dubofsky, *Labor in America: A History*, 4th ed., Arlington Heights, Ill. 1984, pp. 116–19, 138–41; Paul Avrich, *The Haymarket Tragedy*, Princeton, N.J. 1984, pp. 181–86, 429.

58. Hicks, p. 420; Rogin, 'Comment' in Laslett and Lipset, pp. 150–51.

59. Wright, pp. 126–82; Brundage, pp. 178–205; Saxton, 'San Francisco Labor', and *Indispensable Enemy*, pp. 236–38; Kazin, pp. 38, 58. While craft unions were exceptionally strong in San Francisco, and industrial unionism remained dominant and prestigious in the mining industry to which the city was closely linked. Kazin, p. 19, notes that San Francisco, in which the 'old' immigration proliferated, was relatively untouched by 'new' immigration – with the exception of Asian immigrants, who were excluded from union participation.

60. Mink, pp. 45–68; Saxton, *Indispensable Enemy*, pp. 273–78; Jensen, pp. 256–57; John Higham, *Strangers in the Land: Patterns of American Nativism, 1860–1925*, New York 1963, pp. 50, 71–72, 112, 163–64.

61. 'Omaha Platform', July 1892, in Hicks, pp. 439–44; Mink, pp. 129, 143–44; Saloutos and Rogin, in Laslett and Lipset, pp. 134–56; Dulles and Dubofsky, pp. 170–73; Jensen, pp. 259–60.

62. Shannon, *Socialist Party*, pp. 25–28, 35–37; Paul Buhle, *Marxism in the USA from 1870 to the Present Day*, London 1987, pp. 71–79.

63. Jensen, pp. 291–308; Richard L. McCormick, *The Party Period and Public Policy: American Politics from the Age of Jackson to the Progressive Era*, New York 1986, pp. 58, 175–76; Stanley L. Jones, *The Presidential Election of 1896*, Madison, Wis. 1964; Mink, pp. 116–17, 131, 135–39, 155. Mink argues that the craft union commitment to closing Chinese immigration led to an alliance with the Democratic party, which set the precedent for the long–continuing political schism of the American working class. While I have difficulty with Mink's tendency to conflate 'racism' into 'nativism', I find her interpretation of labor politics and the immigration issue persuasive. See my review in *Amerasia Journal* 14:174–77.

64. U.S. Bureau of the Census, *Historical Statistics of the United States from Colonial Times to 1957*, Washington, D.C. 1957, p. 682. Jensen, in his chapter 'How the Midwest Was Won: Money, Morality and Pluralism in 1896', pp. 269–308, demonstrates the real value of ethnocultural data when synthesized with economic and ideological analysis. 1896 is generally taken to be a 'critical election'. Study of 'critical elections' – beginning with V.O. Key's famous essay, 'A Theory of Critical Elections', *Journal of Politics* 17:3–18 – has been serviceable to historians by identifying and describing the political disjunctures that

have ushered in new party systems. The weakness of critical election and realignment theory in my view has stemmed from a determination to explain critical elections and realignments within the political apparatus itself rather than as the results of developmental crises in the socio–economic structure at large. See, for example, Walter Dean Burnham, 'The Periodicity of American Critical Realignments', and 'The Movement toward Depoliticization: The "System of 1896" and the American Electorate', pp. 11–33 and 71–90 in *Critical Elections*, 1970. The same criticism could be made of William E. Gienapp, *The Origins of the Republican Party, 1852–1856*, New York 1987, which is, nonetheless, an extremely impressive work. Gienapp offers the most up-to-date statistical treatment of religious and ethnocultural factors in voting and of the actual behavior of critical elections and party realignment; see his summation, pp. 444–46. Richard L. McCormick has provided balanced reappraisals not only of ethnocultural interpretation, but of critical elections and realignment theory as well: *The Party Period*, pp. 1–88 and 197–227.

65.   William Henry Harbaugh, *The Life and Times of Theodore Roosevelt*, New York 1963, pp. 50–100; Theodore Roosevelt, *The Rough Riders*, [1899] New York 1961; Virgil Carrington Jones, *Roosevelt's Rough Riders*, Garden City, N.Y. 1971.

66.   Harbaugh, pp. 105–7; Roosevelt, *Rough Riders*, p. 14.

67.   Roosevelt, *Rough Riders*, pp. 14–15, 19.

68.   Ibid., pp. 16–17.

69.   Ibid., p. 19. For the regimental 'Muster–Out Roll', pp. 150–85. Jones, pp. 282–340, lists occupations.

70.   Roosevelt, *Rough Riders*, p. 146.

71.   Ibid., pp. 16–17.

72.   Ibid., pp. 28, 73–74.

73.   Ibid., pp. 22–24.

74.   Ibid., pp. 87, 92.

75.   Journal of Horace Wayman Bivins, in Herschel V. Cashin et al., *Under Fire with the Tenth U.S. Cavalry*, [1899] New York 1969, pp. 58–61.

76.   Ibid., pp. 61–62, 74–76; T.G. Steward, *The Colored Regulars in the United States Army*, Philadelphia 1904, p. 245.

77.   Jones, p. 279; Cashin, p. 147; Edward A. Johnson, *History of Negro Soldiers in the Spanish American War and Other Items of Interest*, [1899] New York 1970, p. 39.

78.   Roosevelt, *Rough Riders*, pp. 94–96. A similar version of this account had appeared in an article by Roosevelt in *Scribners Magazine*, April 1899: Willard B. Gatewood, Jr., *Black Americans and the White Man's Burden*, Urbana, Ill. 1975, pp. 241–43; Johnson, p. 40.

79.   Roosevelt, *Rough Riders*, p. 96.

80.   Presley Holliday, 22 April 1899, to New York *Age*, as quoted in Johnson, pp. 41–46; Gatewood, *Black Americans*, pp. 202–3.

81.   Thomas G. Dyer, *Theodore Roosevelt and the Idea of Race*, Baton Rouge, La. 1980, p. 79, citing Hermann Hagedorn, ed., *The Works of Theodore Roosevelt*, New York 1925, 8:157; Harbaugh, pp. 15, 17–23, 32–33, 47. See also Owen Wister, *Roosevelt: The Story of a Friendship*, New York 1930, *passim*.

82.   Harbaugh, pp. 70–71, on Roosevelt's class attitudes and 'partly instinctual' anti-labor responses, p. 120; see also Dyer, pp. 1–20, 31. Dyer, pp. 33–38, stresses the influence of Lamarckianism on Roosevelt. This had the effect of modifying biological determinism by admitting morality and moral choice as factors in explanations of white racial superiority. Harbaugh refers to Roosevelt's inclination to 'reform Darwinism', pp. 327–28.

83.   Roosevelt, *Rough Riders*, p. 146; Harbaugh, pp. 17, 327.

84.   Roosevelt, *Rough Riders*, p 22; Dyer, p. 81; see also Dyer, p. 84, quoting Hagedorn, ed., *Works*, 10:92.

85.   Bivins in Cashin, pp. 74–76. On African-American support for the war in its Cuban phase, see Gatewood, *Black Americans*, pp. 64–101. The sympathy of African Americans was strengthened by the fact that many Cubans were known to be of African descent: Gatewood, pp. 16–19, especially on 'the mulatto general Antonio Maceo, whose exploits received full coverage in the Negro press', p. 17. See Johnson, pp. 8–9; William Hilary Coston, *The Spanish American War Volunteer*, 2nd ed. rev., [1899] Freeport, N.Y. 1971, pp. 160–65. Also, Willard B. Gatewood, Jr., *'Smoked Yankees' and the Struggle for Empire: Letters from Negro Soldiers, 1898–1902*, Urbana 1971, pp. 3–13 and *passim*.

86. New Orleans *Times Democrat*, 19 March 1899, as quoted in Coston, pp. 55–56.

87. For Roosevelt's vacillations on this question, see Dyer, pp. 100–101, and Gatewood, *Black Americans*, pp. 202–3, 242–44.

88. On the first page of *Rough Riders*, Roosevelt wrote: 'While my party was in opposition [i.e., 1893–97] I had preached with all the zeal and fervor I possessed, our duty to intervene in Cuba and to take the opportunity of driving the Spaniard from the western world.' And on page 2: ' ... of course Senator Lodge and I felt precisely alike; for to fight in such a cause ... was merely to carry out the doctrines we had both of us preached for many years.' Shortly before the Cuba landings, Senator Henry Cabot Lodge had written to inform his friend Roosevelt that President McKinley was 'now fully committed to the large policy that we both desire': Roosevelt, *Rough Riders*, pp. 11, 12; Henry Cabot Lodge to Theodore Roosevelt, 24 May 1898, in *Selections from the Correspondence of Theodore Roosevelt and Henry Cabot Lodge, 1884–1918*, New York 1925, 1:300.

Conclusion

The project put forward in the Introduction was to develop an ideological explanation, covering the nineteenth century, for racial differentiation in the United States. Because ideological explanation places white racism as its principal operative factor, what was required was a demonstration, first, of the continuity of racism; second, that racism and the racial differentiation resulting therefrom together sustained important interests of ruling classes or class coalitions; and third, that white racism was generated and regenerated as part of the process of class conflict and compromise.

With respect to the first and second points, I have endeavored to meet these explanatory requirements by focusing on the legitimizing syntheses of successively dominant political parties, viewed as class coalitions. Already by the end of the eighteenth century, ideas and attitudes of white racial dominance appeared as a distinct component within the ideology of the commercial–landlord oligarchy that had led the colonies to independence. This component provided an apologia for slavery and the expropriation of Indians. It made room for those extortionary practices within Christian fellowship and republican polity. It fortified the National Republican theory of regional alliance by reassuring continentalists North, Central and South that their common enterprise rested on shared perceptions; and by discrediting the city-state localism of their Federalist adversaries.

Lower-class Americans, meanwhile – artisans and yeomen farmers entering politics through extension of the franchise – claimed their own birthright in racism as a means of reducing the economic and social distance that separated them from the upper class. The War of 1812, followed by territorial expansion and rapid economic growth, especially in cotton, led to a division of class interest and class identification within the ruling oligarchy. The outcome was a new party based on the alliance of southern planters with northern and western artisans and yeomen. Jacksonian Democrats took charge of the federal apparatus; and as they did so, white racism moved to center stage in the Democracy's legitimizing synthesis. Validating a positive defense of slavery as well as removal or extermination of Indians, the racist component served to define the boundaries of a white republic from which class gradations would presumably be forever barred.

Ousted from power, the National Republicans struggled to salvage the program earlier proclaimed for them by John Quincy Adams and James Barbour. In defense of their National Republican thesis they improvised the Whig party; but they won few victories. Hobbled by commitments to the politics of deference, Whigs remained virtually defenseless against the mass politics of egalitarianism and white supremacy. Yet as whiggery disintegrated, the Democracy also began to fall apart. Jacksonian racism, despite (or, more accurately, because of) the logical symmetry of its anti-Indian and anti-African thrusts, proved unable to cope with problems of western settlement. While the anti-Indian thrust was opening up western lands to slavery, the anti-African thrust – initially intended as a racial justification of slavery – ended by solidifying yeomen and artisans against the entry of slaves into the territories. This reversal undermined the Jacksonian coalition and set the stage for rapprochement between northern commercial and manufacturing interests and the Free Soil movement. From this marriage was born the Republican party.

After organizing the downfall of the planter class, Republicans harnessed the federal government to industrial capitalism and brought in 'modernization' under forced draft. It might be supposed that such a program would have rendered racial distinctions irrelevant; and certainly one trend of anti-slavery thought pointed in that direction. On the other hand, Free Soil had relied on racial hostility to exclude African Americans, slave or free, from the western territories; while the main phalanx of anti-slavery, led by such exquisite moralists as John Quincy Adams, had long learned to identify planter aristocracy with the African 'heart of darkness'. Beyond Appomattox came the opening of the West. A host of high-minded men, benefactors and philanthropists like John Evans, turned their enormous promotional talents to the extirpation of Indians. Thus for the Republican coalition (as for the Jacksonian coalition preceding it) the racist component never ceased to perform indispensable services within the legitimizing synthesis.

Modernization under forced draft quickly revealed previously unperceived aspects of capitalist industrialization. Hard on the heels of the first industrial depressions of 1873 and 1893 came labor organization, violent industrial conflict; and, in the 1890s, the first hegemonic crisis. This, for the United States, was structured by the prior history of parties and party systems, at the crux of which was the tenuousness of the Republican grip on political power. Emergence of a new class coalition in the 1890s *seemed* imminent. Formally, at least, it was possible. But as I argued in the preceding chapter, white racist ideas and institutions worked against that possibility by inhibiting, within the agricultural and industrial labor forces, any extensive rejection of ruling-class legitimacy.

The argument here recapitulated has been intended to satisfy the explanatory requirements of points one and two above: specifically, to show the continuity of racism as it was renovated, rehearsed, and fine-tuned in mass media and literature; and to show that racism, together with racial differentiations resulting from it, sustained important interests of US ruling classes or coalitions.

The issue posed in point three – that of the generation and regeneration of white racism 'as part of the process of class conflict and compromise' – raises a problem that was touched on and deferred in an earlier chapter. The study shows that lower-class organizations and individuals contributed substantially to the continuance of white racism. Doubtless at the very beginning of the era of African slavery and colonial empire, European ruling classes took the lead in constructing racist ideology. Lower orders – as well as explorers and settlers spreading across the globe – shared willingly, if not equally, in the profits of racial exploitation. To that extent they were complicit in deed and doctrine.

Even more was this the case for the United States during the nineteenth century, given its territorial expansion and economic development. Expropriation of Indian lands transformed yeoman farmers into land barons. Urban artisans, primed with profits from plantation slavery, blossomed into manufacturing entrepreneurs. The wandering typesetter of the 1820s – thanks to war against Mexico – presided over a metropolitan daily by the 1850s. Certainly these were not average transactions, but they point to an upward mobility that makes it difficult to specify the class locations of ideological innovation. For an upper class to preempt lower-class perceptions might prove tactically advantageous. Most major parties in the United States have been coalitions that included lower-class elements. To the extent that significant decisions were made through the electoral process, such elements shared in ruling-class power. The racial component often provided the means for checkmating opponents and coercing, or bargaining with, allies higher in the social hierarchy than themselves. Republican reversal on the Burlingame Treaty offers a case in point, as does the influence of the Free Soil contingent in shaping Republican Indian policies. The focus of this study has turned more than once on the manoeuvering of upper classes obliged to defend class privilege in the arena of mass politics.

The problem at issue does not begin or end with mass politics. Underlying all institutional modes of decision making, including parties and party systems, is the social construction of reality. However much racism may have been pushed from above, there is ample evidence of its lower-class ambience. It could be made to work for the perceived interests of lower classes or segments of lower classes as well as for the ruling classes. No one could doubt, for example, that frontier farmers and land speculators had direct economic interest in Indian removal; or that skilled craft workers benefitted from racial exclusion. Although dissenters in both sectors sometimes called for broader horizons of class or group interest, the 'reality' into which they had all been socialized undercut these objections as unrealistic.

Does such evidence of lower-class involvement in constructing racist ideology contradict the assertion put forward in the introductory hypothesis that white racism serves 'justificatory purposes for dominant groups in the changing class coalitions that governed the nation'? My answer is that it does not, since the hypothesis makes no claim that ruling classes monopolize ideological construction. On the contrary, the definition of ideology I have relied on stresses general social participation. Ideological interpretation understands ideas, ascribed values, and collective behavior as molded by class or social group interest. It does not insist that ideas, values, and behavior patterns necessarily originate from, or can be manipulated only by, a ruling class. Nonetheless, upper classes enjoy obvious advantages in gaining acceptance of *their* constructs, especially with the proliferation of mass media.

That racism sometimes worked to the advantage of lower classes does not mean that it ceased to work for upper classes. Transformation of Indian lands into Free Soil homesteads in no way lessened the value to Republican entrepreneurs of having overthrown the Slave Power. Skilled craftsmen might fortify their trade unions by erecting racial barriers, but it was corporate industry that had the most to gain from smashing the industrial unions. This permeation of a society and culture is what I have tried to convey through case histories like that of George Wilkes; through glimpses into newspapers, theater, and blackface minstrelsy; and especially by tracing the orbit of the western hero from lower-class vernacular beginnings to the annunciation, at the turn of the century, of his imperial mission.

The American working class appears in this study as fragmented and indecisive. So dominated was it by a producer ethic corresponding to artisan and yeoman modes of production that consciousness as a class among industrial workers grew only marginally. Separatist identifications of race and ethnicity, skill and union membership or leadership, claimed stronger allegiance than the unifying identification of class. Early Marxists (as well as some later ones) – focusing on the presumedly prototypical industrialization of England and Western Europe – have tended to exaggerate the transformative powers of class consciousness. They imagined proletarian heroes who, having once grasped as self-evident truth the alienation and solidarity of their class, would act to change the world. In the United States, certainly, it did not work out that way.

Is this study, then, another corroboration of American exceptionalism? I would prefer to place the matter differently. There were in fact substantial grounds for attributing almost superhuman characteristics to the working classes of England and Western Europe. Under the special conditions prevailing at the onset of industrialization in those countries, the labor force moved quickly and massively to class organization. Early Marxists were right to celebrate this transition; their mistake was in supposing it to be normative. In the long span of worldwide industrialization, the American working-class experience will probably prove closer to the norm than that of Western Europe.

Approximately this same prediction was implicit in the definition of ideology adopted in the Introduction. To understand ideology as a purposeful construction of meanings in which all classes participate precludes the notion that proletarians grasped their class identity as self-evident truth. It was upon this epistemological misconception borrowed from the Enlightenment by way of early romanticism that expectations of the leap to revolution were based. Stripped of such illusions, the concept of ideology offers – even to the industrial working class – no privileged access to revolutionary commitment.

Is class, then, neutral with respect to ideological construction? I think not. At certain historical junctures, certain classes or class segments may gain access to uniquely far-reaching views of the human condition. In discussing James Fenimore Cooper's Leatherstocking hero, something like this was what I had in mind. And in certain historical periods, poverty, hardship, and relative deprivation may constrict particular class horizons. Such appears to be the case, worldwide, with working-class perceptions of environmental crisis. Yet in the long run the ancient wisdom seems likely to prevail: a camel will pass through the eye of a needle sooner than a rich man enter the kingdom of heaven. Wealth, privilege, power, tend to narrow the vision of ruling classes and their mercenary retainers. If this is true, far-reaching prospects of the human condition are more likely to be constructed in the ghettoes of great cities and third world barrios (or in the work of intellectuals whose socialization has contained 'organic' links to such experience) than among skilled industrial technicians or within military-industrial complexes.

One final question: Does the demonstration that so much talent and creative energy was poured so effectively into constructing and reconstructing white racism in America bring this study to a despairing

390 The Rise and Fall of the White Republic

conclusion? Short of absolute endings, neither despair nor hope can be absolute; as the opposite ends of a spectrum, they remain relative to one another. The study deals only with the nineteenth century and with the dominant Euro-American culture of the United States. Its line of argument has dictated a primary focus on innovators of racist ideology. But this same focus includes dissenters like Edward Wynkoop in Colorado, or the scattered advocates of working-class racial unity who spoke their pieces hopelessly or defiantly and vanished from the record. More important, perhaps, were those, not so much dissenters as collaborators in the midst of white racial politics, who nonetheless projected broader visions of human possibility. Lincoln would be the prototype of such figures. Within the range of this study, John Quincy Adams and Richard Hildreth serve as examples; Mark Twain and Eugene Debs; blackface minstrels during their social satirical interludes; or even George Wilkes at one brief juncture in his career. In all these cases the ideological constructions seem larger than what was needed merely to house white racism.

We know also that ideological innovators of comparable talent and energy were at work among people of color and that their efforts sustained those minorities against seemingly overwhelming adversity. Given the historical separation of American racial minorities and their distance from the larger world outside, there could be little interchange or reinforcement among them throughout the nineteenth century. And given the complicity of the entire white society in racial exploitation, the ideological constructions of racial minorities would have relatively little impact on white racism itself except to intensify it. Probably the only large exception to this generalization was the role of African-American abolitionists and their input in anti-slavery literature. These *givens* ceased to apply in the twentieth century.

It was suggested in the Introduction that white racism is essentially a theory of history. Theories of history may become self-fulfilling prophecies. Such was the situation of white racism for four hundred years during which the outcomes of the practice came to be taken as proofs of the theory. Theories of history, however, which fail to explain new historical phenomena begin to lose their powers of persuasion. With the First World War came a decisive turning point. A conflict unparalleled in savagery and destruction had been unleashed not by darker and presumably less morally and intellectually reliable races, but by the whitest of the white, and in the very heartland of Western European culture. The revolt of the masses in colonial and dominated regions became in itself a new historical phenomenon that racist theory could not explicate. Since the end of the First World War, Euro-American world hegemony, based ideologically on white racism, has progressively disintegrated.

Science reinforced white racism until about 1915. In modern societies, however, science as a social substructure apparently reproduces groups with ideological motivations to penetrate established, even sanctified, explanatory theories. Science thus approximates the mythic universal solvent, dreaded (and sought for) by the alchemists, because it promised to destroy any container to which it was committed. In the long run, this aspect of science, pushed by its technological sorcerers' apprentices, may bring the human species to a Darwinian termination. Confining our view to less apocalyptic vistas, it seems clear that science in the twentieth century criticized the intellectual underpinnings of racism, consequently diminishing the effectiveness of racism in legitimations of power. Here is an example of science fulfilling, at certain historical moments, the Enlightenment expectation of liberator of humanity. Yet white racism was in part the creation of nineteenth-century science. And since – apart from correspondence to an external reality, itself problematical – science must be ideologically constructed, it would seem improvident to rely on the example just cited as grounds for confidence in science as an autonomous liberating force.

What this study shows, simply, is that white racism in the United States during the nineteenth century was continually constructed and reconstructed out of particular historical circumstances. Given different historical circumstances, different constructions would occur. The study does not prove that ideological construction is *not* totally determined by pre-existing historical circumstances. Neither does it prove that it *is*. But by demonstrating variety and conflict in the construction of racial ideology as well as the superfluity of output over immediate legitimizing functions, the study suggests, I think, that ideological construction may not in the long run be completely predetermined. To the extent that it is not, it offers possibilities for creative constructions, new departures. At the end of four centuries of Euro-American world empire – and four decades into the nuclear era – the long run may not be very long.

Index